The Great Plains during World War II

R. DOUGLAS HURT

The Great Plains
during World War II

UNIVERSITY OF NEBRASKA PRESS | LINCOLN & LONDON

Library of Congress Cataloging-
in-Publication Data
Hurt, R. Douglas.
The Great Plains during World War II /
R. Douglas Hurt.
p.   cm.
Includes bibliographical references and
index.
ISBN 978-0-8032-2409-4 (cloth: alk.
paper)
1. Great Plains—History—20th
century.   2. Great Plains—Social
conditions—20th century.   3. World
War, 1939–1945—Great Plains.
I. Title.   II. Title: Great Plains during
World War 2.   III. Title: Great Plains
during World War Two.
F595.H95   2008
940.53'78—dc22
2007041825

Set in Sabon by Bob Reitz.

*For Ray K. Hurt and the
memory of my mother,
Margaret Jane Hurt,
who lived it*

Contents

Illustrations

Preface

The Great Plains spreads across the vastness of ten states, or at least portions of those states. It is an amorphous region not easily identified because the boundaries change with the definition of the region. Some locate the parameters of the Great Plains by grass species. Others trace the border by annual precipitation averages. Still others use soil composition or the ninety-eighth or one hundredth meridian to locate the eastern boundary. In 1936 the federal government authorized the Great Plains Committee to survey the drought-stricken, windblown plains for the purpose of recommending socioeconomic changes, including soil conservation procedures and wise land management practices. This committee used county boundaries to identify the region. All the various identifying tools are satisfactory, but none are perfect, and only a rough uniformity links them. In all cases the boundaries ebb and flow. Given the sweep of this book, I have chosen to identify the region as one composed of ten states—North Dakota, South Dakota, Nebraska, Kansas, Oklahoma, Texas, New Mexico, Colorado, Wyoming, and Montana. My definition includes scientific and environmental determinants, but I also use political boundaries for structure and manageability. Historically speaking, state boundaries make a difference, even though the borders are arbitrary geographic and political lines, because such boundaries help shape the historical developments that are unique to a specific place or region. State and regional boundaries have a powerful symbolic importance and help determine relationships among people and institutions, that is, society, the economy, and the state. Put differently, place makes a difference, and in this study place is the Great Plains. Essentially, my geographic outline of the region traces the Great Plains from the eastern boundary of the Dakotas, Nebraska, Kansas, and Oklahoma to Dallas before meandering down to the San Antonio area, then heading northwest through Roswell, New Mexico, to Albuquerque and then north along the foothills of the Rocky Mountains. For the most part the Great Plains is a region without large cities, although I include those on the fringe of the Plains, such as Kansas City, Kansas, Omaha, Denver, Albuquerque, and Bismarck.

Although the World War II home front has an extensive national historical literature, and while some scholars have written special-ized studies about cities, states, regions, and race during the war, the history of the Great Plains home front has been addressed only in piecemeal fashion. Moreover, although Gerald Nash wrote two important books on the economic history of the West during the war (*The American West Transformed* and *World War II and the West*), he excluded the Great Plains and instead focused on the Far West, that is, the Mountain and Pacific Coast West. Moreover, many studies exemplify top-down approaches, with the scholarship based on government reports, statistical compilations, and institutional policymaking. In contrast my approach has been to study the Great Plains from a grassroots perspective. In order to do so I read widely from a selection of major state and regional newspapers and con-ducted research in archival collections to learn about home front activities in the Great Plains.

This study emphasizes the region's social and economic history during the war years. The political history of the region during that time merits study, but the limitations of time and space precluded that analysis. Each chapter could easily be expanded into a book centered on the region, yet only in the case of the Indians have sev-eral books been written on the subject. In addition to the political history of the region during the war, more work needs to be com-pleted on the African American and Mexican American experience and the cities and labor unions. Moreover, historians of World War II usually begin their studies with the Japanese attack on Pearl Har-bor on December 7, 1941. I start with the isolationist debate during the late 1930s and the German invasion of Poland on September 1, 1939, which brought the Great Plains into the war in terms of mobilization, industrial production, and social change. Yet, if World War II was a "good war," the question must be asked, For whom? Certainly, the United States contributed, often single-handedly, to the destruction of political and military totalitarianism. But it was not a good war for people of Japanese descent, nor did it substantially change working conditions for migrant agricultural workers or dramatically alter race relations between blacks and whites. Racial discrimination and rent and price gouging indicated some responses that did not conform to the all-for-one-and-one-for-all patriotic publicity of the day. Still, community projects, such as scrap drives, rationing, and practice blackouts, provided residents with shared experiences that, in turn, gave their lives a public significance that they had not experienced before as well as a sense of participation in the war effort.

In analyzing the effects of World War II on the Great Plains and the responses of the region's residents to the war on the home front, I have written a narrative history. I also have written topically within a chronological structure to enable readers to purse a subject from the beginning of the war to the peace that followed. My approach is broad and sometimes necessarily impressionistic. It is a narrative of regional mobilization to help defend the nation and improve the lives of Great Plains residents in the process. Much of this book, then, is the story of the interaction of Great Plains men and women with the federal government and the response of the people in the region to economic and social changes wrought by the war. Certainly, the people of the Great Plains were not mere recipients of federal policies.

World War II was not transformative for the Great Plains, in contrast to the experience of the South and the Far West. It accelerated trends already apparent, such as the expansion of the aircraft industry, surplus agricultural production, and out-migration, but it did not bring revolutionary change, that is, a lasting military-industrial complex. When the war ended, much of the federal defense spending left to enhance military research, development, and building activities in the Far West, particularly California. Fundamentally, the Great Plains was an agricultural region when the war began, and it remained so at war's end. Even so, the total effect of the war on the region was, at least temporarily, significant. Military and industrial construction created boomtowns that taxed city services and mandated new attention to city planning backed with federal dollars. The aviation industry expanded rapidly, as did the number of military bases in the region, all of which meant jobs and large payrolls, which, in turn, meant disposable income. Among the previously underemployed, white workers found multiple job opportunities, while African American and Mexican American workers confronted continued discrimination, unskilled positions, and unequal wages, conditions much like those they experienced in the South. Moreover, the war opened doors of economic opportunity for women, but many of those doors closed quickly when the war ended. Still, the people of the Great Plains had welcomed the federal government during the 1930s, so the arrival of new agencies and programs did not cause a conservative political backlash among them. They were accustomed to receiving federal dollars for various projects. World War II enabled the federal government to increase its financial support for the region even more, particularly for construction, jobs, and agricultural commodities, and residents of the Great Plains welcomed it.

My purpose has been to allow the residents of the Great Plains to speak so that we can hear their words and see the days and years through their eyes and minds. I wanted to tell the story of the daily concerns of ordinary people who have become part of the nation's World War II history. At the same time, this is neither a history of unbounded support for federal policies nor a coming-of-age saga similar to that of the Far West during the war years. It is not the history of unbridled economic and social change. It is not a story crafted in black-and-white absolutes. Certainly, the war years were a time of prosperity that provided the economic boom to lift the region from the economic morass of the Great Depression as New Deal programs had not. But in the Great Plains the war years were also a time of racism, the denial of civil liberties, and greed as well as personal self-interest to the point of selfishness and hope against hope that the wartime largesse would last. Put differently, the history of the Great Plains during World War II is the story of patriotism and bonding and perseverance in homes, towns, and cities as well as on the job, but it was not a time of unmitigated self-sacrifice and stellar personal commitment.

I am grateful for the support of many people who helped make this book possible. Travel to archival collections remains essential for any historian even in the age of Web-based research. I could not have completed the project without a research fellowship from the Carl Albert Congressional Research and Studies Center at the University of Oklahoma and a fellowship from the Center for Digital History at the University of Nebraska through the Plains Humanities Alliance as well as a travel grant from the American Heritage Center at the University of Wyoming. Iowa State University also aided my research with a Big XII Faculty Fellowship and a research grant from the Council on Scholarship in the Humanities. Purdue University provided essential travel and research support.

I am appreciative of the help that I received from the staff at the Nebraska State Historical Society, the Kansas State Historical Society, the Oklahoma Historical Society, the University of Nebraska Library, the Purdue University Library, the Iowa State University Library, the Western History Collections and the Carl Albert Congressional Research and Studies Center at the University of Oklahoma, the Wyoming State Archives, the Wyoming State Library, the University of Wyoming Library, the American Heritage Center at the University of Wyoming, the Southwest Collection at Texas Tech University, and the University of Central Oklahoma Library. The interlibrary loan departments at Iowa State University and Purdue University provided timely and essential help.

I am particularly indebted to Megan Birk, Stephanie Carpenter, Alexandra Kindell, Sara Morris, Cameron Saffell, Trevor Soderstrum, and Cherilyn Walley, who provided loyal, dedicated, and skillful assistance. Ed Birch in Oklahoma City provided an essential photograph of the Tonkawa prisoner-of-war camp. Lynda Lynn aided my photograph search in the files of the *Daily Oklahoman*. Don Pisani read an early proposal and provided perceptive, helpful comments.

As always I am thankful for the support of my wife, Mary Ellen, who understands the historian's need for time to travel, write, and reflect.

The Great Plains during World War II

ONE | Reluctance

World War II became the pivotal event in twentieth-century American history, after which life seemed more complex and dangerous than ever before, both at home and abroad. The political, economic, and social changes wrought by the war, such as the centralization and regulation of economic affairs from business to agriculture by the federal government, new roles for women and minorities in American life, and the world leadership of the United States, remain. Certainly, the relationship of the federal government to individuals and the way people perceive freedom and security as well as the public good changed as a result of World War II. Yet those transformations were not readily apparent during the 1930s as the nation teetered on the threshold of a new world war. Moreover, the necessity to enter the European war, once it began, and prior to the Japanese attack on Pearl Harbor, was not obvious to most men and women who lived in the Great Plains. Although they would become staunch, unflinching patriots in pursuit of victory after the attack and following the declaration of war on the United States by Germany and Italy, their enthusiasm for international affairs and foreign policy that could drag the nation into war ran cold.

Indeed, the Great Plains had a well-known reputation for supporting isolationism by the time Germany, Italy, and Japan began threatening world peace during the 1930s. *Isolationism*, of course, is a slippery term, and its meaning can be less precise than apparent. For the people of the Great Plains *isolationism* meant everything from the complete withdrawal from world affairs to noninterventionist internationalism that supported economic and political suasion abroad in order to aid the interests of the United States—all short of war. For others, it meant neutrality in the sense of simply not taking sides in the quarrels of other nations. Collectively, these groups can be termed *isolationist* because they wanted a foreign policy that would categorically keep the nation out of foreign conflicts.[1]

Certainly, by the late 1930s the Great Plains had a reputation for being more isolationist that the rest of the nation. In this region, plains men and women frequently recalled George Washington's admonition to avoid entangling alliances, and they considered Europeans largely incapable of keeping the peace. The people of the Great Plains favored *defense*, but they could not precisely define what the term meant or the context in which it should be applied. By 1939, like most Americans, they favored a British and French victory if war came, but, unlike most Americans, they could not agree whether the United States should provide military support to ensure success because such action would be nonneutral and could easily draw the nation into the war. They believed, however, that the military should be strong enough to prevent an attack. Some even favored a fortress America approach to foreign policy in which the nation withdrew from all world affairs and became impervious to invasion. For most men and women of the Great Plains, isolationism in some degree seemed a logical solution to avoid world problems that constantly led nations to war.

The reasons for this isolationist sentiment among the people of the Great Plains are complex, and they are influenced by a host of causes such as ethnicity, education, Republican partisanship, rural residency, economics, and religious beliefs. Many farmers in North Dakota, for example, feared an internationalist foreign policy because eastern capitalists would make them an "economic goat" while earning billions from defense contracts. These farmers believed that they had been "farmed by a capitalist class" during the Great War. This strongly held opinion overshadowed any sympathy for Germany based on national or ethnic heritage. Overall, however, the people of the Great Plains were isolationist because they did not want their sons, brothers, fathers, and husbands killed or maimed on European battlefields. Even the German-Russians favored isolationism because they hated war, not because they feared the United States would commit them to fighting against their homeland. Moreover, plains men and women were more concerned about domestic economic policy that would end the Great Depression and improve their standard of living after more than a decade of want. They preferred a federal government that would solve domestic problems rather than engage in foreign affairs.[2]

Comparatively speaking, the northern Great Plains states gave the strongest support to isolationism, with North Dakota arguably the most isolationist state in the region. Kansas and Nebraska followed as the next most isolationist, with South Dakota and Wyoming close behind. Colorado, New Mexico, Oklahoma, and Texas were the least isolationist Great Plains states, with Montana somewhere in between. In the Senate and the House, then, the core area for isolationism on the Great Plains extended from North Dakota to Kansas, and party affiliation apparently had minimal effect on voting behavior, although Republicans tended to support isolationist issues more frequently than Democrats and rural people were more isolationist than urban residents.[3]

During the 1930s, then, the men and women who lived in the northern Great Plains expressed an overwhelming sentiment for isolationism, including the variations of noninterventionism and neutrality. By holding this belief they were little different from most Americans, who felt betrayed by the European powers at the Paris Peace Conference in 1919. They adamantly believed that the United States should avoid all European disputes. Like most Americans, they favored trade with other nations, but nothing more. Few plains men and women believed that the United States had any obligation to become involved in international affairs, and certainly not foreign wars. They remained convinced that the Atlantic and Pacific oceans provided nearly all the national security the country needed. The current strength of the army and navy would provide the remaining protection against attack. They saw no reason to depend on alliances or military power to ward off potential enemies and ensure peace. Rather than worry about distant enemies and entangling al-

liances, Great Plains men and women confronted economic hardships brought by the Depression. The loss of jobs, low agricultural
prices, little manufacturing, and the multiplier effects of each on the
creation of want, uncertainty, and fear in daily life occupied their
attention and took their energy.[4]

In 1938, when Adolph Hitler annexed Austria and occupied the
Sudetenland before seizing Czechoslovakia in 1939, Great Plains
residents became alarmed. Like most Americans, they responded by
strongly voicing their belief that the United States should do nothing, other than declare its sympathy for the European democracies.
Central Europe and Germany were far away, and Americans were
safe, particularly those who lived deep in the heart of the nation.
The Europeans, once again, merely savaged each other's throats,
and they should be let alone to solve their own problems.

In January 1939 more than thirty teams of local businessmen in
Bismarck, North Dakota, solicited funds for the relief of displaced
Jews, particularly those who had been forcibly removed from Germany and Austria and released at the Polish border without adequate food, clothing, or shelter. Raising money, of course, was
far different from advocating interference with Germany's policies
against the Jews and expansionist designs. In May, Senator John
C. Gurney from South Dakota reported that "numerous" constituents had urged him to support a strict neutrality law that would
deny the president discretionary enforcement powers and prohibit
"foreign entanglements." One constituent argued that the United
States could not oppose Germany since Great Britain had acquired
its empire by "aggression." Another wrote, "The people are looking
to our congressmen to keep the U.S. out of war with Europe." South
Dakotans generally believed that the United States needed to focus
on solving domestic economic problems and that it did not have any
business interfering in European affairs. As one Aberdeen resident
observed, "We have no business in Europe. Let us mind our own
business." A Gallup poll taken at the time found that Coloradoans
believed that the United States again would be "played for a sucker"
by Great Britain and France in another European war.[5]

Hope, of course, springs eternal. On August 30, 1939, the editor of the *Salina Journal* in Kansas predicted that war would not come. He reasoned that Germany would not attack Poland because Italy would not support Germany. If Italy joined the fight with Hitler, he reasoned, "France would try to sever northern Italy and the British navy would decimate its cities." Moreover, neither Russia nor Japan would support Germany against Poland, and Hitler's advisers opposed war. Since the democracies of the world already condemned Germany for its oppressions and aggressions after Hitler took power in 1933, and since the German people now understood the danger to peace, he argued, "the chance that Germany will risk war grows less as each day passes." At the same time, Germany's prospects grew dimmer for seizing Danzig, the Polish Corridor, and its own lost colonies. He professed, "Everyday it appears to be just a little bit more certain that Hitler has gambled for big stakes—and lost." A day later he wrote, "Unless the wiser and better informed Mussolini can stop him [Hitler], he will soon be in a position where his own ignominious retreat becomes the only alternative to war." The next day, Germany invaded Poland.[6]

On September 3, the first Sunday following Germany's invasion of Poland, and with Britain and France now in the war, ministers across the Great Plains led congregations in prayers for peace. In Texas, Governor W. Lee O'Daniel urged loyalty to President Roosevelt. He would be Americans' "earthly guide" while they let "true patriotism reign supreme" during this time of crisis. Education officials in Texas did not think that the war would affect college enrollments. In Salina, Kansas, residents responded to the war with the belief that Britain and France must fight but that America should remain "aloof." Yet a "depressing fatalism" seemed to weigh heavy on their minds because they feared the United States would eventually be drawn into the war, just as it had been during the last European conflict. Everyone seemed to express the desire to "keep out" and "stay out," but all Salina residents, as well as everyone across the Great Plains, worried about the response of Italy and Russia and what it all meant for their lives.[7]

In Bismarck delegates to the national convention of the American Legion urged neutrality because the loss of American lives during the First World War had been "fruitless." A. D. McKinnon, the commander of the North Dakota Legion, proclaimed that war could easily be avoided because "there is no geographical or economical reason for us to go into it." Yet this sentiment was not universal across the Great Plains. In Kearney, Nebraska, for example, members of the Cosmopolitan, Rotary, and Kiwanis clubs favored changing the Neutrality Act of 1937 to remove the embargo on the sale of arms and move to a cash-and-carry basis, provided the nation remained neutral. A poll of *Kearney Daily Hub* readers found them divided on cash-and-carry, but many reasoned that such a policy would be truly neutral because all belligerents would be treated alike. One resident spoke for many when he said, "My idea is cash on the barrel, and let them get home with it if they can." He also advised that Americans should "keep [their] mouths and pocketbooks shut." Even so, from Abilene, Texas, to Bismarck, North Dakota, enlistments in the army and the navy dramatically increased as the War Department began strengthening its forces and as many Great Plains men sought the excitement of serving at a time when war seemed a real possibility.[8]

Three weeks after the war began, however, Senator William J. Bulow of South Dakota reported receiving letters opposing repeal of the arms embargo by a ratio of sixteen to one. His constituents feared that repeal would lead to war, but some advocated support for Britain and France through cash-and-carry in the form of food and clothing because they favored the Allied cause and because such a policy would boost employment without risking American lives and property. Others worried that this approach would let the moneyed interests lead the nation into a world war once again. Still others contended that, with a $40 billion national debt, largely resulting from New Deal programs during the Depression years, the country could not afford war. Not only would American entry into the conflict substantially increase the national debt; it would lead to regimentation, and even totalitarianism, at home. These critics argued that a balanced budget and attention to domestic affairs offered enough problems to keep the government busy.[9]

Soon after Germany attacked Poland, Bula Swartz of Tulsa, Oklahoma, spoke for many when she wrote to Senator Elmer Thomas,

saying, "European countries have always had their quarrels and probably will continue to have them until the end of time. America has
nothing to fear from foreign invasion. . . . America's danger is from
within." For her, Nazis and Communists in the United States posed
the greatest threat to national security, and they had to be "weeded
out." She concluded, "May the good work of the Dies committee
continue." By the late 1930s, then, most Americans, Great Plains
residents included, considered isolationism, or at least noninterventionism, an article of faith. Between 1935 and 1939, polls by the
American Institute of Public Opinion indicated that large majorities
across the nation believed that everything possible should be done
to maintain neutrality. Interestingly, these polls revealed a new concept of neutrality. Most Americans now hoped that neutrality would
mean restricting commerce, particularly in war materials, with belligerents instead of demanding traditional rights such as freedom
of the seas, defended by diplomacy and force of arms if necessary.
Although a majority of respondents sympathized with Britain and
France, 71 percent of those polled in October 1939 opposed policies
that risked war, and they believed that the United States had made a
mistake when it entered the last conflict.[10]

When Germany invaded Poland, most Americans, Great Plains
residents included, wanted to stay out of the war. By December, a
Fortune survey found that residents of the northern plains remained
the most opposed to war "under any circumstances," and 45 percent of those polled favored only cash-and-carry trade with the belligerents. The people of the Great Plains, however, began to split
about how the nation should respond to the war. The isolationists
quickly voiced opposition to the provision of aid that might commit
the United States to an Allied victory, as happened, they believed,
in 1917. Only a few, such as Kittie Sturdevant in Oklahoma City,
advocated maximum support for Britain and France. In a letter to
Senator Elmer Thomas she concluded, "Since November 11, 1918,
we have only had an armistice. . . . The present affair is the breaking
of that armistice on the part of Germany and the more we can do to
help the Allies eliminate the Nazi mind from off the face of the earth,
the more we will be serving humanity and keeping faith with the

ones we lost in France." For her, "Germany ought to have been laid waste" during the last war rather than treated magnanimously at the Paris Peace Conference. Yet, while the isolationists of the Great Plains disagreed with her position and advocated remaining aloof from the new European war, many residents supported President Roosevelt's incremental commitments to Britain and Russia because they still hoped against hope that the United States could remain out of the conflict.[11]

The desire of the isolationists to remain uncommitted to the Allies had been influenced by the Nye Committee of the U.S. Senate, which in 1934 investigated the reasons for America's entry into World War I and lambasted the Woodrow Wilson administration for committing the nation to war for economic purposes. Senator Gerald P. Nye represented North Dakota, and the findings of his committee placed the blame for America's entry into the war on the bankers, financiers, and munitions makers who, motivated by greed, helped commit the United States to a foreign policy that inevitably led to armed conflict in order to protect their investments and guarantee enormous profits, albeit with the lives of American men. Nye arguably held stronger isolationist views than many residents of the Great Plains, but he had considerable support. On October 3, 1934, when he called war "incorporated murder" and the "makers of machinery of war the incorporates," his words reached sympathetic ears across the region, although even his most ardent admirers must have winced at his lack of proof. Nevertheless, when the final assessment of the Nye Committee appeared in seven parts during 1935 and 1936, Great Plains residents essentially believed that it reported the truth, and they did not want the nation dragged into a new war for the selfish, economic purposes of a corporate America.[12]

In addition to shaping public opinion in the Great Plains, the Nye Committee played a major role in the passage of the Neutrality Act of 1936. This legislation expanded a similar act of the previous year that authorized the president to embargo munitions, that is, prohibit their sale or transport to belligerents, after he proclaimed that a state of war existed between them. The Neutrality Act of 1936 also prohibited loans and credits to belligerents except for ordinary commercial transactions. In Nebraska Senator George Norris supported Nye and the isolationist position among Great Plains residents by saying, "We cannot take sides." Congress agreed, and the Neutrality Act received approval by a voice vote in the Senate and passage by the House 353–27.[13]

When the American First Committee organized in September 1940, Nye became a popular speaker on the organization's behalf. He advocated America for Americans and attributed war to a failure of political leadership. The Japanese attack on Pearl Harbor destroyed the America First Committee and ended Nye's public career; that is, he was not reelected in 1944, and political observers attributed the loss to his uncompromising isolationist position prior to Pearl Harbor. Yet, before the Japanese attack, when most Great Plains residents thought about the possibilities of a new European, not an Asian, war, many agreed with Nye's isolationist views. Moreover, when the United States entered the war, his work helped prevent the profiteering that characterized industrial mobilization during World War I. Nye served as a vocal opponent of President Roosevelt, whom he and many other isolationists in the Great Plains believed was maneuvering the country into war. Ultimately, Nye, like other Great Plains residents, supported war after the Japanese attack and the declarations of war against the United States by Germany and Italy a few days later.[14]

Other Great Plains leaders voiced isolationist sentiment, although not as uncompromisingly as Nye. His colleague from North Dakota, Lynn J. Frazier, who served in the U.S. Senate from 1926 through 1940, also advocated isolationism. Frazier supported international trade so long as American foreign policy did not place the nation in a position that would lead to war. He, too, like many plains men and women, believed that only trouble could come from entangling alliances, collective security commitments, and international organizations, such as the League of Nations. Moreover, he argued that military appropriations and preparedness could lead only to an international arms race that made war inevitable. In 1939, Frazier said, "In my opinion, it has largely been the example set by the United States Government that has caused the world scramble for increased armaments on the part of all the great nations of the world." He concluded, "We are making preparations for war." He opposed not only military appropriations during the late 1930s but also the Selective Training and Service Act of 1940 and compulsory military training in wartime, and he also advocated scrapping the army and the navy.[15]

Few Great Plains residents would go that far, but they agreed that the assets of the United States should be used to end the Depression, not strengthen the military. North Dakota farmers needed federal aid in the form of feed and seed loans to help overcome drought and crop failures as well as policies that would improve the agricultural economy. They did not need expenditures for battleships, armor, and munitions that would ultimately commit their sons and daughters to a foreign war. North Dakotans also agreed with Frazier that the United States had the moral responsibility to champion peace, freedom, and prosperity for all nations and that disarmament, even unilateral disarmament, offered the key to peace and security, not re-armament. Frazier also considered the Kellogg-Briand Pact of 1929, also known as the Treaty of Paris, a seminal event in the history of civilization because it renounced war as an instrument of national policy and advocated settling conflicts by peaceful means. Idealisti-cally, the Kellogg-Briand Pact made war illegal, but Frazier believed that it offered great hope for the people of the world. Frazier, like Nye, served as a strong isolationist voice from the northern Great Plains.[16]

To the South in Kansas, Senator Arthur Capper also advocated his own brand of isolationism, but in contrast to Nye and Frazier he considered himself an internationalist who opposed war. Capper, for example, supported reciprocal trading agreements and the Good Neighbor policy toward Latin America, but he did not want the extension of these programs to Europe or Asia. Capper's isolation-ism sprang from Washington's admonition to avoid entangling alli-ances and Jefferson's embargo policy prior to the War of 1812. He opposed any buildup of the army and navy because buildup would lead to war. As Capper saw it, the country needed a military only for the defense of American shores. He agreed with the report of the Nye Committee and called war "a cursed thing—the world's greatest foolishness." He wrote that the Nye Committee rendered "a most valuable public service in bringing to light the excessive profits of war and preparations for war that go to munitions makers, so-called merchants of death." Capper was a mild-mannered man, but his pen could sting.[17]

On November 11, 1937, Capper introduced a joint resolution with Congressman Louis Ludlow of Indiana calling for a national referendum before any declaration of war, except in response to invasion. Capper supported the Ludlow Resolution as an answer to President Roosevelt's October speech in which he advocated the quarantine of aggressor nations to keep the peace. When Congress voted on the Ludlow Resolution in January 1938, the Kansas delegation in the House (excepting the Democratic senator George McGill), along with Senator Capper, voted for it. Although the resolution did not gain congressional approval, Secretary of State Cordell Hull later reflected that it "seemed a disastrous move toward rigid isolation-ism."[18]

The vote of the Kansas delegation indicated strong pacifist and isolationist sentiments that also reflected the opinions expressed in newspaper editorials about the *Panay* affair, the bombing and sinking of the *Panay*, a U.S. Navy vessel, by Japanese planes on December 12, 1937, during the undeclared Sino-Japanese War of that year. At the time of the attack, the *Panay*, a patrol vessel of the Asiatic fleet, was taking American embassy officials from China via the Yangtze River. Capper, for one, made his isolationist position clear when he said, "I do not believe there are hardly any Americans who really hold that it is our destiny to try to settle affairs in the Orient, nor that it is our duty to police the world." He argued, "If we should start out on such a job, we simply engage in a series of wars, wars without end, such as the people of the Old World have had as far back as we can read history." Most Kansans and people of the Great Plains agreed and supported the total withdrawal of American forces from the Far East to avoid war. At the same time they, like many Great Plains residents, expressed great hostility toward Japan for its militarist and expansionist foreign policy.[19]

Capper, like Nye, opposed the Neutrality Act of 1937 because it gave the president too much latitude regarding cash-and-carry. The act also did not go far enough toward keeping the nation out of war, and Capper had opposed the neutrality legislation of 1935 and 1936 for the same reasons. He preferred strict, mandatory neutrality, a position based on the findings of the Nye Committee. Like other isolationists, he believed that, if a stringent neutrality act could prohibit American ships from entering war zones, mandate cash-and-carry restrictions on all trade with belligerents, prohibit private loans to warring parties, and authorize federal control over the exportation of war supplies, the United States could remain at peace. He did not believe that a new European war would jeopardize American security, as long as the nation remained truly neutral. Kansans and many residents of the Great Plains agreed.[20]

When Germany invaded Poland, Capper argued that the United States could save civilization only through pursuing peace and neutrality. He contended that American participation in the war would substantially increase the loss of life and property, foster dictatorship at home, substantially increase the national debt, and cause a postwar depression. Moreover, intervention would not prevent future European wars, which seemed inevitable and of no concern to Americans. Nye and Capper led a "peace bloc" in the Senate that opposed rescinding the arms embargo to aid Britain because such an act would be nonneutral and lead to war with Germany. Capper and the other Great Plains isolationists simply could not understand that the war involved American interests. Even so, Capper spoke for most of his constituents by advocating a neutrality policy that would prevent American intervention in foreign wars. From the mid-1930s until the Japanese attack on Pearl Harbor, he supported the nationalization of the munitions industry, small appropriations for the military, an embargo on guns and other military equipment, and the limitation of profits during wartime. Many Great Plains residents shared his "isolationist proclivities," placed great store on neutrality legislation, and believed that war could be legislated out of existence. One Kansan wrote to Governor Payne Ratner voicing his opposition to the supply of munitions or credits to European nations at war with Germany. Only strict neutrality would keep the United States out of war. "The proposals and course of the President," he wrote, "are positively mad." Interventionists, however, labeled Capper and others who supported him "ostrich-isolationists" and "peace-at-any-price pacifists."[21]

Congressman William Lemke of North Dakota shrugged off such criticism. Speaking in the House of Representatives he said, "The Nation is dizzy with war propaganda. The munitions manufacturers and the war lords are again in the saddle, riding high, wide, and reckless on the crest of false propaganda—reckless with the public's conscience and other people's agony." The "munitions manufacturers" and the "war lords" were attempting to "monopolize patriotism" while "wrapping the flag of glory around themselves and making millions out of the blood and the tears and the agony of an agonized world." Lemke wanted to stop them with a neutrality act that prohibited the sale of war matériel of any kind, to any nation, at any time.[22]

When President Roosevelt called Congress into special session on September 21, 1939, to revise the Neutrality Act of 1937 in response to Germany's invasion of Poland, many Great Plains people feared the worst. Roosevelt asked Congress to repeal the arms embargo and approve the expired cash-and-carry provision of the act to permit aid for Britain and France. The president argued that this policy would keep the nation out of war. Many Oklahomans, however, expressed their desire to retain the embargo provision of the Neutrality Act. Clarence E. Snow near Oologah, Oklahoma, wrote Senator Thomas, saying, "I say keep Hands off the other People. Don't get us Poor Devils at the Gun Bairl just cause some one wants to make money." Like Senator Capper in Kansas, another constituent advocated nationalizing the munitions industry to prevent the greed that would lead to war. From Tulsa, Bula Swartz reminded Thomas, "America's greatest interest is very definitely to remain at peace." She wrote, "To remain at peace is more important than economic interests or our right to the high seas under International law." Like many Great Plains residents who had been influenced by the Nye Committee, she held, "Everyone knows now that the World War was purely an economic war and that this talk of saving the world

for democracy was only propaganda to incite the people to war."
Many Oklahomans agreed and opposed lifting the embargo because
they believed that such action would lead to war. For them, only
neutrality would save the nation.[23]

But not all agreed. Some, such as Garnet Stone, a farmer near Yukon, Oklahoma, advocated repeal of the Neutrality Act. Although
he did not favor the commitment of American troops to the conflict,
he supported using the navy to help Britain and France complete
an "unfinished job." He did not worry about wartime profiteering
and wrote, "Let's quit aiding Germany and Japan against our own
interest, and against the interest of Morality and Humanity." He
confronted these matters with a directness that few plains residents
were prepared to emulate. In Oklahoma City, Kittie Sturdevant, the
state chairman on legislation for the Oklahoma Federation of Business and Professional Women's Clubs, reflected the opinion of many
women who favored repeal of the arms embargo, which she considered a matter of "simple female logic." Armament sales to Britain
and France would boost the workforce, strengthen the economy, and
help the Allies fend off a "mass of gangsters." Moreover, she argued,
America would have sold armaments to Britain and France during
peacetime, so why not when they were fighting for their existence?
Like Stone, she wanted to stay out of the war. But, she wrote, "we are
more profoundly concerned about staying on the side of right and
law and order." Aid to the Allies, she contended, meant the chance
"to lessen the opportunities for Nazi attack on us." She contended,
"The more England and France can kill off abroad, the stronger fight
they can put up abroad, the fewer we will get over here." Above all,
she reasoned, "We believe the embargo should be repealed and that
we should sell supplies cash and carry as long as that works and figure out something else when that fails." Other Oklahomans favored
strengthening the armed forces sufficiently to "repel an invasion of
the Americas by any nation or group of nations" as long as Germany and Japan maintained a military that menaced the peace of
the Western Hemisphere. Still others considered the Neutrality Act
"un-neutral" and "un-American" and believed that the convoy of
war matériel to Britain would lead to war.[24]

Not all opinions about repeal of the arms embargo were as realistic as those expressed by Senator Thomas's constituents. Some Great Plains residents exhibited gross naïveté, if not ignorance, when they contended that the European democracies or even the people under German hegemony did not deserve American help. By Armistice Day 1939, most Great Plains people believed that, despite the failure of the First World War to ensure European democracy, the "wild goose period" under Hoover, and the Depression years, they had sufficient reason to give thanks and be content. Senator Nye agreed and blamed the Allies for Hitler, charging that Hitler was the baby of Britain and France and that the United States had no obligation to "nurse their baby." Nye still spoke for more Great Plains residents than he probably realized.[25]

In Montana, the Democratic senator Burton K. Wheeler also opposed repeal of the arms embargo and warned about the danger of entering a new European war. In the debates over revising the Neutrality Act, he made the riveting remark that the American people "do not want to see the bodies of their boys hung on the Siegfried Line." In contrast, Senator James E. Murray supported the president's request, even though he had been an isolationist in relation to the World Court and military appropriations. Wheeler, however, remarked, "Perhaps I am too idealistic, but I cannot conceive that the American people, in their idealism, desire to put guns and powder and bombs into the hands of any people with which to kill others." Even so, the cash-and-carry provision clearly indicated that Roosevelt had listened to the isolationists because it showed that the United States would not, at the moment, pay a high price to stop Hitler. Plains men and women favored victory by the European democracies, but at the lowest possible cost in matériel and at no expense, that is, sacrifice of their sons and daughters. Nor did they believe that the United States should build up its own military strength even after Germany overran Poland because a lull in the fighting soon descended over Europe. In November, when Congress passed the Neutrality Act of 1939, which acquiesced to the president's request, the men and women of the Great Plains hoped for the best. Indeed, the Neutrality Act was hardly neutral because it favored Great

Britain, which had a merchant fleet capable of trading according to those cash-and-carry terms as well as a navy ready to protect it.[26]

William Allen White, the newspaper editor in Emporia, Kansas, however, offered a voice in opposition to isolationists such as Senators Nye and Capper. Early in 1940 he organized the Committee to Defend America by Aiding the Allies. Instead of advocating isolationism, White's organization supported aid for the Allies short of war, proposed exchanging destroyers for bases, and advocated convoying merchant ships to England. When France fell on June 22, 1940, the German victory stunned most Americans, but the Roosevelt administration heeded White's advice because only Great Britain remained in the fight against Germany. The public wanted to stay out of the conflict, but the danger had escalated and threatened the United States. With the fall of France, White and his committee provided an articulate voice about the proper response to German aggression. By providing aid to Britain short of military involvement, the United States could, White believed, pursue a policy of self-defense that would keep the British fleet between Europe and the East Coast and permit the American navy to safeguard the Pacific. White favored sending destroyers, guns, and other military equipment to Britain to keep the war from American shores. Not all Great Plains people agreed. Although they opposed Germany, many believed that White's proposal would not protect the United States but, rather, draw it into the conflict.[27]

Speaking for himself and the Committee to Defend America, White, however, opposed revising the Neutrality Act to permit the carrying of contraband, that is, guns and munitions, into the war zone on U.S. ships. He maintained the belief expressed two years earlier that "we should say that any nation having cash to pay can find the goods on the dock if she will come and get them. Briefly this policy might be called 'the dollar on the barrel head and the barrelhead on the dock.'" White wrote, "War would defeat the need for which our committee is organized to defend America by aiding Great Britain and would bring on a thirty year conflict." This view soon represented a more isolationist view than the interventionists on the committee favored, and on January 1, 1941, White resigned because the committee, he believed, now took the nation in the direction of war. White could not support the interventionists beyond supplying aid, and he knew the people of the Great Plains essentially agreed with his position.[28]

Senator George W. Norris of Nebraska, the last surviving senator of the group that had opposed American entry into World War I, also supported repeal of the arms embargo to aid Britain and France. As early as 1934, Norris feared the increasing international tension, writing, "Much as I dislike to say it, it looks to me as though we are doomed to another world war, in spite of the lessons taught by the past." Although Norris supported the neutrality acts of the 1930s, the actions of Germany, Italy, and Japan increasingly caused him to question the wisdom behind that legislation. Although he had worried that the repeal of the arms embargo would lead to nonneutral actions by the United States—the selling of munitions to one side and not the other—by 1939 he had changed his mind. In September he argued, "When we must help one side or the other by our action or non-action, we would be less than human if we did not cast our influence in favor of the right against the admitted wrong." He explained his position to William Allen White, saying, "When we consider Hitler, we must reach the conclusion that his doctrine, his aim, is repulsive to every sense of justice and humanity." Despite favoring aid to Britain and France, however, Norris did not believe that his position on the repeal of the arms embargo would draw the nation into war. Rather, he argued that a strong navy would keep the enemy from American shores. In his view, America could cast its support for "humanity and civilization" but remain out of the conflict. Moreover, a boycott could be personal, not governmental, and Japan would ultimately modify its aggressive actions. A year earlier Norris had written that, if the American navy ever became inferior to the Japanese fleet and the United States refused to trade with her, "some bright morning, we would wake to find ourselves at war with Japan." He urged the government to prepare for an attack "as may come from Japan or from a combination of nations similar to Japan."[29]

Norris, of course, put principle before politics because most Nebraskans favored some form of isolationism, noninterventionism, or neutrality and he understood that isolationist sentiment prevented Roosevelt from carrying Nebraska in the presidential election of 1940. Perhaps Norris's position can be explained by saying that, compared to other isolationists, he looked more to the future than to the past regarding the formulation of American foreign policy. Certainly, Norris was not as concerned as many isolationist politicians in the nation and Great Plains with the centralization of power in the presidency. Norris did not distrust federal power or President Roosevelt, whom he believed sincerely desired to keep the nation out of war. Most of his Nebraska constituents could not have disagreed more.[30]

Certainly, the Nebraska congressman Carl T. Curtis disagreed with Norris. Curtis considered the Roosevelt administration's efforts to aid the European democracies as an attempt to divert public criticism from its domestic policies. In March 1939 Curtis asked, "What has happened in the last few months that imperils the safety of the United States? Who is it that is about to invade or attack us? What foreign nation has issued threatening statements concerning the United States?" Answering his own questions he said, "When we trace down this war hysteria we find that it originates with high officials in the administration. It is the New Deal's spokesmen who have sounded the alarm." Curtis further accused the administration of fostering hatred to help shape public opinion for war against Germany. He cynically wondered, "If the present administration had not made such a mess of every problem that it has undertaken, including the farm program, unemployment relief, and recovery, would there be any necessity for this so-called war hysteria[?]" In the Great Plains Curtis was not the only one to hold this position.[31]

Fear and cynicism became the order of the day. In Peabody, Kansas, two Capper constituents accused the president of inciting war hysteria for his own personal and financial gain. "Everything for his own selfish ends," they wrote, "so that he may become more powerful." In Pierre, South Dakota, the American Legion sent a resolution to Congressman Francis Case urging the federal government to avoid entangling alliances, to let European nations solve their own problems, and to "mind its own business," although the Legionnaires did not specify what that meant. Great Plains residents increasingly believed that aid to Britain and France "short of war" ultimately would lead to an American commitment of money and men.[32]

The fall of France did not convince most Great Plains people that the United States should intervene or provide military aid to save Britain. Nevertheless, on June 20, 1940, two days before the French collapse, Senator Edward R. Burke of Nebraska introduced a bill that authorized the first peacetime military conscription. Both Franklin Roosevelt and Wendell Wilkie supported the Burke-Wadsworth Bill, as it became known during the presidential campaign. Most Great Plains residents found fault with the bill, although a majority of the region's voters aged twenty-one to twenty-five favored a draft of twenty-year-olds for one year, an opinion consistent with that held nationally. When discussion of the peacetime-draft bill circulated in the newspapers, however, the opposition became vocal and consistent. In Nebraska one mother wrote to Congressman Karl Stefan, saying, "We mothers *are depending* on our Senators & Congressmen to *defeat* any Draft Bill (Sen. Burke's) or compulsory training bill, and keep our sons at home." Senator Capper also opposed the draft bill during the Senate debates because he felt that a peacetime draft was unnecessary and that it would create a "militaristic spirit" and a "militaristic cast" in America. "It is not necessary," he said, "to Prussianize the young men of America." Capper, like other Great Plains isolationists, would support war and a draft only after an attack on the United States. In August 1940 the National Farmers Union, which claimed to represent more than one hundred thousand farm families, primarily in the Great Plains, also opposed the Burke-Wadsworth Bill. Robert Handschin, the union spokesman, contended that a draft would disproportionately affect "the class of young men and young women whom we represent—the lower income farmers and their boys of military age." The union's executive board sent every member of Congress a letter opposing the Burke-Wadsworth Bill signed by union officials from seven Great Plains states.[33]

Capper claimed that he received "upwards of 6,000" letters, tele-grams, petitions, and memorials from constituents against enactment of the conscription bill. He believed that this opposition came from individuals, veterans, and church, farm, and business organizations in the cities and towns and from fathers, mothers, and young men. Capper considered the bill a "mistake" and vowed "never to vote for it." He spoke for the ardent isolationists in Kansas and across the Great Plains when he said, "I think that compulsory military service in peacetime is a step toward dictatorship, a long step toward ending our representative form of government." He also believed that peacetime conscription was "a step toward war, a step toward waging war for the sake of war." He favored a defense program without "compulsory military training or conscriptive practices." Clearly, Capper considered a selective service act or draft a provoca-tive measure. And, in words that resonated with most people in the Great Plains, he said, "It may turn out to be a step toward partici-pating in a war that I still believe is not our war." Isolationists in both political parties agreed.[34]

When the Burke-Wadsworth Bill came to a vote on August 28, 1940, Senators Capper, Nye, Norris, and Wheeler, as well as Wil-liam J. Bulow of South Dakota and Edwin C. Johnson of Colorado, among others, opposed it. Senator Bulow refused to support it be-cause his father and other immigrants had fled military conscription when they came to the United States. Senator Norris declined to sup-port it because peacetime conscription mirrored policies in the total-itarian systems abroad. Indeed, Norris believed that the bill would "put this country on a road which means the ultimate destruction of democracy." Wheeler advocated a nationwide referendum on the draft since the bill's supporters claimed that it was necessary to pre-serve democracy. Alva B. Adams of Colorado opposed the bill be-cause of the expense involved and because the United States was not confronted with an immediate threat. He also contended that the bill gave the president too much power. James Murray of Montana objected because the United States needed a "professional army like Hitler has, made up of men . . . intensely trained and . . . equipped . . . with the most modern military machinery." In Murray's view,

"A conscript army made up of youths trained for a year or two, compared to Hitler's army, is like a high school football team going up against the professional teams like they have in Chicago and New York." Senator Nye considered any argument that the United States faced a military threat "laughable." He contended, "About the only argument the friends of conscription have been able to come up with is that Hitler is going to get us if we don't watch out, and probably by tomorrow morning, or anyway come harvest time."[35]

When the bill passed by a vote of 58–31, with Great Plains senators generally opposing, it went to the House. There, Clifford Hope of Garden City, Kansas, expressed the views of many Great Plains people when he said that peacetime conscription was unnecessary for self-defense or the defense of the Western Hemisphere. Hope believed, "The only possible excuse for building up a large conscript army is for offensive use elsewhere." Peacetime conscription meant that the United States was contemplating war. For him, there could be "no other possible justification." He feared that passage of the Burke-Wadsworth Bill might saddle the nation with peacetime conscription and a perpetual dictatorship. Certainly for the Republican isolationists in the Kansas congressional delegation, peacetime conscription meant war. On September 8, the Kansas delegation, except for the Democrat John M. Houston, opposed the bill, and the House passed it by a vote of 263–149, with the Great Plains states mostly voting nay. When the conference committee reported the bill on September 14, Senators Capper and Reed voted against it, but Houston supported it in the House. The Nebraska and North and South Dakota congressional delegations also opposed the bill, but Thomas of Oklahoma and Carl A. Hatch of New Mexico voted yea. By a vote of 47–25 in the Senate and 233–124 in the House, the Burke-Wadsworth Bill became the Selective Training and Service Act when Roosevelt signed it into law on September 16, 1940.[36]

The arguments made against the Selective Service Act by the Kansas delegation serve as an example of the isolationist sentiment, particularly among Republicans across the Great Plains. There, the Burke-Wadsworth Bill was thoroughly discussed in the newspapers, on the radio, and on the street corners. It generated more public controversy than any pre–Pearl Harbor measure, even Lend-Lease, because it touched every family. But it did not come easily or with the support of most people in the Great Plains. Without question, however, it helped prepare the nation psychologically and militarily for war.[37]

Essentially, the isolationist arguments made by Capper, Nye, their congressional colleagues, and the residents in the Great Plains who supported them centered on fears of militarism and dictatorship akin to the situation prevailing under the Axis powers. Capper and his supporters warned that, in peacetime, military conscription would create a military society and erode basic freedoms that would be difficult to regain. Until Pearl Harbor these fears sustained the arguments of the isolationists in the region. Indeed, the opposition of Great Plains congressional representatives to the Selective Service Act serves as an example of isolationism in the Great Plains. This isolationist sentiment also can be traced through polling statistics. For example, during the twelve-week period when the House considered the Burke-Wadsworth Bill, the Gallup, Roper, and Cantril polls reported that American public opinion supported peacetime military conscription by margins ranging from 52.6 to 69 percent, but 90 percent of the Kansas congressional delegation opposed it. By doing so they reflected the views of their constituents, but not those of the country.[38]

In 1940, then, most Great Plains residents preferred either isolationism or neutrality that favored Britain. (The latter, of course, was not neutrality at all, but it still was not considered interventionism.) They agonized over the passage of the Selective Service Act and the extension of the draft by one vote a year later as well as the decision of Congress a month before Pearl Harbor to permit armed merchant vessels to carry cargoes directly to belligerent ports. They hoped for the best, all the while dreading the worst, portions of which seemingly came in ever-increasing doses. In August 1940, for example, Congress authorized the president to call the National Guard and other reserves to active federal duty for one year, and in early September President Roosevelt, by executive agreement, provided fifty overage destroyers to the British for rent-free bases from Newfoundland to British Guiana. During the presidential election that followed in November, the isolationists generally voted for Wendell Wilkie, the Republican presidential candidate, while the interventionists supported Roosevelt. The president used his victory to submit the Lend-Lease Bill to Congress in January 1941. He contended that the security of the United States could no longer be guaranteed by providing military supplies to the British on a cash-and-carry basis because the British needed more aid than they could afford. Now support would be increased by eliminating the matter of monetary sales. War materials would be loaned or leased to Britain, which would return those materials or pay for them after the war. Although Congress did not approve the Lend-Lease Act until March 1941, Great Plains men and women understood that such aid violated neutrality, but many supported it because it offered another chance to keep the nation out of war.[39]

When Roosevelt argued that the Lend-Lease Bill would contribute to the national defense, Capper adamantly spoke against it, and the response of the Kansas congressional delegation serves as an example of the remaining isolationist sentiment on the Great Plains. Capper, like his fellow Kansans in Congress, knew that the Lend-Lease Act would commit the United States to the survival of Britain, and six of the seven-member Kansas delegation in the House of Representatives opposed it. William P. Lambertson of Fairview called Lend-Lease the "most extraordinary, and in my opinion unconstitutional, delegation of legislative authority that has ever been proposed by any President in peacetime or wartime." If it was approved, he believed, the public would soon realize that "they have been stripped of their freedom and that they have been led as a blind-folded and deceived people step by step into war." For Lambertson, the Lend-Lease Bill provided "a complete pattern for a military dictatorship in this country just as perverted and arbitrary as any dictatorship existing anywhere in the world today." Clifford Hope argued that the new war in Europe "arose over matters concerning which we have heretofore assumed no responsibility and over which we have no control." He clearly expressed the view of the isolationists that the American people "do not want to make this our war." For Hope, the danger of the Lend-Lease Bill was clear. "In the end," he said, "the powers granted in this bill mean power to get us into the war. It is almost incomprehensible that such powers should be delegated by a legislative body in a democracy in peacetime." Representative Frank Carlson of Concordia charged, "It is the American people who will have to pay the bills incurred by this legislation. They will have to die on foreign soil and possibly on the battlefields of every continent if we are to police the entire world." Only John M. Houston, a Democrat from Wichita, supported the bill. After the House approved the Lend-Lease Bill by a vote of 260–165, Capper continued the isolationist attack in the Senate and pledged that he was "unilaterally opposed" to the bill, in part because it granted "unlimited dictatorial powers asked by President Roosevelt himself."[40]

The Lend-Lease Bill proved divisive in other Great Plains states. In Montana, for example, Senators Wheeler and Murray voiced opposing views. Wheeler called it the "New Deal's triple-A foreign policy" that would "plow under every fourth American boy." Senator Murray responded, saying that Wheeler made an "appeal to passion and hate." Wyoming's newspaper editors and citizens supported President Roosevelt's desires to aid Britain, and Senators Joseph C. O'Mahoney and Harry H. Schwartz and Representative John J. McIntyre, all three Democrats, supported the Lend-Lease Bill. O'Mahoney argued that it was "the most effective available means" to enable the United States to save, if not restore, European democracies. Senator Schwartz agreed, saying that all "needed boats, airships, guns, and other implements of war, farm products and other assistance" should be provided to Great Britain before time ran out.[41]

Other Great Plains isolationists, however, opposed the bill, including Senators Nye, whom *Time* magazine called the "U.S. Senate's most rabid isolationist," and Usher Burdick of North Dakota. In May Nye reaffirmed his opposition to President Roosevelt's foreign policy and his own commitment to isolationism when he told a home-state radio audience, "Put it down as a fundamental truth: If we get into this war it will not be because the President tried to keep us out." Without doubt many members of the House and Senate from the northern and central Great Plains states believed that they voiced the isolationist wishes of their constituents by voting nay on the Lend-Lease Bill, but the isolationists were not in the majority, either among the politicians or among their constituents. Ultimately, on March 8, the Senate approved the bill by a vote of 60–31. The House then agreed to forgo a conference committee and approved the Senate version by a tally of 317–71. Roosevelt signed the bill on March 11.[42]

By June 1941 Kansans retained a deep desire to avoid the conflict if possible. In contrast many Oklahomans favored aggressive action and participation if need be. The disjuncture in the public attitude toward the war can be traced to political differences. The Democratic Party ruled in Oklahoma, while the Republican Party dominated Kansas. Also, Kansans had voted for Franklin Delano Roosevelt in 1936, but they drifted back to the Republican Party during the following years. In 1937, when President Roosevelt indicated that a quarantine might be good for Japan, Kansans were shocked, but Oklahomans agreed. Kansans worried about America's increasing support for Britain; Oklahomans did not. Kansans were disturbed about the cash-and-carry provision of the Neutrality Act, but Oklahomans accepted it as good policy. During the 1940 presidential election Kansas supported the Republican nominee, Wendell Willkie. Oklahomans voted for Roosevelt. Texans, who supported Roosevelt and the Democratic Party, also favored aiding Great Britain immediately and worrying about the legality of such action later.[43]

Although many Great Plains residents supported Roosevelt's leadership, they hoped that his policies would keep the peace. When Russia joined the war after Germany attacked in June 1941, however, many Wyoming residents had difficulty supporting Lend-Lease aid for a Communist state, but the editor of the *Lander Daily Post* reminded readers, "Extension of aid does not mean that we endorse communism spread outside of Russia." Still, the people of Wyoming wanted to stay out of the conflict. If they were not ardent isolationists, they at least supported noninterventionist or neutral policies. In September 1941, after President Roosevelt authorized the navy to fire on German and Italian ships in waters under the protection of the United States if threatened, the *Wyoming State Tribune* assured readers that this policy would not necessarily lead to war since "the very word war does not mean what it used to mean." After German submarines torpedoed the U.S. destroyers *Kearny* and *Reuben James* off the coast of Iceland in October, isolationist sentiment in Wyoming largely disappeared. Congressman McIntyre reported polling showing that his constituents approved naval action to protect American interests and an expeditionary force "if necessary." By early November the editor of the *Sheridan Press* believed that war with Germany would come soon and wrote that the "arguments of the isolationists seem less and less realistic or repressive." On November 11, however, the *Casper Tribune-Herald* found public opinion still divided with a small group favoring isolation and a similar group supporting intervention. The third and largest group believed that "the emergency demands the delivery of war material to the Allies."[44]

The Japanese attack on Pearl Harbor quickly ended these divisions over foreign policy. December 7, 1941, found Capper in Topeka, and he missed voting on the war resolution against Japan. He informed the Senate, however, that he supported the declaration of war, and he pledged his support to the president. Capper, like the other Great Plains isolationists, had underestimated the Japanese threat, and the neutrality acts had proved insufficient to insulate the United States from world affairs. In the end idealism succumbed to harsh reality.[45]

News about Germany's attack on Poland arrived as the people of the Great Plains slept. In Kearney, Nebraska, the staff of the *Daily Hub* received phone calls at 2:00 a.m. telling them to report to the office in order to prepare an extra edition. At 1:45 a.m. radio station wow in Omaha, which had a United Press wire service line to Kearney, had received the news and informed the *Hub*. When the town awoke, word about the new European war created "mildly intense excitement" among the residents, an excitement that they expressed, in part, with a "buying panic" at local grocery stores.

Sugar, flour, navy beans, lard, and pork (the latter always in demand by the military because it was the only meat that could be easily preserved) quickly disappeared from grocery store shelves. Although food prices increased, Leonard Williams, the chairman of the Chamber of Commerce, did not believe the rise "exorbitant," and he did not foresee a food shortage. After several days hoarding decreased, food prices dropped to previous levels, and the "war market" ended. Even so, the renewed war clearly frightened many Great Plains residents, and some began preparing for worse news.[46]

Indeed, the possibility of America's entry into the war remained on their minds. A Gallup poll among Amarillo residents showed that 88 percent favored military action if Germany attacked Canada, while 85 percent favored a military response if Germany struck Cuba, the Panama Canal, or any country within fifteen hundred miles of the United States. These percentages clearly favored the use of the army and navy in case of an invasion of the Western Hemisphere by a European power, and only Germany, they believed, had that capability. These local polls showed greater support for military action than did national polls, which showed 73 and 72 percent of the population, respectively, favoring the use of the military in the two invasion cases outlined above. Amarillo residents also emphatically believed that the United States should uphold the Monroe Doctrine by aiding any South American country attacked by Germany. In this case, too, they favored the use of military force at a higher rate, 69 percent, than the national average, 53 percent. Amarilloans apparently saw a clear danger to the United States if Germany moved militarily against Canada or the South American nations. Yet everyone in the plains understood that the time was fast approaching when "isolationists, interventionists and America first fans and the hopelessly bewildered" would need to make a decision that would affect them and their country.[47]

Many states now organized defense councils to coordinate all efforts regarding industry, agriculture, and natural resources. In Kansas, Governor Ratner believed the international situation to be as dangerous as that during the Revolutionary and Civil wars, and he urged the public to support the national defense program without equivocation and political bickering. Great Plains residents also received chilling word from Colonel Edward I. Wilbur, the acting civilian defense director for the Seventh Army Corps, when he admonished them to be alert even though they lived in the plains. If war with Germany came, he warned, the enemy might choose to strike the most weakly defended region. If so, the Great Plains would be open to a "wave of incendiaries" against local industrial plants and grain elevators. City officials in Cheyenne took such warnings seriously. Fire Chief Ed Taylor reported that a response to an aerial bombardment of the city would require twelve to fifteen 1,000-gallon-per-minute pumper trucks and six to eight ladder trucks with life nets to deal with the resulting fires and rescues. But Cheyenne had only two 750-gallon-per-minute pumpers and one 1,000-gallon pumper on order, and the city could not afford hundreds of thousands of dollars to purchase the needed equipment. In Dallas officials also worried about aerial bombing, in part because the fire department was not prepared to fight thermite and phosphorous firebombs. Cotton warehouses and oil tanks made the potential threat even more serious because both were highly inflammable. Critics demanded a plan of action, and Dallas officials developed contingencies to safeguard the waterworks and sewage facilities to prevent sabotage. One observer noted the sense of public apprehension, saying, "Sabotage work in this section of the country is not believed at all beyond the bounds of probability by those who have given the matter serious study."[48]

By autumn 1941 the isolationists had clearly lost support. Most Great Plains residents favored aid to Britain short of war. In Montague, Texas, when William H. (Alfalfa Bill) Murray, the former governor of Oklahoma, spoke on behalf of the America First Committee and charged the Roosevelt administration with hurrying the nation into war, he received heckling, not applause. When the county sheriff rose at the conclusion of Murray's address to say that he favored all-out support for Hitler's enemies, the crowd cheered. A month later Governor John E. Miles of New Mexico urged the people of his state to think about their responsibilities for national defense. Everyone sensed that war would soon be upon them whether they favored it or not. Across the Great Plains the FBI also began holding training programs for law enforcement officers to provide instruction about espionage, sabotage, subversive activities, air raids, black outs, looting, the downing of enemy aircraft, gas contamination, and evacuations in time of war.[49]

In early December 1941 many people of the Great Plains assumed that war had become a certainty. But others, such as Wyoming's Senator H. H. Schwartz, believed otherwise. He reassured his constituents, saying, "I don't think there will be any war yet for some time. . . . We will continue to freeze Japanese assets . . . to prevent them from obtaining war materials . . . and they will have to abandon their 'new order' in East Asia. I think Hitler will fold up next year. . . . Germany is going to crack up for sure." The *Sheridan Press* printed its December 7 edition before news of the Japanese attack on Pearl Harbor. The editor, too, expressed cautious optimism that the United States could avoid war, writing, "Barring the occurrence of an inflammatory incident involving representatives of the United States and Japan, either intentionally or accidentally, it seems hardly likely that actual war between the two countries will break out in the near future."[50]

Of course, optimism and discussions about isolationism, interventionism, internationalism, and neutrality could not prevent war from coming. Even so, the people of the Great Plains were surprised when it came, not with an invasion by Germany, but with a Japanese attack on Hawaii, far away in the Pacific Ocean. On December 7, William DeLoach in West Texas heard the news, and he wrote in his diary, "Japanese blow up." Two days later he confided, "The war news is real bad. Japan is still trying to slip up on us again. I think all Japs that is not proven good ought to be rounded up and cut their heads off." Martha Rohrke, a seventy-one-year-old widow in Hoskins, Nebraska, confided to her diary, "We are all so sad about our U.S.A. being in war with Japan. It seems the whole world is filled with hate and all the world is involved." A reporter for the *Casper Tribune-Herald* wrote for her Tuesday column, "All Sunday afternoon and through the night, we sat at our radios, stunned by the stark, horrible news coming to us over the air. By Monday, we had our mixed emotions pretty well in hand. We're still concerned, plenty worried, but we're not quite so frightened and we're carrying on."[51]

Across the Great Plains people responded with shock, bitterness, and a desire for retaliation and revenge. Isolationism, noninterventionism, and neutrality had not protected the country. On Monday morning, December 8, they listened to President Roosevelt ask Congress for a declaration of war against Japan. In Kansas Governor Ratner asked the mayors of thirty-six cities and towns to place their municipal airports on wartime emergency status and assign extra guards around the perimeters to prevent sabotage. In Wyoming Governor Lester C. Hunt also urged the operators of essential industries to guard against sabotage. Officials in many cities across the Great Plains quickly found something to watch. In Cheyenne United Air Lines officials tripled the guards around the airline's facilities, provided employees with identification badges, and withdrew visiting privileges. The state highway superintendent ordered a twenty-four-hour watch on all bridges, and the mayor of Casper placed guards around the waterworks. Near Oklahoma City authorities closed Lake Overholser to all fishing and boating and placed armed guards toting shotguns, rifles, and pistols in lookout towers and on patrols to safeguard the dam, and the water department cleared all brush from below the reservoir to eliminate possible hiding places for saboteurs. City workers put up a barbed wire fence around the water filtration plant, and armed guards patrolled the perimeter. Authorities also blocked all roads leading into the Bluff Creek water project, allowing only authorized personnel to proceed, since the sabotage of the local water facilities seem a natural move for the Japanese. Although cynics questioned such actions, Oklahoma City officials replied that no one expected the Japanese to attack Pearl Harbor. On December 8, news of air raid sirens blaring in San Francisco reinforced the sense of danger in the Great Plains.[52]

At the University of Oklahoma and Oklahoma A&M, students listened to President Roosevelt ask Congress for a declaration of war against Japan. At the field house on the Norman campus, where three thousand students gathered to hear the address, one observer noted, "There was no energetic outbreak and not even all the students applauded." One reporter noted that on "Monday the university campus was tense and serious . . . in marked contrast to the day war was declared in April, 1917." The students, like other Great Plains residents, knew that Japan had attacked the United States. The seriousness of the situation gave them pause, but they knew that the foreign policy choices for the United States had become remarkably simplified—attack or surrender.[53]

In Colorado Governor Ralph L. Carr gave the deathblow to any lingering sense of isolationism when he said, "We have been attacked. Our boys have been murdered. Our very future is at stake." Great Plains men and women knew that he was right, and the declaration of war on the United States by Germany and Italy four days after the Pearl Harbor attack reinforced their conviction. They felt less clear about what the next year and the war would bring. One thing was certain, however; the people of the Great Plains were no longer isolationists.[54]

TWO | The Work of War

The summer of 1939 brought both fear and opportunity to residents of the Great Plains. Europe hurtled toward war, and no one seemed able to prevent the coming violence. Most Great Plains residents hoped to avoid it, but nearly everyone saw the economic advantages for themselves as well as for their state, region, and nation. Although in May 1940 President Roosevelt asked Congress for $1 billion to build fifty thousand planes, the United States did not enter a wartime economy until mid-1941, by which time Congress had appropriated $60 billion for defense spending. Moreover, the conversion of peacetime to wartime industries did not proceed at full pace for another year nationwide, and it had no management until 1943, when the Office of War Mobilization was created. Even so, many Great Plains businessmen had begun giving thought to a wartime economy before Germany struck Poland. Soon the term *defense industries* became part of the common parlance. Plains residents understood that the federal government would set the pace and parameters of this economy.[1]

In late June 1939 South Dakotans anticipated the development of huge manganese deposits in the central portion of the state if war came and if Congress appropriated money under the pending Strategic War Materials Act. Steel production for defense required manganese, and South Dakota had large fields, a cash-poor population, and a public willingness to bring workers into the state to stimulate the multiplier effects of a new mining economy. Opportunity beckoned, but only until it was learned that South Dakota had low-grade manganese and a form different from that used for steelmaking. In the Black Hills residents also anticipated the possibility of opening closed mines as well as digging low-grade ores such as iron, zinc, and lead, the prices of each having increased rapidly after Germany invaded Poland.[2]

The new European war also brought increased railroad traffic and employment. In Wyoming freight traffic shipped over the Union Pacific Railroad increased from 12 billion ton miles in 1940 to 22 billion ton miles in 1941, with annual increases during the course of the war. Passenger miles also increased on the railroad, from 39 million in 1940 to 86 million in 1945, when approximately nine thousand employees collected a monthly payroll of $2.6 million. The Colorado and Southern-Burlington lines also added men, and local trucking companies reported an increase in business. Soon after Germany crossed the Polish frontier the manager of the Cheyenne Credit Bureau predicted a good economy for the duration of the war.[3]

Wyoming, however, gained little manufacturing during World War II. It garnered fewer than five hundred new workers for manufacturing jobs between April 1940 and June 1943 and only nine hundred by the end of the war. In 1941, when a special train of officials crossed the country to inform businesses how to secure government contracts, it did not stop in Wyoming. Congressman John J. McIntyre observed that it passed through the state "like a cat through a dog show." A year later Senator H. H. Schwartz called federal attention to Wyoming's coal and water resources and criticized the government for ignoring the state when it came to defense contracts, saying, "This power could be used if through some fortuitous circumstance, the Office of Production Management and the War Department should be able to locate the state of Wyoming as a part of the union of states situated in an area not accessible to enemy attack." In many respects Wyoming, like most Great Plains states, was left out of the wartime economic windfall for businesses and individuals alike. The state had little hope of attracting war industries because of high freight rates, inadequate labor supply, and insufficient power, water, and capital, and most federal contracts went elsewhere, although United Air Lines developed a bomber modifica-

tion center in Cheyenne during 1942. There, United employed sixteen hundred workers on three shifts, half of them women.[4]

Like Wyoming, other Great Plains states failed to benefit from
the rush of defense industry contracts. In November 1940 Governor
John Moses traveled to Washington DC to promote North Dakota.
He particularly sought waiver of the "200-mile rule" imposed by
the army to prevent for security reasons defense contracts from being let to manufacturers and industrialists within that range of a
foreign border. Governor Moses stressed the abundance of skilled
and semiskilled workers, few labor difficulties, lignite for the extrac-
tion of nitric acid for explosives, and water. He particularly wanted
munitions and anhydrous ammonia plants and an activated carbon
facility to make filters for gas masks. By April 1941, however, North
Dakota still had not received any defense work. North Dakotans
sensed that they had been bypassed and would fail to profit from
the war. South Dakota and Montana experienced similar difficulties,
with contracts that totaled only $128,000 and $12,000, respectively,
by spring.[5]

In the central plains, the Kansas Industrial Development Commission increased its efforts to lure businesses to the state, particularly
"farm chemurgy," that is, manufacturing and industrial production
firms that produced goods developed from agricultural commodities
in order to make the "industrial sun of the state as bright as its agricultural luster." In Kansas Governor Payne Ratner appealed to President Roosevelt to locate defense industries in the state, arguing that
its men would be lured away if war work remained confined in the
East. Defense industries would balance agriculture, which remained
the state's most important industry, and they would "establish an
industrial future" that would greatly relieve the perennial problem
of low incomes, which resulted from depressed agricultural prices,
which resulted from surplus production and limited markets.[6]

On the southern plains, Texans anticipated increased payrolls
from war-related industries, particularly oil and agriculture. In Amarillo, the Chamber of Commerce aggressively sought a munitions
factory, an airplane manufacturer, and a military training camp, and
the members were only slightly disappointed when federal officials

informed them that the city could not have everything. In Denver, on the western edge of the plains, businessmen wanted a leading airplane manufacturer, and they planned to send a "hard-headed" financier to Washington to discuss the possibility of constructing such a factory with congressmen. They wanted at least five thousand workers and an $8.5 million payroll to help the city contribute to the national defense. Chambers of commerce in other Great Plains cities had similar visions.[7]

Contracts caught nearly everyone's attention. By June 1940 the federal government had approved a host of defense contracts across the Great Plains—136 in Texas; 37 in Colorado; 24 in Kansas; 18 in Oklahoma; and 1 in New Mexico—and each plant needed workers. As the federal government prepared to authorize even more war industry contracts, the Hall-Aluminum Aircraft Corporation in Dallas anticipated $100 million in orders for bombers and fighter planes and the construction of an $8 million factory employing five thousand workers. The president of the Chamber of Commerce estimated that this plant would add twenty-five thousand residents to the city. Just as important, he observed, "It is the opening wedge in the big-time industrial development of the Southwest—our first concrete evidence of the industrial decentralization impetus coming out of the national preparedness program." When North American Aviation announced plans to build a $7 million factory to employ twelve thousand skilled workers in order to fill a $72.8 million contract, the door seemed to close on the hard times of the Great Depression for Dallas.[8]

In Nebraska, the state Advertising Commission voted to spend part of its $50,000 allocation to lure war industries to the state, and it pitched Nebraska as "unexcelled" for railroad and highway transportation as well as natural gas, low taxation, and intelligent workers, particularly in the "strategic" Platte Valley. Newspaper editors assured Nebraskans that the isolated Platte Valley could be protected by Fort Warren, Wyoming, near Cheyenne, and Fort Robinson, in western Nebraska, if a hostile power gained a foothold in Mexico or Canada. Soon, federal contracts arrived in Nebraska for planes, small arms, and ammunition.[9]

FIGURE 1. Wichita became a major city in the Great Plains for the construction of bombers. The aircraft industry employed thousands of workers and created an economic boom for the city. This assembly line at Beech Aircraft shows the large-scale, mass production that helped defeat the Axis powers. (Kansas State Historical Society)

Overall, however, by 1940 military plane production still languished, taking only 8.7 percent of the combined appropriations for the army and the navy. The German attack on France in May and its fall in June 1940, however, caused President Roosevelt to seek rapid expansion of the armaments industry, and the Reconstruction Finance Corporation began loaning money for expansion of aircraft manufacturing. Soon, the aviation industry "boomed" in Wichita, Tulsa, Oklahoma City, Dallas, and Fort Worth despite an alleged "curtain of secrecy enforced by governmental agencies for the protection of military information." Tool-and-die and specialty machine shops also expanded production to supply the aircraft plants and increase their payrolls and profits. During the summer the War Department targeted Wichita for the production of B-29 bombers, and the aircraft firms of Boeing and Beechcraft gained $11.2 million in army and navy contracts. By autumn Boeing, Beech, and Cessna had orders for $53 million in airplanes, and these firms anticipated new contracts totaling $121.5 million. As the federal government appealed for speed, the plants operated nearly twenty-four hours a day. City officials expected the employment of more than 7,000 new workers within a year, which would cause a population increase of 20,000–30,000 new residents in the greater metropolitan area. By early October the population projections for the city alone had been revised to reach 120,000 by the end of the year, up from the then-current population of approximately 115,000. Payrolls for old and new residents meant greater "spending power" in the Wichita area. Some observers believed that the further development of the aircraft industry was "assured for years to come." The war, then, offered not only economic opportunity but also a chance to fundamentally and permanently restructure the state's economic base.[10]

By mid-October 1940, Kansas led the Great Plains states in army munitions and supply contracts, but it had received only 5.7 percent of the federal money allocated for defense contracts among all forty-eight states. Overall, Kansas paled in comparison to California, which led the nation with $209.3 million in defense contracts, or 40 percent of the $2.1 billion allocated thus far. Kansans were happy to have the contracts for the aircraft companies, but the state could offer little besides airplanes to the army because, like the other Great Plains states, it did not have arms factories, steel mills, or engine plants. Still, Kansas had space and a skilled workforce, and Boeing planned to expand production to build one Stearman training plane every ninety minutes.[11]

Only skilled workers need apply, and the industry urged the un-skilled to take a training course before they migrated to Wichita. For the moment most of the aircraft jobs went to men because the companies hired workers with experience. The arrival of a female workforce would wait more than a year. By the end of 1940 the Kansas State Employment Service had placed more than fifty thou-sand workers in defense industries. W. B. Harrison, the president of the Union National Bank in Wichita, reflected, "The entire com-munity is vibrant with new life and activity." He anticipated that the economy would boom through 1941 and perhaps a bit longer. When the European war ended, he believed, Wichita would be an "industrial city," which meant "prosperity of a sound type."[12]

By late December 1940 Denver also welcomed the news that the federal government would build a small arms and ammunition plant, which the Remington Arms Company would operate, west of the city. Observers expected the Denver Ordnance Plant to receive $100 million in contracts, provide ten thousand jobs, and ease, if not solve, the area's employment problem. On January 4, 1941, the War Department announced plans to purchase land, construct buildings, and buy equipment. Managers anticipated hiring two thousand women once the plant became operational. All skilled workers would be hired through unions to prevent labor trouble. The contractors and unions agreed to a wage of $0.72 per hour for unskilled and $1.65 per hour for skilled workers, and both groups understood that no strikes would occur during construction. Few workers or managers worried about money until union electricians, steamfitters, and plumbers held out from signing contracts, demanding double overtime, and ironworkers sought $22.88 per day for weekend and holiday work.[13]

While both sides talked, construction continued, and no paralyzing strike similar to the stoppage of production lines by the United Automobile Workers in Detroit in the spring of 1941 impeded completion of the plant. When production peaked with nearly twenty thousand employees, mostly unskilled, who worked three shifts during the summer of 1943, Denverites were certain that hard times had ended. Similarly in Nebraska, on February 14, 1941, the Glenn L. Martin Company signed a government contract to build an aircraft assembly plant at Fort Crook near Bellevue and Omaha. This government-owned plant would cost $10 million and employ as many as twenty thousand workers. Every month the Martin Company would assemble one hundred B-26 medium bombers whose destinations were the British and the American military.[14]

With the passage of the Lend-Lease Act in March 1941, President Roosevelt committed the nation to becoming the "great arsenal of democracy." Federal dollars began flowing to defense industries, particularly for weapons, aircraft, and munitions. The Roosevelt administration asked Congress for $7 billion in Lend-Lease spending and $13.7 billion for the army and navy during 1941, an increase from the $2.2 billion appropriated for the military in 1940. Much of this spending flooded into the large industrial centers. As a result, unemployment quickly decreased to less than 10 percent, aided by the draft, and the economic hard times of the Great Depression began to disappear with the arrival of regular and substantial paychecks. City and state chambers of commerce as well as congressmen and senators continued to lobby for defense contracts for their towns and states though the summer and fall of 1941, driven by the rapidly degenerating relations with Germany and Japan that increasingly made the prospect of war a certainty. The Great Plains, however, remained largely overlooked, in part because it did not have much industrial or manufacturing infrastructure for a wartime economy. The people of the Great Plains wanted their share, but much of the federal largesse went elsewhere.[15]

By 1941 Nebraskans complained about federal neglect. The residents of Hastings, Grand Island, and Kearney particularly groused when the military selected Wahoo as the location for an ordnance plant, and many lobbied to have it moved farther west into their area. By November Senator George Norris became so frustrated with the squabbling over the few defense contracts gained for Nebraska that he complained, "If the Nebraska people are going to object every time a site is located, because it is not located in some other place, then we ought to . . . ask the government not to do anything in the way of national defense projects in the state of Nebraska." Norris's admonishment had no effect on Nebraskans, who continued to complain that they had been left out of all plans to make the nation ready for war. Greed mixed with patriotism prevailed.[16]

Once the United States officially joined the war, however, military needs expanded rapidly, and towns that had been bypassed with defense contracts received new opportunities to participate in the wartime economy. In central Nebraska, for example, business leaders and city officials welcomed the announcement by Senator Norris that the federal government planned to build a munitions plant between

FIGURE 2. The naval ammunition depot at Hastings boosted the local economy, but a large increase in population pitted outsiders against locals. Race relations between African Americans and whites deteriorated. Segregation, price gouging, and discrimination would not abate until peace came and most of the workers and servicemen and women moved away. (Nebraska State Historical Society, RG 0809:47)

Grand Island, Hastings, and Kearney. Yet, while delighted with the news, Kearney residents worried that the plant would be built east of Grand Island and, therefore, diminish the economic benefits for them. But, when Grand Island received the nod, residents reveled in the news that construction costs might reach $28 million and payrolls $100,000 per day, seven days per week. The location had adequate electric power, good transportation, and an able workforce, and was sufficiently isolated from large populated areas should explosive accidents occur. Almost immediately, the Grand Island munitions plant became known as the Cornhusker Ordnance Plant. Construction began on March 24, 1942, with the first bomb poured in mid-November. Observers anticipated the arrival of ten thousand workers in the city of sixteen thousand. The navy also announced approval for an ammunition depot near Hastings. This ordnance plant would cost $45 million and serve as an assembly plant and storage depot.[17]

At the same time, Nebraskans envied the success of Kansas, which, in late 1941, optimists were calling an "industrial giant" for securing defense contracts. Kansans had good reason to relish their newly improved economic conditions. Soon, the Sunflower State ranked sixteenth in national defense contracts and garnered five defense contract dollars for every dollar generated by "normal" manufacturing. In September Governor Payne Ratner told the members of the Kansas League of Municipalities, "Even if we must make nuisances of ourselves, we should make it so hot in Washington that they will give us more defense work, if it is only to keep us quiet." Only Nevada had a higher ratio of defense to nondefense business. Oklahoma was nearly as fortunate and received defense contracts worth nearly three times the value of all manufactured articles in 1939. Those in the know said that the best possibilities for securing war industries depended on contacts with the federal departments that dealt with ordnance and the air corps. Most ordnance projects, they thought, required at least five thousand workers and a location near a densely populated area, while aviation usually required space for the establishment of army airfields and the employment of several thousand workers plus military personnel. Money could be made given the right contacts.[18]

In late 1940 the Consolidated Aircraft Corporation in Tulsa had received military contracts for the production of four-engine bombers, and in February 1941 Oklahomans rejoiced over the news that the Douglas Aircraft Company would operate government-built plants in Tulsa and Oklahoma City. At that time the War Department authorized the expenditure of $16 million for an army air corps depot that would employ twenty-five hundred civilian mechanics and aircraft workers in Oklahoma City. The construction jobs required to build the facility were an added benefit. Oklahoma City also received $1 million to construct a dock for seaplanes at nearby Lake Overholser. By early January 1942 Oklahoma had received $250 million from defense contracts, particularly for the Chouteau powder plant, the bomber factory in Tulsa, and the Midwest Air Depot in Oklahoma City (originally the Oklahoma City Air Depot, later Tinker Field), while the businesses involved with the production of aviation gasoline, meat, flour, zinc, cement, and cotton for munitions worked at full capacity to fill government orders. In contrast, by the end of the year North Dakota had secured only $6 million in war contracts. The largest, for $1.5 million, went to Swimaster Manufacturing to produce inflatable life belts, while smaller manufacturers scattered across the state made canvas covers for shovels and guns and ammunition pouches as well as machine parts.[19]

By early January 1943 officials in Oklahoma City expected the construction of the Douglas plant to cost $20 million and employ twenty-seven thousand workers for the building of cargo planes. The estimated annual payroll ranged from $35 to $40 million. The poverty-stricken, windblown Dust Bowl and Depression days seemed long ago and far away. By January 1943 North Dakotans had also received approximately $13.5 million in defense and construction contracts. Although federal funding still lagged, state officials expressed gratitude for this good fortune. Still, small-scale manufacturers had great difficulty getting federal contracts because military procurement officials preferred working with a relatively small number of large-scale corporations. As a result many businessmen and women worried that the plains states did not receive their fair share of the defense contracts. One contemporary remarked, "The states with the best string-pullers are profiting." Since Oklahomans had the propensity to change their congressmen regularly, they lacked committee seniority and, ultimately, lost defense contracts because of their weak influence in Congress. Moreover, Oklahoma's congressmen jealously guarded their districts and failed to work on behalf of Oklahomans statewide to garner war industry contracts.[20]

In South Dakota the editor of the *Rapid City Daily Journal* observed, "The lack of specific defense industries in the state is something for congressmen and chambers of commerce to cry about." But he saw a silver lining to that black cloud. He contended, "The bigger the defense boom gets . . . the harder will be the fall when the present emergency is over. Because there is no big influx of labor into the state, there will be no serious unemployment problem later. There will be no acute housing situation and no serious dislocation of rents." This view can be attributed to a sour grapes mentality, but it rang true.[21]

FIGURE 3. At Tinker Field, near Oklahoma City, these workers repaired a bomber. This fast-paced repair work became known as a "beehive industry" as workers swarmed over the planes. (Western History Collections, University of Oklahoma Libraries)

Although agriculture remained the major industry on the Great Plains, during the spring of 1941 industrial production and payrolls increased rapidly in the cities where defense contracts gave the local economies a new life. In Wichita, for example, the aircraft industries anticipated adding three hundred employees per week to their payrolls. Only the increasing inability of the plane manufacturers to find trained, that is, skilled workers slowed the hiring process. Wichita officials conservatively estimated the employment of nearly 12,000 men and women in the aircraft industry by the autumn (in reality that estimate was surpassed by nearly 2,000 in mid-September). With plane production estimated at $100 million annually, the importance of the wartime aviation industry for this city of 140,000 proved "staggering." Residents did not want to call their economic bonanza a "boom" for superstitious reasons that might invite contraction, if not collapse, but they began referring to Wichita as the

"Air Capital." By June 1941 new contracts for the building of B-17 Flying Fortress bombers added to the luster of Wichita as the aviation hub of the nation.[22]

By Pearl Harbor federal officials considered Wichita one of the "hottest" defense industry boom cities. Using 1937 for an employment index of 100, manufacturing employment there reached 324, second only to San Diego. Between October 1, 1940, and September 1941 employment in Wichita's aircraft industry increased from 3,500 to 14,500 workers, or more than 400 percent in less than twelve months. Prior to 1941 Wichita had been primarily an agricultural service center, but it now held $326 million in defense contracts, mostly for aircraft production. On December 9, 1941, two days after the Japanese attack on Pearl Harbor, President Roosevelt announced a seven-day workweek for all war industries in order to increase production. As a result Great Plains men and women did not need to look beyond the region to find employment, although the lure of California always proved compelling and irresistible.[23]

Although Congress established the Small War Plants Corporation in June 1942 to aid small-scale manufacturers in pursuit of military contracts, it could not overcome military preferences and the production ability of large-scale corporations. As a result the Great Plains continued to be overlooked. The people of the region considered military contracts to be their opportunity to gain economic stability and security, but the federal government and military procurement officers wanted rapid expansion and production, and, with few exceptions, they did not believe that the Great Plains could deliver.[24]

Still, by the end of 1944 defense industry contracts had revitalized the economy of the Great Plains. In Kansas, for example, these contracts totaled $3.4 billion. These funds did not include expenditures for the Olathe Naval Air Station, the synthetic rubber factory under construction in Topeka, food contracts, and contracts under $50,000. With the average national distribution at $1,507 per capita for defense industry contracts, the Kansas average of $1,937 ranked the Sunflower State tenth in the nation. Still, only 43 of the state's 110 counties shared the spending, with Sedgwick leading with $1.8 billion in contracts, primarily for Wichita's aircraft industry. Kansas ranked thirteenth in the cost of military facilities, fifteenth in the cost of industrial facilities, and eighth in the cost of aircraft facilities. Only California, Michigan, New York, Ohio, New Jersey, Connecticut, and Indiana exceeded Wichita in the value of aircraft plants. Almost every military and industrial facility in Kansas was a direct outgrowth of the war.[25]

In the Great Plains subcontractors also received great economic benefit from federal defense-related contracts, particularly those that sold welding supplies, food, office equipment, paper boxes, and canteen items as well as plumbing and heating supplies, hardware, gas and oil, cement, and building materials. During the last half of 1940, for example, Kansas received $97.9 million awarded to seventy-two primary defense contractors in twenty towns. No one knew the number of subcontractors from across the state who tapped into that funding, but the major contractors helped spread the wealth. In Omaha the Goodyear Tire and Rubber Company and the Chrysler Corporation subcontracted to make parts for the bombers produced by the Martin Company, and officials in New Mexico worked to speed the subcontracting process in the state in order to reach full employment. The multiplier effect of federal defense contracts seemingly knew no end, and those contracts substantially increased industrial construction, production, and services in the Great Plains.[26]

Equally important, small machine shops that did not have defense contracts faced closing for a lack of materials. In order to remain open small-scale businesses needed subcontracts. Large-scale manufacturers with capital and credit seemed to acquire all the defense contracts. Some observers thought that the "pinch" of materials, such as sheet metal, might last as long as a decade, even if the war ended within the year. The fortunate seemed to get bigger. In September 1941 the Oklahoma Office of Price Management estimated that subcontractors held $50 million in contracts. By December Oklahoma's defense contracts jumped from $20 to $300 million. For others, however, time seemed to be running out. The have-nots wanted in.[27]

Skilled workers also wanted jobs, and they had the first opportunities for war industry employment in the cities of the Great Plains. By summer 1940 a host of vocational-training programs, some with federal support, emerged in the states. In Colorado the state director for vocational education announced plans to aid the defense industry by providing federally funded training for workers who had previous industrial experience, such as welders, riveters, and sheet metal workers, many of whom relied on the Works Progress Administration for support. In the second phase individuals without skills from previous industrial employment would receive training for specific positions, such as operating precision grinding machines and making shell cases. This training would be provided through the vocational schools and state colleges and "open many fine opportunities for young men who are uncertain about their future." Similar vocational-training programs soon developed in the other Great Plains states. In North Dakota, for example, during the summer of 1940 workers who had previous experience as aircraft mechanics, machinists, welders, auto mechanics, and electricians received training at Wahpeton. Nevertheless, because North Dakota did not have an aircraft manufacturing plant, after training the young men were recruited by eastern companies and left the state, five hundred alone following the harvest in 1941.[28]

Increasingly, colleges and universities provided training for war industry jobs. Amarillo College, for example, offered night classes for specialty positions in engine repair and sheet metal work. In Wichita, training classes expanded, particularly for sheet metal work and welding, often with round-the-clock classes. The Japanese attack ended any fears that capable men and women would not be able to find employment. Federally funded job-training programs for positions as machine tool operators and welders went on a twenty-four-hour, seven-day schedule in Denver, Omaha, Stillwater, and other towns and cities.[29]

Vocational training in the schools and by agencies as well as within industries proved popular, and the War Manpower Commission (WMC) supported it throughout the war. By Pearl Harbor the Labor Division of the National Defense Advisory Commission effectively mobilized the support of labor, government, industry, and private institutions for vocational-training programs and facilities. Training, however, involved more than preparing the workforce for wartime jobs. In Kansas, the Industrial Development Commission held training sessions to "school" local manufacturers about the procedures for selling "defense products" to the army and navy. The training targeted small-scale manufacturers who could not compete with large-scale industries in the bidding process but who could gain lucrative subcontracts, particularly for food processing and meat-packing products.[30]

By August 1942 the labor pool had diminished considerably in many parts of the Great Plains, as it had across the nation. In Colorado Governor Ralph L. Carr believed that the "manpower reservoir" would be exhausted within six months, and he urged a coordinated effort by state and national agencies to train the handicapped and men and women as old as sixty for defense industry jobs. In mid-October the Works Progress Administration began closing projects in Oklahoma because the defense industries scattered across the state enabled people on the relief rolls to find work. Some fifteen thousand people trained for jobs in the defense industries in Oklahoma City, particularly for the Douglas aircraft assembly plant, and the U.S. Employment Service placed one thousand workers monthly in the city between January and October 1942.[31]

Men and women no longer searched for jobs as in the past. Now, jobs, in the form of employers, sought them. As the draft took the young men, and as war industries attracted women and men ineligible for military service, mining jobs went unfilled. By late summer 1943 Governor L. C. Hunt of Wyoming believed that the shortage of coal miners was critical and that winter supplies for industries and homes might be exhausted. By October the labor shortage proved so great in Dallas that the WMC prevented companies operating there from receiving additional government contracts because it doubted that the orders could be filled. Throughout the war the draft-induced male labor shortage caused problems for small-scale businesses. In many companies only elderly men and women remained.[32]

Despite the relative prosperity in the Great Plains during World War II, businessmen often resented the high wages paid by the federal government (e.g., at the naval ammunition depot in Hastings) because they were unable or unwilling to compete. In 1944, for example, the navy paid civilian workers a base wage of $0.74 per hour for a fifty-four- to sixty-four-hour week and time and a half for overtime, with sick leave and vacation time, among other benefits. In town, clerical and sales workers earned about $0.50 per hour from private employers, and they wanted pay equal to that earned at the depot. In Grand Island merchants also complained that workers initially carned about $0.50 per hour at the Cornhusker Ordnance Plant but received an increase to $0.70 an hour when the government moved to ensure pay-scale equity across the nation for federal employees. In town workers received only $0.30 per hour. Businessmen in Grand Island responded by extending their hours into the evening to capitalize on the disposable income from high wartime wages, but others complained throughout the war that they could not compete for workers with the ordnance plant.[33]

While workers found jobs, drew large paychecks, and deposited their earnings, they often experienced problems with labor unions. In the aircraft factories, for example, the union shop prevailed with federal support. Workers often found that job announcements by subcontractors required the potential employee to join the union. Many common laborers had to pay fees of $16.65 up front, but some unions permitted annual membership fees of $50 for carpenters and $100 for ironworkers, electricians, and pipe fitters to be paid through installments, after a down payment. A receipt for payment of membership served as a work permit. Monthly dues took more from paychecks. Plains men and women, whose familiarity with unions extended no farther than reading about strikes in the newspapers, often preferred to avoid association with them, but they had no choice. Labor unions essentially functioned as employment agencies. Those seeking work in the major defense industries, where the unions controlled the shop floor, did not get hired if they refused to join. In the defense industries the right to work meant the freedom to join the union.[34]

Unions in the major industries often did not emphasize national unity, giving more attention to local wages, hours, and benefits. In

Oklahoma, for example, unions affiliated with the American Federation of Labor (AFL) refused to honor membership in the Congress of Industrial Organizations (CIO), and a bitter contest between the two labor organizations developed in Tulsa over the control of workers at the Douglas Aircraft Company. At the Douglas plant, union workers also walked off the job for a day in December 1942 to protest regulations that prohibited them from working more than twenty hours of overtime per week.[35]

Nationwide work stoppages and strikes in the railroad and mining industries received scant sympathy among the American public. By 1943 South Dakota lawmakers, perhaps anticipating the Taft-Hartley Act of 1947, passed what may have been the first "right-to-work" law in the nation, and Colorado approved a similar statute about that time. Both limited union activities in the workplace. Early in 1943 the Kansas legislature also grappled with a bill that imposed stringent regulations on labor unions. It required unions to register with the state corporation commission and submit financial reports. It also banned sit-down strikes, secondary boycotts, jurisdictional strikes, political contributions, and monopolization of the labor market, that is, closed and union shops. In Texas the state legislature also passed legislation regulating the assessment of union initiation fees. The fight between the CIO and the AFL over worker memberships at the North American Aviation plant near Dallas gave many antiunion state legislators pause because they feared the collective-bargaining power of unions at a time when the nation's existence seemed at stake. When General Lewis B. Hershey, the director of the Selective Service System, canceled worker deferments and threatened immediate induction into the army, the North American strike ended.[36]

Managers, however, had little influence regarding interunion rivalry because the Wagner Act of 1935 gave workers the right to organize and bargain collectively. In Dallas, when the CIO's International Union of Automobile, Aircraft, and Agricultural Implement Workers won the vote, the workers demanded a collective-bargaining agreement and presented their demands to North American. Workers at the Globe Aircraft Corporation in Fort Worth, however, cast an 80 percent vote favoring representation by the International Association of Machinists, an affiliate of the AFL. In June 1942 the National War Labor Board announced the "maintenance-of-membership" rule, which provided that any employer who operated under a union contract would automatically enroll new employees in that union unless the worker requested otherwise. By requiring employers to support a union shop, the rule defused many potential labor problems, but the unions also gave up power in deference to the state.[37]

In mid-February 1943 manufacturers with government contracts breathed a sigh of relief when the War Labor Board for the Southwest ruled that it would not hear any cases involving a work stoppage over wage disputes. Some plains residents, however, believed that the most "irresponsible" unions were associated with industries where confrontations with management had existed for many years, and they realized that labor would have a voice in postwar manufacturing. Most workers on the Great Plains did not care because they were not enamored with unions. The workers in the Great Plains defense industries did not have a tradition of unionization. Many war industry workers who held their first industrial jobs were ambivalent at best about worker solidarity, wage guarantees, seniority rules, grievance procedures, and union loyalty. Essentially, they wanted to work without strings attached and earn a regular paycheck. Strikes worried them, and they tended to see their employers, rather than a union, as the guardian of their interests, particularly women and blacks.[38]

Even so, in early May 1944 many Nebraskans were surprised when about 25 percent of the unionized electrical workers struck power plants over a wage dispute. These plants supplied power across the state, including service to four ordnance plants, three prisoner-of-war camps, and eight air bases. Nonunion employees kept the power plants operational with only minimal disruptions in service. When management threatened the strikers with the loss of their jobs, most returned to work. Before the war ended employees of the Colorado Fuel and Iron Corporation also launched a wildcat strike over a $0.05 per hour wage increase and working hours. Although a board of arbitration denied the demands, labor problems still festered when the war ended. Yet labor problems on the Great Plains paled in comparison to labor problems across the nation, where, by late June 1945, some fifty thousand workers had engaged in strikes and work stoppages. Many workers in the Great Plains distrusted labor unions, and the war years did not provide sufficient time for strong unions to develop among the war industries in the region, particularly those functioning as subcontractors. Moreover, labor unions in the Great Plains generally adhered to the informal "no-strike" pledge that national union leaders gave to the president in 1941. The Smith-Connally Anti-Strike Act (War Labor Disputes Act of 1941) also gave some protection against strikes by requiring a cooling-off period and a worker vote before a strike. On the Great Plains few wartime strikes occurred, and, like those across the nation, those that did occur were wildcat strikes conducted by relative few workers. Other workers usually came forward to take the place of strikers. When employees of the Bismarck Grocers Company, a wholesale firm, struck for higher wages in December 1941, for example, the manager received forty applications for employment.[39]

The war affected every aspect of daily life long after the fighting ceased. No city on the Great Plains connected to a defense industry remained unchanged. Towns that struggled with population losses prior to Pearl Harbor enjoyed an economic boom and confronted the host of problems that went with it. The economic effects of the war, then, proved paradoxical for the Great Plains. Wartime jobs, high wages, and disposable incomes kept restaurants crowded and stores filled with shoppers. Hotels put out no-vacancy signs. Taverns and theaters thrived. New residents bought newspapers for the housing ads. People wanted the war to end but the economic good times to last because this was the first prosperity that many had known. At the same time small towns without war industries often declined still further as young men and women left for the military and the war industries. One Nebraskan observed that on Saturday night the people on the streets in the small towns gave the impression of "an outing from an Old People's Home." If World War II was a good war in terms of fighting dictatorship and oppression, and while it ended the Great Depression, it was not entirely a time of milk and honey. If the war was an economic golden age for the nation, it was a tarnished brass age for the Great Plains.[40]

Certainly, the war brought a strong economy to the region. The war's multiplier effect on the Great Plains paid handsome dividends. The production of planes, munitions, navy landing craft, and other large and small military supplies from parachutes to dungarees to prefabricated buildings kept the defense industries at high productivity into 1945. Indeed, World War II made an "industrial mushroom" of Wichita, Oklahoma City, Dallas, and Denver. In the Great Plains, the major war industries grew and prospered even without access to an industrial labor market. The men and women who worked on the production lines came from the farms, from behind store counters, from cafés, and out of the kitchens. They had skillful hands, a willingness to learn, and a disciplined work ethic. The regional cities with war industries, then, functioned as giant magnets that pulled workers from the crevices of the farms and small towns with a force they could not resist. Although federal war money went only to a relatively few cities in the region, many plains men and women could not escape its pull.[41]

By 1944 Great Plains residents anticipated the end of the war with optimism and foreboding. They wanted peace, but they worried about an economic collapse when the war ended. Thousands of men and women would return to the plains from the military and need jobs at the same time the war industries would be closing or converting to peacetime production. Planners who looked ahead during the spring of 1944 projected major unemployment problems. A commission appointed by Texas governor Cole Stevenson forecast the immediate unemployment of some forty-five thousand workers in Dallas alone but projected quick peacetime adjustments, particularly as 40 percent of the female workers were expected to be laid off or quit, thereby opening jobs for returning service men. Those who could not find employment would be encouraged to seek jobs on the West Coast, where they were "urgently needed." In Wichita city planners expected that 66 percent of the semiskilled workforce would remain after the war. Men constituted 60 percent and women 40 percent of that group. Among the workers who intended to remain in Wichita, 80 percent ranged in age from twenty to forty-nine. Consequently, the provision of housing for men and women mostly of family-rearing age would become a major postwar problem. These young, rural, semiskilled men and women were little different from those who sought opportunities in California during the war years, but, in contrast to the western migration, these wartime migrants to the Great Plains cities primarily were white rather than African American, Mexican American, or Indian.[42]

Across the region, newspapers ran optimistic columns about the organization of committees to study the postwar economy with the intent of keeping the industries that had emerged during the conflict or luring new manufacturing to the region. Senator Pat McCurran of Nevada headed a congressional committee that suggested that the Great Plains, or at least the southern portion, was strategically important for the location of defense industries because its expansive geography and low population would prevent the clustering of important industries in highly populated areas and, thereby, protect them from attack. This dispersal would also promote a balanced industrial and national economy. Moreover, the argument went, the war had provided trained workers in Texas and Oklahoma and an industrial and manufacturing infrastructure that could easily be converted to peacetime production. In Texas and Oklahoma manufacturing could tap markets in Mexico and Latin America. The future offered the possibility of progress rather than the certainty of recession. Denverites expressed similar optimism when they learned in late December 1944 that 166 major defense contacts, totaling $20 million, had been awarded to city manufacturers during the year and that 100 subcontracts totaling more than $1 million had been placed with smaller plants. Now that the war had made Denver a manufacturing city, few officials and businessmen and-women saw any reason to change the economic base.[43]

Yet economic loss could not be avoided when the war ended. Great Plains residents who had come to rely on the war industries could only hope that the economic pain of reconversion would not be too great. The numbers, however, did not look promising. In Wichita the collective workforce that had relied on the aircraft industry during its peak in December 1943 totaled sixty thousand, and the payroll tallied $100 million annually for $1.3 billion in contracts. Both aircraft workers and management hoped postwar needs for military planes would keep them employed. But, as the military canceled contracts, employees of the contractors and subcontractors began losing their jobs. When the Beechcraft Company planned to release three thousand employees by the end of June 1945 because of War Department cutbacks following VE-Day, officials incredulously anticipated little dislocation for workers because many Beechcrafters had been working "purely for patriotic reasons and wish[ed] to return to their homes at the first opportunity."[44]

In early July 1945 the aircraft industry payroll still reached $9 million per month in Wichita, and no one expected it to collapse, but nearly everyone anticipated some economic downturn when Japan finally surrendered. In early August 1945 fifteen thousand workers at the Douglas plant worried about job losses rumored to come at any moment. On August 7, one day after Hiroshima disintegrated from the dropping of the first atomic bomb, the plant resembled a ghost town, forewarning of an impending shutdown. Ten days later some twelve thousand workers had lost their jobs. By late August the $45 million Douglas plant stood essentially empty. At the end of the year only six thousand aircraft employees built planes in Wichita. With similar layoffs and contract cancellations at the Douglas plant in Tulsa as well as at the Champion Refinery at Enid and the Continental Oil Company at Ponca City, economic analysts expected a loss of $91.5 million annually to Oklahoma's economy. Although the army agreed to take over the Douglas Aircraft Company in Oklahoma City to help expand military operations at nearby Tinker Field, no one expected more than half the twenty thousand employees at Douglas or the fifteen thousand civilian workers at Tinker to regain employment.[45]

Moreover, the war did not bring a long-term revival to other areas in the Great Plains, where most defense industries also shut down and laid off workers when the fighting ceased. In mid-August 1945, for example, Kaiser Industries in Denver released forty-five hundred workers. Other layoffs followed at the Rocky Mountain Arsenal or ordnance plant. Observers hoped that many women would leave the workforce, thus softening the blow. Chamber of Commerce officials believed that Denver and Colorado could meet the postwar demand for jobs but at lower wages. In Dallas by VE-Day approximately seventy-one thousand defense industry and federal agency workers expected to lose their jobs, with the corresponding payroll loss of $27 million annually. With civilian employees of the military averaging $2,685, war agency employees $3,070, and employees of the older agencies about $2,300 annually, few expected private businesses to pay as well as the federal government. The result would be great competition for considerably lower-paying jobs in private business. Some observers hoped that the industrial profits earned during the war would enable a conversion of both large-and small-scale businesses with a minimal amount of hardship. States such as Wyoming, North Dakota, Montana, and New Mexico, however, that did not have major wartime industrial centers confronted few problems converting to peacetime production. Overall, however, the wartime economy of the Great Plains faded rapidly.[46]

The Pacific Coast, not the Great Plains, became the major region for the production of aircraft during as well as after the war. The West, not the Great Plains, had a larger labor supply and served as the location for research and development. California was the big winner of postwar government contracts, although subcontracts for Wichita, Oklahoma City, and Tulsa plants proved profitable. Certainly, the wartime aircraft industry helped diversify the economy and workforce of the Great Plains, benefiting everyone except black workers, who, if they were hired at all, often found themselves in janitorial positions. North American Aviation, for example, refused to hire black workers even if they had training.[47]

World War II provided Great Plains communities the economic opportunity to leave the Great Depression behind, but it did not benefit all towns and cities equally, or even proportionally, and some saw no benefit at all. Many towns that sought an ordnance plant or even subcontracts saw lucrative defense funding going elsewhere. Many men and women found relatively high-paying jobs, but those positions often required relocation from the farms and small towns to the cities. This demographic change for labor had consequences for those left behind. Many towns experienced an acute shortage of plumbers, carpenters, and electricians, for example, as those skilled workmen took jobs with defense construction projects far beyond their hometowns. Small projects and repairs took longer to complete and service, if they were completed at all. As a result homeowners learned to get by or fix things themselves.[48]

Other problems developed from the war. Worker population increases of enormous scale caused immediate problems with school districts. Defense industry towns wrestled with the problems of insufficient classrooms, buildings, and teachers. The federal government helped alleviate some difficulties by providing grants for school construction, but the war strained the education system throughout the cities and towns to which industries or military bases attracted workers, many of whom brought school-age children with them. In some areas, such as that of Oklahoma City, the large influx of workers required schedule adjustments for the bus and trolley lines.[49]

Although carpenters, plumbers, and bricklayers had more work than ever before, more workers meant more traffic, and city councils necessarily added more police officers and more expenses to strained budgets, particularly in towns near military bases, such as Roswell, New Mexico. Automobile traffic and safety became a problem in the war industry cities, and law enforcement officials established speed zones near bases to slow people down on highways where few people had hurried before. By mid-June 1942 the disposal plant in Wichita could not handle the increased sewage, and city officials worried about the resulting health hazard and bad odor in nearby housing areas when it necessarily began dumping raw sewage into the Arkansas River. City officials blamed the federal government and asked for funds to fix the problem. War industry workers living in trailer camps outside the city limits of Amarillo dug four hundred pit toilets for outhouses by late September 1942, and county officials could not provide sufficient staff to ensure sanitary inspection. In the cities that attracted defense industries, female workers struggled to find day care for their children. Demands on the telephone system increased. In Wichita Southwestern Bell Telephone grappled to provide service for the one thousand long-distance calls placed daily by mid-February 1943. In Billings, Montana, by the end of March the number of telephones installed during the past year increased by 830, while the number of water, natural gas, and electric power accounts also rose as workers moved into the city.[50]

Other problems developed from wartime economic expansion. In spring 1942 the seven hundred people in Eudora, Kansas, learned that the federal government planned to build a $5 million munitions plant nearby, but not everyone considered the decision a blessing. Eudora had only one police officer and a volunteer fire department with only one truck. Store owners welcomed their new prospects, but others believed that the town might be hurt by increased traffic as well as the substantially expanded needs for health care, education, recreation, safety, and utilities, all of which cost money and required more people to administer, thereby further exacerbating the problem and probably requiring a property tax increase. Most plains men and women had never experienced such hassles.[51]

In addition, high wages, coupled with rationing, meant a pent-up demand to catch up with the purchase of consumer goods when the war ended. In July 1944 a survey conducted at Wichita University indicated that two-thirds of the city's defense workers had saved 10 percent of their wages and that an equal number had savings bonds. They had already used one-fourth of their savings to pay off old debts and mortgages. The survey indicted that postwar purchases would be primarily determined by women, many of whom had worked during the war. An overwhelming 80 percent of those surveyed wanted to buy refrigerators, radios, stoves (both gas and electric), washing machines, vacuum cleaners, and sewing machines, while 50 percent of the respondents want to purchase rugs, mattresses, living room and dining room furniture, air conditioners, and furnaces. One in three respondents wanted to purchase a new automobile, while 10 percent of the defense industry workers wanted to buy or build a house. Although consumer prices rose 30 percent from 1938 to 1945, expectations such as these promised to fuel inflation across the Great Plains when the war ended.[52]

World War II also created a military-industrial complex where the federal government, the military, and the industrial community became mutually supporting and useful allies. Yet, compared to that of the Far West, the wartime economy of the Great Plains remained remarkably undiversified. While federal funds in the form of defense contracts boosted manufacturing in some areas of the region, federal agencies awarded two-thirds of wartime contracts to the five hundred largest corporations in the nation, none of which called the Great Plains home. These companies had access to large labor pools for their assembly lines as well as research staffs that could adapt to contingencies. As a result the Great Plains experienced economic discrimination compared to the Far West.[53]

Certainly, the West Coast proved nearly irresistible. Despite the migration to the defense industry cities in the Great Plains, nearly 50 percent of the 8 million people who moved into the trans-Mississippi West between 1940 and 1950 settled along the Pacific Coast, particularly in California. While California gained 3.5 million people in the decade following 1940, the Great Plains lost 3 percent of its population. Although, like western cities such as Phoenix and Tucson, cities in the Great Plains or on its fringe, such as Albuquerque, Colorado Springs, Dallas, Denver, Rapid City, and Tulsa, grew, owing to the location of nearby military bases, the Great Plains states experienced neither dramatic change in its ethnicity-based social structure nor corresponding urban stresses owing to labor migration.[54]

At the same time the turnover in the defense industries often exceeded 50 percent and occasionally reached 100 percent during the course of a year. At the Martin bomber plant near Omaha absenteeism reached 6 percent and the turnover rate 52 percent by late 1944, compared to the national average turnover rate of 82 percent in manufacturing industries. Male employees, such as those working at the zinc smelters in Amarillo and Dumas, Texas, could not quit without the permission of the U.S. Employment Service. Workers who failed to acquire a certificate of separation from the agency could not be rehired by another employer. Workers who left their war industry jobs without authorization soon found themselves classified for the draft and immediately available for military service. Employers worried that they could be fined if they hired workers who shifted jobs without a certificate of authorization (the fine was $1,000). Industry officials in the Great Plains hoped that these regulations would slow, if not prevent, the flight of workers from the region to even higher-paying jobs in California and the Pacific Northwest.[55]

In contrast to the West Coast, particularly California, the Great Plains states were poor cousins when comparing dollars received for defense contracts and military installations. By March 1945, for example, North Dakota had received only $9.6 million out of $225 billion in defense contracts nationwide. Major manufacturing and the expanded use of natural resources did not occur in North Dakota during the war. Even so, per capita annual income in the Flickertail State increased dramatically—from $340 to $1,401—between 1940 and 1948. At the same time, per capita income in Kansas rose from $423 to $1,133. In Nebraska it jumped from $890 to $1,184 for that period, and in Oklahoma it climbed from $366 to $1,144 annually. Similar increases occurred in other Great Plains states. Even so, World War II did not reshape the Great Plains economy. Although it created an economic boom for the region, unlike in the Far West that boom did not last in the Great Plains because federal largesse eventually left the region, whereas it stayed and expanded on the West Coast. While the Far West emerged with a diversified economy, a progressive image, and a self-confident population, the Great Plains made only marginal economic advances. The petroleum and aircraft industries remained solvent, but postwar cutbacks kept the region in a near colonial economy, one based on primarily agriculture. The Far West emerged from World War II as a land of opportunity, and those who sought it passed over the Great Plains much as they had nearly a century earlier.[56]

While new urban areas emerged in the Far West, no Great Plains city became an economic and manufacturing hub for postwar America. Service industries grew, but that growth not comparable to that in the Far West, where the military-industrial complex boomed. Nor did a science and technology complex emerge on the Great Plains from the war. Indeed, no Silicon Valley would attract investment, business, federal contracts, new innovations. Although some postwar research and manufacturing complexes developed in Albuquerque, Denver, and Lubbock, the defense industry centered in the Far West, not the Great Plains. Postwar federal spending essentially skipped the Great Plains for the Far West. If World War II gave the Far West a new economic structure, it was merely an economic flash in the pan for the Great Plains. When most of the military installations and defense industries closed, not to mention the prisoner-of-war camps, nearby towns suffered a substantial drop in income. During World War II, then, the federal government made the economy of the Great Plains, and it took much of it away when the war ended. Comparatively speaking, little federal money remained to fund the postwar economy in the Great Plains, as it did in the Far West.[57]

The people of the plains states wanted to maintain their wartime gains. No one wanted to slip backward economically. The Kansas Industrial Development Commission, for example, hoped to keep the state's industrial gains by promoting Kansas as a state that offered a skilled workforce that did not strike as well as abundant power, transportation, housing, and raw materials. Chambers of commerce hoped that the decentralization of manufacturing would continue to benefit the Great Plains states when the war ended. Only time world tell, but, what the war had given, the peace threatened to take away. No one wanted to return to the prewar days of unemployment, scant payrolls, and a low standard of living. The war had created a vibrant economy, major demographic change, and new employment patterns, among other changes. Born of war, only a new conflict could restore the economic gains of World War II. It was not long in coming.[58]

THREE | Women at Work

Women took a host of jobs outside the home during World War II. Between 1940 and 1945 the number of women in the workforce expanded by more than 50 percent, from 11.9 to 18.6 million, for 37 percent of all workers. Approximately 75 percent of these newly employed women were married, and nearly 50 percent of all women took employment at some point during the war. High pay, patriotism, and increased status drew them to the defense industries. At the Cornhusker Ordnance Plant in Grand Island, Nebraska, women worked at every job (including pouring liquid TNT into bomb casings), except the most physically demanding positions. Overall, female industrial workers understood that they filled traditionally male jobs and would lose them when the war ended. Even so, World War II gave many Great Plains women their first job outside the home. Most liked the freedom, independence, and money.[1]

Women did not immediately enter the industrial workforce, however. When the war began, employers believed that the male labor supply would remain adequate, and they doubted the physical and mechanical ability of women to handle many defense industry jobs. By late 1942, however, the labor situation had changed dramatically, and employers welcomed female workers. Nationwide, women responded in great numbers. At first they were mostly young, unmarried, and unskilled. Great Plains women constituted part of this group, although the records do not clearly indicate their numbers other than to suggest that thousands held wartime positions. As the war progressed, female workers tended to be married with husbands in the military and older, with approximately half over thirty-five years of age by the end of the war.[2]

In January 1941, the Cessna Airplane Company employed only six women to work in the electrical department. After a month on the job they wired a half dozen instrument panels per day where two men had wired one every three or four days. The supervisor of the department attributed their productivity to nimble fingers compared to men. Cessna officials admitted that they were experimenting to determine whether women could do the work, and some believed that, if the United States entered the war, women would be needed to keep the defense industries producing. By February more than seven hundred women waited for admittance to the National Defense Training School in Wichita in order to learn sheet metal work, woodworking, and blueprint reading. At the same time the School of Medicine at the University of Oklahoma suffered a severe loss of faculty, nurses, and staff, and the medical director of the university hospital urged women to "take advantage of the opportunity to serve and receive training." Across the Great Plains officials counted the registered nurses in their hospitals and clinics and asked whether they would accept military assignments immediately or only in an emergency. The U.S. Public Health Service anticipated that many older nurses would be needed at home if the younger professionals joined the army or the navy.[3]

Although the training programs lagged, some Great Plains women anticipated that the United States would eventually become involved in the war, and they began preparing for it. They understood that, if war came, many men would necessarily leave their industrial jobs and that, if women were trained, they could qualify for high-paying positions. In Oklahoma City some women enrolled in the Oklahoma Aircraft School, where they learned the craft of riveting and that the terms *dimple* and *dolly* had nothing to do with sex appeal. Other women studied radio repair and drafting. Moreover, during the summer of 1941 the National Defense Training School in Wichita finally accepted a special class of twenty-four women to be trained specifically for employment at the Cessna aircraft plant, where they would make wood ribs for planes. If the eight-week class

FIGURE 4. Women entered the war industry workforce because employers needed their labor not only to replace men who had joined the military but also to meet production and repair schedules mandated by federal contracts. This photograph shows the first all-female engine repair crew at Tinker Field, Oklahoma. (Western History Collections, University of Oklahoma Libraries)

proved successful, more women would be trained. Soon, Wichita women enrolled in courses at local high schools under the national defense training program. There, vocational instructors taught various skills, particularly riveting, around the clock in three shifts. On completion of the course, these women qualified for immediate employment in the city's aircraft industries.[4]

By late August 1941 many Kansas women had taken jobs in the aircraft factories. Economic observers believed that more women would be needed if the war continued, particularly if the United States became involved in the conflict. On the production line of the Stearman bomber and trainer plant in Wichita, about fifty women cut and sewed fabric for wings and motor and cockpit covers. One former waitress liked the "nice clean place to work," and she made more money than she had waiting tables. At the Cessna, Beech, and Culver Aircraft plants women held specialized production jobs that did not require physical strength. Although no women conducted heavy factory work, such as operating lathes, welding, riveting, or running power presses, line supervisors believed that they could do those jobs with little difficulty if the situation required. In September the National Youth Administration also offered welding classes to women in Arkansas City, Kansas, and Bismarck, North Dakota, with the intent of qualifying them for industrial jobs within three months. The instructors proclaimed that "women make fine welders." When they finished their training, the women had abundant opportunities for employment.[5]

After the United States entered the war, women who wanted to participate in voluntary war-related work organized under the auspices of the American Women's Voluntary Services, Inc. In Denver the organization anticipated the drafting of female nurses and urged other women to enroll in training classes for nurses' aides to help staff the hospitals after the nurses left for the armed forces. The Voluntary Services also sponsored training sessions for women to learn auto and truck repair and to fly planes. In Amarillo the hospitals offered refresher courses for nurses who had been out of the profession for some time to relieve the "possibility of insufficient nursing service during the emergency." In Omaha Red Cross women took an auto mechanics course designed to help them make simple repairs and diagnose problems. Most of the course involved changing tires, putting on chains, and cleaning spark plugs and clogged gas lines.[6]

Training sessions of all sorts, but especially medical, could be found in the larger Great Plains towns during the early months of the war. In Bismarck the Council on Civil Defense organized training sessions for women to become nurses' aides. Except in "very special cases," however, these women had to be American citizens. Certainly, the war also increased the demand for nurses, whose numbers nationwide proved inadequate as early as December 1941. In the war industry towns hospitals often suffered overcrowding and a lack of skilled and professional employees. In 1942 Congress attempted to enhance the training of nurses by passing the Labor-Federal Security Appropriation Act to fund nursing education on an expanded scale, but the program, which was administered by the U.S. Public Health Service, attracted few students. As a result Congress acted again and approved the Nurse Training Act, or the Bolton Act, which became law on July 1, 1943. The act created the U.S. Cadet Nurse Corps and authorized the federal government to subsidize training by paying tuition and monthly stipends as well as providing uniforms and supporting postgraduate refresher courses. In Nebraska twelve of the thirteen hospital schools met federal guidelines to participate in the program, and administrators enrolled 1,986 students from 1943 through 1945. Most of the graduates took jobs in Nebraska. The Bolton Act required all graduates to remain active, that is, employed as nurses, until the war ended. Only the St. Joseph's Hospital School of Nursing in Alliance accepted second-generation Japanese American, or Nisei, students. No African American students received admission to the Nebraska Cadet Nurse Corps.[7]

Funding from the Bolton Act enabled many hospitals in the Great Plains to expand nurses' training programs in a way that would not have been possible without the war accelerating. The war and the Bolton Act, then, gave many Great Plains women an opportunity to further their education and pursue a career. Some women who participated in the Cadet Nurse Corps program, however, believed that hospitals accepted the trainees because they needed the students to staff the hospital wards in lieu of trained nurses, thereby saving money while the institution accepted federal funds. Many women in South and North Dakota apparently joined the Cadet Nurse Corps for patriotic reasons, but others took advantage of an economic opportunity born of war. One South Dakota woman recalled, "I could be a teacher or a secretary. I chose the Cadet Nurse Corps mainly because of financial reasons, not necessarily patriotic, more practical."[8]

Early in 1942 women could train in Kansas City, Kansas, to assemble radios, but they had to be between eighteen and twenty-six years of age with at least two years of high school education. In Wichita, however, women confronted age, marital, and educational restrictions for training programs, and the housing shortage meant that local women had the best chance to gain employment. Within months the Works Progress Administration (WPA) in Topeka offered a twelve-week course in sheet metal work and airplane riveting for women between the ages of eighteen and forty who had an eighth-grade education. During their training they received "regular WPA wages for women." Boeing officials, however, remained uncertain about the ability of women to perform jobs that had been traditionally associated with men. Southern Methodist University rejected that view and offered free drafting courses for women. After twelve weeks of study they could be placed immediately in local aircraft plants, such as at North American Aviation in Dallas.[9]

Women who took short vocational courses through various training programs, such as the Works Progress Administration in Cheyenne, local schools in Wichita, Kansas City, and Oklahoma City, or colleges in North Dakota, received quick employment on completion of their work. By mid-January 1942 women had taken many specialized positions in the Great Plains aircraft plants, where they worked "men's jobs" and received "men's pay," that is, $0.60 per hour at entry with an automatic increase to $0.75 per hour after three months of successful employment. The gendered structure of the division of labor began to crack.[10]

By early 1942 the aircraft companies in Wichita were hiring essentially all the women who applied, provided they were between the ages of twenty-one and thirty-five and weighed no more than

135 pounds. These characteristics, officials believed, would enable the women to learn the required skills and negotiate small, cramped work spaces in airplanes—a perception that continued to stereotype women. War industry employers, such as the Douglas Aircraft Corporation in Oklahoma City and Tulsa and Consolidated Aircraft in Dallas, hired women because they were "more dexterous with their fingers" and because they were not eligible for the draft. Some critics, however, charged that many employers and government officials believed that women excelled at repetitive jobs that required finger dexterity and patience and, therefore, relegated them to the least-skilled jobs.[11]

Many women apparently did not care about the stereotyping or the marginalization of their work in the defense industries. One reporter noted, "Waitresses, stenographers, beauty operators, even housewives, are flocking into the factories drawn by a combination of patriotism, adventurousness—and the $27.50 weekly starting wage." The aircraft industries did not object to paying equal wages to women because they could recover that expenditure with cost-plus contracts. Even so, although women held traditionally male jobs in the aircraft plants, such as drafting, metal fabrication, and riveting as well as the operation of shear, brake, roller, and drill presses, some assembly-line positions were still considered "feminine jobs," such as upholstering and making parachutes. Four months after Pearl Harbor one Bismarck reporter succinctly observed, "The question is no longer 'What jobs can women hold?' but 'Will the number of women who voluntarily shift from peacetime jobs be enough to fill the need of expanding war industry?'" Male workers in the airplane plants did not seem to resent the new female employees.[12]

To ensure as little turnover as possible the airplane manufacturers preferred single women without children or married women with husbands in the service. One reporter noted that these women would tell their grandchildren one day that they built the planes to help "whip the Japs." In Fort Worth, however, an initial reluctance to hire older women for jobs in the aircraft industries prevailed as late as July 1942. Consolidated Aircraft hired only women between the ages of twenty and thirty, although clerical workers could be older. Shop foremen, one observer wrote, thought that women older than thirty were "too bossy," that they created "friction" among the younger women, and that they got "surly" about taking orders. Other aircraft plants in Fort Worth, however, considered older women "tasteful and pliable enough" for defense training schools and hired women as old as forty-five. Soon, women at Consolidated worked on the longest assembly line in the world, where they built B-24 bombers. At Consolidated supervisors reported that female workers had greater patience with detail and handled repetitive jobs without losing interest better than male workers. Female employees also proved themselves more eager to learn and more willing to ask questions than male employees. Although this view also continued to stereotype women with certain feminine skills and relegate them to jobs that became the industrial equivalent of "women's work" at home, supervisors believed that production increased substantially in departments where a large number of women worked.[13]

As the war progressed, more women were needed to replace men in almost every occupation. In March 1942 Western Union in Denver began hiring women to deliver telegrams to replace "boy messengers" who left for defense industry positions or the military. In Salina, Kansas, and Billings, Montana, female taxi drivers took to the streets for the first time, and some residents considered their employment another indication that women continued to infiltrate the male world. Amarillo women also drove taxis, worked as butchers, and staffed all positions at the Victory Theater except for the operation of the "picture machine." They also worked at the Coca-Cola Bottling Company, where one observer noted, "They wear coveralls and sling large cases of Coca-Cola around with all the ease of yesterday's housewife shuffling cards." At the First National Bank a woman replaced a man who left for the military. There, she kept the "general ledger," allegedly one of the most important jobs in the bank. Women replaced other men in the bank, reportedly operating "complicated" business machines. At the *Amarillo News and Globe* women began work in the editorial and photography departments. The Ford dealer also began hiring women, observing, "If women can build airplanes they can repair Ford cars."[14]

In McCook, Nebraska, the Burlington Railroad hired women to clean engines, and the male workers called them "beauty operators." Whether these women accepted the moniker with good humor remains unknown, but they looked forward to "fat paychecks." The Dallas Railway and Terminal Company also hired female streetcar and bus drivers because the draft, enlistments, and the war industries had created a severe worker shortage. The female drivers would receive the same pay as men for performing the same jobs, including work on the night shift. Women operated the streetcars in Oklahoma City, and they had better safe-driving records than the men, which one official reported kept them from maintaining schedules as well as male drivers. In Colorado Springs, on the western edge of the Great Plains, the director of the local employment service reported that businesses that made deliveries preferred women because they were easier on tires, a major concern now that truck tires had become nearly irreplaceable. In Oklahoma women with pharmacy degrees proved highly employable for the first time in drugstores, hospitals, and laboratories. W. D. Peterson, the secretary of the State Board of Pharmacy, welcomed their employment but doubted that they could stand on their feet as long as men.[15]

In the summer of 1942 the personnel director at Beech Aircraft reported that the women hired from Wichita and the surrounding small towns and farms had a work ethic and an ability little different from the men hired from these areas, which he believed resulted from being born in the Great Plains. A less romantic observer, however, attributed the number of women hired to the company's secretary-treasurer, Olive Ann Beech, who insisted that women could do practically any job in the plant and was most responsible for the company's policy of equal pay for women who held traditionally male jobs. At that time women constituted approximately 8 percent of the welders at Boeing. More than half the women who worked at Boeing came from farms and small towns and understood the need for hard work. At Will Rogers Field, near Oklahoma City, women held positions as sheet metal workers, and management expected to place them in other areas of plane maintenance as the number of male employees decreased. Some women also worked on ground

FIGURE 5. This all-female repair crew worked to remove the fairing and hose connection on a B-25 bomber at Tinker Field in Oklahoma. War industry jobs offered women income and independence that few had experienced before the war. (Western History Collections, University of Oklahoma Libraries)

crews. In Oklahoma City the Douglas Aircraft Company actively hired women for its cargo plane production lines. C. C. Pearson, the general manager, reported that by November 1942 women constituted one-third of the workforce and that they had shown particular ability at tasks involving "accuracy, dexterity, patience and judgment." Still, the total number of women working on aircraft production lines nationwide remained small, at least for the moment. In June 1942, for example, about four thousand women worked on the production lines in eleven aircraft plants, and 45 percent of those employees worked in California. Moreover, women averaged lower wages. In factory (including munitions and armament) work nationwide women averaged $0.60 per hour, while men earned $0.10 more for such work by mid-1942. In the aircraft industry, however, entry-level wages were equal for men and women, with the same rate increase for each group after six months.[16]

In the autumn of 1942 the Great Western Sugar Company factories in Scottsbluff and Gering, Nebraska, and Billings, Montana, hired women for the first time, and, if they proved satisfactory, the management planned to employ more to alleviate the manpower shortage. Similarly, at Billings, the U.S. Weather Bureau hired female observers to replace men. In reality this occupational and social gain proved less significant than it appeared because men still controlled the weather forecasts. One observer wrote, "The girls are permitted only to look at the weather." On a less sexist note, in mid-November the Boeing Airplane Company announced that it would hire one thousand women between the ages of twenty-one and forty at $0.50 per hour and send them to a national defense training school to learn sheet metal work and machine shop procedures. After completing a short course they would be hired by Boeing at $0.60 per hour. One observer noted, "At Boeing you can find hundreds of housewives performing sheet-metal work with all the zest and enthusiasm they formally displayed when polishing up their best silverware for an afternoon party."[17]

Few Great Plains women, of course, ordinarily spent their afternoons hosting parties, but many sought jobs in the aircraft industries. By late 1942 more than two thousand women reportedly "invaded" the Glenn L. Martin bomber plant at Fort Crook near Omaha. Although before their employment an estimated 90 percent had never been near machinery other than sewing machines, electric mixers, and vacuum cleaners, they operated drill presses, lathes, milling machines, and hydraulic presses and competed equally with men at electrical installation and welding. They, too, worked the same hours, at the same jobs, and for the same pay as men. One observer noted their dedication, ability, and toughness, saying, "They ask no quarter and are given none." Still, Great Plains airplane manufacturers professed that the women who entered production work supplemented rather than displaced men.[18]

Even so, women quickly proved capable of conducting their work and rivaled potential male employees for jobs. By late 1942 women also began replacing men in the meatpacking plants in Montana. The packinghouse managers believed that two women could replace one man for every job except for the slaughter of cattle and hogs, from which they were prohibited. One observer noted, "The boys are marching out and the girls are marching in." The same observer reported that, in Billings, "petticoat troops are making forced landings in business and industry, and the situation is in hand." In Cheyenne, the local employment service urged women to take jobs and encouraged them, saying, "Any healthy, willing housewife or another woman can be trained for factory work." With three hundred jobs for women available in August 1943, the employment service put out desperate calls for women.[19]

The work of women changed in other ways. Besides women from small towns and farms taking war industry jobs, so many women in cities were taking newly created civil service positions related to the war effort that secretarial schools were unable to meet private employers' demands for replacements. The women who enrolled at the secretarial schools tended to be older housewives who chose to return to paid employment. Hotels also began employing women in their business offices and at reservations and customer service desks. In Oklahoma City waitresses soon enjoyed receiving "generous" tips from soldiers and sailors, particularly officers, from the nearby bases, most of whom came from the North and East, where people readily practiced that custom. A waitress could easily make $10 and sometimes $20 per day in tips, a considerable amount compared to the $10 per week wage job. These women hoped that their Oklahoma customers would soon adopt that practice.[20]

Defense industry and other wartime jobs such as these changed the labor dynamics across the Great Plains. In Oklahoma, for example, so many women flocked to jobs in defense industries, primarily located in Oklahoma City, that cafés and restaurants experienced a shortage of waitresses. In Salina, Kansas, and Cheyenne, Wyoming, gas station owners replaced the male pump operators who had left for better-paying war-related jobs with "pretty girls." Other women participated in the war by running family businesses, such as lumberyards and printing shops, after their husbands left for the military. The manpower shortage also necessitated an alteration in gender roles around the house, where men had traditionally assumed the fix-it-person role. With so many men gone, in June 1943 the University of Omaha offered a one-week course on home mechanics for women, where they learned to repair dripping faucets, fix window screens, and replace lamp sockets, among other things.[21]

By spring 1944 "begrimed" women poured molten steel, welded, and operated huge overhead cranes at the Omaha Steel Works. With every available healthy man of draft age already in the service, the number of physically unqualified men, that is, those classified as 4-F, available for war industry work proved insufficient. Only women could fill the open positions. At Omaha Steel as well as the Eaton Metal Products Corporation, Paxton-Mitchell, and the Gates City Iron Works, women helped fill army and navy contracts. They averaged about $0.75 per hour and enjoyed and spent their disposable income. The labor situation, however, had reached a crisis level. At four plants that powdered eggs for the military and the Lend-Lease program, many eggs went uncracked and unprocessed, and local officials of the War Manpower Commission (WMC) called for "emergency" help and urged women to take open positions as their patriotic duty. Management at these plants offered to arrange work schedules between 7:00 a.m. and 10:00 p.m. to meet any woman's needs. In Dallas so many housewives went to work in the war industries that the city's laundries became swamped. Tired women with money to spend preferred to send their laundry out rather than do it themselves, or they had worn out their machines and could not get them repaired or purchase new ones. One-day service quickly became four or five days because the laundries could not find sufficient workers to meet the demand. Some women lamented the shortage of "negro help," a problem for wealthier (middle-and upper-class) women across the nation. In the Great Plains as elsewhere World War II gave African American women only a slight chance to leave domestic service for manufacturing jobs.[22]

Throughout the war black women had a difficult time gaining employment. In 1940 more than half of black women nationwide worked in domestic service. These women earned a median yearly wage of just $246, whereas white women conducting the same work earned $568. In Texas employers rationalized that they did not have time to build segregated restrooms. Or employers promised to hire black women when they had enough applicants to merit a segregated sift, which never materialized. Others claimed that white women would walk off the job if employers hired black women. By the end of the war black women constituted only about 2 percent of all women working outside the home. If the aircraft companies hired women, they preferred white to black. One labor official reported that in Kansas "there is no demand for colored in-plant trainees," and the training programs in 1941 did not include black students. When Senator Arthur Capper attempted to acquire federal funding for a training program for African American women, Congress denied it. Overall, in the Great Plains, as nationwide, black women often became employees of last resort.[23]

As a result, on the eve of Pearl Harbor African Americans remained excluded from employment in the aircraft factories in Wichita. Employment offices based this decision, not on race per se, but on the fact that without training, from which they were also excluded, African Americans were not qualified for defense industry jobs. By 1943, however, the labor shortage in the war industries necessitated the hiring of some black women and men, but the hiring pace proved slow, and resentment by whites remained common. By the end of the war few war industries across the Great Plains employed African American women and men in professional or technical capacities, in part because the black population was smaller there than in other regions with an industrial economy. Nationwide, for example, the number of black women in the workforce averaged 1.5–2.1 million between 1940 and 1944, when 40 percent of African American women worked in some capacity, including 18 percent in industrial jobs. For the most part, black women worked as janitors in the defense industries.[24]

The men who observed women working in the aircraft factories constantly sought affirmation that femininity prevailed despite figure-hiding coveralls, boots, and bandanas. At the North American Aviation plant in Dallas or at Douglas Aircraft in Oklahoma City and Tulsa, one reporter noted that, although female employees could not wear jewelry for safety reasons, they maintained their gender identity by wearing bright socks, when oxfords were permitted, that matched their slacks and head-covering bandanas. He also noted that hair bows sat "perkily on short hair cuts." Although the women did not powder their faces, they all wore lipstick as "brightly as [they wore] their identification badges," which led the reporter to conclude that "women will be women." In Wichita one observer noted that women "dolled up in snappy uniforms" to drive taxicabs. Even so, most women who wore overalls did not attempt to be "glamorous" while working on the aircraft assembly line, and they were more noticeable because they were women in work clothes and occupied much of the space on city buses as they traveled to and from work at Cessna, Beech, and Boeing.[25]

The industrial demands of war not only provided high-paying jobs for women but also necessitated statutory equity concerning hours worked on the job. Some states still had laws that prohibited women from working at night or shifts of odd hours to ensure that they could be home with their families for supper and the evening hours as well as to protect their health. But the war industries maintained work shifts around the clock, and employers expected women to labor at all hours just like male employees. By mid-1943 the states had dealt with the problem either by changing the laws or, as in Texas, by granting exceptions. In spring 1943, for example, the Texas State Labor Commission conducted hearings and granted exemptions from regulations governing the hours of female employees. It granted six-month permits to Mosher Steel, Hubbard Machine Products, and several other Dallas companies allowing women to work ten hours per day and seventy hours per week. To achieve this exemption the commission held hearings under provisions of a new law granting war industry plants immunity from state regulations prohibiting women from working more than nine hours per day or fifty-four hours per week. At the hearings Texas employers had to show that the public interest merited longer hours and that the health of the women would not be endangered.[26]

The North American bomber plant in Kansas City, for example, required all workers to labor on ten-hour shifts, six days per week,

FIGURE 6. These women were typical mechanics who worked the "line," either building or repairing airplane engines in war industry towns such as Wichita, Dallas, and Oklahoma City. (Western History Collections, University of Oklahoma Libraries)

a policy that caused fatigue and limited family life, particularly for women. In October 1943 North American changed the schedule to two ten-hour shifts five days per week, with the possibility of scheduling a weekend off. By March 1944 Nebraska prohibited women from working more than nine hours per day without a special permit to help safeguard family and home life. In Kansas women could not work longer than nine hours per day or 49.5 hours per week. Colorado, New Mexico, Montana, and Wyoming limited the workday to eight hours and the workweek to forty-eight hours, while Oklahoma and Texas imposed limits of nine and fifty-four hours, respectively. South Dakota also permitted a ten-hour workday and a fifty-four-hour workweek. Across the nation, women typically worked a forty-eight-hour week with one day off.[27]

As women took jobs in war industries, child care became a problem. In January 1942 Oklahoma's Committee on Care of Children urged women not employed outside the home to volunteer for child-care services, a plea that still left many children without adequate care. Indeed, working mothers desperately needed day care or extended school services. The Oklahoma Public School District worked to meet this need by gaining federal funds to hire extra teachers for afterschool supervision of children whose parents, particularly mothers, could not remain at home or meet them after school. Often in the Great Plains the child services for workingwomen proved inadequate, particularly when school ended in the spring. Working-women who had older children often confronted problems of juvenile delinquency because they necessarily left their children unsupervised after school. At the same time women could earn $1,500 per year as civil service employees at army bases near Wichita, Dodge City, Garden City, Pratt, and Winfield, Kansas, while "inspectorettes" who worked in the aircraft plants earned as much as $2,000 per year with the possible enhancement of 21 percent more pay for overtime work. These were opportunities and wages that few Great Plains women had dreamed would be available to them. Afternoon-bridge-playing women did not need this income, but usually women with small children took it if they could arrange child care.[28]

For many women, however, employment was not only an opportunity to earn a high income but also a chance to participate in the war. Work of any kind, but particularly in the defense industries, gave women the opportunity to take part in a war that all knew would change the world. Early in 1943 the personnel manager at the Nebraska Ordnance Plant in Meade reported that women constituted 33 percent of the employees and that they were more patriotic, more stable, and less given to complaining than the male workers. Although absenteeism occurred more frequently among female employees, their turnover rate was less than the men's, and the company preferred absenteeism to turnover. The absentee rate for women in the Wichita aircraft industry also exceeded the rate for male employees because family obligations often made their work schedules impossible to maintain, particularly if they worked the second or third shift. At the same time absenteeism among women at the Denver Ordnance plant was, allegedly, nearly nonexistent.[29]

By July 1943 women constituted 30 percent of the fifty-four-thou-
sand-person workforce in sixty-four of Nebraska's largest essential
industries, except the railroads and construction, although a few
women also worked in those fields. Many more women had taken
less essential jobs, such as office and retail workers, or labored on
a farm. At the Glenn L. Martin Company women constituted more
than 40 percent of the bomber plant's employees, which made Glenn
Martin Nebraska's largest employer of women. Even so, 83 percent
of the women hired held positions with the lowest classification, as
drill operators, bench electricians, and maintenance staff as well as
clerks, cafeteria workers, and "general helpers." They averaged $96
to $172 monthly, but they had a higher turnover rate than men,
perhaps owing to family responsibilities.[30]

At the same time women constituted 42 percent of the workforce
at the Douglas Aircraft Company in Wichita. And Douglas officials
expected that women would soon constitute 70 percent of their
employees. At the Oklahoma City air depot (later Tinker Field) 32
percent of the ten thousand employees were women, and officials
predicted that they would eventually constitute 50 percent of the
workforce. At the Amarillo Army Air Field women applied for a
host of jobs, including flight-and mechanical-training instructors.
An airfield spokesman said that they were "anxious to do something
worthwhile for their country." In Dallas the director of the WMC recognized that women provided the largest potential labor pool and
urged women to enter the city's defense industries to meet the labor shortage, which approached 8,000 workers. Already more than
6,300 women constituted 60 percent of the labor force in the local
aircraft industry. Similarly, at the North American plant in Kansas
City 9,125 women constituted 39 percent of the workforce building
B-25 bombers. These percentages for female workers in Great Plains
airplane manufacturing mirrored national averages.[31]

By February 1944 women constituted 35 percent of all war workers in Denver, and approximately 40 percent of the women above
the age of fourteen had entered the labor force in some capacity in
the Dallas/Fort Worth area by early spring. By December women
constituted 43 percent of the workforce in Wichita. By March 1945

women had replaced men on the production line of the Rocky Mountain Arsenal in Denver, except at four stations where bombs required lifting. The women on the production line filled bomb casings with an incendiary mixture, checked bomb weights, inserted detonation devices, painted the bombs, and nailed them in cases, all the while operating under the axiom, "The women make 'em and the men drop 'em." Those women who made bombs earned $35 to $39 per week, and they constituted 70 percent of the workforce.[32]

For many Great Plains women work equaled participation and patriotism, and many took this opportunity to be a part of the war through their labor. Women in the defense industries also believed that their work would help win the war. Certainly, patriotism played a major role in their decisions to seek employment during World War II. Without a doubt they made a major contribution to their household income and in many ways redefined the place of women in the workforce, a redefinition that would have social, educational, and economic ramifications in the postwar years. In many respects "womanpower" in a nontraditional form had come to the Great Plains.[33]

Early in 1944, women's groups in Dallas and Wichita met to discuss the employment of women once the war ended and industrial production and the economy returned to peacetime conditions. Generally, they accepted the idea that servicemen should have their old jobs back, but they wanted to keep many positions in transportation and communications, especially those that had opened because of the wartime manpower shortage. Those who held jobs, particularly women, worried about the loss of employment now that they had entered the workforce. Many women knew that they had been hired only for the duration of the war, in part because they held traditional male jobs. But many women had no desire to give up the sense of purpose and fulfillment that working outside the home gave them, nor did they want to lose their paychecks and their independence when the war ended. Women who previously held lower-paying jobs in retail sales and housekeeping particularly wanted to keep their defense industry employment. In April 1944 a survey by the Wichita

Chamber of Commerce indicated that 26 percent of the city's work-ingwomen hoped to retain their defense industry jobs. This finding surprised the many men who had assumed that female war work-ers would eagerly and voluntarily leave their jobs and return home when the war ended. Some worried that women might keep their wartime jobs and that their returning husbands would be forced to go on the government dole. The war apparently had emancipated many Great Plains women in ways few had anticipated.[34]

Still, many women felt no regrets and returned home to begin families and pursue the expected way of living, never to take outside employment again. By 1946 the number of women in the workforce nationwide had declined from 19.1 to 16.9 million, or from 36.5 to 30.8 percent of all workers. Many women left unwillingly, either let go by their employers or pressured by husbands who did not want their wives to work. One woman who left a job at an aircraft plant recalled, "Society looked down on women who worked out-side the home." Certainly, the traditional, patriarchal view of work-ingwomen held sway after the war ended. Unmarried women who needed to support themselves and who remained in the workforce usually took unskilled, low-paying jobs as secretaries, cashiers, and salesclerks. Often, they felt pressured to leave their defense indus-try positions before they received termination notices. One aircraft worker remembered the expectations for her to quit, saying, "All the talk both inside the plant and in the newspapers encouraged women to give up their jobs for returning veterans."[35]

In January 1945 the Colorado and Denver Business and Profes-sional Women's Club sought legislation to ensure postwar hiring and salary practices that treated women equally with men as well as make discrimination against women in personnel relations ille-gal. One Colorado woman put the problem succinctly, saying, "We don't want to be legislated into our homes. We can be lured there by the right men, but we want the right to work." She considered any attempt to remove women from the workforce nothing less than a "Fascist idea." Plains women in the war industries as well as other occupations customarily relegated to men would contend with the same issue of equal pay for equal work as well as nondiscriminatory hiring practices for decades after the war, but the war had given women opportunities, and they demanded a voice thereafter concerning their place in the workforce. For many Great Plains workingwomen the employment and earning opportunities created by World War II would be halcyon days not soon to come again.[36]

Yet not every plains woman agreed. In Dallas one club woman professed, "Every girl would rather have a home and children than a job." Many men held this same belief—that a woman's place was in the home and not on the production line. Similarly, in Omaha a chapter of the Veterans of Foreign Wars (VFW) asked married women who held "men's jobs" to give them up if their husbands held full-time employment, a request based on the premise that such women denied a man the opportunity to provide for his family. If they did not surrender their positions, the VFW predicted, another depression would ensue. The VFW, however, did not explain the economic logic on which it based that resolution, and most Omaha women ignored it. Seniority rules and preferences for veterans, however, along with social and spousal pressure, forced many women from their wartime jobs. In the Great Plains the curtailment of government contracts also pushed women out of wartime employment. Although many women kept their jobs in the war plants into July 1945, their days there were numbered.[37]

Wartime work brought large paychecks, thus giving women more economic freedom and independence as well as the opportunity to contribute to the family finances for the first time. Women with children, those with husbands in the military, and those who remained single all needed the money. In addition earned income gave plains women greater influence in the financial decisions of their families and empowered them as never before. Most important, the war provided employment opportunities that did not end with the war. When peace came, many women moved down in terms of job earnings and status, but they also moved on, that is, remained in the workforce. Great Plains men might not have liked the expanded presence of women in the workplace, and many were troubled by the lack of clear distinctions between men's and women's work, but the war had changed these relationships for all time. Thereafter, Great Plains women would question gender restrictions. Romona Snyder, who went to work for Boeing in Wichita in 1942, assessed the achievement of women working in wartime, saying, "We more or less came out from under man's thumb." Still, few women advanced to supervisory positions in the war industries, and few could voluntarily work overtime or the night shift if they had families.[38]

When the war ended, the Great Plains returned to prewar conditions in many ways. Certainly, the war provided new employment opportunities for women, but many jobs disappeared when the defense industries closed. Women lost high-paying jobs that had given them independence, and many had no alternative but to return to domestic life and labor. For women who worked in the defense industries, however, their contribution to the war had another real and often overlooked significance. One reporter noted it clearly when he observed that the women who repaired and installed guns at the Oklahoma City air depot dispensed "death with a feminine touch."[39]

In retrospect, mobilization for war required a major conversion of peacetime industries and a draft for the armed forces. As a result women necessarily took jobs traditionally identified as men's, such as riveting and welding. Even so, the WMC and the Office of War Information, which were responsible for recruiting women and gaining the public acceptance of women's employment in the defense industries, always assumed that these women would work only until the war ended. Women, of course, had worked and held manufacturing positions since the beginning of the industrial age, but never on the scale mandated by World War II. Although thousands of women took jobs across the Great Plains, like their sisters nationwide they remained identified as wives and mothers who labored hard but kept their femininity and maintained their charm and glamour. At the same time the federal government did not concern itself with women already employed in underpaid and low-status jobs. Rather, it glamorized the movement of housewives to the defense industries and transformed them into the symbolic Rosie the Riveter and Wendy the Welder even though most workingwomen in the Great Plains and across the nation did not labor in defense industries.[40]

The Office of War Information invariably stressed a sense of patriotism rather than the opportunity to earn high wages as the major reason housewives left their homes for the workplace during the war. On vj-Day, when the war ended, women constituted 47 percent of the workforce at the Douglas Aircraft plant in Tulsa. When Douglas began hiring for the war effort, approximately 70 percent of the first four thousand new employees were women. Although a local reporter contended that most of the women who worked at Douglas during the war did so for "reasons of patriotism," he did allow that some women considered aircraft industry work an opportunity to add to the family's income. He did not expect many of these women to seek new employment after their release from Douglas when it began shutting down on April 9, 1945. Still, the loss of a payroll worth $1 million per month, about half of which was earned by women, would "jolt" the community. Certainly, women often worked for money rather than patriotism, but many did so from necessity, having lost disposable income when their husbands left for military service. Women also worked to help end the war as quickly as possible and bring their husbands and sons home so that they could leave the factories and return to their homes satisfied with a job well done during an emergency. In this context, then, they worked for patriotism and love, which remained acceptable, nonthreatening social boundaries governing the relationships between men and women, particularly within the context of women's loyalty to and support of men.[41]

Nationwide surveys conducted between 1943 and 1945, however, indicated that between 61 and 85 percent of female workers, and between 47 and 68 percent of married female workers, wanted to remain employed after the war, some for financial reasons, others to keep what they had gained. A Women's Bureau survey of ten defense areas showed that 75 percent of the women employed in 1944–45 wanted to keep working, preferably in their current jobs, but in Wichita only 61 percent planned to continue on the job, the lowest proportion of women wanting postwar work. By late 1944, a nationwide survey conducted by the Family Economics Bureau of Minneapolis, Minnesota, indicated that seven of ten women planned to keep their jobs after the war. A follow-up sample by the *Omaha World Herald* indicated that about the same percentage of female wartime workers in Omaha intended to keep their jobs. Great Plains women who took jobs in war industries enjoyed the extra income if they were married as well as a new independence, and many women had no intention of returning to domestic housework. Some people, however, believed that, if they did not give up their jobs and return home, the divorce rate would rapidly accelerate because men would reject sharing housework. Children would be raised by hired women and girls, and the family home as it was then known would disappear. Even Mother's Day might be abolished. All worries about the collapse of society remained moot, however, until the war ended.[42]

Still, most women nationwide, including those living in the Great Plains, remained housewives. Of the women who worked, only 16 percent were employed in defense industries, partly because their husbands did not want them working in those situations. Approximately 75 percent of all women old enough to work did not hold jobs when the war began. Most women returned to domestic life when the war ended, and they preferred lives as wives and homemakers to lives as defense industry employees. Moreover, no more than 2 million, or about 10 percent, of employed women worked in defense industries nationwide, although about half a million labored in the aircraft industry. Of the 33 million women at home nationwide during 1941, seven of eight remained there in 1944, the peak year of wartime employment. Many middle-class women simply rejected blue-collar jobs and, more important, preferred to stay home, where they believed they could best aid the war effort by nurturing the family. They remained homemakers, and their husbands preferred this role for them. Moreover, the war segregated women in certain jobs, such as secretaries, store clerks, and bank tellers, and most middle-class women could afford to quit these jobs or accept termination at the end of the war. Blue-collar female workers who wanted and needed to keep their high-paying jobs often lost their work and income with peace. In the end World War II did not produce many long-term economic and social gains for workingwomen.[43]

World War II did, however, enable the permanent occupation of women in the labor force on an unprecedented scale, both in government and in civilian work. Indeed, the war gave Great Plains men and women new and considerable employment opportunities. Although women in defense plants sometimes complained that they worked harder than men, women over forty years of age were happy to get jobs because employers often discriminated against them because of their age, contending that they were too old to learn the job, too slow on the production line, and too susceptible to accidents. Many understood, however, that they would be paid less because they were women. Most important, the war opened a host of jobs previously closed to women. Yet neither Rosie the Riveter nor Wendy the Welder were typical wartime women in the Great Plains or across the nation. Moreover, the women who stayed home received little or no recognition for their efforts to take care of their families. In addition, few defense industries welcomed women until 1943, when few male workers were available. When the war ended, the status of female workers had not improved much from the prewar years. They remained cheap labor and a reserve force that could be easily exploited regarding pay, hiring, and promotion. In 1944, for example, female industrial workers nationwide averaged $31.21 per week, compared to $54.65 per week for men. When the war ended, many women remained employed, although at lesser jobs. Even so, they helped provide the basis for postwar economic growth, which included more jobs for women. Most Americans made no commitment to altering their values regarding workingwomen, so little changed, and women returned to low-skilled, low-paying, dead-end jobs traditionally identified as "women's work." Yet those Great Plains women who worked outside the home during World War II were subtly and sometimes profoundly changed. Thereafter, they had different expectations about work, independence, and self-worth. In this sense World War II left an indelible mark on the Great Plains. But it was a mark more felt than seen.[44]

FOUR | The Home Front

The Japanese attack on Pearl Harbor and the subsequent declaration of war on the United States by Germany and Italy gal-
vanized the men and women of the Great Plains against the Axis
powers. The official entry of the United States into the war quickly
muted the voices of isolationism. Mobilization for the war and victory became the watchword of the hour as plains men and women
rallied to support the nation with a personal and communal sense
of purpose. No one could question their patriotism, nor would they
question America's entry into the war. The enemy had to be defeated, and the region had to help win the war and adjust to life in
wartime. Although no one knew the precise nature and extent of the
adjustments that would be necessary, plains men and women prepared to sacrifice for the good of the nation. The people of the Great
Plains would do their part.

On December 8, 1941, North Dakota and other Great Plains
states began organizing Home Guard units to provide protection,
particularly against Japanese sabotage. In Bismarck members of the
American Legion and of the Veterans of Foreign Wars, state highway patrol officers, highway department employees, and the local
police took up positions to guard the municipal airport. Governor
John Moses proclaimed a "state of unlimited emergency" and announced that he would establish a home guard of fourteen companies, composed of eight hundred men. He made that decision in
conformity with a statute authorizing the governor to organize a
military force when more than 50 percent of the state's National

Guardsmen had been called into federal service. With some three thousand of North Dakota's guardsmen absorbed into the army, Governor Moses considered the state unprotected from the dangers within. The legislation authorizing a home guard, however, made no provision for support. Without funding for the guard, Moses appealed to each community where Home Guard units were organized to provide uniforms. The War Department promised rifles and other equipment. The governor urged men between the ages of eighteen and forty to join the Home Guard.[1]

Similarly, in Colorado Governor Ralph L. Carr urged the state legislature to increase the Denver unit of the Home Guard from two hundred to six hundred men and to authorize units for other Great Plains towns, such as Pueblo, Trinidad, and Sterling. Although the guardsmen enlisted for only one year and they would not be paid, they would be available for quick deployment to combat sabotage, quell rioting, and guard military and industrial establishments. Quickly, several hundred men between the ages of twenty-five and fifty-five applied. Most had previous military experience. The Denver Racing Pigeon Club donated five hundred carrier pigeons to the Home Guard to carry messages between headquarters in Denver and units in other towns if the enemy invaded and destroyed communication lines. While these efforts seem conceived in hysteria, many plains residents felt fear and anxiety after Pearl Harbor, and the organization of Home Guard units to defend against Japanese and German saboteurs indicated a seriousness that seems an emotional overreaction only in hindsight.[2]

Although the mayor of Salina, Kansas, thought the possibility of a Japanese attack on his city "improbable," several days after Pearl Harbor he planned a civil defense organization, in part to "prepare for any eventuality," even air raids. Soon, members of a Civil Air Patrol (CAP) unit flew above the city and the surrounding area and watched the local power and pipelines. CAP units organized in other towns across the Great Plains. In Amarillo men above the age of sixteen could join, learn to fly, and patrol the Texas Panhandle for Japanese and German saboteurs. In Oklahoma women joined the CAP because, in the words of one reporter, it "offered more exciting work than knitting."[3]

Civilian defense committees also organized in towns across the Great Plains. The *Omaha World Herald* reminded its readers, "If you see the whites of their eyes, then it will be too late to start preparing for civilian defense." But even before Pearl Harbor civilian defense committees appointed air raid wardens, planned for medical emergencies in time of attack, and practiced blackout drills. In June 1941 Roswell, New Mexico, residents conducted blackout drills in a celebratory spirit and even invited the singing cowboy/movie star and Roswell native Roy Rogers to participate. They planned for bombers from the army air base at Albuquerque to simulate enemy aircraft and give civil defense air raid wardens practice spotting them. Although only one Flying Fortress made the run, everything worked according to plan, and the blackout gave residents a "thrill." In early September New Mexico conducted the first statewide blackout, primarily because Fiorella H. LaGuardia, the national director of civilian defense, believed that its sparse population and border-state status made it "potentially the section thru which an invasion of the United States might be initiated."[4]

Across the Great Plains other towns practiced blackout drills. In mid-December 1942 a blackout test failed in Denver because the air raid warning siren malfunctioned. Nevertheless, the city darkened at 9:00 p.m. because citizens had been told via newspapers and radio announcements to turn off their lights at that time. Similar tests in Colorado, Kansas, Nebraska, and North and South Dakota proved successful, but Cheyenne, Casper, and Wheatland in Wyoming struggled to get it right. The *Wyoming State Tribune* reported the shortcomings of a blackout drill held in Cheyenne on July 8, 1943, saying, "Consider your self bombed to death last night!" Residents had, apparently, confused the blackout and the all-clear signals and brightened rather than darkened the city when the sirens sounded. Earlier, Omaha police arrested individuals who did not comply with blackout drills, and the municipal court fined them $100 each plus court costs. Blackout drills and practice for air raids continued in Cheyenne, Omaha, Wichita, Bismarck, and other Great Plains cities throughout the war. Wichita, however, exempted defense industries from mandatory participation.[5]

Schools also practiced air raid drills, and local newspapers published drawings of enemy bombers so that the public could learn to recognize them in case of attack. Omaha school administrators touted the ability of their students to reach designated air raid shelters in ten minutes. In Wichita air raid wardens distributed four-page booklets describing the appropriate action if the city came under attack. With an eye to making a dollar born of the war, in mid-June 1942 the Wichita Association of Insurance Agents began selling "bombardment and war damage insurance." The fine print in the contracts prohibited claims for losses due to blackouts, sabotage, capture, seizure, pillage, and looting. Fires caused by German or Japanese bombers would be covered, provided the buyer did not have other fire insurance.[6]

Great Plains residents did not consider their isolation a protection from enemy attack. Earnestness characterized their response and indicated their fears. In Wyoming some residents urged officials to study the feasibility of using mines and caves for shelter in times of enemy bombing. In Casper one resident complained, "Have we got to wait until lives are needlessly sacrificed before we at least begin to plan air raid shelters?" In Nebraska the American Legion helped the state's Advisory Defense Committee plan an air raid warning system that included spotters using telephones to report enemy attacks to district headquarters for further relay to the army at Fort Crook. Little more than a month after Pearl Harbor air raid wardens in the Texas Panhandle attended training courses in Amarillo, sponsored by the Texas State Department of Public Safety and the FBI, where they learned to prepare for a German air attack, extinguish fires from incendiary bombs, and administer first aid. Although training to help plan for a gas attack indicated preparation to fight the last war, in truth no one knew what the Germans and Japanese might do. Still, everyone expected the worst.[7]

The war also brought a flurry of volunteerism to the Great Plains, particularly among women. Some joined the Red Cross and assembled packages of bandages for the combatants before the United States entered the conflict. In an effort to maintain neutrality, in October 1939 the Dallas chapter sent those bandages to Red Cross units in England, France, and Germany. In Denver women volunteered to collect cash donations on street corners to aid civilian war victims in Europe and somehow keep Denver "War-Free." In Wichita women in the Red Cross collected clothing and medical supplies for "beleaguered Norway and defeated Poland." Although few Wichita residents were of Polish descent, many area residents had Norwegian and Swedish ancestry, and their desire to provide aid can be linked to both cultural ties and "moral repugnance" to German aggression.[8]

In January 1941 some Oklahoma women volunteered to join the state's Women's Ambulance and Transport Corps in case war came to the southern Great Plains. Although age limits prevented women younger than eighteen or older than forty-five from joining, by July 250 women in Oklahoma City who worked as beauticians, stenographers, and businesswomen signed up. At the first meeting, held in the Federal Building, a reserve army officer gave a lecture on the duties of an infantry battalion, reconnaissance methods, and defense against tanks and aircraft. He also provided instruction on map reading because he did not believe that the women volunteers knew the streets of Oklahoma City or could reach Norman if the highway was blocked. After this useless, if not embarrassing and derogatory, session, someone announced that the next meeting would emphasize ambulance driving and techniques for moving the injured. Despite the absurdity of the meeting, it inspired women in Ada, Blackwell, Duke, Elk City, and Okmulgee to seek this opportunity, and the Oklahoma chapter of the National Patriotic Council assumed responsibility for organizing state chapters of the Women's Ambulance and Transport Corps. By early February 350 women had enrolled in the Oklahoma City chapter alone.[9]

Volunteerism, particularly for women, became a patriotic activity during the war. Women volunteered for the Red Cross, hospital work, and social activities for military men and women on trains or stationed at nearby bases. In railroad towns such as Aberdeen, South Dakota, for example, women volunteered to serve sandwiches, milk, and coffee to soldiers and sailors on trains that made whistle-stops. At Aberdeen women from approximately forty nearby towns within a seventy-five-mile radius donated their time to the canteen located

FIGURE 7. These servicemen and -women enjoyed coffee and sandwiches at the North Platte Canteen in Nebraska. Female volunteers, here and in other railroad towns, often set up tables at the station to greet and feed military men and women as they changed trains. The North Platte Canteen served several thousand military personnel every day during most of the war years. (Nebraska State Historical Society, RG 1331-52)

in the depot of the Chicago, Milwaukee and St. Paul Railroad, preparing food, washing dishes, and raising money. The local organizers joined the United Services Organizations (USO) and the Red Cross to meet the trains. The women operated the canteen seven days a week and gained an envied reputation in 1943 by serving free pheasant sandwiches after a local farmer delivered a number of the birds to the canteen. The pheasant sandwiches became so popular that local residents pooled their gasoline and shotgun shells and organized pheasant hunts to keep a local locker supplied. Helen J. Bergh, who worked at the canteen, remembered that the military personnel on the trains could not believe that all canteen food was free to them. "Evidently," she reflected, "most of them came from areas where people are not as open-handed as they are in South Dakota."[10]

FIGURE 8. Women who lived near military bases often volunteered as dance partners for the soldiers and sailors at post and community social functions. These young servicemen and volunteer civilian women enjoyed a dance at the opening night of the Soldiers Recreation Center in Leavenworth, Kansas. (Kansas State Historical Society)

In Lubbock, Texas, a group known as the "Hub-ettes," composed of "young ladies of the community," organized to provide wholesome recreation at dances and other social functions for the soldiers at the nearby army air base. The young women would be under the supervision of the Coed Committee of the Lubbock Defense Recreation Council. They called themselves "Hub-ettes" because, by the Defense Recreation Council's own admission, Lubbock served as the hub of the Great Plains. These young women primarily functioned as dancing partners and friendly companions and were admitted to USO social functions on the base only by invitation. The girls had to be eighteen years of age or older to participate. If they attended Texas Technological College, they had to return directly to their dormitories on leaving dances. While they essentially served as hostesses, they were to be "charming, interesting, and wholesome," brandish "sincere smiles," and discard "husband seeking complexes." In Great Falls nearly eight hundred women volunteered to be "victory belles" or dancé partners for the army men from nearby East Base at USO dances, while young women in Albuquerque trained to be hostesses at the USO club. Although male volunteers registered to serve in a variety of capacities from fire and police protection to civil defense, block captains and health-care providers, women's organizations in the Great Plains played an active, gendered role in the war effort.[11]

Community commitments to the war effort also became evident with the number of scrap metal and other drives. Soon after the war began the Office of Production Management urged the collection of scrap metal for the "victory program." Quickly, Great Plains communities organized scrap metal drives and also collected rubber and paper, and local newspapers frequently published photographs of donors and volunteer collectors before various scrap piles. Although scrap drives began before Pearl Harbor, they became a major wartime activity. During the summer of 1942 in Billings, Montana, the city scrap metal committee urged businessmen to pile their junk curbside for pickup, encouraged participation by announcing that "each pile of junk in front of each business establishment will be a badge of the owner's patriotism," and set a goal of collecting one thousand tons or twenty railroad cars of scrap metal. In the autumn so much scrap metal had been collected in Great Falls that some observers questioned whether the military really needed it. Soon, "junk dealers" became particularly valued citizens for collecting and sorting metal from scrap drives and shipping it to smelters, where federal officials required the payment of the highest prevailing price, at least for aluminum. Sales to the smelter were made under the auspices of the city or town that sponsored the collection drive, with the earnings restricted to use for civilian defense. Coercion in the name of patriotism became common across the Great Plains.[12]

In Nebraska Joe W. Seacrest, the state salvage chairman, took a gentler approach to both collection and patriotism, saying that the salvage of scrap metal was the "job of every man, woman and child," and he urged teachers to organize their students to help col-

FIGURE 9. During the war these Oklahoma children participated in a school-organized scrap drive. Across the Great Plains children collected scrap in towns and on farms and sent thousands of tons to smelters for ultimate reuse as guns, tanks, and planes. (University of Central Oklahoma Archives/Special Collections)

lect it. Commitment, however, sometimes lagged, and in October Seacrest criticized some Nebraskans for showing "apathy, indifference, and selfishness" for their lack of participation in scrap drives. Similarly, after a scrap drive in Oklahoma City few people volunteered their trucks to haul the metal away, and county officials had to rely on army, Works Progress Administration (WPA), and state highway trucks to carry the loads. The state director of scrap collection criticized Oklahomans, saying that the transportation problem indicated a lack of commitment and the admission that "civilians can't and won't do the job," and he called for "more sacrifice from everyone." Clearly, Oklahomans and Nebraskans understood the concept of comparative sacrifice, and many apparently believed that they had contributed enough time and effort to war-related activities or that someone else would make the sacrifice and save them the effort. By autumn 1942 enthusiasm had begun to wane for collective action and self-sacrifice.[13]

Scrap drives became venues for competition between schools, classes, service clubs, towns, counties, and states. In Ellis, Kansas, high school students competed by class to determine which could collect the most metal. The 253 boys and girls who participated collected 420,954 pounds, or more than 210 tons, of scrap metal in October 1942. The students had set a quota of 100 pounds each but exceeded it by more than sixteen times, for 1,664 pounds per student. The enthusiasm of the sophomores carried the day, and they won the competition by collecting 104 tons, which earned them a day off from school. The school treated everyone else to a free movie. Nebraskans showed so much enthusiasm for the drives that they earned the sobriquet "scrap happy."[14]

Virtually all forms of metal, such as license plates, door knockers, dishwashers, and cannons from courthouse and statehouse lawns merited collection for recycling into iron, steel and other metals for the military. Copper and brass as well as lead and zinc from automobile batteries also became sought-after metals. The University of Oklahoma Press donated all the engraved metal plates for its books, some dating to 1900—several thousand pounds of copper and brass in all. Not only was the press contributing to the war effort; it was, according to the director, freeing up needed space as well. In Oklahoma and Wyoming tax commissioners helped save metal by authorizing windshield stickers to replace metal license plates during the war. Automobile dealers also used the scrap drives to unload junked cars, but transport to the smelters by local governments or organizations proved difficult. Amarillo residents even took up some streetcar tracks, and Nebraskans ripped up abandoned railroad tracks—with permission from the state office of the Interstate Commerce Commission—for shipment to smelters.[15]

Agricultural papers also urged Great Plains farmers to collect discarded machinery for scrap drives, arguing that they had enough junk metal to build battleships. In August 1942 the *Nebraska Farmer* challenged Cornhusker readers to contribute a ton of scrap from every farm. In Nebraska, however, farmers received criticism early in the war for not contributing to the scrap metal drives after some contended that they were too busy. This caused one critic to charge

FIGURE 10. Local groups, such as the Boy Scouts, participated in scrap drives. City and school officials often awarded prizes to the group or organization that collected the most scrap. In August 1943 these Boy Scouts collected scrap metal at a junkyard in Lincoln, Nebraska. (Nebraska State Historical Society, MacDonald Collection, RG 2183-19430811 [5])

that farmers were "a bit slow sometimes to realize how important a little thing can be." In late August the Junior Chamber of Commerce in Billings, Montana, held a scrap campaign that included nearby farmers. Members used their own trucks to circulate through the countryside and collect scrap iron or "junk" from local farms, and officials overseeing a scrap drive in Sheridan, Wyoming, gave a $50 war bond to the rancher who contributed the most metal.[16]

Overall, Great Plains farmers supported scrap drives and responded to such patriotic appeals as, "Let's gather that scrap to slap the Jap," and, "Get your scrap into the Fight." In Wyoming agricultural scrap brought $0.40 to $0.50 per hundred pounds, or approximately $10.00 per ton, from licensed scrap dealers, or it could be donated to the American Legion or the Red Cross. Besides contributing to the war effort and earning some income from scrap, farmers also gained the added benefit of cleaning up their farms by removing used implements, tractor wheels, and other junk that they normally parked or tossed in an isolated portion of their farms.[17]

Occasionally, however, patriotic enthusiasm achieved success at the expense of the material culture of the past, that is, the region's history. In April the Wyoming Stock Growers Association protested the removal of the cannons from the statehouse lawn for scrap. Russell Thorp, the secretary of the association, poignantly observed, "Why do we sit back and permit things to be destroyed that stand for our traditions? . . . Why do we have to destroy things that create interest in and respect for the very ideals that we are now fighting to preserve?" All to no avail. The state's salvage officials sent the cannons to a smelter. In December 1943 the War Production Board (WPB) in North Dakota seized thirty tons of scrap metal on a farm near Belfield. A steam engine not used since 1930 had no apparent historical significance at the time, and, saying that it "could not be classified as a farm implement by any stretch of the imagination," the regional chief of the WPB sent it to a smelter. At the same time a Kansas farmer had three hundred tons of scrap in the form of tractors, machinery, milk cans, and "material of a kindred nature" seized by a deputy U.S. marshal.

Indeed, the public viewed farmers with large junkyards as unpatriotic, and local officials seized their scrap in the name of the federal government. In December the WPB also gave farmers the option of selling their scrap or losing it to seizure. When farmers balked, the government moved forcefully, if not quickly, to take it. Most Great Plains farmers cooperated and avoided a visit from law enforcement authorities with seizure papers in hand. Patriotism served as the primary factor motivating participation in the scrap drives.[18]

Drives collecting wastepaper, tin cans, and cooking fats also occurred across the plains in conjunction with scrap metal and rubber drives. Women primarily organized the collection of tin cans, newspapers, cooking fats, and silk stockings. In Albuquerque, Bismarck, Denver, and Cheyenne salvage committees urged housewives to wash vegetable cans and crush them with their feet to help save space on city trucks during a collection drive. The State Salvage Committee of the WPB in Nebraska urged women to collect these materials to help with the war, and in October 1943 the Women's Division of the State Salvage Committee adopted the slogan: "A ton of scrap for every Nebraska Service Man." One Nebraska woman urged women in the state to stop making soap because that chore was unpatriotic. She complained to the committee, "The woman who makes soap to-day, when fats are needed for medicines and for ammunition tends to sabotage the war effort."[19]

Plains women also organized war bond drives, often conducting door-to-door campaigns. Essentially, these women operated on the premise that, if they could do nothing else, they could raise money that would help shorten the war. Bond drives sponsored by the Treasury Department, states, and towns became popular, patriotic occasions that volunteers, particularly women's organizations, often scheduled in conjunction with important events, such as Navy Day celebrations. In late April 1942 the war bond drive committee in Colby, Kansas, secured pledges ranging from $1.00 to $1.50 per month per person for the purchase of stamps and quickly gained commitments of $150,000 for the war fund. In Salina, Kansas, the Metro Club sponsored a campaign to sell defense stamps and bonds. Anyone who purchased as little as a $0.10 stamp could hammer a nail into a coffin labeled "Herr Hitler." In Cheyenne, Wyoming, schoolchildren received war stamp books so that they could purchase stamps one day each week. When they filled their books, they could exchange them for a war bond that cost $18.75 and returned $25.00 on maturity.[20]

Bond and stamp sale campaigns remained popular throughout the war. The symbolic act of buying bonds or stamps helped build community spirit and created a sense of participation in the war effort as well as contributed funds to the federal government. Service groups catering to all interests and ages as well as businessmen and newspaper carriers also became involved in selling bonds and stamps furnished by the postmaster. Even Boy Scouts and Girl Scouts sold stamps. In July 1942 the Girl Scouts in Billings began selling war stamps in $0.10 and $0.25 denominations. They optimistically intended to raise $3.2 million to cover the estimated cost of building four bombers for attacks on Tokyo. Celebrities sometimes aided the bond drives. In mid-September the movie stars Stan Laurel, Oliver Hardy, Dick Arlen, and Jean Parker attended a dinner for bond buyers in Bismarck. Admission was open to all who wore a $1 boutonniere made by the local Red Cross, the boutonnieres being much like the poppies the organization made for Armistice Day. Throughout the war, then, Great Plains residents, like others across the nation, purchased bonds that contributed to financing the war. Bond purchases, however, primarily served to keep inflation under control by siphoning off disposable income as well as enabling participation in the war effort, guarding against loss of purchasing power in the event of a postwar depression, and helping banks reduce savings accounts on which they paid interest.[21]

In addition to these volunteer efforts, the federal government encouraged so-called victory gardens to help people supplement their diets with fresh fruits and vegetables, which could not be rationed because they spoiled quickly. In Oklahoma the Future Farmers of America began planting victory gardens and canning the produce as organizational projects in the summer of 1942. The state Extension Service published pamphlets to help people raise gardens, can vegetables, and maintain a balanced diet through the use of garden products. The Extension Service also encouraged Great Plains residents to establish community and school gardens. Officials, however, warned against overexuberance and, to avoid waste, urged gardeners to plant only vegetables that they liked and only in quantities that could be consumed. Victory gardening became an obligation with its own military terminology, pests, for example, becoming a "fifth column" and "saboteurs" that would "invade" and "destroy" the vegetables. In 1943 the Colorado state Extension Service reminded everyone that gardening was not a hobby but a patriotic duty. Victory gardens provided a tangible outlet for patriotism while producing food from one's labor. In Kansas Governor Payne Ratner sent certificates in recognition of their participation in the war effort to people who raised victory gardens. Still, not every farm or household had a garden, and not every victory garden was well tended.[22]

Amarillo donated ten acres to the Council of Parents and Teachers for a victory garden that would help supply the school lunch program. WPA workers tended the garden and canned the vegetables. The city provided water for irrigation. In Bismarck the WPA allocated $37,000 to help lay out irrigated victory gardens along the Missouri River, and the Dakota National Bank offered cash prizes for the best gardens. The bank's real motive, however, was to profile the value of irrigation agriculture to encourage large-scale development and lending in the area. Throughout the war Great Plains newspapers carried victory garden columns to help readers increase their production of vegetables, and county Extension Service agents also provided advice. In June 1943 the golfing women of Omaha reportedly had given up the game, or at least significantly cut back on their rounds, for the duration of the war because their work in victory gardens and as volunteers took time previously allocated for the links. Throughout the war, then, victory gardens served as a symbol of patriotism and enabled Great Plains residents to participate in the war effort by helping alleviate food shortages. Nationally, victory gardens produced more than 40 percent of the nation's vegetables, and they became a common sight across the Great Plains.[23]

Throughout all these activities daily life went on with attendant perennial concerns. In Oklahoma, for example, the Methodist Church used patriotic rhetoric to fight its ongoing war against the sale of beer in the state. Methodists sought repeal of the "beer bill" because alcoholic beverages were the "worst fifth columnist in America." For the Methodists beer fostered "moral diseases," and it was as dangerous as any Axis power. The Oklahoma Baptists, not to be outdone, sought the prohibition of beer and liquor on military bases in the state. With only 3.2 percent alcohol beer legal in Oklahoma, however, demand for whiskey sent the price soaring to $4 per pint, confirming the proverbial more bang for the buck. Oklahomans had war industry money to spend and a whisky thirst but no opportunity to purchase whiskey legally. Oklahoma's governor, Leon C. Phillips, provoked a controversy by asking Congress to stop the sale of liquor on federal property because the state's constitution prohibited the sale of alcoholic beverages. Phillips's messianic and moralistic support from the state's temperance forces temporarily brought an end to liquor sales at Fort Sill, much to the displeasure of the officer corps. State officials argued that they had to stop liquor trucks from reaching the fort because these deliveries traversed Oklahoma's highways. Army officials charged that state law did not apply to federal property. Governor Phillips, apparently not having much to do or playing to the dry voters, charged that the army circumvented state law by using airplanes to fly liquor into the post.[24]

During the war one reporter wondered whether Omaha was becoming "a city of playboys and party girls as a result of war hysteria" and because the defense industries fattened checking accounts. Drinking had increased, and some thought night work at defense plants had created a new class of "morning drinkers." Bartenders reported that their customers often switched from beer to whiskey, indicating that they had more money to spend. Bars once popular with college students now attracted army personnel, and more mature men and women replaced the previous youthful clientele. Female drinkers, whom bartenders classified as members of the "lonely hearts club," also became frequent patrons.[25]

In Oklahoma, however, the war nearly ended the bootleg liquor business because so many bootleggers either joined the military, took jobs in defense industries, or sought other employment because of gasoline and tire shortages. County sheriffs predicted that sugar rationing would further contribute to the decline in bootlegging. As early as March 1942 the sheriff of Caddo County reported that his territory had had a 40 percent decrease in bootlegging since Pearl Harbor. The town of Ada, however, quickly earned the reputation for providing the "fastest telephone whiskey service in the state." A phone call brought a quick delivery because the remaining bootleggers did not want to lose business. As a result, in the words of one contemporary, "Every customer gets practically personal service, and the bootlegger is afraid if he doesn't hurry, you too, will change your mind and buy a defense bond." Despite the decline of bootleggers, Oklahomans near the Texas line had easy access to package liquor stores in the Lone Star State. Some bootleggers complained, however, that too many of their customers had joined the military to remain in the moonshine business. Coloradoans, in contrast, allegedly "spurred by uneasiness caused by the approach of war," drank more liquor in 1941 than they had in the previous year.[26]

The daily strain of wartime also affected romance or the lack of it. By summer 1940 the number of marriages increased, often breaking records. Observers attributed the jump in marriage applications to the draft, and the divorce rate dropped. In Wichita, however, one district court employee predicted an increase in failed marriages, in part because the average age of couples applying for marriage licenses was twenty-two for men and twenty for women, compared to the national average of twenty-five and twenty-one, respectively. This lower age for men may have reflected their desire to avoid the draft, which at that time still protected married men from induction into the military.[27]

By late 1943 the divorce rate in Dallas had skyrocketed. Observers attributed the increase to the economic independence of women in the war industry. They could afford divorces without alimony and exercised their freedom when they thought best. In the past, experts contended, poverty prevented women from seeking a divorce, but in wartime Dallas divorces were "inextricably linked to money." The experts also contended that men with "well-stuffed wallets" were prone to moral recklessness, which, along with the uncertainty of war, created a "don't-give-a-damn" attitude, and divorce often resulted. In Dallas one judge attributed the increase in divorces to "war and its hasty, passion-prone marriages," particularly involving "soldier-husbands," with "infidelity, jealously, and whiskey" contributing to broken marriages.[28]

In Omaha a survey of married women in mid-May 1943 indicated that nine of ten who had married during the last eighteen months believed that they had made the right decision, although women who married prior to the war urged postponement until the conflict ended. Wartime separations, however, soon cooled passions. By late summer 1944, 1,018 petitions for divorce set a new record. Marriage counselors believed that the increase in divorces resulted from the separation of servicemen and war industry workers from their wives, from more women working and becoming independent, and from married men and women who worked with each other in war industries becoming "infatuated" with each other. Marriage experts in Nebraska believed that the trend would continue as more "war marriages" hit the "rocks" and that the decline in applications for marriage licenses could be attributed to a new law requiring examination for venereal disease before a license could be issued.[29]

Certainly, across the nation the war caused family stress that often ended in divorce. In April 1944 the Bureau of Labor Statistics estimated the dissolution of 3 million marriages since the war had begun. Between 1940 and 1944 the divorce rate rose from sixteen to twenty-seven per hundred marriages, that is, from 16 to 27 percent. In 1944 Oklahoma County, with Oklahoma City its center, granted 4,096 divorces, up from 2,400 in 1942 and 3,500 in 1943. By May 1945, 975 divorces had already been granted, and the county attorney's office reported receiving sixteen to seventeen divorce petitions daily. Men and women on the Great Plains who married during the war years struggled with the same problems of separation, reassessment, and remorse as others across the nation.[30]

Some optimists argued that war could strengthen marriages, although they admitted that wives had the major responsibility for saving wartime unions by writing letters, confessing mistakes, and sending cookies as well as conveying their "enthusiastic interest in homemaking," including practice at preparing meals. But these old-fashioned views had little appeal for many women. Instead, many plains women took advantage of wartime opportunities—employment, financial independence, and social freedom, the latter of which also involved sexual liberty. In the towns and cities near army and navy bases, soldiers, sailors, and workingwomen had money to spend at bars and restaurants, and they lived for the moment and changed gender protocol between the sexes. Young women, separated by time and space from husbands, boyfriends, and families, often took advantage of a laxity in customary moral behavior. Biological need and a desire for a good time occasionally ended with unwanted pregnancies or venereal diseases, but most young women continued to pursue their new lifestyles. One Oklahoma moralist, however, reminded all who would listen, "Of all morale destroyers the philandering of wives is the deadliest." Less was said about the sexual affairs of men away from home. One female correspondent urged Oklahoma women with wandering eyes to stay "extremely busy." More than one plains woman, however, succumbed to temptation, spurred on by a snappy uniform, money in the pocket, and a live-for-the-moment atmosphere.[31]

The war also contributed to increased juvenile delinquency, particularly in defense industry towns, where parents or a mother worked away from home all day or where the father served in the military. A psychologist at the Billings Polytechnic Institute warned that war caused "intensive activity," which affected children and led to juvenile delinquency. He urged parents to know where their children were as well as what they were doing at all times as long as the war lasted. In Dallas experts blamed an unstable home life for almost all juvenile delinquency. The chief probation officer of the juvenile court attributed the increase in burglary, robbery, and sexual promiscuity to a war psychology that devalued human life and property and taught "hatred, violence, and destruction." As a result children developed a belligerent attitude, particularly in single-parent homes where mothers had had little experience disciplining their children when their husbands left for the military.[32]

By April 1943 Dallas authorities worried about the outbreak of sexual promiscuity among girls, but the morals of boys apparently did not register the same concern. In towns with defense industries or near military bases or training camps, the Texas Social Welfare Association (TSWA) reported a nearly 58 percent increase in sex offenses, by which it generally meant prostitution, during the past four years, compared to an increase of 24 percent for other juvenile crimes. The TSWA attributed the increase in sexual promiscuity to the "influx of population, overcrowding, and the prevalence of honky-tonks, which compete with inadequate recreational facilities of a constructive nature." The TSWA also blamed the problem on the tendency of young women to learn from older women, particularly because, on their arrest, the police often placed them in cells with prostitutes. The TSWA contended that juvenile delinquency also stemmed from a lack of parental guidance and a breakdown of social values attributed to the war, which fostered an "I don't care" philosophy. By midsummer the juvenile delinquency rate in Dallas had increased among adolescents from broken homes but also among boys and girls from wealthy neighborhoods. Truancy, drinking, auto theft, vandalism, burglary, and fighting became increasing problems among the young. Some observers believed that juvenile delinquency emanated from adolescents adopting the "live-for-today" attitude of adults.[33]

In Denver, where juvenile delinquency, particularly gang activity, increased, Judge Phillip B. Giulliam of the juvenile court urged mothers to stay home rather than take war industry jobs. He acknowledged, "There are . . . times when women cannot refuse to take jobs in war activities, but the welfare of the home and children must be considered as of prime importance." In Wichita the courts saw an increase of charges for truancy, petty larceny, burglary, and sex offenses among children of working mothers. There, the Women's Legion Auxiliary urged women with small children to forgo employment because they could contribute more to the "morale on the home front by staying home and looking after their youngsters." By so doing they would help prevent juvenile delinquency. The auxiliary also contended that the women who played bridge in the afternoons should take jobs in the war industries so that the women with children could stay home. Marion Gibson, the chief probation officer in Omaha, believed that the number of fathers and mothers who worked and left their children unsupervised created a "particularly dangerous situation." By late 1943 juvenile delinquency had increased sharply in Billings. In January 1944 Oklahoma City's Junior Chamber of Commerce also issued a report on the city's "acute" juvenile delinquency problem. The Recreation Committee charged with studying the problem reported, "Our youths have felt themselves unimportant and have become emotionally upset." Parents had become too busy to supervise their children, and truancy, sexual promiscuity, drinking, and burglary resulted. The committee recommended the creation of teen centers in the local junior and senior high schools to provide constructive outlets for free time.[34]

Wartime crime rates increased among young people in other areas. In Taos, on the western edge of the southern Great Plains, 18 percent of all arrests during the first nine months of 1943 were of young adults under twenty-one years of age. Most of those arrests involved eighteen-year-olds. No one explained the cause in the newspapers, but residents became vocal in their demands for law enforcement among this age group. In Wichita school officials attempted to thwart delinquency problems among the junior and senior high school students by organizing the Sons of Victory. The organization sought volunteer men to serve as surrogate fathers for boys whose parents had left for military service. These volunteers ate lunch with their assigned students, played sports with them, and otherwise spent time with them during the weekends. Later, the Daughters of Victory also organized to provide emotional support for girls.[35]

In retrospect, the parental neglect of children often resulted from necessity rather than choice. Women who took defense industry jobs spent most of their days and sometimes their nights away from home. As a result the "latch-key" children felt neglected, became bored, and occasionally got into trouble because they were not supervised. Overcrowded schools did not help the social situation, and the employment of teenagers, some experts contended, exposed them to "special moral hazards." Others argued that the war permitted "specific biological urges" from being "held in check by convention." In general the experts considered the promiscuity of girls a moral problem but, because of venereal disease, that of boys a medical problem. Overall, the people of the Great Plains were not really different from others across the nation. The war years were a time when the young seemed irresponsible and self-indulgent, with too much money to spend and a lack of self-discipline. In 1942, for example, the Cheyenne Ministerial Association investigated rumors of increased juvenile delinquency in the city and concluded that it was "just about normal and what we can expect under present-day conditions." Most towns imposed curfews to help alleviate the problem.[36]

Education also became a daily concern for the people of the Great Plains. Many public school teachers quit their poor-paying jobs for higher salaries in the war industries. As early as February 1942 a teacher shortage emerged across the Great Plains. In Sedgwick County, Kansas, the Wichita aircraft industries drew the teachers like a siren, and thirty of sixty-eight rural schoolteachers had resigned for the next year by mid-April. In Montana school principals worried that the draft of male teachers into the military would require the employment of more female teachers, but vacancies might remain for industrial arts and boy's athletics, among other courses and activities traditionally taught or supervised by male instructors. Many Oklahoma school districts quickly experienced a loss of teachers. With entry-level teaching positions paying only $1,000 in Oklahoma City and $1,400 in Tulsa, better-paying jobs were to be had for the asking, easily boosting annual income by $1,000. In the autumn the Oklahoma Education Association predicted a shortage of four hundred to five hundred industrial arts teachers because they could command salaries from 50 to 100 percent above their school compensation in the war plants. With trainees for various defense industries in Oklahoma City earning $90 per month with a guaranteed job on completion, schoolteachers' salaries had little appeal for mobile young men and women.[37]

When teachers broke their contracts midyear, school boards protested to the federal government that it had lured them away. In Nebraska school superintendents charged the federal government with "enticement" because government-supported war industries easily paid twice the salaries of the state's teachers. As a result turnover climbed as high as 50 percent in many school districts, and teachers had little remorse about walking way from their contracts if better-paying jobs emerged elsewhere. The Nebraska Association of County Superintendents joined with the Association of School Boards and Executives and the Nebraska Educational Association to advocate revoking teachers' licenses for one year if they broke their contracts. By the autumn of 1943 approximately fifteen hundred rural schools had closed in Nebraska as a result of the teacher shortage.[38]

Similarly, in Amarillo one observer noted that a "terrific" teacher shortage threatened the future of high school football at the smaller schools. One Oklahoma school superintendent, faced with the flight of teachers from his classrooms, argued, "It should be made clear to teachers that it is their patriotic duty to stay on the job." In Roswell, New Mexico, the school board increased teachers' salaries and hoped that the "pay and the patriotic opportunity" would have a "positive appeal." Money to be made in the war industries, rather than dedication to teaching or patriotism, clinched the decisions of most teachers who left their positions. By February 1943 20 percent of the teachers in the twenty-three schools of Dallas County, Texas, had left for the military or war industries. The usual reserve of teachers had evaporated, and one observer noted that only the patriotic remained. Yet, with teachers earning only $100 per month, $90 after deductions, for a total of $810 for nine months, those who lived on that salary for the year averaged only $67.50 per month. Little wonder that so many left for higher-paying jobs. Other problems also developed. By mid-October 1942 scores of children whose parents worked in the Wichita defense industries had moved into a 604-unit trailer camp near the Veteran's Hospital. Their school district consisted of a one-room school, and the Wichita schools did not have room for them. The county superintendent of education, Adel F. Throkmorton, called the situation that the children faced "hopeless."[39]

The draft and defense industry jobs also pulled male students away from colleges and universities. Most college administrators could not accurately predict the number of students who would arrive for the fall 1941 semester, but all expected fewer students and less tuition revenue. By mid-March 1942 nine institutions of higher education in North Dakota experienced a collective loss of 23 percent of the male enrollment from the previous year. Nebraska's twenty-three state teachers colleges and denominational schools lost 25 percent of their enrollment by the fall semester of 1943; many of these students had been training to become teachers. Similarly, when the spring semester began at South Dakota State College in 1942, male enrollment declined, and the president informed the governor that additional state support might be needed. By fall enrollment had dropped by 95, to 1,132 students, and it continued to decline until only 245 women and 102 men enrolled for the 1944–45 academic year.[40]

Moreover, few of the teachers who left would return, and the schools that closed would not reopen. The war changed everything, including the structure of school systems and districts, the design of instruction, and teacher training and placement. Certainly, the war brought about curriculum changes, and high schools often became more vocationally oriented. The public also expected the schools to support community activities, such as scrap and bond drives. Moreover, the war also disrupted normal school activities. In West Texas, for example, athletic coaches and band leaders were reportedly as scare as the unemployed. More teachers who had been granted temporary wartime certification entered classrooms to help meet the desperate need. Academic standards often declined, teaching loads increased, and teacher turnover rates remained high. In terms of education the war wrought havoc on many local school districts, particularly those with a large number of rural schools. By the time the war ended, the one-room country school on the Great Plains had largely become an institution of the past. Urban schools did not close, but they did become severely crowded in defense industry cities because the federal government did not provide funds for new buildings unless the schools reached 200 percent capacity.[41]

World War II brought, among other things, a serious housing problem to the Great Plains. Immediately, the war forced city planners to address the housing shortage in areas where defense industries and military posts drew both civilian employees and military personnel. No Great Plains defense industry city ever gained control of its housing problem, but no city could afford to ignore it. Although shortages of materials became a constant problem, once the federal government designated a city or town a "national defense housing area" contractors theoretically could secure building materials for the construction of housing for military officers. City councils, chambers of commerce, and state politicians worked hard to ensure that their communities received this designation. In January 1942 Denver's city council began planning a hundred-unit housing project that would be devoted exclusively to army officers stationed at Lowry Field. The War Department requested this construction, and the Federal Public Housing Authority guaranteed the loans. In addition to appreciating the needed extra housing, the city fathers relished the $600,000 addition to the property tax rolls. In Denver the realty board worked to convert vacant stores into apartments for defense industry workers. With an estimated seventy-five thousand additional housing units needed, the pressure to provide it proved enormous.[42]

At the same time Roswell, New Mexico, was designated a defense housing area, and work began on 250 housing units for air base families and defense workers. Contractors used private capital to finance their construction projects, but the ability to acquire the building materials proved even more important. In Fort Worth the Consolidated Vultee Aircraft Corporation attracted many single women as workers, but the city had few suitable apartments given the mores of the day. As a result the company built two-story barracks or dormitories with federal funds. Known as "liberator" or "victory" villages, these studio apartments, with the bathroom down the hall, helped meet the housing needs of fifteen hundred workers. Most single female workers in the Dallas/Fort Worth area became borders in private homes or rooming houses.[43]

The provision of adequate housing proved no small task. In Oklahoma City the projected workforce of at least thirty-one thousand at the Douglas Aircraft Company and the Oklahoma City air depot (later Tinker Field), which would increase the payroll by as much as $45 million annually, created an incredible demand for housing. The Chamber of Commerce estimated a population increase of fifty thousand from those two military projects alone, and that translated into the need for prefabricated houses, which the federal government intended to purchase for defense workers. By late January 1942 the population of Wichita had increased by twenty-five thousand since 1940, with only 4,000 new housing units being built, the majority by private contractors. Observers believed that private industry would need to build 3,500 homes and the federal government finance the construction of twice that number to avoid a housing crisis. By mid-March the Southern Mill and Manufacturing Company worked to provide 1,860 prefabricated houses for a government housing project in Wichita, and city and federal officials planned a new housing area for 10,000 units south of town. The Sedgwick County Taxpayers Union, however, organized to block the extension of sewer and water lines as well as fire protection into the newly incorporated and developing industrial and residential areas, but the city government essentially ignored it, in part as a patriotic duty, and in part because it needed more property tax revenue.[44]

In Dallas the housing shortage became so critical that the city contemplated the denial of new war industry contracts because the needed workers would not be able to find places to live. Prefabricated houses and trailers seemed to some observers to be the solution, but little improvement occurred. By mid-1945 the housing shortage in Dallas, Wichita, and Albuquerque had become the most critical in the history of those cities. Wichita and Albuquerque officials reported "zero" housing available, while Dallas authorities announced, "The situation now is the worst ever." In these cities the pressure for housing came not only from war workers but also from returning veterans, government employees, and military personnel. Denver officials relaxed zoning regulations to permit more homeowners to rent rooms to workers and the wives of servicemen recuperating at Fitzsimons Army Hospital.[45]

Small towns experienced similar problems. In Salina homeowners rented their backyards to trailer owners, but even here crowding occurred, and the city commission prevented property owners from parking more than two trailers in their backyards for living purposes. By midsummer 1942 in Mead, Nebraska, the town's population of 260 braced for the arrival of as many as 9,000 men to work on the construction of an ordnance plant. Once the project was completed, as many as 4,000 workers would be employed. Since the plant would, no doubt, be temporary, the best solution to the housing situation seemed the provision of train transportation and staggered shifts that would enable workers to leave via rail when the next shift arrived. This system would permit workers to live in nearby cities and towns rather than require the construction of houses or apartments that would be abandoned when the war ended.[46]

Cultural problems also developed. By early March a number

of workers with trailers had arrived in Mead, and, although they tended to be skilled, married workers with children, one contemporary noted that they "suffer under the suspicion of local people, who are inclined to dismiss all such roving workers as trash." In Amarillo a newly arrived wife with her army husband had her first rent check denied at a local bank. When she went to the bank to inquire about the problem, the manager told her "curt and cold" that she had signed the signature card "Dellie Hahne" but signed the check "Mrs. Dellie Hahne." She remembered the incident forty years later as an "immediate cold, contemptuous dismissal": "I was an outsider." Similarly, in Fort Worth a landlord advertised an apartment for rent with restrictions that read: "No street-walkers, home wreckers, drunks wanted; couples must present marriage certificate." In May 1942 Casper, Wyoming, also experienced a serious housing shortage when construction began at the army air base. Petroleum refinery workers and military families kept the housing demand high and the housing supply short in Casper throughout the war. Families with children experienced considerable difficulty locating housing because landlords did not want them, particularly in Casper. In Cheyenne many landlords refused to rent rooms to women with babies, and across the Great Plains housing officials in war industry cities urged homeowners to rent individual rooms if possible. Property owners in Salina, however, often discriminated against army wives because they preferred workers whom they believed would stay longer.[47]

Other problems occurred. In 1940 Bellevue, Nebraska, for example, a town of 1,184 residents, did not have paved streets, streetlights or signs, or sewers or storm drains. On December 6, when residents learned that a bomber assembly plant would be located at nearby Fort Crook, everyone knew that the proposed workforce of twenty-seven thousand would transform the community. Omaha officials a dozen miles away had worked hard to secure the plant, and President Roosevelt wanted the plains states to receive defense contracts to dampen complaints that the federal government ignored them during World War I. Omaha seemed a likely source for labor and housing, but property values also increased in Bellevue. City lots that sold for $15 prior to the arrival of the Glenn Martin bomber plant shot up in price to $825 in 1941. Bellevue officials quickly attempted to implement a zoning plan to avoid "discord and confusion." In February 1941 the town hired an engineer and an attorney to assess community needs and draft codes and ordinances. Bellevue officials particularly worried about controlling the number of trailer homes because they would decrease property values and give the community a transient quality. By April Bellevue officials had zoned the town for future growth, separated the trailer camps from the better homes, and established building codes that met Federal Public Housing Authority requirements for loans. Bellevue also secured assistance from both the WPA, to improve the sewers and streets, and the Public Works Administration, for a better water system, a health center, a new elementary school, and an expanded high school. In January 1942, when the bomber plant began operation, the town boomed with new residents and money, but the streets remained unpaved and were often muddy, a state of affairs that led to the ouster of the council members in April 1944.[48]

Omaha officials were not enamored with Bellevue and Sarpy County zoning plans, and they moved to take that responsibility, much to the displeasure of county officials because the tax base fell within their jurisdiction. Almost immediately, Omaha and Sarpy County officials began arguing over which entity had responsibility for zoning around the bomber plant. County officials in particular wanted to protect residents "from infiltration of the gambler, the bootlegger, and women of shady occupation" as well as to ensure attractive offers to other companies. They took especial offense when Omaha's mayor suggested that they did not have the experience to handle the job. County sympathizers advocated home rule, guaranteed by the legislature, and accused Omaha officials of trying to extend their authority across the state. Ultimately, the state legislature took responsibility for the zoning because the two polities could not agree and discussions degenerated into acrimony. An unintended consequence of this war-driven fight over zoning authority was the extension of state legislative power over issues that heretofore had been local in nature.[49]

Limited available housing restricted the recruitment of labor throughout the war. By spring 1942 in Amarillo, for example, the demand for "desirable living quarters" exceeded supply, and trailer homes began to dot sections of the city. But, with lumber supplies frozen for all building except war plant construction, city officials contemplated the erection of temporary "duration dormitories" for defense industry workers and military families. Chamber of Commerce members feared that, without adequate housing, defense workers would go elsewhere, and the "no-children" rule generally invoked by landlords did not help. Except for the establishment of trailer camps and tent cities near war industry construction projects, no one had an immediate solution for the housing problem in Amarillo. Similarly, as late as June 1945 the Goodyear Tire and Rubber Company in Topeka needed more workers, but it had exhausted the local labor pool, and it did not believe that an adequate number of workers could be found until the housing problem was solved. Without adequate housing outside recruiting proved futile. The company needed 500 workers immediately and, by August, another 250 workers, with an additional 100 per month for the next four months. The resulting housing-driven labor shortage held production at the plant to only 39 percent of capacity.[50]

Housing shortages caused rents to shoot up, with Office of Price Administration (OPA) rent controls quickly following. By late February 1942 rents in Wichita had increased from $30 to $45 per month since January, but federal officials considered the escalation within the realm of fairness. In Salina residents complained that rents had increased from $35 to $70 per month within three weeks because of housing pressures created by the construction of the Smoky Hill Air Base. By summer OPA officials, however, had held meetings across the plains about rent hikes. Soon thereafter, the agency froze rents, much to the displeasure of property owners who rented apartments and houses.[51]

Although the federal government declared Cheyenne and Casper "defense rental areas" and requested landlords to voluntarily freeze rents at March 1, 1942, rates, many landlords ignored the edict. One contemporary complained that landlords charged "all they can get."

As a result the OPA issued maximum-rent regulations. By April 1943 landlords complained that the rent freeze was "working a hardship on scores of property owners, including old couples, and old ladies who have small rental properties which represented their life savings and their only present source of income." Throughout the war landlords in Casper and Cheyenne considered themselves abused by the OPA, but the freeze remained in place.[52]

In Hastings rents also doubled, going from an average of $35 to as much as $70 per month almost immediately after Pearl Harbor, and ordnance depot workers charged landlords with gouging. Lieutenant Commander W. B. Short, who oversaw construction of the depot, called the rent increase "decidedly not Christian." Rate increases also affected locals, who not only resented the intrusion of the depot workers but also sometimes had to take second jobs to pay their increased rents. There were eight thousand workers at the naval ammunition depot at its peak, and, since war industry workers had a reputation for being "good spenders," landlords operating on the premise that money should be made when the opportunity prevailed considered them fair game for exploitation. Not all landlords gouged their tenants, but the OPA accused some in Bismarck of being "overly ambitious." In reality rent controls established by the federal government on December 1, 1942, benefited landlords because they kept rates reasonable. As a result renters could afford to pay, and eviction problems were avoided, but these benefits were not always apparent to landlords who wanted to charge all the market would bear.[53]

Despite the general can-do attitude and spirit of self-sacrifice for the war effort, the home front on the Great Plains had its dark sides. Tolerance for conscientious objectors faded quickly, and some ended in jail for rejecting the draft. As early as May 1940 law enforcement officers at Waxahachie, near Odessa, Texas, had to rescue more than fifty members of the Jehovah's Witnesses from a ranch house where they had fled from an angry mob because they had refused to salute the American flag and pledged that they would not fight for the United States and because they attempted to distribute antiwar literature. Although one member attributed their rescue to divine intervention, law enforcement officers jailed them with twenty other conscientious objectors for their own protection. The county attorney reported that they would remain in jail until they saluted the flag, although no charges were filed against these West Texans. As the town "fairly seethed with indignation over alleged insults to the United States flag," a grand jury convened in Ellis County to hear evidence against them, including accusations that they were Nazi sympathizers and that they had insulted the flag. With a mob congregating outside the jail and threatening to take matters into its own hands, the town reportedly was ready to blow "like a case of TNT." The prisoners, including a few children, filled the entire second and third floors of the county jail and taxed the resources of the sheriff's office. Ultimately, passions cooled, common sense and the law prevailed, and they were released.[54]

In central Kansas the Mennonites also experienced intimidation and violence. Kansans showed no tolerance for conscientious objectors who refused military service. In 1939, at the outbreak of war, residents in Newton renewed their anti-German hysteria from World War I and directed it against the local Mennonites. In September the city commission asked the U.S. Justice Department to investigate rumors that "certain disloyal or un-American organizations, specifically the German-American Bund, [had] been active in or near Newtown." Edmund G. Kaufman, the president of the sectarian Bethel College, responded by affirming the loyalty of the Mennonites and urged everyone to remember the Sermon on the Mount. With the declaration of war against Japan came an increase in insults to and the alienation of the Mennonite community. By early April 1942 the intimidation included smearing yellow paint on Mennonite businesses. Although the Selective Service Act of September 1940 excused from military service anyone who, "by reason of religious training and belief, is conscientiously opposed to participation in war in any form," conscientious objectors could meet their wartime service obligation by conducting work of "national importance under civilian direction," such as soil conservation and hospital work. Still, prejudice against them prevailed.[55]

Almost 50 percent of the Mennonite men drafted in Kansas opted for duty in the Civilian Public Service, while another 18 percent accepted noncombat military duty, for a considerably higher percentage than peace church members nationwide. In Kansas county draft boards willingly extended conscientious objector classification to the young Mennonites, but the non-Mennonite community was less tolerant. In August 1944 twelve Mennonites traveling by bus from Hutchinson to Leavenworth to take preinduction army physicals were subject to beatings by the nonpacifists on board. In South Dakota some conscientious objectors among the Hutterites, Mennonites, and Jehovah's Witnesses also suffered persecution that led to jail sentences for their refusal to register for the draft. In Alma, Nebraska, a resident with a German surname awoke one morning to find his front porch splattered with yellow paint, although there and in Oklahoma the Seventh-Day Adventists avoided trouble because they willingly served in the military's medical corps, which enabled them to maintain noncombat conscientious objector status. Overall, however, conscientious objectors on the Great Plains endured occasional physical and mental intimidation as an outgrowth of intolerance, but they were not subjected to mass violence.[56]

Despite the intolerance exhibited by some against conscientious objectors and ethnic minorities suspected of disloyalty, the people of the Great Plains committed themselves to the war effort and made the personal adjustments mandated by rapid changes in wartime society. Personal feelings and symbols of patriotism were important. A sense of unity and individual commitment prevailed as Great Plains residents contributed to the war as it was fought on the nation's home front. Like it or not, the war affected the lives of everyone. For the people of the Great Plains, then, the war became all consuming. Almost everyone in the region wanted to participate in some way. In late September 1941, for example, the Kansas Association of Insurance Agents met to discuss the effect that the still-distant but rapidly approaching war could have on clients, businesses, and themselves. Topics of discussion included claims resulting from high blood pressure caused by stress, industrial accidents resulting from increased and rapid production, and automobile accidents resulting from more old cars on the highways, all attributable to the war. Similarly, the Lotos Club in Lincoln, Nebraska, which served as a social club and an organization for the discussion of art, history, music, and literature, now folded bandages, made clothing, and sent money to the British War Relief Fund. In Norman, Oklahoma, the Blue Star Mother's Club prepared surgical dressings for the Red Cross. By spring 1942 nearly every mundane activity now had some association with the war. In Denver Mrs. Amos C. Sudler, the chair of the Women's Home Arsenal Committee of the Salvation Army, announced that "indiscriminate house cleaning this spring will be almost as bad as sabotage," and she urged women to "clean house for victory." In Amarillo the local editor observed that "nothing stirs patriot fever like good martial music," and the municipal band agreed to an on-call status to play at rallies and public meetings whenever city and community defense officials sought their services. The band's conductor, Robert Louis Barron, asked his musicians to volunteer for this "defense job" to help keep up morale in Amarillo.[57]

Yet intense emotional and physical commitment on the home front could not be sustained. As piles of scrap metal, tires, and newspaper became common sights across the Great Plains, enthusiasm for collective efforts and symbolic acts waned. By late summer 1942 civilian defense training for volunteer air raid workers, auxiliary firemen, and ambulance drivers slowed as the immediate threat of attack and sabotage dissipated. Volunteer and home front projects such as victory gardens and bond and scrap drives faded, particularly after 1944. In Rapid City, South Dakota, women, not men, registered for civilian defense duty, and many areas remained understaffed. Late in the war many Great Plains residents considered civil defense work a waste of time, and one contemporary in Wyoming urged residents not to plan civil defense programs "beyond the realm of credulity," given the state's geography and proximity to the actual fighting.[58]

Certainly, the construction boom and the defense industries gave a host of workers employment and disposable income. In urban areas stores often remained open on Monday nights, and banks offered evening hours at least one day each week. Night spots and "hot spots" operated around-the-clock unless local officials imposed a curfew, as they did in Wichita. One observer noted, "To hear the groans you would think that the strip tease was an essential industry. It seems now that most of the morale on the home front is built up between midnight and morning." Other subtle changes occurred. Although almost everyone welcomed the construction of wartime housing, contractors often struggled to get needed materials, particularly lumber, and they usually rushed their jobs, particularly if they fell behind schedule because of material shortages. Housing built for the federal government often proved shoddy. In Salina, Kansas, for example, housing promoted as temporary soon became permanent and lowered the property values of nearby private homes.[59]

Moreover, population migration to the cities with war industries continued to cause infrastructure problems. In Oklahoma City, for example, by the end of the war the primary goal of the city government was to expand its sewer system. This system had been designed for 75,000 residents as early as 1910, but it now served 225,000 people. Breaks became common, with corresponding health and odor problems. By mid-May 1941 miles of new homes built at the rate of thirty-five houses each week lined new city streets in Wichita. With an average of twelve men working on each house, the building tradesmen reportedly were "reaping a golden harvest." Grocery stores and gas stations opened to service the new workers, and automobile traffic became a major problem for city officials.[60]

For families that did not lose sons or daughters or see them injured, the conflict was a good war. The people of the Great Plains experienced prosperity, a quickened pace in living (largely job driven), and a sense of commitment for the common good. Even so, war-imposed sacrifices were often met with complaint and sometimes resistance and rejection. In the end the people of the Great Plains would sacrifice for the home front war, but it would be a comparative sacrifice. They would do their part, but they did not want to sacrifice more than those living in other regions. If they believed that the wartime hardships of the home front were not shared equally, they complained loudly and often ignored or willingly violated regulations. In many respects the manner in which they dealt with rationing was both their brightest and their darkest hour.

FIVE | Rationing

News of a new European war brought a spike in domestic prices for residents of the Great Plains. By September 7, 1939, only six days after Germany invaded Poland, food prices had escalated. Housewives complained and wanted local, state, and national officials to protect them from profiteering, hoarding, and speculation, which would affect the cost of "necessities." As housewives lined up to make needed or wanted purchases, wholesalers and retailers blamed them, not the war, for price escalation. Demand, not supply, they contended, caused a 50 percent jump in prices for sugar, meat, butter, and lard. In the months ahead, as the nation converted from peacetime to wartime industries, consumers experienced spot shortages of certain goods and foods. Prices steadily escalated but eventually leveled off in late October 1941 after increasing about 8 percent from the previous year. Harry Chrysler, the secretary of the Colorado Retailers Association, believed that prices would rise no further, saying, "I can't see where there will be any radical advance in the average food prices, because we are already at the peak, or very near it." He did not believe that workers had sufficient buying power to feed inflation, and the nation remained at peace.[1]

When the United States entered the war, however, everything changed. In January 1942 Congress approved the Emergency Price Control Act, which gave the Office of Price Administration (OPA) the authority to set maximum prices on most commodities and rents and rationed products. In April the OPA attempted to control rapidly rising prices by issuing its General Maximum Price Regulation. This dictate froze most prices at the highest level reached in March. Consumer prices, however, continued to rise, for an 18 percent increase between 1941 and 1943, but the OPA eventually gained control of inflation. The agency also attempted to institute a rationing program. It hoped that price controls and rationing would keep costs under control and guarantee a "fair share of goods made scarce by war" for everyone. Rationing was also meant to be a symbolic, patriotic action demonstrating public commitment, a sense of community, and democratic obligation and, as such, giving people an opportunity to contribute to the war effort. As a result the family dinner table and the local gas station became domestic war fronts.[2]

With the loss of 97 percent of the nation's rubber supply to Japanese conquests in the Far East, the OPA quickly and strictly limited the purchase of rubber tires. In late December 1941 tire rationing began with the opening of state and local rationing boards. Theoretically, new tires could not be purchased, unless they were destined for medical and emergency services. Counties received tires and tubes by quota based on the number of vehicles registered, and the boards determined who could purchase them. In order to buy a new tire a motorist first had to have the old tire checked by a certified dealer. At no charge the dealer would decide whether the tire should be retreaded or replaced. If a replacement was needed, the motorist received a certificate for presentation to the rationing board, which would review the case and, the motorist hoped, issue another certificate authorizing the purchase. Appeals could be made to state tire-rationing boards. Local defense councils appointed the tire-rationing boards, which state officials or the governor's office then approved. All members of the rationing boards took an oath to become agents of the United States. In order to aid the tire-rationing program, the American Automobile Association asked its members in Colorado, Wyoming, and New Mexico to reduce family driving by 50 percent to save tires and launched a "budget your mileage campaign."[3]

Across the Great Plains tire theft and the sale of stolen tires soon became a problem, and retreads became standard replacements. Police and sheriff's departments urged drivers not to park their cars outside overnight and to record the serial numbers of their tires as well as lock their trunks. Gas stations and tire dealers also offered to register tires and provide proof of ownership, but a black market quickly developed for tires. Kansans made matters worse because many did not understand the need to ration tires, or, in fact, believe that there was a need to ration them, even though the state rationing board labeled fast drivers, that is, those who drove over forty miles per hour, "unpatriotic" because they wasted rubber.[4]

As tires wore out with little chance of replacement, abandoned cars, or at least undrivable cars, began to appear parked on city streets, to the annoyance of more fastidious residents. Individuals who purchased or sold tires without the approval of county rationing boards received heavy fines in federal court—if they got caught. Tire rationing also had a multiplier effect. Without new or even used tires scarce or nonexistent, and with metals primarily diverted to the military, drivers bought few cars. Automobile dealerships often converted to war industries. In Wichita the showroom of the Oldsmobile dealer became an office of the U.S. Employment Service. The rubber shortage also forced schools, such as those in Cheyenne, to restrict or cancel athletic, music, and other school activities because rationing boards approved tire replacements for school buses only for the purpose of transporting students to class. In Salina, Kansas, when the city rationing board allotted tires and tubes, the fortunate recipients had their names published in the local newspaper, along with the number of items received, such as one truck tire, one tube, or one passenger tire. Even so, little evidence indicates that tire rationing caused Great Plains residents to limit automobile travel substantially until near the end of the war.[5]

Plains residents tended to drive more than federal officials had assumed they would, perhaps because of the vast distances between the places they wanted to go. In Salina during spring 1943 the tire shortage became so critical that the county ration board ruled that anyone who received a speeding ticket would be denied new tires. In Kansas as well the state highway patrol sent county rationing boards copies of tickets issued to speeders and reckless drivers, who because of their infractions were prohibited from purchasing recapped tires. Drivers on the road for pleasure trips could have their names legally reported to the boards for the same purpose. In Denver reckless driving and tire hoarding became grounds for losing gasoline ration books. One important benefit of tire rationing beyond diverting more rubber to the military, however, emerged when the state compiled statistics on traffic fatalities. With speed limits reduced, federal, state, and local police officials reported fewer accidents and deaths than usual.[6]

Oil production also quickly became critical for the nations involved in the war. By 1939 Japan was consuming 46 million barrels but producing only 3 million barrels annually. The United States supplied about three-fourths of that oil—until President Roosevelt imposed an oil embargo in July 1941. The loss of this market proved inconsequential for the United States because the American petroleum industry fueled the Allied war effort. Still, prices increased. By May 1941 the demand for petroleum products by the defense industry and motorists increased by 15 percent. Crude oil prices jumped $0.10 per barrel in Kansas, Oklahoma, Texas, and New Mexico, bumping prices to $1.25 per barrel in Kansas and Oklahoma and $1.29 per barrel in Texas and New Mexico. Allied needs and high prices stimulated increased production and "wildcatting," that is, the search for new wells by independent operators. In 1941 production in the Texas Panhandle reached a record 27.9 million barrels, up from 26.7 million the previous year. The Texas Railroad Commission set production rates for oil and natural gas in the state. Texas, with half the known oil reserves in the United States, provided the lead for other states concerning production guidelines. Major expansion could not occur, however, because the military needed steel to build airplanes and tanks, making it difficult for the petroleum companies to procure enough steel to build the new derricks, drills, and pumping equipment they needed. Still, by 1942 the number of oil wells in the Texas Panhandle had increased by approximately 12 percent since 1940, from 4,788 to 5,378. The Office of Production Management, however, also limited the number of wells to one per forty acres, not for conservation purposes, but to prevent a steel shortage in the war industries. Producers argued that geologic lay-

FIGURE 11. In 1939 oil wells reached the outskirts of Oklahoma City. During the war Great Plains residents complained about gasoline rationing because they believed that the federal government limited sales in the region to meet the needs of others, particularly in the Eastern United States. This photograph looks west and north near the intersection of Byars and Reno. (Western History Collections, University of Oklahoma Libraries)

ers, not acreage, determined how many wells could be drilled in an area, but antiquated equipment as well as policy reduced both drilling and pumping capacity during the war. By 1943 drilling crews incurred shortages of replacement parts, bits, drill pipe, and engine parts.[7]

As late as June 1941 many Great Plains residents did not believe that an oil or gasoline shortage would affect them. One Nebraska editor reported that the oil industry could produce far beyond demand and that, while a shortage existed along the Atlantic seaboard, it stemmed from transportation problems and shipments to Great Britain. By August gasoline supplies still seemed more than adequate for the foreseeable future. In January 1942, then, when gasoline rationing began in the East because of transportation and distribution problems that prevented adequate supply, plains residents were surprised. And, when the OPA applied gasoline rationing to the Great Plains, they were angry. In Kansas a group of state legislators called it "nonsensical, unjustified, and asinine" as well as a real and basic threat to the Kansas war program, economic life, and business activity. Great Plains refiners produced gasoline in abundance, and large reserves remained untapped, they argued. For Kansans gasoline rationing could not be justified for economic or practical reasons. Most Great Plains residents agreed, particularly after they learned that one oil field near McPherson produced more than 8 million barrels of crude in 1942 and that geologists estimated the underground pool at more than 70 million barrels. In Denver drivers quickly circumvented OPA gasoline rationing through the black market. They knew that a phone call to their gas station for a "quickie" would lead to several gallons delivered to their homes, much like bootleg liquor during Prohibition, and at similarly "exorbitant prices."[8]

On December 1, 1942, when the Petroleum Administration for War (PAW) issued a nationwide gasoline-rationing policy, drivers with a car sticker received only four gallons per week, reduced to three the next year and two in March 1944. Everyday drivers received an "A" ration book, while "B" ration books went to people who commuted more than six miles per week to war industry jobs. "C" ration books went to individuals in "essential" occupations, such as doctors, veterinarians, and government officials. County rationing officers distributed the ration books on driver registration, at which time drivers certified that they did not own more than five tires for each passenger car. Additional tires had to be sold to the Office of Defense Transportation. As complaints mounted the editor of the *Daily Oklahoman* reminded readers, "You should be willing to shoulder some personal hardship under these new conditions, so don't complain unless you really have a kick coming." Great Plains drivers had never confronted gasoline shortages before, and they disliked the restrictions that rationing imposed on their freedom. Even so, pleasure driving nearly ceased.[9]

To help save gasoline, oil, and rubber state officials also asked motorists to limit their speed to forty-five miles per hour and to drive less. In 1942 the state legislature in Oklahoma and the Texas Highway Commission required drivers to observe speed limits as low as thirty-five miles per hour because voluntary compliance had failed on the relatively low-trafficked and isolated roads in the expansive, even desolate southern plains. In July state highway officials estimated that nearly 78 percent of Coloradoans exceeded the recommended speed limit of forty miles per hour. Most drove between fifty and sixty. In North Dakota Governor John Moss asked residents to drive under fifty miles per hour, and by early 1944 South Dakota slowed traffic to forty on highways. Several months later, on the Wyoming plains, the superintendent of the state highway department complained that "few" drivers observed the thirty-five-mile-per-hour speed limit and that a "good many" exceeded sixty miles per hour regularly, but he attributed the speeding to out-of-state drivers, as did officials in Colorado faced with a similar situation. In Kansas Governor Ratner and, later, Governor Schoeppel asked residents to observe thirty-mile-per-hour speed limits. Travelers, however, observed that Kansans, particularly war industry workers, flagrantly violated those requests. Governor Schoeppel lamented, "It is pretty hard to compel people, by law, to do something if they do not want to do so as law abiding individuals." He saw no hope of slowing them down with a "strict law." For most Kansans patriotism was one thing, but their preoccupation with time and space in the form of distance was quite another, especially once they were in their automobiles.[10]

Great Plains residents, however, complained less about the speed restrictions and more about gasoline rationing because they believed that crude oil production and supplies could meet all automotive needs. As a result they did not give universal cooperation to the federal government's gasoline-rationing program. Denverites particularly balked at registering for ration books because they, too, did not believe that gasoline was in short supply. Soon, a black market for gasoline coupons developed, particularly in Kansas, where farmers sold or traded gasoline coupons intended for the purchase of tractor fuel to owners of passenger cars. Gasoline ration books also became the objects of theft by criminals who operated black markets for the acquisition of gasoline. By late 1943 counterfeiters allegedly from

FIGURE 12. Gasoline rationing affected the people of the Great Plains in many ways. Family drives and vacations essentially disappeared until the war ended. In 1942 horse power replaced engine power on this milk wagon in Nebraska. (Nebraska State Historical Society, MacDonald Collection, RG 2183-19430811 [5])

the East began selling gasoline ration books in Kansas, Oklahoma, and Texas. Gasoline sold improperly was known as "black gas," that is, black market gasoline.[11]

The shortage of gasoline in the Great Plains stemmed from quotas placed on refineries by the PAW in order to increase the production of aviation fuel and supplies for the East Coast. In August 1943 the PAW established new gasoline quotas for the Great Plains by lowering supplies 15 percent, or "appreciably" below the rate of consumption. Although gasoline had been rationed nationwide since December 1, 1942, in order to preserve rubber, the agency now argued that consumption had increased in the region while production had declined, the decline being due to military demands on the refiners for higher-octane aviation fuel and the increasing need for fuel oil by war industries. Moreover, pipelines had been completed to enable the transport of more gasoline to the East and, thus, more equitable distribution.[12]

During 1943 in the Dakotas, Nebraska, Kansas, and New Mexico, the PAW tightened its gasoline-rationing program by reducing the value of all passenger car coupons to three gallons and lowered the gasoline allowances for workers who qualified for more fuel because they commuted to essential war industries. The PAW wanted to use this new rationing policy to limit average automobile driving to five thousand miles per car annually. The plains states governors reacted angrily and sought a repeal of the new regulations. Governor Schoeppel of Kansas called the new policies "terrible blunders" and "stupidity" caused by a lack of "foresight and judgment." Governor M. Q. Sharpe of South Dakota appealed to President Roosevelt and Harold Ickes, the head of the PAW, to delay the reduction in gasoline until after the wheat harvest because of the vast distances within the region traveled by custom cutters and other agricultural workers. Ickes, however, argued that the cutback was necessary because production had declined in many oil fields in the Great Plains and because petroleum tankers remained in short supply owing to losses from enemy attacks in the Atlantic. Gasoline production for domestic use also lagged because of insufficient railroad tank cars, inadequate labor (owing to the draft), low wages in the oil fields compared to the war industries, low pricing at the wellhead, and wartime price freezes (which discouraged wildcat drilling).[13]

The most important reason for the decline in gasoline production for automobiles, however, was military need. In 1940 approximately 37 percent of each forty-two-gallon barrel of crude oil was manufactured into automobile gasoline. In 1943 that percentage fell to 25 percent. Put differently, a gasoline shortage did not exist because Great Plains oil companies could not pump enough oil. Rather, government policy demanding production for military uses and the equalization of automobile gasoline for East Coast consumers caused fuel shortages in the plains. Ickes promised, however, that the farmers in the Great Plains would be treated fairly and receive "adequate" gasoline for their farm operations. Even so, refineries owned by farmers' cooperatives, such as those at Phillipsburg and

McPherson, Kansas, found that the large-scale refiners with aviation fuel contracts received the crude needed to meet agricultural demands. In fact the crude oil allotments for the large-scale refiners were higher than the amount of crude they received. By mid-September 1943 the cooperatives sold all the automotive gasoline they produced each day. No supplies existed, and some farmers ran out of fuel and could not get more. The PAW suggested that the refiners purchase the shortfall in allotted crude oil from Texas, but the Kansas cooperatives complained that they would have enough oil if the big companies did not send Kansas crude to refiners in Oklahoma, Missouri, and Illinois for the production of aviation fuel.[14]

Governor Schoeppel complained to Ickes that refineries operated by farmers' cooperatives did not qualify for a "primary war plant" rating and, therefore, could not acquire the crude oil needed to remain in business. He argued that the oil wells in Kansas pumped at full capacity and that the problem was not one of production but one of allocation. In order to ensure the success of the state's refining industry, he requested an increase in crude oil allocations to refiners that supplied agricultural areas. Ickes replied that military needs had top priority and that "non-war" refiners received equitable treatment by getting 80 percent of their "normal" crude oil supplies. Moreover, with two-thirds of the Kansas refiners classified as "war plants," he did not see a serious problem. If the refiners wanted more oil, they could buy it from Texas.[15]

Not until 1944, however, did the PAW, which coordinated federal and state petroleum policies, seek increased production to meet greater military demands resulting from the long-range bombing of Germany and planning for the Normandy invasion. The PAW now authorized one well per twenty acres and sought the drilling of 24,000 new wells nationwide. As a result, the number of wells in the Texas Panhandle increased to 5,901, with production of 33.4 million barrels in 1944, the peak year. Although the number of Panhandle oil wells increased to 6,052 in 1945, the end of the war brought production cutbacks to 31.7 million barrels for the year. Although the OPA set ceiling prices for oil that enabled refineries to make a profit, the prices for crude oil at the wellhead differed across the southern plains because crude oil has varying qualities, depending on impurities in the oil. Ultimately, Texas produced as much as 44.6 percent of domestic petroleum during the war. Moreover, throughout the war the state, not the federal government, retained control of production and planning for the postwar years, and the Texas Railroad Commission and other state oil agencies successfully countered federal attempts to regulate the oil industry.[16]

During the war, then, the Great Plains oil companies protested gasoline rationing by arguing that it would destroy their industry, and many station operators believed that rationing would put them out of business. Everyone proclaimed support for the war effort, but most Great Plains residents believed that the government was asking them to do too much. They compared their needs to those of others and concluded that they were being asked for a disproportionate sacrifice. Indeed, comparative sacrifice often seemed unbalanced and unfair to Great Plains residents. In December 1942 the editor of the *Amarillo Globe* captured the problem of comparative sacrifice best when he wrote, "Some people feel that Washington's ration formula as applied to the big cities of the East isn't fair in this part of the country; and that just as much rubber could be saved if the regulations were modified and tailored to fit our way of life in the wide open space." The Potter County ration board responded by announcing that the employees of certain government agencies, including the U.S. Soil Conservation Service and the state comptroller's office, could not have supplemental gasoline rations that exceeded those of private individuals engaged in similar work. When Mark McGee, the OPA chief in Texas, supported the county ration board, contending that mere employment by federal, state, or city governments did not entitle anyone to additional gasoline, the controversy quickly ended because residents believed that "western justice" had protected their interests. Plains men and women would make a patriotic sacrifice, but that sacrifice could not give comparative advantage to people in other regions or special groups. Patriotism was one thing, but personal convenience often superseded it.[17]

Food also became an essential component of federal wartime rationing policy. To aid the war effort the OPA attempted to develop a rationing program that would curb consumption yet give all consumers some choice in and control over food purchases. This intention resulted in the issuing of ration books (containing either coupons or stamps) distributed each month by local ration boards and a complicated point system for using them for the purchase of food. Large families, for example, received meat coupons with more points than smaller families. At grocery stores meat had coupon or point prices and cash prices. Consequently, families with a large number of points each month could more easily meet their food needs without spending cash, something that other consumers needed to make purchases. Local boards administered the rationing program, while the OPA set policy and determined procedures. At first many Americans considered rationing a necessary evil, but Great Plains residents soon took major issue with the food-rationing program, and many felt little guilt about violating rationing policy.[18]

On the Great Plains sugar and beef became the two most important foods rationed during the war; both were high-status foods, the consumption of which gave people a sense of personal success and comfort. During this era consumers also considered sugar a high-energy and nutritious food. Although sugar from beets remained plentiful, much of it went to processing plants for conversion into alcohol, which was used in the manufacture of smokeless powder, and supplies for the table dwindled. Soon sugar bowls disappeared from restaurants because owners could purchase only 80 percent of the amount bought in February 1941, and, when asked for sugar, waitresses often stirred a mere teaspoon into a cup of coffee. In April 1942, with supplies rapidly diminishing, sugar rationing began for retailers and wholesalers, whose allocations depended on a formula that factored purchases and sales since November 1941. Restaurants received 50 percent of the sugar used in March. Thereafter, all purchases required the presentation of ration stamps that limited the amount. Grocers, for example, could exchange one hundred stamps for one hundred pounds of sugar from wholesalers.[19]

Sugar rationing for consumers began on May 5, 1942. Schools across the Great Plains served as registration sites for the acquisition of ration stamps. Registering consumers for the sugar stamps proved no small task, but in Bismarck volunteers considered this work a "patriotic duty" and just as important as more "dramatic jobs." Denver schools closed for several days so that teachers could register some 340,000 residents for ration books. At the time of registering, heads of households had to declare how much sugar they had at home. The OPA allowed two pounds of sugar per family member. If they declared more, sugar registering officials deducted the appropriate number of stamps from their ration book. Thereafter, each person could purchase approximately half a pound of sugar per week, or about half of the prewar level of consumption. Sugar rationing did not prove onerous for most people in the Great Plains. Farm families could apply to local ration boards for a four-week supply because of the difficulty involved in getting to town regularly. Women who canned and preserved vegetables and fruits could apply for ten to twenty extra pounds in season. Local newspapers printed the application forms so that readers could see how to complete them correctly.[20]

Great Plains residents took sugar rationing in stride, but beef rationing soon generated considerable complaint—and criticism and violation of OPA policy. No one in the Great Plains anticipated meat rationing when the war in Europe began. Great Plains consumers considered beef a daily food and preferred red meat, considering it a source of good nutrition. Some nutrition experts warned that morale would decline if consumers could not purchase red meat. But OPA policy was intended to encourage sacrifice, particularly when it came to rationing beef. As late as mid-April 1941, however, few people expected beef shortages, rationing, or runaway meat prices. F. E. Mollin, the secretary of the American National Livestock Association, informed Great Plains cattlemen that federal officials assured him that "the American meat industry would be given its full opportunity to contribute to the defense program." Although cattle raisers got their wish for higher prices and increased government purchases, consumers soon experienced meat shortages at the butcher shops and grocery stores, shortages that ultimately led to rationing. By spring 1942 meat prices in Oklahoma had risen 19 percent since the war began. Before the end of the year, Denver experienced its first meat shortage because packers preferred to sell to the military and to the Lend-Lease program, which paid higher prices for meat than consumers did because of government-imposed ceiling prices.[21]

Early in 1942 government officials urged the public to voluntarily limit its consumption of meat to 2.5 pounds per week, that is, to 130 pounds per year. Yet this amount exceeded the average 126 pounds of red meat consumed annually from 1935 to 1939. Still, the amount was less than the 141 pounds consumed on average in 1941, an increase that had been stimulated by high disposable income from defense industry jobs and abundant cattle production. Federal officials contended that meat rationing was necessary to curb civilian consumption and ensure that soldiers and sailors received 1 pound of meat per day, or 365 pounds per year, or about 2.5 times the average civilian consumption.[22]

Through the autumn of 1942, Great Plains cattlemen looked to Washington with "apprehensive eyes" as rumors spread about the inevitability of meat rationing and cattle quotas for packers. People with cold-storage lockers began stocking up, that is, hoarding meat even though the August slaughter was 10 percent greater than the previous year. Secretary of Agriculture Claude R. Wickard anticipated meat rationing and recommended "meatless days" to limit civilian consumption. The *Dakota Farmer* urged cattle raisers to help alleviate the situation by killing, cutting, and curing their own meat. Almost immediately after Secretary Wickard's announcement, packers and wholesalers began "upgrading" lower cuts of beef to command higher prices. The fact that USDA officials were estimating a domestic and military demand of 27 billion pounds of beef for 1943 but that there were only 24 billion pounds in the supply chain, coupled with high wartime earnings and disposable income, caused them to fear that beef prices would escalate beyond control despite the Emergency Price Control Act.[23]

By October 1942 the meat supply for civilians had declined by 20 percent. Meatpackers urged grocers to manage their meat supplies so that workers who shopped late in the day would have something to purchase. In Amarillo spot shortages occurred, and livestock producers, processors, retailers, wholesalers, café owners, and consumers joined the Chamber of Commerce in calling on the OPA to allocate more beef for the Texas Panhandle. There, a population increase, spurred by the defense industries and with military purchases, had depleted the meat supply to less than one pound per person per week. The OPA had allotted Amarillo only 80 percent of the beef supply for the last quarter of 1941, and consumers in the Panhandle wanted the area designated a "war area" and the beef supply increased. A month later federal officials asked the public to begin the first week of December by adding a meatless day to family and restaurant menus. Government officials and nutrition experts urged the public to eat less red meat and more poultry, fish, milk, and eggs, but most Great Plains consumers wanted beef.[24]

While consumers complained about an anticipated meat-rationing program, Great Plains cattle producers favored it if rationing would prevent the government from designating meatless days, similar to those experienced during World War I. OPA plans to ration meat, however, proved difficult to perfect because meat could not be handled like sugar or any other commodity. Red meat, whether beef, pork, or lamb, has many grades as well as choice and cheap cuts within each grade. No one knew what portion of an individual's beef quota should be composed of which cuts. The Great Plains livestock associations held the position that meat rationing would be unnecessary if the OPA adjusted price ceilings so that both producers and packers could make a profit. Great Plains cattle producers believed that meat production was as much a war industry as the manufacture of tanks and planes and that the rancher was entitled to a profit, in this case from more cattle sales. Secretary of Agriculture Wickard, however, favored meat rationing.[25]

In January 1943, as the beef supply tightened, consumers in Lincoln, Nebraska, actively bought "bootlegged" or "meatlegged" beef, that is, non–federally inspected beef from small slaughterhouses. These consumers had found a loophole in the OPA rationing and price-control program by purchasing a quarter or a half of beef from a slaughterhouse, then asking a local butcher to cut and package it. These sales were in addition to the number of cattle officially allocated for slaughter in the area. The black market in meat now became a problem in the Great Plains. Butcher shops in the small towns across the region also became the worst offenders because they purchased a few cattle from local stock raisers, slaughtered them, cut the meat, and sold it for whatever price they could get. The federal government did not have enough inspectors to track and punish these illegal sales. The slaughter of cattle by small-scale producers who operated beyond the law was, in the minds of government officials, depriving the military of needed food to help fight the war.[26]

Packers attempted to absolve themselves of blame for the meat shortage crisis in the Great Plains by blaming the OPA, which limited the number of cattle slaughtered for civilian consumption. While packers and the OPA bickered, many butchers' meat cases remained empty or stocked with black market beef. Grocers and butchers in Albuquerque, however, did not expect a meat shortage, provided consumers were not "picky and choosy" about kinds and cuts of meat. Yet, with retailers receiving only 70 percent of their prewar meat supplies, shortages became inevitable. Still, Albuquerque consumers reportedly accepted this "with a smile." They smiled less in February 1943 when the OPA rolled back the maximum price that processors could charge for cut beef to $0.20 per pound. But packers claimed that it cost $0.24 per pound to process beef, and in response they stopped buying beef until they could make a profit. In April New Mexicans learned that forty thousand cattle were ready for slaughterhouses but that many packers had closed because they had met their quotas. Many Oklahoma packers also closed because their costs still exceeded the allowed retail price of beef. Some packers pledged to stop buying and slaughtering cattle until the federal government permitted them to make a profit. One observer noted, "The situation was perfect for a flourishing black market." Meatpackers continued to complain about pricing and processing regulations until the end of the war.[27]

In February 1943 the OPA issued a war ration book that contained red stamps or points that entitled consumers to purchase specific amounts of meat monthly. Meat points were valued according to USDA grades, scarcity, and demand. Meat rationing followed on

March 29 because OPA officials believed that, without rationing, price controls would prevent lower-income consumers from purchasing meat. The OPA rationing regulations allotted each person twenty-eight ounces of meat per week, at a time when the wealthiest third of the nation consumed approximately five pounds per person per week and the poor often could not purchase one pound weekly. In turn butchers nationwide received detailed instructions from the OPA describing methods for cutting meat to ensure uniform standards and the receipt by consumers of fair value when exchanging their stamps. After considerable exasperation on the part of packers, livestock men, and consumers, and after the agency sent a pamphlet to butchers containing minutely detailed instructions for cutting meat, Senator Hugh Butler of Nebraska called the OPA directives "nutty." "It shows," he contended, "what a bunch of young lawyers do when they meet up with a beef chart." While critics of the OPA complained, meat continued to disappear from butchers' display cases, and the agency told packers to make more frankfurters by using soybeans, potatoes, and cracker meal for filler.[28]

Although meat supplies to grocers and butchers became critically short during spring 1943, the black market boomed, and the government extended the rationing program to include canned and processed meats. Nationwide, farm-slaughtered beef constituted an estimated 12 percent of the civilian supply, and it kept cold-storage lockers filled from sales where no exchange of ration stamps occurred. Overall, approximately 20 percent of the civilian meat supply came from black market sources because the federal government took approximately 60 percent of the prime and choice cuts of beef and 80 percent of the utility grades for the military and the Lend-Lease program. Since retailers had a beef allocation equivalent to sales in 1941, they could seldom meet demands in 1943, in part because the large-scale packers took approximately 25–30 percent of the slaughtered cattle for military sales. In North Dakota some restaurants responded to the beef shortage by allegedly purchasing illegally slaughtered meat, either "knowingly or unknowingly."[29]

Soon, talk of meatless days bordered on hysteria, and it damaged public morale, at least according to the American Meat Institute, which called the daily consumption of meat a "symbol of democracy" and the "New Ammunition." When several restaurants began designating "meatless" days, the Colorado Stock Growers and Feeders Association protested that restaurants did so only to offer cheap meat substitutes at high prices instead of meals with meat. Cattle producers wanted their "army of livestock" to furnish at least half of the daily protein needed to keep men and women energized for work in the war industries. They also wanted moderate production costs and no restrictions on prices.[30]

The Colorado Stock Growers and Feeders Association worried that black markets for beef would soon develop in the state because consumers could not buy enough beef. The result would be twofold. First, cattlemen would not receive fair prices through the normal sales process, and, second, black markets would encourage cattle rustling. Yet equity required meat rationing, and the OPA intended to ensure that meat was rationed by prohibiting slaughterhouses from processing more cattle for family consumption than they killed during any three-month period in 1941, which the OPA set as the base year. In March the Wyoming Stock Growers Association warned its members to increase their vigilance because cattle rustling, illegal sales, and unauthorized butchering had increased. Moreover, livestock raisers were subject to legal action if they slaughtered cattle and either gave beef away or sold it, and slaughterhouses faced suits if they processed more cattle than permitted under federal regulations. By late winter 1943, however, black markets for beef existed from coast to coast. Law-abiding butchers could not compete with the black market in beef, which operated in flagrant, but profitable, violation of the law. One Kansan likened black market beef to Prohibition era bootleg whiskey and beer, saying that it was better than no beef at all.[31]

By spring 1943 everyone on the Great Plains seemed unhappy about the OPA meat-rationing program. Consumers complained that rationing would not solve the problem of inadequate beef supplies because too many black market cattle went to grocers and butchers. Cattle raisers charged that OPA slaughter quotas remained too low for the civilian market and that meat rationing caused the overstock of their ranges because they could not sell all their cattle when ready for market. The major packers groused that cattle prices, which were unrestricted, advanced above OPA price ceilings for the sale of meat and that, consequently, they could not make a profit because they paid more for cattle than they received for cut beef. Still, some plains livestock raisers did not care whether a local slaughterer house processed their beef and sold it to butchers on the black market as long as they could sell more cattle. In general consumers wanted beef and willingly paid high prices for it, no matter government regulations.[32]

The USDA attempted to slow, if not curtail, black market sales by warning consumers that such beef had often been processed under unsanitary conditions and that only licensed individuals or companies could provide a safe product. The protection of public health, of course, was not the goal. Rather, the government was attempting to prevent beef from bypassing the distribution process for meat intended for the military and the Lend-Lease program. While government officials sought to end the black market for beef, cattlemen enjoyed high prices and, often, illegal sales. By July 1943 observers in North Dakota expected black market sales in beef to expand greatly. Herds grazed near most towns, and cattle could be easily slaughtered and the meat sold without government authorization or inspection. Indeed, as one contemporary observed, "It would take an army of inspectors to stop it." Some observers, however, criticized Great Plains consumers who bought black market beef because they refused to change "normal habits or make any sacrifice in order to help win the war."[33]

By mid-1943 meat meant hamburger across Great Plains. Residents had become accustomed to hamburger during the Great Depression because it was cheap, and they had learned to like it. Knowledgeable observers of the OPA's slaughtering and rationing program believed that meat shortages would disappear in the Great Plains if the government permitted the increased production of hamburger that could be achieved by using more parts of bulls and old heifers normally saved for canning and lunch meats as well as by permitting the price of hamburger to increase, thereby making it more profitable. By the end of 1943 the price of hamburger had increased substantially. In Denver, for example, the cost had risen 250 percent in two years.[34]

The OPA responded to the meat shortage by lifting quota limitations on slaughterers for two months, beginning September 1, 1943, in areas where consumers had more coupon points for the purchase of meat than there was meat available, provided the slaughterhouses had sufficient labor to process the animals. Although the OPA did not reduce the number of ration points required for the purchase of specific grades of meat, Dallas housewives looked forward to purchasing more and better grades of beef with their ration coupons as a result of the OPA's ruling. At the same time the Reconstruction Finance Corporation began subsidizing slaughterhouses to ensure that they remained in business. In Oklahoma slaughterers had received $200,000 in subsidies since June 1943. These subsidies enabled them to pay the prevailing high market prices for cattle, sell meat at fixed OPA ceiling prices, and still earn a profit. Great Plains consumers appreciated this government program.[35]

As a result in Omaha—where officials of the major meatpacking companies (Cudahy, Swift, Armour, and Wilson) had complained that insufficient labor prevented them from quickly processing the livestock brought to market—more workers were needed. Before Pearl Harbor, these packers employed approximately five thousand workers, but by September 1943 nine thousand workers could not keep up with the killing and cutting of thousands of cattle. The Omaha packers needed at least seven hundred more employees. With livestock producers marketing more animals to take advantage of high wartime prices, one packer processed 13 million pounds of meat in just one quarter of 1942 and 25 million pounds during one quarter of 1943. Additional workers were needed not only because producers marketed more livestock but also because the federal government now required the removal of the bone so that more meat could be shipped more efficiently in railroad cars. The packers hoped that more women would apply for jobs. They also hoped to lure men from nonessential work. With wages high, although inequitable (men started at $0.70 and women at $0.59 per hour), considerable overtime pay could be earned. With 8 million head of livestock slaughtered in Omaha since the war began, the city had become the major meatpacking center of the Great Plains.[36]

Early in 1943, with the OPA unable to meet its minimum quotas for the civilian market, a slaughterhouse in Kansas City began supplying horse meat to a café in Ardmore, Oklahoma, which advertised it as a "U.S. Government Inspected" special on the menu. Although the "Filet of Whirlaway" for $0.85 received a judgment of acceptable from customers, the reactions from consumers in Dallas bordered on moral horror, and they indicated that Texans regarded horses too highly to eat them unless they got "mighty hungry." Across the Great Plains most consumers rejected horse meat as an alternative even though meat shortages occurred, such as that in Chaves County, New Mexico, where in March 1943 meat supplies fell thirty thousand pounds per month below rationing quotas for residents in Roswell and other towns.[37]

Through 1943 cattle raisers and consumers continually complained that even in the "beef bowl," that is, the Great Plains, the purchase of the weekly allotment of two pounds of beef per person proved impossible. With approximately 5.5 million servicemen and-women allotted one pound of meat per day, and with the military and the Lend-Lease program needing 6 of 25 billion pounds annually, cattle producers could not match supply with demand even though some 18.7 million cattle had been slaughtered since Pearl Harbor. The problem, of course, was twofold. First, cattle could not be increased as easily as seeding more acres to wheat or corn for greater production the following year. Cattle fattened on grain in feedlots reached market at twenty to twenty-two months of age and weighed about 1,100 pounds, while grass-fed cattle reached market in fifteen to eighteen months but averaged only 750 pounds. Second, the Allied countries depended on the United States to meet their food needs. Cattle raisers could not produce beef fast enough to meet that need, especially when coupled with domestic and military consumption. Prices escalated, and packers demanded price controls, while livestock producers wanted prices set by supply and demand.[38]

The packers were caught in a price squeeze between the regulated

retail prices for cut meat and the unregulated prices they paid to producers for cattle. Great Plains cattlemen had the ear of the farm bloc
in Congress, which refused to set price ceilings for live cattle. When
the Roosevelt administration rolled back prices to September 1942
levels, many stockmen sold cattle to slaughterers and butchers on the
black market and ignored OPA regulations for cattle sales, slaughtering, wholesaling, and retailing, while the "red market," which involved upgrading low grades of meat for sale at ceiling prices, also
became prevalent across the nation. In the southern Great Plains,
where beef was abundant, grocers often sold hamburger "pre-cut."
By selling beef as steaks and roasts, and usually from black market cattle, at a higher price under a different rubric, they at least
avoided blatant violation of OPA ration regulations. Overall, many
cattle producers, wholesalers, retailers, and consumers honored OPA
meat regulations by noncompliance.[39]

Black market sales of beef continued throughout the war. By
1945 a large-scale black market in Colorado provided consumers
with expensive but plentiful beef, and the OPA could not stop it.
County sheriffs in eastern Colorado reported rustlers from Kansas
and Nebraska bringing cattle to Colorado for sale to restaurants,
taverns, and grocers. The OPA warned that these cattle might be dis-
eased or have been slaughtered under unsanitary conditions. It also
threatened to seek court orders to open cold-storage lockers. If officials found meat for which no points or stamps had been paid,
they would prosecute violators in court. Few Great Plains consumers worried or cared about these OPA regulations and threats. By
late April the OPA in South Dakota reported that the black market
in meat had reached "alarming proportions" and involved the sale
of millions of pounds of meat to consumers and restaurant operators. To solve the problem Montana senator Mike Mansfield urged
the federal government to include more horse meat in foreign food
relief. He contended that horse meat had a high protein content and
that consumers considered it "highly palatable." He did not, however, urge American consumers to eat horse meat. Rather, by sending horse meat abroad, more beef would remain at home to be sold
through legal channels.[40]

By May 1945 local packing companies in Cheyenne sent 80 percent of their meat to the military, and consumers experienced severe shortages that ration stamps could not alleviate. With little beef in grocers' meat cases black market sales remained the only alternative. One Cheyenne resident predicted, "We'll all be vegetarians by August." Consumers wanted larger cattle quotas for slaughter by packers, but the OPA made matters worse by setting beef quotas for small-scale packers at 75 percent of 1944 levels, while large-scale packers essentially sent most of their beef to the military. As a result consumers ate less beef, and the rationing system could not distribute it equitably if the packers could not provide it. In Oklahoma many small-scale packers closed because they could not afford to remain open with a smaller cattle kill. The OPA, however, in fact hoped that these often non–federally inspected packers would close and that cattle processed by them would be forced to federally inspected plants.[41]

In June 1945 the OPA attempted to end the black market for meat in the Great Plains by increasing the slaughter quotas for federally inspected packers and by channeling that meat to civilian consumers while also increasing inspection staff to enforce pricing and purchase policies, but to no avail. When Great Plains residents saw thousands of cattle grazing in pastures and on rangelands, they charged that "swivel chair theorists in Washington" had developed a rationing and pricing policy that kept beef from family tables. The Colorado Stock Growers and Feeders Association reported "an enormous surplus available" and urged the elimination of the beef-rationing program. In Salina, Kansas, the mayor urged Governor Schoeppel to treat the cattle kill by small-scale, non–federally inspected plants as a states' rights issue, take control of the meatpacking industry, and provide "Kansas meat for Kansans."[42]

Meat supplies remained so short across the Great Plains in early July 1945 that the majority of restaurants in Rapid City, South Dakota, announced "Meatless Saturdays." Denver restaurateurs also threatened to close in protest of the OPA's "artificial" meat shortage, particularly beef. Denver housewives, however, sided with the OPA because they wanted more beef but didn't want to have to pay restaurant prices to get it, and they called the proposed strike "unpatriotic." Even so, consumers worried that OPA ration policy encouraged livestock raisers to sell their cattle for high prices on the black market for distribution in other regions. Denver restaurateurs, however, charged that cattle grazed in abundance on the plains but that OPA-imposed shortages, with half the war over, Germany having by this time surrendered, apparently remained to "appease Stalin and Franco." Some charged that the OPA intended to force Great Plains residents on the "British diet of Brussels sprouts." Others blamed Congress for the beef shortage because it gave the OPA the authority to establish meat rationing. One restaurant owner claimed that the beef shortage made him too mad to speak, but he spoke anyway, saying, "We need a revolution in this country, and, by God, right now." Comparative sacrifice became for consumers, restaurateurs, and cattle raisers an all-consuming issue.[43]

In June 1945 Congressman William F. Hubbard of Hugoton, Kansas, complained about the "distressing meat shortage" in his community to H. O. Davis, director of the OPA. The wheat harvest had begun, but the markets had little meat, and the restaurants were serving meatless meals to the harvest hands. Hubbard reported, "Farmers hoped to depend on restaurants to feed harvest men as farm women are in the fields." This indicates another problem—the shortage of agricultural labor. State senator Elmer E. Euwer of Goodland agreed. Local restaurants did not have beef to feed harvest crews. Cattle abounded on nearby pastures, but OPA regulations prevented the local packers from butchering. Restaurants also lacked sufficient points to purchase more beef even if it became available because they had met their quotas. Euwer pleaded with Governor Schoeppel to get the OPA to loosen its meatpacking regulations to save the wheat harvest. Schoeppel responded to appeals such as this by saying that, as long as 75 percent of the slaughtered meat in federally inspected plants went to the government, consumers could only hope for the best. OPA director Davis, however, blamed Kansas farmers for the meat shortage because they withheld cattle from market, hoping to drive up prices, but he granted emergency ration-point allowances for restaurateurs in western Kansas.[44]

On August 13, one day before Japan accepted terms for surrender,

Colorado cattle producers urged the quick removal of point rationing on all meat, especially on lower grades of beef, and the elimination of all meat rationing as soon as supplies warranted. They also wanted the removal of all quotas for slaughterhouses. The 1.8 million cattle on Colorado's ranges meant that the beef herds in the state were 34 percent larger than before the war. Unlimited meat sales at free market prices would put more beef on consumers' tables and enhance producers' and packers' profits beyond wartime gains. The Kansas Livestock Association agreed and wired President Harry Truman and the state congressional delegation to complain that the packers had met their quotas and could not process any more cattle. They wanted a greater cattle kill to stimulate the sale of both live cattle and cut meat. The OPA responded two weeks later by lifting controls that determined how many cattle a packer could slaughter. Housewives, however, did not quickly find more meat in their butchers' cases because the packers did not have enough workers to handle the increased production. As a result consumers could purchase only as much meat as their ration points allowed, thereby continuing wartime consumption patterns. In Denver the packing plants operated at only 40 percent of capacity in early September. Only time—and men and women returning from the armed services and seeking jobs—would solve the problem.[45]

In retrospect, although rationing ensured the most equitable distribution of beef, it also encouraged black markets. Consumers with disposable income quickly found producers and slaughterers who were willing to accept cash for beef. Moreover, the problem of black market sales of beef did not end when Secretary of Agriculture Clinton P. Anderson terminated the meat-rationing program on November 23, 1945. Great Plains cattle raisers agreed that the rationing program had given order to cattle sales, ensured equity in distribution and consumption, and helped maintain high prices for producers and low prices for consumers, but they now anticipated even higher prices and larger sales driven by an affluent postwar society.[46]

The people of the Great Plains, like Americans across the nation, accepted rationing and price controls as necessary evils, but they resisted OPA bureaucracy and seeming incompetence when they were flooded with ration books, coupons, and stamps for food and gasoline and certificates for tires as well as complicated and frequently changing point systems and a host of rules for rationing. Little wonder that many people ignored rationing and price controls and participated in the black market. The people of the Great Plains coped, but they were not prepared to sacrifice more than others, and their grievances became the most vocal in relation to the rationing of beef and gasoline. Even so, most would have admitted that price controls limited inflation and that rationing ensured a steady food supply for the military and adequate food at home.[47]

Like other Americans, then, Great Plains residents complained about rationing, sometimes violated its regulations, and endured the hassles and aggravations associated with it. But their sacrifice was not great. Rationing, whether of food or materials, became an annoyance on the Great Plains home front, but it was never a hardship. Great Plains residents shared rides to work and complained about low speed limits, and they made meal adjustments because they had no choice, but, compared to the alternatives that civilians faced in Europe and Asia, their sacrifices remained few and easily manageable. Moreover, OPA rationing programs brought benefits as well as sacrifices. Rationing boards needed clerical and other office staff to administer the many rationing and pricing programs. Moreover, the tire shortage kept shoppers close to home, and local merchants, such as those in Ponca City, Oklahoma, benefited, not retailers in cities that required a considerable drive to reach, such as Oklahoma City or Tulsa. Despite threats of prosecution, fines, and imprisonment, when retailers ignored OPA price regulations, they had little to fear because few violators of price regulations ever had sanctions applied against them. Moreover, the few OPA inspectors could not monitor the widely scattered merchants in the small towns and cities across the Great Plains.[48]

As a result Great Plains residents violated OPA regulations without remorse. In many areas of the Great Plains the black market, especially for gasoline, tires, and beef, became a profitable business, and it aggravated shortages. For some people wartime shortages seemed a continuation of the days of making do or doing without during the Great Depression, and everyone soon learned the routine of standing in line, but a sense of patriotism helped keep social control during government-imposed deprivation. No one starved on the Great Plains during World War II, although many experienced some inconveniences. Most Americans did without a few things, but real discontent occurred only when people believed that they were being asked or compelled to sacrifice more than others. When Great Plains residents thought about their situation in terms of comparative sacrifice, many often rationalized an excuse to violate the law. Plains residents were willing to do their share, but they did not want to sacrifice when others violated the rules. The matter of comparative sacrifice determined their patriotic judgments, whether in relation to government policy or in relation the activities of their neighbors. All things considered, then, rationing was the greatest hardship the Great Plains people experienced during the war. Yet, when they compared their sacrifices, or, more appropriately, inconveniences, with those of people in other regions, they frequently concluded that they endured more than their fair share.[49]

SIX | The Farm and Ranch Front

B y 1939 farmers in the Great Plains began to emerge from the Great Depression and the drought-stricken and dust-laden years of the 1930s. New Deal agricultural programs, particularly those of the Agricultural Adjustment Administration (AAA) and the Commodity Credit Corporation, provided much-needed income for farmers who participated in acreage-reduction and price-support programs. Nearly normal precipitation had returned to the southern Great Plains. Wheat and cotton surpluses, however, exceeded foreign and domestic demand, and farmers continued to complain about low prices. Indeed, government officials believed that the most serious agricultural problem involved finding ways to increase farm prices and, thereby, income. Unless the demand for agricultural products dramatically increased, many Great Plains farmers confronted chronic poverty, flight from the land, and dependence on government payments, that is, subsidies, for their livelihood.[1]

As Great Plains farmers listened to the radio and read the newspaper reports of impending war, they were of two minds. Nearly all farmers wanted the United States to stay out of any new European war. They dreaded the loss of life, particularly their sons who joined the military, and they remembered the reports of the Nye Committee, which attributed the First World War to greed. Equally important, they remembered the federal government urging farmers to increase production and the collapse of the agricultural economy when the war ended. Farm men and women had no desire to live through another collapse, but many also saw the war, and the associated increase in demand, as a needed opportunity to decrease agricultural surpluses and increase farm prices. If the United States could stay out of the conflict, the war could work to the advantage of farmers in the Great Plains.[2]

As early as January 1939, however, Secretary of Agriculture Henry A. Wallace believed that the production-control and price-support program of the AAA was too expensive for taxpayers and too restrictive for farmers, and he advocated a new processing tax on cotton and wheat to finance parity-income payments and the soil conservation program. Defense spending and politics, however, prevented Wallace from pursuing this goal before Germany invaded Poland. As a result the New Deal agricultural programs remained in effect, although Republicans increasingly supported an agricultural policy that would fix prices at home and dump surplus at world market prices, which essentially meant a recycling of the McNary-Haugen plan of the 1920s. Observers believed that Congress would soon appoint a committee to give further study to the agricultural problem. No matter the solution to the farm problems of overproduction and low prices, one agricultural editor in Oklahoma spoke for most Great Plains farm men and women when he wrote, "Our destiny is at home, here in the Americas." If war came, the United States should stay out of it, and Congress should keep the president from bringing the nation into it.[3]

During summer 1939 farmers and government agricultural officials went about their business as usual. The Farm Security Administration, for example, received applications from tenant farmers, sharecroppers, and farm laborers who sought loans to enable them to purchase their own farms over forty years at 3 percent interest. County AAA officials made loan and insurance plans for the 1940 crop year. The Prairie States Forestry Project continued tree planting to help prevent wind erosion in designated areas, and the Rural Electrification Administration labored to string power lines and revolutionize farm life. When the European war began, however, farmers, government agricultural officials, and farm editors quickly turned their thoughts to matters of production because Britain and France would surely need American commodities. Although most farmers favored peace and American neutrality, many also believed the war would increase farm prices. Surpluses would disappear as foreign demand increased to cover production losses where armies fought in once-bountiful fields. As a result wartime production would end the need for AAA acreage reductions, and commodity prices would rise with demand. One Kansas optimist ventured, "A lot of joy and profit may be the lot of the farmer." Isolationists, however, worried that any war boom for agriculture would be followed by "inevitable depression" similar to the collapse of farm prices after World War I. They also argued that British and French markets would be limited because of a lessened ability to pay, because of Canadian and Argentine competition in those markets, and because the warring nations had stockpiled ample reserves. The large resources of the federal government's Commodity Credit Corporation also indicated no need to increase agricultural production by changing the acreage-control program for 1940.[4]

In early September, when the war began, wheat prices rose to their maximum daily limit on the Chicago Board of Trade, bringing $0.89 per bushel, the highest price since March 1938, but still below the parity price of $1.12 per bushel. In Cheyenne, Wyoming, consumers made a run on sugar, flour, and lard in the grocery stores in anticipation of higher food prices and shortages. Within days wholesalers increased the price of sugar to $135 per hundredweight, while flour from wheat harvested in Colorado and Wyoming rose to $150 per barrel. Lard jumped 2.5¢ per pound. Some grocers began limiting purchases of these food items because wholesalers could not promise resupply for weeks. Some observers expected the federal government to intervene and institute price controls. Sugar beet growers particularly anticipated reaping high prices and good profits from the crop that was nearing harvest. One Wyoming observer contended, "The beet grower will get the lion's share of price advances." But he also astutely noted, "As a whole the war which is bringing distress to Europe is improving the outlook in Wyoming . . . and the prospects are for even greater improvement in the future, providing, of course, that the war continues, and nothing is done by the national government to clamp down on the American producer, as some local experts fear may be done." These words soon became prophecy.[5]

As farmers prepared to seed their 1940 wheat crop, USDA officials in Washington DC cautioned them to stay within the AAA acreage allotment because supplies held by the Commodity Credit Corporation exceeded national demand and wheat remained uncompetitive on the world market. Cotton farmers, however, expected surplus stocks to diminish and price increases owing to wartime demand. Secretary of Agriculture Wallace saw no need to abandon New Deal agricultural policy because acreage allotments, that is, limitations, and price-supporting commodity loans ensured economic stability in agriculture and protected against any postwar collapse in farm prices. All warnings urging caution, however, quickly faded as most Great Plains farmers saw the war as an opportunity to recoup their economic losses of the past decade. When the war was only four days old, one south plains editor noted, "All commodity markets are on a runaway basis. Grains go up the limit on the opening of the market. Buyers are making a wild scramble to load up before further jumps in price." If the war did not end soon, he and others expected farm prices to escalate even higher, in part because war-related industrial jobs would increase consumer income and the consumption of agricultural commodities. Moreover, many observers expected a long war, which would mean "a heavy draft on American farmers for foodstuffs." The *Nebraska Farmer* noted that a prolonged war would also bring "prosperity" because the warring nations would turn to the United States for agricultural commodities and it would capture markets once held by the belligerents.[6]

In Kansas Governor Payne Ratner advised farmers to maintain, rather than expand, production, and he urged them to use wartime price increases to pay off existing debts and save for the war's "aftermath." Many Great Plains farmers believed that wartime price increases would be temporary, the post–World War I collapse in farm prices having been indelibly imprinted on their minds. Little more than a month after the war began, then, Great Plains farmers hoped for both neutrality and high wartime prices. Their political conservatism, distrust of international affairs, and economic sacrifice during the 1930s drove their attempts to have things both ways. At the same time they worried about the peace and continued to support the AAA acreage-control programs that guaranteed profitable, if not always adequate, prices. They preferred to keep a guaranteed income rather than forsake the federal safety net and engage in speculative maximum production while gambling on high domestic free market prices. With farm prices only about 6 percent above their prewar level by November, most Great Plains farmers believed that commodity prices still remained too low and that, if the war did not boost farm income, Congress would need to increase subsidy payments.[7]

Some Great Plains farmers believed that the price of wheat and corn increased during the autumn because drought hindered planting and germination while "peace threats" in Europe brought down prices. Those who thought that the war would be fought on the Eastern Front and spare the rich agricultural lands of Western Europe also argued that, because they were prohibited by U.S. law from buying on credit (a vestige of the last war), Britain and France would purchase food from nations that granted credit and, thereby, save their gold to purchase munitions, not food, from the United States. Moreover, cotton sales had not increased abroad. In general, then, those plains men and women who wanted to avoid war continued to argue that it would not benefit farmers economically. If substantial price increases did not result from war, E. A. O'Neal, the president of the American Farm Bureau Federation, told the Kansas Farm Bureau members, "Our democracy is going to fall unless farm commodity prices, industrial prices and industrial wages are brought into parity relationship." Until farmers achieved income parity with industrial workers, he contended, "agriculture must continue to ask for a government appropriation to keep its income within striking distance of parity." Put simply, many agricultural leaders expected more help from the federal government to improve their standard of living than they did from any economic benefits brought by the new European war.[8]

Not everyone agreed. Representative Marvin Jones, a Texan and the chairman of the House Committee on Agriculture, as well as Congressman Clifford Hope from Kansas, who served as the committee's senior minority member, believed that a "full-fledged conflict" would quickly deplete the reserves of agricultural commodities and eliminate the need for "huge federal subsidies." In response to this view as well as to advice to trim spending, President Roosevelt advocated reducing many farm subsidies on the basis of the expectation that agricultural prices would quickly increase to 75 percent of parity, if not more. As the war deepened, however, many Great Plains farmers took a wait-and-see approach before expanding production. Other Great Plains farmers were more optimistic. In November wheat brought $0.87 per bushel on the Amarillo market, an increase of $0.15 per bushel since July. With approximately 10 million bushels supported by the Commodity Credit Corporation at a price of $0.50 per bushel, wheat farmers had achieved paper gains of $1.5 million over the loan rate offered under the federal program. Many wheat farmers in the Texas Panhandle, however, chose not to sell and waited for prices to go still higher because of the drought and the war. Some anticipated a price of $1 per bushel by spring, which would be "gravy for the farmers," and they planned to plant more wheat.[9]

Even so, when the new year began, many Great Plains farmers, such as those in North Dakota, did not believe that grain prices would dramatically increase because of the "tremendous world surplus" of 5.3 billion bushels. In the United States the carryover from 1939 reached 101 million bushels. One North Dakota agricultural official contended, "The granaries of the world are overflowing with wheat, and Europe is expanding rather than contracting its acreage." These large reserves could not be easily or quickly consumed by people or livestock. Many agricultural experts believed that the best course of action was for Great Plains farmers to limit production through the AAA acreage-control program, thereby increasing prices, rather than expanding production to take advantage of temporary higher wartime prices. This advice seemed best to many who still argued that the war had caused a decline in the foreign sale of agricultural commodities because Britain and France were spending more for armaments than for American farm commodities, particularly wheat, beef, and cotton from the Great Plains.[10]

In early spring 1940 the *Nebraska Farmer* reported that the war had not "lived up to the expectations of those who looked for a boom in exports of farm products." Although a "modest" 15 percent increase in foreign and a 35 percent increase in domestic demand for agricultural commodities brought a 2–4 percent price increase for 1939, one-fourth of the American export market had been closed by Germany or the British blockade. Moreover, agricultural sales to Britain had declined because the British preferred to buy from nations that usually sold to Germany and from within the empire. By late summer 1940, then, only government buying, commodity loans, and export subsidies kept farm prices from falling as a result of the loss of foreign markets. While famine began to ravage Europe, surplus food supplies remained in the United States. Some Great Plains agricultural experts believed that the farm problem would not be solved until the war ended.[11]

In the meantime a bitter winter and the British blockade brought food shortages to Germany. Although the Germans had sufficient wheat for bread, fresh vegetables became hard to find, and potato storage pits froze in the fields. No citrus fruit reached the market, and the meat ration had been reduced to one and a quarter pounds and the egg ration to one per person weekly. Fats, oils, and dairy products were "very scarce." Some observers believed that hunger alone might force Germany to expand the war in order to bring it to a swift conclusion. If so, what effect would it have on Great Plains farmers? No one knew the answer, although opinions ranged from good to no effect at all. When Germany seized Denmark in April 1940, some optimists believed that the British would now buy more American pork. Although the Neutrality Act of 1939 limited foreign sales to a cash-and-carry basis and the Johnson Act of 1934 prohibited government loans to nations in default on previous war debts, Great Plains farmers still hoped that some trade accommodations could be made to enhance agricultural sales. As wheat farmers harvested their crop during the summer of 1940, the war still seemed to many farmers to be a hindrance to higher prices because of lost markets, because of British food rationing, and because of British policy of purchasing food from nations that otherwise traded with Germany. Even so, farm income had increased. One Great Plains editor, however, believed that American foreign policy had created an "unnecessary enemy" by prohibiting the sale of scrap iron to Japan, thereby "cost[ing] cotton farmers one of our best customers."[12]

Great Plains farmers also worried about the government's plan to draft men aged twenty-one to twenty-six because of the agricultural labor problem it would create. Officials in the USDA's Office of Defense Relations considered agricultural deferments a "difficult" problem because the army assumed that farm boys were already skilled at repairing and operating a variety of motor vehicles and, thus, could with minimal training easily operate tanks, armored cars, and self-propelled artillery. After Pearl Harbor the Selective Service System planned to register all men aged eighteen to sixty-five and expected men aged nineteen to forty-five to be eligible for service. Although local draft boards also received instructions to limit farm deferments, Great Plains farmers expected the agricultural labor shortage to worsen. In autumn 1942 Congress approved the Tydings Amendment to the Selective Service Act, which permitted draft boards to defer agricultural workers "essential to the war effort" until replacements could be hired. Quickly, the Tydings Amendment became the basic rationale for farm deferments. By January 1944 the Selective Service System had taken most of the young men from the farms, and, when the agency announced that it intended to call all farm men aged eighteen to twenty-six for physical examinations, parents quickly complained to the highest government officials who could, they hoped, prevent it from doing so. In Kansas one farmer wrote to Governor Andrew Schoeppel about the effect of the draft on agricultural workers, saying, "There just isn't any one to be had at any price." He hoped that the governor could keep his son on the farm.[13]

Discontent over agricultural deferments remained until the war ended, with Great Plains farmers supporting deferments and residents of urban counties resenting their higher quotas to compensate for farm deferments. By March 1944, for example, General Lewis B. Hershey, the director of the Selective Service System, wanted to draft all farmers and their sons whose agricultural production did not "substantially exceed" family consumption or add to the nation's food supply. Men who received agricultural deferments could not leave their farms without permission from the local Selective Service office. Any deferred farmers who took part-time jobs or left for defense industry positions would be classified for induction even if they had dependants. The labor shortage, however, became so serious in Kansas that the state Selective Service director authorized deferred farmers to seek temporary employment with war industries, meatpacking plants, and railroads during slack periods on the farm. This policy, however, was not adopted regionwide.[14]

While Great Plains farmers worried about the draft, they also took advantage of opportunities created by increased military spending for preparedness. In Oklahoma, for example, farmers found a ready market for their horses and mules at Fort Reno, which served as the largest of the army's three remount stations. During the first six months of 1941 the army planned to purchase more than eight thousand horses and mules from farmers in Oklahoma and Texas. At the same time farm income in the southern plains had jumped 3.3 percent from a year earlier because of the greater consumer spending that resulted from increased employment. In South Dakota farmers anticipated a $50 million increase in guaranteed price supports as a result of AAA plans to encourage farmers to increase production for defense purposes, especially to provide food for Britain. USDA estimates indicated that British demand would require a 6–8 percent increase in milk and a 10 percent increase in egg production nationwide. In New Mexico poultrymen also attempted to follow the USDA's "eggs for defense program" by stocking henhouses to capacity and improving feeding and grading practices. In May the soldiers at Lowry Field near Denver consumed more than 13,000 pounds of butter and 138,000 half pints of milk, all to the delight of the Denver Dairy Council, which supported the industry's slogan "Make America Strong by Making Americans Stronger." Incremental gains, however, proved too few and insignificant for H. G. Keeney, the president of the Nebraska Farmers Union, who told members, "The farmer is the 'forgotten man' in the hysteria of war preparations." He believed that the farm economy could be improved only with cooperative buying and selling through the organization. In contrast the Farm Bureau wanted a 100 percent parity-price loan rate for the duration of the war, up from the approved 85 percent rate. Senator Elmer Thomas of Oklahoma even suggested setting parity prices by legislation rather than basing them on a comparative formula of exchange values.[15]

By late spring 1941 Great Plains farmers were caught between the past and the present. New Deal agricultural policy still governed their lives and economic fortunes. The USDA advocated cutting wheat acreage nationwide from 55 to 50 million acres in order to maintain prices, expanding the marketing-quota provisions of the Agricultural Adjustment Act of 1938, and increasing the penalty to $0.10 per pound for farmers who sold more than their quota of cotton. Vice President Henry A. Wallace appealed to farmers to make their desire for high prices secondary to the national interest. Secretary of Agriculture Claude R. Wickard urged farmers to make "war on greed" and forgo demanding 100 percent parity-price-supporting loans. Great Plains farmers, however, did not believe their desires for higher agricultural prices unpatriotic in view of the labor strikes that had paralyzed many industries and the war-mobilization movement from January to mid-June. Many farmers considered organized labor leaders nothing less than "professional agitators, some of them Communists and Bundists . . . robbers, gunmen and racketeers." One remarked, "Who ever heard of a farmer going on a sit-down strike?"[16]

While Great Plains farmers believed that they were more patriotic than striking workers, they also knew that the war had changed their lives and that it would continue to do so for years to come. Sugar beet growers anticipated increasing production and higher prices. In Wyoming G. L. Ammon, a sales manager for the Holly Sugar Corporation, contended, "Sugar is truly crystallized sunshine." In Sheridan, Worland, and Torrington Holly Sugar refining plants produced 1.5 million bags of sugar annually, employed thirteen hundred workers, who processed beets from thirty-seven hundred acres, and generated $700,000 of income, which field-workers contributed to the local economy. Farmers and refiners considered sugar a "vital food stuff" that occupied "a unique position from a defense standpoint." Wyoming farmers also increased their acreage of beans by 215 percent, dairy cows by 8 percent, chickens by 7 percent, egg production by 13 percent, and hog production by 16 percent. Stable feed prices and a guaranteed government market encouraged these increases for commodities considered "vital foods." Many farmers agreed with the agricultural official who said, "There is no reason why our prosperity should not continue to increase even during post-war times."[17]

Indeed, by late summer 1941 Great Plains farmers could not escape the fact that war paid. Agricultural prices gave farmers 25 percent more purchasing power than they had had a year earlier. Farm experts expected another 25 percent increase in 1942. In South Dakota commodity prices averaged 103 percent of parity in mid-July, compared to 75 percent the year before. At the same time the index for prices paid by South Dakota farmers increased from 122 to 125 during that same period. Even so, their cash farm income increased from $38.2 million in 1937 to $56.6 million by mid-1941, in part because of hog, dairy, and poultry price supports. One South Dakota editor observed, "Agriculture is embarking on another period of great change." In Kansas farmers received a $24 million boost from cash sales and government payments during the first six months of 1941, for an income total of $144.4 million. Great Plains cotton farmers, however, complained that the war had cost them their markets in France, Great Britain, and other European countries. A. B. Conner, the director of the Texas Agricultural Experiment Station, said, "If the British go down to defeat, it will cost the South and Texas dearly." Some cotton farmers in Texas and Oklahoma contemplated shifting to cattle production to take advantage of higher prices for beef. Great Plains farmers wanted more.[18]

In early September 1941 the optimism of many farmers increased when Secretary of Agriculture Wickard called for "the largest production in the history of American agriculture to meet the expanding food needs of this country and nations resisting the axis." His call for expanded production, however, did not include wheat and cotton because large reserves of those commodities still remained under the control of the Commodity Credit Corporation. Sugar beet growers could now plant as much acreage as possible, but wheat farmers would be required to reduce their crop by 2 million acres, and cotton farmers were authorized to plant only about the same acreage in 1942 as they had the preceding year. Great Plains farmers eagerly participated in the new AAA wheat program because they wanted a guaranteed income now that wheat-acreage allotments had decreased, production declines having been overcome by higher prices. One observer noted the principle, "If you can't beat 'm jine 'em." E. J. Mahoney of Dorrence, the president of the Progressive Agriculturists of Kansas, a group organized to support the AAA wheat-reduction and price-support and marketing-quota program, believed, "We would be getting about 25 cents a bushel for our wheat if it were not for the fixed price established under the AAA." Instead, wheat prices were "flirting with the dollar mark."[19]

While commodity sales and farm programs remained their two main sources of agricultural income, Great Plains farmers were concerned about price controls. Nearly all expected farm income to emerge as a "bone of political contention," and they feared that, representing as they did only one-fourth of the country's population, they did not have the political power in Congress to guarantee their interests. They need not have worried. On the eve of Pearl Harbor the farm bloc convinced Congress to approve liberal ceiling prices for farm commodities and accept the proposition that federal price fixing would be used to support farm prices. This policy would guarantee that the government would not single out farm prices for domestic controls but would permit farmers a fair return. With this congressional backing, Great Plains farmers anticipated profiting from the European war, which some considered a "stimulant." Essentially, they wanted the prices of their commodities to float upward uncontrolled while a price floor of at least 85 percent of parity mitigated rampant price increases for operational costs and consumer goods.[20]

Federal policy to increase agricultural production in order to feed Great Britain despite the German blockade also meant that the United States took a major step toward war because the government would not let German submarines send the commodities of Great Plains farmers to the bottom of the ocean. President Roosevelt attempted to ensure that policy by issuing a "shoot-on-sight" order in late September 1941. Yet not until the Japanese attack on Pearl Harbor on Sunday, December 7, 1941, did the United States become committed to a war that it had been drifting toward since September 1939, if not earlier. By Thursday, December 11, 1941, wheat prices on the Chicago futures market reached $1.30 per bushel. Extension Service officials at Oklahoma A&M set a goal of 176,400 farm gardens for the state in 1942, an increase from 127,050 in 1939, to contribute to the national "food for freedom" campaign. They also urged every farm family to produce at least 75 percent of its food needs to remain as independent as possible during the war. By late December the army served as the main buyer for flour produced from wheat raised in the Great Plains. The time of waiting was over. Great Plains farmers now committed to meeting government production goals, but they still demanded, more adamantly than ever, guaranteed fair and equitable prices. The farm-price index now reached 143 or 42 percent higher than the year earlier.[21]

By early January 1942 Great Plains farmers knew that the entry of the United States into the war against Germany and Japan would dramatically increase their income. The improved agricultural economy already played a major role in increasing the deposits in the North Dakota State Bank to $34 million, higher than they had been in its twenty-three-year history. One Oklahoma editor proclaimed, "The war has made the farmer almost the most important person in the county, and farming has become as essential a war-time business as the manufacture of airplanes, tanks, guns and ammunition." In Topeka members of the Kansas Veterinary Medical Association met in convention and addressed the need to keep food animals healthy to help ensure the food supply and win the war.[22]

In Colorado, Nebraska, and Montana the Great Western Sugar Company offered growers contracts for the 1942 crop that it alleged provided "the highest division of proceeds in history," and it assured farmers prices ranging from $9.14 to $9.98 per ton. In Wyoming one observer urged farmers to "Beat 'Em with Beets" since the state had been "crying for a defense industry." Sugar beet production and refining offered an opportunity to help win the war and earn "a lot of honest dollars while doing it." Across the Great Plains farmers made plans to increase crop production. In Texas, however, cotton acreage declined to 82 percent of the allotment for 1942. Low prices, compared to wheat and grain sorghum, and labor shortages encouraged farmers to reduce cotton acreage. Even so, by September 1942 some farmers in West Texas anticipated harvesting the largest cotton crop in their history. William DeLoach in Lamb County, Texas, pulled 231 pounds and his wife 131 pounds of cotton in a day. He noted in his diary, "My hands are tired tonight." In the southern plains cotton farmers harvested the crop by pulling the bolls rather than picking the lint because it was faster and, in the absence of labor, cheaper.[23]

Increased demand and higher commodity prices also caused land values to soar. By mid-August 1942 in Wyoming, for example, land prices had doubled since 1939, from $62 to $125 million. Grazing land that sold for $1.00 to $1.50 per acre during the 1930s now brought $3.00 to $5.00 per acre, while dry (nonirrigated) farmland that had sold for $5.00 per acre in 1935 now brought $15.00 per acre. J. C. Mohler, the secretary of the Kansas Board of Agriculture, however, warned farmers to "have the cash when you buy more acreage" in order to be free from debt when the war ended. While Secretary Wickard proclaimed that "food will win the war and food will write the peace," Great Plains farmers operated on the premise that "it is equally bad defense to over-produce as it is to under-produce." Even so, the *Farmer-Stockman* proclaimed, "Oklahoma and Texas farmers are helping to plow under the Japs and Germans who would destroy the free people of the world!" Plowing and planting meant profits, but by May 1942 the Roosevelt administration advocated general wholesale and retail price ceilings fixed at March levels. Great Plains farmers feared the worst. They did not support price ceilings, unless the federal government planned limitations on wages. If the government did impose ceiling prices, it should, they believed, also establish price floors, that is, fair prices below which a commodity could not fall. This issue was not resolved until October 1942, when Congress approved the Steagall Amendment to the

Emergency Price Control Act, which authorized farm prices at 90 percent of parity for two years after the war ended not only to aid farmers but also to control inflation.[24]

As the war progressed, increased production and higher prices boosted farm income. New Mexico agricultural prices reached their highest level in twenty years. By February 1943, with an index at 182 percent of the parity base from August 1909 to July 1914 and 33 percent higher than on January 15, 1942, farmers paid an index price of 158 for needed goods. South Dakota farmers also ended 1942 with $240 million, their highest cash income since 1928, while Nebraska farm income increased 60 percent, for an approximate total of $500 million, up from $307.4 million in 1941. The war paid for Great Plains farmers.[25]

But they wanted more. J. Walter Hammond, the president of the Texas Farm Bureau, argued that agricultural prices had to increase further to ensure parity with the cost of goods that farmers purchased. Higher prices, he reasoned, would increase production and prevent food shortages, not merely enable farmers to accumulate wealth. Higher agricultural prices would also allow farmers to pay better wages and, thereby, lure workers back to the fields from war industry jobs. Until they were able to do so, labor and machinery shortages would prevent maximum production. Even so, the federal government removed all acreage restrictions for 1944 and urged farmers to "plant every acre." Some observers, however, feared another great plow-up of wheat that would lead to a return of the Dust Bowl. Colorado farmers planned to increase their sugar beet production by 34,000 acres, that is, to 175,000 acres, if the price warranted and wheat acreage by 20 percent to 1.6 million acres. One contemporary noted that, with the removal of federal production controls for the 1944 crop year, "only price ceilings, subsidies, and floors remain to remind [farmers] that Washington still has a hand in agriculture."[26]

Great Plains farmers learned, however, that they could not take advantage of food rationing by selling home-canned fruits and vegetables. On March 1, 1943, the Office of Price Administration (OPA) ruled that anyone, including farmers, who sold processed goods had to register and collect ration stamps whenever they made a sale. Cotton farmers in Texas and Oklahoma also learned that, because the federal government had not declared cotton a war crop, the price would remain low and, thus, that they would earn less income. They argued in response not only that cotton was a fiber crop but also that it produced seedcake and oil, which provided important proteins when used in livestock feed. Cotton farmers also championed drought-resistant cotton, the seed and oil of which were essential for the prevention of famine. If they exaggerated their claims, their motives were clear.[27]

Great Plains farmers also knew that the demands of the military and the war industries would take their sons, daughters, and hired workers from the fields, and agricultural economists told them what they already knew—that machinery would improve their efficiency and production and reduce labor costs. The acquisition of agricultural machinery, however, posed a major problem for Great Plains farmers throughout the war because military needs for iron, steel, and rubber superseded those of the agricultural community. In Kansas a hint of this problem emerged during late August 1941, when some farmers reported to the state Land Use Planning Committee that the national defense program had created "serious shortages" of machinery and skilled mechanics. USDA officials as well as implement dealers urged farmers to make their own repairs. These problems would soon become major difficulties.[28]

In mid-January 1942 Great Plains farmers learned that machinery companies could manufacture approximately 83 percent of their production in 1940 as provided by "Schedule A of Limitation Order L26." This federal regulation mandated the quotas for the manufacturing of all farm implements and tools. In March 1943 Secretary Wickard reported that the farm machinery situation was "very bad." Rumors about the rationing of farm machinery spread across the plains, although no one had any idea which agency might supervise such a program. Some observers believed that the federal government would impose a quota system dictating how much machinery farmers could purchase during a year. The USDA urged farmers to stock up on commonly needed replacement parts, and implement dealers across the plains worried about the loss of their businesses.[29]

Shortages of farm implements, particularly tractors, combines, and corn pickers, forced Great Plains farmers to pool resources as equipment broke down or wore out. By mid-summer 1942 H. O. Davis, the rationing director for Kansas, told farmers, "This is more than a question of 'neighboring,' it is a question of patriotic service for the country." He did not believe that farmers would receive even 40 percent of the new machinery allocated for planting and cultivating in 1943. Many Great Plains farmers shared equipment during the war, but as their incomes increased they actively sought the purchase of new or used implements. They preferred the freedom of action that came with ownership rather than relying on shared work. Before the war ended the lack of replacement parts forced some farmers to idle equipment, and other farmers returned to horse-drawn implements, such as mowers, in the absence of needed tractor power. In Kansas many high schools opened vocational agriculture shops to farmers who needed to repair machinery but did not have the necessary tools, such as welders and forges. Vocational agriculture teachers provided help and advice and also offered night classes on equipment maintenance and repair.[30]

In mid-September 1942 Secretary of Agriculture Wickard issued a temporary order rationing all farm machinery, effective in late November, and authorizing the creation of county rationing committees under the administration of the AAA. Wickard's order classified farm machinery into three groups. Equipment in the first group, such as combines, corn pickers, and grain drills, could not be purchased from a dealer without a certificate from the committee verifying that the purchase was essential. Equipment in the second group, such as electric motors, could be purchased with the farmer's certification that it was essential for his production needs. Only equipment in the third group—hand tools and small pieces of horse-drawn equipment—could be sold without restriction. Wickard hoped to have a permanent rationing plan for farm machinery completed as soon as possible. Great Plains farmers had not purchased much machinery during the years of the Great Depression because they did not

FIGURE 13. These young farmers proudly display their tractor and combine in Allen County, Kansas, about 1940. During the war technology helped farmers overcome labor shortages and keep their operations productive and profitable. (Kansas State Historical Society)

have the money or the financing. As a result most entered the war years with old or worn equipment. Although wartime agricultural prices soon gave them the financial ability to purchase new equipment, little could be found because, owing to the lack of steel, iron, and rubber, manufacturers could not produce even their allocations. Great Plains farmers had little choice but to make do, a lifestyle that they knew all too well.[31]

In North and South Dakota implement dealers could not keep pace with demands for repair work. In New Mexico farmers complained that the manufacture of farm machinery had been cut to a "dangerous minimum" and that they could not see the government's reasoning when officials ask them to increase production but denied them the implements to do so. One reporter noted that they were getting the job done only by using "words not found in the dictionary." Government price controls prohibited dealers from selling used implements for more than 85 percent of the original price if they were less than a year old, or more than 70 percent of the purchase price if more than a year old, to protect farmers from paying "excessive" prices. Used implements sold by individuals at farm auctions, however, were not regulated, and in South Dakota used equipment reportedly brought "fabulous prices," as much as eight times their original cost at farm sales. Rolls of used fence wire brought $0.92 per rod, compared to the prewar price of $0.45 per rod. Most Great Plains farmers hoped to keep their machinery in good repair until the manufacture of more agricultural machinery and falling prices permitted new purchases. As agricultural implements wore out most Great Plains farmers relied on neighbors to help with the work, such as harvesting wheat by combine and plowing with a tractor.[32]

In addition to an inadequate supply of agricultural implements, farmers confronted a severe shortage of rubber tires. With rubber supplies from the East Indies (which supplied 98 percent of the world's rubber) cut off, and with synthetic rubber still in the experimental stage, inadequate supplies soon plagued farmers, who needed new tires for the trucks, tractors, and other equipment. By September 1943 farmers could purchase tires only as spares. In order to prevent farmers and motorists from using their rubber tires unwisely, the federal government instituted gasoline rationing, although motor fuel was never in critically short supply. The government planned to use the county agents to administer the gas-rationing program, which soon became the "sorest spot among farmers." One observer noted that the reaction among farmers to sugar and coffee rationing "appeared inconsequential in the disturbance they caused" compared to their reaction to gasoline rationing. Tire rationing also upset farmers. In January 1942 William DeLoach, a farmer from the Texas Panhandle, complained, "I will have to quit going to town if I have no business. Can't get any more new tires now."[33]

County war boards, however, could authorize the purchase of farm machinery without further approval on application by the farmer. Such purchases were to be made from the allocations authorized by the federal War Production Board (WPB) to each state. In

FIGURE 14. Farmers who entered the war with modern equipment, such as this tractor, combine, and pickup truck, reaped large profits from wheat and other crops whose prices escalated during the war. Only the lack of gasoline, tires, and spare parts prevented Great Plains farmers from using their mechanized equipment the most efficiently. (Western History Collections, University of Oklahoma Libraries)

1943, for example, South Dakota received an allocation of 112 large combines, 279 small combines, 8 threshing machines, and 200 grain binders for sale through various dealers during the year. The state rationing boards then allotted the equipment to the counties. Farmers living in one county technically could not purchase implements in another county, but enough farmers filed applications to purchase implements that the AAA office in Salina, Kansas, issued a warning that certificates were not to be used as a "hunting license." When a farmer needed an implement, he had to locate a dealer who had it and apply to the county rationing board saying that he was "reasonably certain" that the dealer would sell it to him if the board provided a certificate authorizing him to make the purchase. In Dallas the agricultural labor shortage, unlimited production, and the needs of the armed forces and civilian population kept the Dixie Cotton Chopper Company working around the clock to manufacture sugar beet thinning machines. In March 1943 the Great Western Sugar Company in Denver ordered 2,250 machines, but the manufacturer did not have the iron required to build them. These machines could thin ten acres per day, compared to the half acre per day that could be thinned by a man with a hoe at the rate of $35 per acre, and farmers wanted them.[34]

The farm machinery supply problem eased in mid-October 1943 when the federal government reduced from ninety-one to thirty-one the number of implements that required purchase certificates from county boards. Among those items taken off the list were combines, corn pickers, and cotton strippers. The federal government also authorized implement manufacturers to increase production to 80 percent of 1940 levels. Dealers did not, however, receive a host of new implements quickly because the manufacturers of gears, crankshafts, and other parts worked to fill military contracts, and planting capacity remained limited. The manufacturing of bailing wire, however, fell, and extension agents urged farmers to save their used wire for smaller bales the next year. In Nebraska dealers, county machinery committees, and state AAA officials agreed to form an advisory committee to help the state AAA office responsible for rationing make a case for more farm implements. The AAA had allotted Nebraska 854 corn pickers for 1944, down from 1,131 in 1943, and considerably fewer than the 3,300 requested from the total U.S. allotment of 15,900 corn pickers. Nebraska farmers also needed 3,000 side delivery rakes for haying and harvesting dry beans, but they received an allotment of only 355. Manufacturers could distribute 80 percent of the machinery allotted directly to dealers, and the advisory committee intended to gain as many implements as possible from the 20 percent held in reserve for emergencies by the War Food Administration (WFA).[35]

By 1944 the military demand for iron and steel had eased, and the WPB and the WFA authorized a 250 percent increase in the production of farm machinery. These new farm implements, of course, would take time to reach Great Plains farmers. In January 1944 Fred Johnson, the Phelps County, Nebraska, farm machinery ration chairman, asserted that at least 20 percent of the tractors in the county needed to be replaced. By February the AAA, not the USDA war rationing boards, controlled the rationing of farm machinery at the state and local levels, although some farmers considered this a "distinction without a difference." In the meantime they confronted immediate and serious problems. In the southern plains the shortage of labor for the cotton harvest reaffirmed the pressing need for a mechanical cotton harvester. Cotton growers hoped the WPB would authorize the materials needed to build cotton strippers in Dallas and Wichita Falls. Whereas the average worker could pick only between 150 and 250 pounds of cotton in a ten-hour day on the Texas plains, stripping machines could collect six to ten bales, that is, as much as 5,000 pounds. Cotton strippers cost about $1,000, but advocates believed that a farmer could pay for a stripper in one season with the money saved by not hiring workers. A farmer in Crosby County reported that he usually paid workers $27.50 per bale to pick cotton but that a mechanical stripper cost him only $2.10 per bale. With the cost of harvesting constituting about half the expense of producing a cotton crop, farmers needed mechanical help to reduce labor costs, and they anxiously waited for the WPB to authorize the manufacture of new strippers, but they waited in vain.[36]

In June 1944 the AAA machinery-rationing officer in Nebraska informed farmers and dealers that the state would receive between fifteen and eighteen hundred tractors but that they would be rationed to communities with the greatest need and to farmers who agreed in writing to do custom work for others if allowed to purchase a new implement. In the southern Great Plains county AAA machinery-rationing boards averaged three applications per available combine. In Oklahoma, which had 5.1 million acres in wheat, compared to 3.8 million acres in 1943, the shortage of combines for the harvest became acute. The availability of farm machinery had not improved by 1945, and it would not until the war ended.[37]

Despite the machinery shortage the USDA asked Great Plains farmers to plant as much wheat as possible for the 1944 harvest. Farmers considered this request their opportunity to make even more money. One editor thought that the mandate would "ensure no weakening of the food links in the victory chain." For the first time in more than

two decades Great Plains farmers had discretionary, that is, disposable, income. They saw no disjuncture between profits and patriotism, and the large crop of 1943 became a "dream come true" with
"mortgages and loans paid and money in the bank." On the plains
near Denver wheat farmers reaped thirty bushels per acre, twice the
normal harvest, and sold it for $1.20 per bushel. Production and
prices such as these would earn a farmer $10,000 from 320 acres of
wheat. Many farmers, particularly tenant farmers, planned to use
their wheat income to buy land, and they intended to save until new
washing machines, refrigerators, and radios reached the market after the war. Others planned to pay off their debts, usually land mortgages. In late July 1943 Howard Lindfors, the owner of the Farmers'
Elevator in Strasburg, Colorado, reported farmers selling from eight
to ten thousand bushels of wheat daily for "spot cash." Most of the
wheat was destined for flour mills rather than government storage.
In 1943, as farmers nationwide anticipated unlimited production
for the next year, they grossed their largest income yet in American
history—$19.7 billion. Great Plains farmers shared this wealth. In
Nebraska, for example, farmers earned a record of more than $668
million, including government payments, while South Dakota farmers earned $244 million from crops, for a $10 million increase over
earnings in 1942. Kansas farmers earned $731 million, the second
highest income garnered in the state's history. The war years were
good years for farmers in the Great Plains.[38]

By 1943 one-fourth of U.S. agricultural products went to the war
effort. Approximately 75 percent of the food supplies shipped abroad
went to Great Britain, while Russia received 20 percent. Military and
Lend-Lease needs took about 13 percent of the food produced in the
United States. When the WFA dampened the optimism of farmers by
proposing limiting the sugar beet crop for 1944, Governor Vivian
of Colorado urged farmers to plant all the beets possible, "up to the
greatest volume they can to obtain contracts from factories." Vivian believed that Colorado's farmers should "plant all they desire of
whatever crops they choose, and market it for the best price they can
get through legal channels." Great Plains farmers needed freedom,
not quotas and regulations, because "individual freedom" would win

the war on the home front, not "theories and dictation." Marvin Jones, who was in charge of the WFA, quickly backed down, or at least proclaimed that he had no intention of limiting sugar beet production, and he suspended marketing quotas for cotton in 1944.[39]

In early 1944, then, Great Plains farmers anticipated another good year with "war prices" and high incomes. Although many became increasingly concerned about labor shortages, the USDA having encouraged them to produce 5 percent more food, as well as about a possible postwar economic collapse, they tried to remain optimistic about postwar spending and the Allies' food needs. Agricultural editors urged farmers in the southern Great Plains to seed more cotton because it was the "surest money crop." Cotton aided the war effort because, in addition to the fiber, the crop provided livestock forage supplements, which would help increase cattle production and, thus, food for humans. Cotton also provided "balance," that is, diversification, for grain and livestock farmers. In the central and northern Great Plains farmers planned to expand their wheat and sugar beet crops. Amid rumors that the war with Germany would end in 1944 and the rationing of food products in 1945, farmers felt secure because postwar price-supporting loans at 90 percent of parity would be available for two years after hostilities ceased and because Europeans would need more American farm commodities during the rebuilding process.[40]

By January 1945 experts expected the farm machinery shortage to ease relatively soon given the progress made in winning the war. When more machinery became available, it would alleviate the continuing problem of insufficient farm labor. Still, experts also now expected consumer income to decrease between 10 and 15 percent with industrial cutbacks and a decline in military buying after the defeat of Germany and another 10–20 percent once Japan surrendered. European food relief needs would, they still hoped, help them keep prices from falling precipitously. With the farm-price index at 180 percent of the 1909–14 average, however, Great Plains farmers enjoyed unprecedented prosperity, and they did not intend to go backward. Economic experts estimated that in the two years following the war Kansas farmers alone would spend more than $50 million on machinery, improvements, and household wares.[41]

Yet there were problems. Great Plains farmers, who had avoided the draft because they had been granted agricultural deferments or because a physical disability prevented them from passing the necessary medical exams, continued to have their patriotism questioned via "neighborhood gossip." Government demands for Great Plains farmers to increase food production no longer gave them recognition as honorable and necessary participants in a war effort for survival. Indeed, young farm men received considerable community pressure to join the military rather than continue "shirking" their wartime obligations. Although the conflict, then, remained a good war in terms of national principles and honor, it had shades of goodness, and Great Plains farmers often found their patriotism questioned if they were of draft age but did not volunteer for the military.[42]

In addition, while Great Plains farmers enjoyed higher incomes during the war, many worried about the continuing loss of their sons and daughters to urban areas. They hoped that laborsaving machinery, automobiles, radios, and electrification would help make life more comfortable, thus encouraging the younger generation to stay on the farm. By the end of the decade, however, these conveniences had not stemmed the flight from the land. Agricultural income did increase, but agricultural costs rose faster. Many farmers attempted to maintain their profits by expanding their operations, often by purchasing land from neighbors. As a result, fewer farms existed at the end of the war than at the beginning. Many young servicemen and-women and many young people on the production lines could not return to their childhood farm homes because those farms no longer existed. As the number of farms decreased and farms grew in size, the farm population fell. Between 1940 and 1945 the northern and central Great Plains suffered a 14.7 percent and the southern Great Plains a 25.1 percent decline in farm population.[43]

By the end of the war farm policy also became a matter of daily and often bitter discussion. The Farmers Union (FU) remained the representative organization for many small-scale farmers and, for some observers, an organization still tinged with 1930s radicalism. The FU supported a postwar policy based on the notion that high industrial employment would create an even greater market for agricultural commodities. It also called for the government to support "family-type" farming at the expense of large, commercial units, overlooking the fact that its small-scale members were commercial farmers. In addition the FU favored computing farm family labor at the rate of $0.60 per hour and employing the resulting figure in a price-support formula in production agreements so that farmers would know in advance what they would be paid for various commodities. The FU also proposed extending the Tennessee Valley Authority to the Missouri Valley and advocated government health care, a 100 percent capital gains tax on land sold on speculation (to prevent the inflation of land prices), and federal aid to schools that was based on need. Moreover, the FU supported the continuation of the school hot lunch and food stamp programs to help decrease food surpluses and boost agricultural prices.[44]

In contrast the American Farm Bureau Federation reflected the wishes of the larger-scale, more prosperous Great Plains farmers, and it sought less government involvement in agriculture and an end to restrictions on crop production, although it supported the continued use of mandatory commodity loans and price supports. The Farm Bureau also favored expanding foreign and domestic commodity markets in order to increase farm income, and it sought a host of tax reductions. The policy differences between the FU and the Farm Bureau would be fought over for the remainder of the twentieth century, and Great Plains farmers would be central to the debate on the crafting and changing of farm policy, in part because they had profited so handsomely from World War II. Similarly, in November 1944 the members of the New Mexico Farm and Livestock Bureau, meeting in Albuquerque, heard President W. P. Thorpe remind them about strength in numbers and urge farmers to "keep their organizations abreast of the times." Thorpe cogently observed, "There is abundant evidence that the power we possessed in the old days will not be great enough to do the job ahead." He urged the cattle and dairy associations to join the Farm Bureau in order to consolidate agricultural political power because farm unity, not division, would protect all agricultural interests.[45]

Although Congress had guaranteed agricultural prices at 90 percent of parity for two years after the war ended, the USDA did not have a long-term program for the future. Great Plains farmers, then, had some security that high wartime prices would prevail, but they worried about a collapse of farm prices similar to that which followed World War I. Many Great Plains farmers anticipated the return of New Deal–type acreage controls. Even so, the war years had been a time of "milk and honey" for Great Plains farmers. By the end of the war the gross farm income reached an index of 248 (1919–14 = 100). Net income on a typical Great Plains wheat farm in Kansas, Oklahoma, and Texas rose from $558 in 1939 to $6,700 in 1945, for an increase of 1,102 percent. Cotton farmers in Oklahoma and Texas averaged $997 in 1939 and $2,894 in 1945, for an increase of 190 percent. Wheat and livestock farmers in the northern Great Plains averaged $704 and $4,620, respectively, for a 556 percent combined increase in earnings. Great Plains farmers had no intention of allowing postwar economic and farm policy to let them fall from prosperity to the want and hopelessness of the past. They had done their part to produce more food than ever before to meet military and domestic needs during the war. They had earned considerable unused disposable income, and they intended to maintain their economic gains.[46]

News that Germany had attacked Poland also brought immediate and unparalleled economic prosperity to the livestock raisers in the Great Plains. Three days after the invasion cattle prices in Kansas City spiked from $0.25 to $0.50 per hundredweight higher, depending on the class of cattle marketed, with choice, heavy heifers bringing $10.65 per hundredweight, the highest price of the year. Traders attributed the price rise to stockmen withholding cattle from market in order to see what effects the new European war would have on the demand for agricultural commodities, including beef, while hoping for still higher prices. In Wyoming cattlemen believed that the new war meant "a jingle of more coin in the old jeans" because food prices would quickly increase. Indeed, the value of cattle, sheep, and hogs in Wyoming was estimated at $14 million more on September 7 than a week earlier. Quickly, the multiplier effect influenced the livestock economy. Wyoming ranchers and farmers who raised hay, the state's primary cash crop, now refused to market it in anticipation of higher prices. With hay selling at $5 to $6 per ton, many remembered that it brought twice that amount during the First World War.[47]

Because speculators were preying on Wyoming stockmen who were "not in touch with the actual market value of their livestock," the Wyoming Stock Growers Association (WSGA) also urged its members to sell cattle at markets beyond the state where they could receive the highest prices. One newspaper reporter cogently observed, "As a whole, the war which is bringing distress to Europe, is improving the outlook in Wyoming and other farm states, and the prospects are for even greater improvement in the future providing, of course, that the war continues, and nothing is done by the national government to clamp down on the American producer, as some local experts fear may be done." By late September, however, the economic excitement over the war had disappeared from the livestock markets. Farmers and ranchers who had held their stock in hope of receiving even higher prices began to ship cattle to market because they needed to maintain a cash flow and pay their bills. They had little choice but to consider the price acceptable, although they would always want more money for their cattle.[48]

By January 1940 beef cattle brought the highest prices since 1930 and, with few exceptions, the highest profits since 1920. To take advantage of high prices, livestock raisers began culling nonproducing heifers no matter their quality while retaining their best breeding stock in anticipation of still higher prices. In South Dakota ranchers and farmers began organizing livestock improvement associations to help them learn the best techniques for upgrading their cattle and improving their pastures. But Sam O. Hyatt, the president of the WSGA, told members, "I do not believe that you stockmen, rugged individualists as you are, rightly want too much theory in getting an efficient and profitable livestock production." By this he meant government regulation. He reminded members that "in such time of semi-panic it is more than ever necessary to keep our feet on the ground"—because the war could easily increase the public debt and require higher taxes. A "sane, careful," economical defense program, including food, would best serve the nation. At the same time the WSGA joined the Institute of American Meat Packers in supporting a major advertising campaign to encourage the public to eat more beef.[49]

While beef producers increased their herds, high wartime prices brought the return of an old problem—cattle rustlers. Whereas in the nineteenth century rustlers drove their stolen cattle to isolated ranches in the daytime, in the twentieth they struck at night, rounding up cattle for transport to distant market via trucks. If the cattle had not been branded or earmarked, and if the slaughterhouses, such as the Armour Packing Company in West Fargo, North Dakota, did not ask questions about ownership, the cattle could be slaughtered, butchered, and transported to grocers' display cases before the grower missed them. To help combat the rustling problem the WSGA stressed the importance of registering brands and inspecting cattle at major railroad loading points and markets. It also warned members that the Billings Live Stock Commission Company and the Pierce and Midland Packing Company in Montana and the Union Livestock Commission, the Platte Valley Commission, the Alliance Livestock Commission, and the Cook Packing Plant in Nebraska were unreliable because they bought branded cattle but did not require proof of ownership. Auction sale barns in South Dakota, Colorado, and Idaho also proved "undependable" when it came to ensuring that they purchased cattle from the rightful owners or helping the rightful owners receive their money if their cattle were sold illegally by someone else.[50]

As in the past the WSGA sent inspectors to shipping and market points, but, instead of arming them with revolvers, it supplied them with cameras to photograph altered or disputed brands. Calling the new breed of rustlers "rubber-tired" bandits, the WSGA sought to achieve brand inspection beyond Wyoming by working with other states to coordinate inspections and develop uniform regulations. The WSGA wanted all buyers to require the seller to provide a bill of sale proving ownership of the cattle marketed. Otherwise, the brand should be recognized as prima facie evidence of the rightful ownership. With 1,888 brands registered in Wyoming alone, however, the inspection task proved labor-intensive and difficult and the brand book something that no longer fit in an inspector's back pocket. Even so, increased vigilance brought the rightful owners the proceeds from the illegal sale of 2,792 cattle and 308 horses during the fiscal year 1940.[51]

In 1940 WSGA members agreed with A. A. Smith, the president of the Colorado Stock Growers and Feeders Association, who told them during their annual meeting in Lander to maintain the independence of their organization. Smith warned these conservative cattle producers, "With the world situation as it is, and the growing menace of war and the urgent need of national defense, the time is coming, if not here, when an expression of disapproval of any governmental program will brand one as a traitor." A year later, however, Charles A. Myers, president of the WSGA, said, "We want all agricultural groups to cooperate because while the cattle kings and sheep barons at different times in the past have felt that they were holier than thou, nevertheless the time has come when agriculture as a whole must co-operate in order to hold its own with other groups." Myers was, of course, referring to organized labor. He also reminded the organization that it had had a cooperative relationship with the Farm Bureau for many years and that it needed to continue that relationship for "mutual advantage," particularly for gaining access to congressional delegations as talk increasingly turned to meat rationing, price controls, and marketing allocations.[52]

By 1941 Great Plains cattlemen enjoyed their profits at the expense of the war-torn European nations. When Secretary of Agriculture Wickard and Roy C. Wilson, the head of the Kansas office of the AAA, however, asked cattlemen in the Sunflower State to expand their herds and use feed grains stored on their farms under the price-support program of the Commodity Credit Corporation to produce more beef and, thus, meet increasing domestic and Lend-Lease demand, they hesitated. They worried that increased production, along with possible government price controls, would work to their detriment. The Nebraska Stock Growers Association, meeting in Ogallala in mid-June, scoffed at the request of Lord Woolton, the British food administrator, that the United States institute meatless days to conserve food supplies for England. Great Plains cattlemen also opposed any price limit on hides, which they considered discrimination without a similar ceiling on prices for shoes and other leather products. They also claimed that tariff reduction would put them at a serious disadvantage at the conclusion of the war, when the United States would become the "dumping ground of the world."[53]

Like crop farmers, livestock producers feared that the economy would collapse after the war, just as it had after World War I. Consequently, from the beginning of the war they always looked to the end and beyond, as well as to the moment, when considering their response to any policy that affected their profits. Great Plains cattle raisers also distrusted the Department of Labor and considered the leadership of many labor organizations "unpatriotic, selfish, and corrupt" for calling strikes in industries essential to the national defense. Earl H. Monahan, the president of the Nebraska Stock Growers Association, also revealed the gender prejudices of the day by calling for a "he man" to lead the Department of Labor instead of Francis Perkins.[54]

At the same time President Myers professed that the WSGA's members were patriots, not pacifists, and pledged to help fight the war with "every weapon," including beef, at his command. In this regard the organization reluctantly agreed to approve the importation of canned beef from Argentina because the military had a greater demand for meat than livestock raisers could meet and to oppose it would have subjected cattlemen to criticism that they placed personal gain above the national interest. The WSGA also affirmed its record as the "champion of states' rights, the champion of the rights of the individual, whoever he may be." By "states' rights" Myers meant the return of federal lands protected from sale under the Taylor Grazing Act to the states for rent or sale. His view of individual rights, however, did not include rights for Communists. Although Myers held that the WSGA would not "take advantage of the serious situation in which this country and the world finds itself to-day to feather our own nests . . . neither will we permit any communists to gain a foothold in our organization." Given the interest of the membership in reaping high profits from cattle sales and the dearth of Communists in Wyoming—and the even fewer Communists who might have contemplated taking over the organization—the WSGA succumbed more to the former possibility than to the latter.[55]

At the annual meeting of the WSGA held at Worland in early June 1941, the members heard F. E. Mollin, the secretary of the American National Livestock Association, warn that beef prices had to be kept reasonable; otherwise, a "run-away cattle market" would bring price controls and decrease the profits of cattle producers who expanded their herds to surplus proportions. The Wyoming cattle raisers, like other Great Plains beef producers, also worried that any tariff reduction under the Reciprocal Trade Agreement Act would be instituted merely to keep other nations, particularly South American nations, tied to the Allied effort. But a tariff reduction would also permit the dumping of foreign beef on the American market after the war. This problem became perennial, and the secretary of the WSGA soon claimed, "We find our Department of State running up and down the tariff wall like a breachy steer looking for a hole in the fence, striving to find a means whereby they can bring in Argentine meat." In Kansas Governor Payne Ratner agreed and added that high tariffs were needed because the agricultural states had not yet benefited from the war to the extent that industrial areas had profited.[56]

Little more than a month after Pearl Harbor, Grover B. Hill, the assistant secretary of agriculture, addressed the American National Livestock Association in Salt Lake City and told cattle producers, "Your job is the production of the most vital and necessary food known to man." In order for soldiers to fight they needed meat, and Hill urged stockmen to keep a constant flow of high-quality cattle headed toward the slaughterhouses. On the Great Plains the drought had ended, feed supplies remained ample, and prices held high. But, Hill warned, cattle producers should not get greedy and overstock their pastures and rangelands. He reminded the stockmen that grass and human consumption were limited, and he urged them to market more cattle by culling old heifers from their herds but not to produce more animals. Other livestock leaders had reminded cattle producers to avoid overexpansion in reaction to the rise in beef prices because the government would radically reduce defense spending when the war ended and consumers would have less income to buy beef. Hill urged them to raise more grass than cows. The National Livestock Association also asked the federal government to terminate all payments to livestock producers under AAA programs because participation required cattle reductions and they could now make more money without government price supports than with them.[57]

While livestock producers contemplated various management practices, the number of cattle increased in the Great Plains. By January 1, 1942, Wyoming cattlemen raised 877,000 head, an increase of 50,000 since a year earlier, and the value of these cattle rose from $37.5 to $49.3 million, while the average value per head rose from $45.50 to $56.30. In Nebraska the number of cattle also expanded from 3 to 3.2 million head, the values of which "materially increased," from $43.10 to $53.80 per head. On the Billings market choice steers brought as much as $11.50 per hundredweight. Cattle carcasses brought as much as $12.10 per hundredweight at the major markets in Oklahoma, the "highest reported prices on record." In Oklahoma City the Wilson and Armour meatpacking companies reported busy days packaging boneless, frozen cuts for the army and the navy, cuts being easier to transport and store than carcasses. This cutting method would continue to be used after the war for provisioning grocery stores, and it eliminated the need for local butchers.[58]

By summer 1942 cattle producers worried about ceiling prices and enjoyed their profits, but they complained that the Selective Service System was the "biggest single threat to the industry" because it drafted the workers needed to put up hay and tend cattle. The WSGA warned of economic collapse unless the government classified ranch labor as "skilled and critical" and, thereby, exempt from the draft. In West Texas a representative of the Selective Service System met with ranchers to assure them that local draft boards would safeguard their interests when determining whether young men were more useful on the farm or ranch than in the army. In October, when the War Manpower Commission announced that the Selective Service System would request local draft boards to defer livestock producers and workers because they were "necessary men" for whom replacements could not be found, cattlemen gained some optimism. The USDA also pledged to work with the U.S. Employment Service to locate livestock workers; however, cattlemen continued to complain that the draft took their hired hands, hindered their efficiency, and restricted their profitability.[59]

By late 1943, then, Great Plains ranchers experienced a shortage of cowhands as a result of the draft, enlistments, and flight to higher-paying wartime jobs. In December the Matador Land and Cattle Company in West Texas had five thousand calves unbranded owing to the labor shortage. The New Mexico Cattle Growers Association claimed that, while the federal government asked it to increase production by 17 percent, local draft boards took all cowhands without dependents and that ranchers would, therefore, necessarily be forced to reduce the size of their herds because they did not have the men to tend them. One observer in Lubbock noted that Texas cowboys had joined the military to begin "dehorning those Japs and Nazis," and a survey of sixty-six ranchmen in West Texas showed that they operated with only two-thirds of their normal labor. The cowhand deficit was met, in part, by ranchers' wives, who proved themselves invaluable because they could "rope, ride, cut, and brand as well as the men do." But, with the turnover rate among hired labor reaching 50 percent during the past year, and with substitutes consisting of "old men and young boys," livestock received less care.[60]

Wyoming cattle producers, led by Governor Nels H. Smith, also complained that they needed more rubber tires than the government rationing program allowed in order to truck their cattle to market. By late July 1942 the rubber shortage was so severe that officials canceled the Sheridan-Wyoming Rodeo because cowboys, ranchers, and fans could not afford to use their precious rubber tires to attend. Other, more serious and long-dreaded problems also emerged during the summer. In July meat shortages began to worry eastern consumers, and they anticipated "real shortages" by fall and winter if Great Plains stockmen reduced sales in response to ceiling prices on cattle. Although cattle production increased nationwide from 8 billion pounds of beef and veal in 1939 to 10 billion pounds in 1942, much of that produced in the Great Plains, consumer prices escalated, and shortages soon occurred. Moreover, OPA-imposed price ceilings on cut meat had an immediate effect on the quality of beef marketed by Great Plains cattle raisers. With packers unable to get top dollar on the best grades of "dressed beef," the government grade of "prime" disappeared from meat counters. Packers could not sell the best cuts for a profit because of the high prices they paid for cattle, and many stopped buying grain-fed cattle that would grade "prime." As a result both the demand and the price for grass-fed cattle that graded lower when butchered increased. This shift in marketing hurt cattle feeders in the Midwest who bought range-or grass-fed cattle to fatten with corn before sale. On September 8, 1942, the OPA also decided to put the entire meat industry, except retailers, under licensing control to prevent packers and wholesalers from upgrading cuts of dressed meat and evading price controls. Moreover, to guarantee adequate meat for the military and the Lend-Lease program, the OPA restricted the amount of meat that slaughterers could distribute to civilian retailers between October and December 1942. They could provide only 80 percent of the beef, 75 percent of the pork, and 95 percent of the lamb distributed during that same period in 1941. Moreover, the OPA urged consumers to restrict meat consumption to two and a half pounds per week per adult. The OPA believed that this amount more than met minimum dietary standards, but it warned consumers to expect meat rationing in 1943.[61]

At the same time full employment and military spending soon threatened to spur inflation, and meat prices escalated because Great Plains cattlemen could not meet demand. Congress and the Roosevelt administration responded by instituting price controls and rationing, but these regulations proved difficult to enforce, and beef prices continued to rise. As a result, on October 2, 1942, Congress approved new price-stabilization legislation, and the OPA followed the next day by placing ceiling prices on selected foods, including beef. Great Plains cattlemen welcomed the price ceilings on feed grains, but they complained that ceiling prices on beef did not allow for differences between grades. They also worried that ceiling prices on live cattle would soon be imposed because ceiling prices on dressed beef had not effectively kept prices from rising to an index price of 107 by 1943. At the same time competitive bidding for cattle forced prices so high that packers often suffered a loss when they sold the beef. Oklahoma cattlemen soon complained that any government attempt to roll back ceiling prices on beef at grocery stores would be nothing less than an "appeasement policy" for John L. Lewis.[62]

When the WSGA met at Lusk in early June 1943, President Myers welcomed the delegates by proclaiming, "The cloven hoof of our most ruthless bureaucrat, Secretary Ickes was never more plainly in evidence than in the proclamation creating the 221,000 acre national monument in Teton County." Myers wanted the Jackson Hole area reserved for "comely white-faced cattle" rather than tourists. He also believed that the federal government should give fifty thousand men who had an agricultural background and who worked as federal employees the choice of joining the military or working on a ranch or farm. The WSGA also advocated the immediate furloughing of military men to harvest hay because high school boys were fully employed and cattlemen believed that town women were not adapted to work on the livestock and hay ranches. This demand soon became common, and livestock producers voiced it for the remainder of the war because they believed that federal policy discriminated against them regarding the labor market.[63]

WSGA officials also believed that the war would be won in 1944 and that the postwar rehabilitation of Europe, Asia, and Africa would keep prices high for only another year before a decline began. Consequently, with an eye on the bottom line they urged association members to use their income from high cattle prices to pay their debts rather than buy war bonds. WSGA members agreed, and they continued to oppose suggestions for price ceilings on live cattle, in part because they wanted to avoid bureaucratic control from Washington. They argued that, because cattle buyers gave livestock many grades, fixed pricing would be complicated, arbitrary, and unfair. Moreover, with more cattle on the rangelands than ever before, with unreasonable quotas limiting the slaughter for civilian consumption, and with meat rationing for civilians set at unreasonably low levels, black market sales would continue. The members of the Texas and

Southwest Cattle Raisers Association also opposed ceiling prices on live cattle. They argued that ceiling prices could not be enforced and that price limits would retard livestock production. In addition ceiling prices would create insurmountable administrative problems and encourage the spread of black markets. Certainly, they would "damage morale," that is, keep cattlemen from earning as much as possible from escalating wartime prices.[64]

Cattlemen's fear of income loss seemed warranted when, in late October 1943, they were "surprised and disappointed" to learn that Fred Vinson, the director of the Office of Economic Stabilization, planned to fix live cattle prices at levels ranging from $7.45 per hundredweight for bulls that would be processed into bologna to $16.00 hundred per hundredweight for cattle that would grade "choice." OPA officials had for some time advocated price fixing for live cattle because beef ceiling prices applied only to meat sold at the grocery stores and escalating costs reduced the profit margins of slaughterers. Meatpackers had to pay these fixed prices for cattle in order to receive a government subsidy ranging from $0.50 to $1.45 per hundred pounds, depending on grade, that helped them remain profitable. The Matador Land and Cattle Company, the Colorado Stock Growers and Feeders Association, and other Great Plains ranchers and feeders quickly criticized the price ceilings on live cattle because they wanted cattle producers to receive their fair share of escalating prices and profits. Nevertheless, the OPA announced ceiling prices on live cattle effective December 1. Cattle raisers responded to the ceiling-price order by flooding the markets with cattle to receive the highest possible price before fixed prices became effective, particularly for grain-fed animals. By December the cattle flood had passed, and the pens along the North Canadian River at Oklahoma City stood nearly empty, while the stockyards in Fort Worth also had fewer fat cattle than usual.[65]

By 1944 cattle raisers also complained that meat shortages occurred because the profits from grain-fattened cattle were too low and labor costs for the feedlot operators too high. Consequently, cattle feeders did not buy their stockers, and more livestock had to be fed on the grasslands, which produced a lower grade of beef. The

Colorado Stock Growers and Feeders Association contended that consumers could have adequate beef if the OPA permitted purchases of lower grades of meat, such as hamburger, without ration points. Ultimately, the OPA, fearing continued meat shortages because of rationing, surprised stockmen, slaughterers, butchers, and the public in early May 1944 by removing the ration points required to purchase all beef except steaks and roasts.[66]

The black market for beef continued, however, through 1944, and in July 1945 the OPA attempted once again to end it by announcing a "rigid ceiling" of $17.50 per hundredweight for live cattle. Cattle producers, however, did not believe that the higher price would deter "black market thieves" because consumers had more income to spend for meat and supplies remained scarce. Cattle producers contended that the black market for beef could be eliminated only if the government provided consumers with high rather than low grades of beef. Ultimately, the OPA increased live cattle prices to $18 per hundredweight to placate cattle producers. Retail butchers in New York City, however, complained that they could not make a profit unless live cattle prices fell to $14 a hundredweight. OPA officials believed that meatpackers could pay the $18 per hundredweight ceiling price for live cattle and still make a profit, and it contended that no packer had to pay that price, only that that price could not be exceeded.[67]

In 1945, despite the increase in ceiling prices, Great Plains cattlemen remained dissatisfied with government livestock policy. The New Mexican A. D. Brownfield, the president of the American National Livestock Association, criticized the OPA for being "entirely consumer minded." George A. Cross, the president of the WSGA, agreed. He opposed any ceiling prices on live cattle as a "detriment to Wyoming stockmen" and "one of the most vicious things that could be forced upon us." The WSGA argued that ceiling prices for cattle would not be equitable until prices were fixed for "everything that goes into the making of fat cattle." Cattlemen wanted prices to rise as high as the market would bear. They believed that ceiling prices did not give feeders enough profit and discouraged them from buying grass-fed cattle from Great Plains stockmen for fattening. As a result, less high-quality beef and fewer pounds of beef overall reached the market. If ceiling prices on live cattle could not be avoided, livestock producers wanted the OPA to set a price floor below which prices could not fall.[68]

Clearly, the war aided cattle producers. With 99 percent of the workforce employed by 1945, up from 85 percent in 1940, weekly wages increasing about 50 percent during that same period, and prices rising only approximately 30 percent, consumers had more disposable income for beef. During the war, beef prices rose from an average of $7.95 per hundredweight in 1940 to $12.41 per hundredweight in 1945. Great Plains cattle producers had not reaped such profits since 1918, when World War I drove prices skyward. In Montana, for example, gross income for cattlemen rose 144 percent from 1940 to 1948, while costs increased only 96 percent, owing primarily to cattle prices increasing 225 percent during that period. High prices kept a large number of cattle on Great Plains range-and pasturelands. In 1945 the Great Plains states grazed and fed 24.5 million head, a figure that declined only slightly, to 24 million head, by 1949. Cattlemen used their wartime earnings to pay off mortgages and other debts. Besides raising more cattle during the war, livestock producers also became more attentive to improved breeding, feeding, and range conservation management practices, and they raised more feed and improved the veterinary care of their herds. Although Great Plains cattle raisers, for example, still preferred handsome, white-faced Herefords, in the deep southern plains they increasingly adopted the heavy, heat-and pest-resistant Santa Gertrudes.[69]

Over the course of the war the number of farms in the Great Plains, most of which produced livestock, decreased from 1.1 million in 1940 to 1 million in 1945. At the same time farm and ranch sizes increased. In the northern Great Plains, for example, the average ranch expanded from 3,559 acres in 1940 to 3,667 acres in 1945. While cattlemen increased their acres, the rate of tenancy decreased during the war. In western North Dakota, for example, the number of cattle ranches jumped from 19.5 to 28.6 percent of the operating units between 1940 and 1945, the number of landowners and part owners also rose, from 63 to 84 percent, and tenant operations decreased from 36 to 16 percent of all cattle producers (among the forty-two cattle ranches studied), primarily because ranchers had more purchasing power to acquire land. Small, family-operated cattle ranches and farms, however, dominated the cattle industry across the Great Plains. Few large-scale corporate operations remained. The Swan Land and Cattle Company of Wyoming, the Bell Ranch in New Mexico, and the Matador Land and Cattle Company and the King Ranch in Texas began selling land because, despite high cattle prices, such sales proved more profitable.[70]

Overall, Great Plains ranchers and farmers enjoyed high wartime cattle prices. In 1941 ranchers and farmers received an index price of 125 (1938–40 = 100) for the sale of their cattle. By the end of the war that price averaged 171, and it rose still higher during the remainder of the decade. At the same time retail prices paid for all commodities rose only from 112 to 136. Index prices that slaughterhouses paid rose during that same time period from 121 to 164, while retail meat prices increased from an index of 108 to one of 115. Clearly, cattle producers and packers benefited from wartime demand, and ceiling prices and rationing did not cause them economic hardship. With the income index for industrial workers increasing from an index of 161 to one of 319 by 1944, before declining to 273 in 1945 as a result of nearly full employment, a longer workweek, often with overtime pay, and higher wages, increased demand and disposable income ensured profits for cattle producers. The income index for nonindustrial or white-collar workers, however, only slightly exceeded farm index prices received for beef. Federal subsidy payments to livestock slaughterers helped keep beef affordable for nonindustrial workers. The federal government intended the meat-subsidy program to reduce or prevent wholesale meat prices from rising by encouraging slaughterers to buy livestock for slaughter at ceiling prices because the subsidy would enhance their income. Meat-subsidy payments to slaughterers began in June 1943, with cattle bringing from $1.10 to $1.50 per hundredweight. These subsidy payments increased periodically throughout the war, and by August 1945 they reached nearly $3 per hundredweight for the best grades of beef, while the lower grades brought slaughterers

$1 per hundredweight. By the time the subsidy payments ended, the federal government had spent more than $500 million to encourage slaughterers to buy cattle despite ceiling prices for meat sold to consumers.[71]

Great Plains cattle producers strongly opposed government price controls and rationing programs, just as they had opposed and resented most government regulations in the past, and, along with the meat processors, they looked forward to "killing" the OPA when the war ended. Ultimately, they played a major role in achieving that goal, but not before they had profited from both the war and government regulations. Still, if cattle raisers on the Great Plains had had their way, they would have taken high wartime prices and unlimited production in order to capitalize on the increased disposable income of consumers who wanted more and better beef than they had had in the past.[72]

During the war the Montana Livestock Association also pledged to "gladly make the effort needed to assure victory in order that we may preserve liberty and freedom in and for our nation." Of course, high beef prices and minimal federal regulations made this patriotic commitment easier. Throughout the war, however, they complained about federal cattle policy on pricing and marketing, wanting assurances but no regulation, and they remained largely independent challengers of government policy to the end. Even so, high wartime prices, generally adequate rainfall, pasture, and feed (with a few exceptions), and improved range management enabled cattle raisers to profit, pay off mortgages, and purchase land. Essentially, Great Plains cattlemen advocated federal aid and protection of the livestock industry and the reduction of regulations on livestock producers. Great Plains cattle raisers, then, patriotically supported the war effort, but on their own terms.[73]

In retrospect, then, when the war began, farmers and ranchers optimistically hoped that the new conflict would benefit them. Increased federal demands for greater production meant more money. During the war Great Plains farmers and ranchers favored maximum production and prices and minimum regulations. The Emergency Price Control Act had guaranteed agricultural prices at 110

percent of parity for the duration of the war, but Great Plains farmers considered this provision a price ceiling rather than a supportive
policy. They were, however, grateful for the 90 percent floor price
guarantee for two years after the war guaranteed by the Steagall
Amendment, even though most farmers considered it too low. Still,
Great Plains farmers sometimes ignored official policy limitations
and paid monetary penalties for exceeding acreage and marketing
regulations, and 1943 became the year when they achieved "all out"
production for the first time.[74]

Overall, however, farmers and ranchers benefited economically
from the war. They paid off debts, retired mortgages, bought land,
and saved. Nevertheless, they worried that agricultural prices might
collapse to the guaranteed 90 percent of parity level as provided
by the Steagall Amendment, or about 20 percent below levels prevailing when the war ended. They hoped that a postwar recession
would pass quickly and that the international demand for American
agricultural commodities would mitigate any major price and income declines. Most farmers and ranchers wanted more money and
labor during the war years, and, while they received the former, they
continued to complain about not getting the latter. Indeed, agricultural labor became a perennial problem for Great Plains farmers and
ranchers. It involved the complex interaction of wartime employment, military induction, and race, not to mention class, gender, and
cost. While they grappled with the agricultural labor problem, Great
Plains farmers and ranchers agreed that war paid.[75]

SEVEN | Agricultural Labor

World War II brought unprecedented prosperity to Great Plains farmers but also considerable uncertainty and problems regarding agricultural labor. By 1940 many young men and women were leaving the farms for high wages and regular hours in war-related industries in the cities of the region. After 1940 thousands of young men left the farms and rural communities for military service, and by 1942 farmers experienced a serious labor shortage for the harvest of their wheat, sugar beet, and cotton crops. Great Plains farmers attempted to solve their labor problems by drawing on the workforce that remained—students, housewives, and businessmen—but this solution proved inadequate and unreliable. Consequently, farmers quickly demanded deferments for their sons and hired workers from local draft boards, supported the Bracero Program (which allowed Mexican nationals to work legally in the United States), and, to a limited extent, accepted the organization and deployment of the Women's Land Army (WLA).

Even though some men and women left the farms for the factories in the cities after the European war began, a farm labor surplus stemming from technological change, government programs, and the Great Depression continued to occupy the attention of economic planners in the USDA. Secretary of Agriculture Henry A. Wallace maintained that too many people still lived on farms and earned an income too meager to provide them with an adequate standard of living. Although the Selective Training and Service Act, which President Roosevelt signed on September 16, 1940, together with the increasing buildup of the defense industries, soon removed many of Wallace's surplus farmers from the land, USDA officials believed that farmers would have enough labor for planting and harvesting to maintain the current level of production in 1941. Still, farmers would need a large number of migratory agricultural workers to meet their labor needs, particularly in areas near towns and cities with defense industries, where they could not compete for long-term labor. By December 1941, for example, Kansas war industries employed 26,623 workers, but the state Board of Agriculture estimated that at least 75,000 workers would be so employed the next year, resulting in a decrease of the farm labor supply to 51 percent of demand by July 1942.[1]

At the same time spot agricultural labor shortages began affecting farmers in the northern Great Plains. In mid-April 1941 Tracy N. Shaw, the director of the Wyoming Employment Service, and officials in the USDA anticipated a 15.7 percent shortage of farm and ranch labor during the spring and summer. Each spring "transient workers" from Kansas, Nebraska, and the Dakotas migrated to Wyoming to work in the sugar beet and hay fields, but they had not yet arrived because more-appealing job opportunities existed in their own states. Farmers in Colorado and Montana also experienced agricultural labor shortages, and Shaw did not believe that outside workers would be available because they had gone to war industries or been inducted into the armed forces. Shaw urged all men who desired farm or ranch work to register at the nearest employment office and announced that they would be hired quickly. In the meantime he told farmers and ranchers to take what they could get. Roy Sheer, Wyoming's state labor commissioner, agreed and anticipated a shortage of three thousand farmworkers for the state. In South Dakota, despite higher wages the farm labor shortage became so acute in 1941 that Charles Newell, the state's director of unemployment compensation, asked the Civilian Conservation Corps (CCC) to release its young men for work in the wheat fields, and the Works Progress Administration (WPA) agreed to shut down projects in the wheat areas to help farmers employ needed workers. The WPA also ordered its local offices to remove from its rolls those people who refused farm employment.[2]

In June 1941 some farmers also complained that their sons had been drafted at a time when they needed them the most. Secretary of Agriculture Claude R. Wickard responded by warning the Selective Service System that the national defense program "has drawn heavily upon the supply of farm labor and maintaining the adequate supply of farmworkers for production of essential foods required for national defense is becoming a serious problem." The Selective Service System responded by notifying local draft boards that they could defer men for sixty days to help with the wheat harvest. In August Congress also attempted to ameliorate the effects of the Selective Service Act on farmers. Originally, the law required all men twenty-one to thirty years of age to register for the draft, but Congress amended it to exempt farm laborers over twenty-seven, provided the farmer who employed them produced more food than just that consumed by the people living and working on the farm. The registrant also had to prove, or at least convince his local draft board, that he was necessary to the farm operation and could not be replaced without substantially decreasing the farm's production.[3]

Still, some areas of the Great Plains did not experience farm labor shortages during the early war years. In Oklahoma, for example, farm leaders and government agencies projected an adequate labor supply for the wheat harvest that would begin in May 1941, even though the labor supply was "going down fast" owing to the draft, industrial expansion, and the widespread movement of potential agricultural workers to learn trades in the towns and cities. With a 10 percent drop in the agricultural labor force since January 1, the wage rate had risen from $2.00 to $2.50 per day compared to the previous year. Although some farm leaders and government officials worried about the future, Tom W. Cheek, the president of the Oklahoma Farmers Union, assured members that a labor shortage would not develop. "We've got plenty of unemployed workers eager for a job," he said. Cletus Hamilton, the acting director of the state employment service, contended that the agency could provide farmers with the twenty thousand workers needed for the harvest because the nation was not at war. South Dakota farmers and employment offices also believed that they could manage the labor force adequately to prevent all but temporary, spot shortages of agricultural labor. After the attack on Pearl Harbor in early December, however, all men between twenty-one and forty-five years of age had to register for the draft. Within the next few months thousands of young men entered the military through the enlistment or the draft process, but the Selective Service System exempted agricultural workers in areas identified by the USDA as experiencing labor shortages resulting from military inductions.[4]

In western Kansas, however, grain sorghums remained in the fields in mid-January 1942. One farmer reported that because of inadequate labor, "most of the crop is just where the binder left it. There has been heavy snow and much of the feed is spoiled." In Colorado the agricultural subcommittee of the state's defense council recommended the creation of labor exchanges to pool labor and facilitate the movement of workers from areas of surplus to locales in need. It also urged the state to work with the Selective Service System to defer "vital skilled farm workers during the planting and growing seasons" as well as requesting school superintendents to dismiss students earlier in the spring, in exchange for a brief summer session, and schedule a late-starting autumn term to provide sugar beet farmers more workers. When the Denver office of the U.S. Employment Service, however, announced a plan to form schoolchildren into companies and battalions of what was to be called a "junior victory army" to work on farms during the summer, it stirred a "hornet's nest" of opposition among educators and parents, who called the plan "a direct copy of Hitler's schemes for regimenting the youth of Axis countries." One educator called it a "pure steal from totalitarianism—even down to the armbands the employment service wants our youth to wear." Although he professed that the junior and senior high school students in the Denver area would willingly help farmers, he considered armbands that included an insignia and school colors, daily radio communication between leaders concerning student work assignments, and transportation to the fields on school buses not to be the "American way."[5]

By spring 1942 J. C. Mohler, the secretary of the Kansas State Board of Agriculture, expected patriotism and a sense of community commitment and obligation to solve the farm labor problem. "Kansans won't stand by and allow wheat to go unharvested for lack of hands," he contended. When the "show down" came, he believed, rural communities would furnish emergency workers: "Merchants will lock their shops, the town banker, minister and teacher—folks who know what the wheat harvest means—will go into the fields." As it turned out part of his prediction came true, but not enough to meet the labor needs of Kansas farmers. Soon, farmers experienced their first labor shortage since 1928. Some nine thousand workers were needed in a twenty-two-county area of southwestern Kansas to help with the wheat harvest. As a result wheat farmers paid harvest wages of $5 per day for common laborers and $7 per day for combine operators, plus room and board, for the highest harvest wages since the record wheat crop of 1931.[6]

In late May the U.S. Employment Service announced that it could no longer meet farm labor shortages by transferring workers from one state to another. As a result it informed farmers in Colorado, Wyoming, and Montana that they should, in part, meet an anticipated shortage of ten thousand agricultural workers caused by a 40 percent increase in sugar beet acreage, and a corresponding 40 percent decrease in the number of agricultural workers, by hiring women and children. South Dakota farmers also expected to meet half their summer labor needs with shared work, 40 percent from nearby towns, and 10 percent from other localities. The sugar companies anticipated paying $28 per acre for all work, including topping, for a 25 percent increase. In Nebraska wages for hired farmworkers increased by 50 percent from the previous year, averaging $44.25 per month with board or $57.50 without it. Workers at the Cessna airplane plant in Wichita, however, easily earned $40 per week, and the company drew 80 percent of its workforce from nearby farms.[7]

Early in 1942 Nebraska senator Hugh Butler also demanded that the Selective Service System defer all farm youths from the draft. Director Lewis B. Hershey responded by asking local draft boards to give careful consideration to farm boys and agricultural workers who sought deferments. The USDA also agreed to establish county war boards that would provide information on the agricultural labor situation to local draft boards, although these war boards would not make recommendations or interfere with the classification of registered men. Senator Butler approved of these efforts but called the farm labor shortage "acute" because of the draft and the fact that the defense industries paid wages that farmers could not afford. He also complained that many farmers could not receive help from the WPA, the CCC, or the National Youth Administration, noting that one farmer near Ponca, Nebraska, reported that men on the WPA rolls wanted $80 per month, plus room and board, before they would leave the agency to work on a farm. Butler responded by recommending the termination of the WPA and other government relief agencies for the duration of the war, thereby forcing men on the relief rolls to accept farmwork when a lack of pecuniary rewards or patriotism kept them from accepting agricultural employment. In North Dakota, however, WPA workers had no choice. In the spring of 1942 the state administrator of the WPA mandated that every man employed in the agency who was capable of farmwork had to accept such employment "promptly when it is offered to him under satisfactory conditions." Since more than six thousand WPA workers had volunteered to help with the last harvest, he believed that "the vast majority of project workers were ready to do their patriotic duty on the farm again." But he also held that "refusals to accept employment at decent wages and under favorable conditions cannot be tolerated by the WPA." Similarly, in Oklahoma the WPA announced that workers on its rolls would be required to take agricultural work if the employing farmer offered the "prevailing community wage."[8]

By late summer 1942 the farm labor shortage became so serious in North Dakota that Governor John Moses asked Hershey to defer all registrants who were "actually engaged in farm labor." Great Plains agricultural leaders and politicians made similar requests, noting that the adoption of gasoline-powered tractors made the sons of farmers skilled workers who could not be easily replaced because they, rather than their fathers, had learned to service and repair those implements. Workers unfamiliar with tractors and other tractor-powered machinery, they argued, could not replace the sons of farmers, and production for the war effort would necessarily suffer. Governor Moses complained to the Selective Service System that, since North Dakota did not have any war industry, and because 75 percent of its people depended directly on agriculture for their living, it needed to keep farmers' sons and agricultural workers at home until October 1 to help with the grain harvest. While the governor waited for a reply, the daily farm labor wage rose to $4 per day for potato pickers. Yet, despite the agricultural labor shortage in North Dakota, farmers in the Williston area refused to hire Indians who were available for work because of prejudice. Ultimately, in September 1942 Hershey responded and asked the USDA to identify critical areas where the agricultural labor supply was insufficient and promised to limit the draft of farm boys in those areas, if possible.[9]

By 1942, then, farmers could not compete with defense industry wages, and the military was taking many potential workers away. As a result, sugar beet growers in Montana and Wyoming, among others, who produced "white gold" struggled to harvest their crops. With an estimated eighteen hundred workers needed in Montana, five hundred in Wyoming, and three hundred in South Dakota, Blaine Ferguson, the president of the Sugar Beet Growers Association, contended that the crop would freeze in the ground for want of harvesters, and he urged the federal government to "initiate a policy of drafting for farms." Clearly, unusual conditions brought suggestions for unusual solutions and made these Great Plains farmers, who usually decried government interference, seek federal help.[10]

In late October 1942 some farmers received the news they had wanted for some time when the Manpower Division of the War Department announced that the Selective Service System would no longer draft workers considered essential for livestock, dairy, and poultry production. At the same time farmers were urged to "accept women for more general farm work." Dairy farmers, however, doubted that many city women would volunteer for agricultural work yet believed that farm women were already "doing about all they can." The farm labor problem also involved more than gaining temporary workers. The most difficult farm employment task involved hiring skilled workers as year-round help. Moreover, draft deferments for workers on dairy and livestock farms protected them from military service only as long as they stayed on the farm. If they quit those agricultural jobs, they had to have the permission of their local draft board, or they would be subject to immediate military service. This policy applied to married men with children as well as single workers as young as eighteen years old. At the same time the Selective Service System informed draft boards that agricultural workers who moved from a "necessary" farm to a "non-necessary" farm could also be immediately inducted into the military. Equally important, the draft waiver meant that agricultural workers had to remain on the farm, often at wages half those earned in the war industries. In Kansas the Selective Service System directive apparently encouraged some farmworkers to quit and seek employment in the Wichita aircraft industry before their employment became frozen on a farm. In the end farmers, not hired men, primarily requested deferments for agricultural workers.[11]

Farm policy critics argued that, while agricultural prices had increased dramatically, agricultural wages remained below war industry wages because the government ensured high prices and profits for the war industries while keeping the ceiling on farm prices too low. The result was "rank injustice." Yet, when the federal government removed the wage ceiling for agricultural workers in late 1942, the move had little effect because most farmers already paid all they could afford for labor. At the same time the federal government did not clarify which farms it meant when it singled out livestock, dairy, and poultry farms, but in South Dakota the state Selective Service director told draft boards to "consider as such a farm, any farm, that can be remotely interpreted as being one of the three."[12]

While the agricultural labor shortage worsened in the Great Plains, the United Cannery, Agricultural, Packing and Allied Workers of America attempted to use the wartime labor shortage to enhance its organizational strength in the sugar beet fields of the northern Great Plains. In August 1942 this Congress of Industrial Organizations union proposed a plan to the Farm Security Administration (FSA), the Farmers Union (FU), the Mountain States Beet Growers Association, and the Great Western Sugar Company that would permit it to organize in the sugar beet factories and secure agreements between the field-workers and the farmers. The union contended that such organizational and contractual planning would enable it to guarantee the labor supply, train workers, and serve as a clearinghouse to assist farmworkers.[13]

Efforts to organize agricultural labor, if only through crew leaders who contracted with farmers to supply workers, brought strong opposition in New Mexico. In March 1943 the New Mexico Farm and Livestock Bureau charged that "labor racketeers" were making exorbitant wage demands designed "to build up union dues and fatten their own salaries." As a result they kept essential workers from the farms and ranches, interfered with the war effort, and endangered the lives of American boys on the battlefields. In response the bureau sponsored a bill in the state legislature to regulate the activities of unions by requiring that they register with the secretary of state and that their officials be U.S. citizens and resident in New Mexico for at least one year. Agricultural unions would also be taxed 2 percent of their gross receipts, and they would be forbidden to make contributions to political campaigns. The bureau insisted that the bill would not interfere with "lawful strikes or collective bargaining."[14]

Most nonskilled farmworkers did not need coercion or union organization to help farmers in time of need. During June 1942 in Montana buses with volunteers ran daily from Helena to Townsend, where the U.S. Employment Service distributed the workers to farmers who needed help in the sugar beet fields. The Helena office of the employment service organized a "Keep 'Em Growing" campaign and planned to draw on patriotism to encourage doctors, lawyers, merchants, housewives, stenographers, and schoolchildren to aid farmers for the current wage rate and, thereby, meet spot labor shortages thorough the summer and autumn. With Montana's farmers lacking 26,000 hired workers, or about 30 percent of the total number of laborers required for 1942, they desperately needed help. More than 450 volunteers, including women and girls as well as businessmen and miners, met the challenge and blocked and thinned sugar beets near Sheridan, Wyoming, during the summer. Volunteers also helped farmers shock barley and wheat in Colorado. The Longmont Cham-

FIGURE 15. The agricultural labor shortage became so severe that the U.S. Employment Service and the Extension Service urged urbanites to volunteer their labor, particularly at harvest time. This crew of businessmen from Lincoln, Nebraska, shocked grain on a nearby farm. (Nebraska State Historical Society, RG 1161-206)

ber of Commerce organized the workers and, although the workers did not accept wages, asked farmers to estimate the value of the work performed and contribute that amount to a local defense organization or the Red Cross. Members of the Junior Victory Army, aged fourteen or older, also picked berries and beans on truck farms near Denver, for which they received a piece rate that totaled about $2 per day for eight hours of work.[15]

In the southern Great Plains cotton farmers also struggled to meet their labor needs. In Harding County, New Mexico, farmers contended that 75 percent of the workers had departed by September. Joe C. Scott, the president of the Oklahoma State Board of Agriculture, together with other agricultural leaders, urged farmworkers to be "reasonable" in their wage demands and recommended a $1.25 wage for picking one hundred pounds of cotton. He deplored "labor piracy," that is, luring workers from one farm to another with the offer of higher wages. Scott estimated that 46.3 million man-hours would be needed to pick Oklahoma's 828,000-bale cotton crop. If workers used the "snapping" rather than the "picking" method, which left more trash in the fiber, 27.4 million man-hours would still be required.[16]

The construction of military bases and employment at the bomber and ordnance plants, airbases, ammunition depots, and flying schools further drained the agricultural labor supply in the Great Plains because the construction and war industries paid considerably higher wages than farmers. In Kansas farmers typically paid from $40 to $60 per month with room and board for year-round help and $3 per day for seasonal harvest hands. By autumn 1942, however, they were paying $5 per day for inexperienced workers, and they could not find enough even of these, in part because the aircraft industry in Wichita paid as much as $12 per day. The acquisition of temporary harvest labor, then, became a problem, but, more important, year-round labor disappeared, particularly for dairy farmers. In Kansas consumers began to experience milk shortages because some three hundred dairy farmers had sold their herds for lack of labor to maintain them. By the end of the year many dairy herds in the Great Plains had been sent to the slaughterhouses, and USDA officials worried that a nationwide milk shortage might occur during 1943.[17]

Moreover, a farm labor study indicated that industry had depleted farm labor by 35 percent owing to higher wages and shorter hours, and one agricultural official contended that the harvest of feed crops could be completed only by women and boys, "both rural and city alike." The Kansas Labor Commission responded by issuing an emergency order to allow the employment of women on farms for more than the maximum hours permitted by law. At the same time Governor Payne Ratner contended that high school and college students and government employees should be drafted to work on farms because the autumn labor shortage created "a most serious emergency" for farmers. The state director of the FSA also proclaimed, "A lot of energy is going to waste on the football field." Arguing the point that "an idle Kansas farm aids the axis as surely as a shutdown in a vital war plant," Ratner recommended the cancellation of all athletic events in the high schools across the state until the war ended. Others also supported a draft to provide agricultural labor. Desperation caused unusual responses to the shortage of farmworkers, but more rational minds ultimately prevailed. In Washington Paul V. McNutt, the War Manpower Commission

(WMC) chief, told the House Agricultural Committee that he disliked terms such as *labor draft* and *labor conscription*, in part because of "certain constitutional questions." In the end nothing came of this recommendation, and Great Plains farmers had to solve their labor problems with the workers available.[18]

As 1942 drew to a close the USDA urged greater agricultural production during the next year. A continued labor shortage, however, still threatened production goals. At the same time the Office of Economic Stabilization (OES) exempted farm wages from a general wage and salary freeze because it considered them "substandard" compared to wages paid in the war industries. The OES declared that no ceiling would be placed on agricultural wages until the secretary of agriculture determined that such a ceiling should apply. In addition it ruled that agricultural wages could not fall below the highest rate paid between January 1 and September 15, 1942, without the secretary's approval. These rulings were intended to help farmworkers who earned less than $2,400 annually while encouraging all agricultural workers to remain on the farms. Although the OES believed that this policy would help farmers keep their workers, it also increased their costs and affected their ability to pay workers.[19]

In late November, while the OES planned to initiate its new agricultural labor program, farmers from twelve western states, including Wyoming, New Mexico, Montana, Kansas, and North Dakota, met with Secretary Wickard in Denver, and they were in an angry mood. There, a government official presented a seven-point agricultural aid program that included the movement of workers from nonessential to essential farms and from subsistence to commercial operations. This latter ideal harked back to the New Deal days of state planning and the movement of workers through Resettlement Administration and FSA programs because it also involved combining subsistence farms under one operator to achieve commercial production. By the time Secretary Wickard appeared before the farmers they had drafted their own plan for solving the agricultural labor problem. It included drafting workers to work on farms as well as issuing uniforms to farmworkers "to show they are as important in total war as the Marines in Guadalcanal." Wickard could give them no more encouragement than to urge the production of more food as a "patriotic obligation," even though continued labor shortages would make that work difficult. He also advocated the hiring of more women and older men.[20]

While Great Plains farmers planned for 1943, however, the Selective Service System established the agricultural production requirements needed to defer a full-time "essential" farmer or agricultural worker at sixteen war units. For example, the care of 16 milk cows or 240 beef cattle equaled sixteen units and would defer one man, while fifteen acres of wheat equaled only one war unit. Other crops were assigned unit points that could be applied to the total needed for a deferment. If a farmer whose production accounted for fewer than the number of units required for the deferment of two men had a son who was draft age and wanted him deferred, either he had to increase his units, or his son had to take outside farmwork. As 1942 ended farmers and ranchers put pencil to paper and inventoried their production by acres and livestock in order to calculate how they could keep their sons and, in some cases, themselves on the farm. No war units were given for raising upland cotton on the southern Great Plains if the fibers were less than one inch long. Still, local draft boards were not to consider the directive a "rigid yardstick," and they could apply either a higher or a lower standard. This cotton regulation excluded the deferment of seasonal workers unless more than one farmer employed them.[21]

Farmers continued to demand changes in the draft system and the provision of military furloughs to ensure adequate agricultural labor, but the War Department staunchly opposed such a policy. In January 1943 Great Plains farmers received some relief when the Selective Service System reduced the number of production units needed to qualify for a farm deferment from sixteen to eight, after strong criticism of the original plan. The new guidelines also provided for the deferment of anyone engaged in legitimate agriculture. Prior to this change in the regulations only a "key man" on the farm could receive a deferment. Essentially, any agricultural work would now be considered a "war job" and, thereby, qualify a farmworker for a deferment, provided that he produced crops and livestock essential to the war effort. Local draft boards would make this determination. Paul V. McNutt, the director of the WMC, and the newly appointed director of the War Food Administration (WFA), Chester Davis, also announced that they would seek mobilization of a 3.5 million volunteer "land army" for seasonal work on farms across the nation. Local extension agents would recruit workers not employed in defense industries and ask them to work on farms and accept "regular farm wages," even if below the pay of their regular jobs, as a contribution to the war effort. McNutt also advocated a forty-eight-hour workweek to achieve "maximum production with what we have," but farmers immediately wondered whether work beyond that amount would require them to pay overtime. No one knew the answer.[22]

Cynics thought the proposal absurd not only because "back-to-the-soil patriots" would be unskilled but also because farmers could not provide the necessary housing and "hygienic arrangements." Instead, they proposed "farm furloughs" whereby military men would be released from their duties during critical agricultural periods, such as planting and harvesting, to provide farmers with the needed labor. Farmers would pay the prevailing wage rate directly to the Department of the Treasury, and the soldiers would receive their regular army pay. Farm officials could apply to the commandant of the nearest military post for a specific number of men for farmwork, and he would release them for temporary work. President Roosevelt liked the plan and approved it in late February 1943. The army, however, opposed it and had already declined a request from Secretary Wickard to provide soldiers to help farmers with the wheat harvest in South Dakota during 1942. At the same time, Senator Gerald P. Nye of North Dakota advocated reducing the size of the army to ensure an adequate farm labor supply. The Kansas Farm Bureau also offered its own variant of the furlough plan. It contended that twenty-five years of experience were required to produce a skilled farmworker, and it wanted the army and navy to transfer those men who had it back to farms. Those workers would remain in uniform, that is, part of the military, and form a "great land army." The Kansas Junior Chamber of Commerce also asked Governor Schoeppel to seek furloughs for all Kansas farmers in the army and navy from June 15 to July 15, 1943, to help with the wheat harvest.[23]

In Colorado Governor John C. Vivian also told Secretary Wickard that farmers could not meet their labor needs by employing city and town children above fourteen years of age, as the USDA and President Roosevelt recommended, because they had "neither the experience nor the capacity to do this work." Even so, he urged school officials to release these students to help with the spring planting. Vivian also appealed to Secretary of War Henry L. Stimpson for the release of all Coloradoans who had been drafted from farms, ranches, and dairies, and who were still in the continental United States, to help with spring fieldwork. Vivian called the drafting of such men "short-sighted and blundering." The governor also called on all Colorado men who had left farms, whether as owners or as workers, since Pearl Harbor to leave their jobs and return to their farms. He did not, however, explain how these men could return to the "identical farms, which they left," but he urged them to do so as a "patriotic duty."[24]

Contending that 75 percent of the labor needed on Colorado farms in 1943 had to be recruited out of state, Vivian attempted to solve the agricultural labor problem by ordering a halt to the induction of all Colorado farmworkers into the armed forces. He did so under his power to administer the Selective Service Act in the state as provided by federal law. Colorado senator Edwin Johnson called the governor's plan "brazen demagoguery at its worst." Federal Selective Service officials ignored the governor's order. Vivian, however, continued to demand a "blanket deferment for agricultural labor" by Selective Service officials in Colorado. If local draft boards did not support him, he would issue executive orders deferring farmers on the induction lists on an individual basis. Vivian charged that a lack of response by Selective Service officials indicated that "they must be confused." Nebraska governor Dwight Griswold, however, opposed "blanket deferments to any class of people or kind of worker," but Texas farm leaders supported Vivian's idea and organized the National Agricultural Council to support the deferment of farm labor.[25]

While Governor Vivian took his stand during the spring of 1943, the USDA attempted to give system and order to the recruitment and employment of agricultural workers. The agency's major objectives were to keep a cadre of experienced farmers and agricultural workers on the land and encourage the return to the farm of workers who were not employed in essential defense industries and who had agricultural expertise. USDA officials also wanted to mobilize a "U.S. Crop Corps" of 3.5 million men, women, and children from the towns and cities for full-time, seasonal, and temporary farmwork, particularly at harvest time, and provide transportation and housing for farmworkers recruited beyond local and state areas. On April 18 the WMC assisted by prohibiting anyone engaged in farmwork from leaving agriculture for a higher-paying job. Although this prohibition or regulation could not be enforced, the WMC hoped that it would discourage employers from hiring farm people, including women. The WMC also asked men aged eighteen to forty-five who were classified as 4-F, that is, physically unfit for military service, and others thirty-eight years of age or older who had farm experience and who were not employed in war industries to take agricultural employment; the latter would also face immediate induction if they refused and lived in counties suffering an acute farm labor shortage.[26]

In addition, on April 29, 1943, Congress passed Public Law 45, which established the Emergency Farm Labor Program. This legislation gave the Extension Service in each state the responsibility for recruiting, transporting, and placing agricultural workers. The Extension Service would also work with the U.S. Department of Education in seeking recruits for two new programs: schoolchildren for the U.S. Crop Corps's "Victory Farm Volunteers" and female agricultural labor for the WLA. Moreover, the agency would arrange transportation and housing for workers recruited in other states. The USDA's plans called for the WFA to handle the recruitment of foreign workers, conscientious objectors, and Japanese evacuees in war relocation centers, and it would use the FSA to coordinate the transportation and housing of foreign and out-of-state workers.[27]

This legislation, however, failed to protect workers from discriminatory practices and bad treatment, particularly in Texas. In the Lone Star State the Farm Labor Office of the Extension Service in College Station had responsibility for routing and placing farmworkers within the state. Although officials in the Farm Labor Office worked diligently to locate and place agricultural workers, it could not guarantee adequate housing and sanitary facilities. In West Texas these deficiencies became serious when some farmers housed migrant workers in barns and chicken coops. These workers confronted similar problems in town. During the 1944 cotton season, for example, Lubbock officials prevented migrant workers from using public facilities for bathing and toilet needs. In Lamesa the toilets in the City Hall were locked at noon on Saturdays, and gas stations often refused access. As a result the migrant workers experienced unsanitary conditions, and an epidemic of dysentery developed among them that soon spread to the public schools. Without bathing facilities personal hygiene deteriorated, and, when cotton pickers went to nearby towns on Saturday afternoons, they often found themselves barred from cafés, barbershops, and theaters. In Big Spring law enforcement officers stopped trucks carrying workers heading for town during the cotton season and warned them that stopping there meant arrest. This policy kept the migrant workers passing through Big Spring, but they often kept going, leaving the area entirely, all to the detriment of nearby farmers who needed their labor. Many of these migrant workers were Mexican Americans from South Texas, and they preferred to avoid discrimination and seek employment beyond Texas.[28]

Across the Great Plains the Extension Service also organized state and county farm labor advisory committees, composed of leading farmers and representatives of cooperating state and federal agencies, to conduct the daily operations of recruiting and placing farmworkers. Structurally, on the local level the county agent became the director of the farm labor program. As head of the county farm labor committee the agent worked with the county chairman of the state farm labor commission, vocational agricultural teachers, school superintendents, county commissioners, Boy Scout leaders, chambers of commerce, county chairmen of the USDA war boards, the FSA, and the U.S. Employment Service. The locally controlled organizational structure gave farmers a place to request labor and enabled an organized approach to recruitment and placement that met local needs while adhering to general policy made in Washington.[29]

In April 1943 Congress also authorized the USDA to organize county agricultural wage boards under the direction of the Extension Service and the land-grant colleges. These county wage boards replaced the state wage boards operated by the FSA. They determined prevailing wages for specific agricultural operations, such as picking cotton, harvesting wheat, or topping sugar beets. The county agent also served as the chairman of the wage board, which essentially became a subcommittee of the county farm labor advisory committee, which acted on behalf of the state Extension Service and the WFA. The county wage boards were composed of local farmers and representatives of local government agencies. These wage boards collected information through public hearings and surveys about wages for agricultural work and announced the "prevailing," that is, the most common, wage for a specific job in the county or area. They then submitted their wage recommendations to the director of the state Extension Service for approval, after which the recommended wages became the suggested rate for agricultural labor in the area. The determination of prevailing wages became difficult because wages for seasonal work and piece-rate employment made generalization or averaging problematic and because projecting farm wages for work that was not yet begun but for which agricultural laborers were needed became nearly impossible. The boards had to balance the interests of the farmers and those of the workers to ensure the necessary labor supply, but the composition of the boards made them more sympathetic to the farmers than to the workers.[30]

Even so, the county wage boards provided fairly reliable information for both agricultural workers seeking jobs and farmers seeking workers. Usually, the prevailing wages for specific agricultural labor in a county became the minimum wage that workers both expected and trusted to be "fair" or "unexploitative," provided that it was not less than $0.30 per hour or the equivalent for piecework. The county wage boards did not attempt to narrow the differences between agricultural and war industry wages, equalize wages between regions, or eliminate high wages. Rather, they merely ensured minimum wage standards for a specific area. Farmers, however, usually considered these rates to be maximum wages, thereby fixing the rate for the duration of employment, rather than permitting fluctuation for higher pay if labor supply conditions changed. In practice the "area of employment" usually involved several counties, occasionally the entire state, and sometimes parts of several states. Wyoming and Montana, for example, were designated as employment areas for the purpose of determining the prevailing wage rate for sheepherders, while parts of Nebraska, Wyoming, and Montana were considered to be a single area of employment for the determination of a prevailing wage scale for Mexican nationals, or braceros, employed to work in the sugar beet fields. In every case, however, similar economic and labor conditions enabled the boards to determine reasonably uniform wages, and the boards had sufficient flexibility to reconcile policy with daily farm labor needs.[31]

By June 1943 rumors of a food shortage made the already "acute" farm labor shortage even more critical. In Dallas the mayor provided twenty men, "hardened to toil," from the city payroll to help area farmers, while the Coca-Cola Company provided a similar number. The Dallas County Commissioners also granted a week of paid vacation to all road and bridge employees who would use the time to work on farms in the county. These volunteers were joined by members of the Twenty-ninth Battalion of the Texas State Guard of Dallas, who took hoes to the johnsongrass invading the cotton fields and detasseled corn. The Dallas Chamber of Commerce asked business leaders to release their employees for fieldwork, and it was "perturbed over the lackadaisical attitude of most business firms and industrial interests" toward its call for help. Few Dallas businessmen volunteered to chop cotton, but one observer noted that twenty lined up to tee off on the first hole of a golf course on a Saturday morning, which caused one farmer to reflect, "It ain't near as hard to chop cotton as it is to chase a golf ball around." No one was shamed into leaving the links for the cotton fields, where farmers reportedly were willing to accept "city workers" and pay them $0.25 an hour, or $2.00 per day, to chop cotton or bale hay. Similarly, farm labor officials in Wyoming urged Cheyenne businessmen and their employees to spend their summer vacation working on a farm within a fifty-mile radius of the city. One New Mexico critic, however, observed, "The idea [that] the average volunteer can trip out to the fields and make a real hand is so foolish as to inspire pity that policy makers could be so dumb." In Nebraska one county agent reported that interest in farmwork among schoolboys and-girls lagged, while a survey of high school students in Oklahoma City clearly indicated that most had no intention of working on farms for patriotic reasons because they could earn from $80 to $250 per month in various city jobs. Notices that Oklahoma County farmers needed four hundred workers drew only a "scanty response" from high school students.[32]

To the north W. W. Murray, the president of the North Dakota Federation of Labor, resurrected the idea of a furlough for Flickertail State farm boys during the harvest season, and he requested 15,000 military men to help with the spring wheat harvest. This request achieved some success because the army sent 250 men from Sioux Falls, South Dakota, to Casselton, and the others were expected for deployment in groups of 200 to help farmers who had at least 120 acres of wheat to shock. Only two farmers could pool their acreage to meet the required minimum, and they had to pay the U.S. Treasury the rate of $0.60 per hour for each man. These wheat farmers also anticipated that the soldiers would stay for threshing time. The army, however, permitted them to remain for only twenty days, but, in addition to helping ease the farm labor problem, the army purchased all its perishable foods locally, thereby boosting the local economy. Meat and other rationed food allocations were charged against the army's allotment so that its food needs would not affect rationing to local consumers. Ultimately, approximately 5,600 soldiers arrived in North Dakota from military bases in Nebraska, Colorado, South Dakota, Kansas, and Texas as well as Wisconsin and Illinois. In South Dakota 350 soldiers from Camp Phillips, Kansas, also helped harvest wheat near Lake Preston and Salem. South Dakota's Governor, M. Q. Sharpe, attempted to solve the farm labor problem for the wheat harvest by exempting all harvesting equipment, including trucks, from taxation, by reducing other fees if the implements originated in Texas, Oklahoma, or Kansas or any other state to the south, and by exempting senior citizens from deductions in their state and federal retirement checks if they worked for a farmer.[33]

By the time the harvest season for wheat, cotton, sugar beets, hay, vegetables, and other crops ended in 1943, most farmers had learned that, if they wanted a job done, they had to do it themselves or rely on local labor. A survey indicated that, when Kansas farmers hired workers, approximately 71 percent were local in origin, an increase from 67 percent a year earlier. The governors, agricultural leaders, and farmers in the Great Plains states continued to blame their labor problems on the draft even though the Selective Service System had been lenient about granting deferments for farm operators and workers. In Kansas, of 12,081 single men deferred as "a necessary man in his civilian activity," 6,626, or 55 percent, were farmers, compared to the 26 percent who worked in the aircraft industry. In addition to demanding agricultural deferments and furloughs, farm leaders also wanted higher agricultural prices in order to guarantee the greater profits that would allow them to pay higher wages and, thereby, stem the flow of workers to the defense plants. Generally, farmers believed that the federal government outbid farmers for workers by providing cost-of-production-plus-a-fee contracts for the production of war matériel, thus enabling manufacturers to pay high wages because they could recover all costs and make a handsome profit. As a result farmers paid higher wages and worked longer hours to help make up for the labor shortages. In Oklahoma, for example, farmers paid $3 to $7 per day during the wheat harvest in 1943 for scoopers and truck and tractor drivers and $5 to $10 per day for combine operators, plus room and board. In Kansas farm wages had tripled since 1933, with the average worker earning $81.20 per month, or $59.60 per month with room and board, by early 1944, up from $70.25 for unboarded and $51.25 for boarded farmworkers in January 1943. North Dakota farmers averaged the longest workday, at 13.6 hours by September. Farmers in the other states averaged at least twelve hours, while the national farm work-week averaged seventy-two hours.[34]

Despite the agricultural labor problems, crops did not rot in the fields. The white migrant labor force that followed the wheat harvest from Texas to North Dakota found steady work, and braceros, Japanese internees, prisoners of war, soldiers, women, and school-children as well as farmers' sons and other workers who received agricultural draft deferments helped farmers meet their labor needs. Even so, all these sources provided only stopgap solutions to a problem that persisted into 1944. As the draft increasingly took men for military service, the local and itinerant labor pool declined rapidly. In South Dakota agricultural officials reported that migrant labor fell 25 percent in 1943 from the previous year and that the state faced another 25 percent reduction in 1944. If the agricultural labor situation became critical, county agents planned to request the state Extension Service to declare their counties "emergency areas" to qualify for Mexican nationals, Japanese evacuees, prisoners of war, and interstate workers.[35]

In February 1944, with the War Department planning the invasion of Europe as well as the Italian campaign requiring more soldiers, the Selective Service System announced an immediate review of all farmworkers who had deferments to determine whether they were fulfilling their obligations. With some 1.7 million men holding farm deferments nationwide, the Selective Service System told draft boards that only those men who produced by their "own personal and direct efforts" at least sixteen "war units" a year, that is, an increase from an adjusted eight war units in 1943, could remain deferred. Men who were not fathers could keep their deferments if they qualified, but their cases would be reviewed every six months. Men with farm deferments who were fathers would no longer be deferred in a separate class because they had dependents. Henceforth, only agricultural productivity mattered. Anyone who did not contribute his allotted production would be subject to the draft.[36]

This policy made the farm labor situation worse. By early 1944, few workers remained on north Texas farms. When the Dallas Agricultural Club met in late February, Congressman Hatton W. Sumners called the farmers in attendance the "most distressed-upset dirt farmers I ever saw." On one three-mile stretch of road where fourteen farmers had raised cotton, only five remained; nine had left for work in defense plants, four of the five who remained were over fifty years of age, and only one had a hired hand. Little wonder that in 1943 farmers planted only sixty-eight thousand acres of the county's eighty-six-thousand-acre cotton allotment. This acreage reduction affected the production not only of cotton for fiber but also of cottonseed for cattle feed, particularly for area dairy farmers, who supplied the Dallas market. No one seemed to know how farmers would plant cotton, put up hay, plant onions, or tend dairy herds. In South Dakota farmers had expected to increase by 2 percent their productive acreage (primarily in grains) by using old machinery and family labor and by paying workers as much as $100 per month, up from $40 per month before the war, but they could not find sufficient help.[37]

At the same time some factory workers began moving back to agricultural labor because they believed that farm employment gave them the best chance of maintaining their deferred status. By late March 1944 at least 300,000 war industry workers had returned to farms nationwide because the Selective Service System aggressively sought men under twenty-six who held nonagricultural jobs. With 563,000 men under twenty-six who were not fathers deferred for agricultural work, compared to 348,000 men in other occupations, many young men believed that they could avoid the draft by becoming farmworkers. But, with the Selective Service System intending to draft more than 1 million men by July, the deferred status of all unmarried young men became jeopardized. Moreover, in spring 1944 the Selective Service System dropped the production-unit guidelines for deferments and gave local draft boards the authority to determine whether a farmworker merited deferment by producing a "reasonable amount of food stuffs." This change in the regulations meant that the sons of farmers, part-time farmers, and seasonal farmworkers who were under twenty-six probably would lose their draft deferments.[38]

Texas farmers considered this policy change a "staggering blow."

In Kansas farmers complained to the governor that they would be forced to dispose of their livestock, particularly dairy cattle, if their sons no longer received deferments. One farmer suggested the drafting of union workers because they labored fewer hours and had the propensity to strike. The governor's office invariably replied that the federal government made draft regulations and that the state could not protect the sons of farmers from the draft. Texas farmers also complained that white workers asked for $4 to $6 a day and that blacks wanted $5 per day for their children. Many agricultural workers also went to town on weekends and never returned. The Dallas County Farm Labor Committee also charged that the local office of the U.S. Employment Service actively and intentionally worked against farmers by permitting building contractors to classify "common labor" as semiskilled, enabling common laborers to earn more under wartime wage guidelines. The objection was that, because they were operating under cost-plus-a-fee government contracts, contractors could easily afford such extra costs as higher wages, thus attracting more workers, whereas farmers, who had no way to recoup extra costs, could not.[39]

In Oklahoma and Kansas officials reported that farm labor needs could be met only by using, schoolboys and-girls, businessmen, and "rural and town women," but, when harvest time came for the wheat crop, wages of $10 per day with room and board attracted few volunteers. North Dakota agricultural officials did not expect a return of the 5,600 soldiers who helped with the harvest in 1943, but the state received an allotment of 2,600 combines, up from 700 the previous year, to ease the situation, along with a return of custom combine crews from the south. Even so, farmers in the Flickertail State needed 15,000 workers during the harvest season. Sugar beet farmers had contracted for 1,200 braceros, while potato growers had arranged for the importation of 600 Jamaicans, but the labor shortfall remained considerable.[40]

Indeed, Great Plains farmers considered the agricultural labor supply "tight" as they entered the harvest season. In Texas cotton farmers did not make it through the harvest season without difficulty. In June 1944 Dallas County farmers had 70 percent less labor than a year earlier, and county agents and employment services had great difficulty recruiting agricultural workers. In Dallas they developed a system whereby they sent fifty-nine recruiters to various street corners every morning during the picking season to hire workers and transport them to farms. With pickers earning at best only $5 for a day's work, the recruiters found few takers. Moreover, school leaders continued to inform agricultural officials and labor recruiters that their children would not pick cotton even if they were released from school. With "fear in their hearts" that they would not be able to harvest their cotton, most farmers offered a wage of $2 per hundredweight, but they still had few takers. With a heavy crop producing as much as a bale per acre, many farmers saw themselves eventually plowing under their crop for want of pickers. In Oklahoma cotton farmers paid only $1.50 per hundredweight for picking and had similar problems attracting workers.[41]

At the same time farmers in South Dakota offered the highest wages ever—averaging $92.50 per month with board, compared to $78.75 a year earlier—but they could not employ enough corn pickers. Farmers who were lucky enough to have been able to purchase a mechanical corn picker under the farm machinery–rationing program quickly found that the machine exacerbated their labor problem because a two-row corn picker could fill a wagon with sixty bushels every thirty minutes but two men could not haul and unload corn fast enough to keep up with the machine. Officials from the Agricultural Adjustment Administration who supervised the agricultural machinery–rationing program urged farmers to form "picking rings" and share the use of a corn picker. In this way they could collectively provide the labor necessary for the mechanical corn picker to work efficiently and meet their own labor and picking needs.[42]

The farm labor situation became worse in early January 1945 when the Selective Service System authorized the drafting of farmworkers "to the full extent permitted by the law," which essentially meant the reclassification of all farmworkers between eighteen and twenty-six years of age. In some locations, such as Ness County, Kansas, animosity developed between large-and small-scale farmers over the draft because the small-scale operators believed that the sons of the large-scale farmers received favored treatment from local Selective Service offices while their sons were drafted as "canon fodder." Others charged the local Selective Service boards with favoritism, saying that deferments depended on "who they are." In Colorado farmers insisted that Governor Vivian prevent the reclassification and drafting of these workers because that order violated the Tydings Amendment to the Selective Service Act, which permitted the deferment of agricultural workers between eighteen and twenty-six years of age if continuously employed in food production and if no suitable replacement could be found. Vivian's previous confrontation with the Selective Service System, however, had chastened him, and he now only voiced support for the farmers while admitting that he did not have any authority to help them. In late February Weld County, which produced wheat and cattle, had only six farmers still deferred. By 1945, then, Great Plains farmers complained that the federal government penalized them for their efficiency and productivity and that they could not do more with less. They particularly believed that Selective Service officials did not consider their aging population and old machinery. Farmers wanted their sons at home because they had little hope of employing skilled or knowledgeable farmworkers otherwise, and they worried that, if their sons left, they would not return to the farm.[43]

By April 1945 farmers in South Dakota were paying farmworkers $127 per month without and $96 per month with room and board, the highest wages on record. These monthly rates were nearly four times the five-year average from 1935 to 1939. In North Dakota farmers paid between $0.65 and $0.75 per hour, plus room and board, for threshing and $0.65 per hour for shocking grain, while potato harvesters received $0.10 per bushel, or $0.08 with board. They also paid $0.40 per hour for general farmwork during slack periods or on rainy days. Even so, they could not attract enough agricultural workers.[44]

When Germany surrendered on May 8, 1945, Great Plains farmers still worried about acquiring adequate farm labor even though they would be employing fewer workers than ever before. Peace in Europe encouraged them to anticipate a speedy conversion of the war industries to provide more tractors and combines as well as the release of soldiers, many of whom would return home and take agricultural employment. Even so, Kansas wheat farmers entered the harvest season with only 35 percent of the prewar labor supply, although farm leaders expected 30,000 women to help with the harvest, a number similar to 1944's. With the war against Japan still fully engaged and the Selective Service System warning that farmers over twenty-six could expect induction eventually, no solution to the farm labor shortage appeared imminent. A month after the surrender of the Japanese, the agricultural labor problem persisted on the Great Plains. In some areas it was more severe than ever before. In Kansas some farmers solicited married couples in the hope that such an arrangement would make year-round employment more desirable. With the release of approximately 100,000 men per month from the armed services by late October 1945, however, many farmers hoped that their agricultural labor problems were at an end.[45]

As white workers migrated from the fields to the military and the defense industries, Great Plains farmers sought Mexican and Mexican American workers. During the early twentieth century sugar beet farmers in Colorado and Nebraska had used Mexicans and Mexican Americans to thin the plants after seeding as well as cultivate the crop two or three times with hoes and pull the beets from the ground after a machine called a "lifter" loosened the soil. Then, these workers cut off the tops with a knife and piled the beets for transport to a nearby sugar refinery. Farmers necessarily recruited workers for this "stoop" labor twice each year; cultivation ran from April to July and harvesting from October to December. The sugar beet companies in the central and northern Great Plains helped by recruiting workers from Mexico, Texas, and New Mexico, especially sending agents to Fort Worth and San Antonio. Recruiters and farmers referred to these workers as "Mexicans" and "greasers." Sugar beet companies, such as the Holly and Great Western, encouraged the recruited workers to settle near the plants and urged farmers to provide some work during the slack season to keep them nearby. The sugar companies in Colorado, Wyoming, Montana, and Nebraska succeeded in this effort, and several thousand Mexican workers lived in communities organized by the beet companies, while others located in Denver, Billings, and Cheyenne during the off-season. Both recruiters and farmers believed that Mexicans would provide the stoop labor that white Americans rejected.[46]

In 1939, when the war began and industrial opportunities began to pull white workers away, beet growers in Montana hired approximately forty-four hundred Mexican workers from out of state. As more young men began to leave agricultural work after the passage of the Selective Service Act in September 1940, a group called the Texas Dirt Farmers Congress met in San Antonio on July 22, 1941, and approved a resolution calling on the federal government to provide immediate relief of the agricultural labor shortage by authorizing the importation of Mexican workers. Through the summer Texas farmers on the southern plains continued to lobby the state's congressional delegation to develop a program for the importation of workers from Mexico. When the United States entered the war, many industries also lowered race and nationality barriers, and sugar beet growers quickly experienced a tightening of the labor supply at a time when the federal government asked them for maximum production. As the military and war industries lured workers from the fields, the farm labor shortage became severe.[47]

In January 1942 Secretary of Agriculture Wickard recognized a looming agricultural labor shortage, particularly in the sugar beet fields of the Great Plains. New Mexico cotton farmers also urged their congressional representatives to modify or rescind immigration laws to permit the entry of Mexican workers to chop and pick cotton. In June Nebraska farmers needed workers to thin and block sixty thousand acres of sugar beets. This task required about one laborer per ten acres, or approximately six thousand workers. Governor Dwight Griswold reported a labor shortage of one thousand workers and the inability of local offices of the U.S. Employment Service to solve the problem. Sugar beet growers in Nebraska and Wyoming and cotton farmers in New Mexico hoped that Mexican workers would be available to help with the harvest, but no one believed that they could be obtained in a timely manner. Federal officials also hesitated to permit the entry of Mexican agricultural workers into Texas because they feared that farmers would use them to exploit native Mexican American workers. Moreover, federal officials believed that Mexican workers would not be needed until the domestic labor supply became exhausted, by which time they hoped that Mexican authorities would consent to sending agricultural workers to the Lone Star State.[48]

By summer 1942, however, severe agricultural labor shortages developed in California and the northern Great Plains. As a result of these labor needs and difficulties representatives of the State Department and Mexico began negotiating an agreement to import Mexican workers, known as braceros, an agreement that became effective on August 4, 1942. Officially known as the Farm Labor Transportation Program, it became commonly known as the Bracero Program. The agreement defined the standards, procedures, and methods for the recruitment, transport, and employment of, as well as the provision of housing, health care, and repatriation for, Mexican workers. It also prohibited discrimination. By serving as the official employer the FSA avoided direct worker-grower contracting and hiring, which had proved easily susceptible to abuse. Mexican officials supported temporary migration to help improve the economic condition of the country's workers, alleviate its unemployment problems, and aid the war effort, but they were concerned about wages, working conditions, and race relations, particularly since Mexicans had experienced abusive treatment at the hands of farmers in Texas. The FSA supervised the program from August 1942 to April 1943. Thereafter, the WFA oversaw it as part of the Emergency Farm Labor Program, but the WFA proved less fastidious in the enforcement of wage and housing regulations than the FSA.[49]

Most Great Plains farmers who needed workers supported the Bracero Program because it provided essential workers, but they complained about government regulations. Texas farmers, however, considered the Bracero Program an infringement on their "free market rights" because they could no longer hire directly from Mexico on their own initiative. After Congress passed the Tydings Amendment to the Selective Service Act in the fall of 1942, which authorized draft deferments for essential agriculturally workers, Selective Service boards in the south Texas plains threatened to draft all Mexican American workers who would not pick cotton for a wage of $1 per day. Force failing to gain the needed workers, Texas farmers sought braceros in 1943, but the Mexican government refused permission until Texas ended discrimination and segregation and guaranteed fair treatment for all Mexicans. Texas farmers, then, circumvented the Bracero Program by illegally recruiting and hiring workers from Mexico. Given the porous border and the high Mexican unemployment rate, Mexican officials could not prevent it. These illegal workers, however, did not enjoy even the minimal protections and guarantees that the braceros did. Even so, thousands of Mexicans or "wetbacks," that is, illegal agricultural workers, labored in Texas during the war. Still, Texas farmers wanted braceros not only because they were willing to pick cotton but also because their presence helped keep wages low—if they could be imported in sufficient number. Although Texas classified Mexicans as white in the Caucasian Race Resolution of 1943, which was designed to convince Mexican officials that the state would not tolerate discrimination, few Texans accepted the resolution's premise of equality. Mexican officials also remained unconvinced and until 1947 refused to authorize the employment of braceros in Texas because of "racial prejudice and discrimination." At the same time Mexican American workers complained about the Bracero Program because Great Plains farmers used it to keep wages low and drive away domestic, that is, native-born, workers, including them.[50]

While U.S. and Mexican officials negotiated the bracero agreement, Wyoming sugar beet farmers wanted Mexican workers. Cotton farmers near Roswell, New Mexico, also believed that Mexican workers could solve their labor problems. With the fall harvest looming in mid-September, these farmers needed three thousand pickers, but few were available locally or from other areas. One observer commented on the labor shortage, saying, "The sensible thing to do in this emergency would have been to draw the entire number from the vast reservoir in Old Mexico, their return after the picking was done to be supervised by the government. That was the sensible thing to do therefore it wasn't done." As a result, he contended, "It is quite thinkable that the planters will have to pay a heavy penalty from late picking or no picking at all." With Colorado farmers reportedly paying higher wages than cotton and pinto bean pickers could earn in New Mexico, agricultural labor migrated north. Cotton farmers confronted the task of picking the crop themselves because the state employment service could not supply workers when, in the parlance of the field, "there ain't none." Not long after approval of the Bracero Program, many New Mexico farmers believed that the importation of labor hindered their efforts to produce as much cotton as possible. Before braceros could be employed the FSA had to certify a shortage of American workers in a given area. By late September the agency had not yet provided that certification, and the cotton harvest had begun, with farmers paying $1.50 per hundredweight. Cotton farmers near Las Cruces anticipated an $8 million crop and a need for fifty-two hundred pickers, and they criticized the U.S. Employment Service and FSA for subservience to obstructing union labor racketeers and lack of cooperation.[51]

John P. Murphy, the manager of the Albuquerque Chamber of Commerce, told cotton farmers that they would need to solve their labor problems with American workers because the importation of braceros involved too much "red tape" and because the agreement with Mexico limited Mexican workers to picking long-staple cotton, rather than the short-staple variety grown in New Mexico, which had not been declared vital to the war effort. Murphy also told chamber members, "The business man who helps get labor for cotton farmers will be working to bring thousands of dollars into his own trade channel." With the agricultural economy inextricably linked to the broader economy, businessmen could reap the certain benefits of the war effort by assisting the recruitment of agricultural workers. Some farmers who raised long-staple cotton, however, hoped that their labor problems would soon end because they began entering into contracts for braceros through the FSA. But they had to pay those workers $4 per hundred pounds and contract for a minimum of one hundred pickers, which limited this labor relief to large-scale farmers. Even so, transportation delays prevented the braceros' timely arrival.[52]

Ultimately, Wyoming sugar beet farmers welcomed the braceros, provided that they arrived quickly, worked hard, and left immediately on completion of the harvest. Mexicans had migrated to Wyoming for work in the sugar beet fields since the early 1900s. They were good workers who did not cause trouble, the growers and sugar companies quickly stereotyped them as people who would work long and hard for low wages and not complain, and they were well suited for sugar beet work because they came from rural areas. Although the USDA, through local county war boards, set the wage rate for sugar beet work in Nebraska, Colorado, Kansas, Wyoming, North Dakota, and Montana at $9.50 to $11.00 per acre for blocking and thinning, $3.00 per acre for the first hoeing, and $2.00 per acre for each subsequent cultivation, few local or white migrant workers sought this backbreaking work.[53]

By early 1943 the bureaucratic process required for farmers to receive braceros still impeded their use in New Mexico. One critic reported that hundreds of thousands of Mexicans wanted to work on American farms and that the wages paid would be "rewards of the highest sort." "But," he continued, "restrictions have tied up this labor so that it is almost useless and cannot be had except in rare instances." At the same time farm leaders in Colorado demanded the importation of as many as ten thousand farmworkers for 180 days. They wanted Mexican labor by April for planting sugar beets because Mexican workers had "proved their adaptability and shown their desire for seasonal farmwork in Colorado." These sugar beet growers also requested permission from the USDA to withhold $3 per acre from the earnings of field-workers to force them to stay on the job between the thinning and the harvest seasons. Although this coercion threatened to decrease the number of workers who signed contracts, sugar beet farmers believed that it would ensure the needed labor force at harvest time.[54]

In March 1943 USDA officials urged Colorado farmers to request braceros immediately through agency war boards to ensure, so far as possible, adequate Mexican labor. When Mexican Americans from the Dallas area began their annual migratory trek to the sugar beet fields of the northern Great Plains, one observer attributed it to "free transportation, food and housing along with the Mexicans' own whimsy and desire for travel and new places," rather than the $17 per acre that they expected for thinning and blocking. Only several hundred braceros reached Wyoming for the fall harvest in Goshen, Washakie, Sheridan, and Platte counties because the growers in California contracted for most of the Mexican workers and because of insufficient planning. Ultimately, approximately 1,150 Mexicans worked in Colorado's sugar beet fields, while 2,975 labored in Montana's beet fields and wheat harvest.[55]

Soon after the completion of the sugar beet harvest in 1943, agricultural and sugar beet company officials began planning for the importation of braceros in 1944. By that time, however, the farmers, the sugar beet companies, and others in Wyoming were subjecting the braceros to the same discrimination and racist practices that they had experienced in Texas. In Worland businesses refused service to them. When the Mexican government threatened to remove them and cancel contracts for the arrival of other braceros, the Farm Bureau asked the merchants to let them trade in their stores. Governor Lester C. Hunt and the sugar companies also worked to provide entertainment in local communities, but the relationship between the whites and the braceros remained uncertain and tense, if not outright discriminatory. Disputes over the payment of wages, particularly for piecework, brought many bracero complaints to the Mexican Consulate in Denver, as did the fact that farmers paid workers from Oklahoma $5 per day but the braceros only $4 per day for the same work. Wage discrimination such as this hindered efforts to recruit more braceros for employment in Wyoming, and Mexican officials continued to threaten the denial of permission for them to work in the state. Caucasian Texans, then, were not the only people in the Great Plains to discriminate against Mexicans and Mexican Americans. These groups commonly confronted segregation in restaurants, movie theaters, barbershops, and other public places. In Kansas and Montana, for example, businesses frequently posted signs that read "no Mexicans allowed." In general the braceros and the Mexican Americans lived in poverty and experienced segregation and hostility across the Great Plains. Most white residents of the region considered them racially and culturally inferior. When the war ended, racial discrimination by whites and resentment by the braceros characterized relations between the two groups.[56]

Yet, while not willing to accept braceros as the equals of local, white workers, sugar beet farmers readily admitted that they performed more labor than inexperienced workers, such as schoolchildren and businessmen, because they were more experienced and efficient. They also believed the braceros were, in fact, ideally suited for "stoop labor," probably because so few other workers would take these jobs. Some agricultural officials in Kansas, however, believed that language problems made it "virtually impossible" for farmers to use Mexican workers. North Dakota farmers also complained about the inability of Mexican nationals to speak English and their lack of experience handling heavy machinery. Even so, they considered them honest and commended their work ethic at haying, shocking, and threshing time as well as in the sugar beet fields.[57]

In 1944 Colorado farmers anticipated the arrival of eighty-seven hundred braceros for spring farmwork and an additional thirteen hundred by harvest time for the sugar beet crop. During that year approximately three hundred braceros in South Dakota proved "outstandingly effective" harvesting small grains but "fell considerably below American standards" picking corn. These braceros, however, complained about irregular pay and lower wages than they could earn in California. Sugar beet farmers, however, did their best to recruit and retain braceros. In July braceros at work in the sugar beet fields of western Nebraska could be identified from afar by their sombreros. Ranging in age from twenty to fifty, few spoke English, although the younger men who had worked in California spoke "understandable English." In Wyoming, however, where nearly one thousand braceros worked in the sugar beet fields, livestock raisers considered them "unreliable," a judgment based primarily on racial prejudice.[58]

In Nebraska the Extension Service reported that braceros could learn any farm job with little training and supervision. Although the braceros had never picked corn, the Fillmore County agent observed that they were accustomed to working with their hands, which gave them an advantage over "most unskilled workers." Moreover, he noted, "The Mexicans have been found to be cleaner and more courteous than most transient domestic workers." He also reminded employing farmers, "They, like any other worker, need to go to town at least once a week." He also urged farmers to feed them well to gain maximum work and remember to employ more than one bracero because few spoke English and group support was important.[59]

In April 1945 W. E. Dittmer, the Extension Service farm labor supervisor for South Dakota, planned to prepare "Mexican dictionaries" or phrase books to help farmers explain such jobs as lambing, harvesting, threshing, and corn picking to bracero recruits and improve communication with them. The extension nutritionist also offered advice to the farm women who cooked for them. By the end of the war Great Plains farmers considered the braceros hard, diligent workers but treated them patronizingly. Moreover, from the beginning the Farm Bureau considered the program "utterly impractical" because it applied minimum wage laws, the National Labor Relations Act, and the Fair Labor Standards Act to agricultural labor. Farm Bureau officials believed that the program had been developed by "social experimenters" in the FSA. The Farm Bureau, the National Grange, and the National Council of Farmer Cooperatives wanted the federal government to provide Mexican labor but not require farmers to obey contractual regulations regarding minimum wages and maximum hours. These organizations collectively complained to Congress, "Under the guise of the war effort a social revolution is being perpetrated upon the American people." In New Mexico many farmers considered the Bracero Program too "loaded with red tape and unnecessary expenses to be practical."[60]

In retrospect sugar beet farmers needed Mexican nationals in their fields, but the growers, the sugar beet companies, and the local communities treated them as inferiors, ignored discrimination against them, and relegated them to the lowest level of employment. Like all agricultural workers, the braceros never enjoyed the economic and social status of farmers or the legal and legislative protection afforded laborers in manufacturing and industry. Most had no alternatives, or at least migrant labor was their best opportunity to earn a living.

Essentially, the Bracero Program made the federal government the overseer of a twentieth-century version of indentured servitude. One government official called it "legalized slavery." Overall, between August 1943 and August 1945 approximately twenty thousand braceros worked in the Great Plains, where they served as an important part of the labor force. They helped harvest sugar beets, corn, and potatoes, shocked and threshed grain, put up hay, and worked in a variety of vegetable fields, all of which helped farmers provide food for the military and public and earn handsome profits from wartime prices. Yet Great Plains farmers used them to minimize wages, and local merchants often subjected them to discrimination, all the while proclaiming their support for the war effort.[61]

By autumn 1941 the draft and the war industries had drawn many farmworkers from the fields and ranches across the Great Plains. Soon, the agricultural labor shortage would become much worse, but, by October 1, 1941, the USDA reported that the number of farmworkers had already declined by 200,000 nationwide from the previous year. Confronted with a labor problem that had no male solution, some agricultural officials, state politicians, and women's organizations began considering a female solution, that is, considering women, from both farm and town, as a collective agricultural labor pool. Eleanor Roosevelt also considered the agricultural labor problem an opportunity for women to aid the war effort. Roosevelt, who in addition to being the president's wife served as the assistant director of the Office of Civilian Defense, suggested the replacement of male farmworkers with a "women's land army." These "farmerettes" would help harvest crops and assist with other farmwork. The WLA would be modeled after a similar program instituted during World War I, under which farm families took women into their homes to help with agricultural work. Moreover, with town women of all ages working on British farms, Roosevelt contended that American women "can if necessary do what other women of the world are doing," if they received training.[62]

The response from the Great Plains was not encouraging. R. H. Vater, a member of the Kansas State Board of Agriculture, considered a corresponding suggestion from the USDA that farmers hire "town girls" to help with agricultural work "the silliest thing" he had ever heard of: "Our wives would run them off the farms, even if they were so foolish as to consent to come." Yet, with the farm labor supply meeting only about half the demand in Kansas even though wages had reached the highest level in twelve years, more farm women necessarily left their homes and gardens to milk cows and perform, in the words of USDA and State Board of Agriculture officials, "light chores and light field work." By May 1942, however, the wheat harvest loomed, and Kansas farmers recruited thousands of "women and girls" from nearby towns to drive tractors and operate other harvesting machinery. In some communities farm implement companies offered free instruction in tractor operation to women, who reportedly "enthusiastically" took these courses. But Harold Lewis, the director of farm replacement for the state employment service, observed that Kansas farmers "don't have much truck with the suggestion from Washington that city women and college co-eds be trained to do the outside chores." However, they accepted, even expected, the help of their wives and daughters. By the autumn, one reporter noted, farm wives conducted as much labor as possible, usually by driving tractors and baling hay "until their backs ached and the moon rose." Similarly, farm women held at least 20 percent of all agricultural jobs in North Dakota.[63]

In Grady County, Oklahoma, however, the Farm Board recommended that all individuals sixteen years of age or older, including women, register for agricultural work, such as chopping cotton and cutting, hauling, and stacking alfalfa. At the same time farm "women folk" in South Dakota reportedly worked alongside their men. The state Crop and Livestock Reporting Service noted that as of April 1942 women constituted 17 percent of farmworkers in the state, which, it contended, showed that farmers depended on women to replace men who left for the armed forces or factories. Women and girls also constituted approximately 10 percent of all Nebraska farmworkers, or approximately 16,400 female workers. Those women, along with other family members, constituted 88 percent of the total number of farmworkers, while hired hands contributed only 12 percent of that labor force. By August one Nebraska observer reported that "hundreds" of women and teenage girls helped solve the acute labor shortage by working in the potato harvest, detasseling corn, and putting up hay, and farmers appreciated these "victory workers." In the autumn officials from the U.S. Employment Service canvassed the neighborhoods of Roswell, New Mexico, to recruit women to pick cotton, even for half a day, but only about twenty accepted this work.[64]

In late 1942, while farm women struggled to provide needed labor, M. L. Wilson, the director of extension work at the USDA, appointed a committee of home economists to consider the ways in which nonfarm women could be utilized for agricultural labor. Planning in the USDA to establish the WLA then quickened in January 1943, and on February 3 Secretary of Agriculture Wickard asked the Cooperative Extension Service to develop and supervise "a program for the organized recruitment and utilization of nonfarm women for the appropriate types of farmwork wherever practicable; also for cooperation with and rendering appropriate assistance to other groups sponsoring and organizing activities along these lines." Although the American Farm Bureau Federation, the FU, and the Grange opposed the organized recruitment of nonfarm women for agricultural employment because they lacked experience, knowledge, and training, in April Congress appropriated funding and authorized the Cooperative Extension Service and the state Extension Service to create the WLA. Florence Hall, an experienced USDA employee, became the head of the WLA. The state Extension Service had the responsibility of appointing state leaders for recruitment and organizational work. These individuals would work under the state farm labor supervisor and especially closely with the county and home demonstration agents and the employment service to recruit, train, and place women on farms, primarily to serve as temporary labor. The WLA had an official uniform composed of blue denim overalls, jacket, and cap and a "tailored powder-blue sport shirt," but few women purchased it because they worked only several weeks a year.[65]

The WLA functioned as a decentralized organization within the Emergency Farm Labor Program and as part of the U.S. Crop

Corps. It had few employees and only a meager budget—$150,000 for 1943. It sought 60,000 women for agricultural employment (10,000 for year-round and 50,000 for seasonal work), and 300,000 for part-time work, that is, daily or weekly employment, nation-wide. Enrollment was available to any woman at least eighteen years of age who produced a doctor's certification of good health. The Women's Bureau recommended limiting recruitment to communities in areas where farm labor shortages were expected, in order to avoid transportation and housing problems. It also recommended making sure that local farmers were willing to use WLA volunteers before recruiting anyone, in order to avoid damaging volunteers' morale. Each volunteer had to be willing to work on a farm continuously for at least one month. Year-round workers would receive training for three to six weeks at a state agricultural college or some similar institution. Women who enrolled as seasonal help would receive less training, but still enough to prepare them for work and "life on a farm." Agriculture and home economics teachers would provide the training. This instruction was intended, in part, to "save the un-trained city women many embarrassing moments" when they took farm jobs. It would also help the WLA volunteers free farm women as quickly as possible for work that required the operation of ma-chinery.[66]

Women employed in the WLA would receive the prevailing local wage for farmwork. Despite earning wages that were lower than those paid in cities, WLA officials believed, "women with a lively interest in plant and animal life" would find "the experience on the farm . . . invaluable." The state Extension Service planned to "select the women having the best chance of making good as farm workers for the Land Army." A farmer interested in hiring WLA volunteers could contact his county agent, who would locate the women best suited for the situation from the WLA's local and state labor pools. The county Extension Service would monitor volunteers' employment to ensure their adjustment to farm life and the provision of adequate living quarters and sanitary facilities. Florence Hall addressed farm-ers' skepticism about hiring town women, saying, "Farm families will accept the workers in the spirit in which they come—the spirit

FIGURE 16. Women, usually the wives and daughters of farmers, conducted
a variety of agricultural labor to replace hired workers and sons, brothers, and
relatives who served in the military. The Women's Land Army attempted to
recruit town women for farm labor but achieved only mixed results because
farm women often did not trust town women to do the required work
properly. In 1943 these women took a water break from detasseling corn in
Nebraska. (Nebraska State Historical Society, RG 2183-1940307228 [2])

of service to their country." Great Plains farm men and women appreciated patriotism, but they questioned whether nonfarm women
were up to the physical labor involved in agricultural work.[67]

These concerns proved accurate. Owing to the low wages, the absence of child care, and farmers' reluctance, the WLA attracted few
recruits among town women—so few that in October 1943 farm
women became eligible to join. This decision enabled WLA officials
to count far more women as participants and claim at least numeri-
cal success. Indeed, from 1943 to the termination of the program in
1945 as many as 2 million women became part of the WLA. Women
participated primarily in states where fruit and vegetable farmers traditionally used women in work crews. In the Great Plains farmers
customarily had not hired women for seasonal, that is, harvest, work,

and recruitment proved difficult. In Nebraska, for example, Extension Service recruiters reported that farmers willingly accepted the work of their wives and daughters in the fields but that they were "reluctant" to hire nonfarm women except in crews. They preferred to hire town women to perform housework and provide child care, thus freeing farm women for fieldwork. Nonfarm women, however, did not find this work attractive or consider it a contribution to the war effort, preferring higher-paying jobs in town or work in defense plants.[68]

WLA recruiters visited schools and women's groups and canvassed neighborhoods to enlist women. Once enlisted, women attended short courses at colleges across the state where they learned to tend poultry, milk cows, and conduct other chores. In 1943, however, the Oklahoma Extension Service did not organize any recruiting campaigns for the WLA because farm women had replaced their sons and husbands as much as possible to avoid the payment of high wages to "inexperienced hands." In Oklahoma women—most from the farms but a few from the towns—played a major role in completing the wheat harvest. One observer noted, "These are women of prosperous wheat farms. They are mostly educated, refined women. . . . Many arc young college girls, out of school for the summer." In Oklahoma county agents also reported that farm women helped meet the agricultural labor shortage by milking cows, hauling the milk to market, and threshing peanuts. In Kansas farm women and girls, along with a few town women, drove an estimated 50–75 percent of the tractors and trucks in some areas during the wheat harvest.[69]

To the north women detasseled corn and pitched hay in South Dakota, shocked wheat in North Dakota, and harvested potatoes in Wyoming, where the number of women driving tractors soon became "very noticeable." In Nebraska women also drove tractors to cultivate corn, and they harvested grain as well as picked corn. In Colorado women constituted 23 percent of the farm labor force, helping with every type of work except the "heavier field work." Most of these women, however, were family members, not nonfarm, that is, urban or town, women. While at least 20,000 women worked on Kansas farms during 1943, primarily during the wheat harvest, 90 percent were farm reared. Overall, women performed approximately 6 percent of the work on Kansas farms that year, up from 3.6 percent in 1942. Even so, Kansas farmers used 6 percent fewer workers in 1943 than the year before. They compensated, in part, by using more women, particularly to haul wheat directly to the elevator to save labor scooping into bins on the farm. Similarly, the Emergency Farm Labor Program placed nearly 3,200 women on South Dakota farms, but only 359 were enrolled in the WLA, and most of these female agricultural workers were farmers anyway. Not all farm women, of course, felt that they were suited for fieldwork, believing that their gender made them weaker than men. Although these women seem to have been in the minority, one such Nebraska woman advised Eleanor Roosevelt to try scooping wheat before she suggested that young girls perform that work at harvest time.[70]

Other women were more willing. In July 1943 the farm labor committee of Mitchell County, Kansas, reported, "Many women and girls . . . filled application forms for jobs, and we placed them in jobs as truck drivers and in homes to do home work while the farmer's wife helped in the field." In Mitchell County forty women drove grain trucks from the fields to the elevators for their principal "man-relieving" job. Governor Schoeppel "praised" the women who worked during the wheat harvest for the "fine way" in which they helped meet the labor shortage. By the end of the crop season more nonfarm women had worked in agriculture across the Great Plains than previously, but most of the female agricultural workers were the wives and daughters of farmers, and most operated machinery (trucks and tractors), most commonly hauling grain. For the remainder of the war farm women helped their husbands and fathers by driving tractors to pull combines and plows as well as by hauling grain to storage bins or local elevators or performing basic maintenance on equipment. Occasionally, these women had volunteered for the WLA.[71]

During the war, however, the WLA reportedly sent "hundreds" of nonfarm women into the fields of Nebraska and Colorado to detassel hybrid corn. One reporter noted, "These girls are not just temporary help, like transient harvest hands, but permanent parts of the rural American landscape." In 1945, out of a female agricultural labor force of 40,000, 10,000 nonfarm women were employed by Kansas farmers to drive wheat trucks and help their wives with domestic duties. These women helped replace the 215,000 men between the ages of eighteen and thirty-five, 60 percent of whom were farmers, who had joined the armed forces, and they reportedly helped save the wheat crop, plowed stubble, and planted corn. In South Dakota women planted potatoes and corn, put up hay, and harvested wheat, and in Oklahoma, North Dakota, and Wyoming they drove tractors to help cultivate and harvest the sugar beet, potato, and wheat crops. Consequently, the work of women on the farms proved crucial across the Great Plains.[72]

Still, Great Plains farmers generally considered women "reserve labor" for fieldwork and sought their aid only when absolutely necessary. Great Plains ranchers, particularly in Montana, generally considered women, especially urban women, unsuitable for many jobs. Moreover, few farm women wanted city women working in their homes. They preferred to exchange work with their neighbors, for example, preparing meals at harvest time, and to neglect nonessential tasks. In addition, although black women had always been acceptable for picking cotton, many Great Plains farmers had mechanized their operations with tractors and other heavy equipment that took skill and experience to operate safely and efficiently. These farmers were skeptical about hiring women, particularly nonfarm women. They preferred to entrust their machinery to their wives and daughters or other farm women because they had at least some knowledge about the operation of various implements. In general Great Plains farmers were "suspicious" of "city-bred" women and doubted whether they were "worth their board and keep." Consequently, while many women registered at employment service offices for agricultural work, farmers hesitated to hire "girl aids," other than family members, relatives, or friends. Farmers usually doubted that town women could hold up to exhausting farmwork, particularly because the women who worked in the fields were also expected to cook meals for the harvest crews. Consequently, the women working on Great Plains farms generally were, first, the farmers' wives; second, their live-at-home daughters; third, the daughters who had moved away but could get two weeks' vacation to help; fourth, relatives; fifth, friends; and, last, town women.[73]

In addition Kansas farm men believed that town men were more efficient and physically able to operate agricultural machinery than town women, and they preferred them for agricultural work. In the absence of town men Great Plains farmers preferred farm women for the operation of machinery because they allegedly were more "adaptable, capable, and all-around more efficient for driving heavy machinery." One Kansas farmer called his sister "ace-high on the tractor." In South Dakota, through local implement dealers the state Extension Service operated "tractor schools" for women where they received instruction about driving, maintenance, engine components, and safety. International Harvester dealers provided similar training and called their students "Tractorettes." Farm women did not mind operating machinery, but they wanted schools where someone, other than a family member, would teach them operational and maintenance skills, such as turning a tractor-drawn combine in the field or changing spark plugs on a truck. Short farm management courses for women at the University of Nebraska also proved popular, and chambers of commerce sometimes sponsored a "tractor school" with enrollment open to farm and nonfarm women.[74]

No one can say precisely how many women worked on Great Plains farms as part of the WLA, in part because the records are imprecise and inconsistent. Thousands of women, however, labored on farms across the Great Plains, but they were so widely scattered and worked so "unobtrusively" that few people were aware of their contribution to the war effort. In 1945 the WLA became known as the Women's Division of Farm Labor Program to give it a friendlier, if not participatory, image and because agricultural leaders did not believe that women would be needed in the fields once the war ended. Even so, the women employed on farms by the WLA or placed there by the U.S. Employment Service, acting on behalf of the Emergency Farm Labor Program, usually gained the respect of their male employers, and most farmers welcomed their return the next year, particularly for chopping cotton, cultivating crops with tractors, and hauling grain. By the end of World War II women in the WLA had become the agricultural equivalent of Rosie the Riveter. Many women who worked on Great Plains farms, particularly nonfarm women, did so from a sense of patriotism, despite the consistent reluctance of farmers to employ them.[75]

In retrospect the WLA was one part of the federal Emergency Farm Labor Program. As an organization that recruited, enlisted, and placed nonfarm women in agricultural positions in the Great Plains and nation, it achieved only modest success. In Nebraska, for example, women constituted less than 40 percent of the agricultural labor force during the war. Still, farmers tended to accept urban women once they had demonstrated their ability to conduct agricultural work. And by the end of the war women provided more than half of all agricultural labor in South Dakota. In Kansas, for example, in 1945 approximately 20 percent of the women who worked on farms for the WLA came from nonfarm backgrounds, but they seldom operated heavy machinery; only farm women were trusted with that responsibility. However, as a movement that encouraged nonfarm women to leave their homes and jobs and farm women to abandon their kitchens, chicken yards, and gardens for work in the wheat fields, dairy stalls, and hay meadows, the WLA served as an important symbol of collective unity and patriotic sacrifice. Yet in the Great Plains women conducted a considerable amount of agricultural labor, just not as part of the WLA, which from its inception never served as a highly organized agency that systematically and efficiently placed women in agricultural work. Moreover, while farm men approved of nonfarm women helping their wives with domestic chores, farm women often did not want town women in their homes. At best, farm women treated the WLA volunteers as "hired girls" who did not know very much. Farm women considered fieldwork a matter of course and willingly accepted it as a responsibility and a necessity. In the end farm women, not the WLA's town recruits, made the greatest contribution to agricultural work in the Great Plains during World War II.[76]

In June 1945 the wheat harvest brought another problem for farmers. In Kansas, with thousands of migrant workers and custom cutters entering the state, a food shortage occurred in some areas. In Harper a restaurant refused a farmer's order for eighteen sandwiches because he did not have enough ration points to qualify for the food, and most workers entered the state without ration books. With harvest hands eating four meals per day, an adequate food supply became the most urgent need, not the number of farmhands, gasoline, or combines available. In Tribune four restaurants could not provide the three thousand meals required daily by harvest hands in Greeley County, and some of those hands returned home. Chickens from local farmers were not available to the restaurants because farmers preferred to sell grain for high prices rather than feed it to chickens, for which they received lower prices.[77]

In Ashland, Kansas, three cafés and a "hamburger joint" each closed one day per week because they did not have enough meat ration points to stay open. With many farm women at work in the fields farmers depended on local restaurants to feed their harvest hands. With the harvest approaching the owners believed that they would need to serve five hundred meals per day, but, when they requested extra ration points to acquire the needed meat, the Office of Price Administration (OPA) immediately mired them in bureaucracy by requiring advance registration of the name of the work crew leader and the number of men he would hire. Compliance with this regulation was, of course, impossible, and they complained to the governor. The OPA, however, charged that farmers were responsible for meat shortages because they were "reluctant" to market cattle and hogs until prices increased, even though Kansas pastures were allegedly "bulging with cattle." Other small towns in western Kansas experienced similar problems, and Governor Schoeppel sent the state director of the OPA to investigate. After several restaurants closed for lack of food and harvest workers went to bed hungry, most threatened to leave the area. The OPA, then, moved quickly to increase the food allotment to the cafés. Ultimately, the OPA extended emergency meat ration points to nearly two dozen restaurants in western Kansas to help meet the food needs of the harvest hands.[78]

Fortunately, this problem remained isolated in western Kansas, and it did not become an issue across the Great Plains, in part because farmworkers remained in short supply, but also because the OPA permitted an increase in the amount of beef that could be slaughtered in areas affected by a large influx of out-of-state workers. Slaughterhouses could apply for permits to increase the cattle kill, and in North Dakota the meat supply jumped 15 percent. If restaurants could prove that patronage had increased by 20 percent, the OPA would authorize a 25 percent increase in their food allocations. Farmers who fed their employees also received additional points from local ration boards to permit the purchase of more food to feed their workers, but not for longer than sixty days.[79]

Moreover, while some farmers sought greater protection from the draft, their sons believed that agricultural deferments would bring them discredit in the community because they would be perceived as "slackers." In fact many who received agricultural deferments suffered recrimination and often received advice to be patriotic and "show your colors, like the rest of the boys." Apparently, some farmers intimidated members of local Selective Service boards to ensure deferments for their sons. Early in 1943 the chairman of the Cheyenne County, Kansas, draft board wrote that he believed that farmers had been fairly treated and that he hoped that he could continue to serve on the board "without pressure from any group and without fear." The fact that he felt compelled to mention it suggests that he had felt that intimidation.[80]

In general Great Plains farmers sought federal agricultural labor programs that would easily and cheaply move workers into their neighborhoods. They wanted braceros and Mexican American workers, but they treated them as second-class citizens. For the most part they rejected the WLA if the workers sent to their farms did not have agricultural backgrounds or farm experience. If the United States had faced total mobilization, however, the reaction of Great Plains farmers to federal agricultural labor policies would of necessity have been far more accepting. Instead, Great Plains farmers, who needed workers, often found fault with the efforts of the federal government to provide them with workers, primarily because they wanted government aid on their own terms and without regulations and limitations. Personal convenience, economic self-interest, and conservatism trumped patriotism in the bountiful grain, cotton, sugar beet, and hay fields in the Great Plains.

EIGHT | Military Affairs

The German invasion of Poland brought fear and anxiety to the people of the Great Plains. The memory of World War I, with the wanton sacrifice of lives by incompetent commanders, mud-filled trenches, and betrayed promises for peace and democracy, rekindled an old xenophobia. But it also caused many Great Plains residents to think about military preparedness. By the autumn of 1939 European and Asian affairs had become so dangerous, volatile, and ominous that mere wishing would not make them go away. Many plains men and women clearly saw war coming, a war that the United States could not avoid, and they mobilized in many ways for the national defense. Yet, while a new war threatened the tranquility of their lives, it also promised economic opportunity.

While the nation drifted toward war, military preparations began on the national, state, and local levels, often in modest ways. After the Munich Crisis in late 1938, for example, Major General H. H. "Hap" Arnold, the chief of the army air corps, announced the Civilian Pilot Training Program—to be administered by the Civil Aeronautics Authority (CAA)—which would provide pilots for the army. Arnold reasoned that American forces would soon be involved in a new war and that the army would need thousands of pilots. In November 1938, as a result of army and CAA cooperation, the Spartan School of Aeronautics in Tulsa received authorization to begin training pilots, including men in the Canadian and British air forces, under this program. The Darr School of Aeronautics also contracted through the federal government to train British pilots in Ponca City.

A host of other civilian schools also opened for business once federal financial support became available. In January 1941, for example, the newly established Oklahoma Air College began training pilots at the rate of one hundred every ten weeks at an airfield near Mustang and Yukon, and in October the W&B Flying School contracted to provide pilot training for the army at Chickasaw. Many of these schools continued to offer flight training under military supervision after the United States entered the war. One pilot who trained at the W&B Flying School remembered, "The school was a fun thing for all of us since it was not very 'military,' and at the time, the Oklahoma College for Women was close by." Another remembered that the civilian instructors at Chickasaw, many of whom were ex-barnstormers with extensive experience, were more patient than the army flight instructors. After six weeks of training the civilian instructors let their students solo. On graduation the newly minted pilots could qualify for basic military flight training at Randolph Field, near San Antonio. The CAA also began classes in Amarillo, administered by the Amarillo Air Service, to train ferry pilots for Lend-Lease activities through the Civilian Pilot Training Program. In Clovis, New Mexico, a flight instructor believed that the Civilian Pilot Training Program would stimulate business in what otherwise looked like a "dull season."[1]

As early as August 1939 some university leaders, such as Henry Garland Bennett, the president of Oklahoma State University, also saw the inevitability of war and began positioning their institutions to offer patriotic support and garner economic rewards. Bennett, for example, sought support from the CAA for the training of pilots at the university. The program would operate independently of the ROTC program, but its graduates would be eligible for commissions in the army. Male students, preferably engineering majors who had completed their freshman year, were eligible to apply. When the first class of forty cadets enrolled in late September, another inauspicious but important step had been taken in a Great Plains state to address the military threat that loomed before the nation. For this effort the university received a federal stipend of $300 per flight student. In 1939 the CAA also operated a civilian flight-training program at

FIGURE 17. Long before the Japanese attacked Pearl Harbor city officials and entrepreneurs with access to airports anticipated a new war and vied for contracts to provide flight training for American and British flyers. In Miami, Oklahoma, the British Air School used these planes to train pilots. (Western History Collections, University of Oklahoma Libraries)

Texas Technological University in Lubbock, and the University of Wyoming coordinated the training of civilian pilots in Cheyenne, Laramie, Wheatland, and Sheridan under the CAA program.[2]

In June 1940 the CAA announced that it would expand the federal government's pilot-training program in Colorado, Kansas, Nebraska, South Dakota, and Wyoming to provide 2,250 pilots during the summer. This would be double the number trained during the previous twelve months. Only college students or graduates could apply for the pilot-training program, which included seventy-two hours of ground work and thirty-five hours of flying time, eighteen of those hours solo. At Kansas Wesleyan in Salina thirty students quickly passed their physical examinations and enrolled in a summer flight-training course. In Nebraska eight colleges offered summer pilot-training programs. By November eighteen civilian schools also offered ten-week introductory pilot-training courses. The college students, like the others who trained at the federally sponsored schools, received their pilot's license and could go directly to army air bases for advanced training. In January 1941 the army planned to train nearly 800 pilots at San Antonio's Randolph Field as part of its effort to prepare 7,000 pilots nationwide by June. By November 1942 the army offered these civilian pilots an officer's commission if they would enlist.[3]

At the same time that the CAA began an extensive pilot-training program to aid the military, the Civilian Air Patrol (CAP) organized a post in Amarillo that was open to all men and women over sixteen years of age. The CAP intended to provide courier service, guard local airports, tow targets for aerial gunnery practice, and patrol the area in search of the enemy. Two hundred pilots quickly joined the CAP at the organizational meeting held in the Crystal Ballroom of the Herring Hotel. Other Great Plains states organized CAP units for the same purposes. No one expected the CAP to go to war; rather, its mission was to provide liaison work, mapping, traffic control, and patrol duties in time of emergency.[4]

While civilian pilots trained for military or quasi-military service, various forms of State Guard units also prepared for war. Although under a presidential directive the National Guard doubled the drill periods to eight per month by November 1939, some Great Plains residents hoped that the intent was to keep the nation out of war through preparedness rather than to enter it. In Kansas the first organized military response to the new European war occurred after the government called the National Guard into federal service on December 23, 1940, and the forty-eight hundred Kansas guardsmen soon left for a year of artillery training at Camp Robinson, near Little Rock, Arkansas. Once the National Guard became absorbed into the U.S. Army, the Kansas legislature responded on April 15, 1941, by resurrecting the State Guard. During World War I Kansas organized a Home Guard to foil labor demonstrations and German espionage as well as permit patriotic participation in a military organization for those too old or unable to qualify for regular military service. Now that the Kansas State Guard was reorganized, military authorities viewed it with a jaundiced eye, considering it "solely a state military organization," in part because it could not be called into federal service.[5]

The departure of the Kansas National Guard for federal service also left behind many senior officers who could not pass the army's physical examination, and some would soon became members of the First Infantry Regiment of the Kansas State Guard. In Salina registration of World War I veterans for the State Guard began in May 1941, with officers of the American Legion taking charge. The registrants completed forms on which they listed the kinds of jobs they could perform during an emergency, such as police work and firefighting. On May 8 a major recruitment campaign began to enlist 1,360 guardsmen and 120 officers, aged twenty-one to fifty for the ranks and under sixty-five for the officer corps. Thirty-three towns participated in the recruitment process and began military training, including instruction in signal communication, protection against chemical agents, and methods of and formations for suppressing domestic disturbances. Each company would be located at a National Guard armory, with the unit designated by locality, such as Dodge City, Wichita, and Garden City. Men eligible for the army were not prevented from joining the State Guard, but they were not encouraged to enlist. The state adjutant general preferred veterans of World War I and the National Guard or those with ROTC experience. By June twenty-one states had organized similar Home Guard units, and the War Department proclaimed that the "status of each member is that of a lawful belligerent as a soldier in the military service of his state." Even so, the State Guard served primarily as paramilitary units dedicated to maintaining civil order.[6]

In Kansas the State Guardsmen wore khaki shirts and pants, black ties, and blue-and-yellow shoulder patches during the summer and green gabardine uniforms with green-and-yellow patches in the winter, the patches meant to distinguish between units. The guardsmen drilled without pay. On July 1, 1943, however, the state legislature authorized compensation at the rate of $0.60 per month for privates and as much as $2.50 for captains who participated in weekly drills. Regularly scheduled meetings included lectures on chemical warfare by the chemistry teacher at the local high school and exercises in scouting and patrolling. In Sabetha the town's guardsmen reportedly would use their skills to solve a tactical problem "under simulated combat conditions . . . if weather permits." More sensible and realistic use of State Guardsmen occurred when they replaced National Guardsmen during civil emergencies, such as aiding the evacuation of flood victims, checking levees, and guarding property.[7]

Similarly, in Texas on February 14, 1941, the State Guard organized to replace units of the National Guard that had been incorporated into the army. In May men between the ages of sixteen and sixty-five trained at Amarillo in "up-to-the-minute" fighting techniques, with emphasis placed on "guerilla and commando tactics in both attack and defense," and they took machine gun practice along the Canadian River. By mid-December the Panhandle battalion drilled intensively with rifles but without uniforms, although four hundred matching shirts had been ordered from the Works Progress Administration (WPA) "sewing room" in Amarillo. Future plans involved discussion about handling traffic in emergency situations. Texas legislators idealistically believed that the State Guard would provide internal security, assist in training men for the regular service, and form a military reserve. With companies in Amarillo, Borger, Pampa, Dumas, and Dalhart, the men took their responsibilities seriously and resented being called "Boy Scouts," "Tin Soldiers," and "Saber-rattlers" who liked to "play soldier" for two and a half hours each Tuesday night, usually at a local school.[8]

The war, of course, brought out the best and the worst in human nature, including silliness and absurdity, just as it did in other regions. In June 1941, for example, not satisfied with the State Guard, Governor W. Lee O'Daniel of Texas asked President Roosevelt for permission to allow the Lone Star State to form its own army, navy, and air force, independent of the United States but financed with federal money and administered by a Texas defense commission. Governor O'Daniel, also a candidate for a U.S. Senate seat, contended that a Texas military force was needed "to stop any nation or combination of nations from coming into the United States from the South." O'Daniel, a flour salesman who became governor with the aid of the slogan "Pass the Biscuits Pappy" and a hillbilly band, argued that a Texas military would be operated "just the same as if we were still the Republic of Texas." President Roosevelt denounced O'Daniel's plan as a less than helpful idea.[9]

After failing to gain federal approval for the creation of an independent military for Texas, in late 1941 Governor O'Daniel and the legislature created the Texas Defense Guard Air Corps. With the twenty-two planes of the Eleventh Squadron located at Amarillo, Lubbock, Borger, and Pampa, Defense Guard pilots had the responsibility to patrol the Panhandle and the, surrounding area. Some local residents hailed the guard as the "first military aviation unit ever organized in the Texas Panhandle." Originally, enlistment was restricted to pilots who owned their own planes, but officials soon recognized that this standard was too high and opened the ranks to licensed pilots.[10]

Certainly, State Guard units across the Great Plains enabled many men who could not qualify for regular military service to participate in a paramilitary organization during the war, and they also provided the occasional public service. The war, however, required a far greater public commitment than patriotic enthusiasm masquerading in a quasi-military uniform, and that commitment came after the virtual invasion of the Great Plains by the military, which saw the blue skies, "pool table flat" land, and isolation of the region as ideal for pilot training on a massive scale. On June 26, 1940, President Roosevelt signed the First Supplemental National Defense Appropriation Act, which provided $1 billion to the War Department for military mobilization, including $84 million for the construction of army airfields, military housing, and coastal defenses. By autumn the president's Advisory Commission to the Council of National Defense recommended the construction of military bases between the Rocky and the Appalachian mountains. By that time Great Plains chambers of commerce and congressional delegations were hard at work attempting to gain their share of any federal appropriations because military installations meant jobs and payrolls and the opportunity to leave the hard times of the Great Depression.[11]

Local chambers of commerce, congressmen, and governors, among others, saw the coming war as a great economic opportunity, and they lobbied the War Department long and hard for the establishment of military bases, training camps, airfields, and hospitals in their neighborhoods or states. During World War I the Great Plains had not shared the wealth created by industrial mobilization because the majority of the contracts for war-related production went to eastern companies. This time, however, the political and business leaders in the plains states were not about to defer wartime prosperity to other regions. In October 1940, for example, the "military board" of Kansas recommended Wichita for the site of a new National Guard air squadron. To encourage the army to locate a new squadron in Wichita, city officials offered it a long-term lease for space at the municipal airport, while the state promised to build the required hangar, at an estimated cost of $500,000, with WPA funds and labor provided under the national defense program. These efforts proved successful, and by midsummer 1941 150 men of the 127th Observation Squadron of the National Guard made Wichita their home base. Similarly, the Oklahoma City Chamber of Commerce began efforts in fall 1940 to locate an air base for bombers at the municipal airport. Senators Elmer Thomas and Josh Lee, along with Representative Mike Montgomery, worked to gain congressional approval. By mid-March the army assured Oklahomans that it would locate an air depot near Oklahoma City. With construction costs exceeding $21 million and nearly fifteen thousand workers employed, Tinker Field (as the depot was known after 1942) became a bomber repair and modification site that contributed significantly to the military-sponsored economic boom in Oklahoma.[12]

In October 1940 thirty-two hundred cadets moved into new barracks at Lowry Field near Denver, and the army planned to spend $13 million to establish a major "cadet training center" for pilots, bombardiers, and photographers. The army also anticipated a major construction program to expand both Lowry Field (with a new "cantonment") and Fort Logan, at an estimated cost of $612,000. Although this economic stimulus to the Denver area was a mere pittance of the estimated $47.5 million that the War Department planned to spend for its "urgent" housing needs alone as it prepared for war, this project and others in the Great Plains brought large payrolls for civilian workers into the region. From the beginning, then, the new European war had important economic benefits for the Great Plains. Some of the expenditures came through the WPA, which required the hiring of unemployed workers.[13]

Similarly, in Texas Midland's Mayor M. C. Ulmer traveled to Washington DC in spring 1940, reportedly visiting "government departments" in an effort to link the local airport with the national defense program. Town leaders also organized a "National Defense Committee" for "the promotion of all things necessary for the national defense," and the committee declared war on the "totalitarian powers, or all enemies of France and England." The committee also urged residents to send letters to their congressmen and senators urging them to stop Hitler by supporting a strong national defense. This activity caught the attention of the War Department, and in July army officials arrived to examine the municipal airport, the Chamber of Commerce treating them to a dinner at the Scharbauer Hotel afterward. The officers liked Midland's "strategic location," but the War Department did not announce its selection of Midland for an airfield for pilot and bombardier training until early June 1941. The army's offer to lease the airport for $1 per year did not trouble city officials because the military planned to spend more than $5 million to establish the air base that would provide a monthly military payroll of more than $1 million.[14]

The influx of federal dollars into the Great Plains for military construction occurred quickly because the army required the completion of some projects within ninety days. On January 3, 1941, the federal government authorized the Douglas Aircraft Company to occupy a government-built plant in Tulsa. In April the army also selected fourteen hundred acres near Lubbock as the location for the Advanced Twin-Engine Training School, with an initial allocation of $4.6 million for construction, and the work began in August. Ultimately, sixteen hundred workers completed the project within 120 days. After several name changes the site became the Lubbock Army Air Field in April 1943. In June 1942 Lubbock also became home to the South Plains Army Flying School, which trained glider pilots, and the War Department spent $3 million for the construction of a glider field north of the city. With the construction of these airfields local residents realized that they had "smashed squarely into the middle of the National Defense picture."[15]

Similarly, in early August 1941, the residents of Roswell, New Mexico, were ecstatic when they learned that the army would build a permanent air base nearby. One resident told a local reporter, "We'll date everything in the future on the basis 'Before the Air Base' and 'After the Air Base.'" Another called the decision the "biggest thing that ever happened to Roswell," although another resident qualified that exuberance by contending that the air base was the greatest thing that had happened to Roswell "since the first artesian well came in." Everyone agreed, however, that the establishment of the base meant "good times ahead." Residents realized that Roswell would never be the same, but few cared. With the monthly payroll projected to be as high as $400,000 for three thousand army personnel, they anticipated making money. Moreover, estimates for construction costs soon escalated from $6.5 to $14.5 million. H. A. Poorbaugh, the chairman of the Chamber of Commerce Housing Committee, wanted the construction money for housing to go to local builders, saying, "Houses must be built now, and we want them built by home people and not by outsiders."[16]

To the north, in Kansas, the army developed sixteen air bases, and the economic rewards for area residents proved significant. The congressional delegation, the Kansas Industrial Development Commission, and local officials began work as early as June 1941 to gain airfields for army training purposes. At that time the Chamber of Commerce in Garden City also sought the location of a base for training British pilots. Although the Royal Air Force did not appear in western Kansas, the Garden City Chamber of Commerce felt well satisfied with the army's completion of a $9.2 million air base on May 25, 1943. Only occasionally did Kansans refuse to cooperate by objecting to the sale of their land for air bases, an action that forced the federal government to obtain title through condemnation proceedings in court.[17]

The War Department, however, did not locate all the airfields in Kansas with care. In Ellis County the army acquired 1,840 acres through a condemnation order for land near Walker on which it intended to locate a base with ten-thousand-foot runways, and it planned to lease acreage for gunnery and bombing ranges in nearby counties. It did not, however, pay attention to a report of the state geologist that judged the site unsuitable for water supply. Of course, the wells soon proved insufficient, and water had to be obtained from Hays through a twelve-mile pipeline. Morale flagged at the Walker Army Air Field from the time the first military personnel arrived on November 11, 1942. Hays and Russell were the closest large towns, but each had only a few thousand residents. Adequate housing proved an even more difficult problem than providing recreation for the soldiers and civilian employees. By the time the number of army personnel peaked at the base in August 1944, at 5,936 officers, enlisted personnel, and civilians, a bad relationship had developed between the airfield and the surrounding communities, particularly Hays, with vituperative exchanges over matters of inadequate housing and recreational opportunities. Part of the problem can also be attributed to a disagreement over the naming of the base. Hays residents wanted the base named the Hays-Walker Army Air Field, but Walker citizens protested, and the army sided with them. Hays residents, however, took considerable satisfaction in knowing that many of the men hired to complete the $2 million project spent their paychecks in Hays, the county seat.[18]

The U.S. Navy also came to the Great Plains to train pilots. When the war began, a Naval Reserve base already operated at Fairfax Field, the municipal airport at Kansas City, Kansas, and the navy quickly began a year-round pilot-training program there during winter 1939. With the declaration of war, however, the navy needed a larger training facility because an increase in transport traffic and the location of the North American Company's B-25 bomber plant at the site crowded things and made training hazardous. Consequently, in January 1942 the navy purchased land near Olathe and soon began constructing a new airfield, including three five-thousand-foot runways and five outlying fields. On completion the Olathe U.S. Naval Air Station provided primary flight training for cadets and quarters for traveling officials. The mission of the Olathe Air Station changed, however, on September 10, 1943, when it became responsible for training transport pilots and providing support facilities for the Naval Air Transport Squadron, which operated medical flights to equalize the patient load at the various navy hospitals across the country.[19]

In summer 1942 the navy also approved the establishment of a base at Hutchinson, Kansas, as part of its plan to train thirty thousand pilots annually. Good drainage, access to railroad and highway transportation, fuel, natural gas, and electric power, open country, the availability of land for outlying fields, a favorable climate for flying during most of the year, and a nearby liberty port persuaded the navy to select the twenty-five-hundred-acre location. The Hutchinson Chamber of Commerce helped lure the navy to the area with a promise of adequate housing (which proved false) and the use of the state fairgrounds, which had bunking and food facilities for one thousand men, as well as the lease of the municipal airport for $1 per year for training purposes until the main station and runways could be completed. The efforts of the Chamber of Commerce proved the decisive factor in the navy's decision to locate a base near Hutchinson.[20]

Although Amish farmers owned most of the land needed for the navy base, these conscientious objectors reportedly proved "highly cooperative" and willingly sold their land to the government. The War Department saved demolition time by allowing the farmers to remove or salvage their buildings. The navy also leased nearly four thousand acres from fifty-five farmers for the duration of the war plus six months to provide outlying practice fields. With the land purchase price of $378,000 and the annual rent of outlying fields at $25,600, plus an expenditure of $12,306 to local farmers for crop liquidation and damages, the economic boost to the local economy proved immediate, and it would become more important when the sailors arrived for staffing and training.[21]

Although the facility was officially commissioned as the U.S. Naval Reserve Aviation Base on October 23, the navy changed its name to the Hutchinson U.S. Naval Air Station on January 1, 1943. By that time the aircraft industry in Wichita had proved an important source of skilled labor, and the navy recruited many employees capable of servicing aircraft for duty at Hutchinson. At the same time, however, the quality of the men began to decline as recruits arrived from outside the immediate region after the navy stopped enlisting men for service at a specific base in mid-November 1942. Personnel problems almost immediately occurred when 275 sailors arrived from Dallas, Texas, on February 15, 1943. Navy policy dictated that, when a new station needed a complement of men, established bases would help meet that need. Such a practice proved beneficial to the older stations because commanding officers rounded up the undesirables—a routine known as "cleaning out the brig"—and sent them to their new home. As a result many of the discipline problems at Hutchinson came from malcontents and troublemakers from other bases. Soon, they kept the line long at the captain's mast.[22]

Kearney, Nebraska, also provides a good example of a community's efforts to gain an army base and to deal with the advantages and problems that the base's presence created for the town. In 1940 Kearney, Grand Island, and Hastings formed the Central Nebraska Defense Council to convince the federal government to locate defense establishments in central Nebraska. The Kearney Chamber of Commerce also appointed six subcommittees to write a report lauding the town's benefits for distribution to every federal agency that considered sites for defense projects. By early 1941 Kearney and North Platte were lobbying the War Department to bestow the title *national defense airport* on their civilian facilities. This designation would enable the airport to serve as a storage depot for newly constructed planes that rolled off the assembly line at the Fort Crook bomber plant near Omaha and Bellevue. Kearney, however, did not have a civilian airport meriting consideration by the military for this designation, so city leaders held an election in April to authorize the sale of bonds worth $60,000 to finance a new airport. Kearney's voters approved the bond issue, and the WPA pledged to fund the additional $300,000 necessary to build an airport suitable for modest military purposes.[23]

Although pleased with the bond issue, residents became even more excited about the possibilities of the military buildup when the War Department announced in September 1941 that the army planned to locate an aviation school in western Nebraska. The locations under consideration were Kearney, McCook, Grand Island, and North Platte. With one thousand cadets expected in each class, the monthly payroll generated by the aviation school would exceed $1 million. As a result the work to improve Kearney's airport quickened because most people believed that North Platte had the advantage of its better airport in the attempt to lure the military. On December 12, 1941, four days after Congress declared war against Japan, the WPA began working around the clock to finish the Kearney airport. Construction progressed much more slowly than city officials desired, but the two asphalt runways, each more than four thousand feet long, and the hangar were completed by summer, and the town dedicated the airport on August 23, 1942.[24]

Town officials and residents were startled to learn less than a month later that the army wanted Kearney but not its airport. On September 1, 1942, the army announced that it had selected Kearney as the site of a primary training facility and that McCook and several other towns would provide satellite airfields. Although the benefits of this new designation would be great, Kearney's residents were stunned to learn that the army wanted the new airport torn up and a larger one built in its place. In this case, however, bigger was better, the larger base requiring two thousand workers for construction. Real estate agents, grocers, restaurant owners, dry cleaners, and other businesspeople anticipated a significant boost in their standard of living.[25]

Nebraskans, of course, were as patriotic as anyone on the Great Plains, and they supported the war effort. Kearney's mayor, for example, noted that several farm families had lost their homes to the new construction, but they were "taking it like good Americans." Soon, a thousand men labored to remove the new asphalt runways so that thicker, concrete runways could be laid to support heavy bombers and to build hangars and other buildings. After completion of the Kearney Army Air Field on February 1, 1943, B-17 pilots began making practice bombing runs on ranges south of Broken Bow and at smaller ranges near Ansley, Berwyn, Callaway, and Arnold. Still, the mayor warned that outlandish increases in rents damaged Kearney's reputation with the army, and he admonished, "We will have to do our part or Kearney will fumble her one chance to help with the war effort." Essentially, Nebraskans, like other plains men and women, wanted to make money while they had the opportunity.[26]

Similarly, in Casper, Wyoming, Chamber of Commerce members, city officials, and the Natrona County commissioners led the effort to gain federal approval for an army base, and Senators H. H. Schwartz and Joseph C. O'Mahoney argued their case in Washington, including the city's promise to appropriate $20,000 to lay a waterline to the base site, wherever it might be. In spring 1942 the army selected a site eight miles west of Casper for a new airfield. The Casper construction firm of Rognstad and Olsen received the contract for the buildings and subcontracted much of the work for the $10 million project to other Wyoming firms. Almost immediately, the economy of Casper left the lethargy of the Great Depression behind as four thousand workers arrived to erect buildings, install water-and sewer lines, and lay streets and runways. Electricians, welders, and mechanics also plied their crafts. They, too, drew their paychecks and spent money. During 1942 the civilian employees who worked at the airfield earned more than $2.5 million in wages. By October deposits in Casper's two banks set a record of $14 million; a year later those deposits reached $17 million. Activated on September 1, 1942, the Casper Army Air Base provided training for crews of high-altitude, heavy bombers, that is, B-17 (Flying Fortress) and B-24 aircraft. When the first troops arrived, a group of local women served them a hot meal in a mess hall because the army's cooks were scheduled to arrive only on a later train. During the first two weeks troops were there, town and army officials coordinated a welcoming dance at the base, with fifty women from Casper serving as hostesses and dance partners. Casper provided space in town for clubs for officers and noncoms and a servicemen's center, all of which soon became popular with the troops. Fort Warren, near Cheyenne, also began rapid expansion in 1940, when the army committed $5.1 million for construction to accommodate as many as ten thousand men, up from thirty-five hundred, at this quartermaster replacement training center.[27]

Although contractors, workers, and businessmen welcomed the federal contracts, labor problems frequently developed immediately. In December 1940 union workers protested the use of WPA labor on the $391,860 runway project for the army at the municipal airport in Oklahoma City. The law, however, prohibited the WPA from negotiating for the employment of union labor, and, although the building trades objected to contractors hiring nonunion workers, the construction went ahead. In South Dakota carpenters, who were members of the American Federation of Labor (AFL), refused to accept work from contractors ten days after construction began on an air base at Rapid City because the Associated Industries, a group representing local businessmen, advocated an "open shop" policy for all employers. While the labor union threatened to seek jobs out of the area, the executive committee of the Associated Industries claimed that work at the air base preceded on schedule with nonunion workers hired from other areas.[28]

In May 1942, at Salina, Kansas, the AFL required all workers employed by contractors at the Smoky Hill Army Air Base to have a union card, and the organization strictly enforced the closed shop. Common laborers paid $15.00 and heavy machinery operators $60.00 in initiation fees, plus $2.25 per month for union dues. In Cheyenne labor union leaders also announced that contractors on the Fort Warren expansion project would honor a "closed shop." As a result, all workers had to join the appropriate union before they could begin their jobs at the fort. Not only did this requirement give the unions control of the labor force supported by military contacts, but it also brought money into their treasuries. The local Teamsters Union, for example, required its workers to be in good standing in the organization, that is, dues paid up, and mandated that teamsters who worked in the jurisdiction of Cheyenne's local transfer their membership to the local and pay its initiation fee. Nonmember workers would have their paychecks garnished $0.50 per day until their membership fee had been paid to the Teamsters. With initiation fees ranging as high as $100, a considerable amount of money, which translated into power, was at stake. The Teamsters gave hiring priority for jobs at Fort Warren to applicants from Laramie County, then workers from other counties in Wyoming, and last out-of-state workers. Out-of-state contractors also could bring only administrative and a few technical staff with them to ensure employment for as many Wyoming men and women as possible.[29]

With the Fort Warren expansion project estimated to require three thousand workers, the army created "one of the greatest labor shortages ever faced in Cheyenne" when the construction quartermaster sent out a call to the Wyoming Employment Service for carpenters, plumbers, electricians, and heavy equipment operators. The expansion called for 266 buildings that would serve as a "junior Ft. Warren" and function as a "self-sustaining city under military rule." In addition the army planned to spend $100,000 to convert stables into garages for the repair of the equipment of the two new National Guard artillery regiments scheduled to arrive early in 1941. By February 1941 4,546 workers, including 1,400 carpenters, labored feverishly to expand the post, but neither Cheyenne nor Wyoming could provide the required number of carpenters, and 900 had to be recruited outside the state.[30]

Cheyenne officials worried, however, that area realtors were charging excessive rents for houses and apartments. They reasoned that, if rents were not reasonable, the federal government would develop its own housing project, with a resulting "drastic effect upon rental rates for already existing property." Or the military might take the project elsewhere because the War Department had warned that it would not tolerate profiteering in Cheyenne and the established scale had to be observed when renting property to commissioned and noncommissioned officers. The army's warning quickly influenced the Chamber of Commerce and local realtors to locate reasonably affordable housing for the officers to "protect Cheyenne's interests."[31]

Price gouging, however, occurred in all military boomtowns, and it became a perennial problem. In Salina, Kansas, the competition between civilian workers employed and soldiers stationed at the Smoky Hill Army Air Field enabled some landlords to profit from sudden prosperity. There, a bunk in a basement commonly brought $5 per week, while a "sleeping room" earned the owner $8 per week. Furnished five-room houses rented for $75 to $100 a month, but in July 1942 no such properties remained on the market. Rents skyrocketed so quickly that the army invoked a general order in September freezing them in all defense areas. As late as November 1944 the commander at Bismarck's municipal airport complained that rents paid by some of his men took half their monthly pay of $80. The Office of Price Administration (OPA) responded by promising to consider a rent-control edict.[32]

Kearney and other towns, however, at first essentially ignored the OPA, and rents continued to escalate as thousands of workers and their families arrived seeking employment on base construction projects. By October 1942 the town's population had increased by 25 percent. The shortage of housing and high rents brought mounting complaints from construction workers, which brought intervention by the federal government. In March 1943 an official from the Rent Division of the OPA arrived and determined that federal rent controls needed to be imposed. As a result, on May 1 landlords received notice that within sixty days they were to roll back rents to the rates charged on March 1, 1942, within sixty days or suffer fines and other penalties. The OPA also established a rent-control office in the city hall to monitor the situation. Landlords in Grand Island, Fremont, Wahoo, Sidney, Alliance, Omaha, Lincoln, and Hastings also had federal ceilings placed on their rental rates.[33]

In Cheyenne residents also welcomed the opportunity to capitalize on the expansion of Fort Warren, just as other plains towns welcomed the establishment or expansion of bases in their locales. The army wanted to expand Fort Warren with an expenditure of $9 million, in part using the WPA for construction to accommodate sixteen thousand men, including the 188th Field Artillery unit of the South Dakota National Guard, and to train quartermasters. Here, as elsewhere, the workers and soldiers invigorated the economy by renting apartments, purchasing used cars, buying groceries, using laundry and dry-cleaning services, and patronizing restaurants and movie theaters. Indeed, the monthly military payroll of $1.3 million in mid-1942 exceeded the industrial payroll for Wyoming. In April 1942 the *Wyoming Eagle* estimated that one-third of the people on

Cheyenne's streets during the evenings were soldiers and that soldiers constituted two-thirds of the shoppers on Saturday nights. So
many soldiers occupied the streets on Christmas night in 1943 that
Cheyenne authorities asked the post commander to call them back
to the base to prevent trouble from developing among the holiday
revelers.[34]

Cheyenne merchants depended on the soldiers for their prosperity, and the military men and women stationed at Fort Warren believed that the businesses gouged them. In July 1942 one soldier
complained, "Cheyenne seems to have strayed from the cow trail
to the gold trail." Greed, he contended, governed relations between
the business community and the soldiers. "From this camp, upon
which you have come to depend so much," he wrote, "come more
and more complaints because some of our merchants belong to the
tribe which believes that a soldier and his salary are soon parted and
why not speed the parting? Being an army town today is not only
an honor and an asset but a national responsibility." This problem
continued into January 1945, when the post commander appointed
his adjutant to work with officials from the OPA to help enforce
government price-control policy and asked the soldiers to report any
instances of overcharging.[35]

Social problems as well as economic opportunities also arrived with
the military in the communities located near the army and navy
bases. In February 1943, for example, when the first contingent of
black soldiers arrived in Casper to provide maintenance services,
city officials felt compelled to establish a colored men's service center because the town, like the base, was segregated. Only one restaurant served the black soldiers, and their recreational opportunities were limited. The army periodically attempted to deal with low
morale among the black soldiers at Casper by providing two-day
passes and transportation to Denver. Similarly, at the Smoky Hill
Army Air Field near Salina, Kansas, officials practiced racial segregation while addressing the social needs of black soldiers. In August
1943 the Booker T. Washington Center made arrangements for the
entertainment of African American soldiers in "Negro homes," and

FIGURE 18. African American men stationed at military bases in the Great Plains often socialized with black women who volunteered to attend segregated dances. These African American women boarded a bus that stopped in nearby towns to transport them to a social event at the Colored Recreation Center in Junction City, Kansas. (Kansas State Historical Society)

it planned a dance at the city's Memorial Hall to which young black women from Salina and other towns, such as Wichita, McPherson, Great Bend, Lyons, Hoisington, and Abilene, were invited. The public was invited to "spectate" at the dance.[36]

Similarly, when black troops arrived at Midland, Texas, in January 1942, given the military and social traditions of the time, they were segregated into service and quartermaster units. The black soldiers also had their own mess, housing, and service club on the base and a segregated USO club in Odessa. Racial clashes did not occur on the base, however, until a "colored" squadron of fifty WACs arrived in early 1945 to replace white men at the base hospital. Trouble came almost immediately because the black WACs resented being restricted to serving as orderlies and cleaning women. Army regulations held that women could not be assigned to menial labor, which the black

WACs considered included orderly and janitorial duties. After a white civilian nurse referred to a black WAC as a "nigger," eighteen African American WACs refused to work until threatened with army discipline.[37]

The racial problems at the Midland Army Air Field developed because the black WACs were "northern negro women or women who ha[d] lived in the North the greater apart of their lives" and they had not endured the kind of discrimination that they experienced in the army and in West Texas. The army reported, "It is unfortunate but true that discrimination exists in Texas against all negroes, whether in uniform or not." When the white civilians and soldiers who worked at the base hospital provoked trouble for the black WACs, who reportedly had a "different" orientation, they caused many "vexing problems" for the airfield administrators. As soon as the black WACs received assignments other than orderly and janitorial work at the hospital, however, they readily adjusted to their new home and performed their duties, and racial confrontations subsided, with the exception of "off post incidents."[38]

When on February 2, 1943, Kearney officials learned that black troops would soon be stationed at the airfield, they too believed that the African American soldiers required segregation to ensure the social order. Quickly, they selected a building to provide separate but equal services, as the army demanded, but this action caused a public uproar. The problem was not that black servicemen would come into Kearney for recreation and spend money during their leisure time. Rather, it was the location of the club. Kearney officials had selected a building across the street from the Methodist church, whose members, at least in theory, prided themselves on abstinence from alcoholic beverages. Although white soldiers were not served beer at the town's USO service center, they could purchase it at a nearby tavern. Black soldiers did not have that option because Kearney was a segregated town and they could not enter white establishments. Consequently, the army insisted that the city permit the sale of beer to black soldiers at their club. Quickly, the clergy in Kearney joined the Methodists and the Allied Dry Forces in protest, and the War Recreation Board refused to permit the sale of beer at the black

FIGURE 19. Many Great Plains residents confronted their racial prejudices when the military arrived in force. Segregation required the separation of whites and blacks in all areas, both civilian and military, such as at this USO Club in Lincoln, Nebraska. (Nebraska State Historical Society, MacDonald Collection, RG 2183-1945 0922 [2])

servicemen's club. The army did not wait long to deal with the situation. In April it threatened to declare the city off-limits to all officers and enlisted men, both single and married, if black soldiers were not served beer at their club. This gave city officials reason to pause and rethink their public policy. Without much deliberation they decided that the economic benefits of the air base to the city far outweighed the moral concerns of the clergy, and they quickly located a new building where the black servicemen enjoyed free beer until a liquor license could be obtained for the club.[39]

With that problem solved, another emerged. Because no black people lived in Kearney, an African American Hostess Club could not be easily organized to provide female companionship and dance partners for the soldiers. Although the wives of the black soldiers and women from the USO in Lincoln and Omaha occasionally provided companionship, many dances became stag parties because women failed to arrive. To help resolve this problem, the commanding officer authorized frequent convoys to Omaha for those black soldiers who had a few days of leave.[40]

The July 1944 racial "disturbance" at the naval ammunition depot in Hastings, Nebraska, provides another example of the discrimination that African Americans often confronted in the Great Plains during World War II. Although a board of investigation attributed it to "improper administration," that is, a lack of leadership on the part of the navy officers who supervised the black servicemen involved, as well as to "some of the low-class and ignorant type of negro personnel" assigned to the depot, discrimination against black servicemen and their families proved the root cause of the trouble. The Hastings depot produced approximately one-third of the ammunition used by the navy, and it employed 7,584 civilians and 2,089 military personnel. Of this force 1,458 black enlisted men worked in labor or "ordnance battalions." They washed casings for ammunition and loaded shells as well as loading and unloading freight cars and trucks with powder and ammunition and conducting cleanup work, all under the supervision of black leaders in segregated work parties. About 500 blacks civilians also lived in the vicinity, and 383 of them worked at the depot. The wives of the black enlisted men constituted about half the civilian African American workforce.[41]

Like most Great Plains cities and towns, Hastings had a predominantly white population. When approximately one thousand African Americans arrived, town residents were uncertain about how they should treat them. It was not that they were not prejudiced; they were, but previously the small African American population of about seventy in twelve families did not require special considerations. Rather, the problem was that the white population of Hastings was unprepared to practice segregation on a grand scale. The town did not have separate recreational facilities and other establishments dedicated to serving blacks alone. As a result, when black servicemen arrived, racial tensions were quickly sparked, flaring into several altercations between blacks and whites at the depot.

Many of the families of black sailors stationed at the depot, for example, lived in converted Civilian Conservation Corps (CCC) barracks, known as Prairie Village. These quarters were located within the fenced-in depot grounds. Each Saturday a military or civilian inspector visited the black apartments and awarded a pennant to the keeper of the "cleanest and neatest" one, but white apartment dwellers living elsewhere under the jurisdiction of the Federal Public Housing Authority evidently did not undergo those inspections. In addition Hastings real estate agents generally agreed to refrain from selling or renting to blacks property north of the railroad tracks that divided the city. African American civilians resented this redlining as a form of discrimination, and most black newcomers continued to live in the federal housing areas or trailer parks. Housing for African American families always remained inadequate and a "sore point" among the black civilian population.[42]

In general, Hastings residents practiced discrimination, but not uniformly. Owners of grocery and merchandise stores welcomed black servicemen and civilians. Theaters admitted blacks and did not require segregated seating, and the schools were integrated. Little discrimination occurred on the buses operating between the depot and the housing areas because almost all the riders were black. Disturbances usually resulted from white southerners who objected to riding with African Americans, but no "set policy" of black/white segregation ever applied to the bus service. Restaurants, taverns, bowling alleys, and the Winter Garden Dance Pavilion, however, "effectively discouraged the negro trade by one means or another." If black sailors received service in beer parlors, bartenders often required them to drink from a bottle rather than a glass. Black servicemen resented these discriminatory practices and the lack of recreational facilities in town. At the depot black sailors were served from segregated lines in the mess hall, and blacks and whites ate at segregated tables, which caused further resentment among the African American servicemen. They were also denied admittance to some recreational facilities at the depot unless they received a pass stating that they had a legitimate business, not a recreational, reason for being on the premises. Whites, of course, had unrestricted access. Inadequate recreational facilities for black sailors in Hastings meant that they earned liberty about once every nine days, compared to three nights in four given white enlisted men.[43]

These problems eventually triggered fighting among blacks and whites at the barracks area on June 10, 11, and 14. One sailor was arrested but, during transport to the brig for "disobeying his orders and assuming an insolent attitude," approximately twenty men forcibly freed him from the control of the master-at-arms. The black sailors then retired to their barracks without further incident, except for "insolent and disrespectful remarks generally directed at some of the Naval Barracks officers." The next day, however, a group of black sailors refused to board the navy buses for work. And, at an afternoon meeting in the gymnasium at which the commanding officer intended to quiet the discontent and restore order, black enlisted men heckled him. The next day the commander received an interdepot letter signed "The Boys" that demanded "better respect" for the black enlisted men.[44]

The tension at the depot intensified when, during the evening of June 14, the Shore Patrol detained a black sailor for intoxication and placed him in the brig. When a group of sixty black sailors appeared at the Shore Patrol office, an altercation occurred, and five more men were detained but then released. As animosity increased black sailors began talking about taking matters into their own hands, as in "we're going to clean the place out." By June 17 rumors had spread through Hastings that the black sailors were going to take over the depot on June 19 to coincide with their celebration of congressional action in 1862 to end slavery in the territories of the United States. In the meantime navy and city officials began an investigation. They quickly discovered that the black sailors experienced discrimination, wanted "respectable night spots" in downtown Hastings where they could take their wives and a hotel to accommodate visiting parents, wives, and girlfriends in town, a "negro petty officers' club" at the depot so that the black officers would not have to "associate with negro enlisted men," more liberty and "equal rights with whites in regard to frequency and length of time on liberty," the elimination of restrictions on patronage at such public places in Hastings as restaurants, cafés, beer parlors, bowling alleys, and dance halls, a black chaplain with officer rank (although they would accept a white one), and the elimination of favoritism in promotions and punishments at mast. On reviewing the complaints the commanding officer promised to obtain a white chaplain, establish an petty officers' club, "clean out" the Cabin in the Sky, a "negro tavern" in downtown Hastings, and make other improvements.[45]

Immediately after the "disturbance" the navy authorized a board of investigation to determine what happened and offer solutions to prevent a recurrence. On June 20 the investigating board attributed the disturbances to low morale encouraged by a "weakened system of discipline," a situation that had been brewing for some time. The black enlisted men believed that the commanding and ranking officers were inconsiderate and disrespectful and denied them their "equal rights." The lack of recreational facilities, the fact of discrimination by owners of hotels and cafés in Hastings that "catered to the white trade," and "favoritism to certain negro enlisted men" generally characterized the complaints and findings of the investigating board. At the same time the board determined that, while the white residents of Hastings had been unprepared to provide segregated housing and recreational facilities, they had "largely adjusted themselves to the situation as a wartime measure." They reached this epiphany after realizing the financial benefit of the depot to the community. Even so, townspeople were concerned about the association of whites and blacks, "the prevailing immorality, the occasional knifing, the disorderly conduct at the negro restaurants and beer parlors," and conflict between "white and colored" at the housing areas because it might lead to injury of whites and rioting. The navy also held that segregated barracks were needed for "reasons of military necessity."[46]

Although the navy's investigation board did not find any known houses of prostitution, it determined that "a normal amount of immorality among negros" existed and that "amateur negro prostitutes" competed with more experienced "free-lance negro prostitutes" in several places in the black section of town, noticeably along First and South Hastings streets, despite the efforts of local law enforcement officers to prevent black and white women from selling sex. The investigating board also determined that the commanding officer had lost the respect of the black enlisted men and that he was unable to enforce discipline. And it recommended the relief of two officers and several courts-martial for fighting and disobeying the lawful order of a superior officer, among other rulings. The commanding officer and a black chaplain were also relieved of their duties. When a new commanding officer assumed responsibility for the depot on July 20, 1944, he tightened disciple, enforced regular drills, and applied uniform punishments for black and white sailors at the captain's mast as well as providing transportation for black families wishing to attend the Hamilton Methodist Church on Sundays. He also shipped out the 125 "outstanding trouble-makers and habitual mast offenders" and those who had participated in the June disturbances or who were "suspected as possible agitators" as well as strengthening the Shore Patrol to help ensure order at the depot and in Hastings. On August 5 he also authorized the transport on navy buses of 175 "negro girls" from Omaha to provide partners at a USO dance to boost morale.[47]

In retrospect, not since the late nineteenth century had so many black soldiers (and now sailors and WACs) been stationed in the Great Plains, and racial difficulties quickly developed. The problem in the Great Plains, however, was not that racism emerged but, rather, that the residents were unprepared logistically to act on their beliefs. But they soon adjusted to wartime annoyances and learned to segregate on a large scale and discriminate both overtly and covertly.[48]

Social, and particularly sexual, relationships also changed in the communities near the military bases. Midland, Texas, for example, became known as a "good duty base," one where willing women from the town and nearby Odessa allegedly waited behind every tree, but the punch line went, "There aren't any trees." Wartime pressures on both men and women to live for the day helped loosen sexual boundaries and caused social problems. Affairs between local women who worked on the bases and married soldiers sometimes ended with an unwanted pregnancy and personal and family disgrace. The greatest problem that resulted from the arrival of the army and the navy in the Great Plains became the prevalence of venereal disease, which primarily threatened the civilian population. The spread of venereal disease also challenged the conservative moral practices of most residents of the region, and they wanted someone to do something about it.[49]

As early as July 1940 the U.S. Public Health Service worried that venereal disease would lower the efficiency of the military, as it did during World War I, and Dr. M. C. Keith, the state health officer for Wyoming, urged the "repression of prostitutes" to combat the disease. By early 1941 "scores" of draft registrants in Oklahoma City tested positive for syphilis, for a higher than average rate among the states. Oklahoma residents tested positive at the rate of sixty-one per one thousand, while North Dakota and Nebraska ranked among the lowest, with a rate of seven per one thousand. In Kansas the state Selective Service director provided draft boards with the locations of venereal disease clinics for referral to registrants who had the disease. The Kansas Bureau of Investigation also provided an agent to assist officers at Fort Riley in combating vice and the spread of venereal disease by the prostitutes who preyed on the soldiers who left the post for recreation in nearby Junction City.[50]

In Oklahoma City officials attributed the rise of venereal disease to the "final fling" of young men bound for the armed forces, during which they were "tempted to excesses they formerly did not indulge in, perhaps new attractions in the opposite sex." The danger of war brought a sense of finality to young men and women, and the moment often seemed more important than the future. In Wyoming Ethel M. Ferguson remembered "girls gave themselves to their guys on the last night before shipping out." In North Dakota Governor John Moses proclaimed the first week of February 1942 Social Hygiene Week. Dr. Percy L. Owens, the city health officer of Bismarck, urged the public to fight "vice and venereal disease to protect our workers." In Muskogee, Oklahoma, members of the Junior Chamber of Commerce offered to set a good public health example and submit to a blood test for venereal disease. Although the results were kept confidential, every member tested received an "I am an American" badge to wear. By June the state health department had established sixty-six venereal disease clinics across the state. In Amarillo the nearby army air base brought soldiers and camp followers, and the venereal disease rate escalated. To combat the problem city officials established a clinic for testing, and the police chief organized a vice squad to "round up" prostitutes. A local reporter observed, "Scores of these girls are being arrested, finger-printed, photographed and referred to the health department." In October, when Clint Branden, the Democratic nominee for the state senate for Latimer and LaFlore counties in Oklahoma, proposed mandatory testing for syphilis for everyone over three years of age in the state and the requirement that everyone carry a card proving that such testing had been conducted, most Oklahomans thought that he had gone too far. Others supported his idea to treat infected people who refused treatment for syphilis as felons.[51]

In February 1943 the Oklahoma State Social Hygiene Association urged a major public commitment to "child education" as the best long-term solution to fighting venereal disease. The officer in charge of venereal disease control at Tinker Field near Oklahoma City attributed the problem to "young girls" from the small towns and farms who arrived in town to find work but who also no longer felt constrained by public opinion since they were not at home. In town they met young men who were also way from "home ties and inhibitions." The result was a "perfect opportunity for moral let-down." A local psychologist believed that sexual instincts and desires could be "subliminated" by social activities at the YMCA and churches, although he admitted the lack of this institutional influence on "moral delinquents." In Dallas Major General Richard Donovan, the commanding officer of the Eighth Service Command, contended, "The source of venereal infection is not the Army, but among civilians. Control is chiefly a civilian problem." The Dallas Health Department responded to the growing venereal disease problem by opening a twenty-four-hour prophylactic station at Parkland Hospital, available to both men and women. In New Mexico state board of health officials began quarantining infected people to combat an "alarming" increase in venereal disease near the military bases, such as at Roswell. Although some people advocated legalized prostitution in order to ensure periodic health checks and to keep the prostitutes in brothels and off the streets, the reformers usually had the last word, calling syphilis, gonorrhea, and those who spread venereal diseases "enemy agents within our midst" who worked with the Axis powers. Great Plains residents appreciated efforts to treat venereal disease, but they wanted prevention because their sons and daughters were at risk from a new morality born of war.[52]

Clearly, the infection rate for venereal disease proved startling in the Great Plains. In early 1943 New Mexico ranked first in the nation, followed by Texas, for whites, while among blacks Texas ranked second and New Mexico seventh. In Oklahoma the white population ranked seventh in the nation for syphilis infection, the black population fourteenth. Officials in the Texas Social Hygiene Association, however, did not attribute the problem solely to prostitutes who preyed on the military. The association held, "The rank and file of our men are not being infected by prostitutes; they are being infected by employed and unemployed women and girls in all walks of life, who least suspect that they themselves are carrying the disease." Besides the physical and psychological trauma of venereal disease, health officials worried about cultural degeneration, contending, "Unless the white race become alive to the menace, it will be a matter of time until venereal disease figures will match those of the negro race." They recommended mandatory testing for everyone in the state.[53]

Soldiers, sailors, and marines, of course, attracted prostitutes, who helped spread venereal disease to such an extent that immorality seemed inextricably linked to the military. Prostitution became a particularly serious problem in Cheyenne, where the combination of liquor, soldiers, and women troubled city officials throughout the war. Indeed, prostitutes came with the army and the navy, and they did not leave in great numbers until after the military essentially departed from the Great Plains towns after the war. In June 1943, for example, Cheyenne's mayor, Ed Warren, pledged that the city would curb prostitution after a federal investigator found that a "number of houses of prostitution" operated with impunity in the city. The federal investigator recommended that Cheyenne be declared "out of bounds" for the men stationed at Fort Warren. When the police investigated this charge, however, they could find only rooming houses, not brothels. The federal investigator rejected this finding and again threatened to have Cheyenne declared "off limits" for the servicemen at Fort Warren. He did not know, however, how such an order would affect the soldiers living in Cheyenne. The city attorney called the investigator's proposal a "clearly unconstitutional action" that the city could not authorize. In the end neither the city, the federal government, nor the army took any action, and local businessmen breathed a sigh of relief.[54]

In Tulsa the police commissioner authorized the vice squad to crack down hard on prostitutes visited by the soldiers from Camp Gruber near Muskogee. The local newspaper, however, complained of heavy-handed tactics, and the municipal judge dismissed a number of cases because the police had gathered evidence illegally, by "pussyfooting methods." The police commissioner admitted that a vice squad raid on a rooming house had not been "entirely legal," but, he claimed, he was only utilizing methods advised by federal agents to help curb the spread of venereal disease. He then pledged to abolish the vice squad and, thereby, "insure the prostitutes a wide-open town," Tulsa apparently not wanting law enforcement.[55]

Certainly, venereal disease spread rapidly in the military towns in the Great Plains because of prostitution. Although venereal disease was not unknown in Cheyenne, particularly among the cowboys who worked the ranges and trailed cattle north from Texas to Montana pastures during the late nineteenth century, by November 1942 it had become such a problem that the state health department urged a public education campaign to help prevent its spread because syphilis and gonorrhea led the list of communicable diseases in Wyoming. Although the Office of Community War Services in Washington DC considered the rate of venereal disease in Cheyenne to be "comparatively low" when compared to other army towns, it became serious enough to cause concern among federal authorities. The regional representative of the office contended, "It is the responsibility of Cheyenne, both to the federal government and to the soldier's parents, to make sure that nothing disastrous happens to the soldier which might be avoided by the correction of local conditions." The Office of Community War Services urged Cheyenne officials to close all places of prostitution and to police taverns, restaurants, movie theaters, and hotels where soldiers met prostitutes, colloquially called "victory girls," and provide free examinations, treatment, and places for quarantine.[56]

By September 1943 San Antonio had the worst venereal disease record in the Texas plains, followed by Dallas and Fort Worth. In Dallas 70 percent of the venereal disease cases were among whites, and only 20 percent were attributed to prostitutes, the other 80 percent coming from "nonprofessional women." Major General Donovan demanded that Dallas be cleaned up without delay. City officials considered clearing women from the streets early each evening. By November 150 soldiers were contracting venereal disease weekly, a figure that one observer suspected was less than half the true infection rate. Many Dallas residents feared that the federal government would take drastic action under the May Act, which authorized the FBI to close houses of prostitution and make arrests. If that happened, adverse effects on both civil rights and business were predicted. Dallas public health officials looked to the military to help solve the problem by placing approximately sixty taverns (two black), cafés, and small hotels off limits, and the mayor appointed a committee to deal with the problem, including representatives from the Dallas Hotel Association.[57]

The problems with venereal disease did not improve in Cheyenne. By late December 1943 syphilis had increased 80 percent during the year compared to 1942 and 147 percent compared to the previous five years. The state health department reported that an urgent need existed for a venereal disease preventive education program. Cheyenne police then initiated a crackdown on prostitution that the Seventh Service Command lauded for its effectiveness in sharply reducing the cases of venereal disease at Fort Warren by June 1944. Although civilian and military officials made great progress in slowing the spread of venereal disease among the soldiers, in February 1945 one federal official reported, "The white problem has been licked in Cheyenne, but the disease among the colored is still a problem."[58]

At Kearney venereal disease proved a constant problem, although the rate fell within the middle third of the range for all military bases in the United States. The medical aid at the Kearney Army Air Field included the Venereal Disease Control Council, which operated three prophylactic stations for the distribution of condoms to the servicemen and provided physical examinations and medical treatment. One station operated at the base hospital, another served "colored" men, and a third attended to the soldiers in downtown Kearney. Although all military bases offered the services of "pro" stations during the war, an army inspector judged Kearney's to be "one of the best Prophylactic Stations ever seen." In Hutchinson, Kansas, however, the navy located a station for the distribution of condoms near the police headquarters, and it received little business.[59]

In Kearney officials attributed the problem of venereal disease to the five brothels that operated relatively openly and without much hindrance by the police. There, victory girls from nearby towns, such as Valentine, or faraway places, such as Oklahoma City, found employment. If a woman who had a police record and "no visible means of support" was seen by the police in the company of a soldier, she could be arrested, charged with vagrancy, and given an examination for venereal disease. If she tested positive, she would be sent to the Rapid Treatment Hospital in Omaha. If she did not have venereal disease, a bus ride out of town awaited her on her release. The soldiers arrested for accompanying a prostitute were transferred to the custody of the military police, who took them to a pro station for a checkup. No one questioned whether such force exercised by the state violated civil liberties, although officials acted under the assumption that they were protecting the general welfare. In early 1944, however, the infection rate in Kearney soared, and on February 28 the army imposed a curfew that required all soldiers to return to the airfield by midnight. The curfew lasted only a month, and the number of cases of venereal disease at the airfield again escalated in August 1945. The post surgeon attributed the increase to "excessive drinking and celebrating brought about by the news of the Japanese surrender."[60]

Still, opportunities and dangers created by the war differed among individuals. In November 1941, when police and the army banned soldiers from a seven-block "scarlet" area in Oklahoma City, the prostitutes and retailers who plied their trades complained because both groups lost a considerable amount of money. While participating hotels required the professional prostitutes to show evidence of monthly blood checks, the professional women complained that it was not they who were spreading venereal disease but amateurs, or "beer joint girls," who did not take care of themselves or undergo regular examinations. The professionals also argued that soldiers usually hired the services of the amateurs because they were cheaper. Moreover, both soldiers and prostitutes spent money in the retail stores in the area, and the ban hurt these merchants. Ultimately, the soldiers and prostitutes relocated in the city.[61]

In January 1944 Dallas led the state in venereal disease infection. One local medical official believed that the venereal disease problem had to be solved among blacks before it could be extinguished among whites. By late August Dallas led the Great Plains cities with the highest venereal disease rate. It ranked sixth in the nation among military personnel, a ranking that the army attributed to "good time girls." One police officer complained that lawyers had begun to give the department problems because they were bailing women out of jail before they could be compelled to take a blood test for venereal disease. "It's disturbing and embarrassing," he said, "to have women released a couple of hours after they have been put in jail and before we have a chance to have them examined."[62]

The fear of venereal disease among Great Plains residents led to constitutionally questionable efforts to prevent its spread. In Albuquerque and Dallas city police and county sheriff's officers arrested suspected prostitutes, forced them to undergo testing at a venereal disease clinic, and held them in jail until the clinic reported that they were no longer infected. By spring 1943 the Wyoming Health Department recommended the "internment" of victory girls to curb the spread of venereal disease. Wyoming officials reported that nearly all the soldiers in the state who contracted venereal disease did so from women who frequented taverns and other "hot spots." They too recommended great efforts at public education. In Albuquerque public health officials planned a venereal disease clinic where infected "younger women" would be segregated from "confirmed prostitutes" during the three-month treatment process.[63]

Throughout the war officials in Oklahoma City sent women in "questionable circumstances" to the city clinic for a mandatory venereal disease check. During November 1942 the police made 817 investigations at rooming houses looking for evidence of prostitution. Perhaps these raids were an anomaly because one reporter wrote that the soldiers and sailors who visited Oklahoma City liked "girls with their cloths on" and preferred cookies and milk offered by local hospitality organizations. Another commented that those service organizations sponsored dances that appealed to the military men because the "nicest girls in town are hostesses and partners." By early 1943, however, the commanding officer at the navy aviation school near Norman, Oklahoma, placed eight "night spots" off-limits in Oklahoma City. Although he did not give a specific reason for doing so, his public relations officer reported that the taverns had "failed to comply with standards deemed fitting for naval personnel," which probably meant that prostitutes worked there and that liquor could be obtained there even though Oklahoma was a dry state.[64]

Similarly, by late May 1944 army encampments near Pueblo, Colorado, had contributed to vice and drinking problems in the city that, in the words of Bert L. Beatty, the president of the city council, "approached alarming conditions" that the local police force could not handle. In a desperate attempt to solve this problem a military-civilian council convened and urged tavern and rooming-house owners to place civic welfare above "monetary profits," but little changed. In Denver, however, the police chief claimed that the city had "no moral problems" because it cracked down hard on prostitutes and encouraged amateur camp followers or victory girls to leave town.[65]

By February 1945 incidences of venereal disease outnumbered those of all other communicable maladies in Oklahoma. Military officials believed that 80 percent of the soldiers and sailors with venereal disease in the state contracted it in Oklahoma City, and they urged civilian authorities in the city to "eradicate its cesspool of promiscuous women." A month later public health officials estimated twenty-five to thirty thousand venereal disease cases, both civilian and military, in Oklahoma. They expected the infection rate to increase when the war ended and demobilization occurred. They recommend more money, legislation, and personnel to combat the problem. One contemporary worried, "If in the post-war period there should be even a brief season of greater moral laxity than now prevailing that will produce an extremely distressing situation, for promiscuity already has reached the highest level in our history." The problem occurred, she believed, because promiscuous women could not distinguish between love and lust, and she felt that "loose-living" was a symptom of "mental, emotional, and social disorganization." The solution, she believed, involved a return to the sound teaching of moral values in homes, schools, and churches. Clearly, the postwar world in the Great Plains promised to be both passionate and bleak.[66]

Indeed, by 1945 venereal disease was so bad in Oklahoma City that Governor Robert S. Kerr hosted a conference with representatives from the War Department, the U.S. Public Health Service, the American Social Hygiene Association, and the Social Protection Division of the Federal Security Agency in attendance to discuss the creation of a venereal disease–control program. The conference convened on March 2 and adjourned the following day. Lengthy addresses filled the two days. The recommendations to solve the problem contained nothing new—self-policing by tavern and hotel owners, renewed commitment to high moral standards, and improved education as well as a more forceful crackdown on prostitutes and "promiscuous" women.[67]

By December 1945 public opinion had largely forgotten the venereal disease problem. Most soldiers and sailors left the Great Plains, and military bases closed. Most camp followers also departed, but the victory girls remained. If they did not spread venereal disease, they continued to enjoy their newly experienced sexual freedom, and public pressure to arrest women who visited taverns essentially ended. Still, looking back, Great Plains residents attributed the threat of venereal disease to the arrival of the military and the camp followers who joined them, a witness to a terrible collapse of morality in their neighborhoods caused by the war. While the military bases provided jobs and created prosperity, then, sterility and even death became associational risks that few had contemplated when they anxiously supported the military buildup in the Great Plains.[68]

Drinking and the problems that came with it also upset many residents in communities located near military installations. In 1942 Oklahoma dry forces contested the right of the army to sell liquor at its installations within the state. Governor Leon C. Phillips, "long a traveler on the sands of temperance and a strict dry law enforcer," started the controversy by petitioning the state's representatives to ask Congress to "stop these law violating officers" from selling beer in Oklahoma. Phillips claimed state jurisdiction because beer trucks crossed dry Oklahoma soil before delivering their wet goods to the military bases. In response the commander at Fort Sill halted liquor and beer sales, while the army charged that state officials had no jurisdiction on federal property. Fortunately for the soldiers the federal court quickly resolved the problem in favor of the army. The dry forces also failed to prevent the sale of beer in Oklahoma City because beer retailers continued to meet the demands of the soldiers and sailors. The only concession of the tavern owners to the dry forces was to stop selling beer at 11:15 p.m. to prevent late-night brawling, particularly by sailors. Similarly, in Nebraska the Allied Dry Forces had become particularly alarmed by January 1943 that "strong" beer was being sold near the army bases and particularly on the Lincoln air base. The drys angrily charged that, while the army permitted only beer with 3.2 percent alcohol to be sold, their chemical analysis proved that the beer being sold at the base tested at nearly 5 percent alcohol by volume. The Nebraska dry forces, looking to the past, wanted to solve the problem with national prohibition legislation. In Cheyenne city officials restricted the sale of package liquor to the hours between 2:00 and 8:00 p.m. to reduce drinking on the buses that returned the soldiers to Fort Warren at night. They did not, however, restrict the sale of liquor by the drink in Cheyenne bars.[69]

By June 1943 Dallas had become a major destination for military men on a weekend furlough from Love Field and other bases in the area. Between Friday and Sunday some six thousand soldiers made Dallas one of the largest concentration centers for military personnel on leave in the southern Great Plains. City officials claimed their behavior to be exemplary as they visited friends, relatives, and servicemen's clubs. The military police viewed their behavior somewhat differently, but no less positively, reporting that they averaged only one hundred arrests on weekends, primarily for drinking and fighting in the downtown taverns. The fifty-five military police who worked the downtown area on weekends operated a stockade at Young and Austin streets where they took their inebriated soldiers to sober up. Sheriff Smoot Schmid thought that the soldiers behaved better in Dallas than did civilians who had been away from home for some time.[70]

Social and domestic dislocation also occurred in the military towns when soldiers married local women and left for overseas duty, only to have their wives reconsider their quick commitments, made under the influence of passion rather than cool reason. In Cheyenne the Laramie County Clerk noted that the wives of servicemen overseas received 18 percent of the divorces granted in 1943. The clerk observed, "The main reason for this large percentage in divorces by soldiers' wives seems to be that the man doesn't or isn't able to get home enough." Hasty marriages during the war no doubt caused this situation. "The woman," he reported, "doesn't want to wait for the man because she realizes that she never loved him despite the fact she married him." And, the clerk predicted, the situation would get "progressively worse" as the war continued. The pleasures of the moment appealed to many women in the military towns, and the initiation of infidelity had no gender restriction.[71]

In the end the military bases provided good-paying jobs and steady employment for many men and women in the plains, during both the construction and the operational phases of the bases. Nearby property values and railroad traffic for freight and passengers increased. In Alliance, Nebraska, during 1942, for example, officials delighted at the 50 percent increase in business after the establishment of the army airfield. During a ninety-day period ending in late autumn, the Guardian National Bank gained $1.1 million in deposits. Every town located near a military base on the Great Plains experienced "unprecedented" prosperity during the war years. Certainly, the large military payrolls for soldiers and civilians gave the nearby towns an important economic boost. But many employees, merchants, and city officials gave little thought to the end of the war. Most assumed that any military cutback would affect someone else and that their town would become part of federal plans for the postwar military. As a result, when the war ended and nearly all the bases quickly closed, the million-dollar payrolls disappeared, and those who had become accustomed to good, high-paying jobs suffered severe economic adjustment, almost equivalent to their experience during the days of the Great Depression, when they had little money and not much hope of getting a decent, permanent job.[72]

Without question, however, the economic benefit to communities near military bases on the Great Plains helped break the grip of the Great Depression by providing jobs and creating a demand for goods and services. By June 1943 the army had spent more than $80 million in little more than two years near Oklahoma City alone, particularly at Tinker and Will Rogers fields, Fort Reno, and the Douglas airplane assembly plant. The Douglas plant cost more than $40 million, while the army expended $25 million on Tinker Field. Will Rogers Field required an initial $15 million for construction, and the internment camp at Fort Reno brought $2 million into the area, all of which kept construction workers and mechanics among the civilian population busy and local store owners prosperous. Usually, the flow of money came quickly. In Oklahoma City contractors needed five thousand workers within three weeks to convert part of the municipal airport into an army airfield. With the War Department providing cost-plus-fee contracts to assure speed in construction as well as profit for the contractors, earnings rose rapidly. On a more modest scale, in March 1942 the (CCC) moved its camp from Hondo, New Mexico, to Roswell, where it used its young men to build target ranges, string telephone lines, dig wells, and lay water- and gas lines.[73]

Still, some communities missed the prosperity generated by military payrolls. In 1940, when the War Department announced the imminent closure of Fort Lincoln, North Dakota, the Bismarck Association of Commerce protested because the closure would mean the loss of a large payroll for the city, and Governor John Moses and the state's congressmen and senators worked to prevent it. However, because the per capita expense of maintaining the fort exceeded the average by more than $30 per person, largely because of the climate, the army preferred to concentrate its troops at larger posts to reduce costs. In March 1941, when the War Department made the final decision to close Fort Lincoln, Congressman Charles B. Robertson complained that it was "not consistent with good business."[74]

Certainly, the military buildup on the Great Plains contributed to the war effort. The War Department found the plains appealing for the establishment of military bases, particularly in Kansas, Oklahoma, Texas, and New Mexico, where snow presented few problems. But the northern Great Plains also benefited from the war. By February 1942 the War Department had committed $8.5 million for the construction of an air base for bomber training at Rapid City, and work crews were on the job. A month later the War Department selected Sioux Falls for the establishment of a $15 million army air corps radio school at the municipal airport, including the construction of barracks and a hospital and other facilities for a "little city," all largely due to the efforts of Senators Chan Gurney and W. J. Bulow, Congressman Karl Mundt, and the Chamber of Commerce. The fifteen thousand students scheduled to train there would increase the population of Sioux Falls by one-third. The city anticipated acquiring the necessary eighteen hundred acres, which it intended to lease to the War Department for $1 per year, for $300,000.[75]

By December 1942, after seven months of work, a great stretch of Montana grassland had been transformed into the Great Falls Army Air Field for the training of heavy bomber crews. Satellite airfields had also been established at Cut Bank, Lewiston, and Glasgow, with Great Falls housing approximately three thousand men. By late May 1943 the army had also come to Billings, where it established a training center for aviation mechanics and radio and communications personnel, whose number and length of training the army kept classified. Here, the soldiers rose to reveille at the Grand Hotel, ate their meals at Q's Coffee Shop, and attended training classes at the junior high school.[76]

Air bases also provided training for bomber, fighter, and transport pilots and crews, but no female pilots attached to the Air Transport Command at Love Field near Dallas served as part of the Women's Army Auxiliary Ferrying Squadron and flew bombers and transport or cargo planes to domestic and foreign destinations. While residents welcomed the economic stimulus to the local economy, the army and navy bases brought new concerns, some trivial, such as the tendency of Flying Fortress pilots from Tinker and Will Rogers fields to "buzz" the neighborhoods of Oklahoma City at treetop height, and some serious, such as the spread of venereal disease and racial conflict. Some problems fell between these extremes. Soon after the first cadets arrived at Midland, Texas, on February 6, 1943, for example, ranchers began telephoning the base to complain that fire frequently spread from the practice ranges to their property and that they occasionally lost cattle and buildings to errant or overzealous pilots and bombardiers, the latter of whom called themselves the "hell from heaven" men. Although the army had a process for filing a claim and awarding compensation, these Texas ranchers became contentious over the red tape and the delay in payment, particularly when military officials suggested that some ranchers set fire to their own rangelands because they needed the cash. After the training began at Casper, Wyoming, area ranchers also worried about the safety of their herds, and one complained that a plane had dropped bombs near his house and fired machine guns at his horses. Economic opportunity born of war interrupted normal living patterns for civilians and soldiers alike, and it required social adjustments, if not substantive change.[77]

Still, the military's economic boost to the wartime Great Plains came in many ways. By October 1942, for example, since car, tire, and gasoline rationing had devastated the summer tourist industry in the Black Hills, with business down an estimated 85 percent in the Rapid City area, some residents welcomed the army's plan to build an air base nearby. Merchants anxiously awaited spending on payday. Stanton Neil, the president of the Chamber of Commerce, reflected that, although many residents were not yet "entirely attuned to the fact that the nation is at war," the businessmen saw the construction project in terms of "there may be something in it for us." They were right. After construction began, local businessmen enjoyed their share of the "huge payrolls" for the construction workers and contracts held by local firms, and banks remained open during the evening on paydays to accommodate the workers.[78]

Overall, the military gave the economy of the Great Plains a significant boost. The army and navy air bases created thousands of jobs and multimillion-dollar monthly payrolls. By spring 1944, as the army took as many able-bodied men as possible for the impending invasion of Europe, more civilians were needed to replace servicemen at the bases and hospitals. In May an officer at Fitzsimons Army Hospital in Denver reported, "Under army orders Fitzsimons must replace all its able-bodied military enlisted personnel with civilian employees by June 30." As a result the hospital needed three hundred men and women almost immediately for work in the wards, mess halls, and kitchens. With no age limits imposed or experience required, new employees could learn on the job and earn a beginning wage of $130 per month. The army anticipated that the positions at Fitzsimons would be long-term jobs because more disabled men were arriving from the war fronts every day and because the army expected the hospital to increase its workload as the temporary rehabilitation camps closed after the war.[79]

Moreover, civilian contractors provided services to the military bases throughout the war. Federal funds did not reach the pockets of workers as a onetime injection of money for the initial construction of the installations. Expansion and repair projects kept contractors and workers busy. The army also hired civilians for a host of technical jobs. At Lowry and Buckley fields and Fort Logan several hundred civilians held jobs that paid between $1,620 and $4,600 annually. In July 1943 the army planned to spend $1.5 million to expand the "bomber modification center" operated in Cheyenne by United Airlines, which had already brought a "huge aviation payroll" into the area. Although the number of people employed remained classified, civilians constituted most to the workforce, and 50 percent of them were women. The military bases also meant income for city coffers. Cheyenne, for example, earned more than $100,000 annually for supplying water to Fort Warren.[80]

In some towns radical social changes occurred. In Abilene, Texas, for example, residents confronted the problems created by fundamentalist Christian beliefs and economic opportunity. In January 1941 some residents worried that the pending arrival of construction workers and soldiers who would build and occupy Camp Barkeley would violate the drinking mores of "dry" Taylor County. When the Retail Merchants Association, however, proposed a new ordinance to the city council that would permit movies on Sunday nights, battle lines were drawn. One minister opposed the ordinance, saying, "We should be unfaithful to our trust to the youth in our colleges here if we countenanced the evil of Sunday night picture shows." A resident countered, "Sunday night shows will help keep the boys out of honky-tonks." Another minister objected, saying, "There are not going to be any honky-tonks." This position drew the response, "I had reference to the honky-tonks in neighboring communities." Rumors of a million-dollar monthly payroll for the construction workers and untold millions in earnings once Camp Barkeley had been completed, staffed, and garrisoned no doubt influenced the city council's 3–1 vote in favor of the ordinance to permit Sunday night "picture shows" in Abilene.[81]

Overall, the War Department established dozens of air bases and training facilities in the Great Plains during World War II. Oklahoma alone had twenty-eight army camps and thirteen navy bases. Nebraska had eleven army air bases. By 1945 Great Plains residents had become accustomed to seeing "Flying Fortresses," gliders, and PCBYs, among other aircraft, flying training missions over their neighborhoods. The air bases had become economic pillars for nearby communities, and plains men and women did not want to lose them when the war ended, a matter that many began worrying about as soon as the War Department established the bases. Nearly everyone wanted the base near their community to be designated a "permanent" rather than an "interim" or a "surplus" military installation. When the war ended, some of the bases established during the conflict remained, such as Roswell Army Air Field and the Smoky Hill Army Air Field. Others, such as Fort Riley, Fort Warren, and Lowry Field, predated the war and remained or were only temporarily deactivated, to be reactivated a few years later under another name, such as Reese Air Force Base at Lubbock. But the War Department quickly abandoned the smaller air bases, such as that at Rapid City, and eventually some of the larger bases also closed as military needs and the economy changed. For some civilians who worked at the air bases, their jobs terminated quickly. At the Rapid City Army Air Base, September 21, 1945, marked the last day of work. In Nebraska the state purchased the airfields at Bruning, Fairmont, Harvard, McCook, and Scribner to operate as state airports, while municipal governments acquired the airfields at Alliance, Ainsworth, Grand Island, Kearney, Lincoln, and Scottsbluff for city airports.[82]

In many respects the military presence on the Great Plains was representative of that experienced by other regions. When the military arrived in force, the economy boomed, but the towns and cities confronted a host of problems concerning the provision of adequate services such as streets, sewage disposal, and garbage collection as well as the provision of adequate housing and recreation. Odessa, Texas, near the Midland Army Air Field, tripled in population, from 9,462 in 1940 to approximately 30,000 by 1945. On the eve of the war the city had twelve miles of water pipe; by the end of the war it had thirty-four miles. As thousands of young, single men arrived en masse, social problems often developed, such as the abuse of alcohol, prostitution, and venereal disease. To some extent, of course, every town that supported a military base confronted the problem of prostitution because women for hire have always followed armies. But the blatant solicitation of sex for money and the willingness of many soldiers and sailors to seek prostitutes challenged the morals of the residents in Great Plains communities. Civilian and military police might restrict the practice of prostitution, but they could never eliminate it, and they could do little more than complain and worry about it. The arrival of black troops compounded these problems. Great Plains residents were prejudiced, but they were unprepared to act on their beliefs, and it took time to provide segregated housing and recreational facilities.[83]

Without question the new European war touched every city, town, and village in the nation after Congress passed the Selective Service Act on September 16, 1940. Thousands of men registered for the draft and left home, and many lost their lives. Families felt loneliness when sons and daughters departed for the military, and they suffered life-shattering losses when news arrived that a son had been reported missing in action or killed. In 1944 William DeLoach's son Bill served as an army copilot flying supplies out of Moran, India, to Myitkyina, Burma. On Wednesday, August 23, DeLoach confided in his diary, "The awful blow hit us about 6 p.m. A Mr. Lowrey drove up and said he wanted to speak to me. I went out to his car. He said he had a death message from Washington, D.C. Well, I knew what it was. . . . Sallie knew that something had happened to Bill."[84]

Not every home on the Great Plains suffered the tragic loss of a son, but the location of an army or a navy base brought the war close to those who lived nearby. The military bases enabled many Great Plains residents to participate in the war effort even though they could not qualify for military service because of age, medical, or some other reason. Jobs at the bases, whether they involved packing parachutes, typing, or conducting aircraft or building maintenance, gave civilians the opportunity to feel that they contributed, and they also gave them a daily outlet for their patriotism, anxiety, and need to participate. Certainly, their efforts helped make possible the massive military buildup necessary to defeat Germany and Japan. Moreover, the location of an airfield gave local residents the belief that their town had a greater economic destiny than merely to remain an agricultural service center, that is, farm town, where people sold their cotton, grain, or livestock, bought essential supplies, and waited for better economic times. But the opportunity to change one's destiny carried an uncertain price. The war brought economic prosperity to many towns blessed with a military airfield, but it also created a host of problems that those towns' citizens had never experienced. When the war ended, most of the military towns faded economically, and some, such as Walker, Kansas, nearly disappeared. Whether the economic, social, cultural, and political changes on the Great Plains wrought by the war and the establishment of military bases brought more good than ill, no one could precisely say.

NINE | Internment

By the summer of 1940 fear based on the need for self-protection and patriotism anchored by racial prejudice led many Great Plains residents to restrict civil liberties and impose regulations on personal freedom that they would have rejected in less threatening and more peaceful times. In late June the city commission in Bismarck, North Dakota, unanimously adopted a resolution binding employees on the city's payroll. All present and future employees had to prove American citizenship as well as submit to fingerprinting as a "measure of good government and a matter of precaution in time of world crisis." Mayor N. O. Churchill reported that the rule also applied to the members of the city commission "to insure the Americanism of everyone connected with the municipal government." Naturalization papers and birth certificates would serve as proof, but soon German, Italian, and Japanese names would add a new dimension to discrimination and the violation of the right to equal protection under the law.[1]

In August Postmaster Eugene Bangs in Rapid City, South Dakota, announced preparations to help institute the nationwide registration of all aliens, some 3.5 million, by the Immigration and Naturalization Service (INS). The Alien Registration Act of 1940 authorized local post offices to register and fingerprint aliens fourteen years of age or older. Younger children would be registered with their parents. Failure to report for registration brought a $1,000 fine and six months in jail. Wichita residents learned that the federal government required aliens to answer a host of questions, including whether they had entered the

United States via ship as a passenger, crew member, or stowaway as well as whether they had ever served as a foreign agent or received remuneration for service to a foreign government in a political, public, or policymaking capacity. By early October 829 aliens living in Wichita and the surrounding area had been registered and fingerprinted. In Rapid City the postmaster urged anyone to register if they were uncertain whether they were aliens or citizens because registering did not "constitute an admission of alienship." Small wonder that confusion prevailed as the December 26 deadline approached. In order to make the registering and fingerprinting process easier in Bismarck, officials offered to visit the homes of invalid aliens.[2]

In Wichita many aliens attempted to comply, but "considerable confusion" about their status caused anxiety. Alien women who married native-born men before September 22, 1922, for example, had legal citizenship, but those who married after that date had to present naturalization papers to avoid registration. American women, however, who married alien men prior to September 22, 1922, took the citizenship of their spouses, but those who married after that date could choose their citizenship. Many of the women in both categories, however, assumed that they were citizens of the United States. During peacetime few people cared about these regulations, and it was not until the postmaster explained the law that many women who thought they were legal citizens discovered that they were aliens subject to federal scrutiny. In Wichita, when more than 250 Mexicans learned that the federal government considered them aliens, the application supply dwindled at the post office because they were quick to comply for fear of losing their jobs. This fear was well-founded because aliens had increasing difficulty finding employment even though government officials urged citizens not to consider them dangerous. Postmaster J. B. Riddle in Wichita, however, observed that the government had "full legal and moral right" to require the collection of personal information and the registration of "persons living here as our guests." One employee of the registration and fingerprinting office put it differently, saying that foreigners living in Wichita would be "wearing out their welcome" and might suffer deportation unless they registered as aliens.[3]

The registration of aliens continued during the war but only with difficulty because the federal government also required them to present three recent photographs to obtain certificates of identification. By January 1942 9,902 aliens had registered in North Dakota, 6,957 in South Dakota, and 13,639 in Montana. By late February the *Bismarck Tribune* reported, "All who fail to register may end up in a concentration camp." This threat and the continued registration of enemy aliens, particularly German, became unsettling, particularly in North and South Dakota, where large populations of Germans resided. In January 1943, as distrust grew, Senator Gerald Nyc of North Dakota countered charges that only New Jersey had more Nazi sympathizers than North and South Dakota. Nye staunchly proclaimed the loyalty of Dakotans of German descent and his desire to "wring the very necks of the agitators and prejudice builders." Many Great Plains residents, however, distrusted German aliens.[4]

As the United States moved closer to war federal officials asked some aliens to leave. In December 1940, for example, a German student at the University of Denver, Karl Ludwig Scheuring, whose mother was an American and whose father was a German government official, was asked to depart. Government authorities considered this "self-avowed Nazi" a security risk, someone who, they believed, "as a good Nazi would betray the hospitality of America." Federal investigators reported that "Scheuring was in the habit of being absent from his grandmother's home at night," during which time he engaged in "German activities." His membership in the Nazi Party did not help, and the federal government arranged passage home on a Japanese ship.[5]

Problems such as these indicated that the federal government had made few plans for the treatment of enemy aliens in time of war. It had preliminary plans for the confinement of POWs but virtually no arrangements for the internment of enemy aliens if the United States went to war with the Axis powers. Even so, within twenty-four hours of the attack on Pearl Harbor, the FBI arrested 1,771 enemy aliens. In early January 1942, on federal order, aliens began delivering their cameras, radio transmitters, and shortwave radios to police stations. The order applied to all aliens whether or not their country was at war with the United States, and it was intended to safeguard "the interests of national defense." Still, it did not mean that the government considered all aliens enemies.[6]

Despite previous uncertainty about what should be done with aliens, the day after the attack on Pearl Harbor the Office of the Provost Marshal General authorized the construction of nine internment camps for enemy aliens. On the Great Plains Fort Abraham Lincoln in North Dakota already detained some Germans, who now became enemy aliens, and Roswell, New Mexico, was designated as the future site of an internment camp. The War Department's selection of these sites was based on the need for security and for separation from the civilian and military population and industrial centers. North Dakota and New Mexico seemed like good choices, but, when New Mexicans learned of the plan, they strongly objected. New Mexicans particularly opposed the relocation of Japanese in the state because it was felt that they could not be trusted. The *Roswell Daily Record* succinctly summarized the opposition, saying, "Japanese are not wanted in New Mexico whether they were born in Japan or America. We have enough of a racial problem in the state as it is, not to complicate it any further." Those who opposed Japanese internment camps believed that they acted in the best interest of the state, and the watchword became "Keep the Japs Out." Ultimately, Roswell received a POW camp, and the Japanese went to Lordsburg, beyond the plains area of the state.[7]

In the meantime the federal government designated Fort Lincoln as an alien internment camp for Italian seamen who were charged with sabotage while in American ports or who worked on ships that the federal government confiscated. By January 1942 more than 400 German aliens also lived in detention at Fort Lincoln. These Germans had been arrested across the country and waited hearings to determine their status—continued detention or release. Many of these internees had been businessmen working in the United States or sailors whose ships had been docked at American ports when Germany and Great Britain went to war in 1939 and prevented by the British navy from returning home. Until Germany declared war on the United States in December 1941, the federal government held the Germans as unfortunate guests who remained in the country through no fault of their own as legal aliens. The federal government held the German aliens at Ellis Island before the initial transfer of 220 to Fort Lincoln on May 31, 1941. One observer noted of the 410 Germans that arrived in December that "they are a more sullen, grim and harder collection" than the first group sent there during the spring.[8]

The Justice Department informed the internment camp directors that all internees had the same protection that the Geneva Convention gave prisoners of war (POWs). These provisions prohibited forcing prisoners to conduct work that would aid the war effort. In late April 1943, however, the Justice Department paroled sixty-two German internees who volunteered to work for the Northern Pacific Railroad. The Germans wanted to escape the boredom and confinement of camp life and earn some money, while the Northern Pacific needed workers to help maintain the roadbeds. By July railroad officials were well satisfied with the German internees, and some five hundred Germans had requested permission to join their colleagues on the railroad line. Some hardened Nazis at Fort Lincoln, however, considered railroad work treasonous, and they pressured the internees to remain in camp, but most preferred to work and took their chances with the Nazis.[9]

With the attack on Pearl Harbor on December 7, 1941, relations between the federal government, Caucasian Americans, and U.S. residents of Japanese descent become more complicated than relations with German and Italian aliens. At that time approximately 127,000 people of Japanese ancestry lived in the United States, of which about 113,000 lived in California, Oregon, Washington, and Arizona. Japanese constituted less than 1 percent of the American population and less than 2 percent of the population of California, the state with the most people of Japanese heritage. Of the 127,000 Japanese in the United States, some 47,000 had been born in Japan (98 percent having immigrated before the Oriental Exclusion Act of 1924), and approximately 80,000 had been born in America. (The immigrants were known as Issei, their children as Nisei, and their grandchildren as Sansei.) Those born in the United States had American citizenship, and most had been educated in American schools. The Nisei spoke English outside the home and adopted many American cultural practices. Two-thirds of the Nisei were under twenty years of age, and about 45 percent of the entire group of Japanese were engaged in agriculture as farm owners, tenants, sharecroppers, or workers. They were familiar with racial discrimination, having been discriminated against when it came to such issues as intermarriage, property ownership, and employment.[10]

When the war began, the Japanese who were ineligible for citizenship automatically became classified as enemy aliens, which, according to presidential proclamations on December 7 and 8, made them subject to arrest and internment as well as possible exclusion from military zones. Almost immediately after Pearl Harbor the FBI began arresting Japanese nationals suspected of subversive activities. By February 16, 1942, nearly twenty-two hundred Japanese enemy aliens, that is, noncitizens of Japanese ancestry, had been apprehended. The government froze their assets, prohibited travel, and closed their businesses. It did not distinguish between Issei, Nisei, or Sansei, having announced on December 8 that it did not acknowledge the status of the Nisei as American citizens and intended to treat them as descendants of the enemy. On the West Coast, and throughout the nation, the harassment of the Japanese increased. At the same time fifty-five Japanese residents in Cheyenne, Wyoming, publicly proclaimed their loyalty to city and state officials via a signed resolution.[11]

In order to control this potentially dangerous population the Justice Department created zones around the San Francisco waterfront and the Los Angeles airport in which Japanese were prohibited. Other restricted areas soon followed. At the same time John L. DeWitt, the commanding general of the Western Defense Command, urged the mass removal of enemy aliens and "all Japanese" for internment under guard. Soon thereafter, on February 19, President Franklin D. Roosevelt signed Executive Order 9066 authorizing the secretary of war to create military zones from which certain people could be excluded. General DeWitt moved quickly. On March 2 he designated the western half of California, the western third of Oregon and Washington, and the southern quarter of Arizona as Military Area No. 1, from which all persons of Japanese ancestry as well as all German and Italian enemy aliens were excluded. Ultimately, only people of Japanese ancestry were evacuated from those areas, essentially because of racial prejudice. The Japanese responded vehemently, and few agreed to leave their homes, fearing discrimination and violence, but the federal government forced the removal of nearly 110,000 people of Japanese descent from the western states. In the words of one contemporary, the Japanese increasingly became an "unwanted people."[12]

In March 1942 President Roosevelt created the War Relocation Authority (WRA) to supervise the resettlement of the displaced evacuees. Only Governor Ralph Carr welcomed Japanese evacuees to Colorado and the Great Plains. Some observers believed that this action cost Carr a Senate seat during the next election. Residents in the interior considered the Japanese nothing less than "undesirable enemy aliens" and "potential saboteurs" who should be placed in concentration camps. Since few aliens of Japanese ancestry had the opportunity to relocate voluntarily, on March 27, 1942, the army planned to move them to designated relocation centers from which they could be dispersed to other areas beyond the West Coast. By early June eleven centers had been selected, and two—Heart Mountain, Wyoming, and Granada, Colorado—would confine Japanese evacuees, who would influence the history of the Great Plains. Heart Mountain would house a maximum of ten thousand evacuees and the Granada Relocation Center, commonly known as Amache, eight thousand. Each center would function as a cooperative, and food raised would reduce operating costs.[13]

While the West Coast Japanese moved east to relocation camps, the city of Clovis, New Mexico, worked for the removal of its Japanese population. When the war began, a "colony" of several dozen Japanese lived in Clovis, where some of the men worked for the Santa Fe Railroad. These residents of Japanese descent surprised their Caucasian neighbors by proclaiming, "We are American citizens just as other citizens in this country," when asked their opinion about the attack on Pearl Harbor. The *Amarillo Daily News* reported, "No action of any kind was anticipated to be taken against the colony by either city or state officials, as all the families are held in high esteem in Clovis." Some residents had expected supportive sentiment for Japan, and they were surprised when the Japanese in Clovis considered the attack on Pearl Harbor an attack against them as well as other Americans. Actually, the attack on Pearl Harbor brought threats of violence, including lynching, against the Japanese in Clovis, particularly the railroad workers. The Santa Fe wanted to avoid violence and maintain good community relations, so it fired its Japanese employees. The Justice Department then ordered the Border Patrol to protect the Japanese, and at midnight on January 23, 1942, an armed guard whisked them to an abandoned Civilian Conservation Corps camp that the WRA called the Old Raton Ranch Camp. Located approximately 220 miles east of Albuquerque, the camp confined the Japanese who had been relocated from Clovis. By December 1942, however, the WRA had moved them to other camps in Utah and Arizona because the living conditions at the Old Raton Ranch Camp were so dismal, if not inhumane. The response of Clovis to the Japanese indicated the hostile attitudes that the evacuees from the West Coast would encounter when they reached the Great Plains. After the war none of the thirty-two Japanese internees returned to Clovis.[14]

At the same time the INS established an internment camp at Santa Fe primarily for Issei and stranded Italian seamen. It also established an internment camp at Fort Stanton in Lincoln County, New Mexico. Until March 1945 Fort Stanton primarily held German seamen and nationals. Japanese internees did not arrive until March 1945. Primarily, the INS considered these particular internees "troublemakers" who required segregation from Japanese in other camps. Perhaps so, but the federal government never brought any criminal charges against them.[15]

To the north no Japanese had been sent to Fort Abraham Lincoln, also called Camp Bismarck, and during the first two months of the war officials expected the camp to remain reserved for German nationals and stranded seamen. In early February 1942, however, a group of 415 Japanese arrived by train from the West Coast. On their arrival one reporter noted that they were "ringed by a cordon of federal immigration patrolmen armed with sub-machine guns." He continued, "The little yellow men scrambled from their coaches twenty-five at a time, and were put in guard trucks and rushed out to the internment camp." Each truck left the train station accompanied by a sheriff's car, highway patrolmen, or immigration officials. Observers noted that the Japanese shivered as a sharp north wind cut through their thin clothing. Most of them showed no emotion as they left the train and boarded the trucks. Soon, 1,129 Issei, 282 German seamen, and 107 German nationals were held at Fort Lincoln. Depression and despair gripped internees' lives.[16]

Little more than two weeks later 750 Japanese arrived from California to take up quarters behind ten-foot-high fences that separated them from the nearly 400 German internees. By March approximately 1,100 Japanese lived behind the high wire stockade at Fort Lincoln, and officials in the INS expected the camp population to reach its capacity of 2,000 internees. Yet, as the fear of enemy aliens grew, the *Bismarck Tribune* reminded its readers that out of 5 million aliens in the United States only 1.1 million were enemy aliens and that not all German, Italian, and Japanese aliens should be considered enemies of the United States. Moreover, since the declaration of war only 4,000 enemy aliens, or approximately one-third of 1 percent, had been declared "dangerous" and arrested. Even so, suspicion remained and escalated.[17]

At the same time Fort Sill in Oklahoma became an internment camp for Japanese aliens who had been detained in the Great Plains states, the Midwest, and Central and South America. There, a two-row, twelve-foot-high fence topped with barbed wire and guard towers with .30-caliber machine guns and searchlights enabled shotgun-toting guards to intimidate the seven hundred internees confined there by May 1942. The army could not adequately care for this large number of Japanese, and, with more expected, it moved them to larger quarters at Camp Livingston, Louisiana, by late June. Other Oklahomans also saw opportunity with the establishment of an internment camp. At Stringtown local officials converted an unused state prison for the confinement of Japanese internees and German POWs.[18]

Local residents generally welcomed the camps because they would provide army and civilian payrolls and benefit merchants. In Konawa, Oklahoma, for example, a group of citizens, including the presidents of the Oklahoma State Bank and the First National Bank, drafted a proposal for the construction of an "Alien Camp" by the War Department. The purpose of the camp would be to draw federal dollars from construction and payrolls into this community in Seminole County. Patriotism would, of course, play a role, but economics drove the decision. The report noted, "There are no war industries in this region and any type of a program that would call for laborers would be a much needed project." With one hundred vacant houses and apartments available in Konawa, the location of an internment camp would be as beneficial as the placement of a prison or some other institution nearby, and it would have a multiplier effect on the local economy. For Konawa, the war could pay.[19]

Still, the Konawa proposal, which was supported by neighboring Sasakwa, brought considerable opposition from some residents who believed that the federal government planned to establish a "concentration camp for placing a bunch of aliens or naturalized Japanese people" in their midst. Opponents considered them "undesirables," and Congressman Lyle H. Borne quickly quelled the rumor by saying that the federal government had no plan to establish a camp for aliens in Seminole County, Oklahoma.[20]

In many respects the Japanese posed a far more serious alien problem than the Germans and the Italians because the matter of race became inextricably linked to it, particularly after the United States entered the war and reports of Japanese atrocities reached home from the Pacific Theater. Even before Pearl Harbor, however, many Japanese in Denver proclaimed their loyalty. One Japanese woman from Greeley attributed such patriotism to religion, saying, "Christianity has helped us to a better understanding of the present war situation and is making better Americans of the Japanese young men and women in this country." She also noted, "Families who are not Christians do not always feel as we do about our loyalty and patriotism." Certainly, American-born Japanese who had some exposure to, if not acceptance of, Christianity and American culture considered themselves Americans just as much as German and Italian Americans did. The only difference that affected their treatment was color.[21]

Racism, then, became the foundation for anti-Japanese sentiment in the Great Plains. In Oklahoma City a Chinese restaurant posted a sign saying "No Japs Allowed," even though few Japanese lived in the city. In Denver one Chinese American high school student stenciled "Don't Shoot I'm a Chinaman" on his jacket, while others wore lapel pins with American and Chinese flags crossed in the "V for Victory" symbol and bearing the legend "American Chinese." In Amarillo the only Orientals were Chinese, and they worried about being identified as Japanese. The "Chinese colony" of approximately thirty had a reputation for thrift, and they sent money to family members in China. They were also conspicuously among the first in Amarillo to purchase defense bonds, and they proclaimed, "We are proud to be American-Chinese." The *Amarillo News and Globe* gladly reported, "There is not a single Jap in the city." In Denver two days after Pearl Harbor the Federal Reserve Bank began investigating all Japanese-operated businesses whose bank accounts were frozen by order of Secretary of the Treasury Henry Morgenthau Jr. Although only approximately fifty small-scale Japanese businesses operated in Denver and northern New Mexico, the owners were denied access to their security deposit boxes, to help prevent the removal of funds hidden there, as well as to their bank accounts.[22]

On February 29, ten days after President Roosevelt signed Executive Order 9066, Govern Ralph L. Carr stated that Colorado would accept law-abiding Japanese, Germans, and Italians scheduled for removal from the West Coast. Carr declared, "They are as loyal to American institutions as you and I. Many of them have been born here and are American citizens with no connection with or feeling of loyalty toward the customs and philosophies of Italy, Germany, and Japan." Carr also believed that Colorado was "big enough and patriotic enough" to accept "a handful of undesirables whose presence on the West Coast might prove the difference between a successful invasion and the saving of our country." Carr emphatically argued, "If a majority may seize a minority and place them in jails today then every minority group regardless may expect the majority to treat them the same way."[23]

Most Coloradoans, however, resented and opposed the internment of any Japanese and called Carr a "Jap lover." Governor Carr countered that refusal would indicate a lack of patriotism and willingness to participate in the war effort. Those opposed, however, did not want among them enemy aliens who might acquire property rights, compete with local labor, and create a "constant menace and threat to our peaceful way of life." When Carr learned, however, that the state and the counties would be required to police "Jap evacuees" who worked on Colorado farms, he adamantly objected, declaring, "The Japanese problem still belongs to the federal and not to the state government."[24]

Carr, however, did not speak for all Coloradoans or for other Great Plains governors. At a meeting organized by the WRA in Salt Lake City on April 7, 1942, Governor Nels Smith of Wyoming told Milton Eisenhower, who headed the agency, "If you bring Japanese into my state, I promise they will be hanging from every tree." Smith feared that the Japanese would buy land and overrun his thinly populated state. He favored placing all Japanese in "concentration camps," not "relocation centers." Governor Harlan H. J. Bushfield also objected to the relocation of Japanese in South Dakota, and he refused to permit 675 Nisei to work in the sugar beet harvest because the state could not protect them and only farmers wanted them. Governor Bushfield asserted, "To turn six or seven hundred Japanese loose within the confines of the state without proper military guard at all times would, in my opinion, result in rioting and perhaps even worse." If such a disaster occurred, American prisoners in Japanese hands might suffer retribution. New Mexicans debated the same dilemma. Residents of Albuquerque opposed the internment of Japanese, arguing that the state's population of 530,000 could not absorb thousands of Japanese without creating a "serious racial and economic situation."[25]

Kansans also became contentious. Like Coloradoans and New Mexicans, they did not want Japanese internees. Governor Payne

Ratner ordered roadblocks near the Colorado line and the highway patrol to turn back any Japanese trying to "filter" into the Sunflower State. While the state troopers guarded highways 24, 36, and 40, the Border Patrol watched the lesser roads. Governor Ratner made his opinion clear: "Japs are not wanted and not welcome in Kansas." Ratner had heard reports of "Japanese concentrations" across the Colorado boarder. He worried about the safety of western Kansans, particularly residents in the irrigated Arkansas River valley. The precise danger, other than local hysteria or at least fear, remains unclear. Moreover, the state Board of Regents ruled that Japanese students would not be admitted to the public schools. When the residents of Ellsworth, Kansas, learned that the federal government contemplated locating a "Japanese concentration camp" nearby, the mayor said, "We could put 15 or 20 thousand of those Japs down our mine."[26]

Andrew Schoeppel, who became governor of Kansas in January 1943, struggled with the same problems concerning the Japanese as his predecessor. Local 201 of the United Brotherhood of Carpenters and Joiners of America informed him that they opposed the importation of Japanese to Kansas because they would compete for jobs and also endanger the defense industries. The Wichita Board of Commissioners agreed. The police chief also contended that he could not protect Japanese evacuees. The city manager said, "The temper of the local citizens is such that it would be difficult to handle the situation." The Topeka Building and Construction Trades Council expressed the same hostility to the director of the WRA in Kansas City, saying that it would protest the "use of the Japs in any capacity, and certainly never under the conditions of equality or superiority."[27]

Fear of the Japanese spread across Oklahoma as early as April 1942 after twenty-seven Nisei arrived at Boise City to work for a Colorado seed company. When the rumor spread that a German farmer brought a "bunch of Japs to the Oklahoma Panhandle," local residents voiced their anger to Governor Leon Phillips. But Oklahomans were perplexed when the Japanese quietly pursued their work raising garden seeds rather than practicing subversive activities.[28]

Montana's Governor, Sam C. Ford, worried about the potential presence of several thousand Japanese because, given the "sentiment of our people," he did not believe that they could be given adequate protection. If Japanese families were scattered on farms, they would be isolated and vulnerable to violence. Ford candidly said, "Our people cannot tell an American-born Japanese from an alien, nor has any method yet been found whereby a loyal, patriotic Japanese can be distinguished from a saboteur." Ford worried that, when the casualty reports began arriving with the names of Montana boys, he would "fear for the safety of any Japanese in this state unless the army has provided proper protection." He also demanded assurances that any Japanese evacuated to Montana would be "removed" when the war ended. If they remained, he warned, the "white man will be driven from our fertile farms." He feared that the Japanese might stay and buy land, and they looked different.[29]

While many Great Plains residents contemplated the arrival of Japanese evacuees, the federal government chose Granada in southeastern Colorado for a Japanese relocation center. The nearby camp was called Amache because the post office in Grenada could not handle the volume of mail for the Japanese, thereby requiring a new town name for the postal service. There, on June 12, 1942, workers began to construct a camp on 10,500 acres purchased from private owners. By late August fencing and living quarters had been completed by approximately 1,000 workmen, and Japanese evacuees began arriving. In two weeks 4,492 Japanese had relocated to Amache. The camp director reported, "Trains arrived, usually at night; lighting facilities were extremely sketchy, and families stumbled in the dark, individuals often falling into excavations. . . . Hot and cold water was provided in only a few blocks." The residents of nearby Grenada generally proved friendly, in part because the Japanese had free access to town and they had money to spend.[30]

Ultimately, Colorado, which needed abundant agricultural labor, proved flexible regarding the relocation of the evacuees of Japanese descent. By late October 1942 Amache held some seven thousand Japanese men, women, and children inside a fenced and guarded square mile of dryland, from which, in the words of one observer,

"the native rattlesnake and jackrabbit have not entirely departed."
(In fact some of the early residents killed the snakes and sold the rat-
tles for as much as $1.50 each for souvenirs in order to make some
money.) At its peak the Japanese population at Amache reached approximately seventy-five hundred. Amache occupied a site on the
Arkansas River in Prowers County, which only a few years before
had been in the heart of the Dust Bowl. Military police guarded the
entrance and fence from four watchtowers, but the civilian WRA ran
the camp. One Nisei recalled that Amache was "barren, with no
trees. Just ugly barracks on a hillside." Another remembered, "It
was like a prison camp. Coming from our environment it was just
devastating." At Amache American history was a basic subject in
the school, and the teachers "talked about freedom all the time," the
irony of which was not lost on the high school students.[31]

At Amache the Japanese established their own city government,
lived in barracks divided into apartments, and took their meals in
a mess hall. Although the food proved adequate in quantity and
quality, cafeteria-style meals had an immediate and negative effect
on family life. One reporter noted that "many of the older persons
object bitterly to the community mess" because "family control has
its very foundation in the family meal." Traditionally, mealtime was
structured family time. Consequently, the adults believed that the
community mess hall robbed them of authority over their children,
and they felt angry about it. Japanese cooks prepared the meals,
but the Caucasian American drive for order and efficiency in serving several thousand people three times a day caused serious social
hardship that cut to the core of Japanese culture. The Japanese also
established their own consumers' cooperative as well as a variety of
stores and opened the camp to shoppers from outside on weekends.
Residents passed their time listening to the radio and visiting. Boredom made their lives worse and helped make Amache "as bleak a
spot as one can find on the western plains." The desolation of the
area masked the potential the camp held for great agricultural productivity, but farming required irrigation, and the WRA had no funds
or plans to provide it.[32]

Although the Japanese demanded that the WRA provide plots of land that they could till as individuals in order to sell the produce to camp members for a modest income, Director James G. Lindley rejected the proposal and reminded them that any allocated farm-land would be run by the camp for the camp, that is, by the WRA. Other problems emerged because, if allocated land, Japanese farmers would need to walk to their fields but return to the camp for lunch and dinner and the WRA would not permit them to work longer than an eight-hour day, nor could they work Saturday afternoon or Sun-day. Although experienced Japanese farmers could receive a wage of $16 per month, the WRA's concept of small-scale agriculture to make the Japanese more self-sufficient proved impractical from the begin-ning. Local farmers who understood agriculture on the Great Plains laughed and predicted failure.[33]

The WRA also caused resentment in the white community when it authorized the construction of a new, temporary high school to accommodate approximately six hundred students at Amache. When local residents learned that the superintendent would receive an annual salary of $4,600, or $600 more than the superintendent of schools in nearby Lamar, they questioned the better facilities for the Japanese and the higher administrative salary. Moreover, the high school curriculum at Amache reportedly was "full of the trick subjects of the day—subjects which deal little at all with the three Rs, but economics and music, and painting and the arts." The WRA, however, mandated that, like other Japanese internment camp schools, Amache High encourage the "understanding of American ideals and loyalty to American institutions and . . . train students for responsibilities of citizenship." The Japanese internees also seemed different, and, therefore, untrustworthy, because in the camp they spoke Japanese in preference to English. The camp also appeared far more comfortable than the Japanese deserved to local residents when they learned about the executions of downed American flyers. Some Great Plains residents believed that the federal government should place "enemy Japs" in concentration camps and kill prison-ers if the Japanese executed captured Americans because the "dirty Japs should be given a taste of their own medicine."[34]

Although the Japanese could not be forced to work because they were American citizens who had not committed a crime, and while the Geneva Convention of 1929 prohibited the forced labor of aliens, many Japanese internees wanted to work, if only to get out of the camps. By late January 1943 some Japanese women at Heart Mountain had taken positions as maids in Billings, Montana. Their wages were determined by mutual agreement with the employer, but the employer paid transportation costs. The federal government did not impose travel restrictions on the Nisei in counties designated as work vicinities unless local "peace ordnances" required such regulation. The Japanese work ethic in homes and fields, as well as the organization of an American Legion post and a Girl Scout troop at Heart Mountain and the evacuees' willingness to purchase war bonds and donate to the USO and the Red Cross, gave residents of the northern Great Plains pause. The Japanese Americans were not the enemy they had expected. Even so, many plains residents believed that the WRA "coddled and pampered" the Japanese in the internment camps at Amache and just west of the Wyoming plains at Heart Mountain.[35]

Increasingly, many Japanese feared leaving their camps. At Amache a reporter noted, "Many of the evacuees have become inflicted with a great fear of the outside world." The older Japanese, particularly the Issei, had lost their savings and saw no hope of beginning again, and Coloradoans did not want them or the Nisei to stay. The editor of the *Lamar News* observed, "The Japanese aren't assimilated into society here." Yet the businessmen wanted their trade as long as they remained because they were polite, deferred to whites, and willingly paid high prices. Even so, distrust of the Japanese prevailed among whites. One Lamar policeman observed, "We don't have no trouble with Japs. They're good guys individually. . . . But they're Japanese." The WRA advised the Japanese in Wyoming to forgo skilled work or resettlement opportunities in Denver because "the community already had reached, or possibly passed, its saturation point with regard to the people of Japanese ancestry, and more arrivals would jeopardize the welfare of the entire Japanese-American population."[36]

In late October 1943 the danger posed by the Japanese internees in Colorado seemed obvious when federal agents questioned five Nisei women from Amache concerning their romantic relations with German POWs who worked alongside them on a farm near Trinidad. The FBI investigation continued through the winter, and on May 9, 1944, a federal grand jury indicted three California-born sisters from the group on charges of treason and conspiracy to commit treason in the escape of two German POWs from Camp Trinidad. The indictment charged that the women had given the Germans road maps, railroad timetables, clothing, flashlights, and money and had driven them eighty miles south to Wagon Mound, New Mexico. The POWs then separated from the women and traveled twenty miles on foot to Watrous, where the highway patrol arrested them. The women allegedly had placed a package containing the items in a clump of bushes near their work location. The grand jury did not charge the sisters with espionage because the maps did not have markings of military value. Pictures in the possession of one POW, taken by the women, showed them in "amorous embrace," or, as one reporter phrased it, "kissing and hugging" with the men. The Nisei professed innocence and claimed that the photographs were harmless snapshots. One sister complained, "German prisoners have been escaping right and left from the camp at Trinidad, and I suppose we are to be held responsible for those escapes too." Unable to pay the $7,500 bonds, the women waited arraignment in a Denver jail. At the arraignment the judge referred to the women as Japanese and only once as Japanese Americans.[37]

The trial received broad coverage, and Great Plains residents debated whether the Germans would tell the truth because they believed that Nazis had no moral compunction about testifying falsely. The Germans, however, testified that they wanted to escape only in order to fight the "Hitler gang," and they cast the Nisei women as their benefactors rather than as agents intent on harming the United States. Although the prosecution labeled the women "little Benedict Arnolds in skirts," the defense argued that they aided the Germans because of love. In the end the government could not provide the required two independent witnesses to their allegedly treasonous act. The court, however, convicted the women of conspiring to commit treason. On sentencing one sister received two years in prison for being the "ringleader" and the others twenty months, plus $1,000 fines. At the end of the trial the judge now referred to the Nisei as "American sisters." When government agents transported the women to a reformatory in West Virginia, the case dropped from the newspapers. For nearly a year Great Plains residents had followed it with prurient interest. Most were amazed about the titillating events that transpired in a south plains onion field.[38]

In January 1944 Nebraskans also became upset when they learned that the WRA planned to resettle a large number of Japanese from Heart Mountain to central Nebraska, primarily to provide farm labor. The report proved untrue, but it aroused a latent prejudice. Talk about relocating the Japanese after the war also worried plains residents. The Colorado legislature, although anxious to help farmers with their labor problems, contemplated a special session to consider placing a constitutional amendment prohibiting Japanese from owning property on the November ballot. Opponents feared that such restrictions would be nothing less than the "oppression of minorities," which could easily get out of control, and reasoned that the Japanese in Colorado were too few to threaten anything. This reasoning had little effect on those who argued that, if the Japanese were Americans, they should read English-language newspapers. Although the resolution passed the House, some legislators considered it "dangerous and discriminatory" and wanted no part in a "legislative lynching." Friends of the constitutional process and perhaps of the Japanese were relieved when it died in the Senate. One disappointed senator said of the Japanese, "They are pagan and cannot be assimilated because they won't accept our ways and our beliefs." In the end, however, the Colorado legislature chose reason and law over prejudice, racism, and hatred. The opponents of the Japanese, however, did not give up and continued to pursue placing a constitutional amendment on the ballot via a petition, in part because they learned that many Japanese at Amache did not plan to return to their West Coast homes when the war ended. Not long thereafter Dillon S. Meyer, the director of the WRA, announced that no more Japanese would be relocated to Colorado, and many residents breathed a sigh of relief.[39]

Adams County, Colorado, farmers and businessmen, however, worried that Japanese would remain in the Amache vicinity and buy land. In January 1944 Governor Vivian received a delegation from Brighton claiming that an "alarming" number of Japanese had been buying land in the county during the past six months and proposing a special session of the legislature to pass an antialien land law and prohibit the ownership of real estate by aliens ineligible for citizenship. With naturalization prohibited for Asians the discriminatory intent was clear. Governor Vivian considered such legislation unconstitutional and refused to call a special legislative session. On February 7, 1944, however, the Colorado House established the Constitutional Amendment Committee, which submitted the Anti-Alien Land Law Amendment for an October 29 election. In a vote of 184,458–168,865 the amendment failed, primarily because the majority of voting Coloradans considered it a racist action that violated the American sanctity of property and because they realized that the denial of property rights to the Japanese could lead to the denial of property rights to other ethnic or racial groups in the state.[40]

Plains residents who feared the permanent settlement of relocated Japanese learned in May 1944 that 2,507 Nisei who had left the relocation centers had settled in Colorado while 385 selected Wyoming and 293 Montana as their new homes. Most of the Japanese located in plains cities such as Denver, Pueblo, Billings, Casper, and Cheyenne. This new form of resettlement continued to arouse hatred against the Japanese and spur arguments that they should be denied the right to own property. Coloradoans particularly feared Japanese labor. The Colorado Chamber of Commerce responded, asking the War Department to send the Japanese back to the West Coast because the danger of an invasion had ended.[41]

On December 18, 1944, Great Plains residents learned that the War Department would permit the Japanese evacuees to return home after January 1, citing favorable progress in the Pacific Theater as well as other developments. Westerners worried about the ramifications of the new policy, but many Great Plains residents hoped that the Japanese would leave the region. At Amache approximately 6,000 Japanese remained out of a population of 7,986 in Colorado. Fifty-six Japanese families sent from Amache lived in Sidney, Nebraska, and the men and women worked at the U.S. Army's Sioux Ordnance Depot. The Japanese American Citizens League of Colorado, however, expected most of the evacuees to remain in the state because they had lost their homes, businesses, and other property in California, Oregon, and Washington. In February 1945 some North Dakotans were surprised at the arrival of 650 Japanese at Fort Lincoln. These Japanese had been transferred from the internment camp at Tule Lake in California. By March WRA officials believed that most of the Japanese at Amache would leave Colorado for jobs out of the state and the region because they would have better employment opportunities there. The Japanese who elected to remain in the Great Plains states included 374 in Montana, 502 in Nebraska, 13 in North Dakota, 28 in South Dakota, 256 in Wyoming, and 2,769 in Colorado. Denver became a magnet for many, along with Chicago, Cleveland, Salt Lake City, and St. Louis. Anti-Japanese sentiment remained high on the Great Plains, and WRA plans to close the relocation camps by the end of the year contributed to the feeling of ill will against any Japanese who might choose to stay.[42]

In April 1945 residents of Shelton, Nebraska, angrily shouted their displeasure at WRA officials in a town meeting. The government wanted to place Nisei families in Shelton to work on the irrigated farms in the area. Residents feared the importation of a "colony." Harlie Simmons, the protest leader, told a WRA supervisor that the federal government was "wrong in pushing Japs all over the United States and taking away the rights for which we are fighting." Noah Dean, a local farmer, asked the WRA officials, "If you were living out here [Buffalo City] where the Japs are working what would your attitude be?" One farmer attempted to avoid being blamed for employing Japanese, saying, "These people came here the same as any other people, and I was glad to get them. I spent days trying to get someone else and couldn't." He also reported that the Nisei were "clean and self-depriving" and that they were not "aggressive." Given the hostility toward the Japanese Americans at the town meeting, a spokesperson for the Nisei agricultural workers said that they had no plans to found a Japanese colony there and that they would move away if the residents of Shelton insisted. With the war relocation camps at Amache and Heart Mountain scheduled to close on October 15, many Great Plains residents feared that the ten thousand Japanese from these camps, who would be free to go anywhere in the United States, would in some manner descend on their communities.[43]

Fear of the Japanese quickly dissipated when those at Amache and Heart Mountain who did not return to the West Coast chose other locations than plains communities for their new homes. The closings of both camps passed almost unnoticed. Amache and Heart Mountain became virtual ghost towns while officials decided how best to sell and remove the buildings and other remaining property. At the same time, on Christmas Day 360 Japanese aliens whom government officials considered to be "trouble makers" also left the detention camp at Fort Lincoln via train bound for Portland and repatriation to Japan. The 150 Nisei and 200 German aliens who remained awaited an uncertain future.[44]

Reports of more than thirty Japanese balloons carrying incendiary bombs over Colorado, Kansas, Nebraska, and North and South Dakota had contributed to ongoing mistrust, particularly when rumors spread that the Japanese were testing balloon bombs for bacterial warfare against humans, crops, and livestock. The Japanese launched a balloon campaign because they could not reach the United States with conventional means of transportation. Residents learned that wind patterns made the northern plains most susceptible to attack, although balloon bombs let aloft from southern Japan could strike the central plains, which made the exclusion or removal of the Nisei all the more sensible to Kansans. The thirty-foot-wide hydrogen balloons carried incendiary bombs that the Japanese hoped would create fear and lower morale where they fell. The Japanese sent ninety-three hundred balloons aloft between November 3, 1944, and April 20, 1945. Few reached the Great Plains. Two balloons flew over Denver, and one passed above Fort Collins, but the seventy-pound payloads drifted eastward without causing harm. In February 1945 a balloon landed in a field near Ashley, North Dakota. Soon thereafter an FBI agent collected it for examination by military authorities.

Another balloon dropped without incident near Warsaw. Other balloons descended harmlessly in South Dakota, although one exploded in the sky near Custer. In Kansas a farmer near Bigelow found one in a tree and hauled it to the local post office, thinking it was a weather balloon.[45]

Before World War II ended Nisei college students also experienced welcome and rejection, and Lincoln and Wichita provided examples of each experience. After Pearl Harbor most public universities were unwilling to enroll Japanese Americans, but the University of Nebraska became an exception. In 1940 Nebraska had a Japanese population of 480. Most of the adults worked in the Panhandle's sugar beet fields. During the fall semester before Pearl Harbor eleven Nisei students attended the University of Nebraska. Two additional students joined the university during the "voluntary relocation" period that ended in March 1942. Later that month university officials decided to accept Japanese students who had been cleared by the FBI, met academic standards, professed loyalty, and provided evidence of sufficient financial resources. In Lincoln the Japanese Student Relocation Council met these students on arrival and helped them locate housing.[46]

By December 1942 approximately sixty Nisei attended the University of Nebraska. George W. Rosenlof, the university's registrar, considered them "fine quality young people." At the university the Nisei by their own account received fair and kind treatment, except regarding housing assignments. The housing authorities segregated the Nisei women in the dormitories, and in 1944 the board of regents sanctioned this unofficial policy to avoid "interracial agitation or interracial questions whenever possible." In order to enforce this policy the university identified one dormitory as an international house where it boarded non-Caucasian women—Japanese, African American, and Puerto Rican. For their part the Japanese students attempted to avoid situations of "high social visibility." One student remarked, "All of us have tried to avoid being seen in conspicuous groups and have tried to spread out as much as possible." The American Legion in Nebraska, however, vigorously opposed the admission of Nisei students to the university and passed resolutions calling on the federal government to send all Japanese Americans to concentration camps. Others voiced similar opposition, but they remained a minority. Most of the Nebraskans who paid attention to the school issue took a live-and-let-live attitude, which might be explained, in part, by the large ethnic population in the state, some of whom experienced discrimination during World War I. Japanese American college students considered their education a means to enter mainstream American life and, thereby, minimize discrimination and prejudice. The attrition rate, however, proved high. At Nebraska Wesleyan only ten of twenty-six Japanese Americans finished their degrees, in part because of "horizontal mobility." After the Japanese American students learned their options they frequently transferred to other public intuitions where programs of study more closely matched their interests.[47]

Whatever the reasons for the relatively good treatment of Nisei students at the University of Nebraska, many Kansans projected a hostile attitude toward the admission of Nisei to their colleges and universities. In February 1943 Russell E. McClure, the city manager of Wichita, informed the WRA that Japanese American students should not be relocated to Wichita because they would threaten the city's war industries. Moreover, Wichita's population had mushroomed from 115,000 to 225,000 since 1940, and the city struggled to provide services, including police protection, as it was. The city manger believed that, if Japanese students arrived, trouble would result. In late November 1943, however, McClure learned of the admission of two Nisei to Friends University in Wichita, and he wanted Governor Schoeppel to remove them because their presence had not been approved by the community, that is, the city government. McClure contended, "Since it is the responsibility of the municipal officials to provide for the safety of the citizens of this community, it is our belief that it is unwise to increase our present hazards by the relocation of Japanese to this area." He also did not believe that the Nisei students could be protected because "our citizens will not accept the Japanese and trouble will result." Governor Schoeppel blamed their presence on the WRA, which had placed them at the university on its own authority and without consulting him. The State Board of

Education supported McClure by closing the public schools to any Japanese arrivals. Wichita Municipal University, now Wichita State University, also refused admittance to Japanese evacuees. Fear and ignorance reigned supreme.[48]

With the initial arrival of several hundred Japanese at Fort Lincoln some Great Plains residents saw opportunity, not danger. Quickly, the projected shortage of agricultural labor encouraged many sugar beet growers to inquire about hiring the evacuees to work in South Dakota and Montana. Sugar beet farmers were particularly interested because they learned that the Japanese internees would be wards of the state and that federal officials would supervise them for the duration of the war. Cheap labor that brought with it few responsibilities appealed to these farmers, and the arrival of the Japanese appeared as an opportunity that should not be lost. Similarly, in Nebraska by May 1942 agricultural workers were "steadily seeping away to defense industries." Sugar beet farmers in the North Platte River valley could not employ sufficient Mexican American and Mexican labor, and Governor Griswold welcomed Japanese workers from the relocation centers. But he wanted them isolated and segregated in camps and kept under armed guard to prevent them from harming local residents. Other Nebraskans agreed. C. W. Murphy of York wrote to the governor, saying, "We have no industries in this state that will take care of that class of people and in a few years we will have the same trouble California is now having." If Japanese moved to Nebraska for work, Murphy believed, "they will have to be watched all the time and just think what it would be after years having our children grow up and go to school with that class of children." Griswold also believed that the Japanese "might bring a lot of trouble to the state if they are permitted to enter and be scattered over the farming territory." Even so, by September some one thousand Japanese had volunteered for the sugar beet and potato harvest in Scottsbluff, Morrill, and Sioux counties in Nebraska, but at Governor Griswold's insistence they awaited clearance by army intelligence officers. By November Nebraska farmers were lauding Japanese workers and requested their continued employment through the winter.[49]

In North Dakota a desperate need for farm labor did not overcome racism and efforts to support the hiring of union workers for the agricultural labor force. W. W. Murray, the president of the North Dakota Federation of Labor, rejected the "import of prison labor of various sorts" and adamantly opposed the use of Japanese internees. In June 1942 he noted that the introduction of "Jap labor" into competition with free American labor was a "dangerous step." He opposed the importation of Japanese workers "under any circumstances which will place them in competition with our own laborers." Not only would Japanese workers compete with North Dakotans for farm labor jobs, but also, and more important, he argued, "The possibility that many of these people, if they are brought in now, may stay after the war is over, and the problems which would surely arise in their contacts with our own people [would] far outweigh any benefits which might result."[50]

In Montana, however, 138 Japanese evacuees worked in the sugar beet fields near Chinook and Townsend, with more reported on the way to help with the thinning and cultivating. In Oklahoma one truck farmer in the Washita Valley also announced that he was so desperate for help that he would employ a "right-minded Jap family" if the government had any in his vicinity. At the same time sugar beet farmers near Worland, Wyoming, voted unanimously to accept Japanese labor if it became available. Wyoming farmers were not torn about the use of Japanese agricultural workers because the sugar beet economy could not be maintained without field-workers. By June 1942 Wyoming residents had learned that the federal government intended to "transplant" a large number of Japanese to an internment camp in the Rockies west of Cody and that they could be used for labor in the sugar beet fields down on the plains. Wyoming residents also believed that the Japanese men could dig irrigation canals and conduct other farmwork, and, in the words of one contemporary, "transform the barren plains country into a rich agricultural section." By August farmers in the Lucerne area had contacted their county agent to arrange for Japanese workers to help with the sugar beet harvest. In Colorado farmers also anticipated employing Japanese workers on completion of the relocation center near Granada.[51]

By mid-October Japanese and Mexican workers had harvested most of Colorado's potatoes and moved to the sugar beet fields. Of the 1,260 Japanese workers placed on farms in Colorado, all but 180 harvested sugar beets. Although only a small percentage of the nearly 7,500 men, women, and children at Amache were capable of farmwork, Colorado's farmers considered them good laborers who did not cause trouble. Many farmers expressed an interest in keeping the Japanese as "permanent workers" by special arrangement with the WRA. They also paid farmworkers, including the Japanese, $52.75 per month with board or $81.00 per month without it, while the daily rates were $3.55 and $4.30 with and without board, respectively, for the highest farm wages in Colorado since 1920.[52]

Farmers in the Arkansas River valley in western Kansas, who could not hire enough workers for the sugar beet and onion fields, also increasingly believed that the Japanese could solve their farm labor problem. Still, others considered it "an insult to the people" of Kansas to bring Japanese Americans to the state. Ultimately, Governor Schoeppel approved the use of Japanese internees from Colorado for agricultural labor, provided that they were cleared by the FBI. Schoeppel told Kansans, "Only those [Japanese] who are found satisfactory and dependable will be released from the internment camp. They will be principally American born Japanese." Yet one Kansas farmer expressed the fear of many to Governor Schoeppel, saying, "I have fought for years to keep bind-weeds and other noxious weeds eradicated and these Japs would likely do much damage." The evacuees were, then, for some Kansans as noxious as weeds and potentially dangerous saboteurs. A year later the Douglas County Board of Commissioners wrote Governor Schoeppel, saying that three "Jap families" had moved into Lawrence, a town that had sent approximately twenty-five hundred men and women to the armed services. According to them, "Giving jobs to Japs who became permanent citizens of this community when those jobs should be protected and saved for our boys and girls when they come back does not appeal to our sense of justice."[53]

Another Kansan worried, "Our machinery would not be safe with them as they could easily injure them with sand, dirt, and bolts."

By late March 1943 farmers and officials at the Garden City Sugar Company believed that they would have difficulty recruiting Japanese workers because the Japanese considered the bathing and toilet facilities on southwestern Kansas farms unsatisfactory. Governor Schoeppel responded to the news with disgust, observing that the WRA appeared more interested in meeting the needs of the Japanese than those of the people of the United States, who made the country and who willingly paid taxes to help bring the war to a successful conclusion. Others, particularly those who had sons in the military, did not want to find themselves working alongside any Nisei if they were relocated to their community. In May Roy E. Dillard, the manager of the Country Club Guernsey Dairy in Salina, inquired about the possibility of acquiring Japanese workers from Amache in southeastern Colorado. He also noted, "We are told the Japs in this camp are all thoroughly American and not in the least bit foreign in their attitude, habits, or education." Governor Schoeppel's office suggested that he contact officials in Colorado. Overall, then, remarkable ignorance prevailed in Kansas about the Japanese.[54]

By spring 1943 New Mexico farmers also sought Japanese workers, but they wanted state legislation prohibiting them from leasing or buying land. Still, a rumor that the federal government might permit large numbers of Japanese to settle on fertile land below Elephant Butte Dam in Dona Ana County near Las Cruces brought a storm of protest. The county's Labor Advisory Committee expressed the hostile opinion of many residents, saying that the Japanese could not be trusted because of their ancestry, because their standard of living made them "undesirable," and because the treatment of American POWs made the thought of the relocation of any Japanese there "repulsive." The committee also asked, "If they are unsafe for the coast states, why would they be desirable for location in other parts of America?" In contrast sugar beet farmers in South Dakota eagerly sought Japanese workers, and by late July several hundred Japanese from Amache and Heart Mountain worked in the beet fields of the western part of the state, where they "proved satisfactory."[55]

The WRA required written permission for any Japanese to leave the camp compounds to work for a farmer or some other employer.

Farmers could receive Japanese workers by completing a form indicating the work involved, the duration of the job, the type of housing available, and the wages to be paid. The local office of the U.S. Employment Service received the request and sent it to the regional office of the WRA in Denver, which sent the forms to Amache and Heart Mountain with a request for volunteers. On acceptance by a Japanese worker the agreement became binding, although either the farmers or the workers could terminate it by giving five days' notice. Employing farmers agreed to provide transportation and housing and pay the prevailing local wage. State and local law enforcement officers had to promise protection and the maintenance of law and order. In 1942, when the WRA approved the use of Japanese labor on farms in Colorado, Wyoming, Montana, and Nebraska, farmers in South Dakota appealed to Governor Bushfield to reconsider his refusal to permit their hire for the autumn sugar beet harvest. Sugar beet farmers could plant unlimited acreage, and they needed workers to harvest the crop. They did not care whether the workers were Japanese so long as they did not lose the crop and the high income from wartime prices that it would earn. In the end farmers who needed stoop labor welcomed Japanese workers. Their desire for agricultural profits overcame racism in the Great Plains, at least while the Japanese labored in the fields.[56]

In the internment camps, then, the Japanese were denied freedom of movement, confined to the camp (if they did not have a work permit for off-site employment), and restricted to their residential areas within the camps after dark. Military police guarded the camp perimeters. These "guarded cities" primarily held American citizens, and Great Plains residents believed that those citizens were getting what they deserved because their ethnicity made them untrustworthy and dangerous. They believed that the internees had contributed to the war being waged against the United States in their hearts if not in actual fact, all by cultural association. Overall, the Japanese at Amache lived in purgatory, somewhere above a concentration camp and below the slums, and they existed primarily on rice, carrots, noodles, and cabbage. Although Colorado's governor had taken an enlightened position, saying, "They are loyal Americans sharing only race with the enemy," most Great Plains residents remained skeptical. They believed that the Japanese at Amache, Heart Mountain, and Fort Lincoln, as well as the workers scattered across various farms, businesses, and homes in the region, received better treatment than they deserved. Although employing farmers considered the Japanese hard and reliable workers, most plains residents were glad to see them leave. Culture and skin color perpetuated racist beliefs that would linger in the Great Plains for decades after the war ended. In the words of Kansans, "Once a Jap always a Jap."[57]

TEN | Prisoner-of-War Camps

On July 26, 1943, Jimmie Don Morris, a boy in McLean, Texas, watched with excitement and anticipation as a troop train backed onto a siding at this Panhandle station. Other town residents had gathered as well, exhibiting uncommon interest and some anxiety as the crew unhooked the cars and the engine pulled away. No friends waited to greet the passengers. Instead, armed military guards stationed themselves along the cars as an officer gave the order to disembark. The Afrika Korps had come to West Texas, not as the invincible members of Rommel's army, but as prisoners of war (POWs). Morris remembered, "They still had on their brown uniforms and most were carrying packs, canteens, and empty gun holsters. It was a strange, disturbing sight." Laura Patty Goodman remembered, "Most of McLean turned out to see the prisoners get off the train and load up in trucks. Many citizens felt an uneasiness at having these foreigners so close to their homes." But another girl recalled, "The German prisoners seemed very young and were well behaved."[1]

In Mexia, Texas, on the eastern fringe of the Great Plains, residents lined along Railroad Street to watch 3,250 German prisoners step down from the train. One resident recalled, "The line of prisoners stretched the full three miles out to the camp." The site was impressive and shocking. "Remember," he said, "that we were a town of only 6,000 people, and we had just seen our population increase by 50 percent—and they were foreigners on top of it." In 1944, after the Normandy invasion, Camp McLean received more German prisoners by train. Goodman also recalled their arrival: "They were unloaded and marched around by the cemetery, a distance of three miles or more. I had an uncanny feeling as the men marched by our house. Some of the prisoners dropped out by the side of the road to be picked up by trucks. Seems many had been sick on the train." To the north a resident near Camp Atlanta, Nebraska, recalled the arrival of Italian POWs. She remembered their walk from the train station to the camp as a "pitiful sight," with the men wearing "ragged, dingy shorts" and looking "thin and hungry."[2]

The arrival of Italian prisoners also brought fear and apprehension to the residents of Hereford in Deaf Smith County, Texas. When they arrived by train in April 1943, a nurse employed at the camp recalled, "I expected each Italian to have devil's horns and tail. I was surprised that they were just a bunch of boys the same age as myself." Later, they told her, "We're terrible fighters. We're not fighters at all, we're lovers!" She continued, "After awhile they didn't seem like prisoners." Another resident recalled, "We had a little fury in the back of our minds. We kinda hated them at first. But when you stopped to think that they were somebody's son, somebody's father, you realize they were human beings just like we were. Several of us had fought in foreign countries ourselves. That helped us to give in to the fact that they were caught up in a situation they had no control over, and they were just doing the best they could." A guard also recalled that, while he helped escort the Italian prisoners on the eight-mile hike from Summerfield to Camp Hereford, his detail was thankful that the POWs sang and seemed in good spirits as they walked along, rather than attempting to escape, because the guards did not have bullets for their guns owing to an army error when ordering supplies.[3]

Superficial observations, however, can be deceptive because the War Department designated Camp Hereford as the facility to house the most hardened, that is, ideologically committed, Fascists. Soon, Camp Hereford became the largest Italian POW installation and the only camp reserved exclusively for Italians. POW camps near Amarillo, Big Spring, Dalhart, Dumas, and Lubbock held considerably fewer Italian POWs than Camp Hereford, which accommodated

3,860, or Camp McLean, which confined 2,580. The War Department also held Italian POWs at Camp Carson, Colorado, Camp Phillips, Kansas, and Camp Douglas, Wyoming, among other sites. One German POW at Camp Trinidad, Colorado, also saw his new world through an ideological lens. He remembered, "They transported us like the lowest criminals about which they seem to have plenty of experience in this country. . . . They fear us 'Bad Nazis' so much, but this fear only fills us with pride. . . . Conditions here are indescribable and primitive . . . four of us in a room; no tables or chairs." He complained that Trinidad was "a camp for gangsters or Indians, but not for white men and captured officers." He continued, "After a victorious end of this war, retaliation will be taken."[4]

Few residents of the Great Plains imagined when the war began on December 7, 1941, that thousands of German and Italian soldiers and sailors would occupy a host of POW camps across the region. Indeed, every Great Plains state became the home for POWs; while North Dakota and Montana did not have base camps, both had temporary camps that supplied workers to nearby farmers. Along with the departure of sons and daughters for the armed forces and the construction of army and navy bases, the arrival of POWs brought the war to the Great Plains, and it changed many communities and lives for all time. Some heretofore isolated residents of the plains never lost the uncomfortable feeling caused by the location of a POW camp, often twice the size of their community, near their homes. Most residents, however, ultimately accepted a POW camp as a needed boost to the local economy and a supply source for agricultural labor. Many residents also viewed the German and Italian POWs with sympathy, and the camps would be their only contact with the military during the war.[5]

When the war began, the military had little experience handling POWs. Indeed, the army had not been responsible for large numbers of foreign POWs since the War of 1812 or for any prisoners of consequence since the Civil War. The War Department's first priority, of course, was the training of several million men and women to serve as soldiers, sailors, and pilots to provide for the national defense,

FIGURE 20. The POW camp near Concordia in Cloud County, Kansas, held German soldiers. The economic benefits to nearby communities in terms of jobs and services helped end the Great Depression and stimulated the local economy while providing agricultural labor to compensate for farmworkers who left for the military. (Kansas State Historical Society)

and it did not begin to give serious attention to POWs until September 15, 1942, when the provost marshal general submitted a plan for the construction of POW camps to the Joint Chiefs of Staff. This plan advocated the use of Civilian Conservation Corps (CCC) camps constructed as barracks during the 1930s to house POWs. It also advocated the use of military posts that had available space, such as Fort Sill, Oklahoma, Fort Riley, Kansas, and Camp Carson, Colorado, as well as fairgrounds and tent cities. Soon, the British pressed the United States to help alleviate the problem of caring for POWs after the Allied invasion of North Africa in November 1942, which produced thousands of German and Italian prisoners. Although the Geneva Convention of 1929 provided guidelines for handling POWs, the U.S. Army confronted a major organizational task in administering and operating the POW camps.[6]

The War Department was most concerned about providing security to the areas where POW camps would be located. As a result the department prohibited the location of these camps in the blackout area, called the "zone sanitare," that extended approximately 170 miles from the coastline or 150 miles from either the Canadian or the Mexican borders or near shipyards, munitions plants, or other war industries, to avoid sabotage. The Army Corps of Engineers, which had the responsibility of constructing POW camps in areas where facilities did not exist, also preferred to develop areas located two or three miles from railroads or towns. This distance would enable easy transportation and supply yet minimize the opportunities for escape and sabotage. Isolation, then, became a primary consideration in locating and the Great Plains an obvious location for POW camps. With a standard construction plan for barracks and other buildings that would house approximately three thousand prisoners on at least 350 acres, the POW camps often became larger entities than the nearby towns that served them. The camps included a firehouse, a hospital, a dentist's office, and a host of other buildings, often numbering thirty or more, as well as roads named to commemorate American military heroes such as Ulysses S. Grant, Robert E. Lee, Douglas MacArthur, Davy Crocket, and Sam Houston. The POW camps were utilitarian and spartan, but some Great Plains residents considered them too good for the enemy and sarcastically called them the "Fritz Ritz."[7]

In addition to the main POW base camps, on July 22, 1943, the War Department authorized the development of temporary "branch" camps, also called "side" or "fly" camps. Branch camps were usually designed to house approximately 250–750 prisoners assigned to work details aiding local farmers and others who needed help in the absence of an adequate labor supply. Camp Hereford, for example, served as the base camp for the Texas Panhandle, and it provided workers for branch camps at Fort Sumner and Clovis, New Mexico, as well as at the army airfields in Amarillo, Lubbock, Childress, Dalhart, Big Spring, Dumas, and McLean, where the POWs primarily provided food and laundry services and hired out as farmworkers. Branch camps could be established if a county agent and the director of the state War Manpower Commission (WMC) certified that an area needed workers, that the POWs would be paid the hourly wage prevailing in the area, and that adequate housing existed. The Fort

Meade branch camp, for example, provided agricultural labor for farmers in western South Dakota near Rapid City. At Camp Peabody, operated by Camp Concordia in Kansas, the prisoners and their guards were quartered in tents. At Hays, also administered from Concordia, the men occupied an old seed and tool house on the grounds of the state experiment station, while at Council Grove, supervised by Camp Phillips near Salina, the prisoners and guards occupied a CCC camp. The Army Service Forces administered the POW camps, with the Eighth Service Command in Dallas responsible for the southern Great Plains, the Seventh Service Command at Omaha overseeing the camps in the central and northern plains, and the Ninth Service Command in Salt Lake City administering the branch camps in Montana.[8]

By September 1943 Allied victories in North Africa produced nearly 164,000 POWs, putting great pressure on the Provost Marshal General's Office, the Corps of Engineers, and the War Department to locate suitable campsites and provide the necessary facilities for housing thousands of prisoners. In its haste the War Department often selected campsites without notifying local property owners, business leaders, or congressmen. Frequently, local residents learned about the location of a nearby POW camp by reading an announcement in the local paper. On January 7, 1943, for example, the residents of El Reno, Oklahoma, read that the army planned to establish a POW camp at Fort Reno and that local engineers and contractors would be needed for the $500,000 project. By working feverishly builders had the camp ready by early July, and the *El Reno American* announced the arrival of the "First Batch of Hun Captives." Army secrecy and imposed POW campsites were the rule, but congressmen, city officials, and business leaders, such as those at Hearne and Mexica, Texas, and Grand Forks, Fargo, and Grafton, North Dakota, also lobbied for a POW camp to help boost the economy of their locality and provide needed labor. In these cases public enthusiasm for the location of a POW base or branch camp nearby frequently reached lofty heights.[9]

In fact governors, congressmen, senators, railroads, and chambers

of commerce often lobbied the War Department for the establishment of a POW camp. The construction of POW camps meant work
for carpenters, plumbers, and electricians as well as garbage collectors, clerical workers, nurses, and firemen. The location of a camp
also guaranteed a major increase in business for real estate agents,
apartment owners, grocery stores, florists, cafés, dry cleaners, movie
theaters, and other businesses providing goods and services to camp
military personnel and their families. In autumn 1942, for example,
Trinidad, Colorado, boomed when construction began on a POW
camp. A newspaper reporter wrote, "Every hotel room, house and
apartment in Trinidad is full, every citizen who wants work has a
job and hundreds of new workers and their families have migrated
to the city." Indeed, with the federal government prepared to spend
millions of dollars on the war effort at home, POW camps meant
a significant economic boost to a community, and residents of the
Great Plains took advantage of that opportunity.[10]

The location of a POW camp also became a political consideration.
In January 1943, when Governor Lester C. Hunt learned that the
War Department planned to locate a POW camp at Douglas, Wyoming, he wrote Senator Joseph C. O'Mahoney to suggest political
significance. Hunt noted, "There may be reasons why it is to be
located at Douglas, but it occurs to me that if the camp is an asset to
a community we might well attempt to have it placed in some community where these people who are our friends would benefit." The
government, however, located the POW camp at Douglas, and Italian
prisoners arrived there in August 1943.[11]

Federal funding for the construction of POW camps, then, provided
an important economic lift for area residents by creating construction and service jobs. Although the U.S. Army Corps of Engineers
supervised the construction, civilian contractors conducted most of
the work. At Camp Hereford, for example, the Russell J. Brydan
Company of Dallas served as the major contractor for the $2 mil-
lion project, and the firm of Freeze and Nichols of Fort Worth provided the architectural services. In addition the Sherman and Erbett
Company of Fort Worth laid the water-, sewer, and gas lines, while
the American District Telegraph Company of Texas provided elec-

tric power. Similarly, the Randall Construction Company of Amarillo received the contract to build Camp McLean, while the firm of Olson-Assenmacher of Lincoln, Nebraska, offered the low bid to build Camp Concordia, and the Kansas Power Company provided the electricity. The A. G. Sherwood Construction Company of Independence, Kansas, received the contract for Camp Tonkawa, Oklahoma, while Kay Electric, the local Rural Electrification Administration cooperative at Blackwell, provided the power. Federal spending had rescued the Great Plains during the years of the Dust Bowl and Great Depression, and residents no longer had a moral compunction against participating in federal programs or accepting government money.[12]

At Camp Hereford the economic influence on the town became readily apparent when the daily workforce approached one thousand. Many workers lived in Hereford, Dimmitt, and other communities in Deaf Smith and the surrounding counties, but others came from far away, lived in the barracks, and took their meals in town at a restaurant that contracted with the Corps of Engineers for the food service. At Camp Hereford armed civilian guards provided security until the arrival of the military police on February 16, 1943. At Camp Tonkawa, located about ninety miles north of Oklahoma City, the construction crews ate at Cecil's Lunch, Botkin's Coffee Shop, and the Tonkawa Hotel Café. One resident of Tonkawa recalled, "They hired every farmer in the county that could saw a board or drive a nail. It really perked things up around here." The location of a POW camp in areas where opportunities had been few, then, offered some Great Plains residents a means to make money as well as enabling them to contribute to the war effort. Although some nearby residents worried about their safety at first, others soon resented the seemingly posh accommodations provided the POWs. Betty Stephan, a resident of Hereford, recalled, "They had it much better than we did. They had indoor plumbing, electricity in all the buildings, recreation centers, and a host of conveniences that most of the people in the surrounding area didn't have."[13]

Although the military police provided camp security as soon as possible, with the best men in the armed forces, the POW camps soon

FIGURE 21. On August 15, 1943, this contingent of military police arrived at the Tonkawa POW camp in Oklahoma. German prisoners arrived on August 30, eventually totaling nearly three thousand soldiers, mostly from the Afrika Korps. Ed Birch, a camp guard, recalled that the German cooks prepared better meals than they received at the mess hall, and the guards often exchanged clothing and other supplies for invitations to eat lunch with the prisoners. (Courtesy of Ed Birch)

gained a reputation as a dumping ground for the "superfluous," that is, physically and psychologically unfit, soldiers and "dead-end" officers judged too old or unsuitable for field commands and duty. In late February 1945 the commanding officer at Camp Carson, Colorado, complained that his guards consisted of the "usual surplus of psycho-neurotics and ill-disciplined soldiers." A month later a general POW camp inspection report charged that most enlisted guards generally were of "poor quality and not sufficiently trained for this type of duty." It continued, "The majority of them . . . are incompetent because of physical defects or mental limitations." It also noted that most camps exhibited "an unmistakable laxity in performance of duty by many of the guards." One resident of McLean, Texas, recalled, "The German POWs often showed more discipline and military bearing than the American guards." This situation remained unchanged until the end of the war because many guard units were composed of service personnel who had some disability that kept them from combat duty. The civilians at Scottsbluff, Nebraska, who worked at Camp Atlanta referred to these soldiers as "Sick, Crippled, and Useless."[14]

Overall, however, the guards, many of whom were "middle aged well seasoned men," did their duty, but often without much dedication. As a result some farmers reported that guards occasionally slept in the shade while their prisoners worked in the fields. Near Peabody, Kansas, a farmer reported that, when his POW workers saw an officer approaching, they woke their guard so that he would not get in trouble. In Texas some guards even cleaned their rifles in the presence of prisoners or let their charges handle their weapons. At Camp McLean one local resident obtained a job as a civilian guard watching prisoners chop cotton. He recalled, "I wore my regular clothes, and they gave me a rifle and one bullet. I carried the bullet in my shirt pocket under my badge. I was told that if I shot the bullet, I would have to buy the next one myself." Wayland Smith, who served as a guard at Camp Hereford, recalled (perhaps incorrectly given the hard-core Fascist reputation of the Italian prisoners), "You could have guarded them with a stick just as easy as a shotgun. They were good guys. They were our enemies, but they were good guys."[15]

At Camp Concordia, Kansas, a "Country Club" atmosphere prevailed among the American soldiers, and "the Bar Room was a much better inhabited place than the offices." In October 1943 the army replaced the commanding officer after his wife was shot in the abdomen during a party at the Officers' Club, but not before the camp became known as "the worst prisoner of war camp in the United States." In 1944, however, conditions improved, and Camp Concordia became a model POW camp, particularly for pioneering the establishment of branch camps to provide agricultural labor.[16]

Indeed, once the camps were established, the POW labor program became popular, particularly among local farmers. By mid-1942, the military and the high-paying war industries having drawn away so many workers, some employers began experiencing a labor shortage. On the Great Plains the diminishing of the manpower pool primarily affected farmers, who considered the problem "acute." The Geneva Convention of 1929 provided that POWs could be required to work by their captors, provided that they were physically fit, that they were not assigned work that was "degrading, unhealthful, or hazardous" or beyond their physical capacity, and that no project directly contributed to the war effort, such as the manufacture of munitions. But officers could not be compelled to labor, and non-commissioned officers could be forced to conduct only supervisory work, although individuals in both groups could volunteer to labor. No prisoner could be forced to work longer than civilian employees who conducted the same task. At the camps the POWs usually conducted routine maintenance and clerical tasks, for which they were paid $0.70 per day in scrip in addition to the $0.10 per day to which they were entitled no matter whether they worked or not. The prisoners used the scrip to purchase toiletries, tobacco, candy, shoe polish, and other items at the commissary. Although the rate of compensation compared favorably to an American private's monthly pay of $21.00 in 1941, it was considerably less than the $1.50 per day wage rates earned by "free" or civilian workers.[17]

The army operated on the premise that, the more POWs who worked at the camps, the more Americans who could be sent to the front. Work that contributed to the operation of the camp, such as kitchen duty and maintenance, was not paid labor, however, and the men from the lower ranks conducted it on a rotational basis. At Camp Carson, Colorado, German POWs worked in the laundry, a job for which they were paid. Although the American officer in charge reported that they did good work, he noted that they were only 90 percent as efficient as the civilian women whom they replaced. Camp work that required special skills, such as typing, bookkeeping, and plumbing, or labor contracted off-site was paid labor. At Camp Concordia German POWs also laid bricks and planted trees. They performed similar work at other bases and camps.[18]

Although the noncommissioned officers and privates could be required to work in the camps, as stipulated by the Geneva Convention, some Germans refused to do so or conducted their assigned tasks in the slowest manner possible. In October 1943 the Provost Marshal General's Office authorized camp commanders to meet refusals to work or slowdowns with a "no work, no eat" policy, which usually ended the disobedience. On June 22, 1944, for example, ninety-four Germans at Camp Worland, Wyoming, protested the absence of benches in the trucks that transported them to their work sites by holding a strike. The camp commander immediately placed the strikers on a bread-and-water diet, and the work soon resumed. Most German and Italian POW camp commanders, however, experienced little difficulty with POW workers.[19]

The wartime labor shortage particularly affected farmers and ranchers across the Great Plains. In 1943, however, when, despite government efforts to import Mexican workers, the farm labor shortage seemed desperate, thousands of POWs began to arrive, and on May 1 the War Department announced at the Agricultural Farm Labor Conference in Salt Lake City that POWs could be used to aid civilians who needed workers. Not until August, however, did the War Department and the WMC reached an agreement on the terms under which POWs could be employed. Although POWs were first obligated to provide "essential work" at military bases, any remaining free time could be used to aid civilians, but only on a voluntary basis. Prisoners who could not be fully employed at military bases formed a surplus labor pool, and they could be hired out to farmers, businesses, and industries. After Italy surrendered on September 8, 1943, however, and joined the Allies, Italian POWs were declared "co-belligerents," which removed the restrictions of the Geneva Convention regarding work. They were then organized into "Italian Service Units" and permitted to work in nonessential war industries, but they were not freed.[20]

In the beginning farmers who wanted to hire POWs had to apply to the state office of the WMC, through the local employment office, for a certification of need. After an applicant explained the nature of the work and swore that local workers could not be hired, that the use of POW labor would not lower local wages or diminish opportunities for returning servicemen and-women, that the rights of the prisoners would not be violated, and that job conditions were equivalent to those experienced by local workers, the WMC approved the certification and sent it to the regional director, who on approving the certification sent it to the regional director of the state Extension Service, who then sent it to the War Department for action, action in this case involving instructing the appropriate POW camp commander to provide the requested workers. A local extension agent then determined the number of workers needed by the applicant. The War Department also issued a contract in which the employer agreed to use POW workers only for a maximum of three months. POW workers were not "cut-rate" labor. The minimum off-camp wage was set at the local daily rate, or about $1.50 per day, but the prisoners still received only the authorized $0.80 per day in scrip or canteen coupons, although they could earn more in certain situations. The employer paid the difference to the U.S. Treasury, which credited the earnings to the POWs for collection after repatriation. County farm wage boards, however, often set wages for POWs lower than they did wages for regular hired workers, especially in Texas.[21]

Employers could deduct $0.01 per mile from the wages paid for transportation and $0.05 from the prevailing wage rate for training. Farmers paid the federal government through the county agent within ninety days of the last working day. This bureaucratic process soon proved too complicated, time-consuming, and restrictive. Numerous complaints by farmers ultimately achieved reform in March 1944, when the War Department authorized the county agent in the Extension Service to work directly with farmers to determine their needs, then notify the camp commanders several days in advance so that the appropriate number of prisoners would be ready to work when the farmers arrived to collect them.[22]

The War Department advised farmers to work alongside the POWs, give them rest breaks, perhaps a noon meal, and avoid wearing blue-colored clothing, which served as the uniform for prisoners. Technically, farmers had to contract for at least fifteen POWs because the army could not afford to provide guard details for only two or three men, although in practice many farmers employed fewer. One Kansas farmer believed that the German POWs worked better without guards. The prisoners, however, could not be worked more than ten hours per day, including travel time. As a result, POW labor could not be effectively used much beyond a thirty-mile radius, or about an hour's drive, of the camps. Some farmers who spoke fluent German, however, were removed from the list of eligible employers to avoid any possibility of collaboration.[23]

While the employment process at first proved inordinately bureaucratic and farmers complained bitterly about it, they employed many
POW workers. In December 1943, for example, farmers in Muskogee
County, Oklahoma, used POWs from nearby Camp Gruber to harvest more than four thousand acres of spinach. POWs also dug potatoes in the Texas Panhandle, blocked beets in Nebraska, shocked
wheat in Kansas, and harvested broomcorn in New Mexico. Prisoners, however, were not permitted to drive trucks or tractors or operate other machinery. This restriction prevented their most efficient
use, particularly for plowing and planting crops. Consequently, POW
labor could not be used efficiently in areas where farmers relied on
combines to harvest wheat, such as central and western Kansas, but
they were reported to have been "extremely helpful" where they
used binders to harvest the grain crop and for shocking corn and
sorghum and hauling hay. German POWs from Camp Phillips also
worked for the Shellabarger Mills in Salina, Kansas, where they
unloaded "several hundred" boxcars of grain, which helped relieve
the congestion in the railroad yards. In 1943 farmers near Deming,
Texas, also requested Italian POWs for the potato harvest because
many did not want Japanese or German POWs. Farmers near Artesia, New Mexico, however, sought German POW workers to pick
cotton, and they wanted a branch camp manned by POWs from the
Roswell base camp established nearby. In early September 150 Italian POWs from Lordsburg picked cotton near Las Cruces. Cotton
farmers anticipated employing approximately 1,500 POWs as soon
as the picking season reached "full swing." By late September Italian POWs worked in the potato and sugar beet fields near Douglas,
Wyoming.[24]

Although one reporter observed that Kansas farmers were pleased
with the German POWs and had "an amazing faith in them," he
was uncertain about their good behavior and willingness to help
farmers. He suspected that they considered "American kindness and
compassion" signs of weakness and that they were working while
they waited for "Hitler and his hordes" to rescue them. If Nebraska
farmers worried about being duped, they gave no indication. Instead, they welcomed some two thousand Italian POWs to pick po-

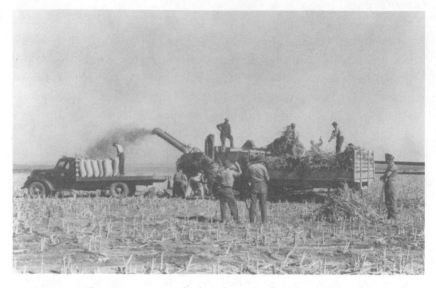

FIGURE 22. German POWs worked at the agricultural experiment station in Hays, Kansas. These POWs are feeding sheaves of milo into a threshing machine and bagging the grain, ca. 1943. (Kansas State Historical Society)

tatoes and top sugar beets during autumn 1943. These POWs picked from fifty to one hundred bushels of potatoes and topped four or five tons of sugar beets per man in six or seven hours, such work falling "considerably short of experienced free [i.e., non-POW] labor," but Nebraska farmers were glad for their help. These farmers also used POW labor to pick and detassel corn, haul hay and manure, harvest apples, cut weeds, fill silos, and perform other jobs. The POWs picked enough corn and cut sufficient ensilage to feed as many as eight hundred beef cattle during the coming winter in addition to repairing fences and spreading fertilizer. With the average age of the German POWs in Kansas reported to be twenty-four, farmers considered them physically fit for "long hours at hard tasks." By the end of the year the WMC considered the use of POW agricultural labor a success, citing Kansas and Nebraska as examples. From Camp Phillips and the branch camp at Council Grove, POWs harvested 4,000 bushels of apples, 7,500 bags of potatoes, 4,000 tons of ensilage, 2,000 tons of hay, and 485 bushels of corn for Kansas farmers.[25]

West Texas farmers particularly welcomed Italian POW labor. Enormous demand and high wartime prices encouraged farmers to produce bumper crops. In Texas, however, the farm labor shortage proved particularly acute not only because the military and the wartime industries took young men but also because Mexican and Latino workers went elsewhere, often to the sugar beet fields in Colorado, Wyoming, and Nebraska, where they received higher pay and better treatment. Consequently, farmers in West Texas, who raised potatoes, onions, carrots, and other root crops, saw Italian POWs as the solution to their labor problem, even a "God-send," although the Italians had a tendency to shout "viva Mussolini" on their way to the fields. Even so, approximately thirty-five hundred POWs conducted agricultural labor in twenty-nine Texas counties alone in 1943. A year later, Italian POWs worked more than three thousand hours during the fall harvest for John Paetzold near Hereford, and they picked cotton, baled hay, gathered pecans, husked corn, cleared land, and cut cordwood.[26]

In the autumn of 1943 Italian POWs arrived in Colorado from base camps in Douglas, Wyoming, and Scottsbluff, Nebraska, to work as agricultural laborers out of branch camps at Greeley, Fort Lupton, Brush, and Loveland. Sugar beet and potato farmers near Greeley thought that the Italians arrived in the "nick of time." German prisoners from Camp Carson near Colorado Springs also arrived at branch camps near Ault and Eaton. During the next three years more than three thousand POWs worked on farms within a hundred-mile radius of Greeley. There, Colorado farmers organized associations that contracted with the army to secure POW workers to top sugar beets. Many of these farmers reported—with considerable amusement—that the Italians often shouted "Mussolini" when their knives severed the beet from the stem. In Greeley the Great Western Sugar Company also contracted with the army for POW workers, dispersing them to farmers under contract to the company. The farmers then paid the Great Western the contract price for harvest workers, and, in turn, the company paid the federal government. The Great Western also helped provide living quarters by aiding the restoration of the unused Horace Mann Elementary School. While the POWs worked in the area sugar beet fields, they also lived in warehouses, high school gymnasiums, and National Guard armories. A host of other Colorado towns had branch camps to aid the sugar beet harvest, and two camps to aid farmers who raised broomcorn were established at Walsh and Elkhart, Kansas.[27]

In Wyoming Italian POWs also helped harvest sugar beets at Pine Bluffs, Albin, Veteran, and Worland in fall 1943. By October the Italians were also harvesting beans and potatoes and baling hay. At Veteran the Goshen County Beet Growers Association contracted for 270 POWs. After the fall harvest Governor Lester C. Hunt spoke for many Wyoming farmers when he wrote about the POW laborers, "I found them working diligently, in a cheerful frame of mind, and they were literally a godsend to the farmers of Goshen County. The agricultural crops of that county are the largest of any county and could not have been harvested had it not been for the labor of these prisoners." The Western South Dakota Farm Labor Association at Belle Fourche also organized sugar beet growers to seek POW labor and the establishment of a branch camp at the former CCC camp at Fort Meade.[28]

Among the German-Russian population in Colorado, particularly in the Ault and Eaton areas north of Greeley, residents met the German POWs with considerable goodwill, not only because of their mutual heritage, but also because local farmers needed workers. The editor of the *Eaton Herald*, however, criticized residents for "lunching" and "coddling" the prisoners, whom he called "Hitler's children." He considered such favorable treatment, "not only undesirable, but detrimental to the morale of our servicemen . . . as well as being the means of encouraging these self-styled German supermen in the belief that overtures of kindness or curiosity, is taken as a sign of inferiority and weakness for the German war machine. . . . Brutality, lust for power and world domination is the code of the Nazi." Despite this admonishment the farmers near Ault and Eaton were glad to have the POW workers, and their wives prepared hearty noon meals for them. In 1944 German POWs helped 291 farmers near these communities harvest crops valued at $712,208 that otherwise might have been lost. Most POWs preferred to work for area farmers because it helped ease their boredom and made time go faster as well as providing the opportunity to earn extra income and perhaps a home-cooked meal. In October 1943 E. E. White, a farmer near Council Grove, Kansas, reported that his wife fed his POW workers every day with "chicken, pie, cake, and stuff like that." As a result he had good, if not enthusiastic, workers.[29]

Great Plains farm families quickly sympathized with the plight of these young men, considered them "real nice," and essentially treated them like local hired workers. Ann Payton Connelly, who worked as a nurse at Camp Hereford, recalled that the Italian POWs were a "God-send to the farmers . . . because we were right then in the middle of a war without enough hands to bring in the crops. And there never was any hint of trying to escape. . . . After a while they didn't even seem like prisoners." One Kansan reflected that the German POWs had to join the army "whether they wanted to or not, just like . . . our boys." And a Kansas ranch woman revealed her sympathy when she said, "I really didn't feel that they were Nazis, but just young men fighting for their country." In September 1944 an army representative admonished the farm women near Peabody, Kansas, to stop mending the prisoners' clothing, driving them to town, and baking them cakes and cookies.[30]

Although the prisoners often worked on many different farms, the men who had been in the camps the longest knew the farmers who provided the best working conditions, and they often asked to be sent to their farms. Near the end of the war one newly arrived German POW at Camp Veteran, Wyoming, found that getting work on a "good farm" proved "very difficult" because seniority in captivity determined who got those jobs. Anglo residents of the Great Plains often treated the POWs better than they did local or itinerant Mexican American farmworkers. At Camp Roswell, New Mexico, for example, one soldier reported, "There was a plumber who came to work in the camp. His name was Gutierrez, and he was Mexican. . . . He was a very nice guy. When he went to the barbershop, he stood in the corner, he did not move, and, as he was 'colored,' he had to wait until all the Whites were done." In Colorado farm women near Greeley, Eaton, and Ault fed the German POWs fried chicken and beer for their midday meals. Imported Mexican workers in the sugar beet fields did not receive this gesture of kindness or special treatment. When, however, the German workers demanded "beer and snacks between meals," the local farmers stopped feeding them.[31]

Even though the language barrier created some problems, many German and Italian prisoners came from rural backgrounds and understood the essential principles of their assigned tasks after a demonstration by the farmer to whom they had been assigned. Still, cultural differences remained, and one farmer no doubt spoke for many cotton farmers in West Texas and Oklahoma when he said that the German POWs did not know "a stalk of cotton from a goddamn cocklebur." Without experience in the cotton fields most German POWs did not pick the daily rate of two hundred pounds expected of "free" labor, averaging only approximately eighty pounds per day. Farmers near Carlsbad, New Mexico, and Mexia, Texas, complained that they picked only sixty to seventy pounds per day, but they harvested a crop that otherwise would have rotted in the fields. Similar complaints prompted the army to permit farmers to scale down wages between 50 and 75 percent for prisoners who lacked the skill or the incentive to pick the expected amount of cotton. Several farmers in Colorado also complained that their German workers loafed on the job and that some took a "sullen attitude." These farmers expected the POWs to block and thin half an acre of sugar beets per day, but they averaged only a quarter. Kansas farmers considered only 70 percent of the Germans to be good workers and the other 30 percent to be "indifferent." In November 1943 one Wyoming farmer, while appreciative of the work provided by a dozen Italians, believed that the prisoners were only about 50 percent as efficient as experienced sugar beet harvesters.[32]

In retrospect no one can say precisely how much POW labor contributed to the agricultural economy of the Great Plains. One farmer who raised irrigated cotton with her husband near Artesia, New Mexico, reflected about the German prisoners who worked on their farm, saying, "The POWs were not enthusiastic pickers, but the 1943 cotton harvest depended almost solely on them." In Wyoming's Goshen Irrigation District Italian POWs from the CCC camp at Veteran harvested 180,000 bushels of potatoes and topped 500 tons of sugar beets. The POWs had also harvested beans, baled hay, and piled beet tops for livestock feed. A year later, in July 1944, Wyoming's Governor, Lester Hunt, contended that the POW camp at Douglas provided "badly needed" labor in all ranch areas. A cattleman near McAlester, Oklahoma, agreed. After he lost his hired workers to better-paying jobs in the war industries, he used forty POWs to help operate his three thousand acres. He reflected, "They been our salvation."[33]

Local farmers never had enough work to employ the prisoners year-round, but from spring to autumn they could never hire enough POWs to compensate for their labor shortages. In June 1944 the demand for POW agricultural labor in the central and northern Great Plains ran six to seven times the manpower available. By June 1945, for example, virtually all the sugar beet growers near Bridgeport, Nebraska, had signed contracts for POW labor from the branch camp established at the fairgrounds. Indeed, in 1945 demand for POW agricultural labor exceeded supply. Certainly, the POWs helped the harvests at crucial times, but Texas Panhandle farmers preferred Mexican American migrants because they worked harder. Local merchants also preferred migrant workers because they earned $12 to $18 per day and spent much of what they earned in the nearby town. The POWs received scrip that could only be exchanged for goods at the camp commissary. Still, by spring 1944 farmers in New Mexico had of necessity come to rely heavily on POW labor. When the state received authorization to employ only two thousand of the sixty-five hundred prisoners that the Extension Service requested, A. E. Triviz, the state supervisor of the Emergency Farm Labor Program, expressed "serious disappointment." In Texas, however, the Extension Service indicated the mixed feelings of many farmers who used POW labor when it reported, "Although their services were not satisfactory in all instances they made a very definite contribution to the relief of the farm labor shortage."[34]

Still, POWs did not have the incentive to work as hard as regular hired workers did. In New Mexico two farmers near Roswell groused that the 150 German POWs whom they employed "weren't really satisfactory labor, but were a whole lot better than nothing." But "it took a big bunch to get anything done." This complaint was well-founded. The German prisoners, who worked primarily in New Mexico's cotton fields, disliked the stoop labor of picking and often "wished all the cotton fields of the area to the devil." Even though the army prepared a booklet entitled *How Cotton Must Be Picked*, German POWs proved reluctant learners. The army, however, contended that their low productivity resulted from poor supervision.[35]

Similarly, a farmer near Ballentine, Montana, who shared a twenty-man crew of German prisoners with his neighbors recalled, "A lot of them didn't even know what a beet was." As a result the Montana Extension Service, along with the sugar companies, organized training programs to teach sugar beet farmers about the best methods for training the POWs for work in the sugar beet fields. In 1945 the Extension Service also published a pamphlet in German entitled *Pulling, Piling, Topping, and Loading Sugar Beets*. One Texas farmer no doubt spoke for many regarding the use of POW workers when he wrote, "I damn sure didn't get them because I wanted to. I just got them because I couldn't do no better."[36]

Overall, the Germans seemed to prefer working to merely serving time. Working also helped them escape harassment by Nazi ideologues. Some Nebraskans, however, remembered Italian POWs stereotypically as "fun-loving and somewhat lazy" and as frequently objecting to farm labor because they were city men. Many Great Plains farmers, however, failed to realize that POW workers had little or no experience at their assigned tasks and no incentive to be efficient or productive. They could earn only $0.80 per day, payable in scrip, and many worked only to avoid punishment for refusing to work or to escape the boredom of camp life. Even so, POW agricultural labor proved essential in many areas of the Great Plains, and farmers used POW workers more than any other employers did.[37]

Not all contracted POW labor, however, worked on farms. In Oklahoma some POWs operated an ice plant for the Santa Fe Railroad. Dumas, Texas, used prisoners for street cleaning and city maintenance projects, but most worked at the smelter of the American Zinc Company. Grain companies employed POW workers to help pour concrete for new elevators, such as those at Pitman, Dimmitt, and Tulia, Texas. In Summerfield, Texas, the Baptist Church used Italian POWs on loan from a farmer for a basement and roofing project. POWs planted shrubs on the state fairgrounds in Albuquerque, and they tended the greens and fairways of the city golf course in Santa

Fe. German POWs from Camp Huntsville, Texas, also established a temporary camp near Madill, Oklahoma, where they, along with others POWs from Camp Tishomingo, Oklahoma, cleared land for the Denison reservoir.[38]

Labor unions, however, often protested the use of POW workers if they competed for union jobs. On April 7, 1944, the Omaha Central Labor Union sent a resolution to the area, regional, and national offices of the WMC in which its members strongly opposed the use of POW labor in the area. The union argued that non-POW labor remained available and that employers refused to hire "colored labor" in violation of Executive Order 8802. In early November Local 120 of the United Packing House Workers of America (UPWA) demanded that POW workers be removed from the Cold Storage Company, calling their presence "intolerable." Other UPWA locals adopted resolutions of support. The WMC then withdrew the plant's certification for POW workers to prevent further difficulty with the union, and the company began a recruiting drive for local workers, threatening, however, to apply for POW labor again if it failed. The New Mexico Council of Carpenters also opposed the use of POW workers.[39]

Security for POW workers proved lax because it was not needed. The prisoners had little reason to escape because they had nowhere to go and Great Plains residents remained unsympathetic to such efforts. Usually, one guard accompanied every ten prisoners to a nearby farm. Escapes were so infrequent that German POWs assigned to farmers near Fort Riley, Kansas, were not guarded. Instead, the army reported, "Soldiers in cars patrol the general area." If a prisoner disappeared, the army instructed the farmer to continue working with the remaining prisoners but to notify the prison camp so that the guards could begin looking for the escapee. The army called this the "perimeter" system and contended that any escapee could be easily caught and that the POWs worked harder if they were unguarded. Warren Prautzsch, a German POW at Scottsbluff, Nebraska, remembered, "Discipline at the branch camp was pretty loose." Harold Lewis, the mayor of Newton, Kansas, worried that POWs who worked beyond the camps without adequate guards in-

FIGURE 23. These German POWs marched in rank and under guard as they arrived at Fort Robinson, Nebraska. Although tensions existed in the barracks among Nazi and anti-Nazi Germans, local residents considered them all harmless young men who served their country and who provided essential agricultural labor for area farmers. (Nebraska State Historical Society, RG 2725-13)

vited an attack by some "hot-headed person." He asked Governor Schoeppel to arrange adequate protection to prevent an "invitation to riots, sabotage, and other acts of lawlessness." Fortunately, no Kansan seems to have attempted to inflict retribution on any of the POWs who worked in the area.[40]

Although POWs had little hope of returning to Europe after escaping, some tried. They did so, no doubt, because they considered it their duty as well as to flee boredom or intimidation by Nazi or Fascist ideologues. Terror behind the barbed wire probably encouraged escapes as much as it did off-base work. The Seventh Service Command also adopted the policy of "calculated risk," by which it accepted the possibility of a few escapes in order to decrease the number of guards needed. At Camp Trinidad, Colorado, and Camp Alva, Oklahoma, German prisoners occasionally obtained, by means that remain unclear, clothing that tailors among them sewed and chemists dyed to resemble American army uniforms. Prisoners who had traveled or lived in the United States instructed those who planned to escape in American slang. One German used these props to impersonate an American lieutenant and literally walked out the main gate at Camp Trinidad. Captured soon thereafter, he was given the traditional punishment for escaping—thirty days in jail on a diet of bread and water. He recalled, "The camp prison was not too unkind. Most of the time, the doors of the cells were left open; we walked around the interior of the prison and chatted. The guards were rather accommodating." After spending a total of 111 days in the Camp Trinidad jail for several escape attempts, he was transferred to Alva, Oklahoma. There, he again escaped, wearing a newly tailored American suit. After the Border Patrol captured him near the Rio Grande River, he spent another thirty days in the jail at Camp Alva. This light punishment—devised because POW spokesmen regularly reported on their condition to the International Committee of the Red Cross, which conveyed that information to the German government—was designed to help protect American POWs in Germany from harsh treatment or even summary execution for attempting to escape. With more than ninety thousand Americans being held prisoner in Germany, the War Department scrupulously honored and enforced the Geneva Convention, providing fair, even lenient, treatment of German POWs, and even protecting them from "acts of violence, insults, and public curiosity."[41]

In order to discourage prisoners from attempting to escape, the camps had a caution line that ran inside the stockade fence. Any prisoner who crossed that line could be shot, although the guards had orders to shout *halt* at least three times before shooting. On October 15, 1943, a guard shot a German POW at Camp Concordia, Kansas, after the prisoner chased a soccer ball across a two-and-a-half-foot fence that served as the caution line. During the course of the soccer game the guards had warned the prisoners several times to keep the ball inside the fence. When Adolph Huebner defiantly kicked the ball across the fence and taunted the guard as he ran to retrieve it, he was shot in the head. In New Mexico a rancher near Artesia shot and killed a German escapee from Camp Roswell and wounded another when he discovered them trying to

start his truck late one night. Two other POWs were also killed trying to escape from Camp Roswell. At Camp Hereford the Italians
dug an eight-foot-deep tunnel that extended five hundred feet into a
field. The guards discovered it, however, after someone noticed that
the prisoners' gardens and volleyball courts had risen noticeably
as a result of newly deposited soil. The largest escape from a POW
camp on the Great Plains, however, came during the early-morning
hours of March 30, 1944, when twelve Germans fled from Camp
Barkeley near Abilene, Texas. The prisoners used a sixty-foot tunnel to avoid the guards and the wire, but all had been recaptured by
April 3. Because escapes from the POW camps on the Great Plains
occurred infrequently, the local press at first treated them with considerable sensationalism. In November 1943 the *Colorado Springs
Gazette and Telegraph* urged readers to help prevent POW escapes
by taking "extra care not to leave explosives in exposed or unguarded places." Most escaped prisoners were soon captured or
returned voluntarily, usually in a few days or weeks, after they got
cold or hungry, and most residents eventually paid little attention to
escapes. No escaped prisoners were linked to sabotage or espionage
activities.[42]

Most German and Italian POWs did not try to escape because
they were well fed and safe from the fighting. For them the war was
over, and they only awaited peace and repatriation. Any danger that
they encountered came from hard-core Nazis and Fascists intent on
forcing ideological discipline in the camps. Nationwide, only 1,073
German prisoners escaped between November 1942 and February
1945. Only a few dozen fled the POW camps in the Great Plains,
and authorities captured all of them relatively quickly. In the Great
Plains distance and its ally hunger made successful escapes nearly
impossible. One German prisoner at Camp Atlanta, Nebraska, recalled that the country seemed "so wide, so big." Colonel Daniel B.
Byrd, who supervised the POW camps for the Eighth Service Command, contended the POWs sometimes attempted to escape because
in some "vague, mysterious way" they thought they could get back
to Germany, because they had a "strong curiosity" to see the country beyond the barbed wire, or because they simply wanted their

freedom. In the end, he observed, "Nazis are stumped by the great distances in the United States and in the southwest."[43]

Although most German POWs were not political ideologues, residents of the Great Plains customarily referred to them as "Nazis." While the German prisoners were invariably nationalists, they differed considerably in their degree of commitment to Fascism and Adolph Hitler's National Socialist German Workers Party. Even so, in February 1943 the War Department ordered camp commanders to segregate "rabid Nazis" from the anti-Nazis to facilitate a reeducation program designed to enhance the creation of a democratic political system in Germany at the end of the war as well as prevent retaliation against both the less than true believers in the camps and their families back home. This was no easy task because Nazi and Fascist officers soon gained control of the camps and instilled discipline and order, which both they and the camp commanders wanted—the Nazis to maintain control over the camps, the commanders to ensure a peaceful, orderly camp. Although camp commanders appreciated a well-run camp that did not cause trouble, the fanatical Nazi and Fascist prisoners coerced the others to follow the party line. Those who questioned the German and Italian war effort or party ideology suffered intimidation, accusations of "disloyalty," and beatings. In June 1944 the Nazis at Camp Mexia, Texas, placed placards in the barracks warning: "He who is not against the Americans will be punished." At Camp Scottsbluff, Nebraska, Nazis beat a fellow prisoner who wrote a letter to his father who lived in the United States because they judged his father "not a good Nazi."[44]

Nazi "vigilantes" even killed some prisoners accused of lacking faith in the party, Fascism, and Hitler and reported the deaths as suicides to the camp commanders. On October 18, 1943, at Camp Concordia, Kansas, for example, the resident members of the Gestapo suspected Captain Felix Tropschuh of informing camp authorities about a planned escape and resented his diary entries that allegedly included "statements against Nazi ideology." As a result the Nazi camp leaders brought Tropschuh before a "court of honor," where he was "expelled from the German community of fellowship" and sentenced to hang. His Nazi executioners then took him to a room with a rope and a chair and shut the door. After he failed to appear at roll call the next morning, a guard found that he had apparently committed "suicide." In early November a Nazi contingent at Camp Tonkawa, Oklahoma, convicted a Corporal Johann Kunze of treason for informing army officials about secret military installations in Hamburg, information that would aid the Allied bombing campaign. Soon thereafter he was found beaten to death with clubs and broken milk bottles. Although five sergeants in the Afrika Korps were later found guilty of murder and executed, intimidation, along with German military discipline, enabled the Nazi leaders in the POW camps to maintain strict control and hamper any propaganda or education programs among the prisoners.[45]

Camp Concordia also experienced another death on January 11, 1944, when a Private Franz Kettner, an Austrian, refused to steal from the camp storeroom. After personal harassment that included booing in the mess hall and physical threats, a kangaroo court sentenced him to death, after which he was found dead in his bunk with his wrists slashed. When the evidence proved conclusive, however, his attackers were sent to the federal prison at Fort Leavenworth, Kansas. These and other incidents of physical brutality and murder by Nazis and Fascists in the POW camps were, of course, not unique to the camps on the Great Plains, but they indicate that, after the War Department and camp officials abdicated control of the POWs to the most fanatical Nazis and Fascists, they could do little to protect the prisoners who were less than full-fledged supporters of National Socialism and Fascism. At the same time even ardent Nazis from the Afrika Korps could find themselves in danger. At Camp Douglas in Wyoming SS troops occupied one compound, and they frequently cut their way into the other three barracks areas housing Afrika Korps prisoners and attacked them for permitting Rommel's defeat. Double fences with guard dogs between eventually brought the needed protection.[46]

On the plains camp commanders could at best segregate the extreme Nazis and Fascists from the anti-Nazi and-Fascist prisoners, that is, those who professed almost any political philosophy other than National Socialism or Fascism. And on July 19, 1943, the War Department ordered all "Nazi leaders, Gestapo agents, and extremists" to be held at Camp Alva, Oklahoma. This order gave camp commanders the opportunity to transfer troublemakers. So many camp commanders took advantage of this directive to clear their camps of troublesome prisoners, rounding them up with a military police "goon squad," that on July 17, 1944, the War Department ordered that only pro-Nazi officers could be sent to Alva, not "reclaimable material among the German prisoners." Even so, by 1945 the army had sent forty-five hundred of the most philosophically committed and hardened Nazis to Camp Alva. The War Department designated Camp McLean as a post for pro-Nazi or noncooperative noncommissioned officers, while it sent hard-core Italian Fascists to Camp Hereford, Texas. German noncommissioned officers were also segregated and assigned to Douglas, Wyoming, Tonkawa, Oklahoma, and Indianola, Nebraska. Disabled POWs went to Camp McAlester, Oklahoma.[47]

The War Department had no experience segregating POWs on the basis of political ideology. Moreover, the anti-Nazis did not readily come forward, and such segregation was not crucial to the war effort. In addition the Geneva Convention guaranteed prisoners the right to choose their political philosophy, and camp commanders could not ban Nazi political thought any more than the Germans could prohibit American POWs from supporting the democratic process. Thus, as long as the POWs did not violate prison policy, military code, or national or state law, and as long as they remained orderly, disciplined, and obedient and willingly participated in the work program, camp commanders let them run their own affairs behind the barbed wire. And camp spokesmen were usually Nazis or dedicated Fascists. As a result intimidation, terrorism, and violence inflicted on the anti-Nazi or anti-Fascist prisoners became a basic feature of the POW camps. Indeed, the soldiers who were not true believers in National Socialism or Fascism became "prisoners among prisoners" and feared for their safety and lives in the camps. The local residents, however, knew nothing about the internal operations of the POW camps, and they would have been shocked to learn about the systematic intimidation practiced by the hard-core Nazis and Fascists near their homes.[48]

In general the Germans and Italians were well treated, neither coddled nor abused, although the Germans complained that the corn they were served was "pigs'" food and that they wanted bread that would "chew longer." The Germans also asked for more potatoes, dark flour, and lard, while the Italians wanted more spaghetti, tomatoes, ketchup, and bread. Occasionally, nearby residents complained that the POWs wasted food and received cigarettes when they themselves had none. Camp commanders became particularly sensitive to this charge when domestic food shortages occurred early in 1944. On July 1 the army ordered a food conservation program for the POW camps that it tightened in February 1945 to include substitutes for sugar, butter, and beef. After VE-Day, however, prisoners complained that their food rations were reduced to near starvation levels owing to charges of ill treatment of American POWs in Germany, exposure of the concentration camps to public knowledge, public demands for the army to stop coddling prisoners, and food shortages in the United States. One German at Camp Bliss, Texas, recalled the retribution, saying, "They wanted to let us know that we lost the war." A farmer near Greeley, Colorado, also remembered, "They was fed awfully bad. . . . They might have been prisoners but they were still human beings." The army, however, reminded residents that the POWs were not criminals but "honorable soldiers" whose treatment would affect American POWs in Germany. Although the POWs experienced a food reduction, it must be kept in perspective. In May 1945 a veteran prisoner told newly arrived Germans at Camp Atlanta, "The food isn't any good any more." But they responded, "Man this is first rate." Another German POW at Camp Robinson, Nebraska, spoke for most of the prisoners when he recalled, "We had good food, hot showers, decent clothes, work, entertainment—the only thing missing was the lack of opportunity to deal with the male hormones." Generally, Great Plains residents did not hold the German POWs accountable for barbarous acts abroad. Although they ultimately considered the German people collectively responsible for the concentration camps and wartime atrocities, they did not hold accountable individual POWs, whom they considered ordinary citizen soldiers.[49]

Ultimately, approximately 374,000 German and nearly 51,000 Italians were held as POWs in the United States. Only a few Japanese POWs reached the Great Plains: 323 at Hearne and 590 at Kennedy, Texas, out of 4,242 in the United States during the war. Most of the German and Italian prisoners were young men with varying degrees of commitment to National Socialism and Fascism. The German POWs in the Afrika Korps were tough, arrogant, and elite, and they knew it. Until late in the war German soldiers generally sympathized with the National Socialist German Workers Party. Moreover, they had become indoctrinated by participation in various youth organizations during the 1930s. Party expectations, including obedience, were not new to them, and they generally accepted government policy and party discipline. At the same time all Germans were familiar with the work of the SS, the SA, and the Gestapo, which regularly spied on the public at home and commonly arrested Germans, not just Jews, for speaking out against the state and being less than true believers. By the mid-1930s the German public understood the real and daily danger of arrest and confinement in a concentration camp. So captured German soldiers knew that they had survived the war. They had adequate food, housing, and medical care, as guaranteed by the Geneva Convention. Even so, the camps also included what can only be called fanatical Nazis, who often, numbers permitting, ran the camps internally and demanded reverence to the fatherland and Adolph Hitler. Failure to show expected enthusiasm and commitment to the war as well as any suspicion that a German soldier was confiding in or being overly friendly with the American soldiers and officers in charge of the camps invariably garnered a beating and sometimes a kangaroo court and an immediate hanging. While German POWs were safe from the fighting, they were not safe from each other.[50]

Indeed, after the D-Day invasion on June 6, 1944, Wehrmacht prisoners tended to be comparatively old and comparatively young soldiers with less or little ideological commitment, "more subdued" than earlier arrivals, and glad that the war was over for them. The

Afrika Korps POWs usually despised them for their weakness and failure. In turn the younger arrivals considered the older prisoners rough and out of touch with reality. One seventeen-year-old at Camp Veteran, Wyoming, thought that the older prisoners used "very dirty language" and had "only three subjects: women, food, going home." Certainly, plains residents learned, as did Americans generally, that the stereotype "all Germans are Nazis" was not true, that distinguishing between Nazis and anti-Nazis could be a difficult task, and that Germans and Italians could be neither Nazis nor Fascists but rather simply nationalists.[51]

By the end of the war local Great Plains residents often sympathized with the German and Italian POWs and considered them family, which was, in fact, true in some cases. On occasion residents attempted to gain the release of their relatives subject to their care. In May 1944, for example, Vincent Bertone of Lander, Wyoming, wrote Governor Lester C. Hunt and requested that his nephew at Camp Hereford be "released or paroled" to him. Naively, he wrote, "I would be glad to assume the responsibility of his entire keep insofar as his living is concerned, and also take the responsibility of delivering him to the proper authorities if and when called upon." The Sons of Italy and the Guylielmo Marconi Society, among other Italian organizations, also distributed sporting equipment and musical instruments to the Italians at Camp Atlanta.[52]

It is this cultural link, or, even, the protective nature of the relationship, between German and Italian POWs and some residents with a similar heritage that makes the POW experience on the Great Plains distinctive for both prisoners and civilians. In addition German and Italian residents of the Great Plains seldom showed animosity toward the POWs, in contrast to others nationwide who considered them coddled and pampered. Overall, the people of the Great Plains treated the POWs with humanity. Yet, while POWs being transported by truck to the branch camps or the fields became a "fairly common sight," they remained a novelty. Near Ault, Colorado, for example, local residents often took drives into the country to watch the prisoners work in the sugar beet fields.[53]

Overall, the POWs provided important, temporary agricultural labor, work that was well suited to their situation because it required little technical skill or special training. Moreover, POW labor shielded farmers from paying potentially higher wages as a result of the labor shortage. Although no precise accounting of labor costs can be made because wages and tasks varied throughout the region, POW workers were cheaper than regular hired workers. Without question the prisoners harvested crops that otherwise would have rotted in the fields, thereby contributing to the efforts of farmers to meet the military and civilian demand for food. Indeed, many farmers sympathized with their plight and gave them food to smuggle back into their camps, and they considered the POWs the "best bunch of boys you saw in your life." A Colorado farmer recalled, "They was a lot better workers than we could get around here." When the POW farm labor program officially ended on June 16, 1946, most farmers who had participated were pleased with the POWs whom they had employed from 1943 to 1946. Still, POW labor did not meet all or even most of the agricultural demand in the Great Plains. It was only a partial solution to a major problem.[54]

Although the POW camps gave Great Plains residents their only contact with the military and enabled those who worked in the camps or employed prisoners to participate in the home front war effort, humanitarianism did not always govern their actions. Indeed, not everyone treated the POWs with compassion and humaneness. One farmer near Reading, Kansas, reportedly struck a prisoner because he did not work fast enough. German prisoners at Camp Roswell, New Mexico, complained that the guards beat them. At Camp Benkelman, Nebraska, the guards often taunted the German prisoners when planes few over, telling them that they were on the way to bomb Berlin. At Camp Carson, Colorado, a spokesman for the Germans charged that a guard threw a tear gas canister into a truckload of prisoners being transported to a work site. German POWs were also required to follow the American courtesy of standing at attention and saluting whenever "The Star-Spangled Banner" was played. At Camp McAlester, Oklahoma, however, the American officer in charge of one of the compounds convinced the prisoners that "Dixie" was "sort-of" a national anthem for which they should also stand and salute. One reporter wrote that he was "rather pleased with the result." At Camp Hereford the guards commonly addressed the Italian POWs, derogatorily, as, "Hey *paesà* [friend]," and called them sons of bitches, bastards, and slaves. Some people always considered the German POWs despicable and derogatorily referred to them as "nasties," although it is impossible to tell whether they used that term out of spite or because of their own poor education.[55]

In time most residents of the Great Plains who opposed the location of a POW camp nearby or who advocated shooting the prisoners, even those who had lost a son in the war, recognized that the prisoners were valuable as farmworkers and that they were harmless young men who had been forced to join the German or Italian army. Most Great Plains residents distinguished between the enemy represented by the German and Italian governments and the young men whom they held captive. Kansans who had contacts with POWs often became less hostile toward the German people, except for the Nazis, and less demanding that the Allies punish them for the war, and they favored a lenient peace. One Kansan reflected, "I think that it [his contact with POWs] mellowed me a lot, and I had a lot more compassion for people who, really, maybe didn't want to go and fight. Maybe they didn't like Hitler either." Another said, "I really didn't feel that they were Nazis, but just young men fighting for their country." Or, as one Oklahoman put it, they were "patriots in their own right."[56]

Wherever the POW camps were established, however, they changed the nearby communities in both dramatic and subtle ways. Many of the "foreigners" who arrived on the Great Plains because of the POW camps were, in fact, Americans. One native of McLean, Texas, recalled, "All of a sudden [on the completion of the camp] we were being invaded by damn Yankees, some from as far away as Chicago. They were walking the streets and alleys, filling the park and were in every café booth." Government money also quickly flowed into local communities when the soldiers spent their pay on housing, groceries, and entertainment, and the camps created a host of jobs for nearby residents, such as secretarial, clerical, carpentry, and postal workers. Still, residents often treated the workers who arrived from beyond their locale as different. The wife of one army sergeant at Camp McLean remembered, "The community was very small. We had to travel by Greyhound bus to Shamrock, Texas, to attend mass. . . . Although the people were friendly enough, we [the camp people] were outsiders."[57]

Above all, the POW camps brought the war home to the people of the Great Plains in a visible and tangible way, for both good and ill. Some residents near the camps took advantage of the newly gained economic opportunity that tested the definition of patriotism. Rent, restaurant, and other prices escalated as much as 50 percent in some towns near the camps. One guard at Camp Hereford recalled, "When we first arrived we could come to town and buy a good T-bone steak for $1.50, then bingo! All at once the price shot up to $2.50 because a lot of us were eating in town." In May 1943 the army placed several cafés and barbershops in Hereford off-limits because they failed to meet military health standards. Town and camp relations further deteriorated when local Baptist and Methodist ministers tried to prevent dancing at the USO club, prompting the camp commander to charge that they were trying to "run a U.S.O. on sewing circle lines." The Catholic bishop in Amarillo, James FitzSimon, even entered the fray, claiming that the camp commander had "encountered a mentality that has been very characteristic of many Texas towns, especially where the Baptists are in power." Eventually, the crisis passed, and the USO at Hereford offered a range of activities for the servicemen and their families, including dances. Some of the less devout Baptists also enjoyed invitations to the camp because, even though the town of Hereford itself remained dry, they could buy beer at the PX.[58]

The POW camps, however, were not entirely an economic blessing. Certainly, they employed local residents and no doubt prevented many of them, particularly older men, from leaving town for work elsewhere. The military payrolls also brought a welcome prosperity for merchants, and the soldiers and civilians brought tens of thousands of dollars in bank deposits and expenditures into the towns each month. This prosperity, however, did not last. By the end of

June 1946, the camps had closed. The War Department began selling the buildings, weeds soon covered the sites, landlords had empty apartments and houses, and civilians who worked at the camps lost their jobs. Merchants quickly missed the soldiers' payday.[59]

Equally important, the POW camps permitted contact between the enlisted men and nearby women. In January 1945 Camp Roswell hosted a dance and invited women from the surrounding towns of Hagerman, Dexter, Artesia, and Roswell. The jukebox spun the records of Tommy Dorsey, Benny Goodman, and Artie Shaw, and a local paper reported that "plenty of girls" attended. But, as one army wife remembered, "It seems that only the very old and the very young lived in McLean. All the young men and women fit for service or factory work were gone. The female teenagers were all shipped off to grandmothers or aunt Tillies, while the army men were so close." At first, she recalled, the soldiers were welcomed, but they soon "made off with the lonely wives of service men and young local women." Thereafter, the army "riff-raff" were "merely tolerated by the community." After the camp closed in July 1945 the guards and the other personnel departed. One resident reflected, "McLean lost most of a generation of its young women who married the camp soldiers and moved away." This compounded the community's loss of a generation of young men. Although the economic impact of the POW camps on local communities proved important and welcome, trailing only that of defense plants and military bases, by the end of the war the camps had often caused serious personal problems and significant social change. Many residents were glad to see them close and believed that their towns had lost much more than they had gained from the presence of POW camps.[60]

ELEVEN | Indians in Wartime

In September 1939 few Indians in the Great Plains considered the ramifications of Germany's attack on Poland and the violent plunge of Europe into another world war. Instead, they struggled with chronic poverty, inadequate health care, and hopeless unemployment as well as education, credit, and land insufficient to enable them to earn a living and assimilate into white culture. Many lived on isolated reservations and spoke only native languages. Few had access to radios and newspapers. These and other problems confronted John C. Collier, who pressed hard to impose his idealistic policies and remake Indian civilization as he thought best. Since becoming commissioner of Indian affairs in 1933, he had brought both hope and division to Indian America through his support of the Indian Reorganization Act (IRA), which Congress passed the next year. The IRA became the tool with which Collier imposed cultural pluralism on the tribes. It achieved his goal of ending the land-allotment process, which had enabled whites to acquire millions of acres of Indian land, and it provided for the return of some land to some tribes for reincorporation in the entity of the reservation. This revolutionary legislation also allowed the Indians to regain and enhance their political and economic control over tribal affairs as well as establishing their civil and cultural rights, although it imposed white political and legal organization on tribal cultures.[1]

Yet not all Indians supported the IRA. On the Great Plains, for example, a Sioux delegation at the Pine Ridge Reservation in South Dakota appealed to the Senate Committee on Indian Affairs for the repeal of the IRA or at least their exclusion from it. Indeed, on the eve of a new war the Sioux full-bloods complained that only the mixed-bloods, that is, "breeds and those who have jobs," supported the IRA. They also charged that Collier had established an Indian court at Pine Ridge and used it to support the Indian New Deal and to deny free speech to those who opposed the IRA. This appeal reflected intratribal political animosities over the expenditure of tribal funds, land-leasing policy, and law enforcement. When the war began, Collier's attempt to impose a "collective democracy" on the Indians met with considerable resistance from many tribes that distrusted new initiatives by the Bureau of Indian Affairs (BIA). Non-Indian detractors also opposed his attempts to promote cultural pluralism rather than the traditional federal polices that sought assimilation and acculturation. These issues, rather than German and Japanese expansion, occupied the attention of the Indians in the Great Plains.[2]

Despite the increasing focus of the Roosevelt administration on the war in Europe and the president's efforts to prepare the nation industrially and militarily for involvement in that conflict, Collier tried to make the best of an increasingly bad situation, one in which solving the problems of Indian America no longer remained a New Deal priority. In 1939 Collier praised the efforts of the Pawnees in Oklahoma, who had established a representative government with two councils, one composed of "old headmen," who had broad authority to act in various areas of tribal interest, and a business council that would handle routine financial and economic affairs. Other tribes had adopted constitutions and bylaws and incorporated for economic and legal purposes. In the Dakotas, Kansas, and Montana tribal groups also formed councils to share administrative duties with agency superintendents. On the northern Plains the Rosebud Sioux revived the "tiospaye," which they hailed as a "natural unit of social action." While Collier and the BIA worked to achieve tribal self-determination and economic independence, factions emerged, and political infighting on some reservations hindered the quick and smooth drafting of laws and legal codes. Indian politics also slowed BIA attempts to address changes in land management, revenue enhancement, and other matters of daily municipal government.[3]

Clearly, Collier and the BIA still had much to achieve. With more than 40 percent of Indian income unearned (over 20 percent from land leases and royalties paid on oil and other natural resources and over 20 percent from relief sources), 22 percent from agriculture, and the remainder for various individual endeavors, the Indian economy in the Great Plains remained weak. In 1940 approximately 82 percent of the 110,875 Indians in Oklahoma lived in rural areas, and 63 percent, or nearly 70,000 Indians, resided on farms. These fourteen thousand farm families practiced subsistence agriculture. They needed technical assistance for the production of feed and forage, the cultivation of gardens, and food preservation. The BIA, however, could not meet these educational needs in Oklahoma or across the Great Plains because of staff shortages and the inability of the Indians to acquire the credit necessary to purchase agricultural equipment, seed, and fertilizer.[4]

Across the Great Plains, however, the federal government provided some economic aid by making direct loans to cooperatives, credit associations, and individuals, such as rural rehabilitation and resettlement loans. The BIA also provided credit through a revolving fund to charter tribal corporations for economic program development, if the tribe could provide security and a guaranteed repayment plan. The BIA also helped Indian men and women find jobs in cities such as Oklahoma City and Tulsa. For the Indian women this meant working as housekeepers and helpers. Among the Kiowas the federal government constructed two canning plants and an irrigation project that supplied water for home garden use. Works Progress Administration (WPA) construction projects involved building hospitals, schools, and roads, but this work provided only modest income. Throughout the Indian community in the Great Plains a Great Depression subsistence mentality prevailed, and the economic prospects and possibilities born of war seemed far away.[5]

On the eve of World War II Congress made matters worse by substantially reducing funding for the Indian Division of the Civilian Conservation Corps, officially known as the Indian Emergency Conservation Work, but commonly called the Civilian Conservation Corps–Indian Division (CCC-ID). The Roosevelt administration's desire to reduce federal spending and the coming of a new European war made funding increasingly difficult for the CCC-ID. In South Dakota the CCC-ID employed 8,405 Sioux and spent more than $4.5 million for conservation work, such as building terraces and check dams to stem the loss of topsoil from water runoff on the Rosebud, Pine Ridge, and Standing Rock reservations. Road construction provided additional work. In Oklahoma the CCC-ID participated in the shelterbelt program of the Prairie States Forestry Project by planting trees on the Kiowa and Cheyenne-Arapaho reservations and Pawnee land in western Oklahoma and on the Potawatomie Reservation in Kansas. Erosion-control projects proved essential because much of the worst soil erosion occurred on heirship land where whites leased the acreage and used it for maximum production without applying proper soil conservation techniques to protect it from wind and water erosion.[6]

Sioux young men primarily found employment with the CCC-ID, the WPA, and the Farm Security Administration (FSA) and the Indian Service, that is, the BIA. These jobs usually involved "made work" as the nation struggled with the Great Depression. State and county governments could not meet their needs and pressed the federal government to allot Indians land in order to force them to become self-supporting, a policy diametrically the opposite of Collier's plan to return allotted and heirship land to the tribes. By 1939, on the Rosebud Reservation all federal relief projects provided an annual per capita income of only $150, and 95 percent of the population received federal relief. At that time the median annual income for Indian men on the reservations averaged only $500, compared to an average of $2,300 for men nationwide. In 1940 average annual family farm income at Pine Ridge averaged $58, whereas the annual income of nearby white farmers ranged from $837 to $1,063.[7]

Moreover, on the eve of the war off-reservation employment could not meet the needs of the Great Plains Indians, and more than 90 percent of Indian families there survived on work relief projects and direct economic aid from the federal government. In 1940 approximately 50 percent of the Sioux at Standing Rock depended on CCC-ID aid, while 97 percent of the population lived on New Deal relief programs. The economic situation on the other Great Plains reservations was little different. Many Indians employed on government projects considered the work their job rather than temporary relief, even though they earned little from it. Despite the considerable success of soil conservation work on Indian land, however, Congress terminated the CCC-ID on July 10, 1942, owing largely to wartime competition for funds. During the nine-year existence of the CCC-ID, more than eighty-five thousand Indians participated in this work relief and conservation program, and $72 million had been expended to restore land on more than seventy reservations.[8]

Overall, CCC-ID work improved grazing and croplands on the reservations. Yet, while the work of the CCC-ID benefited Indian land, few Indians profited from the work projects beyond receiving a paycheck. White renters gained most because they leased Indian land, and white stockmen benefited from the construction of ponds, terraces, and fences as well as pest-and weed-control measures designed to restore and conserve the grasslands. As long as heirship, that is, land inheritance, policy continued to fragment Indian landholdings, the work of the CCC-ID would not benefit many Indian farmers. Moreover, few Indians remained on the land to raise crops and livestock as a result of their experience and training in the CCC-ID. Once the war lured them away many never returned. Declining federal support for conservation work and agricultural improvement, then, kept Indian farmers in a state of subsistence and poverty. In April 1940 the superintendents of the reservations in North and South Dakota met in Bismarck to discuss administrative problems plaguing BIA programs. They emphasized difficulties with agricultural extension and land use programs as well as with the credit programs of the FSA. Everyone essentially agreed that the reservation Indians in the northern Great Plains needed more financial and technical support to develop viable subsistence agricultural operations. Commercial farming remained beyond anyone's expectations.[9]

Other economic problems plagued the Indians in the Great Plains. In Oklahoma, for example, the Osages complained that a strike by the Ohio Workers' International Union against the Mid-Continent Petroleum Corporation and the Cosden Pipe Line Company denied the tribe royalties from its leased land, the Congress of Industrial Organizations union had shut down oil production in Osage County. Although the Osages received a temporary restraining order against the union, union supporters trespassed on Osage land and destroyed oil-pumping equipment, including a pipeline to a refinery in Tulsa that was dynamited. With sales averaging eleven thousand barrels per day, the Osage lost considerable royalty income. Accordingly, the tribal council requested help from the federal government "to terminate such illegal and unlawful trespasses, depredations, destruction, vandalism and interference with the property of the Osages and their employees, lessees and purchasers of their oil, and to prevent any re-occurrence." Relief did not come soon.[10]

The Choctaws and Chickasaws also leased some 370,000 acres of coal and approximately 3,000 acres of asphalt deposits. With coal revenues tallying more than $86,000 annually, many Choctaws and Chickasaws wanted their royalties paid directly to them on a per capita basis rather than to the BIA for disbursement to the tribal council. The Choctaw and Chickasaw tribal council favored selling the land to the federal government or at public auction, bringing new demands for a per capita distribution of the sale amount so that the tribal members could enjoy the benefits during their lifetime. The Choctaw and Chickasaw tribal council also expressed a willingness to accept payment in defense bonds if Congress could not appropriate funding for the sale. Ultimately, tribal officials and the Department of the Interior reached agreement on a price of $8.5 million for 376,000 acres. Congressional and tribal approval would mean that 27,160 allottees among the Choctaws and Chickasaws would receive approximately $300 each, but these headright allotments had been substantially reduced by heirship divisions, thereby sharply limiting the amount any one person would receive. Even so, many Chickasaws had moved from the area and had no intention of returning, and they therefore preferred to sell the land in order to secure much-needed money. By March 1942 the legal hurdles had been cleared for the sale of thirty-five hundred acres of Choctaw and Chickasaw coal and asphalt land to the McAlester Fuel Company of McAlester, Oklahoma. The coal would be used by the Sheffield Steel Corporation at a plant in Houston to aid the war effort.[11]

Wilburn Cartwright, the Democratic representative for the congressional district that included the Choctaw and Chickasaw land, supported the sale. He observed, "The Indians are anxious to sell it and receive per capita payments while they are this side of the happy hunting ground." Additional benefits from the sale would come from the revival of coal mining in the area, the employment of more than a thousand men, and the multiplier effect of a coal-mining payroll among these Indians. The elders among the Choctaws and Chickasaws worried that further delay might bring per capita payments that would do the older Indians "no good" because they would be dead before they received them. Yet the land had not been sold by war's end, although the Choctaws and Chickasaws continued to plead for the money.[12]

At the same time the Five Civilized Tribes increased tribal income by selling oil and gas leases on their land. In 1940 Congress approved the conduct of these sales by sealed bid, in contrast to the customary practice of open bidding at auction, to improve the price received. The price jumped immediately. In 1939 the average price bid openly for the sale of oil and gas leases was $1.78 per acre. In February and March 1940 sealed bids averaged $5.07 and $5.58 per acre, respectively. Indian Commissioner William Zimmerman hailed the new procedure as a "decided benefit to Indian land owners." Wildcat speculators and others strongly opposed this procedural change, but they protested to no avail. This policy continued during the war years with wildcat leases sold on Indian land in Montana, Oklahoma, Wyoming, South Dakota, and New Mexico. Even so, the semblance of fair treatment had required a prolonged fight.[13]

When the war began, agricultural life among the Indians had changed little since the late nineteenth century. The continued division of estates among the heirs undermined any hope of agricultural progress. During the 1930s land sales slowed but never ceased, and the tribal landowners alienated their farms to acquire money in order to survive. Indian farmers also chronically lacked draft animals, equipment, capital, and credit. By the end of the decade most of Indians in the Great Plains had quit farming. In 1939 only 1 percent of the land, or 1,450 acres, remained in private Indian ownership on the Lower Brule Reservation. In addition 59,000 acres in heirship status had been divided into portions too small to enable individual Indian farmers to earn a living. Another 52,000 acres had also been allotted, but the owners did not yet qualify for title. White livestock men primarily rented the land for grazing cattle. With most of the reservation land in North and South Dakota apportioned to Indians in 160- or 320-acre allotments, these holdings also proved too small for any farmer, Indian or white, to profitably cultivate or graze the land. Although the BIA worked to acquire heirship and allotted land from the Indians as well as purchase land from whites for return to the reservations, it had insufficient funds or willing clients. Indian families who owned land through the allotment process often proved reluctant to sell to the BIA and have it returned to tribal control. White cattlemen and farmers also had no intention of selling land back to the agencies.[14]

In the Dakotas and Montana Indian landlords with only modest acreage preferred to lease their land, and subsist on rental and relief income, rather than cultivate their allotted acreage, which had become little more than small garden plots because of the heirship problem. Some Indians, such as those on the Rosebud Reservation, preferred to rent their land and work as agricultural laborers, particularly in the sugar beet fields of eastern Montana. White farmers and ranchers who rented Indian land quickly considered their leases a vested right that could not be disturbed. On the Omaha Reservation in Nebraska and the Cheyenne River Reservation in South Dakota, however, the Indians had begun to use tribal funds to purchase and consolidate land, while the Lower Brule Livestock Association in South Dakota and the Choctaw sheep raising and wool carding project in Oklahoma also offered limited but encouraging examples of Indian cooperative agricultural enterprises. Yet in a misguided rush to the past the BIA's Education Division sponsored a breeding program for Morgan horses at Pine Ridge, Rosebud, Tongue River, and Chilocco to provide horse-drawn transportation in an attempt to overcome the shortage of rubber automobile, bus, and tractor tires.[15]

FIGURE 24. Indian farmers had little access to credit for the purchase of tractors and farm implements. During the war they continued to use horse-drawn equipment and remained nearly forgotten by the federal government. Most Indian farmers practiced subsistence, not commercial, agriculture and missed the lucrative profits that white farmers gained from high wartime prices. This Indian farmer is plowing on the Cheyenne and Arapaho Reservation in Oklahoma. (Carl Albert Center, Congressional Archives, University of Oklahoma)

On the eve of World War II, then, without adequate credit, technology, and training, the Great Plains Indians struggled to provide for their own food needs by farming. Commercial agriculture remained beyond the ability of most Indians. By 1941, the BIA reported, whites were leasing more than 40 percent of Indian land on the Great Plains. A year later every acre of Indian land not used by the tribes was under lease. As a result the Indians were left to their own devices, but without adequate seed, feed, livestock, and equipment, and without the ability to acquire the financing to obtain them. In 1942 agriculture and ranching on the Pine Ridge Reservation declined further when the army purchased 340,000 acres for $0.75 per acre and leased additional land from the Sioux to establish a gunnery range. One Sioux received orders from the reservation superintendent to leave before harvest time, and he complained, "The War Department was ordering us out and the superintendent of the reservation said that we would be shot if we did not leave." Overall, past intolerance of the Indians remained keen in the Great Plains, including by those appointed to protect them. As a result Indian farmers neared extinction.[16]

Moreover, the revolving-credit program of the federal government could not boost cattle raising and the Indian economy on reservations that had lost considerable acreage to allotment, leasing, and subsequent land sales to whites. By 1939 on the Lower Brule Reservation in South Dakota, for example, 94,000 acres, or 40 percent of the reservation's original area of 234,850 acres, had been alienated to whites. At Pine Ridge 1.8 million acres of grazing land offered opportunity for cattle raising, but BIA policy had encouraged leasing to whites. When the war began, Indian cattlemen used less than one-third of the reservation's grazing land. On the Rosebud Reservation Indian cattlemen used only 37 percent of the 826,000 acres of grazing land, while they leased 53 percent of the grasslands to whites and let approximately 10 percent lie idle. Most of the land leased to whites on the Pine Ridge and Rosebud reservations remained in heirship status, with so many divisions that no one Indian controlled enough land to support agriculture or ranching.[17]

In Montana and the Dakotas the BIA worked to stock the Indian rangelands with cattle to achieve economic independence. The BIA helped the Indians organize grazing associations, loaned cattle and money, and supported cooperative marketing. Yet on the Pine Ridge and Rosebud reservations in South Dakota the sixteen thousand inhabitants primarily lived on government aid. These reservations controlled land capable of supporting 100,000 cattle, but only 18,000 head grazed there, and 55 percent of the families lived without livestock. Heirship land made reservations unsuitable for leasing, and land sales to whites further checkerboarded their land base. The secretary of the interior reported that the expansion of the livestock industry at Pine Ridge and Rosebud was "discouragingly slow." The BIA did not have the funds to buy back land sold to whites to block in reservations and permit Indian stockmen to make a profit from grazing cattle, and only by leasing the heirship land to white ranchers and farmers could the Sioux receive even a pittance of income. Moreover, by 1941 the high wartime price of cattle increased the value of the grazing land, thereby making the purchase of land for the Indians even more difficult. Few families controlled enough acreage to operate even small-scale cattle operations.[18]

Still, the BIA had worked with the Sioux to establish cattle associations, and government officials hoped that the training provided for livestock raising at the Pine Ridge Boarding School eventually would help these Sioux become independent cattlemen. The BIA also hoped that the program to provide breeding cattle, to be paid back later through a revolving cattle pool, and improved credit would enable Indians across the Great Plains to establish themselves in the livestock business, use their major resource, the grasslands, so as to obtain the greatest return, and "eliminate the evils of leasing." Successful livestock raising, however, also required the supplemental feeding of hay during drought and winter. Hay and feed crops, particularly west of the one hundredth meridian, required irrigation, but the BIA achieved only modest success in providing irrigation on the Fort Peck, Fort Belknap, Blackfeet, Crow, and Rocky Boy's reservations in Montana.[19]

On the eve of Pearl Harbor, then, the economic problems on the Great Plains reservations remained nearly insurmountable. On the Turtle Mountain Reservation in North Dakota, for example, nearly one thousand families attempted to "eke out" a living as farmers on land that would barely keep two hundred families from starving. The BIA reported that 90 percent of the population at Turtle Mountain depended on the federal government, and officials noted, "The housing on the reservation now constitutes a typical example of rural slum conditions." Similar situations existed across the plains because the reservations had insufficient land to support a living, that is, commercial, agriculture. On the Lower Brule Reservation in South Dakota the government classified 98 percent of the land suitable only for grazing purposes, but it allotted 160 acres to heads of households and by so doing violated, as one observer noted, "every canon of good land use." Only in Oklahoma did some cultural groups, such as the Osage and the Five Civilized Tribes, enjoy greater wealth and assimilation than other Great Plains Indians because they owned land above vast oil, coal, and asphalt deposits and they drew on that wealth, rather than agriculture, for their livelihood.[20]

Education also lagged for the Great Plains Indians when the war began. In Oklahoma the BIA supported only twelve boarding schools and seventeen day schools for twenty thousand children between six and eighteen years of age who had at least one-quarter Indian blood. Approximately three thousand Indian children attended the boarding schools and the Haskell Institute in Kansas. A few others attended public schools. At the Indian schools the teachers enforced strict discipline with harsh punishments. Truancy plagued the Indian school system, and state regulations regarding attendance could not be enforced on Indian land, thereby contributing to an inadequate and negligent education system. Moreover, at schools such as Haskell that children from many tribes attended, Indian cultures blurred, and students became less Sioux, Kiowa, or Cheyenne and more pan-Indian, a phenomenon particularly prevalent among orphans. When the war began, then, the schools contributed as much to cultural disintegration as they did to education.[21]

Moreover, few Great Plains Indians who received vocational training at the reservation schools found employment. In 1939 vocational education at the reservation schools essentially prepared Great Plains Indian boys and girls for jobs that were nonexistent other than the limited positions available with the federal government or missionary agencies. Across the Great Plains the Indian schools stressed vocational training that was at best suitable for farm life and service jobs in nearby small towns. Chilocco was the flagship federal school for agricultural education; half the day there was spent in class and half the day engaged in farmwork. Yet few Indian boys wanted to be farmers, and few had land on which to ply that vocation.[22]

Most Sioux girls had solved their unemployment problems by marrying before the age of twenty and remained on the reservations. The few off-reservation domestic jobs available for Indian women remained unattractive because such employment meant social iso-lation. Little wonder that 95 percent of the Sioux returned from Indian schools to live on the reservations. At Pine Ridge Sioux boys and girls who attended the federal boarding school "unanimously" looked forward to permanent employment off the reservation, but they often returned to the social and cultural comfort of home. Con-sequently, their training as carpenters, mechanics, and shoe repair-men had no lasting influence on Indian life. Given these problems BIA officials believed that cattle raising offered Sioux men the best possibility for a better life and that women should be trained to tend gardens and raise poultry and goats to help ensure economic self-sufficiency.[23]

Unemployment plagued other reservations such as Rosebud, Crow Creek, Cheyenne River, Standing Rock, and Fort Berthold as well. During the war reservation schools in the Great Plains continued to provide instruction on tending gardens to help alleviate food short-ages, but this training remained geared toward subsistence. Given the absence of off-reservation employment for women, BIA officials questioned whether the Indian schools adequately trained Indian girls for life as homemakers. The war, however, soon gave them bet-ter-paying alternatives. By 1941 the national effort to convert to wartime production substantially changed education on the Great Plains reservations. The war brought opportunities, jobs, and in-come to vocationally trained Indian men and women. War industries offered undreamed-of opportunities for many Indians in the Great Plains. The beginning of the war, then, offered promise, hope, and escape. For Indians it could be a good war.[24]

Quickly, the Indians schools located near defense industries of-fered engine repair, electric and acetylene welding, and radio and telephone operation and maintenance. The CCC-ID provided similar training at the Cheyenne River, Sisseton, Standing Rock, Blackfeet, Five Tribes, Pine Ridge, and Standing Rock agencies. In Oklahoma Kiowas at the agency in Anadarko trained in the CCC-ID program to qualify for employment as carpenters, auto mechanics, and survey-ors. Graduates found employment quickly. Heavy equipment opera-tors earned as much as $10 per day. At El Reno, Oklahoma, Indians also worked as mechanics on PT-19 aircraft in the army training program at the local airport.[25]

At the Haskell Institute in Lawrence, Kansas, Indian students learned the craft of electric welding while practicing on an old army bomber as well as the repair of mechanical equipment. Haskell officials also extended the school week to six days and restructured the school year to include three ninety-day semesters so that students could prepare more quickly for jobs in the war industries as well as keep their summers free for agricultural and war-related work. Haskell also offered office training to "mature men" for work in agency offices, schools, and hospitals because so many young men had joined the military, but it, along with Chilocco in Oklahoma and Flandreau in South Dakota, also enrolled women in sheet metal courses. In addition Indian women took shop and business courses. Employers in Tulsa and Oklahoma City specifically recruited Indians, including women, trained at Chilocco and Haskell. Indian women averaged $40 per week when they completed the sheet metal course and took jobs with airplane manufacturers. In Wichita Beechcraft employed Indian women who completed the sheet metal course at Chilocco throughout the war. Other Indian women found employment at ordnance plants in Kansas and South Dakota. When the United States entered the war, the Kiowa hospital doubled its enrollment of students training as nurses' aids and brought them to graduation in six instead of nine months.[26]

Ultimately, some seven hundred Indians acquired jobs in the defense industries in Wichita and Tulsa, while Albuquerque, Denver, Dallas, and Rapid City, among other cities, offered similar opportunities for Indians to improve their standard of living with annual incomes that averaged between $2,000 and $2,500 in urban areas. Although this income was considerably less than the national average, defense industry employers had to pay Indians and whites alike for equal work, and government and private employers classified Indians as white. In Wichita the director of personnel at Boeing's Stearman Aircraft Company reported to the superintendent of the Haskell Institute, "We have been exceedingly well satisfied with the boys you have sent to us." All seventy students enrolled in Haskell's commercial curriculum in June 1943 had received jobs by November. War industry plants in Kansas and Oklahoma now placed standing job announcements at the Indian schools, and on completion of vocational-training programs Indian men and women sought those jobs. Even so, relatively few Indians found jobs, in part because they did not have the financial reserves necessary to travel to urban areas to seek defense industry work. Those who found nonreservation work usually took employment nearby.[27]

Still, America's drift toward war brought promise for the Indians of the Great Plains. In July 1941 the Creek Indian Council appealed to the Oklahoma congressional delegation for help securing an army airfield for bomber training at Okmulgee. James D. Berryhill, the tribal secretary, justified the request, writing, "Many of our people are now out of employment and the location of such a plant here will afford employment for many of our younger members who are in need of such employment." Besides the economic rationale patriotism also drove the Creek request. Berryhill believed, "This will also give our people an opportunity to show their loyalty and devotion to the nation at this time when all good citizens are desirous of doing all in their power to aid in the national defense." Alex Noon, the chief of the Creek nation, and Joe M. Grayson, the tribal chairman, also supported this request, arguing that the Creeks had not received their fair share of defense work. Moreover, the citizens of Okmulgee approved $185,000 in bonded indebtedness to cover the city's expenses in aiding the establishment of an airport and a pilot-training school, all of which would enable the Creeks to do "their full duty in preparing for the defense of our country."[28]

Defense industry jobs offered the first hope that many Great Plains Indians had experienced in their lives. Wartime employment in Wichita, Oklahoma City, and Rapid City as well as Tulsa and Denver also enabled Indian women to cross gender-defined boundaries within tribal communities and assume new work roles as well as personal independence, usually in an urban area. Defense industry employers preferred to hire Indian women because they were not subject to the draft and because they believed that women in general had greater dexterity when it came to handling small parts and more

patience when it came to conducting tedious and repetitive assignments. Employers always preferred women who were "over twenty-
one but not old." Many companies set the preferred age range for the
women they hired from eighteen to forty-five. Soon, Indian women
began to sever cultural ties to their families and tribal communities
as they moved to the cities for wartime employment. Collier warned,
however, that Indian women would be the first workers fired when
the war ended. Other Indian women worked in agricultural labor.
Lakota women from the Rosebud Reservation labored in the sugar
beet fields in Colorado and at a poultry-processing plant in Winner,
South Dakota, because they chose to remain near home or because
they did not have the education and training to qualify for jobs in
the defense industries.[29]

Indians who sought defense industry employment often confronted
racism and a lack of cultural understanding. When Sioux workers
arrived at the naval ammunition depot in Hastings, Nebraska, locals
referred to them as "braves" who were "on the war path." They lived
segregated and isolated lives in tents and congregated in the post office lobby, where as a "federal people" they felt safe. Cultural conflicts, however, involving different ideas about work ethics, absences,
and productivity caused immediate and lasting problems because
employing farmers expected the Sioux to work like the Mexicans,
who had a reputation for speed and continuous labor from morning
until night with few rest periods, while the Sioux worked intermit-
tently but thoroughly. One contemporary observed that the Mexican
workers knew how much they earned each day while the Sioux had
no concept of wages. Although Collier reported that absenteeism by
Indian employees was virtually unknown, this pronouncement was
far from accurate. Without a culture of work in the white tradition
Indian men and women had difficulty arriving at the job on time,
lacked the Protestant work ethic, often spent their pay on liquor and
other luxuries, and occasionally arrived at work drunk. Most of the
Sioux had never worked for whites who operated large-scale businesses or industries. At the same time most whites had never employed Indians. Each held stereotypical views of the other. The Sioux
knew whites from their contacts with agency officials. Their employ-

ment on reservation relief projects led them to believe that whites would demand less than full effort and adjust to Indian work habits. Moreover, the Sioux worked at a slower pace than whites. They also expected personal attention from the company director, careful and frequent explanation of the job, and acceptance of periodic absences from the job without prearrangement.[30]

White employers, however, expected the Indians to work like whites and harbor the same motivations. Essentially, white employers expected Indians, such as the Rosebud Sioux, to be money driven. They also expected punctuality, reasonable explanations for missing work, problems to be solved between workers and foremen, not workers and the company leader, and notice given prior to quitting. White employers who adjusted to Sioux work habits kept their employees, while those who expected the Indians to adjust to white work habits experienced high attrition among their Indian workers. Urban employers particularly found fault with Sioux employees from the Pine Ridge and Rosebud reservations in South Dakota.[31]

The Sioux especially had difficulty making the transition to city life. Many Sioux lost their sense of group identity and security. Indians who left the reservations for city jobs often congregated in slums and confronted great difficulty advancing beyond the fringe of poverty. Moreover, the Sioux kept to themselves off the reservation. The Rosebud and Pine Ridge Sioux remained aloof even from each other even though they lived in the same city slum. Usually, their only contact with the government came in the form of police officers or social workers. Alcoholism and truancy became lasting problems. The Sioux ultimately adjusted to city environments by moving back and forth between the reservations and the urban areas after a few months on a job. Skilled or semiskilled mixed-bloods adjusted best to city life. Sioux full-bloods usually sought off-reservation employment in agriculture, but others from the Pine Ridge and Rosebud reservations often found construction jobs at nearby military bases, such as the Alliance Army Air Base in Nebraska. The Indians who led lives in transit from job to job in urban areas and back to the reservations usually were single men and women or married men.[32]

The Indians who remained on the Great Plains reservations during the war became more isolated than ever before because the rubber shortage affected travel for shopping and school. Many Indians also chose not to seek employment during the war. Among the Rosebud Sioux 45 percent of the unemployed did not pursue employment because they worried about living in urban areas. Some Rosebud Sioux considered work relief a regular job, and many Sioux hesitated to leave the security of the reservations for wartime employment. Financial problems also proved a major obstacle to seeking off-reservation employment. Without money for initial transportation, room and board, and clothing many potential Sioux workers remained stranded on the Rosebud Reservation. Similar situations existed on all Great Plains reservations.[33]

On the eve of World War II many young Indian men registered for the draft or enlisted in National Guard units. When Congress passed the Selective Service Act on September 16, 1940, many young Indian men traveled to Cheyenne, Bismarck, Minot, Williston, and Jamestown, North Dakota, to enlist. When the Selective Service Act passed, Indian translators explained the draft law to the Sioux, and more enlisted. By March 1941 approximately fifteen hundred of seventy-five hundred eligible Indians from Great Plains reservations had registered for the draft. When the United States entered the war in December, even more Indians joined the armed services, for both patriotic and economic reasons, the latter because the military offered a better life in terms of adequate food, health care, and income than they had on the reservations. At Pine Ridge the enthusiasm for enlisting ran so high that elders complained about the age limit—thirty-five years—for "eligible braves." By January 1942 young Sioux men reportedly "jammed" the recruiting offices in Rapid City. By August some two thousand Sioux alone had enlisted. Soon, the departure of the enlistees became the first large-scale migration from the reservations. The War Department did not recruit Indian women, but approximately eight hundred served in the military nationwide during the war. Women students at Haskell gained a reputation for not "sitting and waiting" but joining the armed forces to serve as WACS and WAVES, primarily taking clerical jobs. Job opportunity, income, and status became the most compelling reasons for enlistment. The Lakota women who enlisted usually had been educated at federal boarding schools or mission schools, where the disciplined regimentation helped them adjust to military life better than white women did.[34]

Many young men on the Fort Peck Sioux-Assiniboine Reservation in Montana, whose grandfathers had fought Custer, volunteered for military service. The number of Indian volunteers exceeded Indian draftees in the Great Plains by a ratio of two to one. Some Sioux were so eager to enlist that they brought their rifles to the induction centers. Although Sioux men volunteered in greater numbers than did men from other tribal groups, Indians in Oklahoma also had a high enlistment rate. In Oklahoma two National Guard units successfully recruited Indians from the Chilocco Indian School. Although many Indian men volunteered for patriotic reasons, the military also proved a lure because it provided an escape from the reservations. Military service meant a paycheck. Money sent home bought radios, heaters, and refrigerators. At the same time, however, poor health care, nutrition, and hygiene prevented many Indian men from enlisting. In the Dakotas, for example, the military rejected 50 percent of the Indian men from the Fort Totten and Standing Rock reservations because they failed their physical examinations. On these reservations the Public Health Service reported that forty-two of eighty-four men between the ages of twenty-one and thirty-five were denied entry into the military for health reasons, primarily eye diseases, probably trachoma, and for "nervous and mental ailments." Tuberculosis also plagued the Turtle Mountain Reservation.[35]

Following the American declaration of war in December 1941, many tribes, such as the Cheyenne and the Ponca in Oklahoma, also declared war against Germany and Japan. The Cheyennes criticized the Axis powers as an "Unholy Triangle" that sought "to conquer and enslave the bodies, minds and souls of all freedom loving people." Declarations of war and condemnations of the Axis powers were important symbolic acts that proclaimed the loyalty of the Indians to the United States and encouraged pan-Indian unity against America's enemies. Such actions reaffirmed the tribes' political autonomy and their intent to retain it.[36]

Many tribal members on the Great Plains also returned to their cultural roots and conducted ceremonies to ensure the safety of their young men in the military. The conflict particularly stimulated the Sioux, Cheyennes, Omahas, and Osages to revive their war dances. During summer 1942 the Sioux at Pine Ridge and Standing Rock in South Dakota and the Crows in Montana held a sun dance and prayed for the safe return of their men in uniform as well as the defeat of Germany and Japan. The Pine Ridge sun dance was the first held in fifty-two years, but without the self-inflicted torture that caused the federal government to prohibit it in 1890. The Sioux continued to hold sun dances periodically throughout the war. On August 7, 1945, Chief Spotted Crow at Pine Ridge began the five-day ceremony by offering prayers for a speedy victory and a lasting peace. One Sioux remembered, "The crisp air would carry to us the voices of elderly people singing plaintive war songs about young people who would not return home alive."[37]

The Blackfeet and Crow agencies in Montana offered President Roosevelt all reservation resources to prosecute the war, and the Crow pledged $10,000 in tribal funds to the federal government to pay for weapons. In January 1942 a Sioux tribal council voted to delay payment of a $5 million judgment from the federal government until after the war. The chairman of the council reported, "We will wait patiently for a few more years if it will help our country." In Oklahoma the Cheyennes also dropped all tribal claims against the federal government until peace returned. In a similar show of support for the war the Quapaws donated $1 million earned from zinc and lead leases to the federal government.[38]

In addition the Great Plains tribes supported the war effort by purchasing war bonds and stamps and collecting scrap iron and cooking fats for munitions. As early as January 1941 the Seminoles in Oklahoma organized an "iron for Britain" movement and collected enough scrap iron to fill ten railroad cars. The Uchees and Creeks in Oklahoma bought $400,000 in war bonds, while the Sioux at Cheyenne River and Pine Ridge and the Kiowas, Shawnees, Seminoles, Pawnees, and Quapaws in Oklahoma and the Sioux at the Turtle Mountain Reservation in North Dakota purchased lesser amounts. By 1943 Indian employees of the BIA bought war bonds through the payroll-deduction program, and war stamps paid for admittance to many tribal social gatherings. In 1944 the Lower Brule Sioux sponsored a bond sale at Reliance, South Dakota. The Sioux donated poultry, quilts, horses, and other items to be bid on and used the $22,000 collected to purchase bonds. This participation in the war proved modest compared to the white community's purchase of war bonds, but it symbolized the patriotism of the Great Plains Indians, who considered the United States their country as much as whites did.[39]

In retrospect, however, the Roosevelt administration cared little about the problems of the Great Plains Indians during the war, and critics increasingly attacked the IRA. As the nation prepared for war federal appropriations increasingly went to the military. As a result planning projects declined, programs already in operation lost financial support, and tribal reorganization slackened owing to decreased annual BIA appropriations. Collier also came under increasing attack by political enemies who disliked his messianic approach to Indian reform, which gave little heed to others who had differing opinions and to whites who sought additional Indian land. The assimilationists, which is how Collier characterized the cattle and oil interests, increasingly pressured the BIA to terminate federal responsibility for the Indians and repeal the IRA. Although the BIA received an appropriation of $46 million in 1939, approximately 20 percent of that, or $11.5 million, was emergency funding, and it disappeared after the United States entered the war. Thereafter, BIA funding continued to declined, all to the detriment of the Indians who lived on reservations in the Great Plains.

When the Japanese attacked Pearl Harbor, the Indian New Deal was already in jeopardy. The efforts of the BIA to foster political autonomy, provide financial assistance meant to promote economic independence, and create a legal structure with which the Indians could manage their own affairs had achieved only limited success. In the Great Plains Indian living standards had improved only moderately. Certainly, the Indian New Deal achieved a "spiritual reawaking" among many tribes in the Great Plains, and the policy of assimilation had been forsaken. Yet, when the United States entered the war, the brass ring of Indian self-determination remained beyond the reach of Collier and Indian America. During the war Collier's opponents continually charged that BIA programs designed to foster tribal self-determination, restore religious traditions, and reassert cultural uniqueness promoted segregation rather than assimilation, to the detriment of all Indian people. As Collier's opposition gained congressional support, funding for the bureau decreased, particularly for land purchases, credit, and construction projects. By early 1945 Collier could no longer protect the bureau from his detractors, and in January 1945 he resigned.[40]

By the end of World War II many problems remained for Great Plains Indians. The superintendent of the Crow Reservation advocated legislation that would guarantee "full citizenship rights," credit sources, and adequate education to help the Indians deal with a host of social, economic, and political problems, but to no avail. Indeed, the war brought decline, not progress and prosperity, for Indian farmers in the Great Plains. Oklahoma offers an excellent example of that regression. In 1940 some forty thousand Indian men engaged in agriculture; by 1950 only twenty-two thousand Indian farmers remained. Virtually all lived in poverty because of insufficient land, technology, and training. The other reservation Indians in the Great Plains lived in similar circumstances. Many Indians did not know how to make the best use of irrigation systems. Others failed to rotate crops, apply fertilizer and insecticides, upbreed livestock, or follow the best range management practices. Many who wanted to improve their farming practices lacked the capital and credit necessary for success.[41]

Although World War II caused increases in commodity prices, which benefited Indian farmers who had crops to sell, the Indians did not profit during the war years as they had done during World War I. High livestock prices, which encouraged whites to seek Indian land for leasing, together with fragmented landholdings, the result of the heirship problem, prevented the Indians from consolidating their landholdings to take the greatest advantage of the wartime economy. After 1945 the use of new and improved forms of agricultural science and technology accelerated. Only those Indian farmers who commanded the necessary capital, credit, and managerial ability to apply that science and technology on increasingly large acreages were able to expand production, reduce unit costs, and increase efficiency in the face of surplus production and chronically low prices. As a result fragmented landholdings, leasing, inadequate access to capital, and insufficient technology plagued Indian farmers. Commissioner William A. Brophy recognized that American agriculture had entered a new age and that in the future successful farming would require larger farms, the intensive application of science and technology, and expanded capital investment. Indian farmers had little opportunity to expand or to acquire new machinery, chemical fertilizers, and pesticides, and they did not have adequate credit. Indeed, Brophy noted that the land available to the Indians for agriculture was insufficient in quantity and quality to support them. Certainly, the shortage of agricultural land remained critical.[42]

Congress did not provide additional funding for land purchases; however, the Rosebud Sioux established the Tribal Land Enterprise in January 1944 and used tribal funds to purchase heirship and allotted land for consolidation under tribal control, primarily for ranching purposes. By summer 1944 it managed 30,000 thousand acres. In 1946 many Rosebud Sioux attempted to expand the tribal land base by exchanging more than 20,000 acres of allotted and heirship land for shares in the Tribal Land Enterprise, which by that time managed 60,000 acres for agricultural and grazing purposes and paid a 4 percent dividend. The Tribal Land Enterprise allocated consolidated land in acreage large enough to support viable faming and grazing units. In that same year the Cheyenne River Sioux transferred 120,000 acres to tribal ownership to aid livestock production. Although these transactions designed to increase the tribal base proved small, they were significant because the federal government had not appropriated funds during the war years to acquire land for the tribal base.[43]

For most of the Indians who were not farmers the war also did not bring long-term opportunity. Their economic gains proved marginal and short-term, and economic improvement came at great personal, social, and cultural price. The Indians who left the reservations for jobs in Denver, Oklahoma City, and Omaha, for example, no longer had easy access to the services of the BIA, and the agency cared little about their fate. The war also brought the termination of the BIA's Office of Social Work and the CCC-ID, thereby ending a moderately successful vocational-training and conservation program on the reservations. World War II, then, significantly altered social and economic conditions for the Great Plains Indians. Many veterans found reservation life unacceptable. In the military they had gown accustomed to adequate food, clothing, and shelter as well as medical care, electricity, hot water, and a regular paycheck. Once accustomed to a higher standard of living many Great Plains Indians left the reservations never to return. Others who had entered vocational-training programs, such as those established at the Haskell Institute in Kansas and the Chilocco School in Oklahoma, also departed from the reservations or their communities on graduation. After the war many Sioux continued to seek jobs in Rapid City and Yankton, South Dakota, and Scottsbluff, Nebraska, where they taxed city services and lived in poverty and desperation. At the Cheyenne River Reservation in South Dakota the Sioux tribal council authorized a $25 bonus to 350 veterans as a gesture of appreciation and to lure them back.[44]

Some returning veterans used their military service for political gain, as did whites, and they won election to their tribal councils, such as those at the Lower Brule, Crow Creek, and Pine Ridge reservations. Once they gained political power these veterans usually worked to gain and ensure Indian civil rights. During the war Indian women also began to take an active role on the tribal councils as a result of tribal adoption of the IRA. At Standing Rock in South Dakota a woman chaired the council, and at Pine Ridge a Sioux woman became the first female judge. Usually Indian women who held public office during the war had experience in tribal affairs and held reputations as leaders. When the war ended, however, Indian women, along with their white counterparts, quickly lost their high-paying war industry jobs as employers converted to peacetime production and hired returning veterans in their place. For these women the war brought brief employment, income, and a higher standard of living. But these gains collapsed with the peace. Still, some Indian women remained in urban areas and held "women's jobs," usually as domestics or low-status employees. Others, however, returned to the reservations, where unemployment, poverty, and a marginal standard of living awaited them.[45]

World War II, however, mandated that the Great Plains Indians become part of a world that extended beyond their communities and reservations. Off-reservation experiences and wage work began to change Indian perspectives. Change, however, required organization, and in November 1944 an Indian delegation representing fifty tribes in twenty-seven states met in Denver to organize the National Congress of American Indians. The congress intended to unify Indians for the purpose of preserving cultural values, ensuring treaty rights, and improving the administration of the BIA as well as achieving voting rights, social security benefits, and the adjudication of their claims against the federal government. These and other goals would occupy much of their time in the years ahead.[46]

Certainly, the Indians confronted the war on the Great Plains home front with commitment, hard work, and patriotism. Moreover, the educational and economic opportunities that the war brought them tantalizingly suggested that assimilation, if not acculturation, could be achieved. Wages skyrocketed, training courses proliferated, and migration off the reservations became easier than ever before. By 1944, for example, more that 25 percent of the tribal population of the Sisseton Sioux and Potawatomi had moved to urban areas. Even so, many Indians did not pursue jobs in urban areas because they worried about adjusting to city life. Others found the mental and physical adjustment to urban individualism from reservation communalism too difficult to endure, and they returned. The veterans who had gone away fared much better because they had gained experience off the reservations and knowledge of white society's expectations, norms, and values. Certainly, the war emphasized the need for education, and improved education became a major goal.[47]

The war, then, created a sense of optimism, equality, and opportunity. For many Indians their wartime economic gains introduced them to a postwar world in which they determined their own affairs, free from federal regulations. Indeed, many Indians believed that the BIA no longer met their needs. Moreover, for those Indians who had left the Great Plains reservations the debate over cultural pluralism and assimilation had considerably less meaning than it had before the war. At best the reservations offered cultural security but little more. By the end of the decade, for example, Indian agriculture still lagged. In 1949 Indian farmers averaged only $500 annually, compared to $2,500 for white agriculturists. Yet most reservation Indians relied on agriculture for their income. Commissioner of Indians Affairs John Ralph Nichols reflected on the situation of the Indians in American life, noting that "there are no panaceas or overnight solutions" for the Indian "problem."[48]

When World War II ended, then, most Great Plains Indians remained in rural poverty. Their land base had continued to decline, and commercial farming and cattle raising no longer proved feasible livelihoods. Moreover, despite vocational training for defense industry jobs many Indians returned to their reservations and economic desperation after they lost their jobs during the conversion to peacetime production owing to racism and the preferential treatment of veterans. They also suffered from poor housing, inferior schools, and racial prejudice in addition to an inadequate land base and high unemployment. The Sioux, however, advocated termination of the BIA to ensure tribal autonomy. In addition, by war's end some government officials and alleged friends of the Indians advocated the termination of all government responsibilities for the reservation Indians to force them to acculturate and assimilate in white society and ease the burden on taxpayers. Some congressmen assumed that the Indians would welcome the opportunity to be "Indian Americans rather than American Indians." Republican congressman Karl Mundt of South Dakota favored termination, and in 1944 he hoped that the newly formed National Congress of American Indians would "help effectively in energizing Indians to leave the reservations and become adjusted to new environments." These and other problems boded ill for the Indians in the Great Plains during the postwar years.[49]

The people of the Great Plains had anxiously awaited an invasion of Europe since December 1941, although some did so with apprehension. In January 1945 the Oklahoma City resident Eugene P. Graham, the secretary of the Oklahoma Bankers Association, asked Governor Robert S. Kerr to issue a proclamation calling for a bank holiday on VE-Day. He wrote, "There seems to be considerable apprehension among the merchants of Tulsa that this occasion will create a good deal of excitement as did the Armistice in 1918, at which time considerable property was destroyed." He noted the merchants were preparing the close their businesses and board up windows. When the attack finally came, Gail Carpenter in Wichita wrote, "Our phone rang very early this morning." When the family heard the news, he reported, "The muscles in our stomachs and throats tightened and the color must have gone from our faces." But, "There were no cheers." His family gathered around the table, listened to the "unveiled excitement" of the news commentators, and then spoke the names of the local boys they knew who were in harm's way. That was, he wrote, "a personal matter to us." In Dallas residents followed news about the invasion with "serious faces and playful hearts." There, churches opened their doors early in the morning. At the Highland Baptist Church the organist played hymns in the predawn darkness after the news "flashed over the sleeping city." Soon, nearly one hundred people sat in the pews, listening and praying; more than six hundred faithful trekked to the Sacred Heart Catholic Church. In Nebraska Martha Rohrke, a seventy-four-year-old widow in Haskins, made no note of the occasion in her diary, but her fellow Nebraskan Ruth Vaughn wrote, "D day the long awaited invasion has begun. We were awakened by fire whistles and bells at 6:00 a.m. It has been a world day of prayer. Please dear god—may it end soon."[1]

The war in Europe ended for the residents of the Great Plains with solitude, loud noises, and a feeling of relief. In Wichita VE-Day came and went with little celebration. In Billings, Montana, Kathryn Wright captured the moment as well as anyone. When the war in Europe ended, she wrote, "local residents paused briefly, thankful that half the job was done, then went back to work with renewed determination to hurry the finish." In Lincoln, Nebraska, Beatrice Vaughn also noted in her diary, "V-E day. How thankful we all are to have the suffering and loss of life cease in Europe. The nation is very solemn and thankful but no wild celebration." On May 8, 1945, Denver residents celebrated the defeat of Germany by ringing bells and going to church, but with little outward excitement, following the news from President Truman at 7:00 a.m. Now their thoughts turned to the South Pacific. In Oklahoma City life continued as usual, except for "quiet jubilation." City churches organized special prayer services.[2]

In the netherworld between the dropping of the atomic bombs on August 6 and 9 and the announcement of the surrender of Japan on August 15, Great Plains residents remained uncertain whether the nation was at peace or at war. When the news of the Japanese surrender came from the White House one Wichita resident reported, "Everyone old enough to understand the significance of the announcement immediately felt welling up within him the desire to do something to celebrate. Shouts of joy went up from the neighborhood kids. The air was soon filled with the continuous beeping of auto horns as drivers commenced to express themselves." Gail Carpenter sat in a Wichita church and gave thanks for peace, but solitude escaped the few who sat in the pews. "The songs of praise," he wrote, "the prayer of thanksgiving and the very fitting remarks of [the minister] arose against a noisy background of far more worldly activities." City police closed the main drag of Douglas Street to local traffic for several blocks, and an "effervescent crowd which seemed to include most of Wichita had congregated in the middle of the street which was littered with the waste paper thrown from the windows earlier in the evening." Carpenter remembered, "It was a happy, milling mob of citizens all feeling the urge to do something and not knowing exactly what to do." Images projected by speed and color were indelibly etched on the mind. Carpenter recalled, "A soldier with a glamorous, scantily clad blonde on his shoulders plowed through the crowd with a pack of drooling wolves at his heels." In the alleys liquor of any kind sold for any price. Some men in uniform, "like butterflies flitting from flower to flower, went from one smudge of lipstick to another." But at their own peril. One GI became so enamored with the wrong set of lips that he did not see the accompanying husband. Carpenter remembered, "There was a quick movement and a resounding smack not unlike the sound of a kiss. Once again it was demonstrated that crime does not pay and the stealer of kisses lost all interest in the celebration which had suddenly taken such a painful turn."[3]

Across the Great Plains, residents responded with "shrieking," whistles, and "expressions of amusement and mild wonderment" to the official confirmation that the war had ended. Residents lined railroad tracks to wave and shout the news to passing troop trains. In Denver church bells rang, and the faithful flooded their churches to "welcome peace with reverence." Others swarmed into downtown streets and blocked streetcar traffic. Sam Lusky, a reporter for the *Rocky Mountain News*, observed, "Servicemen kissed their girls and they kissed somebody else's girl and pretty soon everybody was kissing everybody else, and nobody was complaining." One observer reported, "Dignity was impossible and quiet was destroyed for the night." Only a few people noticed others crying in memory of those for whom the peace came too late. In Randolph, Nebraska, Helen Gladys King, an elementary school teacher, noted in her diary, "V-J Day. First thing I cried. I was so glad to hear of Japan's surrender." Her fellow Nebraskan Martha Rohrke now felt sufficient optimism to note the end of the conflict. On August 14, a day before Japanese emperor Hirohito declared the war at an end, she wrote, "The war is over. Thanks to the good Lord word came at noon today and the world is rejoicing." The next day she recorded without complaint, "The people were all celebrating that peace had come with a lot of noise all night."[4]

In Albuquerque the announcement that the Japanese had surrendered was met with silence. One observer reported that people could not believe it. Five minutes passed before the first car horns honked and people ran into the streets. In Roswell the town sirens announced the peace; car horns and ringing cowbells followed. In Albuquerque and Roswell revelers quickly exhausted the food supply in local restaurants ordering celebratory dinners. In Cheyenne crowds began forming in the streets less than five minutes after President Truman announced Japan's surrender. Businesses closed, and horns and whistles created a din that lasted for hours. Cars with streamers of ribbon and toilet paper created traffic jams. One observer noted that residents were filled with joy, bewilderment, and thankfulness, but he also reported a "solemnity that bespoke sorrow" for those who had died. By early evening Cheyenne's streets were littered with paper and a few drunks "who had gotten the largest share of their enthusiasm in liquid form," but nobody cared. He also thought the celebrators should have been more parsimonious with the use of toilet paper owing to the shortage of that item. After watching the crowd he wondered whether the Japanese were remembering Pearl Harbor.[5]

The day after vj-Day war plants began canceling contracts and closing. Men and women soon returned from the armed forces and began looking for jobs. Clerks employed by various state price-control and rationing boards received notice of termination, although the Office of Price Administration (opa) continued rent and price controls. Optimists hoped that postwar road construction, housing projects, and flood-control improvements would provide many new jobs. Many city officials worried about housing shortages, and the Bismarck Association of Commerce contemplated establishing a "trailer town" to meet the housing need until the construction industry could emerge from wartime inactivity, the absence of housing meaning that workers could not be hired to build houses because they had no place to live. The marriage rate soon increased with the return of the servicemen, thereby contributing to the housing shortage. By November 1945 Lester C. Hunt, the governor of Wyoming, called the housing situation in Cheyenne "acute," there being no vacant dwellings. Yet only 25 percent of the anticipated veterans had returned. In Omaha one observer worried that the housing shortage would soon take a toll on marriages and that the divorce rate would climb.[6]

By January 1945 postwar planning—which many people in the Great Plains states and communities had talked about, if not begun, during the early days of the war—intensified. City and town planners grappled with the need for housing, streets, sidewalks, services, schools, and hospitals. Some businessmen contemplated new and larger stores in anticipation of tremendous postwar spending when new supplies of manufactured goods met pent-up demands and unspent wartime earnings. In New Mexico a committee of business leaders urged the state to stress the development of small-scale industries rather than agricultural improvement. The rural population still exceeded the number that the land could support without the development of extensive irrigation. Small industries, the group believed, would take up the expected postwar employment slack. Textile mills, canneries, and dehydration plants could use the agricultural products of the plains for small-scale industrial development and strengthen the state's economy.[7]

Fear of another depression, such as the one that followed World War I, occupied the minds of many Great Plains residents. The failure of small businesses and the success of many large businesses and corporations, fed by wartime government contracts, threatened to create a postwar world where the differences between the haves and the have-nots would be more striking than ever before. Many Kansans, however, hoped that the postwar years would enable the development of industrial products from agricultural commodities, which, in the parlance of the day, they called "chemurgy." With capital ready for investment and abundant agricultural resources, Kansans expected "marked progress" in manufacturing and industrialization after the war. In Texas one reporter noted that manufacturers, laborers, and servicemen anticipated "plucking the recon-version apple as soon as it ripened by European V Day." Planning became the driving force for commercial change across the Great Plains, second only to winning the war. Nearly everyone wanted postwar industrial opportunities as well as pursuing other agendas such as flood control for the Arkansas River in Kansas and the Upper Missouri River valley.[8]

Wichita provides an example of planning challenges for the post-war years. By autumn 1944 the city trailed only San Diego and Long Beach in airplane manufacturing. Between April 1940 and January 1944 employment in Wichita's aircraft industry increased more than thirty-fold, to 53,000 workers, a number that exceeded by 4,000 the wage earners employed in the aircraft industry nationwide in 1939. If postwar aircraft employment fell to prewar levels, only about 10,000 men and women would be employed. Moreover, in spring 1940 the population of Sedgwick County tallied 143,000, but it increased to 195,000 by late 1943. The questions that city planners confronted were obvious. First, how many of these defense industry workers could secure jobs in Wichita after the war ended? Second, what would be the effects of conversion from a wartime to a peace-time economy? City planners worried that without the aircraft industry the city could not provide employment opportunities and the economy would revert to prewar conditions. Without new forms of employment, they feared, workers would go on relief or migrate to other areas. The result would be a postwar period of decline rather than progress and prosperity.[9]

Many planners hoped that construction jobs would help absorb the employment needs of returning servicemen. Workers who had taken jobs vacated by men going into the military, however, right-fully worried that their wartime economic gains would soon be lost. Union leaders argued that reinstatement would violate union senior-ity structures and contracts. School district officials and teachers also worried about their obligations to and the effect of returning teachers. Dedicated teachers who had forgone high-paying defense industry jobs feared that they would be forced out. These problems would not be solved before the war ended.[10]

Although unemployment compensation claims increased during fall 1945, optimism prevailed, especially in the cities where postwar employment opportunities continued to attract men and women with jobs often paying between $3,000 and $4,500 annually. Even so, discrimination against women quickly prevailed. In Denver, for example, women who had entered the labor force with defense industry jobs soon found that they had to take a pay cut, employers arguing that lucrative government contracts no longer created jobs at high wages, especially for women. By early September 1945 some eight thousand workers had lost their jobs in the defense industries of Omaha, with another four thousand layoffs expected. Even before VJ-Day the aircraft plants began curtailing production. By August 14 the line at the U.S. Employment Office in Wichita stretched a block long. Many women willingly left their jobs for preferred domestic duties, but $1.00 per hour wages at the Martin bomber plant for riveters fell to $0.54 per hour and drove many women from that workforce. Other women, however, preferred to work but could not find jobs because of cutbacks.[11]

Gasoline rationing ended abruptly on VJ-Day, and traffic accidents increased. Lines formed at gas stations, but poor tires kept many drivers off the roads. Great Plains residents had felt particularly aggrieved about gasoline rationing, and they believed that they had sacrificed more than others, comparatively speaking, given the oil fields and refineries in the region. State governors had received numerous letters asking for exemptions from gasoline and other forms of rationing, such as that of tires and food. Invariably, they replied that rationing was a federal program beyond state control. Republican governor Andrew Schoeppel of Kansas no doubt enjoyed using such occasions to subtly jab the Roosevelt administration, saying, "Our officers have little to say in the matter," thereby placing the responsibility on a Democratic president. The war also brought subtle but important social change, particularly in relation to rationing. Gasoline and tire rationing, for example, often prevented rural families from attending country churches. Without a sufficient congregation to support them financially, small town and country churches closed or consolidated. Gas rationing might conserve rubber tires, but it also cut state revenues from taxation. As a result highway improvements came to an abrupt halt during the war.[12]

Not everything changed immediately with the peace, but meatless and butterless days were numbered. Men's clothing, however, remained in short supply because discharged military men wanted civilian clothes. The teacher shortage also continued into the coming academic year. In Wyoming school officials hired nonteachers to fill classroom needs, but they essentially served to keep order rather than teach. Many teachers indicted their intent to resign when their husbands returned home from the military. People had no idea when they would be able to buy new cars. By the end of the war, however, the marriage license business boomed at county courthouses as men and women began converting their private lives to peacetime living.[13]

Still, by 1945 Great Plains residents had experienced considerable change. Prisoner-of-war camps loomed near some communities, military bases brought social problems, and war industries created economic opportunities, particularly for women. New oil fields opened, housing shortages continued, and everything from major brands of cigarettes to staples like sugar and beef was in short supply, was rationed, or disappeared from market shelves. Bank deposits increased, and agricultural production expanded. Everyone hoped that the good times would outlast the war and that the inconveniences would rapidly disappear when peace returned. Only time would tell.[14]

When peace came, Great Plains farmers worried that high wartime production would create surpluses beyond the need, even with postwar food aid to Europe. They feared a recession in business activity and employment until the economy could revert to peacetime conditions. They anticipated less consumer purchasing power and falling agricultural prices, and they looked to the federal government for protection. Essentially, Great Plains farmers agreed with Secretary of Agriculture Claude R. Wickard. They supported an agricultural policy designed to enhance farm income through various price-support measures as well as full production, more efficient marketing, a freight rate structure that would equalize or minimize transportation costs for agricultural products, expanded Extension Service programming, an extended school lunch program, and improved rural education and health services. They also wanted the federal government to provide electricity for all rural areas of the Great Plains, more all-weather roads, and federal payments to farmers who practiced soil conservation. The bottom line in their programmatic wish list for agricultural policy, however, involved money from price-support programs that would enable them to maintain their wartime income and standard of living.[15]

Indeed, in 1939, when the war began, farm prices averaged about 80 percent of parity, and per capita farm income had fallen to only 37.5 percent of that of the nonfarm population. Lend-Lease and defense spending, along with improved marketing and civilian purchasing power, quickly helped reduce surpluses, and agricultural prices increased. Many Great Plains farmers returned to the Republican Party, and they wanted their fair share of postwar spending on agricultural commodities. In 1942 Great Plains farmers gained some price protection when Congress guaranteed 90 percent of parity prices for two years after the war officially ended, that is, through the crop year 1948. Democratic senator Elmer Thomas in Oklahoma and Republican congressman Clifford Hope in Kansas strongly contended that farmers were only now beginning to receive the prices and income that they deserved. Indeed, World War II gave most Great Plains farmers their first real prosperity. In 1940 farm prices averaged 105 percent of parity but rose to 123 percent of parity nationwide in 1946. Per capita farm income increased from $245 in 1940 to $655 in 1945. Even so, when the war ended, the per capita income of farmers nationwide averaged only 57 percent of that of nonfarmers. Still, Great Plains farmers had the protection of price guarantees that would maintain wartime income. For them World War II had been a time of milk and honey.[16]

Beyond payment programs to maintain high wartime income and rapidly improving standards of living, Great Plains farmers also wanted their fair share of programmatic funding from agencies such as the USDA and the Bureau of Reclamation. New Mexico sought new irrigation projects. The editor of the *Albuquerque Journal* urged state government, citizens, and the New Mexico congressional delegation to work hard to get them, saying, "We need all the irrigation projects possible in a post-war program." Continued labor and machinery shortages also worried farmers. During the war the number of farms also declined while farms increased in size.[17]

Certainly, World War II gave Great Plains farmers their greatest period of prosperity to date, but, when the peace came, they continued to fret about a postwar depression. They worried about lower prices, diminishing markets, and reduced income as well as unemployment, all of which would trim food purchases. The war had restored agricultural prosperity as the New Deal had not, but Great Plains farmers could not escape the belief that they faced a period of economic contraction. Too many veterans might also return to the farms and contribute to overproduction and correspondingly low prices for agricultural commodities, and per capita income would fall. Peace meant economic problems.[18]

Within days of Japan's surrender Great Plains cattle raisers urged Clinton P. Anderson, the secretary of agriculture, and Chester Boles, the OPA administrator, to abandon meat rationing by September 15 to improve marketing and "knock out black marketers" and also to end quotas for packers to help meet the food needs of returning servicemen and-women. By March 1946 Secretary Anderson urged cattlemen to consolidate their herds and sell animals while demand and prices remained high. He also reminded them that the USDA subsidy paid to cattle feeders would end on June 30 to ease the taxpayers' burden. Although ceiling prices on meat would increase, Anderson did not believe that inflation would result. He also told farmers that they could expect government support at 90 percent of parity prices, as was provided to other agricultural producers for two years after the war. With the public consuming 165 pounds of meat per capita annually by March 1946, and with demand increasing, cattle raisers faced a prosperous future.[19]

On July 1, 1946, the OPA lifted the ceiling price for cattle, which had stood at $17.65 per hundredweight. Within just a few hours choice steers sold for $22.50 per hundredweight, but with few cattle in the feedlots the kill at slaughterhouses did not increase rapidly. By mid-1946 demand so exceeded supply that butchers could not keep meat cases stocked. Great Plains livestock raisers, however, continued to withhold their cattle from market, hoping for still higher prices. As a result Senator Elmer Thomas of Oklahoma, the chairman of the Agriculture Committee, contended that, unless price controls were lifted, legally sold and processed beef would disappear entirely from the market within thirty days, and he observed that the OPA had "practically given up" on the "black market situation." By September cattle prices had escalated to an index of 249, up from 235 a year earlier.[20]

Packers and butchers across the nation experienced the same shortages, but in Omaha, Lincoln, and Kansas City the beef shortage proved particularly serious. Martin Hansen, the president of the Omaha Meat Dealers Association, called it "more critical than during rationing," and the city's packers laid off three thousand workers because their cattle pens remained essentially empty. He complained that speculators bought cattle and withheld them from market, gambling that prices would go still higher. In the meantime black market sales boomed. Most Great Plains cattlemen, such as the members of the Sandhills Feeder Cattle Producers and the Sandhills Cattle Association in Nebraska, did not believe that the nationwide meat shortage would end until the OPA lifted price controls.[21]

By summer 1946 Denver packers contended that "no beef at all can be purchased thru legitimate channels," and they believed that the shortage would continue until autumn. F. E. Mollin, the executive secretary of the American Livestock Association, warned cattle producers at the annual meeting of the Wyoming Stock Growers Association (WSGA) that OPA price ceilings were unfair, and he told the members that the agency was attempting to control profits rather than prices. He believed that the OPA intended the price ceiling to benefit the working class, to the detriment of cattlemen. Mollin predicted that price controls would soon end and that the OPA would collapse by late 1947 for want of need and support. Mollin stated the obvious, noting, "The housewives are getting tired of standing in line. They are beginning to realize that a low meat ceiling, if there isn't any meat to buy, forces them to the black market for meat."[22]

Certainly, "sharply expanded incomes" enabled thousands of

people who had been light meat eaters before the war to purchase beef that they previously could not afford. When the war ended, disposable income and demand remained high, and Great Plains cattlemen wanted to profit without price controls. While the cattlemen withheld their beef from the market, consumers necessarily turned to meat substitutes and blamed cattlemen for the shortages. Rather than continually contesting with OPA efforts to direct a planned economy, the cattlemen wanted freedom to produce and sell as they pleased. Simply put, the Great Plains cattle producers believed that, by employing price controls, the OPA destroyed production and created a meat shortage rather than controlling inflation.[23]

In 1946 Harry B. Coffee, the president of the Union Stock Yards Company of Omaha, told the WSGA, "The price control system was made in Germany during the First World War and was perfected by Hitler. A controlled economy is an essential tool for a dictator and is not compatible with the free enterprise system that made this country great." The danger was significant because price controls, he believed, would "breed further regimentation and tighter control until frustration finally drives the people into the arms of a centralized totalitarian government." Most Great Plains cattle raisers, while conservative, were not this antagonistic to the federal government, although they bore no love for the OPA. They knew that the problem was not the OPA ceiling price, or $17.65 per hundredweight, for choice steers because few graded that high. Rather, the supply problem stemmed from OPA regulations that controlled the wholesale price for which packers could sell meat. Essentially, cattlemen reasoned that, if wholesalers could increase their prices to retailers, they would be able to pay higher prices for live cattle. For Great Plains cattlemen the solution to federal deficit spending and low livestock prices was clear—eliminate price controls and subsidies on livestock and meat, and the black market, which cost consumers more, would be eliminated. Coffee reflected, "The American housewives have always been able to do a better job of controlling the price of food than has the OPA with 30,000 or more employees on the Federal payroll."[24]

Most of the labor for the war industries in the Great Plains came from the farms and small towns in the region. In many areas the population loss occurred quickly. By late September 1942 eighty-seven counties in Kansas reported a population drop over the past year, with Wichita or California the primary destination. The increase in urban population in certain areas had other than economic ramifications. By February 1944 the rapid growth of population in Wichita necessitated dividing the township into two voting precincts. The war, then, changed living patterns in many ways.[25]

Wyoming lost population during the war years. In 1940 the state had a civilian population of 246,000, but that fell to 232,000 in 1945, before climbing again to 256,000 a year later. Overall decreases or increases were not as important as abrupt changes in specific locations. In Cheyenne, for example, approximately 4,500 workers descended on the city to erect new buildings at Fort Warren. Most of these workers departed after a few months. Even so, Cheyenne's population increased by 10,000 residents between 1940 and November 1943 owing to employment opportunities at the defense industries. Moreover, while thousands of women and children left Wyoming with husbands and fathers, thousands of other women and children arrived with the military and defense industries to keep their families together. Many people, who left for jobs elsewhere, particularly the West Coast, never returned to Wyoming. Moreover, Wyoming's greatest loss of population occurred with the migration away from the farms and ranches. In 1940 the agricultural population tallied 72,674, but by 1945 it had fallen 26 percent, to 53,424. Few of those leaving returned, and the population had not recovered by 1950. Taken together, the agricultural population and the "rural" population in towns with fewer than 2,500 inhabitants fell by 7.2 percent from 1940 to 1950, while the state's urban population increased by 54.5 percent during that same period. Clearly, the war stimulated the migration of rural people to the cities. The social ramifications proved profound and lasting.[26]

Between October 1, 1940, and September 1941 approximately 12,800 families moved to Wichita, increasing the city's population by 20 percent, from about 115,000 to about 138,000. During that period Wichita attracted six times more migrants than Baltimore and twenty times more than Philadelphia, even though both cities were important defense centers. Most of these new residents came from the region—54 percent from Kansas, 18 percent from Oklahoma—with an average distance traveled of 135 miles. Only 7 percent migrated 500 miles or more. More than 50 percent of these new residents came from small towns with fewer than 2,500 people, and 10 percent came from "open country." Towns ranging in population from 2,500 to 25,000 people contributed 38 percent of the new population, small cities 9 percent, and cities larger than 100,000 11 percent. Most of these people—89 percent—had never been to Wichita. These newcomers also averaged 24.9 years of age. Only one worker in sixteen was 45 years of age or older, while women constituted 13 percent of the new workforce. The racial breakdown was 98 percent white and 2 percent "colored." Moreover, 56 percent of these families contained only one person, 22 percent two people, and 19 percent three to four people. Overall, then, these new residents were young, rural, and white, primarily from the farms and trade and service industries in the small towns, and entering the workforce for the first time. The airplane manufacturers hired 52 percent of these new residents. Moreover, until late 1942 most black workers qualified only for janitorial positions at the aircraft plants and other war industries. Two-thirds of these new people shared housing. Although some observers considered this migration rate of "spectacular proportions," others recognized that people were arriving faster than the city could absorb them, whether that meant providing jobs or providing housing. Only problems could come from it.[27]

State officials expected 142,000 Kansans to lose their jobs by the end of 1945, but they believed that the unemployment problem would be solved, in part, by the return of unskilled men and women to the farms from war industries because they could not compete with skilled labor for postwar employment. They expected 50 percent of the women in the workforce to return home. The Kansas Industrial Commission hoped to keep the state's industrial gains by promoting Kansas as a place where companies could find a skilled workforce that did not strike as well as electric power, transportation, good housing, and raw materials.[28]

Yet even the aviation city of Wichita lost population in 1944 compared to previous years, a result primarily of the enlistment of men and women in the military but also of entire families apparently moving elsewhere, probably to California, seeking work. By May 1942, among the Great Plains states North Dakota had lost the most residents, for a 16 percent decline, followed by South Dakota, with a 14 percent population drop. Official estimates of population losses were often based on the distribution of ration books between 1940 and January 31, 1944. By 1945 the Great Plains states had lost 3.4 percent of its population, while California's population increased 22.4 percent. Overall, every Great Plains state, excluding Texas, had a population decline between 1939 and 1946 (see app. 1). Considering that most migrants to the West Coast ranged in age from fifteen to thirty-nine, the Great Plains states lost considerable energy from the workforce. The region's leaders, the newspapers argued, had to provide economic development and job opportunities that would keep the young men and women in the plains.[29]

Certainly, the war caused great internal migration as workers sought jobs within their state and region or elsewhere, particularly California. For Oklahoma and Texas the westward migration pattern had already been established during the drought years of the 1930s. Between 1935 and 1940 ninety-five thousand migrants from Oklahoma alone trekked to California in search of a better life, and the Sooner State contributed the largest number to the Great Plains migration process. Most of those emigrants fled rural areas for urban employment. In 1940 white and nonwhite migrants ranged in age from 20 to 35, with a median age of 28.6. During the war years women constituted approximately 60 percent of the migrants, although men roughly equaled women for those 45 years of age or older.[30]

The war also spurred urbanization in the Great Plains, particularly where war industries flourished. In Kansas, for example, approximately 40 percent of the population lived in urban areas when the war began, but that proportion increased to 52 percent by war's end. The war also stimulated the growth of other cities. In 1940 Albuquerque, for example, covered eleven square miles, but this area increased to sixteen square miles by June 1946, largely as a result of the establishment and rapid expansion of the Kirtland Air Force Base and the location of many regional offices of the federal government. Certainly, the war changed the economic and demographic patterns in the Great Plains. In Wichita, for example, only 3 percent of the population relied on industry for a living in 1939. By 1943, however, approximately 50 percent of the population did so, primarily at Cessna, Beechcraft, and Boeing. Yet, what the war had given, the peace threatened to take away. The war had created a vibrant economy, major demographic change, and new employment patterns, among other changes, but no one wanted to go back to the prewar days of unemployment, scant payrolls, and a low standard of living. Yet by the autumn of 1945 some twenty-five thousand workers had lost their jobs in Wichita alone.[31]

Across the Great Plains African Americans had been second-class citizens before the war, and discrimination and segregation governed their relationships with whites. In 1941 an early breach in white-black relations, however, occurred when Kansas governor Payne Ratner supported full African American participation in defense programs. Although war industries offered some job opportunities and improved income, great disparity remained. Black male and female urban workers earned an average income of about $457 per year, whereas white workers' annual income averaged $1,064. By 1944 those averages had risen to $1,976 and $2,600, respectively. When the war ended, many African American workers faced the "last-hired, first fired" principle.[32]

By war's end Great Plains residents could not be proud of their efforts to improve race relations beyond mere tolerance. During the war years, as in the past, African Americans remained socially segregated. Even so, plains residents were unprepared to act on their prejudices and scrambled to provide segregated spaces for recreation and living. Housing for African Americans, most of whom arrived with the military, remained a problem throughout the war in towns that previously did not have large black populations, such as Cheyenne. In 1943 Oklahoma City school officials established a day-care center, then called a "nursery," for black children whose parents worked. Nine other nurseries provided day-care services for whites. In Roswell, New Mexico, the USO built an entertainment center for black soldiers, whom the local newspaper called "colored folks." With black soldiers also came black prostitutes, who caused more social problems.[33]

Across the Great Plains, however, many African Americans committed themselves to winning the war on the home front. In spring 1940 a group organized in Dallas to watch and work against fifth column activities. Charles T. Brackins, the director of the Negro Chamber of Commerce, said, "The Negros of Dallas realize these are dangerous times. All should work together to protect America." Lawrence I. Brochenbury, the editor of the African American *Dallas Express*, agreed, saying, "The only ism known by the American Negro is Americanism."[34]

Discrimination against blacks on the Great Plains, of course, stemmed from long-established social relationships that often became institutionalized as policy, both civil and governmental. In May 1941, for example, four black men in Amarillo attempted to enlist in the army but met rejection when told that no "fighting classifications" were open for Negroes. The local newspaper reported, "The four have good records as citizens and as workmen and are prominent in negro organizations seeking community and race improvement." By September the school district in Oklahoma City sought federal funds to establish a defense training school for blacks where they would learn industrial arts, shoe repair, and vocational agriculture as well as such traditional work as that done in laundries and restaurants. In Salina, Kansas, city officials designated a "black-belt" area and proclaimed it off-limits to whites unless they had family who lived there. But segregation is segregation, no matter the perspective. If the area remained "off-limits" for whites, by implication an even larger area remained off-limits for the blacks stationed at nearby Camp Phillips when they came to Salina. Black soldiers also experienced discrimination by local bus services, particularly with the inconvenient location of segregated bus stops for military personnel.[35]

During the war, then, Great Plains African Americans experienced the same problems of discrimination characterizing race relations across the nation. Segregation in living quarters, employment, transportation, education, and recreation portended widespread civil disorder in the absence of quick, equitable solutions. Essentially, African Americans in the Great Plains and across the country wanted equality before the law. Many whites, however, believed that the achievement of that goal meant or would lead to social equality. Most blacks, however, sought economic and political equality when the war ended. In Dallas some observers believed that the provision of adequate housing for blacks by private groups and the Dallas Housing Authority would help solve racial inequities. By late January 1945 Dallas sought support from the Federal Public Housing Authority to build fifty thousand houses for African Americans, funded through private builders. Yet, as in the case of Hasting, Nebraska, where city officials also operated on the premise that African Americans wanted segregation, particularly in housing, the resources and the organizational ability were not available to meet that goal. Ultimately, an isolated trailer camp often became the black part of town, and federally funded housing projects met only part of the demand.[36]

Moreover, the war years were not kind to the Urban League on the state and local levels. In Lincoln and Omaha, for example, members of the Urban League, which existed to provide social, economic, and educational opportunities for the black community, found themselves at odds with the national Urban League, which demanded greater efforts to achieve equal opportunity for all African Americans, rather than group-directed service activities. The national Urban League wanted the Lincoln and Omaha members to work with local whites to gain equal opportunities in education, housing, and employment. Rather than the Lincoln and Omaha Urban Leagues, for example, providing recreational opportunities to their constituencies, they should be working with the white power structure to achieve equality for all African Americans. As a result many people-oriented services provided at black community centers were terminated, but not without considerable debate between local and national organizations and the generation of factionalism.[37]

World War II, however, presented new challenges for the Urban League in Lincoln and Omaha. By the end of 1941 the Lincoln Urban League (LUL) had abandoned the quiet behind-the-scenes activities of the past. The national Urban League began to address civil rights issues directly and worked closely with welfare agencies to develop a "better understanding of the criteria for local League programs." Still, the LUL attempted to remain "strictly an educational, charitable, and non-partisan and non-sectarian organization." The loss of federal funds channeled through the Works Progress Administration and other agencies, however, created financial problems that the LUL could not overcome. Most of the staff departed, and recruitment of new members languished. By the end of 1945 the LUL's membership was only 803, and more than half of those members were white. Still, the LUL negotiated the use of the YMCA's swimming pools, which signified an important gain for black civil rights, and it committed to advocating equal opportunity, especially open housing, but met little success. Redlining remained the unwritten rule for African American housing in Lincoln. The LUL, however, adjusted its activities during the war years to helping blacks find jobs and improving the quality of employment available to African Americans. Since Lincoln was not a major defense industry town, however, the LUL made little progress gaining more employment opportunities for blacks. Prejudice, local employment conditions, and the lack of assertiveness among individual African Americans, resulting from a tradition of discrimination, slowed economic and social improvement.[38]

The battle against totalitarian regimes, however, encouraged African Americans in the Great Plains and across the nation to intensify their demands for equality. World War II pushed the LUL into a public realm heretofore foreign to its members. Although the LUL failed to end segregation during the war, it began to pursue the national goals of equality in education, housing, and employment, but the organization's past tradition of local service prevented the transition to a major civil rights organization. In fact the new orientation—toward achieving broader social and economic goals—caused many blacks to lose interest in the local organization once it failed to meet community needs, such as providing news about black churches, social events, and public forums where speakers addressed the major issues of the day.[39]

In Omaha the Urban League suffered from lack of membership and black interest when the war began. Compared to the National Association for the Advancement of Colored People (NAACP), it had few achievements to its credit and little money. The Omaha Urban League (OUL), like the LUL, struggled from the loss of New Deal agency funding and the disappearance of voluntary aid as the military and local defense industries took away black men. As thousands of blacks moved to Omaha for wartime employment, housing conditions deteriorated rapidly. At the same time the OUL sought job training and the integration of offices and factories. Executive Director Raymond R. Brown said, "To those of us engaged in social work, the word defense has a broader and deeper meaning than military preparedness. It must include our economic and social democracy." Leadership and economic opportunities enabled the OUL, unlike the LUL, to increasingly advocate civil rights during the war years. The OUL organized the Northside Building Trades Council and placed some 350 black workers on construction projects at the Martin bomber plant. After President Roosevelt issued Executive Order 8802 in June 1941, creating the Fair Employment Practices Committee, the OUL helped individuals and groups who filed discrimination complaints. It also worked with the American Federation of Labor and the Congress of Industrial Organizations to gain the employment of several previously barred black painters at the Mead Ordnance Plant as well as the placement of forty black women at the Armour meatpacking plant.[40]

In 1942 the OUL organized the Race Relations Council to help local groups and demonstrate the need for a smooth transition into new economic and social relationships with whites when peace came. Still, members demanded change. In Omaha the war created a new militancy in the African American community, as it did elsewhere across the nation. The status quo was no longer acceptable. In 1944 an OUL member observed, "Discrimination practices that went unchallenged before were now met head-on by citizens of this community." During the war the OUL worked closely with the NAACP to resolve African Americans' complaints against theaters, restaurants, and drugstores, and it utilized public forums to address the shortage of adequate housing and slum conditions. By the end of the war it was prepared to aggressively pursue civil rights activism and to work to maintain wartime economic gains. It had made the transition from a local recreational or service agency to an increasingly powerful organization that intended to fight discrimination and segregation against blacks, and it had emerged as an organization dedicated to a broad economic and social agenda to be pursued across the entire community. A host of problems remained, but the OUL was ready for new challenges by the end of the war.[41]

In retrospect, then, World War II spurred a major transition in the OUL. When the war began, it, like the LUL, essentially existed to dispense social services. By the end of the war—owing, in part, to the job opportunities at nearby defense industries—it had become a mediator in search of social justice. Until the United States entered the war, the OUL, like the LUL, worked to improve the quality of African American life in the community. By 1945 it sought the inclusion of blacks in everyday social affairs and by so doing became a new advocate for civil rights. Still, the accomplishments of the OUL, while significant, proved limited given the institutional racism that characterized mainstream American life. The OUL secured greater job opportunities for blacks, but many positions required few skills and remained comparatively low paying. Equal employment opportunity would not be realized for decades. Blacks continued to confront discrimination in housing, and Omaha remained a redlined city like others across the Great Plains and the nation. Even so, by war's end the OUL had become a recognized leader in the African American community, owing largely to the social and economic changes that occurred during World War II.[42]

Cracks in the wall of institutionalized racism also appeared at the University of Kansas. Although the university was founded in 1866 as a monument to the abolitionists, the school's white administration enforced segregation in the best Jim Crow tradition. During World War II, however, many students realized that whites and blacks fought Fascism and racial segregation in Europe at the same time as

African Americans did not enjoy full civil liberties at home, including at the University of Kansas. Prior to World War II the university had a long tradition of barring black students from its dormitories. Many professors required black students to sit at the back of the class and denied them participation in student social activities and organizations. By the time the United States entered the war American thought about race had begun to change in subtle ways, encouraged, in part, by President Roosevelt, who linked the fight against Fascism to the preservation of freedom and democracy at home. On January 6, 1941, Roosevelt had introduced his four freedoms—freedom of religion, freedom of speech, freedom from want, and freedom from fear—as goals for all Americans. African Americans and white liberals, however, asked why those freedoms did not extend to blacks, a state of affairs that the Fascists could use to divide black and white Americans. Soon, black servicemen and-women and African Americans employed in the defense industries had greater expectations. Although discrimination and segregation had limited them in the past, the future offered the potential for new and equal race relations. Across the nation African Americans became more vocal about and active against segregation during the war.[43]

The changing racial atmosphere, one conducive to protests against segregation, gained a welcoming acceptance at the University of Kansas. In February 1942 a group of students organized the Fellowship of Reconciliation, an interracial Christian protest group that targeted the segregated restaurant at the university's Memorial Union for reform. At the restaurant black students could sit only at two corner booths. Chancellor Deane W. Malott considered the group as nothing more than "well-meaning, but misguided students," zealous but ineffective. As far as he was concerned they were creating a problem by challenging segregation, but Jim Crow was not the issue. The culprit appeared to be Nazi propaganda. The University of Kansas, he contended, had a social policy of segregation that both blacks and whites observed in peace and harmony; only the Nazis would attempt to upset the university's stable racial boundaries in order to damage the war effort.[44]

The student protesters did not cease and desist. The journalists on the staff of the university newspaper, the *Kansan*, took up the fight from 1943 through the end of the war. They attacked the university's policy of segregation as analogous to Fascism, contending that the University of Kansas "did a good job of practicing what Hitler preached." They sought a "new order" where "racial tolerance" prevailed. African American students supported this goal by joining the newly organized chapter of the NAACP in Lawrence and the NAACP's Youth Council on campus. They demanded equal treatment at the university's food services institutions, in the dormitories, and when participating in varsity and intramural athletics. They also protested "that other discriminatory and segregational practices are endorsed and maintained by the administration of the University against Negro students." The local NAACP chapter demanded that the governor and the legislature investigate "the entire system of Jim Crow and discriminatory practices against Negro students." The NAACP also threatened legal action to end "these unfair and un-American practices at the states [*sic*] leading education institution." Chancellor Malott responded to Governor Andrew Schoeppel, saying that segregation enabled both races to live "side by side without undue hardship" and that the "parents and students of Kansas are not ready to live in intimate contact with the Negro." Chancellor Malott feared, "We are in for considerable trouble because they [black students] have become more aggressive of late."[45]

In 1943 students at the University of Kansas also protested the segregation of blood donated on campus to the Red Cross. In April two students complained, "This policy of the Red Cross . . . defeats the purpose of obtaining the greatest possible amount of blood donations . . .[and] contributes to racial discrimination by imitating the Nazi theory of the Aryan superman." The *Kansan* asked the Red Cross to explain its blood drive, but the Red Cross begged off, citing the need to comply with military standards. At the same time the Men's Student Council and the Women's Student Council merged to form the All-Student Council, which had a provision in its constitution holding that "no regularly enrolled student shall in a discriminatory manner be denied the privileges of membership." Other student groups pledged to "work for equality." At the end of the war the black and white students at the university pursued an aggressive agenda to eliminate segregation on campus. At the University of Kansas World War II became the catalyst that encouraged students to attack the university's Jim Crow policy of discrimination and segregation. Their wartime experiences advocating civil rights boded well for the years ahead.[46]

In Texas wartime logistic necessities began to chip away at segregation on the railroads that passed throughout the state. Soon after the war began the state's Railroad Commission began receiving complaints about race mixing on troop trains. War Department policy required the equal treatment of white and black soldiers in such cases, and they intermingled in the passenger, Pullman, and dining cars. Beauford H. Jester, the chairman of the Railroad Commission, could not prevent the practice but in July 1943 requested that Texas carriers ensure segregated Pullman and dining cars after the war, when federal regulations would no longer affect state railroads. His request, however, met with failure because the railroads became accustomed to the cost-saving nature of integration. After the war railroad companies had no intention of financing separate-but-equal accommodations when one passenger, Pullman, or dining car could easily meet the needs of both black and white passengers. When the war began, the western-oriented railroads already passively resisted the segregation laws of Texas as a matter of financial sensibility. Wartime demands made duplication of services impossible.[47]

As a result, in Texas the Santa Fe, Missouri Pacific, and Missouri-Kansas-Texas railroads did not enforce segregation when their trains crossed onto Texas soil. Moreover, northern blacks refused to accept segregated cars and services. Texas Railroad Commission officials believed that segregated cars would keep the peace, but railroad officials saw only hassle and expense. Moreover, the Oklahoma Corporation Commission refused to help Texas, pleading the lack of authority to regulate the segregated seating of interstate passengers, many of whom were servicemen and-women. When the war ended, the Railroad Commission wanted to "get back to the full meaning and intent of the Texas statutes." The western-based railroad lines ignored the commission. Although the railroads that crossed Texas would have had desegregated services eventually, if only for reasons of cost, World War II pushed them to ignore Jim Crow regulations. Across the Texas plains, then, the war contributed to a new spirit and practice of racial equality. Still, residents of the Great Plains and the nation as a whole did not consider the dismantling of Jim Crow to be a wartime objective. Nevertheless, the war created a new moral, economic, and social awareness. By ignoring segregation policies some people of the Great Plains helped redirect relations between blacks and whites. Although the achievement of full equality remained a distant goal, the battle against segregation in the Great Plains had begun by the time the war had ended.[48]

For most Mexican Americans who lived in the Great Plains World War II was a turning point in their lives. Military bases provided employment opportunities, especially for women, and gave them the chance to leave agricultural work, domestic service, and positions as waitresses and clerical and sales workers. Even so, they increasingly resented daily affirmations that whites did not consider them Americans no matter their place of birth or contribution to the war effort. In Texas Mexican Americans confronted Jim Crow segregation even though the state constitution did not have a separate-but-equal provision for them, and the courts considered them "Caucasian." Even so, politically and sociologically Texas treated Mexican Americans and African Americans much the same; discrimination and segregation ruled their lives, particularly in the countryside, but less so in the cities, where they became more middle-class consumers. As Texans moved from rural areas to the cities, wartime industrialization and urbanization temporarily caused a relaxation of racial segregation for Mexican Americans. Still, in San Antonio, for example, the schools remained segregated, and businesses often refused service. Discrimination proved the rule in relation to real estate restrictions, employment barriers, and police brutality. Mexican American workers qualified only for unskilled jobs and received lower wages than similarly employed Anglos.[49]

Wartime labor needs provided opportunities for Mexican Americans who lived or moved to the cities. Although jobs opened and income improved, few Texans made any commitment to end discrimination. They considered the wartime employment of Mexican Americans merely a temporary necessity. The war years did not change the pattern of discrimination for Mexican Americans in rural Texas, and many chose to migrate to the central and northern plains to work in the fields from spring to autumn, while Texas farmers used Mexican nationals and more mechanization, particularly tractors. When the war ended, fair employment practices by the federal government largely disappeared, and job discrimination returned. When offices of the U.S. Employment Service returned to state control in November 1946, Mexican Americans qualified only for jobs as common laborers and domestic workers. In San Antonio Senator J. Franklin Spears met defeat when he tried to prevent discrimination against Mexican Americans. Still, Texans could not go back to prewar discrimination practices. Mexican Americans had gained economic power in the cities, and few had any desire to return to rural areas and farmwork. Mexican American soldiers returned home and demanded the freedom and equality that they enjoyed in the military, having no intention of tolerating discrimination.[50]

Throughout the war, then, Great Plains residents continued to judge people by the color of their skin rather than by their patriotism, even though one Mexican American from Kansas remembered, "There was no discrimination in the army; we were White." Not so across the Great Plains. When the war ended, Mexican Americans would push hard for the recognition of their civil rights. The economic gain of Mexican workers during the war provided opportunities for postwar economic and social advancement as well as a developing assertiveness.[51]

Other Mexican Americans believed that the war caused dramatic change in their neighborhoods—and not all for the better. One woman attributed the loss of community cohesiveness to the war. Where before the war Mexican American neighborhoods had functioned much like an extended family, the military took the young men, and families sought employment in West Coast industries. Few returned to their homes in the Great Plains. Other ethnic groups moved into the Hispanic communities, and these "strangers" constantly reminded the Mexican Americans who remained about the effects of the war. Soldiers stationed at the Kirtland Army Air Force Base near Albuquerque sometimes married Mexican American women, creating biracial families with Anglo surnames. Social change such as this eroded prewar relationships.[52]

When the war ended, the big federal contracts and expenditures also left the region, in contrast to the Far West, where they remained and increased, creating the military-industrial complex, a phenomenon that did not touch the Great Plains. Not all federal spending terminated on the Great Plains, of course, because the United States did not quickly or completely demobilize. Although many military bases closed, others remained, such as Lowery in Colorado, Fort Riley in Kansas, and Tinker in Oklahoma. Yet most bases closed; some became municipal airports, the unneeded land being sold to farmers. At Pratt and Herington, Kansas, part of the bases became cattle feedlots. Shilling Air Force Base, near Salina, Kansas, operated for some years but eventually closed. Omaha, however, gained the Fort Crook Airfield for its municipal airport.[53]

Many federal agencies remained and contributed federal payrolls to the local economy. The housing industry boomed as it attempted to meet the needs of returning servicemen and-women. Even so, the big money had gone West during the war, and it stayed there. In the Great Plains farming and agricultural service industries remained the backbone of the economy. Military contracts substantially disappeared, and residents confronted an often painful personal and financial adjustment to a peacetime economy. The planned economy, that is, the partnership between government and business in which each benefited, often at the expense of the public, remained strong in the West. During the war many businesses and states were left out of the federal windfall of contracts and money. By 1945, for example, Wyoming had only three hundred more manufacturing workers than it had in 1940. If it is too much to say that the Great Plains returned to a colonial economy with the peace, the region certainly did not progress economically as an equal to the Far West. Rather, a mixed industrial and agricultural economy emerged from the war, replacing what was essentially a farm economy, but, comparatively speaking, the Great Plains paled in comparison to the Far West, where federal largesse had restructured the economy and, with it, the social patterns of the region. World War II transformed the Far West; it left its colonial dependency on eastern corporations behind, becoming a vibrant region that drove the nation's economy.[54]

For the Great Plains World War II increased urbanization and stimulated the social problems that came with it. Out-migration and migration from the farms and small towns to the cities also resulted from the war as men and women, usually young, sought better opportunities elsewhere, often in California. Although economic diversification increased, the people of the region still tended to look to the federal government for solutions to problems or to meet their needs, usually in the form of price-support programs for agriculture and other forms of economic aid. Still, the Great Plains was essentially an agricultural region when the war began, and it remained so when peace returned. The war could not change the dictates of geography. Farms decreased in number, but they also increased in size. The agricultural population also declined as sons and daughters sought better jobs and a higher standard of living in the cities or other regions. Although per capita income increased, the people of the Great Plains remained poor—often in perception and frequently in reality—compared to the people of the Far West. During the war Great Plains men and women accepted sacrifices, but theirs was a deprivation that remained comparative, that is, flexible, as they kept a watchful eye on the response of people in other regions to government-imposed limitations on their lives. For the Japanese, African Americans, and Mexican Americans wartime sacrifice meant far more than temporary, inconvenient deprivation. Racism set the parameters of their lives and governed their actions. On reflection, then, if the war years for the people of the Great Plains could be painted, it would not be a canvas with brilliant colors or one with stark tones of black and white. Rather, the picture would be multiple shades of gray.[55]

Appendix

Table 1

Population (in thousands) [1]			
	1939	1945	Percentage Change
Colorado	1,120	1,071	-4.3
Kansas	1,824	1,793	-1.6
Montana	555	446	19.0
Nebraska	1,318	1,230	-6.6
New Mexico	523	515	-1.5
North Dakota	644	510	-20.0
Oklahoma	2,333	2,195	-5.9
South Dakota	645	539	-16.0
Texas[2]	6,360	6,708	+5.4
Wyoming	248	252	+1.5
California	6,785	9,073	+25.0

[1] Excludes members of the armed forces.
[2] Includes state population not in the Great Plains.
Source: *Statistical Abstract of the United States* (1949), 31.

Table 2

Personal income: Great Plains states[1]				
Total Income (in Millions of Dollars)			Per Capita Income (in Dollars)	
	1940	1948	1940	1948
Colorado	615	1,810	544	1,433
Kansas	756	2,523	423	1,333
Montana	316	876	566	1,616
Nebraska	573	1,909	890	1,814
New Mexico	198	655	373	1,084
North Dakota	218	813	340	1,401
Oklahoma	851	2,390	366	1,144
South Dakota	231	916	360	1,497
Wyoming	151	429	606	1,595
California	5,802	17,633	835	1,752

[1] Texas is not included in this table because so much of the state is not part of the Great Plains, and most of the income from defense industries came from beyond the Plains.
Source: *Historical Statistics of the United States*, 242–45.

Table 3

Manufacturing (money in thousands of dollars)

	1939		1947	
	Number of Workers	Value Added by Manufacturer[1]	Number of Workers	Value Added by Manufacturer
Colorado	23,388	90,330	44,153	286,774
Kansas	30,935	117,391	59,363	461,061
Montana	8,802	38,828	13,606	92,258
Nebraska	18,416	68,139	37,338	260,658
New Mexico	3,219	8,640	6,349	53,486
North Dakota	2,605	10,984	3,823	29,461
Oklahoma	27,642	101,782	44,302	341,027
South Dakota	5,421	19,619	8,062	51,398
Texas[2]	125,115	448,523	242,014	1,727,464
Wyoming	3,351	15,336	4,285	34,957
California	271,290	1,122,545	530,283	3,994,981

[1]Value of manufactured products less cost of materials.
[2]Includes figures for region not in the Great Plains.
Source: *Statistical Abstract of the United States* (1949), 805.

Table 4

Manufacturing expenditures: New plant and equipment
(in thousands of dollars)

	1939	1947
Colorado	6,037	32,189
Kansas	7,346	36,787
Montana	3,046	7,446
Nebraska	3,682	18,402
New Mexico	993	5,431
North Dakota	583	2,250
Oklahoma	5,551	25,504
South Dakota	749	3,371
Texas[1]	48,502	304,944
Wyoming	748	10,235
California	58,860	410,553

[1]Includes figures for the region not in the Great Plains.
Source: *Statistical Abstract of the United States* (1951), 770.

Table 5

Paid civilian employment: Executive branch of the federal government

	December 1938	June 1945	June 1950	June 1950 (Defense Department)
Colorado	8,692	28,839	23,191	5,742
Kansas	8,964	32,455	18,555	3,583
Montana	8,157	9,150	8,564	699
Nebraska	8,979	27,850	15,282	3,378
New Mexico	7,201	16,206	12,595	3,635
North Dakota	3,820	6,047	6,914	718
Oklahoma	10,631	47,878	31,725	16,955
South Dakota	4,691	10,438	8,363	1,020
Texas[1]	27,777	140,899	87,060	38,303
Wyoming	3,095	5,067	5,990	944
California	48,334	317,236	177,136	97,224

[1]Includes figures for the region not in the Great Plains.

Source: *Statistical Abstract of the United States* (1951), 196.

Table 6

Estimated number of women in farm labor through the Extension Farm Labor
Program (seasonal and year-round)

	1943	1944	1945
Colorado	4,075	3,891	2,484
Kansas	663	1,408	392
Montana	1,472	602	713
Nebraska	1,592	1,043	461
New Mexico	1,249	2,234	1,047
North Dakota	4,879	5,600	6,768
Oklahoma	8,231	15,961	18,499
South Dakota	755	1,178	778
Texas[1]	75,707	51,200	53,868
Wyoming	288	268	171

[1]Includes farm women not in the region of the Great Plains.

Source: Rasmussen, *A History of the Emergency Farm Labor Supply Program 1943–47*,
148–49.

1. Reluctance

1. Polenberg, *War and Society*, 4.

2. Wilkins, "Non-Ethnic Roots," 208–9; Cherny, "Isolationist Voting," 294; Smuckler, "Region of Isolationism," 398, 400; Billington, "Origins"; Strout, *American Image*, 203–5; Cummings, "Examination."

3. Smuckler, "Region of Isolationism," 391–92, 396–97, 400–401.

4. Ambrose, *Rise to Globalism*, 11.

5. *Bismarck (ND) Tribune*, January 17, 1939; *Rapid City (SD) Daily Journal*, May 11, 1939; "National Affairs," 16.

6. *Salina (KS) Journal*, August 30, 31, 1939.

7. *Rapid City (SD) Daily Journal*, September 3, 1939; *Amarillo Globe*, September 4, 1939; *Abilene (TX) News*, September 10, 1939; *Salina (KS) Journal*, September 4, 1939.

8. *Bismarck (ND) Tribune*, September 11, 12, November 8, 1939; *Kearney (NE) Daily Hub*, October 3, 6, 1939; *Abilene (TX) News*, September 14, 1939; *Salina (KS) Journal*, October 9, 1939.

9. *Rapid City (SD) Daily Journal*, September 21, 1939; *Salina (KS) Journal*, October 16, 1939; Addis F. Sweet to Elmer Thomas, July 20, 1940, folder 2, box 42, Legislative Series, Elmer Thomas Collection, Carl Albert Center, University of Oklahoma (hereafter cited as CAC).

10. Bula Swartz to Elmer Thomas, September 19, 1939, folder 2, box 42, Legislative Series, Elmer Thomas Collection, CAC; Strout, *American Image*, 203; Gallup and Robinson, "Surveys, 1935–38," 387–89; Jacob, "Influences of World Events," 48; "Gallup and Fortune Polls" (June 1940), 360. Martin Dies (D-TX) chaired the House Committee to Investigate Un-American Activities.

11. "Fortune Survey," 79; Roy Sloan to Elmer Thomas, September 22, 1939, folder 1, box 43, and Kittie C. Sturdevant to Elmer Thomas, September 22, 1939, folder 2, box 42, Legislative Series, Elmer Thomas Collection, CAC.

12. Leonard, "Nye Committee," 21–24; Robinson, *History of North Dakota*, 421–22.

13. Bailey, *Diplomatic History*, 701–2.

14. Leonard, "Nye Committee," 24–27; Larsen, "Gerald Nye."

15. *Congressional Record* 84, pt. 1:376; Erickson, "Prairie Pacifist," 27–29.

16. Erickson, "Prairie Pacifist," 27–32.

17. Socolofsky, *Arthur Capper*, 175–76, 180.

18. Socolofsky, *Arthur Capper*, 176.

19. Larson, "Panay Incident," 243–44; Partin, "Dilemma," 89; Socolofsky, *Arthur Capper*, 180; Larson, "Panay Incident," 233, 236–37, 239.

20. Partin, "Dilemma," 86–88; Socolofsky, *Arthur Capper*, 180; F. E. Spicer to Payne Ratner, September 30, 1939, folder 1, box 14, Correspondence File, 1939–43, Payne Ratner Collection, Kansas State Historical Society, Topeka (hereafter cited as KSHS).

21. Partin, "Dilemma," 86–88; Socolofsky, *Arthur Capper*, 91–92, 179–80; F. E. Spicer to Payne Ratner, September 30, 1939, folder 1, box 14, Correspondence File, 1939–43, Payne Ratner Collection, KSHS; *Congressional Record* 86, pt. 8:8244–45.

22. *Congressional Record* 84, pt. 8:8244–45.

23. Billington, "Origins," 62; Ambrose, *Rise to Globalism*, 26; Clarence E. Snow to Elmer Thomas, September 19, 1939, folder 1, box 43, James Spulock to Elmer Thomas, September 19, 1939, folder 2, box 43, Bula Swartz to Elmer Thomas, September 19, 1939, folder 3, box 42, Mrs. W. F. Smartz to Senator Elmer Thomas, September 25, 1939, folder 2, box 42, and Lillie Sasnett, September 26, 1939, and Mrs. Vernie Sayers, October 7, 1939, folder 1, box 43, Legislative Series, Elmer Thomas Collection, CAC; Mrs. E. J. S. Wilburn Cartwright to Elmer Thomas, October 10, 1939, folder 1, box 43, Wilburn Cartwright Collection, CAC.

24. E. Garnet Stone to Elmer Thomas, September 4, 1939, folder 2, box 43, Kittie C. Sturdevant to Elmer Thomas, September 22, 1939, folder 2, box 42, B. H. Synder to Elmer Thomas, September 24, 1939, folder 1, box 43, and Clyde Sullivan to Elmer Thomas, October 12, 1939, folder 2, box 42, Legislative Series, Elmer Thomas Collection, CAC.

25. *Salina (KS) Journal*, November 11, 1939; *Bismarck (ND) Tribune*, November 24, 1939; Drury A. Wallace to Wilburn Cartwright, May 22, 1941, folder 33, box 7, Wilburn Cartwright Collection, CAC.

26. Spritzer, "Senators in Conflict," 25–26; *Congressional Record* 85, pt. 1:311–12; Ambrose, *Rise to Globalism*, 26.

27. Strout, *American Image*, 215; Tuttle, "Aid-to-the-Allies," 842, and "William Allen White and Verne Marshall," 201–2.

28. "How to Stay Out of War," 91; Smith, "Father, Son, and Country," 42.

29. Guinsburg, "George W. Norris," 477, 479, 483; Lowitt, *George W. Norris*, 252–53.

30. Lowitt, *George W. Norris*, 417; Guinsburg, "George W. Norris," 477, 479–86.

31. *Congressional Record* 84, pt. 2:2187.

32. *Congressional Record* 84, pt. 4:427–28, and pt. 5:4865, 5275–76.

33. "Gallup and Fortune Polls" (December 1940), 714, 716–17; Mrs. K. Shrum to Congressman Steffen [*sic*], June 21, 1940, folder 154, box 18, Karl Stefan Papers, Nebraska State Historical Society, Lincoln (hereafter cited as

NSHS); *Congressional Record* 86, pt. 10:1074–78; Partin, "Dilemma," 93; Clifford and Spencer, *First Peacetime Draft*, 39–40, 146. In July 1940 nearly 42 percent of Great Plains residents polled, compared to 26 percent of Americans nationwide, believed that the United States should not take sides in the European conflict. By September the Great Plains states of Kansas, Nebraska, and North and South Dakota led the nation with 57 percent preferring to stay out of the war rather than aid Britain.

34. Grant, "Selective Service Act of 1940," 196–99; Clifford and Spencer, *First Peacetime Draft*, 84–85, 181; *Congressional Record* 86, pt. 10:10477, 10975–82.

35. *Congressional Record* 86, pt. 10:11142; Clifford and Spencer, *First Peacetime Draft*, 159, 180–81, 208.

36. *Congressional Record* 86, pt. 10:11142; Grant, "Selective Service Act of 1940," 199–202; Clifford and Spencer, *First Peacetime Draft*, 218; *Congressional Record* 86, pt. 11:12160–61, 12227–28.

37. Clifford and Spencer, *First Peacetime Draft*, 4.

38. Burk, "Debating the Draft," 435–36; Grant, "Selective Service Act of 1940," 204–5.

39. Strout, *American Image*, 214–15, 219; Bailey, *Diplomatic History*, 718, 721; Ambrose, *Rise to Globalism*, 30, 32–35; "Gallup and Fortune Polls" (March 1941), 158–59. By November 1940, only approximately 35 percent of the Great Plains residents polled from North Dakota to Kansas, compared to 54 percent of New Englanders, favored becoming allies with Great Britain and sending arms and supplies.

40. Partin, "Dilemma," 94; *Congressional Record* 87, pt. 1:143, 430, 591–92, 607–8; Grant, "Lend-Lease Act of 1941," 73–75, 78.

41. Spritzer, "Senators in Conflict," 27; Larson, *Wyoming's War Years*, 2; *Congressional Record* 87, pt. 2:2178.

42. Grant, "Lend-Lease Act of 1941," 79; Robinson, *History of North Dakota*, 424; Kennedy, *Freedom from Fear*, 474; *Congressional Record* 87, pt. 11 (app.):2190–92; "Gallup and Fortune Polls" (June 1941), 318, 323. In general, Kansans, Nebraskans, and Dakotans feared that the Lend-Lease Bill would lead to war. They led the nation (42 percent compared to 39 percent nationwide) in believing that the United States had made a mistake entering World War I. Nevertheless, 62 percent of these plains residents, compared to 68 percent nationwide, thought that the safety of the United States depended on Britain winning the war. In February 1941 they supported the Lend-Lease Bill slightly less than the nation as a whole, 55 percent compared to 58 percent.

43. *Wichita Eagle*, June 1, 1941; *Dallas Morning News*, August 17, 1940.

44. Larson, *Wyoming's War Years*, 3; "Gallup and Fortune Polls" (Autumn 1941), 482–84, 486. At that time 79 percent of the American public still opposed going to war with Germany, while in the Great Plains states public opin-

ion against war ranged from a high of 82 percent in Nebraska and South Dakota to 71 percent in Wyoming and Texas. Great Plains residents in Kansas, Nebraska, and North and South Dakota also led the nation with 82 percent opposed to sending the army and navy to aid Britain. They were also the least likely to support a convoy of American ships going to Britain, only 33 percent favoring the idea compared to 71 percent nationwide.

45. Partin, "Dilemma," 95; "Gallup and Fortune Polls" (Winter 1941), 687. Although 51 percent of the American public favored measures to keep Japan from becoming more powerful, even if such actions meant war, as late as August 1941 only 42 percent of those polled in Kansas, Nebraska, and North and South Dakota agreed. Fewer plains residents, however, considered themselves isolationists, 60 percent of Oklahomans and 55 percent of those polled in Colorado, Wyoming, Montana, and New Mexico favoring some form of restrictive action against the Japanese. Of course, the disagreements of the past quickly ended with the Japanese attack on Pearl Harbor.

46. *Kearney (NE) Daily Hub*, September 1, 8, 1939.

47. *Amarillo Globe*, October 8, 1939; "Gallup and Fortune Polls" (June 1940), 360; *Salina (KS) Journal*, September 18, 1941.

48. *Denver Post*, April 27, July 19, 1941; *Wichita Eagle*, September 24, 1941; *Salina (KS) Journal*, September 29, October 13, 1941; *Cheyenne Wyoming State Tribune*, March 31, August 1, 1941; *Dallas Morning News*, August 9, September 27, 1940.

49. *Salina (KS) Journal*, October 7, 1941; *Roswell (NM) Daily Record*, November 6, 1941; *Rapid City (SD) Daily Journal*, October, 25, 1941; *Billings (MT) Gazette*, November 14, 1941.

50. Larson, *Wyoming's War Years*, 6.

51. Neugebauer, ed., *Plains Farmer*, 211; Martha Rohrke Diary, entry for December 8, 1941, folder 9, box 1, Martha Rohrke Collection, NSHS; Larson, *Wyoming's War Years*, 6–7.

52. Larson, *Wyoming's War Years*, 8; *Wichita Eagle*, December 8, 1941; *Salina (KS) Journal*, December 8, 1941; *Denver Post*, December 9, 1941; *Cheyenne Wyoming State Tribune*, December 8, 1941; *Oklahoma City Daily Oklahoman* December 10, 1941.

53. *Oklahoma City Daily Oklahoman*, December 9, 1941.

54. *Denver Post*, December 11, 1941.

2. The Work of War

1. Winkler, *Home Front U.S.A.*, 8; Polenberg, *War and Society*, 11; Vatter, *U.S. Economy*, 11.

2. *Rapid City (SD) Daily Journal*, June 6, 21, September 13, 1939.

3. *Cheyenne Wyoming State Tribune*, September 14, 1939.

4. Cassity, "'In a Narrow Grave,'" 6–7.

5. *Bismarck (ND) Tribune*, November 19, 26, 1940; *Rapid City (SD) Daily Journal*, June 9, 1941.

6. *Salina (KS) Journal*, October 18, 1939, July 9, 1940.

7. *Dallas Morning News*, October 8, 1939; *Amarillo Globe*, January 10, 1940; *Denver Post*, May 19, 1940; *Salina (KS) Journal*, May 24, 1940; *Cheyenne Wyoming State Tribune*, May 28, 1940.

8. *Dallas Morning News*, June 26, 30, 1940.

9. *Lincoln (NE) Star*, July 7, 1940; *Omaha World Herald*, August 6, 1940; *Cheyenne Wyoming State Tribune*, August 8, 1940; *Wichita Eagle*, February 1, 1941; *Denver Post*, February 3, 1941.

10. *Wichita Eagle*, June 9, 15, July 30, September 22, October 2, 13, 15, 1940; Nash, *World War II and the West*, 68; Vander Meulen, "Aircraft Industry."

11. *Wichita Eagle*, October 15, 16, 1940; *Denver Post*, December 29, 1940. Of the $2.1 billion in army munitions contracts awarded nationwide, the breakdown in the Great Plains states was as follows: Colorado, $4,591,000 (0.2 percent); Kansas, $121,552,000 (5.7 percent); Montana, none; Nebraska, $2,532,000 (0.12 percent); New Mexico, none; North Dakota, none; Oklahoma, $310,000 (0.015 percent); Texas, $7,443,000 (0.35 percent); and Wyoming, $36,000 (a negligible percentage).

12. *Wichita Eagle*, October 16, December 1, 4, 29, 1940.

13. *Denver Post*, December 21, 1940, January 4, February 2, 12, March 10, April 1, 1941.

14. *Denver Post*, May 6, 1941; Pfaff, "Bullets for the Yanks," 33, 43; Leonard, "Denver at War," 34; *Omaha World Herald*, December 7, 1940; Larson, "Bomber Plant," 32.

15. Kennedy, *Freedom from Fear*, 476–77; *Salina (KS) Journal*, October 4, 1941.

16. Petersen, "Small Town America," 3.

17. *Omaha World Herald*, January 14, February 16, June 11, September 20, 1942; *Kearney (NE) Daily Hub*, February 12, 16, 1942; Wit, "Munitions Manufacture," 151, 153; Petersen, "Small Town America," 4.

18. *Wichita Eagle*, September 21, 24, 1941; *Rapid City (SD) Daily Journal*, January 26, 1945; *Oklahoma City Daily Oklahoman*, November 26, 1941. As late as October 1944, South Dakota had received only $70 million in defense contracts, out of $205 billion nationwide, since June 1940.

19. Vander Meulen, "Aircraft Industry," 83; *Oklahoma City Daily Oklahoman*, February 27, March 1, April 13, 1941, January 4, 1942.

20. *Oklahoma City Daily Oklahoman*, March 17, 1941, January 3, 1943; *Bismarck (ND) Tribune*, December 8, 1942. Oklahomans complained that the state had received only $7.3 million in army and navy contracts by March 1, 1941, but, if the contracts had been awarded on the basis of population, the

Sooner State should have received $120 million in military orders. Oklahomans also complained that Missouri received $333 million in contracts, or forty-seven times more than their state had, even though it had a smaller population and that Texas, which had about three times the population of Oklahoma, received $216 million, or thirty-one times the dollar value of Oklahoma contracts.

21. *Rapid City (SD) Daily Journal*, August 22, 1941.

22. *Wichita Eagle*, March 3, April 6, 20, June 3, 4, 1941.

23. *Wichita Eagle*, September 2, 1941; *Amarillo Globe*, December 9, 1941.

24. Kennedy, *Freedom from Fear*, 622–23.

25. *Salina (KS) Journal*, March 15, 1945.

26. *Oklahoma City Daily Oklahoman*, January 5, March 12, 1941.

27. *Kearney (NE) Daily Hub*, June 6, 1941; *Wichita Eagle*, July 27, 1941; *Oklahoma City Daily Oklahoman*, September 14, December 3, 1941; *Omaha World Herald*, June 8, 1941; *Bismarck (ND) Tribune*, April 21, 1941; *Rapid City (SD) Daily Journal*, August 21, 1941.

28. *Bismarck (ND) Tribune*, July 10, 1940, July 25, 1941; *Denver Post*, June 30, July 8, 1940; *Rapid City (SD) Daily Journal*, February 11, 1943; *Billings (MT) Gazette*, December 11, 1943.

29. *Amarillo Globe*, May 6, 1943; *Denver Post*, December 9, 1941, September 20, 1943, July 16, 1944; *Cheyenne Wyoming State Tribune*, August 31, 1944; *Wichita Eagle*, January 15, 17, 19, 1941; *Oklahoma City Daily Oklahoman*, December 11, 1941; *Omaha World Herald*, December 28, 1941.

30. Vatter, *U.S. Economy*, 43–44.

31. Kennedy, *Freedom from Fear*, 637; *Denver Post*, January 14, October 10, 1942.

32. *Wichita Eagle*, September 2, 1943; *Cheyenne Wyoming State Tribune*, August 11, September 8, 1943; *Dallas Morning News*, October 1, 1943; Tony Reda to Andrew Schoeppel, January 2, 1945, folder 9, box 63, Correspondence, 1943–47, Andrew Schoeppel Papers, KSHS.

33. Larson, "Bomber Plant," 39; Wit, "Munitions Manufacture," 153, 159. In Wyoming bank assets increased by $8.9 million during 1941 owing to wartime earnings. In Hastings bank deposits increased by 100 percent during 1942 and by another 45.6 percent by June 1943, compared to statewide growth of 21.3 percent. Put differently, in 1939 bank deposits in Hastings totaled $4.5 million but by 1944 had jumped to $12.8 million. In Wyoming bank deposits increased 316 percent between June 29, 1940, and December 31, 1945, while in Colorado deposits rose 320 percent during that same period, although most of this increase can be attributed to agriculture, not manufacturing and industry. Even so, Wyoming's per capita income dropped below the national average during the period 1941–45, primarily because the state lacked manufacturing. Overall, however, bank deposits in the Great Plains increased because consumers had little to purchase. See *Cheyenne Wyoming Eagle*, January 27,

NOTES TO PAGES 48–57   413

1942; Russell, "World War II Boomtown," 76; Larson, *Wyoming's War Years*, 102–3.

34. *Oklahoma City Daily Oklahoman*, April 8, 12, 1942.

35. Vatter, *U.S. Economy*, 45; Kennedy, *Freedom from Fear*, 638.

36. *Oklahoma City Daily Oklahoman*, December 10, 14, 1942; Lee, "'Union Threat,'" 123–25; Vatter, *U.S. Economy*, 45; Lingeman, *Don't You Know There's a War On?* 160; *Dallas Morning News*, February 4, March 25, 1943; Kennedy, *Freedom from Fear*, 639.

37. *Dallas Morning News*, February 6, March 22, 1943; Kennedy, *Freedom from Fear*, 641–42.

38. *Dallas Morning News*, February 17, 1943; *Omaha World Herald*, July 4, 1943; Kennedy, *Freedom from Fear*, 639–40, 643–44, 652.

39. *Omaha World Herald*, January 9, May 5, 1944; *Denver Post*, May 16, 18, 31, June 21, 1945; Lingeman, *Don't You Know There's a War On?* 136–37; *Bismarck (ND) Tribune*, July 20, 1941.

40. *Omaha World Herald*, December 3, 1942, July 11, 1943.

41. *Wichita Eagle*, March 11, 1942; *Denver Post*, December 31, 1944; *Dallas Morning News*, January 7, 1945; Lingeman, *Don't You Know There's a War On?* 69; Sloan, ed., "The Newelletters," 66.

42. *Dallas Morning News*, May 12, August 18, 1944; *Wichita Eagle*, April 16, 1944; Nash, *American West Transformed*, 38.

43. *Oklahoma City Daily Oklahoman*, December 4, 1944; *Denver Post*, January 7, 1945.

44. *Wichita Eagle*, May 26, 1945.

45. *Salina (KS) Journal*, June 13, 1945; *Oklahoma City Daily Oklahoman*, August 7, 19, 24, 26, 1945; Vander Meulen, "Aircraft Industry," 82; Baird and Gobel, *Story of Oklahoma*, 402.

46. *Denver Post*, August 8, 15, 16, 17, 1945; *Dallas Morning News*, May 5, 23, 25, 1945; *Bismarck (ND) Tribune*, October 8, 1945; *Cheyenne Wyoming Eagle*, September 6, 1945; *Billings (MT) Gazette*, October 28, 1945; Wit, "Munitions Manufacture," 162; Russell, "World War II Boomtown," 82; Pfaff, "Bullets for the Yanks," 45; Vander Meulen, "Aircraft Industry," 84.

47. Nash, *World War II and the West*, 69, 71–72, 77–78, 90. Between January 1942 and April 1945, West Coast aircraft industries produced 125,823 planes, or 46 percent of the nation's total of 273,528 aircraft, which meant the production of one plane every eleven minutes.

48. *Salina (KS) Journal*, January 3, 1941; *Dallas Morning News*, March 7, 1943.

49. *Denver Post*, April 4, 1942.

50. *Roswell (NM) Daily Record*, January 5, 1942; *Amarillo Globe*, September 27, 1942; *Billings (MT) Gazette*, April 5, 1942.

51. *Salina (KS) Journal*, March 27, 1942.

52. *Wichita Eagle*, July 30, 1944.

53. Cassity, "'In a Narrow Grave,'" 7; Nash, *American West Transformed*, 41; Winkler, *Home Front U.S.A.*, 30–31, 38, 41, 55–56; Koistinen, "Mobilizing the War Economy," 448; Schell, *History of South Dakota*, 299–300.

54. Nash, *American West Transformed*, 30–31; Myrdal, "American Business," 51.

55. Nelson, ed., *Impact of War*, 101; *Amarillo Globe*, September 27, 1942; *Denver Post*, September 1, 1943.

56. Nash, *American West Transformed*, 57, 218; Robinson, *History of North Dakota*, 427; *Historical Statistics*, 242–45; Nash, *World War II and the West*, 218–19, 222–25.

57. Nash, *World War II and the West*, 218–19, 222–25.

58. *Wichita Eagle*, July 18, 1942, July 5, September 2, 1945; Fearon, "Ploughshares into Airplanes," 314.

3. Women at Work

1. Hartmann, *Home Front and Beyond*, 21; Anderson, *Wartime Women*, 4; Allen, "Preparing Women," 393; Wit, "Munitions Manufacture," 155–56.

2. Hartmann, *Home Front and Beyond*, 54; Winkler, *Home Front U.S.A.*, 55–56; Adams, *Best War Ever*, 123; O'Neill, *Democracy at War*, 242.

3. *Wichita Eagle*, January 5, 1941; Johnson, "Uncle Sam Wanted Them Too!" 40–41; *Oklahoma City Daily Oklahoman*, March 9, 1941; *Denver Post*, March 16, 1941; *Bismarck (ND) Tribune*, April 7, 1941.

4. *Oklahoma City Daily Oklahoman*, February 2, 1941; *Wichita Eagle*, August 3, 1941, January 9, 1942.

5. *Wichita Eagle*, August 24, 1941; *Salina (KS) Journal*, September 4, 6, 1941.

6. *Denver Post*, June 25, July 4, 1941, January 6, 1942; *Amarillo Globe*, January 21, 1942; *Omaha World Herald*, July 30, 1942.

7. *Salina (KS) Journal*, April 2, 17, May 26, June 3, 1942; *Kearney (NE) Daily Hub*, April 11, 1942; *Roswell (NM) Daily Record*, April 26, 1942; *Bismarck (ND) Tribune*, April 17, 1942; Fagan, "Nebraska Nursing Education," 126, 133; *Oklahoma City Daily Oklahoman*, May 26, 1942; *Wichita Eagle*, June 12, 1942, January 28, February 21, November 27, 1943; *Dallas Morning News*, April 16, May 9, 1943; Peterson and Rieger, "'They Needed Nurses at Home,'" 124; Brueggemann, "Cadet Nurse Corps," 11–13, 69, 222–23.

8. Fagan, "Nebraska Nursing Education," 135; Peterson and Rieger, "'They Needed Nurses at Home,'" 127, 131.

9. Fearon, "Ploughshares into Airplanes," 307, 311; *Oklahoma City Daily Oklahoman*, April 6, 1942; *Dallas Morning News*, January 1, 1943.

10. *Wichita Eagle*, January 9, 19, 21, May 1, 1942; Macias, "'We All Had a Cause,'" 253, 255; *Bismarck (ND) Tribune*, January 2, 1942.

11. Fearon, "Ploughshares into Airplanes," 304; Hartley, "Crow Family," 91; Rupp, *Mobilizing Women for War*, 152.

12. *Oklahoma City Daily Oklahoman*, March 15, April 5, 1942; Rupp, *Mobilizing Women for War*, 61; *Wichita Eagle*, July 12, November 17, 1942; *Bismarck (ND) Tribune*, April 18, 1942; *Salina (KS) Journal*, April 2, 17, 1942.

13. *Wichita Eagle*, February 19, April 5, 1942; Busse, "'She's a Good Girl,'" 184; Goodwin, *No Ordinary Time*, 369.

14. *Denver Post*, March 8, April 23, 1942; *Salina (KS) Journal*, March 24, 1942; *Billings (MT) Gazette*, August 30, 1942; *Oklahoma City Daily Oklahoman*, April 11, 1942; *Amarillo Globe*, June 21, 27, 1942.

15. Newspaper clipping, *McCook (NE) Gazette*, ca. 1942, folder 1, box 1, series 2, Doris Lucile Minney Collection, NSHS; *Dallas Morning News*, March 29, 1943; *Denver Post*, April 23, 1942; *Oklahoma City Daily Oklahoman*, April 11, 1942.

16. *Wichita Eagle*, July 12, August 23, 1942; *Oklahoma City Daily Oklahoman*, June 4, November 7, 1942; "Your Questions," 3, 7–8.

17. *Omaha World Herald*, October 9, 1942; *Billings (MT) Gazette*, November 15, 18, 1942; *Wichita Eagle*, November 17, 29, 1942.

18. *Omaha World Herald*, December 13, 1942.

19. *Amarillo Globe*, August 22, 1942; *Billings (MT) Gazette*, October 25, November 1, 1942; *Cheyenne Wyoming State Tribune*, December 2, 1941; *Cheyenne Wyoming Eagle*, August 18, 1943.

20. *Omaha World Herald*, April 25, 1942; *Oklahoma City Daily Oklahoman*, June 13, 1943.

21. *Oklahoma City Daily Oklahoman*, September 4, 1941, May 19, June 6, 1942; *Omaha World Herald*, October 25, 1942, June 6, 1943; *Salina (KS) Journal*, December 2, 1941; *Cheyenne Wyoming Eagle*, May 22, 1943.

22. *Omaha World Herald*, April 4, 9, 16, 1944; Lingeman, *Don't You Know There's a War On?* 165, 249.

23. Fearon, "Ploughshares into Airplanes," 308; Hartmann, *Home Front and Beyond*, 60.

24. Fearon, "Ploughshares into Airplanes," 309–10; Jefferies, *Wartime America*, 98; Hartmann, *Home Front and Beyond*, 87.

25. *Oklahoma City Daily Oklahoman*, March 15, 1942; *Dallas Morning News*, November 14, 1943; Sloan, ed., "The Newelletters," 60; *Wichita Eagle*, April 5, 1942.

26. *Dallas Morning News*, June 9, 1943.

27. Macias, "'We All Had a Cause,'" 255; L. H. Dempster to Dwight Griswold, March 27, 1944, folder 109, box 72, Nebraska Department of Labor Records, and Summary of State Labor Laws for Women, August 19, 1944, folder 165, box 75, U.S. Department of Labor, Women's Bureau, Nebraska De-

partment of Labor Records, NSHS; Johnson, "Uncle Sam Wanted Them Too!" 42; Hartmann, *Home Front and Beyond*, 82.

28. *Oklahoma City Daily Oklahoman*, January 17, 24, November 26, 28, 1942; *Wichita Eagle*, January 17, May 13, 29, June 30, 1943.

29. *Cheyenne Wyoming State Tribune*, November 4, 1943; *Omaha World Herald*, March 3, 1943; Johnson, "Uncle Sam Wanted Them Too!" 42; *Denver Post*, April 3, 1943.

30. Ryan, "History of Building D," 27; Larson, "Bomber Plant," 39, 41.

31. *Oklahoma City Daily Oklahoman*, March 8, 1943; *Amarillo Globe*, January 3, 1943; *Dallas Morning News*, September 1, 11, 1943; Macias, "'We All Had a Cause,'" 255.

32. *Denver Post*, February 29, 1944, March 11, 1945; Fearon, "Plowshares into Airplanes," 312; Larson, "Bomber Plant," 41; Leonard, "Denver at War." By June 1944 Dallas women constituted 47 percent of the 102,930–member workforce, compared to 35 percent, or 43,750 women, working before the war. Put differently, women accounted for the 63 percent increase in the total number of workers.

33. *Omaha World Herald*, November 7, 1943; *Oklahoma City Daily Oklahoman*, June 17, 1943; Johnson, "Uncle Sam Wanted Them Too!" 43; *Denver Post*, September 1, 1943.

34. *Dallas Morning News*, February 3, 1944; Larson, "Bomber Plant," 41; Johnson, "Uncle Sam Wanted Them Too!" 45–46; Hartmann, *Home Front and Beyond*, 24.

35. Wit, "Munitions Manufacture," 156; Hartmann, *Home Front and Beyond*, 24; Johnson, "Uncle Sam Wanted Them Too!" 46.

36. *Denver Post*, January 14, 1945.

37. *Dallas Morning News*, March 9, 1945; *Denver Post*, May 25, 1945; Jefferies, *Wartime America*, 104; Hartmann, *Home Front and Beyond*, 68; *Omaha World Herald*, July 22, 1945.

38. Johnson, "Uncle Sam Wanted Them Too!" 48–49; Hartmann, *Home Front and Beyond*, 78.

39. *Oklahoma City Daily Oklahoman*, February 3, 1943; Hartmann, *Home Front and Beyond*, 24.

40. Winkler, *Home Front U.S.A.*, 57; Rupp, *Mobilizing Women for War*, 138–39, 145, 152; Honey, *Creating Rosie the Riveter*, 50; Jefferies, *Wartime America*, 95. Women constituted 26 percent of the industrial workforce in 1940 and 38 percent in 1945.

41. Rupp, *Mobilizing Women for War*, 155; Winkler, *Home Front U.S.A.*, 60; *Oklahoma City Daily Oklahoman*, June 9, 1945; Honey, *Creating Rosie the Riveter*, 52.

42. Hartmann, *Home Front and Beyond*, 90; Winkler, *Home Front U.S.A.*, 62–63; Anderson, *Wartime Women*, 163–64; *Omaha World Herald*, October 8,

1944; *Oklahoma City Daily Oklahoman*, December 20, 1942; Rupp, *Mobilizing Women for War*, 160–62.

43. Jefferies, *Wartime America*, 100–101; Kennedy, *Freedom from Fear*, 777, 781; Adams, *Best War Ever*, 70, 123–24, 134, 144; Campbell, *Women at War*, 216, 237.

44. Hartmann, *Home Front and Beyond*, 15, 78–80, 93–95, 214; Weatherford, *American Women and World War II*, 48–49, 119, 152, 195; Jefferies, *Wartime America*, 96; Winkler, *Home Front U.S.A.*, 58; Anderson, *Wartime Women*, 173, 175, 178.

4. The Home Front

1. *Bismarck (ND) Tribune*, December 8, 11, 1941.

2. *Denver Post*, December 12, 1941.

3. *Salina (KS) Journal*, December 12, 1941; *Amarillo Globe*, January 4, 1942; *Oklahoma City Daily Oklahoman*, January 24, 1942.

4. *Omaha World Herald*, July 30, 1942; Clippings File, Blackouts, box 199, American Heritage Center, University of Wyoming (hereafter cited as AHC); *Roswell (NM) Daily Record*, June 16, 23, 25, 29, 1941; *Rapid City (SD) Daily Journal*, January 29, 1943; *Salina (KS) Journal*, April 9, 1942; *Denver Post*, September 7, 1941.

5. *Roswell (NM) Daily Record*, August 1, 1941; *Denver Post*, September 7, November 15, 17, 1941, December 1, 15, 1942; *Cheyenne Wyoming Eagle*, April 30, 1942; Larson, *Wyoming's War Years*, 72; *Omaha World Herald*, November 7, 1942, February 1, 1943; *Wichita Eagle*, December 13, 15, 1942, May 22, 1943; *Bismarck (ND) Tribune*, December 9, 10, 1942.

6. *Omaha World Herald*, July 30, 1942; *Wichita Eagle*, June 10, 28, 1942.

7. Lingeman, *Don't You Know There's a War On?* 57; *Kearney (NE) Daily Hub*, May 26, 1941; *Amarillo Globe*, January 14, February 6, 1942.

8. *Dallas Morning News*, October 29, 1939; *Denver Post*, May 24, 1940; *Wichita Eagle*, May 5, 1940.

9. Bromley, "Women on the Home Front," 188–89; *Oklahoma City Daily Oklahoman*, January 21, 23, February 6, 1941.

10. Bergh, "Troop Trains," 136–37, 139.

11. Hub-ette Guide to Better U.S.O.-ing, Correspondence, 1942–1949, Lubbock (Texas) USO Records, 1942–1956, Southwest Collection, Texas Tech University (hereafter cited as SWC); *Lubbock Avalanche Journal*, July 29, 1945; *Albuquerque Journal*, January 10, 13, 1943; Furdell, "Great Falls Home Front," 70; Larson, *Wyoming's War Years*, 82–83.

12. *Denver Post*, July 17, September 9, December 18, 1941, October 10, 1942, May 9, 1944; *Bismarck (ND) Tribune*, September 3, 1941; *Omaha World Herald*, December 8, 1941; *Billings (MT) Gazette*, July 21, 22, 1942; Furdell, "Great Plains Home Front," 68.

13. Joe W. Seacrest, chairman, Nebraska State Salvage Committee, school salvage meeting address, September 11, 1942, folder 1 (unboxed), Joe W. Seacrest Papers, NSHS; Leonard, "Denver at War," 36; Joe W. Seacrest, chairman, Nebraska State Salvage Committee, radio address, typescript, October 11, 1942, folder 1 (unboxed), Joe W. Seacrest Papers, NSHS; *Oklahoma City Daily Oklahoman*, September 24, October 6, 13, 18, 1942; *Amarillo Globe*, October 11, 1942.

14. *Omaha World Herald*, July 21, 1942; *Oklahoma City Daily Oklahoman*, October 5, 1942; *Nebraska Farmer*, May 2, 1942; *Salina (KS) Journal*, September 1, October 15, 20, 21, 22, 24, 1942; *Rapid City (SD) Daily Journal*, November 7, 1942; *Amarillo Globe*, October 2, 1942.

15. *Cheyenne Wyoming State Tribune*, April 22, 30, 1943, April 17, 1945; *Albuquerque Journal*, May 5, 1942; *Denver Post*, November 1, December 9, 1942; *Billings (MT) Gazette*, July 21, 1942; Larson, *Wyoming's War Years*, 95–96; *Oklahoma City Daily Oklahoman*, February 3, 1941, July 24, October 1, 1942; *Amarillo Globe*, September 8, 1942.

16. *Dakota Farmer*, September 5, October 24, December 12, 1942; *Nebraska Farmer*, August 8, 1942; *Hereford Journal*, March 1, 1943; *Omaha World Herald*, July 20, 1942; *Salina (KS) Journal*, September 17, 1942; *Billings (MT) Gazette*, August 21, 42; Larson, *Wyoming's War Years*, 93.

17. *Cheyenne Wyoming Eagle*, February 25, March 7, 1942; *Denver Post*, August 30, September 9, 1942; *Amarillo Globe*, May 24, 25, 1942.

18. *Cheyenne Wyoming State Tribune*, April 28, 1943; *Bismarck (ND) Tribune*, December 3, 1943; *Wichita Eagle*, December 25, 1943; *Omaha World Herald*, October 2, 1942.

19. *Denver Post*, July 9, 1941, January 1, November 19, 22, 1942; *Omaha World Herald*, December 5, 1943; *Roswell (NM) Daily Record*, February 23, 1944; *Billings (MT) Gazette*, January 30, 1944; *Dallas Morning News*, July 23, 1944; Larson, *Wyoming's War Years*, 97–100; *Cheyenne Wyoming State Tribune*, May 7, 1943; *Albuquerque Journal*, January 6, 1943; *Bismarck (ND) Tribune*, March 13, 1943; "Bulletin no. 3," War Production Board, Salvage Division, Women's Activities, Emmet, Nebraska, October 30, 1943, and Mrs. Guy Cole to Chairman, Women's Division, State Salvage Committee, Emmet, Nebraska, April 12, 1944, Nebraska State Salvage Committee Papers, 1943–1945, NSHS.

20. *Cheyenne Wyoming Eagle*, January 14, March 1, 1944; *Salina (KS) Journal*, April 25, December 5, 1942, June 15, 1944; *Oklahoma City Daily Oklahoman*, October 22, 1942; *Bismarck (ND) Tribune*, February 20, 1943; Hartley, "Crow Family," 94.

21. *Wichita Eagle*, May 20, 1943; *Bismarck (ND) Tribune*, September 3, 1942, June 16, 1944; *Cheyenne Wyoming State Tribune*, July 25, 28, December 22, 1944; *Billings (MT) Gazette*, August 19, 1941, July 9, 1942, January 18,

1944; *Salina (KS) Journal*, April 2, 1942; *Amarillo Globe*, December 11, 1942; *Roswell (NM) Daily Record*, August 18, 1941; Kennedy, *Freedom from Fear*, 626; Larson, *Wyoming's War Years*, 106; Welsh, "'Back the Attack.'"

22. *Oklahoma City Daily Oklahoman*, July 31, 1942; "Farm Flash," Leaflet no. 7, March 1942, and "Food for Victory," Leaflet no. 6, January 1942, Nebraska Agricultural Extension Service, box 409, series 79-B-1-79-C-1, Val Kuska Collection, NSHS; Vitamins for Victory, Nebraska State Extension Service Report on Victory Gardens, 1942, folder 22, box 20, Correspondence File, 1939–1943, and J. Weber to Payne Ratner, April 29, 1942, Correspondence Received, Victory Gardens, folder 20, box 20, Correspondence File, 1939–1943, Payne Ratner Collection, KSHS.

23. *Amarillo Globe*, March 3, 1942; *Bismarck (ND) Tribune*, April 16, 28, 1942; *Denver Post*, May 3, 1944; *Billings (MT) Gazette*, March 26, 1944, March 25, 1945; *Omaha World Herald*, June 6, 1943; *Albuquerque Journal*, January 11, 1943; Leonard, "Denver at War," 36.

24. *Oklahoma City Daily Oklahoman*, October 18, November 2, 13, 1942; *Albuquerque Journal*, June 10, 1942.

25. *Omaha World Herald*, October 11, 1942.

26. *Oklahoma City Daily Oklahoman*, March 8, 1942; *Denver Post*, April 28, 1942.

27. *Wichita Eagle*, September 1, 1940.

28. *Dallas Morning News*, July 18, December 12, 1943.

29. *Omaha World Herald*, May 16, 1943, August 8, 1944.

30. Winkler, *Home Front U.S.A.*, 51; *Oklahoma City Daily Oklahoman*, March 10, December 17, 1944, May 13, 1945. A study of divorce in the wartime Great Plains has not been written, but a study of divorce in California is suggestive. It found that wars have affected marriages by delaying, accelerating, and undermining them, particularly as a result of military and combat service. The evidence indicates that veterans were more likely to divorce than nonveterans but that, in general, wartime marriages were no more likely to end in divorce than others. See Pavalko and Elder, "World War II and Divorce."

31. *Oklahoma City Daily Oklahoman*, May 6, 1947.

32. *Billings (MT) Gazette*, July 24, 1941; *Dallas Morning News*, May 21, 1943.

33. *Dallas Morning News*, April 7, July 2, 1943.

34. *Denver Post*, December 21, 1942; *Billings (MT) Gazette*, December 26, 1943, December 31, 1944; *Wichita Eagle*, November 22, 1942, June 16, 1943; *Dallas Morning News*, November 10, 1944; *Omaha World Herald*, December 5, 1943; *Oklahoma City Daily Oklahoman*, April 6, 1942, January 25, 1944.

35. *Albuquerque Journal*, February 27, 1943; O'Brien, "Kansas at War," 14.

36. *Billings (MT) Gazette*, December 31, 1944; Polenberg, *War and Society*, 147–50; Adams, *Best War Ever*, 129; Larson, *Wyoming's War Years*, 156–67. Nationally, most crime rates declined during the war because so many young men, the chief offenders, were in the military. See also O'Neill, *Democracy at War*, 250; and Tuttle, *Daddy's Gone to War*.

37. *Wichita Eagle*, April 15, 1942; *Billings (MT) Gazette*, February 4, 1942; *Oklahoma City Daily Oklahoman*, February 25, May 20, December 23, 1942, June 14, 19, 1943.

38. *Lincoln (NE) Star*, February 23, 1943.

39. *Amarillo Globe*, September 1, 1942; *Oklahoma City Daily Oklahoman*, May 17, 1942; *Roswell (NM) Daily Record*, October 23, 1942; *Dallas Morning News*, February 11, 1943; *Wichita Eagle*, October 20, 1942.

40. *Salina (KS) Journal*, September 1, 1942; *Bismarck (ND) Tribune*, March 20, 1942; Gamradt, "Adapting to Serve," 74–75.

41. Morris, "Patriotism and Education," 88, 91; *Amarillo Globe*, May 29, 1942; *Salina (KS) Journal*, February 1, 1945; O'Neill, *Democracy at War*, 217; Gamradt, "Adapting to Serve," 75–76.

42. *Denver Post*, January 20, 1942.

43. *Roswell (NM) Daily Record*, January 20, 1942; Busse, "'She's a Good Girl,'" 173, 180–81.

44. *Oklahoma City Daily Oklahoman*, January 24, April 1, 1942; *Wichita Eagle*, May 27, 1941, January 25, April 21, 1942.

45. *Wichita Eagle*, February 13, 1945; *Dallas Morning News*, July 11, 1943, February 18, 1945; *Albuquerque Journal*, July 27, August 3, 1944; *Denver Post*, February 11, 1945.

46. *Salina (KS) Journal*, July 10, 1942.

47. *Omaha World Herald*, March 8, 1942; Terkel, *"The Good War,"* 119; Lingeman, *Don't You Know There's a War On?* 81; Larson, *Wyoming's War Years*, 138–40; *Denver Post*, June 24, 25, 1942; *Amarillo Globe*, August 2, 1942; *Wichita Eagle*, September 6, 1942; *Salina (KS) Journal*, November 6, 1942; *Oklahoma City Daily Oklahoman*, May 5, 1943.

48. Larson, "Bomber Plant," 32; Simmons, "Public Leadership," 485–88, 491–93, 495–96.

49. Larson, "Bomber Plant," 34; McGlade, "Zoning of Fort Crook," 21–23, 28, 32.

50. *Amarillo Globe*, May 9, 26, 1942; L. E. Spencer to Topeka City Officials, June 7, 1945, folder 3, box 64, and L. E. Spencer to Andrew Schoeppel, August 8, 1945, folder 3, box 64, Correspondence, 1943–47, Andrew Schoeppel Papers, KSHS.

51. *Amarillo Globe*, June 1, 1942; *Wichita Eagle*, February 21, 1942; *Salina (KS) Journal*, June 15, 18, 1942.

52. Larson, *Wyoming's War Years*, 144.

53. Wit, "Munitions Manufacture," 151; Russell, "World War II Boom Town," 77; *Cheyenne Wyoming Eagle*, July 25–28, 1944; *Bismarck (ND) Tribune*, May 1, 1944; *Salina (KS) Journal*, January 3, 1944.

54. *Dallas Morning News*, June 2, 4, 6, 1940.

55. Juhnke, "Edmund G. Kaufman," 48, 51–52, 54–56; Polenberg, *War and Society*, 54.

56. Juhnke, "Perils of Conscientious Objection"; Karolevitz, "Life on the Home Front," 397; Polenberg, *War and Society*, 59; Coffey, *Great Plains Patchwork*, 145; *Omaha World Herald*, December 1, 1940; *Oklahoma City Daily Oklahoman*, February 1, 1941.

57. Minutes, 1935–1944, folder 10, box 1, and Minutes, 1944–1949, folder 11, box 1, Lotos Club Papers, NSHS; *Oklahoma City Daily Oklahoman*, November 15, 1942; *Denver Post*, March 3, 1942; *Omaha World Herald*, December 14, 1941; *Amarillo Globe*, December 14, 1941.

58. *Amarillo Globe*, July 3, October 12, 1942; *Wichita Eagle*, December 4, 1943; *Cheyenne Wyoming State Tribune*, November 16, 1944; Larson, *Wyoming's War Years*, 89, 91; *Rapid City (SD) Daily Journal*, August 12, 1942; Lingeman, *Don't You Know There's a War On?* 761.

59. Sloan, ed., "The Newelletters," 137, 150; *Salina (KS) Journal*, May 11, 1942; *Dallas Morning News*, October 8, 1943; *Omaha World Herald*, September 8, 1944.

60. *Oklahoma City Daily Oklahoman*, August 12, 1945; *Wichita Eagle*, May 5, September 14, 1941.

5. Rationing

1. *Salina (KS) Journal*, September 7, 1939; *Kearney (NE) Daily Hub*, August 19, 1941; *Denver Post*, October 20, 1941.

2. Jefferies, *Wartime America*, 28–29; Schiller, "Reining in the Administrative State," 193; Bentley, *Eating for Victory*, 1, 4, 5.

3. *Amarillo Globe*, January 5, 1942; *Cheyenne Wyoming Eagle*, December 18, 25, 30, 1941; *Denver Post*, December 29, 31, 1941; *Roswell (NM) Daily Record*, January 2, 1942.

4. *Oklahoma City Daily Oklahoman*, June 23, 1942; *Salina (KS) Journal*, May 5, June 23, October 8, 14, 1942; *Amarillo Globe*, August 18, 1942; *Albuquerque Journal*, January 10, 1943; Furdell, "Great Falls Home Front," 71; Karolevitz, "Life on the Home Front," 404.

5. *Oklahoma City Daily Oklahoman*, August 30, December 13, 1942; Sloan, ed., "The Newelletters," 63; *Salina (KS) Journal*, April 1, 23, 1942; *Cheyenne Wyoming State Tribune*, October 15, 1943.

6. *Salina (KS) Journal*, August 17, 1942, May 13, 1943; *Denver Post*, July 20, August 8, 29, 1943; Sloan, ed., "The Newelletters," 57; *Oklahoma City Daily Oklahoman*, July 3, 1942; *Billings (MT) Gazette*, June 23, 1942.

7. Pfluger, "Fuel for Victory," 19–20, 23–24, 35–36; *Rapid City (SD) Daily Journal*, May 20, 1941.

8. *Cheyenne Wyoming State Tribune*, June 5, 1941; *Kearney (NE) Daily Hub*, August 20, 1941; *Salina (KS) Journal*, May 20, October 30, 1942; Larson, *Wyoming's War Years*, 119–20; undated newspaper clipping, folder 10, box 63, Correspondence, 1943–47, Andrew Schoeppel Papers, KSHS; Leonard, "Denver at War," 37.

9. *Denver Post*, October 15, 1942, October 12, 1943, March 14, 1944; *Oklahoma City Daily Oklahoman*, December 1, 1942; *Cheyenne Wyoming Eagle*, October 12, 1942; Cassity, "'In a Narrow Grave,'" 6. For a detailed explanation of gasoline and rubber rationing, see Plan for Mileage Rationing Instructions to Administrators, November 1942, Office of Price Administration, and Local Board Rationing Program, Mileage Program, October 19, 1942, Office of Price Control Administration Collection, Western History Collections, University of Oklahoma.

10. *Bismarck (ND) Tribune*, February 9, 1942; *Oklahoma City Daily Oklahoman*, January 4, 1942; *Amarillo Glove*, October 21, 1942; *Denver Post*, July 27, November 29, 1942; *Rapid City (SD) Daily Journal*, January 16, 1944; *Cheyenne Wyoming Eagle*, September 19, 1944; Andrew Schoeppel to George E. Merilatt, February 5, 1943, folder 8, box 64, and Survey of Supplemental Gasoline Rations by ODT Advisory Committee—Local Delivery—Kansas (1944?), folder 9, box 44, Correspondence, 1943–47, Andrew Schoeppel Papers, KSHS; *Salina (KS) Journal*, August 26, 1942.

11. *Denver Post*, November 20, 1942, September 15, December 3, 1943, March 12, November 25, 1944, May 5, 1945; *Salina (KS) Journal*, January 24, 1944; *Wichita Eagle*, June 2, 1943; *Omaha World Herald*, March 19, 1944.

12. Report on Civilian Gasoline Supply, October 13, 1943, folder 23, box 13, Gubernatorial Papers, Robert S. Kerr Collection, CAC; Printis M. Brown to Andrew Schoeppel, August 13, 1943, and Petroleum War Administration press release, August 13, 1943, folder 11, box 63, Correspondence, 1943–47, Andrew Schoeppel Papers, KSHS.

13. Report on Civilian Gasoline Supply, October 13, 1943, folder 23, box 13, Gubernatorial Papers, Robert S. Kerr Collection, CAC; Prentis M. Brown to Andrew Schoeppel, August 13, 1943, Petroleum War Administration press release, August 13, 1943, Andrew Schoeppel to Paul T. Vickers, August 7, 1943, M. Q. Sharpe to Franklin Delano Roosevelt, August 5, 1943, and M. Q. Sharpe to Harold Ickes, telegram, August 5, 1943, folder 11, box 63, Correspondence, 1943–47, Andrew Schoeppel Papers, KSHS.

14. Report on Civilian Gasoline Supply, October 13, 1943, folder 23, box 13, Gubernatorial Papers, Robert S. Kerr Collection, CAC; Harold Ickes, speech, August 5, 1943, folder 11, box 63, and Howard A. Cowden to Andrew Schoeppel, September 10, 1943, folder 17, box 53, Correspondence, 1943–47, Andrew Schoeppel Papers, KSHS.

15. Andrew Schoeppel to Harold Ickes, September 15, 1943, and Harold Ickes to Andrew Schoeppel, September ?, 1943, folder 17, box 53, Correspondence, 1943–47, Andrew Schoeppel Papers, KSHS.

16. Pfluger, "Fuel for Victory," 37–38; Childs, "State Control of Oil Production," 570, 573, 580.

17. *Amarillo Globe*, December 1, 8, 1943; Sloan, ed., "The Newelletters," 72.

18. Bentley, *Eating for Victory*, 15–17, 33.

19. Bentley, *Eating for Victory*, 86; *Denver Post*, February 10, 1942; *Salina (KS) Journal*, April 28, May 6, 1942.

20. *Nebraska Farmer*, May 2, 1942; *Bismarck (ND) Tribune*, April 25, 27, 1942; *Denver Post*, March 4, May 5, 1942; *Salina (KS) Journal*, April 3, 24, 1942; Bentley, *Eating for Victory*, 102, 198.

21. *Bismarck (ND) Tribune*, April 22, 28, 1942; Bentley, *Eating for Victory*, 92, 95, 98; *Omaha World Herald*, April 14, 1941; *Roswell (NM) Daily Record*, April 28, 1942; *Oklahoma City Daily Oklahoman*, March 22, 1942; *Denver Post*, August 13, 1942.

22. Bentley, *Eating for Victory*, 93, 111; Skaggs, *Prime Cut*, 166–67. By 1945, the public consumed an average of 71.3 pounds of beef per person annually.

23. *Cheyenne Wyoming Eagle*, September 5, 1942; *Dakota Farmer*, September 19, 1942; *Roswell (NM) Daily Record*, September 3, 1942; *Salina (KS) Journal*, September 1, 1942; *Denver Post*, September 25, 1942.

24. *Denver Post*, October 2, 1942; *Amarillo Globe*, October 18, 1942; *Oklahoma City Daily Oklahoman*, November 22, 1942.

25. *Cheyenne Wyoming Eagle*, September 5, 1942.

26. *Omaha World Herald*, January 20, 1943; *Lincoln (NE) Star*, February 22, 1943; *Salina (KS) Journal*, February 13, 1943; *Dallas Morning News*, February 21, 1943.

27. *Salina (KS) Journal*, March 23, 1943; *Dallas Morning News*, March 26, 1943; *Rapid City (SD) Daily Journal*, March 27, 1943; *Denver Post*, March 29, 1943, March 3, 1945; *Albuquerque Journal*, January 1, 8, April 23, 1943; *Oklahoma City Daily Oklahoman*, July 22, 1943; H. M. Booth to Governor Andrew Schoeppel, June 16, 1945, folder 2, box 45, Correspondence, 1943–47, Andrew Schoeppel Papers, KSHS.

28. Lingeman, *Don't You Know There's a War On?* 254–57; J. I. Scholler to Andrew Schoeppel, June 13, 1945, folder 3, box 45, Correspondence, 1943–47, Andrew Schoeppel Papers, KSHS.

29. Lingeman, *Don't You Know There's a War On?* 259, 263; *Cheyenne Wyoming Eagle*, March 4, 1943; *Denver Post*, March 12, 1943; *Bismarck (ND) Tribune*, March 1, 3, 1943.

30. *Cattleman*, October 1942; *Hereford Journal*, December 1, 1942; *Denver Post*, November 13, 1942; *Farmer-Stockman*, June 15, 1944.

31. *Denver Post*, January 12, 18, 1943; *Cheyenne Wyoming Eagle*, February 4, April 11, 1943; *Amarillo Globe*, February 19, 1943; C. E. Feely to Andrew Schoeppel, June 2, 1945, folder 2, box 45, Correspondence, 1943–47, Andrew Schoeppel Papers, KSHS.

32. *Albuquerque Journal*, May 13, 20, 26, 1943; *Dallas Morning News*, March 11, 20, 1943.

33. *Dallas Morning News*, June 26, July 15, 1943; *Bismarck (ND) Tribune*, March 31, June 30, 1943.

34. *Bismarck (ND) Tribune*, July 6, 1943; Bentley, *Eating for Victory*, 19.

35. *Dallas Morning News*, September 4, 1943; *Oklahoma City Daily Oklahoman*, September 7, 1943.

36. *Omaha World Herald*, September 26, 1943.

37. *Roswell (NM) Daily Record*, February 1, March 29, 1943; *Dallas Morning News*, January 28, 1943.

38. *Cattleman*, May 1943; *Omaha World Herald*, June 7, 1943.

39. Bentley, *Eating for Victory*, 36; Lingeman, *Don't You Know There's a War On?* 259, 263, 268; *Cheyenne Wyoming State Tribune*, December 3, 1944.

40. *Denver Post*, February 18, 1945; *Rapid City (SD) Daily Journal*, April 24, 1945; *Omaha World Herald*, July 22, 1945.

41. *Cheyenne Wyoming Eagle*, May 24, 25, 1945; *Oklahoma City Daily Oklahoman*, May 26, 1945.

42. *Dallas Morning News*, June 13, 1945; *Salina (KS) Journal*, June 16, 21, 27, 1945; *Denver Post*, June 17, 1945.

43. *Rapid City (SD) Daily Journal*, July 3, 1945; *Denver Post*, July 3, 24, 25, 27, August 1, 1945.

44. William F. Hubbard to H. O. Davies, June 21, 1945, folder 2, box 45, and Andrew Schoeppel to T. A. Birch, July 27, 1945, folder 2, box 45, Correspondence, 1943–47, Andrew Schoeppel Papers, KSHS.

45. *Bismarck (ND) Tribune*, September 1, 1945; *Denver Post*, August 8, 13, 1945.

46. Schlebecker, *Cattle Raising on the Plains*, 174.

47. Jefferies, *Wartime America*, 30–31.

48. *Salina (KS) Journal*, October 21, 1942; *Bismarck (ND) Tribune*, May 16, July 28, 1942; *Oklahoma City Daily Oklahoman*, September 27, 1942; Sloan, ed., "The Newelletters," 61; *Denver Post*, January 7, 1945.

49. O'Neill, *Democracy at War*, 249; Kennedy, *Freedom from Fear*, 647.

6. The Farm and Ranch Front

1. Schmidt, *American Farmers*, 310–12.

2. *Farmer-Stockman*, May 15, 1939.

3. *Farmer-Stockman*, January 15, May 25, 1939. The McNary-Haugen plan called for a two-price system in which domestic agricultural prices would rise

behind tariff protection while the government sold surplus production on the international market at world prices.

4. *Farmer-Stockman*, September 15, 1939; *Amarillo Globe*, September 3, 1939; *Salina (KS) Journal*, August 22, 24, 30, 31, September 6, 1939; *Cheyenne Wyoming State Tribune*, September 5, 1939.

5. *Salina (KS) Journal*, September 6, 7, 1939; *Nebraska Farmer*, September 23, 1939; *Cheyenne Wyoming State Tribune*, September 6, 7, 1939; *Cheyenne Wyoming Eagle*, September 7, 1939.

6. *Nebraska Farmer*, September 18, 23, December 30, 1939, January 13, 1940; *Farmer-Stockman*, September 15, 1939.

7. *Nebraska Farmer*, October 21, 1939; *Salina (KS) Journal*, September 16, October 19, 26, 1939; *Rapid City (SD) Daily Journal*, September 23, 1939; *Farmer-Stockman*, October 15, November 1, 1939.

8. *Farmer-Stockman*, November 1, 15, 1939; *Salina (KS) Journal*, November 9, 1939.

9. *Nebraska Farmer*, January 27, 1940; *Salina (KS) Journal*, November 10, 1939; *Amarillo Globe*, December 19, 1939.

10. *Bismarck (ND) Tribune*, January 10, 1940; *Farmer-Stockman*, February 1, 1940.

11. *Nebraska Farmer*, August 24, 1940; *Dakota Farmer*, August 10, 1940.

12. *Farmer-Stockman*, March 3, May 15, July 15, August 15, November 1, 1940; *Nebraska Farmer*, June 29, 1940.

13. *Nebraska Farmer*, October 19, 1940, December 13, 27, 1941; Wilcox, *Farmer in the Second World War*, 84–86; Earl R. Cully to Andrew Schoeppel, January 5, 1945, and Adam Diets to Andrew Schoeppel, January 26, 1945, folder 9, box 63, Correspondence, 1943–47, Andrew Schoeppel Papers, KSHS.

14. A. C. Adams to Lyle H. Boren, February 10, 1942, ? to Lyle H. Boren, February 17, 1942, and O. L. Avery to Lyle H. Boren, January 12, 1943, folder 11, box 4, Lyle H. Boren Collection, CAC; *Oklahoma City Daily Oklahoman*, November 12, 1943; *Albuquerque Journal*, March 3, May 12, 1943; *Cheyenne Wyoming State Tribune*, March 31, 1944; *Wichita Eagle*, December 15, 1944; *Denver Post*, February 16, 1945.

15. *Oklahoma City Daily Oklahoman*, January 3, February 13, 1941; *Rapid City (SD) Daily Journal*, April 24, 1941; *Roswell (NM) Daily Record*, April 27, 1941; *Denver Post*, June 8, 1941; *Kearney (NE) Daily Hub*, February 12, 1941; *Farmer-Stockman*, June 15, 1941; *Nebraska Farmer*, June 14, 1941.

16. *Nebraska Farmer*, June 28, 1941; *Salina (KS) Journal*, July 18, 1941.

17. *Wichita Eagle*, July 22, 1941; *Cheyenne Wyoming State Tribune*, August 22, 1941.

18. *Nebraska Farmer*, August 9, 23, September 1, 1941; *Rapid City (SD) Daily Journal*, August 20, 1941; *Salina (KS) Journal*, September 8, 1941; *Dallas Morning News*, June 28, 1941.

19. *Denver Post*, October 29, 1941; *Salina (KS) Journal*, September 8, 12, 13, 15, 21, October 6, 1941.

20. *Nebraska Farmer*, July 26, October 4, November 15, 1941, January 10, 1942.

21. *Bismarck (ND) Tribune*, July 11, 1941; *Cheyenne Wyoming Eagle*, December 23, 1943; *Wichita Eagle*, December 21, 1941; *Nebraska Farmer*, January 10, 24, 1942.

22. *Oklahoma City Daily Oklahoman*, January 4, 1942; *Wichita Eagle*, January 6, 1942.

23. *Bismarck (ND) Tribune*, January 26, 1942; *Oklahoma City Daily Oklahoman*, January 4, 1942; *Wichita Eagle*, January 6, 18, 1942; *Cheyenne Wyoming Eagle*, February 5, 18, July 21, 24, 1942; Neugebauer, ed., *Plains Farmer*.

24. *Cheyenne Wyoming Eagle*, August 15, 1942; *Salina (KS) Journal*, March 9, 1942; *Oklahoma City Daily Oklahoman*, March 15, 1942; *Farmer-Stockman*, April 1, 1942; *Nebraska Farmer*, May 5, August 23, October 17, November 24, 1942.

25. *Roswell (NM) Daily Record*, February 8, 1943; *Omaha World Herald*, January 3, 1943; *Lincoln (NE) Star*, January 31, 1943.

26. *Dallas Morning News*, November 16, 1943; *Denver Post*, March 21, October 7, 1943; *Nebraska Farmer*, July 17, December 18, 1943.

27. *Dallas Morning News*, February 9, 15, 16, 1943.

28. *Kearney (NE) Daily Hub*, March 3, 1942; *Salina (KS) Journal*, August 29, 1941; *Nebraska Farmer*, August 29, December 13, 27, 1941.

29. *Omaha World Herald*, December 11, 1941, January 11, 1942; *Farmer-Stockman*, December 15, 1941; *Bismarck (ND) Tribune*, December 12, 1941; Lyle H. Boren to H. L. Gregory, December 6, 1942, folder 8, box 4, Lyle H. Boren Collection, CAC.

30. *Salina (KS) Journal*, May 20, July 3, 1942; *Kearney (NE) Daily Hub*, June 23, 1942; *Omaha World Herald*, July 30, 1942; *Cheyenne Wyoming Eagle*, January 30, 1942; *Kansas Farmer*, February 21, June 19, 1943; Wilcox, *Farmer in the Second World War*, 55.

31. *Cheyenne Wyoming Eagle*, September 17, 1942; *Nebraska Farmer*, October 3, November 24, 1942; *Kansas Farmer*, September 5, 1942, February 6, 1943; Wilcox, *Farmer in the Second World War*, 55; *Dakota Farmer*, January 24, September 14, 1942.

32. *Dakota Farmer*, December 12, 1942; *Roswell (NM) Daily Record*, June 27, December 16, 1942; *Farmer-Stockman*, March 4, 1943; *Rapid City (SD) Daily Journal*, March 15, 1943; *Omaha World Herald*, February 4, 1943.

33. *Successful Farming*, June 1942; *Salina (KS) Journal*, January 15, 1943; *Dakota Farmer*, June 27, 1942; *Farmer-Stockman*, September 15, 1943; *Kansas Farmer*, June 6, 1942; *Wichita Eagle*, December 4, 13, 1942; *Denver Post*, November 22, 1942; Neugebauer, ed., *Plains Farmer*, 213.

34. *Cattleman*, April 1943; *Rapid City (SD) Daily Journal*, April 22, 1943; *Salina (KS) Journal*, December 29, 1943; *Bismarck (ND) Tribune*, August 2, 1943; *Dallas Morning News*, March 1, 1943.

35. *Farmer-Stockman*, November 15, 1943; *Omaha World Herald*, December 30, 1943; *Lincoln (NE) Star*, January 31, 1943.

36. *Dallas Morning News*, January 12, June 18, 1944; *Rapid City (SD) Daily Journal*, October 20, 1943; *Omaha World Herald*, January 19, 1944; *Farmer-Stockman*, February 15, 1944.

37. *Omaha World Herald*, June 8, 1944; *Farmer-Stockman*, February 15, 1944; *Nebraska Farmer*, January 20, 1945.

38. *Salina (KS) Journal*, July 14, 1943, April 17, 1945; Neugebauer, ed., *Plains Farmer*, 232; *Denver Post*, July 25, 1943; *Wichita Eagle*, January 28, 1943; *Rapid City (SD) Daily Journal*, December 23, 1943; *Nebraska Farmer*, May 20, 1944.

39. *Denver Post*, July 25, 1943; *Cattleman*, August 1943.

40. *Nebraska Farmer*, January 15, 1944; *Farmer-Stockman*, January 15, February 15, 1944; *Cheyenne Wyoming Eagle*, March 25, 1944; *Denver Post*, April 4, 1944; *Bismarck (ND) Tribune*, April 4, 1944.

41. *Farmer-Stockman*, January 15, February 15, 1945; *Wichita Eagle*, January 9, 1945; *Kansas Farmer*, October 21, 1944.

42. *Nebraska Farmer*, May 15, 1944.

43. *Successful Farming*, April 1944; *Nebraska Farmer*, November 18, 1944. Sheridan County, Kansas, provides an example of wartime demographic change in rural areas across the region. There, the farm population dropped from 2,746 in 1940 to 2,667 in 1945, before falling to 2,346 in 1950, for a 15 percent loss during the decade. Many farmers moved into nearby towns, such as Goodland, took jobs, and became part-time farmers, often called "sidewalk farmers." As farmers sold their land and moved away, the number of farms decreased from 705 in 1940 to 584 in 1945. As the number of farms decreased, farm size increased from an average of 812 acres in 1940 to 993 acres in 1945. During the period from 1937 to 1950 the number of farm homes decreased by 20 percent, and 90 percent were moved or demolished. Moreover, of the 1,226 landowners left in 1950 only 470, or 38 percent, lived in rural areas, and they owned only 41 percent of the land. Put differently, by 1950 less than half the farmers in Sheridan County owned their farms and lived on the land. At the same time the price of good wheat land rose from $10 per acre in 1940 to as much as $100 per acre by 1950. Renters constituted 37 percent of farm operators. The farm population was not tied to the land through ownership and was, therefore, mobile, if not transient. Although agriculture remained the major industry of the Great Plains, fewer farmers worked fewer farms, but those farmers who remained worked more acreage than before the war. This feature of Great Plains agriculture resembled a similar trend nationwide, where, between 1940 and 1945, the farm population declined from 30 to

25 million, or from 23 to 18 percent of the total population. At the same time net farm income increased 200 percent nationwide, owing to expanded production and high wartime prices. See Wilcox, *Farmer in the Second Word War*, 99; "100 Years of Farmland Values"; Kollmorgen and Jenks, "Population and Settlement Changes." Between 1940 and 1945 Kansas lost fifteen thousand farms. At the same time Kansas farmers cultivated 5 million more acres, a 22 percent increase. War industries often drew farmers away. In 1942 aircraft companies in Wichita drew 80 percent of their workforce from the surrounding farms and rural areas. Most of these workers would not return to the land when the war ended. See Grant, "'Food Will Win the War,'" 249, 253.

44. *Farmer-Stockman*, July 15, 1944, January 15, 1945; *Nebraska Farmer*, February 3, 1945.

45. *Nebraska Farmer*, February 3, 1945; Grant, "'Food Will Win the War,'" 255; *Albuquerque Journal*, November 25, 1944.

46. *Farmer-Stockman*, September 15, 1945; *Nebraska Farmer*, September 1, 1945; Wilcox, *Farmer in the Second World War*, 249, 253.

47. *Salina (KS) Journal*, September 6, 1939; *Cheyenne Wyoming Eagle*, September 7, 1939.

48. *Cheyenne Wyoming Eagle*, September 7, 1939; *Kearney (NE) Daily Hub*, September 25, 1939.

49. *Nebraska Farmer*, May 4, 1940; *Rapid City (SD) Daily Journal*, April 4, 1940; Proceedings of the Wyoming Stock Growers Association, 1940, AHC.

50. *Bismarck (ND) Tribune*, July 27, 1940; Proceedings of the Wyoming Stock Growers Association, 1940, AHC.

51. Proceedings of the Wyoming Stock Growers Association, 1940, AHC.

52. Proceedings of the Wyoming Stock Growers Association, 1940 and 1941, AHC.

53. *Salina (KS) Journal*, April 7, 1941; newspaper clipping, May 9, 1941, folder 12, box 4, Lyle H. Boren Collection, CAC.

54. *Nebraska Farmer*, June 28, 1941.

55. Proceedings of the Wyoming Stock Growers Association, 1941, AHC.

56. Proceedings of the Wyoming Stock Growers Association, 1941 and 1942, AHC.

57. *Cattleman*, February 1942; *Omaha World Herald*, February 23, 1942; *Hereford Journal*, January 15, July 3, 1942; Proceedings of the Wyoming Stock Growers Association, 1942, AHC.

58. *Cheyenne Wyoming Eagle*, June 25, July 3, 1942; *Nebraska Farmer*, March 7, 1942; *Billings (MT) Gazette*, February 26, 1942; *Oklahoma City Daily Oklahoman*, March 29, May 5, 1942.

59. *Cheyenne Wyoming Eagle*, June 2, 1942; *Billings (MT) Gazette*, July 1, 1942; *Amarillo Globe*, June 11, 1942; *Dakota Farmer*, November 28, 1942; *Cattleman*, December 1942.

60. *Denver Post*, December 16, 1942; *Cattleman*, May 1943.

61. Proceedings of the Wyoming Stock Growers Association, 1942, AHC; *Denver Post*, June 3, July 25, 1942; *Cheyenne Wyoming Eagle*, June 6, July 25, 1942; *Kansas Farmer*, August 15, 1942; *Roswell (NM) Daily Record*, September 4, 1942; *Cattleman*, December 1942.

62. Schlebecker, *Cattle Raising on the Plains*, 170–71; *Dakota Farmer*, December 12, 1942; Ferdie Deering to Chester C. Davis, June 11, 1943, folder 12, box 4, Lyle H. Boren Collection, CAC.

63. Proceedings of the Wyoming Stock Growers Association, 1943, AHC.

64. Proceedings of the Wyoming Stock Growers Association, 1943, AHC; *Farmer-Stockman*, April 15, 1943.

65. *Denver Post*, October 27, 1943; *Salina (KS) Journal*, October 28, 1943; *Nebraska Farmer*, October 20, 1943; *Oklahoma City Daily Oklahoman*, December 1, 1943.

66. *Roswell (NM) Daily Record*, March 15, 1944; *Omaha World Herald*, March 18, 1944; *Denver Post*, April 27, May 4, 1944.

67. *Nebraska Farmer*, January 8, 1945; *Omaha World Herald*, November 10, 1945; *Cheyenne Wyoming State Tribune*, January 10, 1945.

68. *Roswell (NM) Daily Record*, January 12, 1945; *Cheyenne Wyoming State Tribune*, January 10, 1945.

69. Saunders, "Trends," 74–75; Schlebecker, *Cattle Raising on the Plains*, 169, 172, 184–85, 187, 193; Johnson, "Range Cattle Production," 7, 21–22; Dagel, "Ranchers' Adjustments," 88–90; *Cattleman*, January, August, October 1943; *Rapid City (SD) Daily Journal*, March 27, 1943; *Hereford Journal*, March 15, June 15, October 1, 1943; *Nebraska Farmer*, November 6, 1943; Wood, *Kansas Beef Industry*, 281.

70. Schlebecker, *Cattle Raising on the Plains*, 184–85; *Farmer-Stockman*, March 15, 1944; Johnson, "Range Cattle Production," 15, 28, 34–36; Remeley, *Bell Ranch*, 297–99. By the end of the war North Dakota cattlemen operated on the assumption that they needed at least 100 cows to maintain a calf crop sufficient to provide an adequate standard of living, although no one quantified what that meant. Most North Dakota ranchers, however, strove for larger operations, with at least 265 cows and calves, operations that netted an annual average income of $2,952 in 1944 on a total investment of $45,602. Similarly, in southeastern Montana, northeastern Wyoming, and western South Dakota the "average family-operated cattle ranches," which required two men to operate, increased the average number of cattle grazed from 134 in 1939 to 143 in 1945. At the same time the ranches in that area increased in size, from an average of 3,408 acres in 1939 to 3,667 acres in 1945. As these ranches expanded in size and grazed more cattle, gross annual income also rose, from approximately $3,800 to $7,800 during that same period, while net income increased from approximately $1,800 to $4,200. Ranches in this area valued at $15,000 in 1935

sold for $70,000 or more at the end of the war because good weather and high prices made ranchland more desirable and valuable.

A study of twenty-one large ranches in southeastern Montana indicated similar wartime changes. There, ranches that averaged 11,914 acres in 1940 had expanded to an average size of 14,742 acres by 1948. At the beginning of the war, however, ranchers leased an average of 6,268 acres, usually from the Bureau of Land Management, but on average they leased only 5,121 acres in 1948. The increased acreage of these ranches resulted from the purchase of small tracts from individuals or the state, thereby giving the ranchers control over most of the land that they used for grazing. These ranches also increased the number of cattle grazed annually during the same period, from an average of 319 to 428 head. See Gray and Chester, "Cattle Ranching," 4, 7-8, 12, 14; and Saunders, "Trends," 24, 30, 35, 46.

71. Clawson, *Western Range Livestock Industry*, 372-77. Maximum production and guaranteed prices, however, still did not provide sufficient profits to keep many men and women on the farms and ranches. In 1940, farmers nationwide received an index price of 84 (1910-14 = 100) for wheat, 83 for cotton, and 108 for livestock, while their cost of living reached 121. By the end of the war the index wheat price reached 172, cotton 178, and livestock 210, while the cost-of-living index reached 182. Put differently, the index for prices received on all farm products was 95 in 1939 and 204 in 1945. The parity ratio for farm to nonfarm income for 1939 was 82, but it increased to 144 in 1945. At the same time farmers paid an index price for commodities, interest, taxes, and wages of 123 in 1939 and 192 in 1945. The ratio of prices received to prices paid by farmers was 77 in 1939 and 109 in 1945. See *Crops and Markets, 1950*, 123-24.

72. *Crops and Markets, 1950*, 377.

73. *Billings (MT) Gazette*, May 28, 1942; *Cattleman*, January 1943; *Albuquerque Journal*, February 15, 16, 1943.

74. Fite, *American Farmers*, 84-85; Wilcox, *Farmer in the Second World War*, 45.

75. *Bismarck (ND) Tribune*, November 10, 1943; *Nebraska Farmer*, July 7, 1945; *Cattleman*, October 1943.

7. Agricultural Labor

1. Rasmussen, *Emergency Farm Labor Supply Program*, 14; H. L. Collins to Brigadier General M. R. McClean, January 21, 1942, unnumbered folder, box 15, Correspondence File, 1939-1943, Payne Ratner Collection, KSHS.

2. *Cheyenne Wyoming State Tribune*, April 16, 29, 1941; *Rapid City (SD) Daily Record*, June 17, 1941.

3. *Cheyenne Wyoming State Tribune*, May 29, 1941; *Salina (KS) Journal*, May 28, 1941; *Bismarck (ND) Tribune*, July 1, 1941; Rasmussen, *Emergency Farm Labor Supply Program*, 19.

4. *Oklahoma City Daily Oklahoman*, April 20, 1941; *Rapid City (SD) Daily Journal*, June 13, 1941; Wilcox, *Farmer in the Second World War*, 84; Rasmussen, *Emergency Farm Labor Supply Program*, 19.

5. *Salina (KS) Journal*, January 15, 1942; *Denver Post*, January 23, May 2, 1942.

6. *Salina (KS) Journal*, May 11, 1942.

7. *Denver Post*, May 21, 1942; *Rapid City (SD) Daily Journal*, May 2, 1942; *Albuquerque Journal*, May 7, 1942; *Nebraska Farmer*, May 16, 1942; Grant, "'Food Will Win the War,'" 253.

8. *Omaha World Herald*, February 7, 18, 1942; Suggestions for Recruiting, Registering, and Placement of Non-Farm Labor, typescript, n.d., folder 6, box 44, Classification of Registrants in Agriculture, Local Board Release no. 164, Selective Service, November 17, 1942, folder 3, box 44, and North Dakota Plan for Food for Victory, Office of the Governor, Bismarck, North Dakota, March 8, 1943, folder 3, box 44, Correspondence, 1943–47, Andrew Schoeppel Papers, KSHS; *Omaha World Herald*, February 18, 1942; *Bismarck (ND) Tribune*, February 2, 1942; *Oklahoma City Daily Oklahoman*, April 6, 1942.

9. *Salina (KS) Journal*, August 11, 27, 1942; *Wichita Eagle*, August 30, 1942; *Bismarck (ND) Tribune*, July 7, August 8, 1942; *Salina (KS) Journal*, September 18, 1942.

10. *Rapid City (SD) Daily Journal*, March 27, 1943; *Cheyenne Wyoming Eagle*, October 14, 1942.

11. *Salina (KS) Journal*, October 31, December 1, 1942; *Oklahoma City Daily Oklahoman*, November 8, 1942; *Roswell (NM) Daily Record*, November 18, 1942.

12. *Oklahoma City Daily Oklahoman*, November 8, 1942; *Cheyenne Wyoming Eagle*, December 1, 1942; *Rapid City (SD) Daily Journal*, November 13, 1942.

13. *Denver Post*, August 16, 1942.

14. *Roswell (NM) Daily Record*, March 23, 1943.

15. *Billings (MT) Gazette*, June 23, 1942; Moser, "Farm Labor Practices and Conditions," 29; *Cheyenne Wyoming Eagle*, July 23, 1942; *Denver Post*, July 26, 1942.

16. *Albuquerque Journal*, June 13, 17, 1942; *Dakota Farmer*, September 24, 1942; *Oklahoma City Daily Oklahoman*, September 3, 1942. Picking rates were based on the estimate that it took fifty-six hours to pick a five-hundred-pound bale.

17. *Salina (KS) Journal*, September 14, 1942; *Omaha World Herald*, September 24, 1942; *Oklahoma City Daily Oklahoman*, October 9, 1942; *Bismarck (ND) Tribune*, October 23, 1942.

18. *Salina (KS) Journal*, September 23, 29, 30, 1942; *Roswell (NM) Daily Record*, October 11, 1942.

19. *Nebraska Farmer*, December 26, 1942.

20. *Denver Post*, January 3, December 2, 1942.

21. *Nebraska Farmer*, December 12, 1942; *Oklahoma City Daily Oklahoman*, December 5, 1942; *Roswell (NM) Daily Record*, December 15, 20, 1942.

22. D. G. Dodds to Lyle H. Boren, September 18, 1942, and J. A. Ulio to Lyle H. Boren, September 29, 1942, folder 11, box 4, Lyle H. Boren Collection, CAC; *Cheyenne Wyoming Eagle*, January 20, February 18, 1943; *Roswell (NM) Daily Record*, February 2, 1943; *Denver Post*, January 25, March 9, 1943; *Farmer-Stockman*, April 15, 1943.

23. *Omaha World Herald*, February 15, 1943; *Salina (KS) Journal*, February 20, 1943; *Denver Post*, February 20, March 7, 1943; Mrs. T. W. to Andrew Schoeppel, February 9, 1943, folder 2, box 44, and Luke Chapin to Andrew Schoeppel, March 7, 1943, folder 3, box 44, Correspondence, 1943–47, Andrew Schoeppel Papers, KSHS.

24. *Denver Post*, March 4, 23, 25, 27, 28, 1943.

25. *Denver Post*, March 23, 27, 29, 1943; *Salina (KS) Journal*, March 25, 26, 1943.

26. Rasmussen, *Emergency Farm Labor Supply Program*, 19–20.

27. Rasmussen, *Emergency Farm Labor Supply Program*, 41–46, 57.

28. Coalson, *Migratory Farm Labor System*, 68–71.

29. Coalson, *Migratory Farm Labor System*, 3; Moser, "Farm Labor Practices and Conditions," 49–52; Organization for State Farm Labor Program, Kansas, folder 6, box 44, Correspondence, 1943–47, Andrew Schoeppel Papers, KSHS.

30. Liss, "Farm Wage Boards."

31. Liss, "Prevailing Wage Scales," 4, 6–8, 11–12.

32. *Dallas Morning News*, May 27, June 3, 11, 12, 13, 14, 21, 1943; *Cheyenne Wyoming State Tribune*, July 17, 1943; *Roswell (NM) Daily Record*, April 17, 1943; *Kearney (NE) Daily Hub*, May 22, 1943; *Denver Post*, July 6, 1943; *Oklahoma City Daily Oklahoman*, May 19, 1943.

33. *Rapid City (SD) Daily Journal*, July 14, August 9, 10, 11, 1943; *Bismarck (ND) Tribune*, August 16, 1943.

34. *Kansas Farmer*, March 4, 1944; "Large Number of Single Farm Men Given Occupational Deferment," [1943], folder 3, box 44, Correspondence, 1943–47, Andrew Schoeppel Papers, KSHS; *Dallas Morning News*, September 2, October 5, 1943; Harold B. Lewis to Andrew Schoeppel, June 15, 1943, folder 4, box 44, Correspondence, 1943–47, Andrew Schoeppel Papers, KSHS; *Salina (KS) Journal*, February 17, 1944; *Bismarck (ND) Tribune*, October 1, 1943; Harold B. Lewis, To: All Volunteer Farm Replacement Representatives, June 15, 1943, folder 4, box 44, Correspondence, 1943–47, Andrew Schoeppel Papers, KSHS.

35. *Dakota Farmer*, May 13, 1944.

36. *Roswell (NM) Daily Record*, February 17, 1944; *Denver Post*, February 17, 1944.

37. *Dallas Morning News*, January 9, February 29, 1944; *Rapid City (SD) Daily Journal*, March 24, May 5, 1944.

38. *Salina (KS) Journal*, March 25, 1944; *Roswell (NM) Daily Record*, March 27, 1944; *Dallas Morning News*, April 14, 1944.

39. *Dallas Morning News*, May 17, 19, June 3, 1944; Roy E. Morgan to Andrew Schoeppel, January 4, 1944, and W. F. Turrentine to Roy E. Morgan, January 6, 1945, folder 9, box 63, Correspondence, 1943–47, Andrew Schoeppel Papers, KSHS.

40. *Salina (KS) Journal*, April 20, June 17, 29, 1944; *Oklahoma City Daily Oklahoman*, April 27, 1944; *Bismarck (ND) Tribune*, May 6, 18, 1944.

41. *Dakota Farmer*, March 4, 1944; *Dallas Morning News*, June 6, September 29, October 5, 6, 29, 1944; *Oklahoma City Daily Oklahoman*, December 8, 1944.

42. *Rapid City (SD) Daily Journal*, October 13, 1944.

43. *Salina (KS) Journal*, January 5, 1945; *Roswell (NM) Daily Record*, January 4, 1945; *Nebraska Farmer*, January 8, 1945; Z. W. Johnson to Arthur Capper, February 10, folder 5, box 44, John W. Petty to Andrew Schoeppel, January 17, 1945, folder 9, box 63, and David E. Milbourne to Lewis B. Hershey, January 19, 1945, folder 10, box 63, Correspondence, 1943–47, Andrew Schoeppel Papers, KSHS; *Nebraska Farmer*, February 17, 1945; *Denver Post*, February 20, 22, 1945.

44. *Bismarck (ND) Tribune*, July 24, 30, 1945.

45. *Wichita Eagle*, May 6, October 10, 1945; *Salina (KS) Journal*, May 15, 24, 1945; *Nebraska Farmer*, August 4, 1945.

46. Schwartz, *Seasonal Farm Labor*, 103–5, 108–9, 111–12; Rasmussen, *Emergency Farm Labor Supply Program*, 84.

47. Rasmussen, *Emergency Farm Labor Supply Program*, 14; McCain, "Mexican Labor Question," 48; Schwartz, *Seasonal Farm Labor*, 113–14, 117–21; Scruggs, *Braceros*.

48. Rasmusssen, *Emergency Farm Labor Supply Program*, 20–21; O. M. Olson to Dwight Griswold, June 8, 1942, folder 18, box 12, Correspondence, 1942, Dwight Palmer Griswold Papers, NSHS; Scruggs, *Braceros*, 164.

49. Rasmussen, *Emergency Farm Labor Supply Program*, 26–27, 36, 201–3, 208, 214; Jones, *Mexican War Workers*, 1–26; Scruggs, "Bracero Program under the Farm Security Administration," 149–51, 161–62, and *Braceros*, 147; Foley, *White Scourge*, 205; Nash, *American West Transformed*, 53.

50. McCain, "Mexican Labor Question," 49, 50–52, 62, 64; Scruggs, "Bracero Program under the Farm Security Administration," 158; Foley, *White Scourge*, 206–7; Chamberlain, "'On the Train and Gone,'" 438; *Albuquerque Journal*, March 3, 1944; Scruggs, *Braceros*, 247, 249–50, 299.

51. *Cheyenne Wyoming Eagle*, August 14, 1942; *Roswell (NM) Daily Record*, September 9, 11, 22, 1942.

52. *Roswell (NM) Daily Record*, September 25, 30, November 6, 15, 1942.

53. Hewitt, "Mexican Workers in Wyoming," 21–23.

54. *Roswell (NM) Daily Record*, February 24, 1943; *Denver Post*, February 28, March 3, 1943.

55. *Denver Post*, March 22, September 5, November 30, 1943; *Dallas Morning News*, May 13, 1943; Hewitt, "Mexican Workers in Wyoming," 26–27; *Billings (MT) Gazette*, January 23, 1944.

56. Hewitt, "Mexican Workers in Wyoming," 26–27; Oppenheimer, "Acculturation or Assimilation," 432; Moser, "Farm Labor Practices and Conditions," 66.

57. Hewitt, "Mexican Workers in Wyoming," 23, 25; *Rapid City (SD) Daily Journal*, April 27, 1943, June 2, 1944; *Omaha World Herald*, April 27, 1943; *Rapid City (SD) Daily Journal*, September 14, 1944; *Bismarck (ND) Tribune*, July 1, 21, 22, 1944.

58. *Denver Post*, March 23, 1944; *Rapid City (SD) Daily Journal*, February 5, 1945; *Nebraska Farmer*, July 1, 1944; Hewitt, "Mexican Workers in Wyoming," 25.

59. Notes on Nebraska Farming, Nebraska Agricultural Extension Service press release, September 8, 1944, Val Kuska Collection, NSHS.

60. *Rapid City (SD) Daily Journal*, April 21, 1945; *Dakota Farmer*, July 7, 1945; Foley, *White Scourge*, 206; *Albuquerque Journal*, February 24, 1943.

61. Hewitt, "Mexican Workers in Wyoming," 26, 31; Liss, "Farm Wage Boards," 17; Nash, *American West Transformed*, 51; Rasmussen, *Emergency Farm Labor Supply Program*, 226–32.

62. Smith, "Women's Land Army," 82; *Denver Post*, November 24, 1941, February 15, 1942; Carpenter, *On the Farm Front*, 22, 35; Litoff and Smith, "'To the Rescue of the Crops,'" 349.

63. *Salina (KS) Journal*, April 20, May 11, October 7, 1942; Carpenter, "'Regular Farm Girl,'" 170.

64. *Oklahoma City Daily Oklahoman*, April 6, 1942; *Rapid City (SD) Daily Journal*, May 2, 1942; *Nebraska Farmer*, May 16, August 8, 1942; *Roswell (NM) Daily Record*, October 14, 16, 1942.

65. Litoff and Smith, "To the Rescue of the Crops," 351, 355, 357; Carpenter, *On the Farm Front*, 46, 56, 62; Rasmussen, *Emergency Farm Labor Supply Program*, 138; Smith, "Women's Land Army," 82, 84.

66. "Guides for Wartime Use of Women on Farms," 1–6; Carpenter, *On the Farm Front*, 46, 53, 75; Smith, "Women's Land Army," 86–88; Kansas Women in the Farm Labor Program, a Talk by Georgiana H. Smurthwaite, State Home Demonstration Leader, typescript, May 18–28, 1943, and A Call to Farms, typescript, May 10, 1943, folder 6, box 44, Correspondence, 1943–47, Andrew Schoeppel Papers, KSHS.

67. Questions and Answers on the Women's Land Army of the U.S. Crop Corps, May 10, 1943, and Kansas Women in the Farm Labor Program, a Talk by Georgiana H. Smurthwaite, May 18–28, 1943, folder 6, box 44, Correspondence, 1943–47, Andrew Schoeppel Papers, KSHS.

68. Litoff and Smith, "To the Rescue of the Crops," 36, 354–56; Rasmussen, *Emergency Farm Labor Supply Program*, 141–45.

69. Smith, "Women's Land Army," 86; Rasmussen, *Emergency Farm Labor Supply Program*, 144; *Oklahoma City Daily Oklahoman*, June 27, 1943; *Farmer-Stockman*, March 15, 1944; *Kansas Farmer*, August 21, 1943.

70. *Cheyenne Wyoming State Tribune*, May 15, 1944; Carpenter, "'Regular Farm Girl,'" 176, and *On the Farm Front*, 75; *Wichita Eagle*, July 29, 1943; *Denver Post*, July 6, August 3, 12, 1943; *Cheyenne Wyoming Eagle*, April 23, 1942; *Kansas Farmer*, March 4, 1944; Rasmussen, *Emergency Farm Labor Supply Program*, 148; *Rapid City (SD) Daily Journal*, April 21, 1945; *Dakota Farmer*, March 4, 1944; *Nebraska Farmer*, April 18, 1942.

71. News releases, July 9, 11, 1943, folder 7, box 26, Correspondence, 1943–47, Andrew Schoeppel Papers, KSHS; *Salina (KS) Journal*, July 18, 1945.

72. *Denver Post*, July 1, 1945; *Wichita Eagle*, September 11, 1945; Litoff and Smith, "To the Rescue of the Crops," 357; *Rapid City (SD) Daily Journal*, January 14, 1945; Carpenter, *On the Farm Front*, 111, 128, 133; Smith, "Women's Land Army," 88.

73. Carpenter, *On the Farm Front*, 109–10, 118, 176; Smith, "Women's Land Army," 86, 88; Litoff and Smith, "To the Rescue of the Crops," 354–55; *Omaha World Herald*, March 1, 1943; *Oklahoma City Daily Oklahoman*, April 3, 1944; *Dakota Farmer*, September 9, 1944; *Salina (KS) Journal*, January 14, 1944.

74. *Kansas Farmer*, March 4, 1944, September 5, 1945; *Dakota Farmer*, June 9, 1945; *Salina (KS) Journal*, January 14, March 31, April 19, 1944; *Denver Post*, July 1, 1945; Litoff and Smith, "To the Rescue of the Crops," 356; Smith, "Women's Land Army," 88; *Nebraska Farmer*, October 31, 1942.

75. *Kansas Farmer*, June 19, 1943; Smith, "Women's Land Army," 88; Litoff and Smith, "To the Rescue of the Crops," 357; Carpenter, *On the Farm Front*, 128, 134.

76. Carpenter, *On the Farm Front*, 121, 127–28; Rasmussen, *Emergency Farm Labor Supply Program*, 135, 147, 152; *Wichita Eagle*, May 14, 1944.

77. *Bismarck (ND) Tribune*, June 13, 1945.

78. *Rapid City (SD) Daily Journal*, July 17, 1945; *Salina (KS) Journal*, July 16, 1945; T. R. Couthers to Andrew Schoeppel, June 15, 1945, Elmer E. Euwer to Andrew Schoeppel, June 29, 1945, F. Hubbard to H. O. Davis, June 21, 1945, and newspaper clipping, July 24, 1945, folder 2, box 45, Correspondence, 1943–1947, Andrew Schoeppel Papers, KSHS.

79. *Bismarck (ND) Tribune*, August 6, 1945; *Wichita Eagle*, June 17, 1945; *Salina (KS) Journal*, July 2, 1945.

80. Mrs. Fred Porter to Andrew Schoeppel, January 1, 1942, unnumbered folder, box 15, Correspondence File, 1939–1943, Payne Ratner Collection, and J. L. Finley to Dear Sir, February 27, 1943, folder 10, box 63, Correspondence, 1943–47, Andrew Schoeppel Papers, KSHS.

8. Military Affairs

1. Kelley, "Bamboo Bombers," 361–67; *Oklahoma City Daily Oklahoman*, January 8, 1941; *Amarillo Globe*, December 7, 1941.

2. Rulon, "Campus Cadets," 79; Larson, *Wyoming's War Years*, 221.

3. *Salina (KS) Journal*, June 4, 18, 1940, November 12, 1942; *Kearney (NE) Daily Hub*, June 8, 18, 1940; *Denver Post*, November 22, 1940.

4. *Amarillo Globe*, December 22, 1941, January 4, 1942; *Denver Post*, January 20, 1942; *Cheyenne Wyoming Eagle*, February 6, 1942; *Oklahoma City Daily Oklahoman*, November 15, 1942; *Wichita Eagle*, December 11, 1941.

5. *Kearney (NE) Daily Hub*, October 24, 1939; *Salina (KS) Journal*, December 23, 1940; Lovett, "Don't You Know That There's a War On?" 227, 229.

6. *Salina (KS) Journal*, May 28, 1941, June 5, August 9, 1941; Lovett, "Don't You Know That There's a War On?" 230–32.

7. Lovett, "Don't You Know That There's a War On?" 231–33.

8. *Amarillo Globe*, December 18, 1941, May 23, 1943.

9. *Denver Post*, June 26, 1941.

10. *Dallas Morning News*, June 30, 1940; *Amarillo Globe*, December 14, 1941, February 1, 1942.

11. Lovett, "Don't You Know That There's a War On?" 234; Colwell, "'Hell from Heaven,'" 42; Hurst, "Nebraska Army Air Fields," 129–30.

12. *Denver Post*, May 22, 1940; *Oklahoma City Daily Oklahoman*, January 12, 1941; "U.S. Army and Air Force Wings over Kansas," pt. 1; Eastman, "Location and Growth"; Petersen, "Small Town America," 2; *Omaha World Herald*, October 18, 1940; *Wichita Eagle*, October 15, 1940, July 6, 1941; Crowder, "'More Valuable Than Oil,'" 228–40, 245–46.

13. *Denver Post*, September 6, 15, 22, October 16, November 20, December 4, 22, 1940.

14. Colwell, "'Hell from Heaven,'" 13, 15–16, 18–20.

15. *Denver Post*, September 15, 1940; History, Lubbock Army Air Field, pp. 6, 11, 46, folder 38, box 429, Lubbock Chamber of Commerce Records, 1925–1991, "History: Lubbock Army Air Field to 1 March 1944," Lubbock, TX, pp. 6–9, 11, 14, 33, 46, and T. A. Gilbert to Leona Gelin, April, 23, 1942, Correspondence, 1942–1949, Lubbock (Texas) USO Records, 1942–1956, SWC; *Lubbock Avalanche Journal*, June 21, 1992; *Lamb County Leader*, June, 11, 1942; *South Plains Army Air Field Flying Time*, September 7, 1944; "History, Lubbock Army Air Field," 2. The city acquired the land for $50,000, or $35 per acre. The first pilots graduated in April 1942.

16. *Roswell (NM) Daily Record*, August 8, December 5, 1941, August 8, 10, 13, September 1, 1944. The city had to raise $30,000 by public subscription to purchase three thousand acres and the railroad and other easements required; the War Department would then lease the air base for $1 per year.

17. "U.S. Army and Air Force Wings over Kansas," 130, 135–36, 145, 147.

18. "U.S. Army and Air Force Wings over Kansas," 356–59; discussion between the author and Ray K. Hurt, November 1, 2001; *Salina (KS) Journal*, October 6, 1942.

19. Hurt, "Naval Air Stations in Kansas," 352–54.

20. *Salina (KS) Journal*, July 11, 13, 1942; Hurt, "Naval Air Stations in Kansas," 354–55.

21. Hurt, "Naval Air Stations in Kansas," 355.

22. Hurt, "Naval Air Stations in Kansas," 358.

23. Petersen, "Kearney, Nebraska," 119; *Kearney (NE) Daily Hub*, February 1, 4, 1941.

24. Petersen, "Small Town America," 10.

25. Petersen, "Small Town America," 10–11; *Kearney Air Base News*, April 9, 1943.

26. Petersen, "Small Town America," 13–17

27. *Cheyenne Wyoming Eagle*, May 7, 1942; *Cheyenne Wyoming State Tribune*, April 7, 1941, May 7, 1942; Larson, *Wyoming's War Years*, 213–15; Adams, "Casper Army Air Field," 8–9, 12, 14; Jane R. Kendall and Captain Watson, Fort Francis E. Warren—Contemporary History, 1940, typescript, MSS265, H61-30, Wyoming State Archives, Cheyenne (hereafter cited as WSA).

28. *Oklahoma City Daily Oklahoman*, December 20, 1940; *Rapid City (SD) Daily Journal*, April 9, 1942.

29. *Salina (KS) Journal*, May 8, 1942; *Cheyenne Wyoming State Tribune*, November 10, 1942.

30. *Cheyenne Wyoming State Tribune*, November 3, 1940; Larson, *Wyoming's War Years*, 204.

31. *Cheyenne Wyoming State Tribune*, November 20, 1940.

32. *Salina (KS) Journal*, July 15, 1942; *Bismarck (ND) Tribune*, November 2, 1944.

33. *Omaha Weekly Herald*, July 2, 1942; Petersen, "Kearney Nebraska," 120.

34. *Cheyenne Wyoming State Tribune*, September 13, 1940, March 7, May 16, 1941; Jane R. Kendall and Captain Watson, Fort Francis E. Warren—Contemporary History, 1940, typescript, MSS265, H61-30, WSA; *Denver Post*, October 9, 1940; Larson, *Wyoming's War Years*, 211–12.

35. Larson, *Wyoming's War Years*, 211.

36. *Cheyenne Wyoming State Tribune*, February 3, 1943; *Salina (KS) Journal*, August 13, 1942.

37. Colwell, "'Hell from Heaven,'" 68–69.

38. Colwell, "'Hell from Heaven,'" 70.

39. Petersen, "Small Town America," 188–92.

40. Petersen, "Small Town America," 192–93.

41. Lieutenant Joseph W. Jarrett, Study of Negro Racial Situation at U.S. Naval Ammunition Depot, Hastings, Nebraska, July 1944, pp. 1, 3, 30–31, 33, Naval Intelligence Service, Ninth Naval District, NSHS.

42. Jarrett, Study (n. 41 above), 26–28.

43. Jarrett, Study (n. 41 above), 35–37, 45, 52, 55–57.

44. Jarrett, Study (n. 41 above), 12.

45. Jarrett, Study (n. 41 above), 14–16.

46. Jarrett, Study (n. 41 above), 17, 23.

47. Jarrett, Study (n. 41 above), 10–11, 42–43, 52, 54, 75–77.

48. *Cheyenne Wyoming State Tribune*, October 13, 1940.

49. Colwell, "'Hell from Heaven,'" 73; Junge Interview with Joye Kading, June 18, 1992, Oral History Transcripts, no. 1958, WSA.

50. *Cheyenne Wyoming Eagle*, July 5, 1940; *Oklahoma City Daily Oklahoman*, January 29, February 5, 1941; *Salina (KS) Journal*, August 22, September 5, 1941.

51. *Oklahoma City Daily Oklahoman*, February 1, April 3, June 4, October 10, 1942; Ethel M. Ferguson, How I Felt about World War II, typescript, World War II Subject File, WSA; Costello, *Virtue under Fire*, 206–7, 214; *Bismarck (ND) Tribune*, February 4, 1942; *Amarillo Globe*, June 16, 1942.

52. *Oklahoma City Daily Oklahoman*, February 4, 1943; *Dallas Morning News*, February 5, 1943; *Albuquerque Journal*, February 21, 1943; Polenberg, ed., *America at War*, 151.

53. *Oklahoma City Daily Oklahoman*, February 23, 1943; *Dallas Morning News*, February 21, 1943.

54. *Cheyenne Wyoming Eagle*, August 5, 1942; *Cheyenne Wyoming State Tribune*, June 9, 1943; Adams, "Air Age Comes to Wyoming," 24–25.

55. *Salina (KS) Journal*, December 6, 1943.

56. *Cheyenne Wyoming Eagle*, November 11, 1942, August 2, 1945; *Cheyenne Wyoming State Tribune*, June 4, 1943.

57. *Dallas Morning News*, October 12, 1942, September 4, November 14, 1943.

58. *Cheyenne Wyoming State Tribune*, January 5, July 31, 1944, February 20, 1945.

59. Petersen, "Kearney, Nebraska," 122.

60. Petersen, "Kearney, Nebraska," 122.

61. *Oklahoma City Daily Oklahoman*, November 15, 1941.

62. *Dallas Morning News*, January 29, February 3, July 28, August 28, 1944.

63. *Albuquerque Journal*, April 12, June 19, July 28, 1943; *Dallas Morning News*, November 14, 1943; *Cheyenne Wyoming Eagle*, May 27, 1943.

64. *Oklahoma City Daily Oklahoman*, November 9, December 4, 18, 23, January 3, 1943.

65. *Denver Post*, May 25, 1944; Leonard, "Denver at War," 33.

66. *Oklahoma City Daily Oklahoman*, February 8, March 3, 6, 1945.

67. Robert Kerr to Dear Friend, ca. January–February 1945, folder 16, box 14, Gubernatorial Papers, Robert S. Kerr Collection, CAC.

68. Robert Kerr to Owen Amdall, December 17, 1945, Gubernatorial Papers, folder 16, box 14, Robert S. Kerr Collection, CAC; *Oklahoma City Daily Oklahoman*, November 16, 1941.

69. *Oklahoma City Daily Oklahoman*, June 10, 14, 1942; *Lincoln (NE) Star*, November 9, 1943; *Cheyenne Wyoming Eagle*, March 23, 24, 1943.

70. *Dallas Morning News*, June 20, 1943.

71. *Cheyenne Wyoming State Tribune*, January 5, 1955.

72. Larson, *Wyoming's War Years*, 215; Larsen, "Alliance Army Air Base," 240–41.

73. *Oklahoma City Daily Oklahoman*, February 9, 1941, June 13, 1943; *Roswell (NM) Daily Record*, March 23, 1942.

74. *Bismarck (ND) Tribune*, April 10, 13, May 10, 1940, March 19, 1941.

75. *Oklahoma City Daily Oklahoman*, January 4, 1941; *Rapid City (SD) Daily Journal*, February 5, March 28, 1942.

76. *Billings (MT) Gazette*, December 20, 1942, May 30, 1943.

77. *Dallas Morning News*, June 13, 1943; *Oklahoma City Daily Oklahoman*, June 1, 1943; Colwell, "'Hell from Heaven,'" 51, 53, 54, 96; Adams, "Casper Army Air Field," 11, 17–18.

78. *Rapid City (SD) Daily Journal*, October 10, 1942; *Roswell (NM) Daily Record*, May 20, 1945; Petersen, "Kearney, Nebraska," 126. In June and July 1942 Rapid City bank deposits increased 144 and 178 percent, respectively, from those same months in 1941. At Roswell, New Mexico, bank deposits increased from $5.9 million in 1941 to $17.1 million in 1944, while retail sales jumped from $8.2 to $11.4 million. In Kearney, Nebraska, bank deposits increased from $1.7 to $9.4 million between 1940 and 1947.

79. *Denver Post*, May 7, 1944.

80. *Salina (KS) Journal*, September 12, 1941, May 23, 1942; *Denver Post*, April 18, June 5, October 19, 1941, July 4, 1942; *Roswell (NM) Daily Record*, July 5, 1944; *Cheyenne Wyoming State Tribune*, May 24, July 29, 1943.

81. Myer, "Army Comes to Abilene," 107–8.

82. Kelley, "Bamboo Bombers," 375; Pickle, "Aviation History of Big Spring," 27; Hurst, "Nebraska Army Air Fields," 130–31; *Rapid City (SD) Daily Journal*, September 15, 18, 21, 1945; *Amarillo Globe*, November 30, 1941; *Omaha World Herald*, October 16, 1942, December 15, 1945; Background and History

of Reese Air Force Base, typescript, n.d., Lubbock Army Air Field Collection, SWC; *Roswell (NM) Daily Record*, September 2, 1945; *Denver Post*, September 24, October 15, 1945; *Salina (KS) Journal*, August 30, 1944; Larsen, "Alliance Army Air Base," 253.

83. Paulette, "Odessa during the War Years," 20, 28.

84. Neugebauer, ed., *Plains Farmer*, 236–37.

9. Internment

1. *Bismarck (ND) Tribune*, June 25, 1940.

2. *Rapid City (SD) Daily Journal*, August 14, 22, December 4, 20, 1940; *Wichita Eagle*, August 18, October 10, 1940; *Bismarck (ND) Tribune*, August 27, 30, December 20, 1940.

3. *Wichita Eagle*, August 22, 23, 24, 25, December 11, 1940.

4. *Bismarck (ND) Tribune*, January 15, 18, February 11, 25, 1942.

5. *Denver Post*, December 18, 1940, January 9, 1941.

6. *Salina (KS) Journal*, January 8, 9, 1942; *Denver Post*, January 3, 1942.

7. *Roswell (NM) Daily Record*, April 15, 1942; Spidle, "Axis Invasion," 94–96.

8. *Bismarck (ND) Tribune*, April 12, 14, 18, June 2, 6, July 10, 28, August 8, December 12, 1941, January 19, 1942; Christgau, *Enemies*, 7–8.

9. Christgau, *Enemies*, 88–89.

10. Thomas and Nishimoto, *Spoilage*, 1–3.

11. Thomas and Nishimoto, *Spoilage*, 15–18; *Cheyenne Wyoming State Tribune*, December 10, 1941.

12. Thomas and Nishimoto, *Spoilage*, 1–13, 17; Hosokawa, *Colorado's Japanese Americans*, 283–84, 287, 304, 316.

13. Hosokawa, *Colorado's Japanese Americans*, 225–26, 329, 338; Thomas and Nishimoto, *Spoilage*, 15–18, 24–25, 27.

14. Kashima, *Judgment without Trial*, 111–13; Culley, "World War II and a Western Town," 43, 48, 51–53, 57, 61.

15. Kashima, *Judgment without Trial*, 108, 110, 118, 121–23.

16. Kashima, *Judgment without Trial*, 108–9; *Bismarck (ND) Tribune*, February 9, March 20, 1942.

17. *Bismarck (ND) Tribune*, January 20, 28, February 17, 26, March 9, 1942.

18. Warner, "Barbed Wire and Nazilagers," 46; Kashima, *Judgment without Trial*, 115, 258–59.

19. *Bismarck (ND) Tribune*, May 2, 1941.

20. Jackson Brown to Lyle H. Boren, August 14, 1942, and Lyle H. Boren to Jackson Brown, August 20, 1942, folder 21, box 12, Lyle H. Boren Collection, CAC.

21. *Denver Post*, February 23, 1941.

22. *Oklahoma City Daily Oklahoman*, December 19, 1941; *Denver Post*, December 15, 1941; *Amarillo Globe*, December 14, 1941.

23. Hosokawa, *Colorado's Japanese Americans*, 87.

24. Hosokawa, *Colorado's Japanese Americans*, 93; *Denver Post*, March 1, May 27, September 20, 1942; *Roswell (NM) Daily Record*, March 5, 1942.

25. Daniels, *Concentration Camps*, 94; *Rapid City (SD) Daily Journal*, July 3, 1942; *Roswell (NM) Daily Record*, March 5, 1942.

26. *Salina (KS) Journal*, April 2, 4, 1942; *Billings (MT) Gazette*, April 2, 1942.

27. R. E. Carver to Andrew Schoeppel, January 10, 1943, Russell E. Mc-Clure to Andrew Schoeppel, January 11, 1943, and F. E. Black to Ed Leiker, April 7, 1943, folder 13, box 63, Correspondence, 1943–47, Andrew Schoeppel Papers, KSHS.

28. *Amarillo Globe*, April 5, 1942.

29. *Billings (MT) Gazette*, April 30, 1942.

30. Johnson, "At Home in Amache," 5; Yoshino, "Barbed Wire," 36; Hosokawa, *Colorado's Japanese Americans*, 101.

31. Johnson, "At Home in Amache," 5; Hosokawa, *Colorado's Japanese Americans*, 103; *Denver Post*, February 14, 1943; Terkel, *"The Good War,"* 30.

32. *Denver Post*, February 14, 15, 1943; Johnson, "At Home in Amache," 7, 9; *Bismarck (ND) Tribune*, April 3, 1942.

33. *Denver Post*, February 16, 1943.

34. Hosokawa, *Colorado's Japanese Americans*, 105; *Denver Post*, February 18, April 23, 1943.

35. *Omaha World Herald*, September 18, 1942; *Denver Post*, April 27, 30, 1943.

36. *Omaha World Herald*, July 11, 1943; *Denver Post*, August 11, 1943.

37. *Albuquerque Journal*, October 28, 1943; *Cheyenne Wyoming State Tribune*, October 28, 1943; *Denver Post*, August 6, November 7, 1943, May 9, 10, 29, 1944.

38. *Denver Post*, August 6, 8, 9, 11, 18, 1944; *Omaha World Herald*, August 19, 1944.

39. *Cheyenne Wyoming State Tribune*, January 26, 1944; *Denver Post*, February 1, 4, 6, 8, 9, March 30, May 23, 1944.

40. Hosokawa, *Colorado's Japanese Americans*, 115–18.

41. *Denver Post*, May 25, October 31, November 22, 1944.

42. *Denver Post*, December 14, 18, 1944, March 6, 1945; *Rapid City (SD) Daily Journal*, February 16, March 6, 1945; Hosokawa, *Colorado's Japanese Americans*, 238.

43. *Omaha World Herald*, April 7, 1945; *Cheyenne Wyoming State Tribune*, July 15, 1945.

44. *Denver Post*, October 15, 28, November 11, 18, 1945; *Bismarck (ND) Tribune*, December 26, 1945.

45. *Denver Post*, August 8, 16, 1945; *Omaha World Herald*, August 15, 1945; Unsworth, "Floating Vengeance," 21–24, 26–27, 30–31; Larsen, "War Balloons," 104–5, 108–9. In South Dakota balloons dropped near Buffalo, Kadoka, Marcus, Wolsey, Red Elm, Madison, and Belle Fouche and on the Cheyenne Indian Reservation.

46. Wertheimer, "Admitting Nebraska's Nisei," 58–61; Austin, *From Concentration Camp to Campus*, 15–16.

47. Daniels, *Concentration Camps*, 9–10; Wertheimer, "Admitting Nebraska's Nisei," 63, 65, 67, 69; Austin, *From Concentration Camp to Campus*, 61, 114–15.

48. Russell E. McClure, the Wichita city manager, wrote many letters to Governor Andrew Schoeppel complaining about the admission of Japanese students to Friends University and the University of Wichita. See folder 15, box 63, Correspondence, 1943–47, Andrew Schoeppel Papers, KSHS; and *Salina (KS) Journal*, April 2, 1942.

49. *Bismarck (ND) Tribune*, April 10, 1942; *Rapid City (SD) Daily Journal*, February 27, 1942; *Omaha World Herald*, May 13, 1942; Dwight Griswold to H. R. Hewitt, March 2, 1942, C. W. Murphy to Dwight Griswold, March 2, 1942, and Dwight Griswold to A. E. Sheldon, July 10, 1942, folder 217, box 12, Correspondence, 1942, Dwight Palmer Griswold Papers, NSHS; *Omaha World Herald*, September 19, November 12, 1942.

50. *Bismarck (ND) Tribune*, June 15, 1943.

51. *Billings (MT) Gazette*, June 18, 1942; *Oklahoma City Daily Oklahoman*, June 26, 1942; *Cheyenne Wyoming Eagle*, August 14, 1942; *Cheyenne Wyoming Eagle*, January 15, June 16, August 11, 1942; *Denver Post*, September 9, 1942.

52. *Denver Post*, October 14, 1942.

53. Clara Watson to Andrew Schoeppel, folder 13, box 63, Correspondence, 1943–47, Andrew Schoeppel Papers, KSHS; *Salina (KS) Journal*, March 25, 1943; L. H. Griffith, Ed Johnson, and M. N. Penny to Andrew Schoeppel, June 5, 1944, folder 13, box 63, Correspondence, 1943–47, Andrew Schoeppel Papers, KSHS.

54. W. H. Heiden to Andrew Schoeppel, March 29, 1943, Mrs. Lee Erskine to Andrew Schoeppel, March 29, 1943, Roy E. Dillard to Andrew Schoeppel, June 6, 1943, and Andrew Schoeppel to Roy E. Dillard, June 7, 1943, folder 13, box 63, Andrew Schoeppel Papers, KSHS.

55. *Albuquerque Journal*, March 5, May 25, 26, August 14, 1943; *Rapid City (SD) Daily Journal*, July 21, 1943.

56. War Board Memoranda, no. 55, USDA, folder 218, box 12, Correspondence, 1942, Dwight Palmer Griswold Papers, NSHS; *Denver Post*, September

1, 1942; *Cheyenne Wyoming Eagle*, September 2, 1942; *Rapid City (SD) Daily Journal*, September 17, 1942; *Omaha World Herald*, September 18, 19, 1942.

57. *Omaha World Herald*, July 11, 1943; "Uprooted," 27; Avis Atkinson to Andrew Schoeppel, February 12, 1943, folder 13, box 63, and A. R. Parker and Mrs. A. R. Parker to Andrew Schoeppel, August 14, 1943, folder 6, box 64, Correspondence, 1943–47, Andrew Schoeppel Papers, KSHS.

10. Prisoner-of-War Camps

1. Trew, *McLean POW Camp*, 23, 25, 29, 32.

2. Krammer, "Afrika Korps," 235, and *Nazi Prisoners of War*, 44; Trew, *McLean POW Camp*, 25; Remembrances of Mrs. E. B. Fairfield, February 26, 1978, Joseph W. Fairfield Collection, NSHS.

3. Keefer, *Italian Prisoners of War*, 46–47, 61.

4. Wyoming in World War II, Douglas Internment Camp, Clipping File, University Archives, University of Wyoming (hereafter cited as UA); Moore, "Italian POWs," 141; Rogers, "Camp Hereford," 65; Krammer, "Afrika Korps," 254, 256; Keen, "Recreational and Morale Activities," 89; Krammer, "German Prisoners of War," 72, and *Nazi Prisoners of War*, 24.

5. *Oklahoma City Daily Oklahoman*, November 14, 1943; *Bismarck (ND) Tribune*, July 2, 1943; Prisoner of War Camps, Vertical File, WSA; Jaehn, "Unlikely Harvesters," 51; Pluth, "Administration and Operation," 128; Krammer, *Nazi Prisoners of War*, xiii.

6. Lewis and Mewha, *Prisoner of War Utilization*, 84; T. W. Schomburg to Frank R. VanEaton, memorandum, January 5, 1944, folder 29, box 2, Lester C. Hunt Papers, AHC; Krammer, *Nazi Prisoners of War*, 26–27; *Dallas Morning News*, December 6, 1944; Mason, "German Prisoners of War," 198.

7. Krammer, "Afrika Korps," 249–52, and *Nazi Prisoners of War*, 27–28, 33; O'Brien, Isern, and Lumley, "Stalag Sunflower," 184; Ward, *Concordia Prisoner of War Camp*, 2, 4; Trew, *McLean POW Camp*, 7, 10.

8. Howes, "Prisoners at Work," 58; Spidle, "Axis Invasion," 109–10; Krammer, *Nazi Prisoners of War*, 35–36; Worrall, "Prisoners on the Home Front," 32; Rogers, "Camp Hereford," 77–78; *Rapid City (SD) Daily Journal*, November 7, 1944; *Salina (KS) Journal*, August 11, 1943; Jaehn, "Unlikely Harvesters," 51.

9. Krammer, *Nazi Prisoners of War*, 43; *Bismarck (ND) Tribune*, July 2, 1943.

10. Lester C. Hunt to Lt. Col. Gordon Brittan, July 15, 1943, folder 29, box 2, Lester C. Hunt Papers, AHC; Corbett, "'They Hired Every Farmer in the Country,'" 372–73, 381; Pluth, "Administration and Operation," 128; Tissing, "Stalag—Texas," 30; Trew, *McLean POW Camp*, 20, 25; Paschal, "The Enemy in Colorado," 131.

11. Lester C. Hunt to Joseph C. O'Mahoney, January 9, 1943, folder 29, box

2, Lester C. Hunt Papers, AHC; Wyoming in World War II, Douglas Internment Camp, Clipping File, no. 8179, box 199, UA.

12. *Amarillo Globe*, September 27, 1942; Trew, *McLean POW Camp*, 7; Ward, *Concordia Prisoner of War Camp*, 2–3; Corbett, "'They Hired Every Farmer in the Country,'" 378.

13. *Amarillo Globe*, September 27, 1942; Corbett, "'They Hired Every Farmer in the Country,'" 371, 379, 381; Henegar, "Beating Swords into Ploughshares," 16.

14. Krammer, *Nazi Prisoners of War*, 39; Millett, *Army Service Forces*, 371; Jepson, "Camp Carson," 39; Paschal, "Enemy in Colorado," 122; Pluth, "Administration and Operation," 171; Trew, *McLean POW Camp*, 13; Walker, "The Swastika and the Lone Star," 66; Recollections of Mr. Steve Sorok, Joseph W. Fairfield Collection, NSHS.

15. *Omaha World Herald*, June 13, 1943; O'Brien, Isern, and Lumley, "Stalag Sunflower," 192; Tissing, "Stalag—Texas," 29; Trew, *McLean POW Camp*, 30; Henegar, "Beating Swords into Ploughshares," 19.

16. *Salina (KS) Journal*, October 27, 1943; Ward, *Concordia Prisoner of War Camp*, 7.

17. Memorandum of Facts Pertaining to Survey of Worland, Wyoming Prisoner of War Camp, ca. July 1942, unnumbered folder, box 249, and Procedure to Be Followed in Hiring Out Prisoner-of-War Labor, August 14, 1943, Bulletin no. 63, typescript, War Manpower Commission, folder 2, box 264, Joseph C. O'Mahoney Papers, WSA; McKnight, "Employment of Prisoners of War," 63; *Denver Post*, September 1, 1943; *Oklahoma City Daily Oklahoman*, November 14, 1943; Lewis and Mewha, *Prisoner of War Utilization*, 77–78, 103; *Salina (KS) Journal*, July 17, 1943; Mason, "German Prisoners of War," 210; Krammer, "German Prisoners of War," 69.

18. *Denver Post*, September 1, 1943; O'Brien, Isern, and Lumley, "Stalag Sunflower," 188; Mason, "German Prisoners of War," 210.

19. Lewis and Mewha, *Prisoner of War Utilization*, 151; Krammer, *Nazi Prisoners of War*, 108, 112–13.

20. Paschal, "Enemy in Colorado," 130–31; Krammer, *Nazi Prisoners of War*, 85–86; *Rapid City (SD) Daily Journal*, August 28, 1943; Moore, "Italian POWs," 141–42; Krammer, "German Prisoners of War," 69–70.

21. Procedure to Be Followed in Hiring Out Prisoner-of-War Labor, August 14, 1943, Bulletin no. 63, typescript, War Manpower Commission, folder 2, box 264, Joseph C. O'Mahoney Papers, WSA; *Rapid City (SD) Daily Journal*, March 1, 1944; *Oklahoma City Daily Oklahoman*, June 11, 1943; *Salina (KS) Journal*, May 18, August 7, 1943; Walker, "Prisoners of War in Texas," 389–90.

22. Lt. Col. Clyde B. Dempster to Mrs. John Harmon, August 5, 1943, folder 7, box 1, Lester C. Hunt Papers, AHC; *Oklahoma City Daily Oklahoman*, No-

vember 14, 1943; *Wichita Eagle*, December 10, 1943; *Omaha World Herald*, June 13, 1943; *Dallas Morning News*, December 6, 1944.

23. O'Brien, Isern, and Lumley, "Stalag Sunflower," 191; Howes, "Prisoners at Work," 58; Lester C. Hunt to Dr. J. ? Felix, May 17, 1944, folder 29, box 2, Lester C. Hunt Papers, AHC; *Salina (KS) Journal*, May 18, 1943, October 4, 1944; *Oklahoma City Daily Oklahoman*, November 14, 1943; *Nebraska Farmer*, October 7, 1944; Trew, *McLean pow Camp*, 30; Krammer, *Nazi Prisoners of War*, 87–88; Warner, "Barbed Wire and Nazilagers," 42.

24. Krammer, *Nazi Prisoners of War*, 35–36, 89, and "Afrika Korps," 268; Spidle, "Axis Invasion," 110; Worrall, "Prisoners on the Home Front," 32; O'Brien, Isern, and Lumley, "Stalag Sunflower," 193; Howes, "Prisoners at Work," 62; *Salina (KS) Journal*, July 2, 1943; *Albuquerque Journal*, July 20, August 27, September 8, 1943; *Cheyenne Wyoming Eagle*, September 30, 1943.

25. *Kansas Farmer*, November 6, 1943; *Nebraska Farmer*, December 4, 1943, October 7, 1944; *Salina (KS) Journal*, January 21, 1944; Howes, "Prisoners at Work," 62.

26. Nash, *American West Transformed*, 47–48; Keefer, *Italian Prisoners of War*, 61; Tissing, "Stalag—Texas," 25; *Dallas Morning News*, July 6, 1944; Rogers, "Camp Hereford," 76.

27. Worrall, "Prisoners on the Home Front," 32, 34; *Cheyenne Wyoming State Tribune*, November 23, 1943; *Denver Post*, January 28, 1945.

28. *Cheyenne Wyoming Eagle*, September 4, 1943; *Cheyenne Wyoming State Tribune*, October 4, 1943; Lester C. Hunt to Maj. Gen. F. E. Uhl, November 19, 1943, and D. J. Courtney to District Engineer, Denver, Colorado, November 5, 1943, folder 29, box 2, Lester C. Hunt Papers, AHC.

29. Worrall, "Prisoners on the Home Front," 35, 39; Paschal, "Enemy in Colorado," 133; *Salina (KS) Journal*, October 21, 1943; Doyle, "German Prisoners of War in the Southwest," 57.

30. Tissing, "Stalag—Texas," 29; Keefer, *Italian Prisoners of War*, 61; O'Brien, Isern, and Lumley, "Stalag Sunflower," 192; Krammer, *Nazi Prisoners of War*, 92.

31. Paul Stutz Interview, May 20, 1993, Oral History Transcripts, no. 1581, WSA; Krammer, *Nazi Prisoners of War*, 93; *Denver Post*, August 31, 1944; *Cheyenne Wyoming State Tribune*, November 23, 1944.

32. Tissing, "Stalag—Texas," 25–26; *Dallas Morning News*, June 7, 1943, December 6, 1944; *Denver Post*, May 24, 31, 1945; *Wichita Eagle*, September 24, 1944; *Cheyenne Wyoming State Tribune*, November 23, 1943.

33. *New Mexico Magazine* 63 (December 1985): 25; D. J. Courtney to District Engineer, Denver Colorado, November 5, 1943, and Lester C. Hunt to Leonard B. Shaw, July 9, 1944, folder 29, box 2, Lester C. Hunt Papers, AHC; Gansberg, *Stalag U.S.A.*, 35.

34. *Omaha World Herald*, June 16, 1944; newspaper clipping, *Bridgeport*

(NE) Blade, June 7, 1945, Joseph W. Fairfield Collection, NSHS; *Dallas Morning News*, March 16, 1945; Rogers, "Camp Hereford," 79, 98–102; *Roswell (NM) Daily Record*, May 26, 1944.

35. Spidle, "Axis Invasion," 111.

36. Prisoner of War Camps, Vertical File, WSA; Tissing, "Stalag—Texas," 28.

37. Wilson, "Afrika Korps," 366; Bangerter, "German Prisoners of War," 95; Spencer, "Prisoners of War in Cheyenne County," 441; Spidle, "Axis Invasion," 112.

38. Warner, "Barbed Wire and Nazilagers," 40; Walker, "Prisoners of War in Texas," 78; Keefer, *Italian Prisoners of War*, 70; Keen, "Captive Enemy?" 147; Rogers, "Camp Hereford," 76, 101; Spidle, "Axis Invasion," 112; *Oklahoma City Daily Oklahoman*, May 31, June 3, 1943; Tissing, "Utilization of Prisoners of War," 90.

39. Resolution on War Prisoners, Omaha Central Labor Union, April 7, 1944, folder 132, box 67, Nebraska Department of Labor Records, NSHS; *Omaha World Herald*, November 28, 1944; Doyle, "German Prisoners of War in the Southwest," 331.

40. Frank Belcha to William Turrentine, August ?, 1944, folder 6, box 64, Correspondence, 1943–47, Andrew Schoeppel Papers, KSHS; *Wichita Eagle*, September 24, 1944; Warren Prautzsch Interview, September 15, 1975, Joseph W. Fairfield Collection, NSHS; Harold Lewis to Andrew Schoeppel, August 8, 1944, folder 6, box 64, Correspondence, 1943–47, Andrew Schoeppel Papers, KSHS.

41. Rogers, "Camp Hereford," 100; Krammer, *Nazi Prisoners of War*, 120, 142–43, 153.

42. Krammer, *Nazi Prisoners of War*, 126; Ward, *Concordia Prisoner of War Camp*, 161; Spidle, "Axis Invasion," 107; Keefer, *Italian Prisoners of War*, 141; Myer, "Prisoners of War at Camp Barkeley," 137–38; Paschal, "Enemy in Colorado," 134–39.

43. Krammer, *Nazi Prisoners of War*, 130; Paul Stutz Interview, May 20, 1993, Oral History Transcripts, no. 1581, WSA; *Roswell (NM) Daily Record*, March 3, 1944; *Denver Post*, June 19, 1945.

44. Ehrmann, "Experiment in Political Education," 312; *Oklahoma City Daily Oklahoman*, June 3, 1943; Powers, "What to Do with German Prisoners," 46–47; Walker, "The Swastika and the Lone Star," 47; *Dallas Morning News*, November 11, 1943.

45. Krammer, *Nazi Prisoners of War*, 169–71; *Roswell (NM) Daily Record*, July 10, 1945; Warner, "Barbed Wire and Nazilagers," 40.

46. *Oklahoma City Daily Oklahoman*, January 12, 1944; *Omaha World Herald*, January 12, 1944; Krammer, *Nazi Prisoners of War*, 172, 174; Ward, *Concordia Prisoner of War Camp*, 314; Krammer, "Afrika Korps," 276–77; Bangerter, "German Prisoners of War," 79–80.

47. Powers, "What to Do with German Prisoners," 48; Jepson, "Camp Carson," 41; Krammer, *Nazi Prisoners of War*, 178; O'Brien, Isern, and Lumley, "Stalag Sunflower," 185; Krammer, "German Prisoners of War," 70; Walker, "Prisoners of War in Texas," 42; Pluth, "Administration and Operation," 354.

48. Myer, "Prisoners of War at Camp Barkeley," 137; Krammer, *Nazi Prisoners of War*, 186–87; Walker, "Prisoners of War in Texas," 43, 64–70.

49. Spidle, "Axis Invasion," 101; *Salina (KS) Journal*, August 7, 1943; *Denver Post*, November 7, 1943; O'Brien, Isern, and Lumley, "Stalag Sunflower," 190, 193; Harper, "Hereford Prisoner of War Camp," 62; Worrall, "Prisoners on the Home Front," 36–37; *Rapid City (SD) Daily Journal*, January 23, 1945; *Omaha World Herald*, June 13, 1943; *Cheyenne Wyoming State Tribune*, May 24, 1944; Paschal, "Enemy in Colorado," 125; Keen, "Captive Enemy?" 253–62; Pluth, "Administration and Operation," 101, 155–56; *Dallas Morning News*, March 26, July 13, December 3, 1944; Paul Stutz Interview, Oral History Transcripts, May 20, 1993, no. 1581, WSA.

50. Krammer, "Japanese Prisoners of War," 76, 89, and "Afrika Korps," 254; Evans, *Third Reich in Power*, 20–118.

51. *Denver Post*, July 27, 1944; *Dallas Morning News*, December 3, 1944; Recollections of Mr. Steve Sorok, Joseph W. Fairfield Collection, NSHS; Paul Stutz Interview, May 20, 1993, Oral History Transcripts, no. 1581, WSA.

52. Vincent Bertone to Lester C. Hunt, May 24, 1944, folder 29, box 2, Lester C. Hunt Papers, AHC; *Omaha World Harold*, September 19, 1943.

53. Wilson, "Afrika Korps," 367; Bangerter, "German Prisoners of War," 73; *Oklahoma City Daily Oklahoman*, November 11, 1943; Worrall, "Prisoners on the Home Front," 35.

54. Walker, "Prisoners of War in Texas," 394; Paschal, "Enemy in Colorado," 133; Tissing, "Stalag—Texas," 29; Doyle, "German Prisoners of War in the Southwest," 160.

55. O'Brien, Isern, and Lumley, "Stalag Sunflower," 99–100; *World War II and the People of Dundy County*, 7; Paschal, "Enemy in Colorado," 125; *Oklahoma City Daily Oklahoman*, November 14, 1943; Williams, *Interlude in Umbarger*, 23, 119.

56. O'Brien, Isern, and Lumley, "Stalag Sunflower," 192, 195; Wilson, "Afrika Korps," 367.

57. Trew, *McLean POW Camp*, 28, 32.

58. Harper, "Hereford Prisoner of War Camp," 18; Keen, "Captive Enemy?" 87, 89.

59. Corbett, "Interned for the Duration," 65–66; Moore, "Italian POWs," 142.

60. *Roswell (NM) Daily Record*, January 5, 1945; Harper, "Hereford Prisoner of War Camp," 17; Trew, *McLean POW Camp*, 25, 28–29, 33.

11. Indians in Wartime

1. Frank Colbest to Lyle H. Boren, May 20, 1939, folder 7, box 7, Lyle H. Boren Collection, CAC; Collier, "Indian in a Wartime Nation," 29.

2. Black Hills Treaty Council Resolution, April 1938, and Sioux Delegates for the Black Hills Treaty Council and Sioux War Veterans to Lyle H. Boren, May 3, 1938, folder 11, box 7, Lyle H. Boren Collection, CAC; Philip, *John Collier's Crusade*, xiv, 97; Townsend, *World War II and the American Indian*, 15–16.

3. *Report of the Chief of the Office of Indian Affairs, 1939*, 24–26; *Report of the Chief of the Office of Indian Affairs, 1940*, 394.

4. *Report of the Chief of the Office of Indian Affairs, 1939*, 27; Indian Policy in Oklahoma by Type, folder 105, box 10, Legislative Series, Elmer Thomas Collection, CAC; Report of Activities, Oklahoma Agricultural Extension Service, typescript, folder 5, box 6, Wilburn Cartwright Collection, CAC.

5. ? Herrick to Elmer Thomas, July 18, 1940, folder 106, box 10, Legislative Series, Elmer Thomas Collection, CAC; Report of Activities, Oklahoma Agricultural Extension Service, typescript, folder 5, box 6, Wilburn Cartwright Collection, CAC; *Report of the Chief of the Office of Indian Affairs, 1939*, 29–31.

6. Parman, *Indians and the American West*, 45; Clow, "Tribal Populations," 374; ? Herrick to Elmer Thomas, October 19, 1940, folder 107, box 10, Legislative Series, Elmer Thomas Collection, and Report of Activities, Oklahoma Agricultural Extension Service, typescript, folder 5, box 6, Wilburn Cartwright Collection, CAC.

7. *Report of the Chief of the Office of Indian Affairs, 1940*, 369; Clow, "Tribal Populations," 375; Bernstein, *American Indians and World War II*, 15; *Indian Education*, November 1, 1939, 5.

8. Roger Bromert, "The Sioux and the Indian—CCC," *South Dakota History* 8 (Fall 1978): 355.

9. *Bismarck (ND) Tribune*, April 18, 1940.

10. *Pawhuska (OK) Osage County News*, January 20, 1939, clipping, folder 20, box 7, Lyle H. Boren Collection, CAC.

11. *Annual Report of the Commissioner of Indian Affairs, 1944*, 244; Walter Colbert to Lyle H. Boren, June 7, 1939, folder 9, box 7, Lyle H. Boren Collection, CAC; Albert G. Washington to Elmer Thomas, October 19, 1940, folder 107, box 10, Legislative Series, Elmer Thomas Collection, CAC; newspaper clippings, folder 9, box 53, Wilburn Cartwright Collection, CAC; Charles C. Criner to Elmer Thomas, June 5, 1940, folder 107, box 10, Legislative Series, Elmer Thomas Collection, CAC; Mr. Tony Lyons Resolution, August 29, 1942, folder 9, box 7, Lyle H. Boren Collection, CAC.

12. Mr. Tony Lyons Resolution, August 29, 1942, folder 9, box 7, ? to Lyle H. Boren, March 2, 1944, and Calvin ? Jr. to Lyle H. Boren, May 7, 1946, folder 32, box 21, Lyle H. Boren Collection, CAC.

13. William Zimmerman to Lyle H. Boren, June 8, 1940, folder 13, box 7, and Statement regarding sealed bids . . ., folder 17, box 7, Lyle H. Boren Collection, CAC; *Annual Report of the Commissioner of Indian Affairs, 1944*, 243.

14. Hurt, *Indian Agriculture in America*, 191; *Report of the Chief of the Office of Indian Affairs, 1939*, 37, 42; *Indians at Work* 7 (May–June 1940): 2.

15. *Billings (MT) Gazette*, July 4, 1943; *Indians at Work* 7 (December 1940): 2; *Annual Report of the Commissioner of Indian Affairs, 1941*, 423, 426, 452, and *1942*, 244, 246.

16. *Annual Report of the Commissioner of Indian Affairs, 1942*, 241; *Indians at Work* 8 (January 1941): 1; Bernstein, *American Indians and World War II*, 81; Hale, "Uncle Sam's Warriors," 417. In Oklahoma the Kiowas and the Five Civilized Tribes also sold land for military training purposes.

17. *Report of the Chief of the Office of Indian Affairs, 1939*, 37; *Indian Education*, November 1, 1939, 4–5.

18. *Indians at Work* 6 (February 1939): 12, and 6 (June 1939): 15–16, 33–34; *Report of the Chief of the Office of Indian Affairs, 1940*, 375–76; *Annual Report of the Commissioner of Indian Affairs, 1941*, 426; *Indian Truth* 19 (November–December 1942): 3.

19. *Indians at Work* 7 (May–June 1940): 2, and 7 (December 1940): 1; *Report of the Chief of the Office of Indian Affairs, 1940*, 378.

20. *Indians at Work* 7 (May–June 1940): 3; Bernstein, *American Indians and World War II*, 14–15.

21. Report of Activities, Oklahoma Agricultural Extension Service, typescript, folder 5, box 6, Wilburn Cartwright Collection, and Lyle H. Boren to William Zimmerman, November 21, 1939, folder 24, box 7, Lyle H. Boren Collection, CAC; Holt, *Indian Orphanages*, 198–200.

22. Bernstein, *American Indians and World War II*, 15–16; *Indian Education*, November 1, 1939, 7.

23. *Indian Education*, November 1, 1939, 8; *Indian Truth* 17 (December 1940): 8, and 16 (November 1939): 2–5.

24. Lomawaima, *Prairie Light*, 66–67, 72–74, 106–12; *Indian Education*, February 1, 1941, 3–4.

25. *Indians at Work* 8 (May 1941): 32–33; Kelley, "Bamboo Bombers," 366.

26. *Annual Report of the Commissioner of Indian Affairs, 1941*, 410–13, 418, and *1943*, 288, 294–95; Townsend, *World War II and the American Indian*, 172–73; Gouveia, "'We Also Serve,'" 168–82; *Annual Report of the Commissioner of Indian Affairs, 1944*, 247; *Indians at Work* 7 (August–September 1940): 34; *Annual Report of the Commissioner of Indian Affairs, 1942*, 240, 256.

27. Townsend, *World War II and the American Indian*, 67, 181–83; *Annual Report of the Commissioner of Indian Affairs, 1943*, 275; Clow, "Tribal Populations," 378; Bernstein, *American Indians and World War II*, 75.

28. James D. Berryhill to Lyle H. Boren, July 14, 1941, folder 12, box 7, Lyle H. Boren Collection, CAC.

29. Townsend, *World War II and the American Indian*, 178–80, 185; Bernstein, *American Indians and World War II*, 86; *Annual Report of the Commissioner of Indian Affairs, 1941*, 451; *Billings (MT) Gazette*, April 4, 1943; Gouveia, "'We Also Serve,'" 174–75.

30. Russell, "World War II Boomtown," 78; Useem, MacGregor, and Useem, "Rosebud Sioux," 4, 7; Townsend, *World War II and the American Indian*, 182, 185.

31. Useem, MacGregor, and Useem, "Rosebud Sioux," 4; Townsend, *World War II and the American Indian*, 186.

32. Useem, MacGregor, and Useem, "Rosebud Sioux," 4–5; Townsend, *World War II and the American Indian*, 185; Larsen, "Alliance Army Air Base," 241; Bernstein, *American Indians and World War II*, 79, 86.

33. Bernstein, *American Indians and World War II*, 74, 80; Useem, MacGregor, and Useem, "Rosebud Sioux," 2.

34. *Bismarck (ND) Tribune*, September 24, 1940; *Omaha World Herald*, August 10, 1942; *Cheyenne Wyoming Eagle*, July 13, 1940; Bernstein, *American Indians and World War II*, 26, 35; *Oklahoma City Daily Oklahoman*, January 12, 1941; *New York Times*, February 16, 1941; *Rapid City (SD) Daily Journal*, January 14, 1942; Gouveia, "'We Also Serve,'" 159, 164–65.

35. Bernstein, *American Indians and World War II*, 42, 44, 46, 59; *Annual Report of the Commissioner of Indian Affairs, 1943*, 282.

36. *Indians at Work* 9 (May–June 1942): 35, and 10 (July–September 1943): 8, 19; Townsend, *World War II and the American Indian*, 126–327.

37. *Wichita Eagle*, June 20, August 8, 1942; *Billings (MT) Gazette*, August 9, 1942; *Indians at Work* 9 (July–September 1942): 18–19, 21; *New York Times*, August 6, 1945; Townsend, *World War II and the American Indian*, 170.

38. *Billings (MT) Gazette*, January 7, 1942; *Indians at Work* 9 (July–September 1942): 21; Neuberger, "American Indian Enlists," 628; Collier, "Indian in a Wartime Nation," 30; Bernstein, *American Indians and World War II*, 68, 70, 186.

39. *Billings (MT) Gazette*, June 6, 1943; *Oklahoma City Daily Oklahoman*, January 26, 1941; *Annual Report of the Bureau of Indian Affairs, 1943*, 280; *Indians at Work* 9 (March 1942): 21, 31; Samuel, *Pledging Allegiance*, 109; Townsend, *World War II and the American Indian*, 187; Bernstein, *American Indians and World War II*, 66; *Annual Report of the Commissioner of Indian Affairs, 1943*, 274, 280, and *1944*, 238.

40. Bernstein, *American Indians and World War II*, 21; Taylor, *American Indian Tribalism*, 139–50; Hurt, *Indian Agriculture in America*, 191; Prucha, *Great Father*, 993–94; 1004–5; Philip, *John Collier's Crusade*, 208, 210.

41. *Billings (MT) Gazette*, August 6, 1944; Bernstein, *American Indians and*

World War II, 86, 107; *Annual Report of the Commissioner of Indian Affairs,* *1945*, 234, 236, 239; Hurt, *Indian Agriculture in America,* 194.

42. *Annual Report of the Commissioner of Indian Affairs,* 1945, 234, 236, 239; Hurt, *Indian Agriculture in America,* 194; *Annual Report of the Commissioner of Indian Affairs,* 1946, 363–64.

43. *Annual Report of the Commissioner of Indian Affairs,* 1944, 239–40, 1945, 234, and 1946, 364–65; *Indian Truth* 17 (January 1940): 3.

44. Bernstein, *American Indians and World War II,* 21, 134–36, 146.

45. Bernstein, *American Indians and World War II,* 134–36; Gouveia, "'We Also Serve,'" 178–80, 182.

46. Iverson, "Self-Determination," 165–66; Parman, *Indians and the American West,* 121.

47. Bernstein, *American Indians and World War II,* 74; Fixico, *Urban Indian Experience,* 3, 19; Prucha, *Great Father,* 983.

48. Townsend, *World War II and the American Indian,* 193; Parman, *Indians and the American West,* 115; *Annual Report of the Commissioner of Indian Affairs,* 1947, 346, 352, and 1949, 341.

49. Clow, "Tribal Populations," 380–83; Bernstein, *American Indians and World War II,* 109, 112, 122.

12. War's End

1. N. R. Graham to Robert S. Kerr, January 9, 1945, folder 14, box 33, Gubernatorial Papers, Robert S. Kerr Collection, CAC; Sloan, ed., "The Newell-letters," 158–59; *Dallas Morning News,* June 7, 1944; Martha Rohrke Diary, June 6, 1944, folder 9, box 1, Martha Rohrke Collection, and Ruth Vaughn Diary, June 6, 1944, folder 11, box 1, Larry Vaughn Collection, NSHS.

2. *Wichita Eagle,* May 9, 1945; Beatrice Vaughn Diary, May 8, 1945, unnumbered folder, box 4, Larry Vaughn Collection, NSHS; *Denver Post,* May 8, 1945; Leonard, "Denver at War," 38; *Denver Post,* May 8, 1945; *Oklahoma City Daily Oklahoman,* May 8, September 15, 1945.

3. Sloan, ed., "The Newelletters," 258.

4. Leonard, "Denver at War," 39; *Denver Post,* August 14, 15, 16, September 2, 1945; *Billings (MT) Gazette,* December 30, 1945; Helen Gladys King Diary, August 14, 1945, folder 3, box 1, King Family Papers, and Martha Rohrke Diary, August 14, 15, 1945, folder 13, box 1, Martha Rohrke Collection, NSHS; Kennedy, *Freedom from Fear,* 850–51.

5. *Roswell (NM) Daily Record,* August 15, 16, 1945; *Cheyenne Wyoming Eagle,* August 15, 1945.

6. *Billings (MT) Gazette,* October 19, 28, December 30, 1945; *Denver Post,* August 16, September 1, 1945; *Cheyenne Wyoming State Tribune,* September 5, November 13, 1945; *Cheyenne Wyoming Eagle,* September 6, 1945; *Wichita Eagle,* October 7, November 14, 1945; *Omaha World Herald,* December 9, 1945.

7. *Albuquerque Journal*, March 2, 1944.

8. *Albuquerque Journal*, July 24, 1944; *Wichita Eagle*, July 30, August 6, 1944; *Dallas Morning News*, September 2, 1944; Schneiders, *Unruly River*.

9. *Wichita Eagle*, September 24, 1944; Lee, *Farmers vs. Wage Earners*, 245–46.

10. *Bismarck (ND) Tribune*, January 2, 1945; *Denver Post*, September 2, 1945; *Dallas Morning News*, January 1, 1944; *Albuquerque Journal*, April 22, 1944; *Billings (MT) Gazette*, July 8, 1945.

11. *Denver Post*, September 7, 1945; Sloan, ed., "The Newelletters," 258; *Omaha World Herald*, September 2, October 2, 1945.

12. *Denver Post*, August 15, 17, 1945; *Wichita Eagle*, August 16, 1945; folders 8–13, box 63, Correspondence, 1943–47, Andrew Schoeppel Papers, KSHS (for numerous letters of complaint); *Dallas Morning News*, August 19, 1943; *Oklahoma City Daily Oklahoman*, November 15, 1942; *Albuquerque Journal*, June 28, 1942; *Cheyenne Wyoming Eagle*, August 6, 1942; *Omaha World Herald*, January 8, 1942.

13. *Cheyenne Wyoming State Tribune*, October 12, November 13, 27, 1945; *Rapid City (SD) Daily Journal*, September 21, 1945; *Denver Post*, September 5, 1945.

14. *Billings (MT) Gazette*, December 31, 1944.

15. *Dakota Farmer*, October 14, 1944.

16. Fite, *American Farmers*, 65, 80–87.

17. *Albuquerque Journal*, June 9, 1944; *Kansas Farmer*, September 1, 1945; *Denver Post*, June 24, 1945. By spring 1945, for example, the number of farms in Colorado declined from 11,266 in 1940 to 10,594, a 6 percent decrease. At the same time farm size rose on average from 584.5 to 728.6 acres, a 24.7 percent increase.

18. *Omaha World Herald*, September 23, 1945.

19. *Denver Post*, August 18, 1945; *Nebraska Farmer*, March 2, 1946.

20. *Holdrege (NE) Daily Citizen*, July 1, 1946; *Nebraska Farmer*, September 21, 1946; *Lincoln (NE) Star*, April 13, 1946.

21. *Lincoln (NE) Star*, April 13, June 23, 1946; *Nebraska Farmer*, June 15, 1946.

22. *Holdrege (NE) Daily Citizen*, June 29, 1946; Proceedings of the Wyoming Stock Growers Association, 1946, AHC.

23. Proceedings of the Wyoming Stock Growers Association, 1946, AHC.

24. Proceedings of the Wyoming Stock Growers Association, 1946, AHC.

25. *Salina (KS) Journal*, September 25, 1942; *Wichita Eagle*, February 4, 1944.

26. Larson, *Wyoming's War Years*, 134–36; Dean, "Kansas and the World War Experience," 3. When the military population is included, the numbers range from 250,000 in 1940 to 244,000 in 1945, climbing to 259,000 in 1946.

27. *Wichita Eagle*, September 2, 1941; Fearon, "Ploughshares into Airplanes," 304–6.

28. *Wichita Eagle*, August 18, September 9, 1945. By one estimate, between 1940 and 1944 Wichita's population increased 54 percent, from 114,966 to 176,316, while the population of the greater metropolitan area grew from 127,309 to 210,819, or by 65 percent. During that time industrial employment jumped 806 percent, and retail sales rose 355 percent, while bank deposits increased from $559.4 million to $2.3 billion. In July 1945 a Chamber of Commerce survey found that 66 percent, or 35,000, in the industrial workforce wanted to remain in Wichita when the war ended. With an estimated 11,000 veterans returning, business estimated a deficit of 12,000 jobs.

29. *Wichita Eagle*, March 1, 1944; *Rapid City (SD) Daily Journal*, August 31, 1943; *Cheyenne Wyoming State Tribune*, July 25–28, 1944; *Denver Post*, January 1, 7, 1945; Larson, *Wyoming's War Years*, 134–35.

30. Shryock and Eldridge, "Internal Migration," 28–30, 32–33.

31. O'Brien, "Kansas at War," 18, 20; Rabinowitz, "Growth Trends," 63, 65; Fearon, "Ploughshares into Airplanes," 314; Lee, *Farmers vs. Wage Earners*, 213–21.

32. O'Brien, "Kansas at War," 15; Lingeman, *Don't You Know There's a War On?* 164–66; Lee, *Farmers vs. Wage Earners*, 222–25, 232–33, 238.

33. Karolevitz, "Life on the Home Front," 419; *Cheyenne Wyoming State Tribune*, December 15, 1943; *Oklahoma City Daily Oklahoman*, June 23, 1943; *Roswell (NM) Daily Record*, July 16, 1944; *Cheyenne Wyoming Eagle*, August 8, 1944.

34. *Dallas Morning News*, June 2, 1940. For a Southern comparison, see Sitkoff, "African American Militancy in the World War II South."

35. *Amarillo Globe*, May 10, 1941; *Oklahoma City Daily Oklahoman*, September 25, 1941; *Salina (KS) Journal*, October 24, 1942, June 14, 1943; *Cheyenne Wyoming State Tribune*, July 1, 1941.

36. *Dallas Morning News*, November 29, 1944, January 28, 1945; Wit, "Munitions Manufacture," 154.

37. Mihelich, "Lincoln Urban League," 303–4.

38. Mihelich, "Lincoln Urban League," 309–11, 313–14.

39. Mihelich, "Lincoln Urban League," 303–6, 315.

40. Mihelich, "Omaha Urban League," 403, 406–7, 409, 411, 413.

41. Mihelich, "Omaha Urban League," 415–20.

42. Mihelich, "Omaha Urban League," 421.

43. McCusker, "'The Forgotten Years,'" 27, 29, 30–31.

44. McCusker, "'The Forgotten Years,'" 31, 33.

45. McCusker, "'The Forgotten Years,'" 33–35.

46. McCusker, "'The Forgotten Years,'" 35, 37.

47. Osburn, "Curtains for Jim Crow," 411.

48. Osburn, "Curtains for Jim Crow," 411–15; Bernson and Eggers, "Black People in South Dakota History," 263; Sitkoff, "Racial Militancy and Interracial Violence," 662.

49. Montejano, "The Demise of 'Jim Crow,'" 27–35; Guglielmo, "Fighting for Caucasian Rights"; Gerstle, "Crucial Decade," 1293–96.

50. Montejano, "The Demise of 'Jim Crow,'" 35–42.

51. Ávila, "Immigration and Integration," 34–37; Chavez, "Coming of Age," 389.

52. Chavez, "Coming of Age," 385–86, 390.

53. O'Brien, "Kansas at War," 24–25; *Omaha World Herald*, August 5, October 4, 1944.

54. Cassity, "'In a Narrow Grave,'" 5, 7; Dean, "Kansas and the World War Experience," 3; Nash, *World War II and the West*, xii.

55. For a discussion of sacrifice on the national level, see Leff, "Politics of Sacrifice."

Bibliography

Archival Sources
American Heritage Center, University of Wyoming
    Clippings File, Blackouts
    Lester C. Hunt Papers
    Prisoner-of-War Vertical File
    Proceedings of the Wyoming Stock Growers Association
Carl Albert Center, University of Oklahoma
    Elmer Thomas Collection
    Jack Nichols Collection
    Lyle H. Boren Collection
    Robert S. Kerr Collection
    T. P. Gore Collection
    Wesley Disney Collection
    Wilburn Cartwright Collection
Kansas State Historical Society, Topeka
    Andrew Schoeppel Papers
    Payne Ratner Collection
Nebraska State Historical Society, Lincoln
    Alfred A. Thompson Collection
    Cornhusker Ordnance Plant, Grand Island, Nebraska, Clippings Book
    Doris Lucile Minney Collection
    Dwight Palmer Griswold Papers
    Fort Robinson, Nebraska, Records
    Joe W. Seacrest Papers
    Joseph W. Fairfield Collection
    Karl Stefan Papers
    King Family Papers
    Larry Vaughn Collection
    Lincolnettes Papers
    Lotos Club Papers
    Martha Rohrke Collection
    McDonald Studio Collection
    Nebraska Department of Labor Records
    Nebraska State AFL-CIO Collection
    Nebraska State Salvage Committee Papers

Study of Negro Racial Situation at U.S. Naval Ammunition Depot, Hastings, Nebraska, July 1944
Val Kuska Collection
Southwest Collection, Texas Tech University
Clent Breedlove Collection
Lubbock (Texas) USO Records, 1942–1956
Lubbock Army Air Field Collection
Lubbock Chamber of Commerce Records, 1925–1991
Morgan Nelson Papers
Penney Hule Photo Collection
South Plains Army Air Field History
University Archives, University of Wyoming
Wyoming in World War II, Douglas Internment Camp, Clipping File
Western History Collections, University of Oklahoma
Grace E. Ray Collection
Office of Price Control Administration Collection
Prisoner-of-War Camps Collection
Wyoming State Archives, Cheyenne
Fort Francis E. Warren—Contemporary History, 1940
Joseph C. O'Mahoney Papers
Oral History Transcripts
Prisoner of War Camps, Vertical File
World War II Subject File

Published Sources

Adams, Gerald. "The Air Age Comes to Wyoming." *Annals of Wyoming* 52 (Fall 1980): 18–29.

———. "The Casper Army Air Field in World War II." *Annals of Wyoming* 64 (Fall 1992): 6–23.

———. *Fort Francis E. Warren and the Quartermaster Corps in World War II, 1940 to 1946.* Fort Collins CO: Citizen Printing Co., 1994.

Adams, Michael C. C. *The Best War Ever: America and World War II.* Baltimore: Johns Hopkins University Press, 1994.

Allen, Susan L. "Preparing Women for the National Crisis." *Chronicles of Oklahoma* 69 (Winter 1991–92): 392–407.

Ambrose, Stephen E. *Rise to Globalism: American Foreign Policy since 1938.* New York: Penguin, 1988.

"American Institute of Public Opinion Surveys, 1938–1939." *Public Opinion Quarterly* 3 (October 1939): 581–607.

"An Analysis of Newspaper Opinion on War Issues." *Public Opinion Quarterly* 5 (Autumn 1941): 448–55.

Anderson, Karen. *Wartime Women: Sex Roles, Family Relations, and the Status of Women during World War II*. Westport CT: Greenwood, 1981.

Annual Report of the Commissioner of Indian Affairs. Washington DC: U.S. Government Printing Office, 1939–50.

Annual Report of the Secretary of the Interior. Washington DC: U.S. Government Printing Office, 1939–50.

Armstrong, Robert M. "Nebraska and Nebraskans in World War II." *Nebraska History* 24 (July–September 1943): 174–80.

Arndt, Jessie Ash. "Prisoners of War on the Kansas Plains." *Christian Science Monitor*, weekly magazine section, October 16, 1943, 5, 13.

Austin, Allan W. *From Concentration Camp to Campus: Japanese American Students and World War II*. Urbana: University of Illinois Press, 2004.

Ávila, Henry J. "Immigration and Integration: The Mexican American Community in Garden City, Kansas, 1900–1950." *Kansas History* 20 (Spring 1997): 22–37.

Bailey, Thomas A. *A Diplomatic History of the American People*. Englewood Cliffs NJ: Prentice-Hall, 1980.

Baird, W. David, and Danney Gobel. *The Story of Oklahoma*. Norman: University of Oklahoma Press, 1994.

Bangerter, Lowell A. "German Prisoners of War in Wyoming." *Journal of German-American Studies* 14, no. 2 (1979): 65–123.

Bates, Ron. "A Gift of Sacred Art." *Texas Highways* 38 (December 1991): 22–25.

"The Battle for Kansas." *Kansas Historical Quarterly* 13 (November 1945): 481–84.

Bentley, Amy. *Eating for Victory: Food Rationing and the Politics of Domesticity*. Urbana: University of Illinois Press, 1998.

Bergh, Helen J. "Troop Trains and Pheasant Sandwiches: The Aberdeen Canteen in World War II." *South Dakota History* 23 (Summer 1993): 133–41.

Bernson, Sara L., and Robert J. Eggers. "Black People in South Dakota History." *South Dakota History* 7 (Summer 1977): 241–70.

Bernstein, Alison R. *American Indians and World War II: Toward a New Era in Indian Affairs*. Norman: University of Oklahoma Press, 1991.

Billinger, Robert D., Jr. *Hitler's Soldiers in the Sunshine State: German POWs in Florida*. Gainesville: University Press of Florida, 2000.

Billington, Ray Allen. "The Origins of Middle Western Isolationism." *Political Science Quarterly* 60 (March 1945): 44–64.

Blum, John Morton, *V Was for Victory: Politics and American Culture during World War II*. New York: Harcourt Brace Jovanovich, 1976.

Bosworth, Allan R. *America's Concentration Camps*. New York: Norton, 1967.

Bromert, Roger. "The Sioux and the Indian—CCC." *South Dakota History* 8 (Fall 1978): 340–56.

———. "Sioux Rehabilitation Colonies: Experiments in Self-Sufficiency, 1936–1942." *South Dakota History* 8 (Fall 1978): 31–47.

Bromley, Dorothy Dunbar. "Women on the Home Front." *Harper's*, July 1941, 188–99.

Brueggemann, David W. "The United States Cadet Nurse Corps, 1943–1948: The Nebraska Experience." Master's thesis, University of Nebraska—Omaha, 1992.

Buecker, Thomas R. "Mules, Horses and Dogs—Fort Robinson in World War II." *Council on America's Military Past* 16, no. 1 (1989): 34–39.

———. "Nazi Influence at the Fort Robinson Prisoner of War Camp during World War II." *Nebraska History* 73 (Spring 1992): 32–41.

Burk, James. "Debating the Draft in America." *Armed Forces and Society* 15 (Spring 1989): 431–48.

Busse, Carole. "'She's a Good Girl and Loves America, Too': Housing for Women in WW II Fort Worth, Texas." *Essays in History* 12 (1991–92): 174–94.

"The Call To Arms, Kansas at War." Pt. 1. *Kansas History* 15 (Spring 1992): 36–43.

Campbell, D'Ann. *Women at War with America: Private Lives in a Patriotic Era.* Cambridge MA: Harvard University Press, 1984.

Cantril, Hadley. "America Faces the War: A Study in Public Opinion." *Public Opinion Quarterly* 4 (September 1940): 387–407.

Carpenter, Stephanie A. *On the Farm Front: The Women's Land Army in World War II.* DeKalb: Northern Illinois University Press, 2003.

———. "'Regular Farm Girl': The Women's Land Army in World War II." *Agricultural History* 71 (Spring 1997): 163–85.

Cassity, Michael. "'In a Narrow Grave': World War II and the Subjugation of Wyoming." *Wyoming Historical Journal* 68, no. 2 (1996): 2–13.

Chamberlain, Charles D., III. "'On the Train and Gone': Worker Mobility in the Rural Southwest during World War II, 1939–1945." *Southwestern Historical Quarterly* 53 (April 2000): 427–51.

———. *Victory at Home: Manpower and Race in the American South during World War II.* Athens: University of Georgia Press, 2003.

Chavez, Carmen R. "Coming of Age during the War: Reminiscences of an Albuquerque Hispana." *New Mexico Historical Review* 70 (October 1995): 383–97.

Cherny, Robert W. "Isolationist Voting in 1940: A Statistical Analysis." *Nebraska History* 52 (Fall 1971): 293–310.

Childs, William R. "Texas, the Interstate Oil Compact Commission, and State Control of Oil Production: Regionalism, States' Rights, and Federalism during World War II." *Pacific Historical Review* 64 (November 1995): 567–98.

Christgau, John. *Enemies: World War II Alien Internment.* Ames: Iowa State University Press, 1985.

Clarke, Sally H. *Regulation and the Revolution in United States Productivity.* Melbourne: Cambridge University Press, 1994.

Clawson, Marion. *The Western Range Livestock Industry.* New York: McGraw-Hill, 1950.

Clifford, J. Garry. "A Note on the Break between Senator Nye and President Roosevelt in 1939." *North Dakota History* 49 (Fall 1982): 14–17.

Clifford, J. Garry, and Samuel R. Spencer Jr. *The First Peacetime Draft.* Lawrence: University Press of Kansas, 1986.

Clow, Richmond L. "Tribal Populations in Transition: Sioux Reservation and Federal Policy, 1934–1965." *South Dakota History* 19 (Fall 1989): 362–91.

Coalson, George O. *The Development of the Migratory Farm Labor System in Texas: 1900–1954.* San Francisco: R&E Research Associates, 1977.

Coffey, Marilyn. *Great Plains Patchwork: A Memoir.* Ames: Iowa State University Press, 1989.

Collier, John. "The Indian in a Wartime Nation." *Annals of the American Academy of Political Science* 223 (September 1942): 29–35.

Colwell, James L. "'Hell from Heaven': Midland Army Air Field in World War II." Pts. 1–3. *Permian Historical Annual* 25 (1985): 11–42; 26 (1986): 51–90; 27 (1987): 95–127.

———. "Wings over West Texas: Pecos Army Air Field in World War II." *West Texas Historical Association Year Book* 63 (1987): 42–62.

"Completion Report Covering Construction and Completion of Operational Training Unit, One Squadron Station Ainsworth Satellite Field, Ainsworth, Nebraska, War Department, Office of the Chief of Engineers, Omaha District, Missouri River Division, United States Army." Omaha, December 31, 1942.

Congressional Record. 76th Cong., 1st sess., 1939. Vol. 84, pt. 1. Washington DC.

Congressional Record. 76th Cong., 1st sess., 1939. Vol. 84, pt. 2. Washington DC.

Congressional Record. 76th Cong., 1st sess., 1939. Vol. 84, pt. 4. Washington DC.

Congressional Record. 76th Cong., 1st sess., 1939. Vol. 84, pt. 8. Washington DC.

Congressional Record. 76th Cong., 2d sess., 1939. Vol. 85, pt. 1. Washington DC.

Congressional Record. 76th Cong., 2d sess., 1940. Vol. 86, pt. 8. Washington DC.

Congressional Record. 76th Cong., 3d sess., 1940. Vol. 86, pt. 10. Washington DC.

Congressional Record. 76th Cong., 3d sess., 1940. Vol. 86, pt. 11. Washington DC.

Congressional Record. 77th Cong., 1st sess., 1941. Vol. 87, pt. 1. Washington DC.

Congressional Record. 77th Cong., 1st sess., 1941. Vol. 87, pt. 2. Washington DC.

Congressional Record. 77th Cong., 1st sess., 1941. Vol. 87, pt. 11. Washington DC.

Corbett, Edward C. "Interned for the Duration: Axis Prisoners of War in Oklahoma, 1942–1946." Master's thesis, Oklahoma City University, 1967.

Corbett, William. P. "'They Hired Every Farmer in the Country': Establishing the Prisoner of War Camp at Tonkawa." *Chronicles of Oklahoma* 69 (Winter 1992): 368–91.

Costello, John. *Virtue under Fire: How World War II Changed Our Social and Sexual Attitudes.* Boston: Little, Brown, 1985.

Craig, Richard B. *The Bracero Program: Interest Groups and Foreign Policy.* Austin: University of Texas Press, 1971.

Crops and Markets, 1950. Vol. 27. Washington DC: U.S. Department of Agriculture, Bureau of Agricultural Economics, 1950.

Cross, George Flynn. *Professors, Presidents, and Politicians: Civil Rights at the University of Oklahoma, 1890–1968.* Norman: University of Oklahoma Press, 1981.

Crowder, James L., Jr. "'More Valuable Than Oil': The Establishment and Development of Tinker Air Force Base, 1940–1949." *Chronicles of Oklahoma* 70 (Fall 1992): 228–57.

Culley, John J. "A Troublesome Presence: World War II Internment of German Sailors in New Mexico." *Prologue: The Journal of the National Archives* 28 (Winter 1996): 278–95.

———. "World War II and a Western Town: The Internment of the Japanese Railroad Workers of Clovis, New Mexico." *Western Historical Quarterly* 13 (January 1982): 43–61.

Cummings, Tom. "An Examination of the Lubell Thesis: McIntosh County, North Dakota, 1936–1940." *North Dakota Quarterly* 42, no. 4 (1974): 26–41.

Dagel, Kenneth Charles, "Ranchers' Adjustments in a Marginal Environment." PhD diss., University of Nebraska, 1994.

Dalfiume, Richard M. "The 'Forgotten Years' of the Negro Revolution." *Journal of American History* 55 (June 1968): 90–106.

Daniels, Roger. *Concentration Camps, North America: Japanese in the United States and Canada during World War II.* Malabar FL: Krieger, 1981.

Daugherty, Fred A., and Pendleton Woods. "Oklahoma's Military Tradition." *Chronicles of Oklahoma* 57 (Winter 1979–80): 427–45.

Dean, Virgil. "Another Wichita Seditionist? Elmer J. Garner and the Radical Right's Opposition to World War II." *Kansas History* 17 (Spring 1994): 50–64.

———. "Kansas and the World War Experience." *Kansas History* 17 (Spring 1994): 2–5.

Doyle, Frederick Joseph. "German Prisoners of War in the Southwest United States during World War II: An Oral History." PhD diss., University of Denver, 1978.

Doyle, Susan Badger. "German and Italian Prisoners of War in Albuquerque, 1943–1946." *New Mexico Historical Review* 66 (July 1991): 327–40.

Eastman, James N., Jr. "Location and Growth of Tinker Air Force Base and Oklahoma City Air Materiel Area." *Chronicles of Oklahoma* 50 (Summer 1972): 326–46.

Ehrmann, Henry W. "An Experiment in Political Education: The Prisoner-of-War Schools in the United States." *Social Research: An International Quarterly of Political and Social Science* 14 (September 1947): 304–20.

Eicher, Carl K. "An Approach to Income Improvement on the Rosebud Sioux Indian Reservation." *Human Organization* 20 (Winter 1961–62): 191–202.

Erenberg, Lewis A., and Susan E. Hirsch, eds. *The American War in American Culture: Society and Consciousness during World War II*. Chicago: University of Chicago Press, 1996.

Erickson, Neis. "Prairie Pacifist: Senator Lynn J. Frazier and America's Global Mission, 1927–1940." *North Dakota History* 52 (Fall 1985): 27–32.

Ernst, Daniel R., and Victor Jew, eds. *Total War and the Law: The American Home Front during World War II*. Westport CT: Praeger, 2002.

Evans, Richard J. *The Third Reich in Power, 1933–1939*. New York: Penguin, 2005.

Fagan, Michele L. "Nebraska Nursing Education during World War II." *Nebraska History* 73 (Fall 1992): 126–37.

Fearon, Peter. "Ploughshares into Airplanes: Manufacturing Industry and Workers during World War II." *Kansas History* 22 (Winter 1999–2000): 298–314.

Fiedler, David. *The Enemy among Us*. St. Louis: Missouri Historical Society Press, 2003.

Fite, Gilbert C. *American Farmers: The New Minority*. Bloomington: Indiana University Press, 1981.

Fixico, Donald L. *The Urban Indian Experience in America*. Albuquerque: University of New Mexico Press, 2000.

Foley, Neil. *The White Scourge: Mexicans, Blacks, and Poor Whites in Texas Cotton Culture*. Berkeley: University of California Press, 1997.

Foner, Jack D. *Blacks and the Military in American History*. New York: Praeger, 1974.

"The Fortune Survey: XXV." *Fortune* 20 (December 1939): 78–95.

Franks, Kenny A. "'Goodbye, Dear, I'll Be Back in a Year': The Mobilization of the Oklahoma National Guard for World War II." *Chronicles of Oklahoma* 69 (Winter 1992): 340–67.

Fuller, Edward J. "Scrap Drives, New Vocational Courses, and Patriotic Songs: Dallas Schools and Negro Support of World War II." *Journal of the Midwest History of Education* 21 (1944): 173–89.

Furdell, William J. "The Great Falls Home Front during World War II." *Montana: The Magazine of Western History* 48 (Winter 1998): 63–75.

Gallup, George, and Claude Robinson. "American Institute of Public Opinion—Surveys, 1935–1938." *Public Opinion Quarterly* 2 (July 1938): 373–98.

"Gallup and Fortune Polls." *Public Opinion Quarterly* 4 (June 1940): 339–63.

"Gallup and Fortune Polls." *Public Opinion Quarterly* 4 (September 1940): 533–53.

"Gallup and Fortune Polls." *Public Opinion Quarterly* 4 (December 1940): 704–18.

"Gallup and Fortune Polls." *Public Opinion Quarterly* 5 (March 1941): 133–65.

"Gallup and Fortune Polls." *Public Opinion Quarterly* 5 (June 1941): 313–34.

"Gallup and Fortune Polls." *Public Opinion Quarterly* 5 (Autumn 1941): 470–97.

"Gallup and Fortune Polls." *Public Opinion Quarterly* 5 (Winter 1941): 666–87.

Gamboa, Erasmo. *Mexican Labor and World War II: Braceros in the Pacific Northwest, 1942–1947*. Austin: University of Texas Press, 1990.

Gamradt, Crystal J. "Adapting to Serve: South Dakota State College Responds to World War II." *South Dakota History* 36 (Spring 2006): 66–87.

Gansberg, Judith M. *Stalag U.S.A.: The Remarkable Story of German POWs in America*. New York: Thomas Y. Crowell, 1977.

Geiss, Lester H. "Fort Warren's Quartermaster Replacement Training Center." *Quartermaster Review* 22 (September–October 1942): 25–27, 128–29.

Gerstle, Gary. "The Crucial Decade: The 1940s and Beyond." *Journal of American History* 92 (March 2006): 1292–99.

Gluck, Sheena Berger. *Rosie the Riveter Revisited: Women, the War and Social Change*. Boston: Twayne, 1987.

Goodstein, Paul. "The Day the Army Invaded Montgomery Ward." *Colorado Heritage*, 1991, no. 1:40–47.

Goodwin, Doris Kearns. *No Ordinary Time: Franklin and Eleanor Roosevelt: The Home Front in World War II*. New York: Simon & Schuster, 1994.

Gorer, Geoffrey. *The American People: A Study in National Character.* New York: Norton, 1948.

Gouveia, Grace Mary. "'We Also Serve': American Indian Women's Role in World War II." *Michigan Historical Review* 20 (Fall 1994): 153–82.

Graebner, William S. *The Age of Doubt: American Thought and Culture in the 1940s.* Boston: Twayne, 1991.

Grant, Michael J. "'Food Will Win the War and Write the Peace': The Federal Government and Kansas Farmers during World War II." *Kansas History* 20 (Winter 1997–98): 242–57.

Grant, Philip A., Jr. "The Kansas Congressional Delegation and the Lend-Lease Act of 1941." *Kansas History* 14 (Summer 1991): 72–81.

———. "The Kansas Congressional Delegation and the Selective Service Act of 1940." *Kansas History* 2 (Autumn 1979): 196–205.

Gray, James R., and B. B. Chester. "Cattle Ranching: The Northern Great Plains." *Circular,* no. 204. Bozeman: Montana Agricultural Experiment Station, December 1953.

Grove, Wayne A. "The Mexican Farm Labor Program, 1942–1964: Government-Administered Labor Market Insurance for Farmers." *Agricultural History* 70 (Spring 1996): 302–20.

Guglielmo, Thomas A. "Fighting for Caucasian Rights: Mexicans, Mexican Americans, and the Transnational Struggle for Civil Rights in World War II Texas." *Journal of American History* 92 (March 2006): 212–37.

"Guides for Wartime Use of Women on Farms." Special Bulletin no. 8 of the Women's Bureau. Washington DC: U.S. Government Printing Office, 1942.

Guinsburg, Thomas N. "The George W. Norris 'Conversion' to Internationalism, 1939–1941." *Nebraska History* 53 (Winter 1972): 477–90.

Hale, Duane K. "Uncle Sam's Warriors: American Indians in World War II." *Chronicles of Oklahoma* 69 (Winter 1992): 408–29.

Harper, Louise Hooper. "Hereford Prisoner of War Camp." Pts. 1–2. *Hale County History* 16 (November 1986): 3–49; 16 (February 1987): 50–88.

Hartley, Thomas J. "The Crow Family in Hamlin, Texas, 1940–1945." *West Texas Historical Association Year Book* 69 (1993): 89–98.

Hartmann, Susan M. *The Home Front and Beyond: American Women in the 1940s.* Boston: Twayne, 1982.

Henegar, Lucielle. "Beating Swords into Ploughshares: Hereford Military Reservation and Reception Center." *West Texas Historical Association Year Book* 62 (1986): 14–28.

Hereford P.O.W. Camp, 1942–1946. N.p.: n.p., 1988.

Hewitt, William L. "Mexican Workers in Wyoming during World War II: Necessity, Discrimination and Protest." *Annals of Wyoming* 54 (Fall 1982): 20–33.

Historical Abstracts of the United States. Washington DC: U.S. Government Printing Office, 1945–51.

Historical Statistics of the United States: Colonial Times to 1970, Part 1, Bicentennial Edition. Washington DC: U.S. Department of the Census, 1975.

Holt, Marilyn I. *Indian Orphanages.* Lawrence: University Press of Kansas, 2001.

Honey, Maureen. *Bitter Fruit: African American Women in World War II.* Columbia: University of Missouri Press, 1999.

———. *Creating Rosie the Riveter: Class, Gender, and Propaganda during World War II.* Amherst: University of Massachusetts Press, 1984.

———. "The 'Womanpower' Campaign: Advertising and Recruitment Propaganda during World War II." *Frontiers: A Journal of Women's Studies* 6 (Spring/Summer 1981): 50–56.

Hosokawa, Bill. *Colorado's Japanese Americans: From 1886 to the Present.* Boulder: University Press of Colorado, 2005.

———. *Nisei: The Quiet Americans.* Rev. ed. Boulder: University Press of Colorado, 2002.

Howard, James H. "The Dakota Indian Victory Dance: World War II." *North Dakota History* 18 (January 1951): 31–40.

Howes, Cecil. "Prisoners at Work." *Kansas Magazine*, 1944, 57–62.

"How to Stay Out of War: An Open Forum of Opinions on Keeping America Neutral." *Forum and Century* 97 (February 1937): 89–95.

Hurst, Robert. "Nebraska Army Air Fields, a Pictorial Review." *Nebraska History* 76 (Summer/Fall 1995): 129–43.

Hurt, R. Douglas. *Indian Agriculture in America: Prehistory to the Present.* Lawrence: University Press of Kansas, 1987.

———. "Naval Air Stations in Kansas during World War II." *Kansas Historical Quarterly* 43 (Autumn 1977): 351–62.

Iverson, Peter. "Building toward Self-Determination: Plains and Southwestern Indians in the 1940s and 1950s." *Western Historical Quarterly* 16 (April 1985): 163–73.

Jacob, Philip E. "Influences of World Events on U.S. 'Neutrality' Opinion." *Public Opinion Quarterly* 4 (March 1940): 48–65.

Jaehn, Tomas. "Unlikely Harvesters: German Prisoners of War as Agricultural Workers in the Northwest." *Montana: The Magazine of Western History* 50 (Autumn 2000): 46–57.

Jefferies, John W. *Wartime America: The World War II Home Front.* Chicago: Ivan Dee, 1996.

Jepson, Daniel A. "Camp Carson, Colorado: European Prisoners of War in the American West during World War II." *Midwest Review* 13 (1991): 32–53.

Johnson, Judith R. "Uncle Sam Wanted Them Too! Women Aircraft Workers in Wichita during World War II." *Kansas History* 17 (Spring 1994): 38–49.

Johnson, M. B. "Range Cattle Production in Western North Dakota." *Bulletin,* no. 347. Fargo: North Dakota Agricultural Experiment Station, July 1947.

Johnson, Melvyn. "At Home in Amache: A Japanese-American Relocation Camp in Colorado." *Colorado Heritage,* 1989, no. 1:2–11.

Jones, Robert C. *Mexican War Workers in the United States: The Mexico–United States Manpower Recruiting Program and Its Operation.* Washington DC: Pan American Union, Division of Labor and Social Information, 1945.

Juhnke, James C. "Edmund G. Kaufman: Minister of Peace in a World of War." *Kansas History* 18 (Spring 1995): 48–58.

———. "The Perils of Conscientious Objection: An Oral History Study of a 1944 Event." *Mennonite Life* 34 (September 1979): 4–9.

Karolevitz, Robert F. "Life on the Home Front: South Dakota in World War II." *South Dakota History* 19 (Fall 1989): 392–423.

Kashima, Tetsuden. *Judgment without Trial: Japanese American Imprisonment during World War II.* Seattle: University of Washington Press, 2003.

Keefer, Louis E. *Italian Prisoners of War in America, 1942–1946: Captives or Allies?* New York: Praeger, 1992.

Keen, James Richard. "The Captive Enemy? Italian Prisoners of War in Texas during World War II." Master's thesis, University of Texas of the Permian Basin, 1988.

———. "Recreational and Morale Activities in the Hereford Prisoner of War Camp, 1943–1946." *Permian Historical Annual* 29 (1989): 89–108.

Kelley, Leo. "Bamboo Bombers over Oklahoma: USAF Pilot Training during World War II." *Chronicles of Oklahoma* 68 (Winter 1990–91): 360–75.

Kennedy, David M. *Freedom from Fear: The American People in Depression and War, 1929–1945.* New York: Oxford University Press, 1999.

Kirwan, William E. "Escape Tactics of German Prisoners." *Journal of Criminal Law and Criminology* 35 (January–February 1945): 357–66.

Koistinen, Paul A. C. *The Military-Industrial Complex: A Historical Perspective.* New York: Praeger, 1980.

———. "Mobilizing the World War II Economy: Labor and the Industrial-Military Alliance." *Pacific Historical Review* 42 (November 1973): 443–78.

Kollmorgen, Walton M., and George F. Jenks. "A Geographic Study of Population and Settlement Changes in Sherman County, Kansas, Pt. 2: Goodland." *Transactions of the Kansas Academy of Science* 55 (March 1952): 1–37.

Koop, Allen V. *Stark Decency: German Prisoners of War in a New England Village.* Hanover NH: University Press of New England, 1988.

Krammer, Arnold. "German Prisoners of War in the United States." *Military Affairs* 60 (April 1976): 68–73.

———. "Japanese Prisoners of War in America." *Pacific Historical Review* 52 (February 1983): 67–91.

————. *Nazi Prisoners of War in America.* New York: Stein & Day, 1979.

————. *Public Administration of Prisoner of War Camps in America since the Revolutionary War.* Public Administration Series, Bibliography P-626. Monticello IL: Vance Bibliographies, 1980.

————. "When the Afrika Korps Came to Texas." *Southwestern Historical Quarterly* 80 (January 1977): 247–82.

Larsen, Lawrence H. "The Alliance Army Air Base Case." *Nebraska History* 67 (Fall 1986): 239–55.

————. "Gerald Nye and the Isolationist Argument." *North Dakota History* 47 (Winter 1980): 25–27.

————. "War Balloons over the Prairie: The Japanese Invasion of South Dakota." *South Dakota History* 9 (Spring 1979): 103–15.

Larson, Bruce. "Kansas and the Panay Incident, 1937." *Kansas Historical Quarterly* 31 (Autumn 1965): 233–44.

Larson, George A. "Nebraska's World War II Bomber Plant: The Glenn L. Martin–Nebraska Company." *Nebraska History* 74 (Spring 1993): 32–43.

Larson, T. A. *Wyoming's War Years, 1941–1945.* 1954. Reprint, Cheyenne: Wyoming Historical Foundation, 1993.

Lee, James Ward. *1941: Texas Goes to War.* Denton: University of North Texas Press, 1991.

Lee, R. Alton. *Farmers vs. Wage Earners: Organized Labor in Kansas, 1860–1960.* Lawrence: University Press of Kansas, 2005.

————. "Reining in the 'Union Threat': Right-to-Work Laws in South Dakota." *South Dakota History* 26 (Summer/Fall 1996): 121–36.

Leff, Mark H. "The Politics of Sacrifice on the American Home Front in World War II." *Journal of American History* 77 (March 1991): 1296–1318.

Leonard, Robert James. "The Nye Committee: Legislating against War." *North Dakota History* 41 (Fall 1974): 20–28.

Leonard, Stephen J. "Denver at War: The Home Front in World War II." *Colorado Heritage,* 1987, no. 4:30–39.

Levengood, Paul Alejandro. "For the Duration and Beyond: World War II and the Creation of Modern Houston, Texas." PhD diss., Rice University, 1999.

Lewis, George G., and John Mewha. *History of Prisoner of War Utilization by the United States Army, 1776–1945.* Washington DC: Center for Military History, 1988.

Lichtenstein, Nelson. *Labor's War at Home: The CIO in World War II.* New York: Cambridge University Press, 1982.

Lingeman, Richard R. *Don't You Know There's a War On? The Home Front, 1941–1945.* New York: Putnam's, 1970.

Liss, Samuel. "The Concept and Determination of Prevailing Wage Scales in Agriculture during World War II." *Agricultural History* 24 (January 1950): 4–18.

————. "Farm Wage Boards under the Cooperative Extension Service during World War II." *Agricultural History* 27 (July 1953): 103–8.

Litoff, Judy Barrett, and David C. Smith. "'To the Rescue of the Crops': The Women's Land Army during World War II." *Prologue: The Journal of the National Archives* 25 (Winter 1993): 346–61.

Lomawaima, K. Tsianina. *They Called It Prairie Light: The Story of Chilocco Indians School.* Lincoln: University of Nebraska Press, 1994.

Lotchin, Roger W. *The Bad City in the Good War: San Francisco, Los Angeles, Oakland, and San Diego.* Bloomington: Indiana University Press, 2003.

————. "The Historian's War or the Home Front's War? Some Thoughts for Western Historians." *Western Historical Quarterly* 36 (Summer 1995): 185–96.

Lovett, Christopher C. "Don't You Know That There's a War On? A History of the Kansas State Guard in World War II." *Kansas History* 8 (Winter 1985–86): 226–35.

Lowitt, Richard. *George W. Norris: The Triumph of a Progressive, 1933–1944.* Urbana: University of Illinois Press, 1978.

Macias, Richard. "'We All Had a Cause': Kansas City's Bomber Plant, 1941–1945." *Kansas History* 28 (Winter 2005–6): 244–61.

Mason, John Brown. "German Prisoners of War in the United States." *American Journal of International Law* 39 (April 1945): 198–215.

McCain, Johnny M. "Texas and the Mexican Labor Question, 1942–1947." *Southwestern Historical Quarterly* 85 (July 1981): 45–64.

McCusker, Kristine M. "'The Forgotten Years' of America's Civil Rights Movement: Wartime Protests at the University of Kansas, 1939–1945." *Kansas History* 17 (Spring 1994): 26–37.

McGlade, Jacqueline. "The Zoning of Fort Crook: Urban Expansion vs. County Home Rule." *Nebraska History* 64 (Spring 1983): 21–34.

McKnight, Maxwell S. "The Employment of Prisoners of War in the United States." *International Labour Review* 50 (July 1944): 47–64.

McMillen, Neil R. *Remaking Dixie: The Impact of World War II on the American South.* Jackson: University of Mississippi Press, 1997.

Merrill, Francis E. *Social Problems on the Home Front: A Study of War-Time Influences.* New York: Harper & Row, 1948.

Mihelich, Dennis N. "The Lincoln Urban League: The Travail of Depression and War." *Nebraska History* 70 (Winter 1989): 303–16.

————. "World War II and the Transformation of the Omaha Urban League." *Nebraska History* 60 (Fall 1979): 401–23.

Milkman, Ruth. *Gender at Work: The Dynamics of Job Segregation by Sex during World War II.* Urbana: University of Illinois Press, 1987.

Millett, John D. *The Army Service Forces: The Organization and Role of the Army Service Forces.* Washington DC: Office of the Chief of Military History, 1954.

Mills, Walter. *Arms and Men: A Study in American Military History*. New York: Putnam's, 1956.

Milner, Elmer Ray. "An Agonizing Evolution: A History of the Texas National Guard, 1900–1945." PhD diss., North Texas State University, 1979.

Moeller, James C. "Answering the Call: Omaha Jewry and the War Effort, 1941–1945." *Memories of the Jewish Midwest* 10 (1995): 2–7.

Montejano, David. "The Demise of 'Jim Crow' for Texas Mexicans, 1940–1970." *Azltan* 16, nos. 1–2 (1987): 27–69.

Moore, John Hammond. "Italian POWs in America: War Is Not Always Hell." *Prologue: The Journal of the National Archives* 8 (Fall 1976): 140–51.

Morris, James W. "Patriotism and Education in der Vaterland of Texas during World War II." *Journal of the Midwest History of Education Society* 22 (1995): 87–101.

Moser, Dexter H. "A Study of Farm Labor Practices and Conditions in Montana during World War II as Factors in Post War Farm Labor Employment Problems." M.A. thesis, Montana State College, 1946.

Murphy, Henry C. *National Debt in War and Transition*. New York: McGraw-Hill, 1950.

Myer, James M. "The Army Comes to Abilene." *West Texas Historical Association Year Book* 65 (1985): 101–10.

———. "Prisoners of War at Camp Barkeley." *West Texas Historical Association Year Book* 61 (1985): 134–40.

Myrdal, Gunnar. "Is American Business Deluding Itself?" *Atlantic Monthly* 174 (November 1944): 51–58.

Namikas, Lise. "The Committee to Defend America and the Debate between Internationalists and Interventionists, 1939–1941." *Historian* 61 (Summer 1999): 843–63.

Nash, Gerald D. *The American West Transformed: The Impact of the Second World War*. Bloomington: Indiana University Press, 1985.

———. *The Great Depression and World War II: Organizing America, 1933–1945*. New York: St. Martin's, 1979.

———. *World War II and the West: Reshaping the Economy*. Lincoln: University of Nebraska Press, 1990.

"National Affairs." *Time* 33 (April 24, 1939): 16–17.

Nelson, Keith L., ed. *The Impact of War on American Life*. New York: Holt, Rinehart & Winston, 1971.

Neuberger, Richard L. "The American Indian Enlists." *Asia and the Americas* 42 (November 1942): 628–31.

Neugebauer, Janet M., ed. *Plains Farmer: The Diary of William G. DeLoach, 1914–1964*. College Station: Texas A&M University Press, 1991.

"No Bread Today: Wartime Rationing." *Colorado Heritage*, Winter 1995, 29–31.

O'Brien, Kenneth Paul, and Lynn Judson Parsons. *The Home-Front War: World War II in American Society*. Westport CT: Greenwood, 1995.

O'Brien, Patrick G. "Kansas at War: The Home Front, 1941–1945." *Kansas History* 17 (Spring 1994): 6–25.

O'Brien, Patrick G., Thomas D. Isern, and R. Daniel Lumley. "Stalag Sunflower: German Prisoners of War in Kansas." *Kansas History* 7 (Autumn 1984): 182–98.

Okihiro, Gary Y., ed. *Whispered Silences: Japanese Americans and World War II*. Seattle: University of Washington Press, 1996.

"100 Years of Farmland Values in Kansas." *Bulletin*, no. 611. Manhattan: Kansas Agricultural Experiment Station, September 1977.

O'Neill, William L. *A Democracy at War: America's Fight at Home and Abroad in World War II*. New York: Free Press, 1993.

Oppenheimer, Robert. "Acculturation or Assimilation: Mexican Immigrants in Kansas, 1900 to World War II." *Western Historical Quarterly* 16 (October 1985): 429–48.

Osburn, William S. "Curtains for Jim Crow: Law, Race, and the Texas Railroads." *Southwestern Historical Quarterly* 105 (January 2002): 392–427.

Parman, Donald. *Indians and the American West*. Bloomington: Indiana University Press, 1994.

Partin, John W. "The Dilemma of 'a Good, Very Good Man': Capper and Noninterventionism, 1936–1941." *Kansas History* 2 (Summer 1979): 86–95.

Paschal, Allen W. "The Enemy in Colorado: German Prisoners of War, 1943–46." *Colorado Magazine* 56 (Summer/Fall 1979): 119–42.

Paulette, Irene. "Odessa during the War Years, 1941–1945: A Microcosm of the Nation." *Permian Historical Annual* 22 (1992): 15–33.

Pavalko, Eliza K., and Glen H. Elder Jr. "World War II and Divorce: A Life-Course Perspective." *American Journal of Sociology* 95 (March 1990): 1213–34.

Petersen, Todd L. "Kearney, Nebraska, and the Kearney Army Air Field in World War II." *Nebraska History* 72 (Fall 1991): 118–26.

———. "Small Town America Goes to War: The History of the Kearney Army Air Field, 1942–1949." Master's thesis, Kearney State College, 1990.

Peterson, Susan C., and Amy K. Rieger. "'They Needed Nurses at Home': The Cadet Nurse Corps in South Dakota and North Dakota." *South Dakota History* 23 (Summer 1993): 122–32.

Pfaff, Christine. "Bullets for the Yanks: Colorado's World War II Ammunition Factory." *Colorado Heritage*, Summer 1992, 33–45.

Pfluger, James R. "Fuel for Victory: Texas Panhandle Petroleum, 1941–1945." *Panhandle-Plains Historical Review* 62 (1989): 19–56.

Philip, Kenneth. *John Collier's Crusade for Indian Reform, 1920–1954*. Tucson: University of Arizona Press, 1980.

Pickle, Joe. "Aviation History of Big Spring, Texas." *Permian Historical Annual* 39 (1999): 19–34.

Pluth, Edward John. "The Administration and Operation of German Prisoner of War Camps in the United States during World War II." PhD diss., Ball State University, 1970.

Polenberg, Richard, ed. *America at War: The Home Front, 1941–1945.* Englewood Cliffs NJ: Prentice-Hall, 1968.

————. *War and Society: The United States, 1941–1945.* Westport CT: Greenwood, 1972.

Powers, James H. "What to Do with German Prisoners: The American Muddle." *Atlantic Monthly* 174 (November 1944): 46–50.

Prucha, Francis Paul. *The Great Father: The United States Government and the American Indians.* Vol. 2. Lincoln: University of Nebraska Press, 1984.

Rabinowitz, Howard N. "Growth Trends in the Albuquerque SMSA, 1940–1978." *Journal of the West* 18 (July 1979): 62–74.

Rasel, John T. "An Historiography of Racism: Japanese American Internment, 1942–1945." *Historia* 14 (2004): 87–99.

Rasmussen, Wayne D. *A History of the Emergency Farm Labor Supply Program, 1943–47.* Agriculture Monograph no. 13. Washington DC: U.S. Department of Agriculture, Bureau of Agricultural Economics, 1951.

Remeley, David. *Bell Ranch: Cattle Ranching in the Southwest, 1824–1947.* Albuquerque: University of New Mexico Press, 1993.

Report of the Chief of the Office of Indian Affairs. Washington DC: U.S. Government Printing Office, 1939–40.

Riley, Karen Lea. "Schools behind Barbed Wire: A History of Schooling in the United States Department of Justice Internment Camp at Crystal City, Texas, during World War II, 1942–1946." PhD diss., University of Texas at Austin, 1996.

Roberts, William O. "Successful Agriculture within the Reservation Framework." *Applied Anthropology* 2 (April–June 1943): 37–44.

Robin, Ron. *The Barbed-Wire College: Reeducating German POWs in the United States during World War II.* Princeton NJ: Princeton University Press, 1995.

Robinson, Elwyn B. *History of North Dakota.* Lincoln: University of Nebraska Press, 1966.

Rogers, Joe D. "Camp Hereford: Italian Prisoners of War on the Texas Plains, 1942–1945." *Panhandle-Plains Historical Review* 62 (1989): 57–110.

Rooker, Oliver E. "Supplying the Civilians: A Photo Essay of World War II Ration Stamps." *Chronicles of Oklahoma* 69 (Winter 1992): 430–41.

Rosenman, Samuel I., ed. *The Public Papers and Addresses of Franklin D. Roosevelt.* Vol. 9, *War and Aid to Democracies, 1940.* New York: Macmillan, 1941.

Rugg, Harold. "The War and American Public Opinion." *Scholastica* 38 (March 17, 1941): 11–13.

Rulon, Philip Reed. "The Campus Cadets: A History of Collegiate Military Training, 1891–1951." *Chronicles of Oklahoma* 57 (Spring 1979): 67–90.

Rupp, Leila J. *Mobilizing Women for War: German and American Propaganda, 1939–1945.* Princeton NJ: Princeton University Press, 1978.

Russell, Beverly. "World War II Boomtown: Hastings and the Naval Ammunition Depot." *Nebraska History* 76 (Summer/Fall 1995): 75–83.

Ryan, Ted. "History of Building D." *Aerospace Historian* 26 (Spring 1979): 25–29.

Samuel, Lawrence R. *Pledging Allegiance: American Identity and the Bond Drive of World War II.* Washington DC: Smithsonian Institution Press, 1997.

Sanson, Jerry Purvis. *Louisiana during World War II.* Baton Rouge: Louisiana State University Press, 1999.

Saunders, A. Dale. "Trends in Size, Land Tenure, Income, Organization, and Management of Selected Cattle Ranches in Southeastern Montana, 1924–48." Master's thesis, Montana State College, 1949.

Schell, Herbert S. *History of South Dakota.* Lincoln: University of Nebraska Press, 1975.

Schiller, Reuel E. "Reining in the Administrative State: World War II and the Decline of Expert Administration." In *Total War and the Law: The American Home Front during World War II*, ed. Daniel R. Ernst and Victor Jew, 185–206. Westport CT: Praeger, 2002.

Schlebecker, John T. *Cattle Raising on the Plains, 1900–1950.* Lincoln: University of Nebraska Press, 1963.

Schmidt, Carl Theodore. *American Farmers in the World Crisis.* New York: Oxford University Press, 1941.

Schneiders, Robert Kelley. *Unruly River: Two Centuries of Change along the Missouri.* Lawrence: University Press of Kansas, 1999.

Schwartz, Harry. *Seasonal Farm Labor in the United States, with Special Reference to Hired Workers in Fruit and Vegetable and Sugar-Beet Production.* New York: Columbia University Press, 1945.

Scruggs, Otey M. "The Bracero Program under the Farm Security Administration, 1942–1943." *Labor History* 4 (Spring 1962): 149–68.

———. *Braceros, "Wetbacks," and the Farm Labor Problem.* New York: Garland, 1988.

———. "Texas and the Bracero Program, 1942–1947." *Pacific Historical Review* 32 (February 1963): 251–64.

———. "The United States, Mexico, and the Wetbacks, 1942–1947." *Pacific Historical Review* 30 (May 1961): 149–64.

Segal, David R. *Recruiting for Uncle Sam: Citizenship and Military Power Policy.* Lawrence: University Press of Kansas, 1989.

Shryock, Henry S., Jr. "Internal Migration in Peace and War." *American Sociological Review* 12 (February 1947): 27–39.

Shryock, Henry S., Jr., and Hope Tisdale Eldridge. "Internal Migration in Peace and War." *American Sociological Review* 12 (February 1947): 27–39.

Simmons, Jerold. "Public Leadership in a World War II Boom Town: Bellevue, Nebraska." *Nebraska History* 65 (Winter 1984): 484–99.

Sitkoff, Harvard. "African American Militancy in the World War II South: Another Perspective." In *Remaking Dixie: The Impact of World War II on the American South*, ed. Neil R. McMillen, 70–92. Jackson: University of Mississippi Press, 1997.

———. "Racial Militancy and Interracial Violence in the Second World War." *Journal of American History* 58 (December 1971): 661–80.

Skaggs, Jimmie M. *Prime Cut: Livestock Raising and Meatpacking in the United States, 1607–1983.* College Station: Texas A&M University Press, 1986.

Sloan, Charles William, Jr., ed. "The Newelletters: E. Gail Carpenter Describes Life on the Home Front." Pts. 1–4. *Kansas History* 11 (Spring 1988): 54–72; 11 (Summer 1988): 123–42; 11 (Autumn 1988): 150–70; 11 (Winter 1988–1989): 222–39.

Smith, Caron. "The Women's Land Army during World War II." *Kansas History* 14 (Summer 1991): 82–88.

Smith, Karen Manners. "Father, Son, and Country on the Eve of War: William Allen White, William Lindsay White, and American Isolationism, 1940–1941." *Kansas History* 28 (Spring 2005): 30–43.

Smuckler, Ralph H. "The Region of Isolationism." *American Political Science Review* 47 (June 1953): 386–401.

Snapp, Harry F. "Pioneering Women in West Texas Skies: Women Airforce Service Pilots of World War II." *West Texas Historical Association Year Book* 70 (1994): 19–39.

Socolofsky, Homer E. *Arthur Capper: Publisher, Politician, and Philanthropist.* Lawrence: University of Kansas Press, 1962.

South Dakota in World War II. N.p.: World War History Commission, n.d.

Spencer, Ralph. "Prisoners of War in Cheyenne County, 1943–1946." *Nebraska History* 63 (Fall 1982): 438–49.

Spidle, Jake W., Jr. "Axis Invasion of the American West: POWs in New Mexico, 1942–1946." *New Mexico Historical Review* 49 (April 1974): 93–122.

———. "Axis Prisoners of War in the United States, 1942–1946: A Bibliographical Essay." *Military Affairs* 39 (April 1975): 61–66.

Spinney, Robert G. *World War II in Nashville: Transformation of the Homefront.* Knoxville: University of Tennessee Press, 1998.

Spritzer, Donald E. "Senators in Conflict." *Montana: The Magazine of Western History* 23 (Spring 1973): 16–33.

Stahnke, Herbert H. "Ministry to German POWs at Fort Sill, 1943–1946." *Concordia Historical Institute Quarterly* 62 (Fall 1989): 119–24.

Statistical Abstract of the United States. Washington DC: U.S. Government Printing Office, 1949, 1951.

Statistical Supplement to the Annual Report of the Commissioner of Indian Affairs. Washington DC: U.S. Government Printing Office, 1939, 1945.

Stewart, Miller J. "Fort Robinson, Nebraska." *Nebraska History* 70 (Winter 1989): 274–82.

Stout, Robert Joe. "Lend Him a Hand!" *Southwest Review* 69 (Winter 1984): 262–64.

Straub, Eleanor F. "United States Government Policy toward Civilian Women during World War II." *Prologue: The Journal of the National Archives* 5 (Winter 1973): 240–54.

Strout, Cushing. *The American Image of the Old World.* New York: Harper & Row, 1963.

Taylor, Graham D. *The New Deal and American Indian Tribalism: The Administration of the Indian Reorganization Act, 1934–1945.* Lincoln: University of Nebraska Press, 1980.

Terkel, Studs. *"The Good War": An Oral History of World War II.* New York: Pantheon, 1984.

Thiesen, John D. "Civilian Public Service: Two Cases." *Mennonite Life* 45 (June 1990): 4–12.

Thomas, Dorothy S., and Richard S. Nishimoto. *The Spoilage: Japanese-American Evacuation and Resettlement during World War II.* Berkeley and Los Angeles: University of California Press, 1946.

Thompson, Gerald W., Monroe L. Billington, and Roger D. Walker, ed. *Victory in World War II: The New Mexico Story.* Los Cruces: New Mexico State University Library, 1994.

Thompson, Glenn. *Prisoners on the Plains: The German POWs at Camp Atlanta.* Holdrege NE: Phelps County Historical Society, 1993.

Thompson, William Takamatsu. "Amache: A Working Bibliography on One Japanese American Concentration Camp." *Amerasia Journal* 19, no. 1 (1993): 153–59.

Tissing, Robert Warren. "Stalag—Texas, 1943–1945." *Military History of Texas and the Southwest* 13 (Winter 1976): 23–34.

———. "Utilization of Prisoners of War in the United States during World War II Texas: A Case Study." Master's thesis, Baylor University, 1973.

Tolley, Howard R. *The Farmer Citizen at War.* New York: Macmillan, 1943.

Townsend, Kenneth W. *World War II and the American Indian.* Albuquerque: University of New Mexico Press, 2000.

Trew, Delbert. *The McLean POW Camp.* McLean TX: D.R.M., 1997.

Tuttle, William M. "Aid-to-the-Allies Short-of-War versus American Interventionism, 1940: A Reappraisal of William Allen White's Leadership." *Journal of American History* 56 (March 1970): 840–58.

———. *Daddy's Gone to War: The Second World War in the Lives of America's Children.* New York: Oxford University Press, 1993.

———. "William Allen White and Verne Marshall: Two Midwestern Editors Debate Aid to the Allies versus Isolationism." *Kansas Historical Quarterly* 32 (Summer 1966): 201–9.

Unsworth, Michael E. "Floating Vengeance: The World War II Japanese Balloon Attack on Colorado." *Colorado Heritage*, Autumn 1993, 22–35.

———. "The Japanese Balloon Bomb Campaign in North Dakota." *North Dakota History* 64 (Winter 1997): 21–26.

"Uprooted: A Portfolio of Japanese-Americans in World War II." *Colorado Heritage*, 1989, no. 1:12–28.

"U.S. Army and Air Force Wings over Kansas." Pts. 1–2. *Kansas Historical Quarterly* 25 (Summer 1959): 129–57; 25 (Autumn 1959): 334–60.

Useem, John, Gordon MacGregor, and Ruth Hill Useem. "Wartime Employment and Cultural Adjustments of the Rosebud Sioux." *Applied Anthropology* 2 (January–March 1943): 1–9.

Vander Meulen, Jacob. "World War II Aircraft Industry in the West." *Journal of the West* 36 (July 1997): 78–84.

Van Valkenburg, Carol Bulger. *An Alien Place: The Fort Missoula, Montana, Detention Camp, 1941–1944.* Missoula MT: Pictorial Histories, 1995.

Vatter, Harold G. *The U.S. Economy in World War II.* New York: Columbia University Press, 1985.

"Vitamins for Victory." *Colorado Heritage*, Winter 1995, 25–28.

Walker, Richard Paul. "Prisoners of War in Texas during World War II." PhD diss., North Texas State University, 1980.

———. "The Swastika and the Lone Star: Nazi Activity in Texas POW Camps." *Military History of the Southwest* 19 (Spring 1989): 39–70.

Ward, Leslie A. *History of the Concordia Prisoner of War Camp.* Concordia: Kansas Printing House, 1982.

Warner, Richard S. "Barbed Wire and Nazilagers: PW Camps in Oklahoma." *Chronicles of Oklahoma* 64 (Winter 1986): 36–67.

Weatherford, Doris. *American Women and World War II.* New York: Facts on File, 1990.

Weglyn, Michi. *Years of Infamy: The Untold Story of America's Concentration Camps.* New York: Morrow, 1976.

Welsh, Carol H. "'Back the Attack': The Sale of War Bonds in Oklahoma." 61 *Chronicles of Oklahoma* (Fall 1983): 226–45.

Wertheimer, Andrew B. "Admitting Nebraska's Nisei: Japanese American Students at the University of Nebraska, 1942–1945." *Nebraska History* 83 (Summer 2002): 58–72.

"What Did You Do in the War?" Special issue, *Nebraska History* 72 (Winter 1991).

White, Walter. *A Rising Wind*. Garden City NY: Doubleday, Doran, 1945.

White, William Allen. "This Is America: The Middle West Drifts to the Right." *Nation* 148 (June 3, 1939): 635–38.

Wilcox, Walter W. *The Farmer in the Second World War*. Ames: Iowa State College Press, 1947.

Wilkins, Robert P. "The Non-Ethnic Roots of North Dakota Isolationism." *Nebraska History* 44 (September 1963): 205–21.

Williams, Donald Mace. *Interlude in Umbarger: Italian POWs and a Texas Church*. Lubbock: Texas Tech University Press, 1992.

Wilson, Terry Paul. "The Afrika Korps in Oklahoma: Fort Reno's Prisoner of War Compound." *Chronicles of Oklahoma* 52 (Fall 1974): 360–69.

Winkler, Alan M. *Home Front U.S.A.: America during World War II*. 2nd ed. Wheeling IL: Harlan Davidson, 2000.

———. *The Politics of Propaganda: The Office of War Information, 1942–1945*. New Haven CT: Yale University Press, 1978.

Wit, Tracy Lyn. "The Social and Economic Impact of World War II Munitions Manufacture on Grand Island, Nebraska." *Nebraska History* 71 (Fall 1990): 151–63.

Wood, Charles L. *The Kansas Beef Industry*. Lawrence: Regents Press of Kansas, 1980.

Woods, Betty. "'Commando' Cowboys." *New Mexico Magazine* 22 (March 1944): 12–33.

World War II and the People of Dundy County: A 50th Anniversary Album. N.p.: Curtis Media, 1992.

Worrall, Janet E. "Prisoners on the Home Front: Community Reactions to German and Italian POWs in Northern Colorado, 1943–1946." *Colorado Heritage*, 1990, no. 1:32–47.

Wynn, Neil A. *The Afro-American and the Second World War*. London: Paul Elke, 1976.

Yoshino, Ronald W. "Barbed Wire and Beyond: A Sojourn through Internment—a Personal Recollection." *Journal of the West* 35 (January 1996): 34–43.

"Your Questions as to Women in War Industries." Bulletin no. 194 of the Women's Bureau. Washington DC: U.S. Government Printing Office, 1942.